600

Marianne Baumann
43 Berch...
HO.3267 / KE 93%

343

ART THROUGH THE AGES

HELEN GARDNER'S

ART

THROUGH THE AGES

Fourth Edition

REVISED UNDER THE EDITORSHIP OF

SUMNER McK. CROSBY

by

THE DEPARTMENT OF
THE HISTORY OF ART
YALE UNIVERSITY

HARCOURT, BRACE AND COMPANY

  New York

709

G-173A4

COVER ILLUSTRATION: Detail from GEORGES SEURAT, *Sunday Afternoon on Grande Jatte Island.*
The Art Institute of Chicago. (Courtesy of the Art Institute of Chicago, Helen Birch Bartlett
Memorial Collection)

Includes bibliographies.

1. Art — Hist.

I. Title.

The Editors were unable to locate the copyright holders of the following illustrations: 8–13,
8–19, 8–20, 8–56, 8–64, 10–46, 13–3, and 13–9. If the copyright holders will communicate
with Harcourt, Brace and Company, the usual fee for the use of these photographs will be paid.

CONTENTS

INTRODUCTION:

Vocabulary and Principles of Art History   1

ANCIENT ART   31

EUROPEAN ART   187

NON-EUROPEAN ART   489

MODERN ART   649

PREFACE

Helen Gardner's *Art Through the Ages,* since its first edition in 1926, has been a favorite with generations of students in schools and colleges, and the general reader who is interested in the history of art has found it an exciting and informative survey. Miss Gardner's sincere enthusiasm, her broad knowledge and deep humanity have made it possible for the beginner to learn how to see, and to penetrate the seeming mysteries of even the most complex artistic achievements. Every effort has been made in this new volume to preserve her freshness and simplicity of style, and above all her sympathetic approach to individual works of art and to the styles of which they are a part.

Miss Gardner completed the Third Edition shortly before her death in 1948. When new archaeological discoveries and continuing scholarly research indicated the need for a fourth revision, the publishers asked Yale University's Department of the History of Art to undertake the task. It was agreed that individual members of the department would prepare initial drafts of the various chapters in accordance with their special knowledge, but that one member would serve as editor in order to unify the work. Most members of the Yale Department have actively participated in introductory courses which, although they are presented by a number of different lecturers and section leaders, are carefully studied by the group as a whole to maintain unity and continuity. The editor has directed the popular Introduction to the History of Art course at Yale since its inception in 1946.

Although Miss Gardner's organization of the Third Edition provided many opportunities for interesting comparisons and made it possible to study in adjacent chapters what was occurring in different parts of the world during more or less the same historic periods, this organization often obscured the intrinsic qualities and especially the development of the different styles. As our table of contents indicates, we have presented the arts of different periods and countries in a more normal order. The division into Ancient, European, Non-European, and Modern Art and the grouping by periods and countries under these divisions will, we believe, provide a clear and coherent chronological account of the history of art throughout the world.

The Introduction for the Fourth Edition has been revised and expanded, and is presented as a separate section in order to emphasize the importance to the student or amateur of acquiring a vocabulary and of learning how to see.

One of the most useful and popular features of the older editions has been the number and quality of its illustrations. The Fourth Edition continues this tradition. But even eight hundred illustrations has often seemed a restriction to the editors as they surveyed the available material. Omissions have been necessary at times even though mention or rather detailed analysis of a work of art may be included in the text. In many instances in which a choice had to be made the well-known or often-illustrated object or building was put aside in favor of the less familiar.

The eight color plates show, insofar as reproductions can, the fascinating variations created by different techniques and media. We are particularly grateful to Professor Josef Albers and to Assistant Professor Sewell Sillman for producing the example of Goethe's color triangle, which appears as Plate 8.

As in earlier editions rather extensive bibliographies will be found at the end of each chapter, and as before they have been compiled with a well-equipped but not specialized art library in mind. Serious attempts have been made to bring them up to date, and whenever possible an American or recent edition has been cited rather than a foreign or earlier one, in the hope that it might be more readily available. When sources of quotations, or other bibliographical material, appear in the footnotes, only the author, title and page number are given if the item is included in the chapter's bibliography.

The number of maps has been increased in this edition, but the reader must remember that these are not, properly speaking, maps. They should be regarded as charts used to locate the cities, towns, or artistic sites mentioned in the text.

In presenting this new edition the Editor assumes full responsibility for the final text, but its preparation would have been impossible without the cooperation of his many colleagues. In the Department of the History of Art at Yale these include: Professors George H. Hamilton, George A. Kubler, Carroll L. V. Meeks, and Charles Seymour, Jr.; Associate Professor Vincent J. Scully, Jr.; Instructors William R. Crelly, William L. MacDonald, Hellmut Wohl, and Nelson I. Wu. Others who were members of the Department when they worked on the text but who now have positions elsewhere are: Professor J. Leroy Davidson, Chairman of the Graduate Department of the History of Art, Claremont College, Claremont, Calif.; Associate Professors John R. Spencer, Chairman of the Department of History of Art, University of Florida, Gainesville, Fla.; William Jordy, Brown University, Providence, R. I.; Robert Wark, Curator of Painting, Huntington Library, San Marino, Calif.; Ralph T. Coe, National Museum of Art, Washington, D. C.; Richard Brilliant, Fulbright Fellow in Europe. Miss Elizabeth A. Chase, Assistant Professor of Art, and Miss Ann L. Perkins, Research Associate in Classics at Yale, also worked on the original text. Such outside experts as Mr. Beaumont Newhall, Director of the Eastman House, Rochester, N. Y., and Professors Irving Rouse of the Department of Anthropology, Yale University, and Henry-Russell Hitchcock, Smith College, were asked to prepare or comment on the revised text; Associate Professor Charles Comfort of the Art and Archeology

Department, University of Toronto, Toronto, Ont., very kindly revised the pages on Canadian art.

Although the publishers have assumed the responsibility of procuring the illustrations, we are particularly grateful to the staff of the Metropolitan Museum of Art, New York, N. Y., for extensive help in supplying photographs. In other instances credit for the photographs or diagrams are given in parentheses in the illustration caption.

For assistance in typing and in the preparation and checking of the manuscript and proofs we thank the staffs of the Yale Art Library and Yale Slide and Photograph Collections, as well as Mrs. Patricia S. Beach, Miss Barbara Chatfield, Mrs. Susan Collins, Miss Caroline Rollins, Miss Susan Wintringham, Mrs. Marion Wohl, and Jonathan Barnett.

To the Assistant Editor, Mrs. Joy Greene Sweet, my especial gratitude is extended. Her devoted attention to the preparation of the text and the correction of the galley proof; her innate sense of style, taste, and logic have contributed immensely to the achievement of this volume.

SUMNER McK. CROSBY

New Haven, Connecticut
October, 1958

LIST OF COLOR PLATES

Plate 1 EARTH COLORS AND CHARCOAL ON NATURAL ROCK. *Two Bison*. Cave of Lascaux. Montignac, France. *ca.* 15,000 B.C. (Sumner Crosby)

Plate 2 MOSAIC. *Emperor Justinian* (detail). San Vitale, Ravenna. 6th century A.D. (From André Grabar, *Byzantine Painting,* courtesy of Skira, Inc.)

Plate 3 COPPER AND SILVER GILT, PRECIOUS STONES AND GEMS, CHAMPLEVÉ ENAMEL
MEDALLIONS. *The Stavelot Triptych.* A.D. *ca.* 1150. Pierpont Morgan Library.
(Pierpont Morgan Library)

Plate 4 STAINED GLASS. *Signatures of donor guilds: carpenters, cabinetmakers, wheel-makers.* Detail of St. Julian window. Chartres cathedral. 13th century. (Sumner Crosby)

Plate 5 TEMPERA ON WOOD PANEL. St. Peter (detail) from the wing of an altarpiece by Nardo di Cione. 14th century. Yale University Art Gallery. (Yale Art Gallery)

Plate 6 OIL ON CANVAS. *Self-Portrait*. Rembrandt van Rijn. 1658. Frick Collection, New York. (Copyright the Frick Collection, New York)

Plate 7   OIL ON CANVAS. *Bend in the Road*. Paul Cézanne. *ca.* 1900. Collection Mr. and Mrs. Walter Bareiss (Herbert Orth, courtesy *Life*)

Plate 8 COLOR TRIANGLE. Devised by Johann Wolfgang von Goethe. Prepared by Josef Albers and Sewell Sillman, Yale University.

ART THROUGH THE AGES

INTRO-
DUCTION

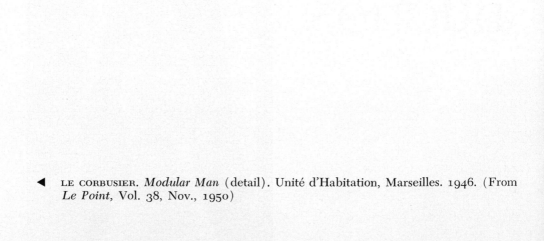

◄ LE CORBUSIER. *Modular Man* (detail). Unité d'Habitation, Marseilles. 1946. (From *Le Point*, Vol. 38, Nov., 1950)

VOCABULARY
AND
PRINCIPLES
OF
ART HISTORY

Our title, *Art Through the Ages*, implies two major concerns: art and history. To discover what art is we shall examine its specific manifestations in the visual arts; and we shall illuminate this study by reference to its constantly changing environments throughout the world from prehistoric times to our own.

A work of art is a unique experience, both for the artist who creates it and for the intelligent observer who benefits by its creation. For this reason art is defined by works of art, not by words about them. Yet some verbal generalizations are necessary, and thus we identify the visual arts as the selective communication of human experience in tangible forms existing as matter in space.

The visual arts, of course, require the ability to see. Yet few of us are

ILLUSTRATION ABOVE. **0–1** PAUL CÉZANNE. *The Card Player.* Drawing. 1892. Museum of Art, Providence, Rhode Island. (Rhode Island School of Design, Providence)

taught how to do this. We are taught to speak, to read, and to write, and even how to play; but only recently have our students been taught how to see.

Many things other than physical blindness limit our capacity or our willingness to see. Most of these impediments are preconceptions or misconceptions. For instance, there is our misleading concept that the visual arts should be regarded as the "fine arts," a translation from the original French *beaux-arts*. By definition such "fine arts" included only those arts which were concerned with the "beautiful," a term to be officially interpreted by the academies and, by implication, only to be understood by the educated and sophisticated. This has led to the assumption that art has little to do with normal, humdrum daily existence, that one must go to a museum or "fine arts gallery" to see art, and that one must have some superior insight or talent in order to "appreciate," enjoy, or understand it.

This concept of an esoteric beauty

as the hallmark of a work of art is a modern misconception. Only since the middle of the eighteenth century has a distinction been drawn between the arts of the past and of the present. Previously, although the monuments of past styles, for example those of Greco-Roman Antiquity, might be extolled and emulated, art was always new, always proposing new solutions for contemporary problems. When a style as original as Gothic was developed, it was referred to as *opus modernum*, or "modern art." Only those generations who have lost faith in themselves and in the future prefer the past to the present; and the school or doctrine which evokes past principles to the exclusion of experimentation and innovation must inevitably stifle initiative. The new or unusual must not be suspect merely because of its "newness." But since new experiences are often difficult to assess, we must be prepared to make the necessary effort — often a very considerable one — to comprehend the unfamiliar in our own times or in other cultures.

Such difficulties often arise from the common belief that a work of art must look like something, either like something we see around us or like something which has existed before — that art should look like something other than itself. Yet it takes but little effort to realize that all art is an abstraction. No matter how meticulous or skillful an artist may be, no matter how desirous he is of producing a likeness of his subject, the painted, carved, or graphic representation will of necessity be a distortion of the original. In other words, all works of art, whether or not they have an image of nature as their subject, are abstractions. Yet the apparent lack of relationship to nature is a common cause for a misunderstanding of the art of today.

But why should art be restricted to certain categories in selecting its material? Today, especially, when our concepts of natural forces can often be expressed only in terms of highly abstract relationships, is it not to be expected that artists should treat, or explore, these relationships in "abstract" colors or shapes? And is it not true that such abstractions may well reveal profound truths about the laws of nature or about man's intuitive processes? The province of art is the order of man's thought and the intensity or strength of his emotions or beliefs. The modes or forms of art must therefore be varied. The challenge to the historian, or critic, of art is the recognition and interpretation of these forms.

The historian of art remembers that each work of art is unique, that it is its own embodiment of truth. In continually searching for relationships between historical events, he may be preoccupied with the patterns of culture, with the growth of civilizations and of the men who define them. He may find such studies fascinating and rewarding, but he must never lose sight of the fact that individual works of art are his basic events, that each must first be comprehended by itself and for itself alone.

A work of visual art, given favorable conditions, may survive centuries, even millenia, in more or less its original condition. This is also true of literature and poetry, especially since the invention of printing, but is not equally true of music or the drama, which vary with every performance. The fact that the visual arts are composed of matter which exists in space — for even a delicate line on a fragile piece of rice paper must be defined as matter in space — gives them an actuality which successive generations may experience.

To convey this experience we must use words, but lack of conformity in interpreting key words, in ways of explaining what is being looked at, often leads to serious confusion. Thus we now turn to the vocabulary available for the analysis and description of the visual arts. The following definitions of terms may not be universally accepted, but they will be a key to understanding this book.

Since the visual arts exist as matter in space, the way in which this matter is organized, the way it exists in, or interprets, space, the way in which it is defined by the light that permits us to see it — these give this matter its *form.*

"Form" has many meanings. We shall use the term in its widest sense: that of total organic structure, of a synthesis of all the elements of that structure and of the manner in which these elements are related and united to create its distinctive character. By "organic" we mean possessed of an articulated structure comparable to that of a human being, in which the relation of the parts involves relation to the whole. It is the form of a work of art which enables us to apprehend it. It is by *formal* analysis that we may identify the properties and qualities of that *form,* if we wish to communicate our reactions to, and understanding of, works of art.

When an artist creates a work of art, he gives tangible, visible substance to his concepts. For this the world offers him innumerable materials. His choice of material, however, is not a matter of chance. Each has its own potentialities and limitations, and it is part of the artist's creative activity to determine whether a certain material is suitable for the expression of his concept and whether he is technically proficient in handling it. The peculiar properties of the material and the processes and tools with which it is worked are vital in determining form. This may be seen in a comparison of the marble statue of *Apollo* from Olympia (Fig. 5–24) with the bronze *Charioteer of Delphi* (p. 31). The *Apollo* is firmly modeled,

0–2 STATUETTE OF A HORSE. Greek Geometric style. Bronze. H. *ca.* 7 in. 8th century B.C. Metropolitan Museum of Art, New York.

with emphasis on broad, generalized planes appropriate to stone and to the sculptor's use of the chisel. The fineness of detail, the crisp, sharp folds of the *Charioteer's* drapery, on the other hand, bespeak the fact that it is made of metal.

Thus we see that another prerequisite to a full understanding of form is experience with, or regard for, those processes and tools with which matter is worked. We must realize that the distinctive technique which every artist develops is his personal solution for the expression of his ideas and emotions. It is the way, for instance, in which his hammer and chisel slowly carve a figure from solid stone, as in Michelangelo's *Bound Slave* (Fig. 0–3), or his fingers and tools delicately model in soft clay, as in Houdon's bust of *Louise Brogniart* (Fig. 10–38), which transforms matter into a work of art. It is when technique liberates from matter its vital forces that it becomes an integral part of the creative process, more than a means to an end. If matter is the substance of art, technique,

0-3 MICHELANGELO BUONARROTI. *Unfinished Bound Slave.* Marble. 1519. Accademia, Florence. (Alinari)

then, is man's ability to infuse that substance with meaning. Before we approach this problem of meaning, however, we must return to form and to the vocabulary used for its definition, first in spatial terms, and then in those of light.

Space is ordinarily considered to be a boundless, continuous expanse within which all material things are contained. Modern science, of course, has added the concept of the time continuum to that of the space continuum; and theories of relativity have greatly enhanced our understanding of such vast terms as universal space or such minute ones as nuclear space. In studying the history of art before the twentieth century, however, we need not consider space in terms other than

Newtonian, for the visual arts up to this time may be adequately described and analyzed in relation to three-dimensional space.

Since one of the major objectives of the visual arts, especially in painting, has been to create an illusion of three-dimensional space on flat, or two-dimensional, surfaces, we begin with a discussion of terms which describe this specific, limited type of space.

The words *area* and *plane* are generally used to refer to the surface of an object. A *plane* is flat. Although its perimeter may be irregular, its area is limited to two dimensions. It may exist at any angle in space, but it is a continuous surface which does not change direction, as is seen in one of the sides of a pyramid (Fig. 2–8). An *area* may also be level; and it is often used to describe a flat space which is enclosed or bounded by something. Bernini had this in mind when he defined the area in front of *St. Peter's* by means of his curving colonnades (Fig. 10–2). In this way *area* implies the limits of two-dimensional space. But an *area* may also undulate, or be curved, as long as only its surface is under consideration. The words we employ to describe the shape, or extent, of a plane or an area are those of plane geometry: square, rectangle, triangle, circle, ellipse, and the like.

Mass and *volume* are terms that also describe the way in which forms limit, or define, space. In contradistinction to *plane* and *area*, however, they describe these forms not in two-dimensional but in three-dimensional space. We must remember, when we use any of these terms in relation to the visual arts, that, although we may be describing the forms themselves, it is essentially the effect of these forms which is of interest to us. For this reason, when we use *mass* to describe the exterior shape of a building, we use the vocabulary of solid geometry: cube, pyra-

0–4 WILHELM LEHMBRUCK. *Seated Youth.* Bronze. 1918. Duisburg, West Germany. (Museum of Modern Art, New York)

0–5 AUGUSTE RODIN. *The Thinker.* Bronze. 1880. Metropolitan Museum of Art, New York.

mid, cylinder, sphere, cone (Fig. 8–18), and our use is akin both to that of the mathematician, who is interested in the extent of the forms, and to that of the physicist, who is interested in the quantity and quality of matter in a given body. In both architecture and sculpture *mass* is the effect and degree of bulk, density, and weight of matter in space. Yet the *mass* does not have to be solid. It is the exterior form of matter in space. It may apply to a pyramid which is essentially solid or to the exterior of *Hagia Sophia*, which encloses vast spaces (Fig. 7–11).

Volume is also descriptive of three-dimensional space. It is the way space is organized by *mass*. It may be the enclosed spaces of the interior of a building. It may also be the intervals of space between the *masses* of a building or of a piece of sculpture, ceramics, or furniture. *Volume* and *mass* are often used interchangeably. But they need not be; and it is often very useful to be able to distinguish between the *exterior* and *interior* forms of a work

of art, as well as between the matter of which it is composed and the spaces that exist around and between that matter. How meager our description would be of such a piece of sculpture as Lehmbruck's *Seated Youth* (Fig. 0–4) if we could not call attention specifically to the *volumes* enclosed by the attenuated masses of the torso, arms, and legs. And how much richer our understanding is when we realize the importance these volumes play in creating the total effect of this statue in comparison, let us say, with another seated figure, that of *The Thinker* by Auguste Rodin (Fig. 0–5).

Other phrases may also enrich our perception and understanding of the intimate association between forms and the space in which they exist. *Closed form,* for example, describes a *mass* limited by space, one whose smooth surfaces are contiguous with space, as in the figure of the Virgin of the *Annunciation* on the west façade of Reims cathedral (Fig. 8–49). *Open form,* to the contrary, allows space to penetrate

0–6 PABLO PICASSO. *Bathers.* Detail. Pencil drawing on white paper. 1918. Meta and Paul J. Sachs Collection, Fogg Art Museum, Harvard University. (Fogg Art Museum)

its mass. Its surfaces are irregular, with deep undercutting or recesses, which create strong contrasts of light and shadow, as in the two figures of the *Visitation* on the same portal (Fig. 8–49). Examples of the two extremes of *closed* and *open forms* [1] may be found in most styles of art. They may represent different moments in the development of a style, as in the contrast between the *Hera of Samos* (Fig. 5–12) from Archaic Greek art, and the *Victory of Samothrace* (Fig. 5–47) from Hellenistic, or Late Greek, art; and they always produce strikingly different psychological effects.

In the definition of mass and volume, *line* is one of the most important, and yet most difficult, terms to comprehend fully. Its definition as the identifiable

[1] For an excellent discussion of these and similar descriptive terms see H. Wölfflin, *Principles of Art History.*

path of a point moving in space is explicit and easily understood by both scientists and artists; but the infinite subtleties encompassed by such a definition are known only to those who have made a special study of drawing or of the graphic arts (see p. 23). A point, in and of itself, defines space; but the limitless variety of its movements, the wide range of characteristics its path may assume, seem dependent only on the personality and skill of the artist, or on the limitations of the implement or medium with which it is made. Whatever its function or character, *line* suggests movement in some direction: vertical, horizontal, diagonal, or curved. The psychological reactions to these different directions are common experience: vertical as positive, horizontal as passive, or diagonal as restless energy. A *line* may be broad or thick (Fig. 15–20). It may be thin, even ephemeral (Fig. 9–40). There is a poetical quality in *line* that invites lyrical description. *Line* also defines space. A *line* may be an edge, in which case we often refer to it as a *silhouette* or simple tracing of the outline of an object (Fig. 15–8). A *line* may also define a *contour* (Fig. 0–6), wherein the modulations express the existence of a mass in space. While a *silhouette* may contribute to the pattern, or decorative effect, of a design, a *contour* envelops space and by its own subtlety creates the illusion of mass and volume.

When a *line* serves as a direction for the organization of other forms in space, it is known as an *axis*. In other words, an *axis* is the organization of the component parts of a building or of any work of art, or of an interrelated group of works, along a given *line* or *lines*. An *axis* suggests, as does *line*, movement in some direction; and these directions have the same psychological intensity as those discussed in the previous paragraph about *line*. We must

0-7 Lines of perspective organization superimposed on *School of Athens* by Raphael. (N. Stetson) Compare with Figs. 0–22 and 9–57.

be prepared, as well, to comprehend the relationship of one *axis* to another. In many instances there may be a single, or dominant, *axis* (Fig. 7–6); but there may also be multiple *axes* (Fig. 6–32), or *axes* radiating from a given point (Fig. 9–70). The significant factors of such *axes* in the organization of architecture, sculpture, and painting will be further elaborated in the following chapters. It is sufficient for the moment to note that *axes* are among the most important factors of coherence in forms as small as a jewel or in areas as vast as the heavily populated Eastern seaboard of the United States, now recognized by urban planners as an organic entity.

Perspective, though it originally referred to the science of optics, is, in its general connotation, a way of looking at things. In reality *perspective*, no less than *axis*, is a method of organizing forms in space. Yet we use *perspective* almost exclusively in relation to ways of creating the illusion of depth or space on a two-dimensional surface. We instinctively think of *perspective* as the rational ordering of space in terms of a single point — a point where those lines converge which mark the diminishing size of forms as they recede in relative distance (Fig. 0–7). But we realize today that this particular system, developed in western Europe during the Renaissance, is only one of several different systems. It is quite correct to speak of the *perspective* of Chinese Sung painting (Fig. 15–18) or of Japanese prints (Fig. 16–19), although they have nothing in common with these Western systems; and we should be prepared to speak of Roman (Fig. 6–16) or other *perspectives*, although we have not as yet been able to discern all the controlling principles then employed to organize the illusion of depth in space.

Two additional words should be included in this general discussion of spatial terms. They are *proportion* and *scale*. Both of them involve measurement and refer to relative sizes of forms in space, but each of them has its own specific meaning. *Proportion* is the mathematical relationship in size of one part of a work of art to others within it, as well as to the totality of all these parts. It implies the use of a common denomination in the measurements of the different parts. As stated by Galen: "[Beauty exists] in the proportions, not of the elements, but of the parts, that is to say, of finger to finger and of all the fingers to the palm and wrist, and of these to the forearm and of the forearm to the upper arm and of all the parts to each other, as they are set forth in the Canon of Polykleitos."[2] (See Fig. 5–30.) But it should be noted that such rigorous systems inevitably tend to develop into rules, or *canons*, which often result in academic formulas, regulating how perfection in the arts may be achieved.

[2] H. S. Jones, *Select Passages from Ancient Writers*, Macmillan, New York, 1895, pp. 128 ff.

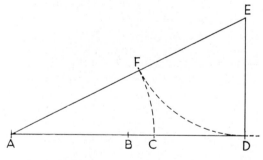

0–8 Diagram of Golden Mean. In order to divide a given line *AD* according to the Golden Mean, first bisect it. Erect a vertical at right angles to *AD* equal in length to *AB*. On the hypotenuse of the triangle (*AE*), locate *F* so that *EF* equals *AB* (or *DE*). On the original line *AD* locate *C* so that *AC* equals *AF*. *C* divides *AD* according to the proportions of the Golden Mean.

There is one such proportional system, however, which has appeared again and again in many different styles. It is referred to as the *Golden Mean* or *Section*. Mathematically it is incommensurable, since its ratio may only be expressed in nonfinite terms: $(\sqrt{5} + 1)/2 = 1.618$ . . . . It is easily arrived at, though, by geometrical means (Fig. 0–8); and such proportions have an aesthetic appeal, a stable, yet never static, effect, which has led artists of varying periods and cultures to employ it in determining basic measurements. It may be seen, for example, in the dimensions of the *Court of the Lions* in the Alhambra (Fig. 13–9) or of the east façade of the *Louvre* in Paris (Fig. 10–32), where the proportions of the lower story to the upper one are according to the *Golden Mean*.

More frequently a given unit of measurement is employed in determining proportional relationships. Such a unit is called a *module* or *modular*. This module may be based on the dimensions of an important part of a building, such as the diameter of a column (Fig. 5–5); on some basic structural material, such as the size of a brick; or on some abstract but commonly accepted unit of measurement, such as the centimeter or the inch, or as with Le Corbusier, on the normal dimensions of man (p. 783).

Scale is also a mathematical relation of the parts or totality of a building or of an object; but in this instance the ratio is *to their use*, or *function*, or to the *size* of the original form. Thus the plan of a building may have a *scale* of one-quarter inch to a foot, a statue may be one-third life size, or a building may be scaled to an elephant or to a penguin (Fig. 0–9), although we usually think of man as the norm for *scale*.

Since every style develops its own particular *scale*, as it does its system of *proportion*, both of these extraordinar-

0–9 PENGUIN HOUSE, London Zoo. Designed by Messrs. Tecton. *ca.* 1934. (F. S. Lincoln)

ily discriminating terms will be constantly referred to throughout the remainder of this book.

The terms we have been discussing are descriptive of forms in space. We must now turn our attention to those primarily concerned with the properties of *light*. The function of *light* as illumination in the world of nature is such a common experience that it is often taken for granted, and there are few who realize the extraordinary variations wrought by *light* alone on our most familiar surroundings, as the hours of the day or the months of the year unfold. Only the artist or those trained to observe closely realize fully the extent to which *light* affects and creates form. The French artist Monet,

0–10 CLAUDE MONET. *Façade of Rouen Cathedral.* Two views. *ca.* 1880. Left, Chester Dale Collection, National Gallery of Art, Washington, D. C. Right, Museum of Fine Arts, Boston. (National Gallery; courtesy, Museum of Fine Arts, Boston)

for instance, painted the reflections in a water-lily pond according to their seasonal variations, and in a series of more than twenty canvases of the façade of the cathedral of Rouen revealed its changing forms from dawn until twilight (Fig. 0–10). If form exists as matter in space, this matter is defined by *light;* and we may even say that in the visual arts *light* is as important to the structure, or existence, of form as is the matter of which it is made.

In the analysis of *light* an important distinction must immediately be made for the realm of art: natural, or sun, light is whole or additive light, whereas the painter's light in art is subtractive light. Natural light is composed of all the wave lengths of the spectrum, visible or invisible. We may disassemble light into the colors of the spectral band; but we could reconstruct natural light only if we could put back together, or reassemble, all the elements contained in the source of this light, the sun. Reflected light (that is, the artist's light) is subtractive, not additive. Most of the colors we see result from the peculiar ability of pigments (as in the pigments of paint or of the human body) to reflect specific segments of the spectrum while absorbing all the rest. The function of a green pigment is to subtract all the light in the spectrum except for green light, which is then reflected to the eye and perceived as green color. One of the disturbing discoveries of anyone who begins to mix paints or colors is that the more pigments are combined, the muddier are the results. In fact, if black is the absence of light in one sense, as a color it is the presence of all pigments. Ideally, if these pigments could be totally mixed they should subtract all light. Actually their mixture never attains more than a dark gray.

The degree of luminosity or rela-

◄ **0–11** Diagram of value relationships. (S. Sillman)

tive intensity, i.e., presence or absence of light, is referred to as *value* in painting, and most particularly in drawing and the graphic arts. A scale of *values* from white to black can easily be developed (Fig. 0–11); and it is interesting to see how colors react on each other, or even seem to change as the relationship between them changes. The center *value* in this diagram remains absolutely constant, although it looks lighter at the top and darker at the bottom. The Italian word, *chiaroscuro* (*chiaro*, or "light," and "*scuro*, or "dark"), refers to *value*, and especially to graduations between light and dark, which produce the effect of *modeling*, or of light reflected from three-dimensional surfaces, as in one of Mantegna's superb drawings (Fig. 0–12).

The name of a color is its *hue* — red, blue, or yellow. Although the colors of the spectrum extend in a continuous band, artists usually conceive of their *hues* as distinct from each other. For this reason there are many different types of color charts, which are helpful in identifying exact relationships and in developing precise terminology or notation of different *hues*, their *tonality*, *intensity*, or *chroma*. These last terms all refer to the relative purity or *value* of a *hue*. A *hue*, or pigment, which is unadulterated may be said to be at its maximum *chroma* or full saturation; and *tonality* refers to the relative degree to which white or dark has been added to a hue, thereby changing its *intensity*. The exploration of color and of the reaction or interaction of colors on each other is the province of the artist and can only be experienced, or really understood, by intense practice and experimentation. One of the more interesting diagrams of these col-

0–12 ANDREA MANTEGNA. *Seven Apostles Watching the Ascension of Christ.* Brush drawing heightened with white. *ca.* 1464. Fogg Art Museum, Harvard University. (Fogg Art Museum)

or relationships is the color triangle devised by Goethe (Plate 8). Red, yellow, and blue, the *primary colors*, are placed in the apexes of the triangle, with the colors which result from their mixing — orange, green and purple, respectively, called *secondary colors* — in between them.[3] The possible gradations or mutations between them are seen in the inner triangles. Those colors which lie opposite each other are the *complementary hues*, such as red and green. Since these are composed of

[3] Perhaps the most striking advantages of this simple triangle are (1) that it separates the lightest and the darkest of the primary hues at the extremes of the base of the triangle and places the middle hue at the apex, which never can occur in a color wheel; and (2) that it also immediately places the secondary and tertiary hues relative to themselves and to the primary hues. These facts and other psychological observations regarding different effects were stated by Goethe and reported by Carry van Biema, *Farben und Formen als Lebendige Kräfte,* Eugen Diedericks Verlag, Jena, 1930.

0–13 Air view of New York City. (Robert Yarnall Richie)

subtractive pigments, they may be said to complement, or complete, each other; for they produce a neutral, or gray, when mixed in the right proportion. Another important property of color is its psychological effect, which always gives rise to tensions, creating spatial relationships. The physical connotations of red and yellow, quite naturally, are *warm;* and those of blue or blue-green are *cool.* For many artists the *warm colors* seem to advance, while the *cool colors* tend to recede. The use of color, consequently, may enhance the illusion of space or may create emotional tensions (Plate 7).

It is also a property of light to reveal the quality of a surface in visual terms. Such a surface may be rough or smooth, hard or soft, shiny or dull; and we refer to this quality as *texture. Texture* is literally the sensuous feeling of such a surface. In painting, different media and different techniques cre-

ate a variety of *textures.* The artist may simulate the *texture* of materials represented (Fig. 9–68) or create arbitrary surface differentiations as part of his design (Fig. 20–48). *Texture* modifies light, and light in turn explores the sensuous quality of matter.

The terms we have been discussing have connotations for all the visual arts. They may be more pertinent in one context than in another, but none of them is restricted to a given technique. As we approach the analysis of architecture, painting, and sculpture, however, certain observations are relevant to each which not only include a number of specialized terms, but also propose ways of looking or methods of analysis.

Architecture is the art of designing and constructing buildings. It may have archetypes in natural forms, such as the cave, a clearing, a forest, or a

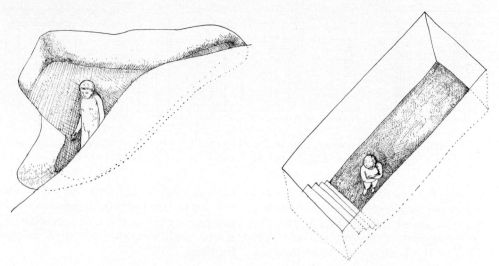

0–14 Diagrams illustrating varying spatial sensations. (After Ernö Goldfinger, *Architectural Review,* November, 1941, p. 130)

mountain; but it also has invented many of its own, such as the pavilion, the pagoda, or the skyscraper. Architecture is man's definition of physical space for his own use; and, since it creates its own environment, independent of nature although it may be in harmony with it, it has a dominating, positive psychological effect.

We first experience architecture directly through our vision, and we react intuitively to the spaces it creates as we move about or live in it. We may be confined or released, passively or oppressively bound by surrounding walls, or challenged and excited by their treatment (Fig. 0–14). Thus the plans of many modern buildings relate the interior with the exterior to create an organic sense of continuity (Figs. 0–15 and 23–14). In a *central* plan — one which radiates around a given point — such as the Pantheon in Rome, we immediately perceive a spatial entity, while the *axial* plan of a Christian basilica (Fig. 7–6) or a Gothic cathedral (Fig. 8–40) organizes space differently by controlling our attention and focusing it at a given point: the altar at the eastern end of the nave.

An architect must be trained as a mathematician and as an engineer. He must also have the sensibilities of a sculptor and of a painter. In establishing the plan of a building, the architect computes his areas and uses the instru-

0–15 MIES VAN DER ROHE. *German Pavilion,* International Exposition, Barcelona. Plan. 1929. (P. Johnson, *Mies van der Rohe,* Museum of Modern Art, 2nd ed., 1953) (See also Fig. 23–14.)

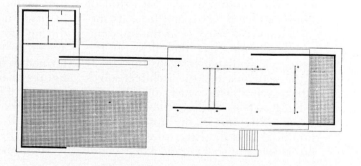

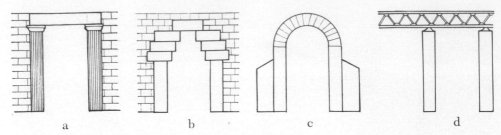

0–16 STRUCTURAL DEVICES. *a.* Post and lintel (cf. Fig. 5–9). *b.* Corbeled arch or vault (cf. Fig. 4–8). *c.* Arch (cf. Fig. 6–23). *d.* Cantilever (cf. Fig. 23–11).

ments of a mathematician. As he resolves the structural problems, he functions as an engineer (Fig. 0–16). In the treatment of the masses and volumes of the building, he must think as a sculptor; and, when he studies the control of lighting, as well as the textures and colors of his materials, he is dealing with light as does the painter (Fig. 8–57). His major responsibilities, however, lie in the manner in which he interprets the *program* of the building, for it is this totality of his efforts and of his abilities which results in the building itself.

Program is not an easy term to explain. It is often defined specifically as the function or use of a building or of a work of art in general, without adequate consideration of the full implications of words such as *use* or *function*. We do not talk in architectural terms when we describe a building simply as a church, a hospital, a railroad station, or a house. Any proposed building presents the architect with its own problems — problems arising from the site, as in the building of the cathedral of Bourges (see p. 256), and from its surroundings, the purpose of the building, the requirements of the client, or the materials available for construction. It is the way in which the architect solves all these problems which must be considered when we use the term *program*. *Program* is the totality of a building. It is the effect of this totality in all its details. *Program* for a build-

ing may be the incentive which prods the architect toward a solution, but program is more than an incentive; it is the total solution embodied in the building.

Sculpture exists, as does architecture, in the three-dimensional space of our physical world, but sculpture is closer to the realm of painting than is architecture. Until recently its preoccupations have been the representation of man and of natural forms in tangible materials, which exist in the same space as the forms of nature. Sculpture may embody in material form the subject of man's visions or of his highest ideals. It has consistently presented images of his deities and of himself in his most heroic as well as in his most human aspects (Fig. 0–17).

Sculpture may be intimately associated with architecture, often to such a degree that it is impossible to disassociate one from the other. Friezes, corbel tables, or moldings which trap light as accents in many forms and in varying degrees may be used sparingly, as in modern architecture, or lavishly, as during the seventeenth century (Fig. 10–8). In these instances it is normally termed *relief* sculpture, in which the figures or forms are attached to a background (Fig. 8–37). Sculpture is called *high relief* if the figures or design project boldly; low, or *bas relief*, if they project slightly (Fig. 3–18).

Sculpture also exists in its own right,

independently of any architectural frame or setting (Fig. 5–14). Then we usually refer to it as *free-standing* or in the round, although there are many occasions in the art of Greece and of the Renaissance when free-standing sculpture is closely allied to architecture. Indeed, sculpture is such a powerful agent in creating a spatial as well as an intellectual environment that its presence in city squares or in parks and gardens is usually the controlling factor in the atmosphere or general effect.

We view sculpture stereoscopically with both our eyes so that we perceive it as mass and volume in space. Some statues are to be seen as a whole — to be walked around. Others have been created for a specific environment and should be viewed only from a restricted angle. Our museum curators and our photographers often overlook the fact that a given piece of sculpture was meant to be viewed from a certain angle or to receive light in a given manner. The frieze of the *Parthenon* (Fig. 5–28), for example, was intended to be seen from below in a very restricted space between the columns of the peristyle and the wall of the cella, where the light on the frieze was reflected from below and was not received directly from the sun. Yet the fragments of this frieze as they are exhibited in the British Museum are only slightly above eye level; and most photographs of them are dramatically lit from above or from the side so that the original effect of the modeling is completely distorted. An equally startling contrast may be seen in Figure 0–18, in which the first photograph is taken directly from the front, as it is now seen in the museum, whereas the second one is taken from below, or from approximately the same angle at which the statue was originally meant to be seen in its niche on the façade of the cathedral of Florence. The sculptor is always aware of these vital factors

0–17 PARTHENON. Athens. Figure from the west pediment, probably to be identified as Dionysos, traditionally known as Theseus. 447–432 B.C. British Museum, London. (Trustees of the British Museum)

when he creates a statue; and they should not be ignored when the work is exhibited or reproduced for our study today.

In sculpture, perhaps more than in any other medium, textures, or tactile values, are important. One's first instinct is, almost always, to handle a piece of sculpture, to run one's finger over its surfaces. The sculptor is aware of this and sometimes leaves surfaces in apparently unfinished condition in order to achieve textural contrasts or visual effects (Fig. 9–74). Of course, such textures are initially part of the intrinsic quality of the material, and for this reason special attention must be given to the type of stone or wood, metal or clay in which the statue is created, as well as to the technique employed.

Two basic distinctions exist in sculptural techniques; and they may be described in terms identical to those used in the analyses of light, although the connotations are different. Carving, for instance, is a subtractive technique in that the final form is a reduction of the original mass. Additive sculpture, however, is built up, usually in clay, around

0-18 DONATELLO. *St. John the Evangelist.* Marble. 1412–1415. Museo del Duomo, Florence. Left, as seen in museum. Right, as intended to be seen on façade of the cathedral of Florence. (Alinari; Brogi)

an armature. The figure is then fired to become *terra cotta* or translated into some other material, such as bronze, cast stone, or even solid stone by the system of pointing. Many casting techniques are extremely complicated, as described by the sixteenth-century sculptor and goldsmith, Benvenuto Cellini, in his *Autobiography*. The opportunity to transform the matter of nature into an expression of man's most exalted ideals is at once the inspiration and the victory of the sculptor.

Related to sculpture in the three-dimensional forms they produce and in certain basic techniques are the widely practiced arts of ceramics and metalwork. But since these techniques are somewhat specialized and have their own distinct vocabularies, they must be described in some detail.

Pottery is shaped clay hardened by heat. It is one of the oldest and most universal of the arts. Most pottery, of course, is utilitarian. But often the quality of its form and decoration rank it as a major artistic medium, as, for instance, Greek vases, Nasca pottery, or Chinese porcelains (see pp. 131, 610, 566). According to the character of the clay and the degree of firing, pottery is earthenware, porcelain, or stoneware. Earthenware, the most common, has a relatively coarse base and is fired at low heat. Being porous, it requires treatment to render it impervious, though sometimes porosity is an advantage, as when evaporation is desired for cooling purposes. Porcelain is made of a fine clay, kaolin, to which feldspathic rock is added. Fired at a high temperature, it becomes vitreous throughout and thus impermeable. Porcelain can be shaped thin enough to be translucent, and when struck it produces a musical tone. Stoneware is of the same nature as porcelain but of a coarser texture, partially vitrified, and with relatively thick walls.

Whatever the character of the base, a general four-step process is applicable to all pottery: the preparation of the clay, the shaping, the decorating, and the firing. First the potter washes and wedges the clay to give it a smooth texture and to free it of air particles, after which he adds any other necessary ingredient, such as the feldspar in porcelain. He is then ready to shape it. If the piece is small, he may shape it with his fingers; or he may build the walls of ropelike coils of clay, which he can smooth with his fingers or some implement, or leave unsmoothed. Another method is to throw the clay on a wheel, shaping it with the hands as the mass revolves. Still another method is to press or pour the clay into a mold, the process suitable for mass production. The third step is drying to a leather-hard condition — hard enough to handle without injuring the shape — and decorating, usually with glaze. Polishing produces a texture which has a decorative quality of its own.

Glazing is one of the most universal methods for securing color, other decorative effects, and imperviousness. *Glaze* is melted glass, which may be transparent or opaque, glossy or mat; and it may be colored by the addition of metallic oxide. The glaze can be poured over the surface of the vessel, painted, or sprayed on; or, if the vessel is small, it can be dipped into the glaze. If the base is coarse, it must sometimes be covered with slip (clay thinned to a fluid consistency), to furnish a base for a transparent glaze.

Painting is another common method of decoration. The design may be painted on the slip and covered with the transparent glaze; or it may be painted over a glaze or done by the wax-painting process. In the latter method the design is painted in wax, and the object is then entirely covered with pigment and heated. As the wax melts off it leaves the original clay. Other decorative methods consist of relief, incising, stamping, or sgraffito — that is, covering the vessel with two coatings of slip or glaze of different colors and then, by cutting a design through the outer coat, producing a two-color pattern.

The final step in pottery-making is the firing. Often only one firing is sufficient; sometimes an extra one is necessary at the decorative stage. A further means of decoration added after firing is luster, a thin, transparent, metallic film which requires additional firing at low temperature, and which produces an evanescent, iridescent effect which may be seen particularly well in Islamic *Rhages* bowls (Fig. 13–16).

Metalwork is the term applied to a widely varied group of objects. All metals share, each to a varying degree, hardness, tenacity, and thus durability; they have opaque and reflecting surfaces. They also, in varying degrees, are fusible, capable of being molded and cast; ductile, capable of being drawn into wires or threads; and malleable, capable of being beaten or hammered into sheets, at times of incredible thinness, as in gold. For ornamentation, chasing or engraving is perhaps the simplest method; *repoussé* is also common. *Repoussé* consists of beating a sheet of metal into a mold of resistant material in such a way as not to break the metal, leaving a pattern in relief on one side and in intaglio on the other (Fig. 0–19). Another decorative process is *damascening*, inlaying in a metal base shapes or figures of other metals

0–19 Cover of the *Four Gospels. ca.* A.D. 870. Gold repoussé and jewels. Pierpont Morgan Library, New York. (Pierpont Morgan Library)

of different color and texture. Still another is *plating*, the coating of one metal wholly or in part with another.

Whereas the forms of architecture and sculpture exist in actual space, the forms of painting exist almost wholly on a two-dimensional surface, and their concern is to create an illusion. This illusion, however, becomes so convincing that we often forget that it is one, and we may tend to interpret painting in terms other than its own, which inevitably results in confusion and misunderstanding. We must resolutely keep in mind that painting is the creation of an illusion (compare for example the two entirely different interpretations of nature presented by El Greco in his *View of Toledo* [Fig. 0–20] and by Cézanne in his *Mont-Sainte-Victoire* [Fig. 20–19]). We must consider

each and every painting as a unique creation if we are to be better prepared to enjoy and ponder the mystery, as well as the magic, of the painter's art.

Painting is inescapably bound to the materials or *media* of which it is made and to the *techniques* which organize this matter. We have already discussed some of the problems relating to the pigments which form the hues on the painter's palette. The material used to bind these pigments to a surface constitute a *medium;* and all media have their own intrinsic qualities as well as their limitations. As in all the arts it is a primary requisite that an artist exhibit mastery of his *medium;* but such mastery by itself does not necessarily produce the greatest art. In the space at our disposal we cannot discuss all the *media* of painting, but we will mention a few to demonstrate their wide variety.

One of the simplest *media* is *pastel,* in which the pigments, in the form of powders, are compressed lightly into sticks. Since these sticks are then applied directly to the paper, like pencils, the medium is usually classified as drawing; but the delicate hues and fine gradations in value are closely allied to painting. In order to bind these powdery pigments to the surface, a fixative must be blown on once the work is finished.

Equally direct, from a technical point of view, is *water color,* in which the pigments are mixed with water and applied to an absorbent surface, such as paper or silk. Since the process of absorption is rapid, the medium lends itself to spontaneous expression with transparent, evanescent effects, but the master of this medium must have a sure eye and a quick hand, since his colors dry quickly and he cannot retouch or repaint an area without spoiling its effect (Fig. 0–21). *Gouache* is water color rendered opaque by the addition of a filler, such as zinc white.

0–20 EL GRECO. *View of Toledo*. 1604–1614. Metropolitan Museum of Art, New York. (Bequest of Mrs. H. O. Havemeyer, 1929; H. O. Havemeyer Collection)

It has more body and dries more slowly than the transparent water color and lends itself to bright color effects and meticulous detail, as in Persian miniatures (Fig. 13–14).

Fresco is painting on damp plaster with water color which becomes chemically incorporated with the surface and thus a part of the wall itself. The wall to be frescoed requires special preparation, usually several coats of plaster, before the final thin coat is laid on. A preliminary drawing, known as a cartoon, has previously been prepared and is then transferred to the moist surface. The colors which a fresco painter can use are limited to those — chiefly the earth colors — not affected by the calcium in the plaster. The technique requires clear thinking and unfaltering workmanship, for once the color is laid on it cannot be altered except by changes or additions made after the painting is dry. Alteration of this sort, called "dry" painting, is subject to the danger of subsequent peeling. Fresco, since it is actually incorporated as a part of the wall, is an appropriate architectural painting technique (Fig. 8–61).

In *tempera* painting the binding medium is egg yolk, or an equally viscous substance. It is a meticulous technique capable of striking effects and exact detail and is normally applied to especially prepared surfaces such as parchment, vellum, or wooden panels (Plate 5). The panel is first covered with linen, on which are laid layers of gesso (plaster of Paris) which are smoothed and polished to an ivory-like finish. On this surface the painter draws his design in detail; he then puts on an underpainting, usually of green for the figures and red for any areas to be covered with gold; finally he adds the individual colors in pigments mixed with egg yolk. As this medium dries quickly, he works with small brushes in fine strokes, a painstaking technique.

0–21 JOHN SINGER SARGENT. *The Pic-
nic*. Water color. *ca*. 1895. Museum of
Fine Arts, Boston. (Courtesy, Museum of
Fine Arts, Boston)

The result is a smooth hard surface
with bright hues and a linear, decorative quality.

Whereas *tempera* is essentially an
opaque medium, oil painting is translucent. Light penetrates the oil and is
refracted so that the surface is luminous and brilliant (Plate 6). As a vehicle for pigment, oil (normally linseed
oil) is slow in drying, allowing the
painter maximum flexibility in apply-
ing his pigments directly on a canvas or
on a variety of prepared surfaces. Since
its mastery in the fifteenth century in
Flanders, oil has been a favorite medium and its possibilities have been explored in many ways by Western artists.

Another important consideration in
looking at a painting has to do with the
way in which we see. We all realize

that we cannot see everything at once,
that our eyes are constantly moving,
constantly scanning the objects of our
attention, which are then rendered into complete images by the intricate
processes of our brain. What we often
forget is that, although the over-all
cone of our vision has an apex of about
60 degrees, the cone of actual focus is
only 1 degree. In other words, as we
look at a picture, we see only a very
small portion of its surface at any one
time, and it is as our eye scans the surface that the image is created. It is,
therefore, another function of the artist
to guide our eyes as we look at a painting, to bring order into what otherwise
might be chaos. This order we speak of
as the *composition*, or design, of a
painting (Fig. 0–22). It is its structure
and may be achieved in many different
ways: by geometric means, by lines or
curves, or by areas related in value or
in hue, which lead our eyes from portion to portion as they construct the image in our brain. Sometimes this order
is immediately apparent and we "read"
the picture easily; in other instances we
may have to search out the order if we
are to understand the artist's message
(see Fig. 20–67 and p. 727). As our
analyses of the different historical
styles progresses, we shall try to discover what types of order distinguish one
style from another; and we shall learn
that the bases for such order are often
keys to different ways of looking at the
world and of understanding the minds
of men.

In painting, as in sculpture, there are
special categories whose technical vocabularies need additional description.
First, there are drawings, and deriving
from them the graphic arts.

Some of the aspects of drawings have
already been described in our discussion of the term *line*. But their elusive
and particular qualities deserve further
mention. The word "draw" as defined
by Paul J. Sachs means:

0-22 A diagrammatic rendering of rhythmical relationships which are one of the unifying factors in the composition of the *School of Athens* by Raphael. (N. Stetson) Compare with Figs. 0–7 and 9–57.

to drag a pen or other instrument over a surface which leaves a mark behind it. To draw is to outline; to delineate; to represent a form or shape by means of light and shade alone or within a simple outline: — in short, to make a picture by such means. An artist's line has fundamental significance when it reveals form or design. . . . To draw lines or outlines is a way to express ideas — the grammar of art. Drawing is, indeed, the fundamental element in all great picture making, just as grammar is the root of all good writing . . . . it is in his drawings that the artist makes his most spontaneous statements, and enables us to follow his thought in the very act of creation.[4]

This may vividly be seen by comparing Cézanne's sketch of a card player (Fig. 0–1) with his painting of the *Card Players* (Fig. 20–20).

Although drawings may be made

[4] Paul J. Sachs, *The Pocket Book of Great Drawings*, pp. 1–2.

with any kind of instrument or substance which will leave a trace, there are several important tools to distinguish. *Pen and ink* has been universally used and in some instances with extraordinary preparation, as in China. *Charcoal* and chalks often enhance a basic drawing and give it tonalities; and *pencil* has been a favorite medium since its invention in the nineteenth century. One of the earliest instruments was a sharp stone, used to scratch a design in bone, as in the prehistoric drawing of a charging mammoth (Fig. 1–5). The favorite sharp drawing instrument of the Renaissance was the *silver point* (a sharp silver stylus) with which the artist drew on parchment or paper which had been coated with a thin colored ground of powdered bone mixed with gum water. The result is a pale gray line which is attractive by virtue of its crispness and clarity.

0–23 ALBRECHT DÜRER. *St. Christopher*. Woodcut. 1515. Yale University Art Gallery. (Yale Art Gallery)

The graphic arts involve the making of prints, and, since many prints can be made from one plate, works of art of the highest quality may often be acquired by the amateur or student at a reasonable price, with excellent opportunities for training one's eye.

Prints, impressions made from plates, vary in kind according to the process by which the plate is made. Though the finished print is usually on paper (and the selection of the paper is important), the work of the artist is concentrated chiefly on making the plate — always, however, with the effect of the print in mind. His materials are a plate of metal, a block of wood, or a slab of stone; tools suitable for each material; paper and ink; and a press or hand tools for printing. There are three important ways of making the plate: relief, intaglio, and planography.

The *woodcut* is the best example of *relief* (Fig. 0–23). On a block of wood the artist draws his design and then with knives and gouges cuts the wood away, leaving in relief the lines and surfaces he wishes to have take the ink.

The block is then inked and covered with a sheet of moist paper which, subjected to pressure, takes the ink from the parts of the plate it touches (the areas in relief), leaving the untouched parts (the areas cut back) in white. In cutting the wood the carver is generally restricted, because of the grain, to a simple direct expression in which the lines and areas are strong and bold, and transitions from black to white are abrupt. Prints in several colors can be made by cutting a separate block for each color, a technique superbly mastered by the Japanese (Figs. 16–1 and 16–20).

In *intaglio,* the second important method, the design is sunk into a plate, usually copper. Engraving, etching, and dry point are the chief examples. In *engraving,* the artist works with a steel graver, the burin, set in a wooden handle. Holding the tool so that its handle rests in the palm of his hand, he pushes it into the plate with enough force to cut the metal; and, according to the pressure and the angle at which he holds the tool, he can make his furrow narrow or broad, deep or shallow. In cutting the metal his burin raises ridges of metal, called burr, along the sides of the furrow; this he usually scrapes away so as to make his line clean-cut. The hardness of the metal and its resistance to his tool tend to produce a precise, crisp line, somewhat inflexible. Gradations of line can be secured by manipulation of the burin, gradations of tone by hatchings, that is, by engraving lines across those already engraved.

In *etching* the copper plate is covered with a protective ground of wax or varnish. In this the design is drawn with an etching needle, or any pointed tool which moves easily and lightly through the ground, exposing the metal below but not cutting into its surface. The plate is then immersed in an acid which etches, or bites, the exposed parts of the metal, acting in the same capacity as the burin in engraving. But the fact that the artist can make his design in a material as soft as wax frees him from the restrictions forced on the woodcutter and the engraver by their mediums and thus makes etching the most facile of the graphic arts in its process and the most capable of subtleties of line and tone. (See Fig. 10–22.)

In both engraving and etching the printing process is the same. The ink is thoroughly worked into the engraved or bitten furrows and the surface is cleaned. A sheet of moist paper is laid on the plate, and together the two are put through a press, where the ink is absorbed from the furrows and thus transferred to the paper.

Dry point is a process akin to both etching and engraving. It is similar to engraving in that the design is cut upon a metal plate by a steel needle; but it differs from engraving in that the burr is left on the plate. The rough surfaces, holding the ink, produce soft, furry lines, richly black. As the needle cuts only lightly into the plate, it can produce a much more delicate and flexible line than the burin in engraving.

The *planographic* process differs from relief and intaglio in that the printing surface is not cut or bitten, but retains its original surface or plane; a chemical action is utilized to make the plate. *Lithography* is such a process. On a special kind of stone which has been cut and polished, the design is drawn with a greasy crayon, or with a brush and specially prepared ink. The stone is then given a chemical treatment which does not affect the drawing but which prepares the rest of the surface to take up moisture. This surface is then moistened. An inked roller is then passed over the stone. The moistened surface repels the greasy ink, which only the lines of the drawing retain, just as the relief lines retain

0–24   HENRI   TOULOUSE-LAUTREC.   *Jane Avril* poster. Lithograph. *ca.* 1890. Museum of Modern Art, New York. (Museum of Modern Art)

the ink in the process of printing woodcuts. Then paper is pressed against the inked stone. Linear and tonal values of great range and subtlety characterize lithographs, because of the freedom possible in making the original drawing (Fig. 0–24).

Much more restricted in their design than the graphic arts are textiles. A textile is any woven fabric. Like pottery, textiles are ancient and universal because of their function — that of a covering. The materials of the weaver are fibers ranging from vegetable to synthetic. First the fibers are spun into threads, fine or coarse depending on their nature. The threads are strung on a loom which may be vertical or horizontal but consists fundamentally of two parallel beams, held firmly apart. These first threads constitute the warp, through which is interlaced the weft (woof, filling). The weaving process involves three fundamental steps: (1)

shedding — raising the warp thread to make a shed, through which (2) the weft is thrown or shot, and (3) battening — beating down the weft threads against the woven fabric. A great variety of weaves results from the manner in which the weft is inserted; for example, plain cloth, tapestry, twill, satin, and damask. Any weave can be enriched with additional weft, as in embroidery, brocades, and pile fabrics.

Textile form is two-dimensional. In the weaving process, the artist makes and organizes his surface at the same time; and in doing this he uses the organizing elements that are two-dimensional: line, areas of color and texture, and light and dark. Texture is one of the most important elements — the actual "feel" of a fabric as well as its visual quality. The smooth lustrous character of satin or linen, for example, appeals equally to the senses of touch and of sight. Even color, as we have seen, is somewhat dependent upon texture, for one hue will have different values in different weaves such as satin or velvet. Intricate patterns, sensed by both the touch and the eye, can be woven in one color alone; and highly complex designs result from combining several weaves and colors. The artist can also produce patterns by painting or stamping a design upon a piece already woven, a process used largely today in machine-made fabrics. *Batik* is another decorative process in which the artist draws his design on cloth — usually white cotton cloth — and covers with wax the areas he wishes to have remain white. He then dips the cloth into a pigment, which the unpainted areas absorb. The wax is then melted off, leaving white the areas it covered. A similar process has already been noted in the decoration of ceramics.

Finally, we turn to problems and words having to do with the meaning of a work of art.[5] At the very start, it will be useful to distinguish between the terms *image, sign,* and *symbol.* A *natural image* is the image which forms make on our retina. It is what something looks like. In a painting, say, of a still life, we recognize the different objects because of their resemblance to certain forms in nature. This is an apple because it looks like an apple. It is the *image* of an apple. It is a one-to-one relationship, and everything would be very simple if the problem of meaning was no more complicated than that. Unfortunately, forms often have very different meanings from the objects they resemble; and there are also possible images other than the natural, or visual, image. There is, for instance, the *conceptual,* or *mental, image* of something. In Chapter 19 on primitive art mention is made of the difference between two portraits of a Maori chief. In one a Western artist painted a portrait of this chief, producing a visual image of the chief's head: his ornaments, tattoos, and other details which he saw. In the other the chieftain produced a self-portrait which recorded only the tattoo marks in a highly ornamental and abstract manner. These were his marks of distinction. They differentiated him from other chiefs and constituted his idea of what he looked like (see p. 633). In our terms the result is a conceptual rather than a natural, or visual image; and the same is true wherever something more, something different, than what we can actually see of an object or person is included in the image.

As civilization has developed and man's ideas have become more and more complex, he has established more and more conventions to embody or to

[5] Unfortunately the word "meaning" has been given so many meanings as to be almost meaningless. An excellent discussion of this problem is in C. K. Ogden and I. A. Richards, *The Meaning of Meaning.*

signify such ideas. These conventions usually involve a given form, which it is agreed will mean a certain thing. Such a form then becomes the *symbol* of something else. The letters, and words, we use here are symbols. We can usually differentiate between certain levels of complexity, and it is often helpful to distinguish between a *sign* and a *symbol,* although, since both of them have meanings other than what they look like, they both qualify as *symbols.* A *sign* has essentially a direct, specific relationship. A single horizontal line (—) is the sign for minus. Two lines intersecting at right angles are a plus sign (+). If the vertical line is extended to form a † we have an entirely different set of meanings, as complex as Christianity itself, and this form is then a *symbol.* We may do the same thing with the ☾ which as a *form* is the *image* of an apple. It may appear drawn on a signboard as a golden apple to identify an inn, and as long as it refers to that particular inn, it is a *sign.* Our experience at the inn may be pleasant or otherwise and immediately the apple may take on other connotations, so that it becomes a *symbol.* Thus in classic mythology the apple which Paris finally presented to Aphrodite was the *symbol* of beauty and love. But for Christians the apple signifies the fall of man; it is the *symbol* of evil.

The study of these images, and of their meanings, is called *iconography.*[6]

[6] In Greek εἰκών (icon, ikon, or eikon) means likeness, image, picture. Although modern critics of literature have revived and given emphasis to this meaning of *icon,* its use in the history of the visual arts has the special connotation of a painting, piece of sculpture, or even of a building which is regarded as an object of veneration. It is in this sense that *icon* is used in this book. For a more detailed analysis of iconography and iconology and their methods, see Erwin Panofsky, *Studies in Iconology.* The important Introduction to these *Studies* has been reprinted in Panofsky's *Meaning in the Visual Arts.*

Such a study, quite naturally, requires an intimate knowledge of the literature, legends, folklore, and thought of any given people or generation, and for this reason is attractive to the erudite, who delight in the discovery of solutions for iconographical puzzles. However, if such a study goes beyond the identification of images and symbols and approaches the interpretation of a work of art as a synthetic expression of an historical moment, then the study is more properly distinguished as *iconological.*

But works of art have as many facets, as many different avenues of approach, as the men who with varying interests or different objectives undertake their study. The *archeologist,* for instance, searches to uncover lost monuments and works of art. With meticulous care and scientific precision he will excavate a site in the hope that sufficient remains will be discovered to enable him to reconstruct a building, a site, or an individual work of art. His task is that of discovery, of recovery, and of assigning accurate historical dates. If he interprets the results of his work, he leaves the realm of pure archeology to enter that of the iconologist and historian of art.

Another approach to the study of works of art is that of the *connoisseur,* who, in seeking criteria for the attribution of a work of art to a given artist, is concerned with the problem of *style.*

Style has two very different meanings. In its generic sense the word indicates a special and superior quality in a work of art. In this sense it is an absolute, since it creates standards which distinguish between superior and mediocre achievements. When a given work of art has *style,* it has attained a degree of excellence which sets it apart. When a work of art belongs to a *style,* however, the connotations are entirely different. "A style" is a development, a coherent grouping of forms united by a reciprocal fitness. For the Greeks it was the proportions of the shaft of a column which defined a style and distinguished between, not the quality, but the coherent vocabulary of forms which constituted the Doric, as distinct from the Ionic, order or style. It is the reciprocal fitness of certain measurements, and of certain ways of interpreting space, which defines Romanesque as a style not to be confused with Gothic; and the same is true of any of the long list of styles with which this volume will be concerned.

The study of individual characteristics and idiosyncrasies by which the personal style of an artist may be determined was developed by an Italian, Giovanni Morelli, in the nineteenth century. He observed that every artist developed a particular way in which to treat such details as the lobe of an ear, or fingernails, or hair, and that once devised, this method was always retained. Such constants in the style of a given individual or in any style are known as Morellian characteristics and often prove to be extremely helpful in stylistic analyses. The *connoisseur* of style,[7] or of a style, must develop a very sensitive eye and a profound visual memory, and yet, since his preoccupations are often limited to details and his judgments are normally formed about a given, more or less limited, historical period, he is often at a loss to assess or to understand the styles of other eras.

It was also in the nineteenth century that, in an effort to reach a fuller understanding of the meaning of art, certain artists, philosophers, and historians turned to the work of art itself and to the creative activity which produced it as the necessary point of departure for an analysis or understanding of art.[8] Since one of their primary concerns was the analysis of form, they are known generally as *morphologists,* a term borrowed directly from the natural sciences. For many, their insistence on the validity of each work of art as an interpretation of the world of nature as well as of the world of ideas, quite apart from any given philosophical system, has provided the least restrictive approach to the entire problem of defining art.

As beginners, it is, perhaps, sufficient that we should be aware of such different approaches to a work of art. But a word of warning is necessary. It is dangerous, particularly at the beginning, to adopt one approach to the understanding of art in favor of another. The true historian will keep his mind open and will when necessary modify his approach to the specific conditions presented by the individual work of art.

Each generation develops a vocabulary and a style of its own, as well as its own interpretation of history. The history of art, like any other historical study, needs, therefore, to be rewritten or reappraised at regular intervals. The vitality of a work of art lies in its provoking new interpretations without undergoing change in itself. This is the life of a work of art, which we have already said is the fulfillment of its program. To learn to see, to recognize and interpret different styles, to learn to experience a work of art, is our aim in this book.

[8] See A. Hildebrand, *The Problem of Form in Painting and Sculpture;* Konrad Fiedler, *On Judging Works of Visual Art;* Heinrich Wölfflin, *Principles of Art History;* and Henri Foçillon, *The Life of Forms in Art.*

Bibliography

Arnheim, Rudolph, *Art and Visual Perception,* University of California Press, Berkeley, 1954.
——, *The Art and Technique of Ceramics,* Brooklyn Museum, New York, 1937.

[7] One of the outstanding connoisseurs of this century is Bernard Berenson, whose studies of *Italian Painters of the Renaissance* are excellent demonstrations of this approach to painting.

Berenson, Bernard, *The Italian Painters of the Renaissance,* Phaidon Publishers, New York, 1952.

Bergson, Henri, *The Creative Mind,* Wisdom Library, New York, 1946.

Blossfeldt, Karl, *Art Forms in Nature,* Weyhe, New York, 1929.

Braun-Feldweg, Wilhelm, *Metall,* Otto Maier, Ravensburg, Germany, 1950.

Casson, Stanley, *The Technique of Early Greek Sculpture,* Oxford University Press, New York, 1933.

Cellini, Benvenuto, *Autobiography,* Modern Library, New York, 1927.

Croce, Benedetto, *Aesthetic as Science of Expression and General Linguistic,* Noonday Press, New York, 1953.

Curwen, Harold, *Processes of Graphic Reproduction in Painting,* Faber & Faber, London, 1949.

Doerner, Max, *The Materials of the Artist,* tr. by Eugen Neuhaus, Harcourt, Brace, 1949.

Durst, Alan L., *Wood Carving,* Studio Publications, New York, 1938.

Edman, Irwin, *Arts and the Man,* Norton, New York, 1939.

Evans, Ralph M., *An Introduction to Color,* Wiley, New York, 1948.

Fiedler, Konrad, *On Judging Works of Visual Art,* University of California Press, Berkeley, 1949.

Focillon, Henri, *The Life of Forms in Art,* Wittenborn, New York, 1957.

Friedländer, Max J., *Art and Connoisseurship,* B. Cassirer, London, 1942.

Fry, Roger Eliot, *Vision and Design,* Brentano's, New York, 1924.

Giedion, Sigfried, *Space, Time and Architecture,* Harvard University Press, 1954.

Goldwater, R., and Treves, M., *Artists on Art,* Pantheon Books, New York, 1945.

Hayes, Bartlett H., and Rathbun, Mary C., *Layman's Guide to Modern Art,* Addison Gallery, Andover, Mass., 1954.

Hildebrand, Adolf, *The Problem of Form in Painting and Sculpture,* G. E. Stechert, New York, 1945.

Holt, Elizabeth B., *Literary Sources of Art History,* Princeton University Press, 1947.

Honey, W. B., *The Art of the Potter,* Faber & Faber, London, 1946.

Hooper, Luther, *Hand-Loom Weaving,* Pitman, New York, 1920.

Ivins, William M., *How Prints Look,* Metropolitan Museum of Art, New York, 1943.

Kenny, John B., *Ceramic Sculpture,* Greenberg, New York, 1953.

Kepes, Gyorgy, *Language of Vision,* Theobald, Chicago, 1944.

Kronquist, Emil, and Pelikan, A. G., *Simple Metalwork,* Studio Publications, New York, 1940.

Le Corbusier (pseud. of Charles E. Jeanneret-Gris), *Towards a New Architecture,* Payson & Clarke, New York, 1927.

Malraux, André, *The Voices of Silence,* Doubleday, 1953.

Mayer, Ralph, *Artist's Handbook of Materials and Techniques,* Viking, New York, 1957.

McMahon, Ames P., *The Art of Enjoying Art,* McGraw-Hill, 1938.

Ogden, C. K., and Richards, I. A., *The Meaning of Meaning,* Harcourt, Brace, 1923.

Opdyke, George H., *Art and Nature Appreciation,* Macmillan, New York, 1932.

Osborne, H., *Theory of Beauty,* Philosophical Library, New York, 1953.

Panofsky, Erwin, *Meaning in the Visual Arts,* Anchor Books, Garden City, N. Y., 1955.

——, *Studies in Iconology,* Oxford University Press, New York, 1939.

Pearson, Ralph M., *Experiencing Pictures,* Harcourt, Brace, 1932.

Pope, A., *The Language of Drawing and Painting,* Harvard University Press, 1949.

Read, Herbert, *Art and Society,* Faber & Faber, London, 1945.

Reath, Nancy A., *The Weaves of Hand-Loom Fabrics,* Pennsylvania Museum, Philadelphia, 1927.

Rich, Jack C., *The Materials and Methods of Sculpture,* Oxford University Press, New York, 1947.

Sachs, Paul J., *The Pocket Book of Great Drawings,* Dell, New York, 1951.

Santayana, George, *The Sense of Beauty,* Dover Publications, New York, 1955.

Scott, Robert G., *Design Fundamentals,* McGraw-Hill, 1951.

Seymour, Charles, *Tradition and Experiment in Modern Sculpture,* American University Press, Washington, D. C., 1949.

Shahn, Ben, *The Shape of Content,* Harvard University Press, Cambridge, 1957.

Sloan, John, *Gist of Art,* American Artists Group, New York, 1939.

Venturi, Lionello, *Painting and Painters,* Scribner's, 1945.

Watrous, James, *The Craft of Old-Master Drawings,* University of Wisconsin Press, Madison, 1957.

Weitenkampf, Frank, *How to Appreciate Prints,* rev. ed., Scribner's, 1932.

Wengenroth, Stow, *Making a Lithograph,* Studio Publications, New York, 1936.

Whyte, Lancelot L., *Accent on Form,* Harper, 1954.

Wölfflin, Heinrich, *Principles of Art History,* Dover Publications, New York, 1950.

ANCIENT
ART

O UR knowledge of prehistory throughout the world derives from the evidence of geology and paleontology, and from man's artifacts. Wherever the art of prehistoric man appears, certain basic similarities provide a common vocabulary; indeed, we might almost call prehistoric art the first and last truly International style. But fundamental and often striking differences distinguish the styles of all early civilizations. The transformation of relatively similar prehistoric cultures into distinctive civilizations is a process still not fully understood, but even the least tutored student may readily learn to identify differences between the arts of the different civilizations.

The civilizations which arose in the lands around the Mediterranean were the cradle of our Western culture, and because our heritage is that of western Europe we refer to these early Mediterranean civilizations as the ancient world. In this section therefore we shall discuss first the art of prehistoric man in western Europe and then the art of the early cultures in Egypt, the Middle East, and the Aegean Sea. Finally we shall discuss the arts of Greece and Rome which in Classical terms constitute the world of Antiquity.

Recent archaeological and linguistic research indicates that the Middle East was the true cradle of Western civilization. But we still treat Egyptian art first because its relative simplicity and stability will enable us to understand the complexity and individualism of the Tigris-Euphrates valley. We shall mark the spontaneity and comparative brevity of the Minoan and Mycenaean cultures, whose people and spirit may be the first properly identifiable as Mediterranean.

In Greece we shall study the first formulation and exposition of the ideals of the Western world. To the order of geometry the Greeks added the concept of beauty in terms of moral values, in perfect equilibrium with the study and representation of man and the world of nature: *mimesis*. With a vigorous Italic and Etruscan background the Romans established the Pax Romana, which brought peace to the Mediterranean basin for more than three centuries. Administrative talent and engineering prowess encouraged the growth of Roman urban complexes, a setting in which the individual competed fiercely. But Romans were also concerned with individual salvation and with the brotherhood of man, which fostered the growth of Christianity — the final contribution of the world of Antiquity to Western civilization.

◄ CHARIOTEER OF DELPHI. *ca.* 475 B.C. H. 6 ft. Delphi Museum. (Alinari)

CHAPTER 1

PREHISTORIC

Paleolithic Art

When in the long development of human life did art first appear? What was its character? Was it childishly crude, or did it reveal any grasp of those fundamentals which underlie all great art expression? To answer these questions, we must turn to prehistoric archeology — the study of the remains of man's activity which date from the period before the invention of writing. We shall start with the time of the first appearance of man, which is known as the Pleistocene.

The Pleistocene epoch began approximately half a million years ago. In Europe, it was marked by at least four periods of low temperature, during each of which a great ice sheet advanced south from Scandinavia over the plains of north central Europe and glaciers spread down from the Alps and other mountain ranges to produce climatic conditions very much like those of Greenland today. These cold periods are known as glacial stages. They were separated by at least three warm, interglacial stages during which the ice receded and the climate in western Europe became comparable in many respects with that in North Africa today. It has been possible to subdivide the final glacial stage into an early and a main advance, separated by a retreat of the ice, and to distinguish a series of intervening fluctuations (Fig. 1–2). These fluctuations ended about 8000 B.C. in Scandinavia, although the withdrawal of the ice had begun earlier to the south.

ILLUSTRATION ABOVE. 1–1 BISON WITH TURNED HEAD. Carved in reindeer horn. From the rock shelter La Madeleine, Dordogne. Magdalenian. Musée des Antiquités Nationales, Saint-Germain-en-Laye. (American Museum of Natural History)

FLINTS

The oldest definite traces of man are from the earliest known glacial stage and the subsequent interglacial stage.

Glacial Stages	Cultural Periods	Paleolithic Traditions and Phases
Postglacial (since 8000 B.C. in Scandanavia)	IRON / BRONZE / NEOLITHIC / MESOLITHIC	
Glacial stage — Later fluctuations / Main advance / Retreat	UPPER PALEOLITHIC	Aurignacian, Solutrean, Magdalenian
Glacial stage — Early advance	MIDDLE PALEOLITHIC	Levalloisian, Mousterian, Micoquean
Interglacial		
Glacial stage	LOWER PALEOLITHIC	Clactonian — Acheulean
Interglacial		
Glacial stage		Abbevillean
Interglacial	?	Flake Tradition — Core Tradition — Blade Tradition
Glacial stage		Eoliths (?)

1–2 This chart (to be read up) shows how geologists and archeologists currently conceive of the relationships between climatic change and cultural development in western Europe.

So far, these remains have been found only in Africa. Many archeologists now think that man originated there; moved northward through the Sahara region, which was probably moist at that time; and crossed the Mediterranean into Europe over then-existent land bridges. The few finds, believed to be implements, of this period in Europe are termed eoliths. They consist of stones which were supposedly picked up and used in their natural state, so that they bear the marks of use, but not of manufacture. Man may at this time have relied primarily upon wooden tools, but, if so, these have not survived the passage of time.

With the beginning of the next stage, man in Europe entered the Paleolithic or Old Stone Age. He produced implements by knocking flakes off stones and by chipping pebbles into shape, but had not yet learned the Neolithic or New Stone Age skills of grinding stone and making pottery. Archeologists subdivide the Paleolithic of Europe into three periods: Lower Paleolithic, Middle Paleolithic, and Upper Paleolithic (Fig. 1–2).

Most archeologists now recognize the existence of two great contemporary traditions of toolmaking in Europe during the Lower Paleolithic period. One, a *Flake* tradition, appears to have been a *local* development. In this tradition, the craftsman selected a pebble, generally one of flint, and, by striking it with a hammerstone, knocked off a succession of thin, sharp flakes. He used these flakes as tools, and discarded the core of the pebble from which the flakes had been struck.

The second toolmaking tradition, the *Core* tradition, is believed to have originated in Africa. Its original, African phases are characterized by tools known as pebble choppers, made by knocking chips off one edge of a waterworn stone in order to sharpen the edge. This Core tradition is so called because the tool is made from the original pebble or core and not from flakes struck off the core; indeed, the chopper still retains the shape of the original pebble except for its sharpened edge.

By the time the Core tradition arrived in Europe, the process of chipping had been extended from the edge of the pebble to cover both surfaces — it is therefore called bifacial — so that the tool no longer retains the original shape of the pebble. In the Abbevillean or first European phase of the tradition the tools are identified as hand axes because they consist of blades which are pointed at one end and were probably grasped by the other end and used either as weapons or perhaps for digging in the soil. In the subsequent, Acheulean phase, the chipping is better done and a second form of tool, the cleaver, with a rectangular rather than a pointed end, is added.

In the Core tradition we may recognize that, of two flints which were cut equally well, one is more pleasing than the other because of a quality of form which has nothing to do with the utility of the tool. Such a feeling for form, for a balance between the *what* and the *how*, we recognize as a fundamental artistic impulse.

Of the physical characteristics of the Lower Paleolithic men who developed the Flake and Core traditions, we know practically nothing. Unfortunately, almost all the inhabited Lower Paleolithic sites of Europe have been washed away by rivers and only the most resistant stone tools have survived the action of water. We are not even certain that these men possessed fire, although it is clear that Paleolithic man in China had fire at this time.

The Middle Paleolithic phase of the Core tradition is known as Micoquean. Micoquean hand axes are the finest of all — smaller, thinner, and beautifully worked over both surfaces. The Micoquean people also made some flake

a   b   c

1–3   SOLUTREAN FLINTS. *a*. Laurel-leaf point. From Solutré. Scale ⅓. *b*. Willow-leaf knife from the Grotte de l'Eglise at Saint-Martin d'Excedeuil, Dordogne. Scale ca. ⅔. *c*. Point or graver from cave of La Marie at Teyjat, Dordogne. Scale ⅔.

tools, but these are not so well made nor are they bifacially worked, for the technique seems to have been copied from that of the Flake tradition with practically no modification.

Middle Paleolithic man discovered the advantages of living in caves and under overhanging ledges of rock, and as a result the vestiges of his culture are much better preserved than those of Lower Paleolithic time. We have evidence that he was a hunter and knew the use of fire. A few crude bone tools have survived in the sites. Some Mousterian people seem to have picked up stone objects and brought them to the dwellings because they had the appearance of animals or birds. These "figure stones," which have been discovered together with obviously manufactured pieces, are evidence of an artistic instinct as well as, possibly, of an early symbolic intent.

Many traces of human burial date from the Middle Paleolithic period. At least one skeleton can be identified as *Homo sapiens,* for it is in every respect similar to modern man. The majority of the finds, however, are of *Homo neanderthalensis,* a more primitive form of man who had a stooping posture, heavy brow ridges, and a receding chin, although his brain was as large as that of modern man.

With the retreat of the glaciers at the beginning of Upper Paleolithic time, the way was opened for new groups of people to migrate into western Europe from Asia and the Near East. These included various forms of *Homo sapiens,* such as the Cro-Magnon race, which overwhelmed the preceding Neanderthal inhabitants.

The Upper Paleolithic newcomers brought with them a new method of making tools which is known as the *Blade* tradition. This was basically an improved Flake technique. The craftsman carefully shaped his core into the form of a prism so that he was able to strike off a succession of long, narrow blades in place of the broad, more irregular flakes of Middle Paleolithic time. In the first and most widespread phase of the tradition, the Aurignacian, the blades were trimmed only on the edges, as in the Flake tradition.

In a subsequent, Solutrean phase the artisans applied the bifacial technique to their blades, producing thin,

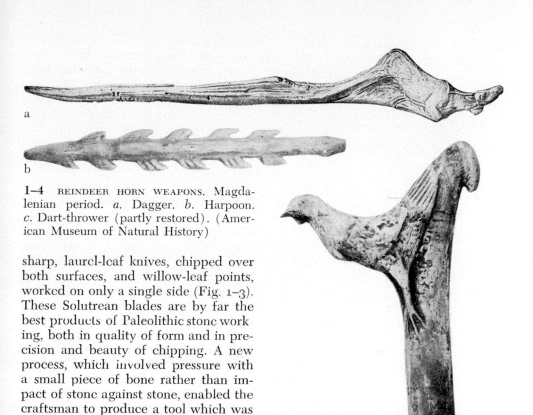

a

b

1–4 REINDEER HORN WEAPONS. Magdalenian period. *a.* Dagger. *b.* Harpoon. *c.* Dart-thrower (partly restored). (American Museum of Natural History)

c

sharp, laurel-leaf knives, chipped over both surfaces, and willow-leaf points, worked on only a single side (Fig. 1–3). These Solutrean blades are by far the best products of Paleolithic stone working, both in quality of form and in precision and beauty of chipping. A new process, which involved pressure with a small piece of bone rather than impact of stone against stone, enabled the craftsman to produce a tool which was even more pleasing to the eye. There is refinement in shape, proportion, and character of the curve, together with a rhythmic movement over the surface formed by the scars of chipping.

In southern France and northern Spain the Solutrean phase was succeeded by the Magdalenian, in which the craftsmen reverted to the custom of trimming only the edges of blades. The same kinds of blades were made as before and, once again, little attention was paid to form and appearance.

Upper Paleolithic man continued to live in caves and rock shelters and to bury his dead there, laying out the body with ornaments and tools for use in a life after death. The bodies were frequently sprinkled with red ocher as is done among many modern primitive people. Man was still primarily a hunter and, by the Magdalenian phase,[1] is

[1] The age of the Magdalenian phase has been determined by the new method of radiocarbon analysis. A by-product of atomic re-

search, this method depends upon the fact that, as living things absorb carbon dioxide from the air, they take in with it minute quantities of a radioactive form of carbon known as carbon 14. Each organism retains the same relative amount of carbon 14 so long as it is alive, but normally ceases to take in any more after death. Instead, the carbon 14 already present begins to disintegrate into nitrogen 14, which is nonradioactive. The rate of disintegration is always the same. Knowing the original quantity of carbon 14 and the rate of disintegration, scientists are able to calculate from the amount of radioactivity still to be found in any organic matter just how long it has been since the organism died. This method has been applied to charcoal and carbonized bone found in Magdalenian sites and has yielded dates of about 14,000 to 9000 B.C. for the Magdalenian phase.

1–5 CHARGING MAMMOTH. Engraved on a piece of ivory tusk. Dordogne. Musée D'Archéologie, Jardin des Plantes, Paris. (American Museum of Natural History)

thought to have clothed himself in skins, which he had learned to sew together with bone needles.

CARVINGS AND ENGRAVINGS

The Aurignacian craftsmen made increasing use of bone, horn, and ivory. This trend was interrupted in the Solutrean phase, with its emphasis upon fine stone chipping, but was resumed in the Magdalenian phase, in which bone, horn, and ivory artifacts are the outstanding products. From these materials the Magdalenian craftsmen fashioned bone javelin points, needles, harpoons, arrow straighteners, batons, and dart-throwers or throwing sticks (Fig. 1–4).

There was a similar trend toward bonework in other parts of the Old World at this time, notably in central Europe, the Ukraine, and southern Siberia, but nowhere did it attain the degree of elaboration and refinement that it did in western Europe. The Magdalenian craftsmen not only made a greater variety of bone artifacts but also decorated them in a more complex and sophisticated manner, sometimes with lines and conventional patterns, sometimes with an animal form. In Figure 1–4*a*, for example, a reindeer has been carved as the handle of a dagger in such a way that the fig-

ure is not "applied" to the surface. Note, rather, how the extended head and neck, the folded forelegs, the raised rump follow the original form of the bone and yet provide an easily grasped handle. To feel such a relationship between the original material and the animal form requires intelligence and sensitivity.

On stone, ivory, and horn, on both flat and curving surfaces the hunter-artist engraved many figures. Some were linear or geometric ornament;[2] a great many were animals. In the *Bison with Turned Head* (Fig. 1–1), we are impressed partly by its striking vitality and partly by the formal beauty expressed by the simplest means. The head is so turned that it is entirely framed by the massive bulk of the body, and its pattern involves a vivid play of curve and countercurve and a surface contrast obtained by the use of incised lines as a decorative convention to indicate the mane. Figure 1–5 shows an infuriated mammoth charging forward. Here is a largeness, a strikingly direct statement of a few essentials, expressed by a line so sure and so economical that it incorporates all details without specifically stating them. The keen-visioned hunter-artist had observed the action of every part of the animal, and with phenomenal memory he transferred the vision, with a sharp flint point, to the piece of horn. In the *Deer and Salmonid* (Fig 1–6) there seems to be a conscious grouping of several figures. The movements of each animal and the forward movement of the group are portrayed by a few essential lines. Even the backward turn of one head, which may represent the animal calling to the herd, helps the artist to integrate the head and antlers with the other figures without overlapping, which seems to have been deliberately avoided, as one notes in

[2] Many of these engraved pieces are fragments and thus their purpose is unknown.

1–6   DEER AND SALMONID. Engraved reindeer antler. L. 5½ in. Magdalenian. From the Cave Lorthet, Hautes Pyrénées. Musée de Saint-Germain-en-Laye. (American Museum of Natural History)

the placing of the fish. These fish may symbolize a stream, while the significance of the two lozenges above the stag is not known.

PAINTING

During the Upper Paleolithic Age, notably in the Magdalenian phase, there are extraordinary expressions of man's artistic abilities. In the caves of southern France and northern Spain are numerous paintings and sculptures, often beautifully preserved and so startling in their effect that it is no wonder they amazed and perplexed their discoverers (Fig. 1–7). These caverns were subterranean water channels varying in length from a few hundred to some four thousand feet and are often now choked, at places almost impassably, by faults or by deposits, such as stalactites and stalagmites. Far inside these caverns the hunter-artist, in utter quiet, engraved and painted on the walls many pictures, chiefly of animals. For light he used a tiny stone lamp, filled with marrow or fat and supplied with a wick, perhaps of moss. For drawing he used chunks of red and yellow ocher, and for painting he ground these same ochers into powder, which he blew on the walls or mixed with some medium, perhaps animal fat. A large flat bone served him as palette; he could make brushes from reeds or bristles; he could use a blowpipe of reeds to trace outlines of figures and to put pigments on out-of-reach surfaces; he had stone scrapers for smoothing the wall, and sharp flint points for engraving. Such was his array of tools.

The artist often used the contours of the cavern surfaces to enhance the realism of his image. In the Two Bison from Lascaux [3] (Plate 1) for instance, the bulging rocks lend mass and even movement to the shoulders of the running animals. By superimposing their rumps and by carefully rendering the

[3] The caves at Lascaux, near Montignac, France, were discovered accidentally in 1941 by two young boys who were playing in a field with their dog. Their ball disappeared in a hole and so did the dog. Soon they could hear barking resounding from below and they found another hole large enough for them to crawl down. Their lighted matches revealed the magnificent animals, now generally regarded as the most remarkable of all prehistoric art.

1–7 CAVE OF LASCAUX, MONTIGNAC, FRANCE. General view, interior. Paintings *ca.* 15,000 B.C. (From *Four Hundred Years of Cave Art,* realized by F. Windels)

legs, the artist has created an additional illusion of space, so forceful that the bison seem to be charging out from the wall.

In a drawing of a *Woolly Rhinoceros* at Font-de-Gaume, there is the same understanding of the animal form, equally convincing and monumental. Here the contour is broken and more varied, and is accented at points as if to suggest the mass of the figure, while short lines indicate hair and serve as rudimentary shading.

The *Reindeer* of Figure 1–8 was first incised on the wall, which had been somewhat smoothed by a scraper; it was then outlined in paint, and finally the details were added, and the figure was modeled in various tones. The image of nature is most convincing. Yet note the line of the back, and the beauty of line as line in the horns. In the painted figure, as in the chalk

drawings, there is a vitality, whether the figure is at rest or in movement, which makes it not a dead image but a living creature.

There is great variety in these primeval paintings, variety both of animal and of pose — mammoth, bison, reindeer, horse, boar, wolf (at Lascaux there is even one unidentifiable animal, covered with spots and with a single long horn). The individual figures are sometimes superimposed, one on another, with no relationship to each other or to the wall space. They may represent the renewed efforts of succeeding generations or they may indicate that the act of rendering an image fulfilled in itself the purpose of the artist. Although most of the animals are depicted singly, there are notable exceptions, such as the *Procession of Mammoths* at Font-de-Gaume; or the herd of deer swimming a river at Las-

1–8 REINDEER. Painting. Cave of Font-de-Gaume, France. *ca.* 15,000 B.C. (Cartaillac and Breuil)

caux. Each painting reflects the keen observation of the hunter-artist, and especially an extraordinary memory for instantaneous poses, whose accuracy has been proved and hardly surpassed by the motion-picture camera of today. Yet this observation was of the selective type. It saw and recorded only those essential aspects which interpret the appearance and the character of the animal, its grace or awkwardness, its cunning or dignity.

The naturalistic pictures of animals are often accompanied by geometric signs, some of which are roof- or comb-shaped, while others consist of checkers, dots, squares, or other arrangements of lines. Several observers have professed to see a primitive form of writing in these representations of non-living things, but more likely they had magical significance. The ones which look like traps or snares, for example, may have been drawn to ensure success in hunting with these devices.

But why were these paintings hidden in dark caverns deep in the earth? Some scholars explain them as expression only, an outlet of an artistic impulse for its own sake in terms of the artist's own environment as a hunter. Others, with more probability and by analogy with practices of primitive peo-

ples of today, see in them a magical purpose. These obscure isolated caverns may have been sacred places, and the bison painted on the wall may have been intended to bring success in the hunt, as the ibex carved on the dart-thrower may have been believed to make the arm more sure and powerful in bringing down the game. The painting of these images may have been part of the psychic preparation of the hunters before they sallied forth from the caves with their crude weapons, just as the images may have been supposed to exert magical compulsion on the animals represented. Whatever the purpose, the artist displayed his keen hunter's knowledge and the sureness of his hand, of his own artistic instinct.

Man also is represented in these paintings. At Lascaux, deep in a shaft, he is shown as a symbol — a stick man — dead or dying during an attack on a mammoth. This may have been a scene commemorative of a disaster. In the caves of Addaura, discovered between 1945 and 1947 at Monte Pellegrino near Palermo, Sicily, there are paintings of men, less intense perhaps in the rendering of natural forms, but interesting for the representation of man in what must have been ritual ceremonies performed with dancelike movements.

1–9 HUNTERS. Paintings. H. *ca.* 4 in. Caves of eastern Spain. (After Obermaier and Wernert)

In southeastern Spain paintings of a different, and not yet entirely explicable, nature have been discovered. They are but a few inches in size and consist of a whole group of figures, both human and animal. Hunting, fighting, and dancing scenes are expressed with great vigor and with an exaggeration of movement that is in distinct contrast to the imposing dignity and serenity of the paintings at Lascaux and Altamira. Note, for example, the contrasts of dynamic movement in Figure 1–9.

SCULPTURE

The animal carvings on the throwing sticks foreshadow the capacity of the

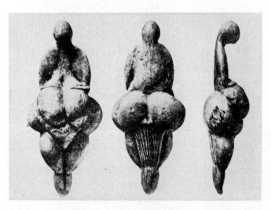

1–10 FEMALE STATUETTE. Ivory. H. 5¾ in. Aurignacian period. Lespugue, France. (Musée National d'Histoire Naturelle, Paris)

Paleolithic artist as a true sculptor. In the Cap-Blanc *Frieze of Animals* life-sized horses in procession, carved in relief ten or twelve inches deep, testify to the same sureness of vision as the paintings, and present the same naturalistic rendering. So also do the clay bisons modeled on the floor of the cavern of Tuc d'Audoubert. In the few extant examples of the human figure, however, a different approach appears. The Willendorf *Statuette* (so called from the cave in Austria where it was found), as well as others (Fig. 1–10), shows a concentration upon the repetition of bulbous shapes, with which the arms are integrated. Such figures are commonly associated with the cult of fertility. In the small *Head of a Woman*, carved from bone, details are subordinated to the basic oval. Thus in sculpture, as well as painting, two divergent views of representation [4] — the realistic and the abstract — are presented. Both of these basic but contrasting concepts have occurred with varying degrees of dominance in the art expressions of all peoples, as we shall have occasion to observe in the following chapters.

[4] See Roger E. Fry, "The Art of the Bushmen," *Vision and Design,* Coward-McCann, 1924, for a discussion of these two contrasting attitudes.

Mesolithic, Neolithic, Bronze, and Iron Ages

(ABOUT 10,000–1000 B.C.)

As the ice of the Paleolithic Age melted in the increasing warmth, the reindeer migrated north, the mammoth and the woolly rhinoceros disappeared, and the hunter-artists vanished. Why and where? These are still unanswered questions. What we do know is that the Ice Age gave way to a transition period known as the Mesolithic. Western Europe became geographically, climatically, and biologically the Europe of today. Man still roamed as a hunter but seemed to have lost the artistic impulses which manifested themselves so vigorously in the Paleolithic Age. His tools were crude. The only art objects which warrant attention in a brief survey are the painted pebbles from Mas d'Azil, which are of interest chiefly, perhaps, as possible examples of an early form of writing.

Cultural evolution in western Europe marked time. But about 7000–6000 B.C. there appeared changes in the Near East which profoundly affected life: the domestication of animals and the cultivation of grain; the appearance of pottery and textiles and, late in the period, of metal. It took over three millennia for these Neolithic innovations to spread from the by now civilized people of the Near East to the peoples of western Europe, but gradually farming and the use of pottery, textiles, and, later, metals spread into Europe.

STONEWARE, POTTERY, TEXTILES

New activities required new tools, which continued to be made chiefly of stone. Some of these, fashioned by the old method of chipping and flaking by pressure, reflect peerless skill in stone-cutting, both in the beauty of their shape and proportions and in the precision and rhythm of their flaking (Fig. 1–11). But a new method of toolmaking, that of grinding and polishing, appeared by means of which man could obtain a smooth surface and a fine cutting edge. By attaching a wooden handle he could then supply himself with a tool comparable to those of modern times.

Some of the domestic demands made by permanent, more secure, and better-equipped homes were met by pottery and textiles. The idea of clay fashioned into a shape and hardened by fire may have been suggested by the attempt to protect a basket from fire by smearing clay on it before placing it over the flames. Neolithic pottery was made by hand, for the potter's wheel was ap-

1–11 DAGGERS FOUND IN DENMARK. Stone flaked by pressure. L. 11½ in. Neolithic. (After Müller)

1-12   NEOLITHIC POTTERY.

parently unknown. It was simple and rugged, sometimes pleasing in shape and proportion, with geometric decoration — concentric lines, spirals, zigzags, dots, chevrons the basic motifs in much of western Europe — well adapted to the shape and often accenting the structural lines and surfaces (Fig. 1–12). Understandably, only a few pieces of textiles have survived, but many objects, such as spinning whorls, loom weights, and bundles of fibers, are evidence of the weaving of cloth and the making of baskets. The latter, together with tools and implements, not only supplied the home but constituted objects of trade. With the interchange of goods came interchange of ideas, more definite social groupings, and a great acceleration in man's development in contrast to the long eons of time consumed in his early advances.

BUILDING

With the growth of communities, social organization, and trade and industry, monumental stone structures appear. *Dolmens* — tombs or monuments to the dead — consisted of several great stones set on end with a large covering slab. Single megaliths, *menhirs,* at times seventy feet high, were set up on end individually, or were arranged in long rows, as at Carnac in Brittany. Their purpose, though not clear, was certainly ritualistic and may have had to do with a cult of the dead or the worship of the sun. Carvings on some of the menhirs and dolmens are essentially incised lines, sometimes producing a symbol of man or decorating a surface with stalks of grain. They are simple and powerful, yet it is difficult to tell when they were carved, and consequently whether they may be accepted as products of Neolithic and Bronze Age culture. Sometimes these huge stones were arranged in a circle known as a *cromlech;* among the most imposing are those at *Avebury* and at *Stonehenge* in England (Fig. 1–13). The circle at Stonehenge consists of an outer ring of immense monoliths capped with lintels roughly cut, just as they came from the quarry, and laid without mortar. Inside is a line of smaller stones; then a broken ring of five pairs of monoliths, each pair with its lintel; and again an inner broken circle of smaller stones, inside of which

1–13   STONEHENGE. *ca.* 1500 B.C. Salisbury Plain, England.

is a large slab which may have served as an altar. In line with this slab to the east is another erect stone, which casts its shadow directly on the center of the slab as the sun first rises in the spring solstice. Astronomical calculations, recently confirmed by carbon 14 tests (see note, p. 37) prove that Stonehenge was in use about 1500 B.C. At Avebury there is a series of concentric circles with connecting curvilinear pathways or avenues (Fig. 1–14). In these arrangements is a feeling for order and symmetry and a varied rhythm — evidence of well-developed ceremonial rituals. Since these structures do not entirely enclose a space, they have often been excluded from the realm of architecture. They are, however, among the earliest human attempts to define a specific environment, distinct from nature, and they reflect their builders' concept of the universe and the forces which control it. Even in their ruined state they possess a solemn majesty, created by heroic human effort and ingenuity.

1–14   AVEBURY CIRCLE (restored after Abury). Avebury, Wiltshire, England.

1 / PREHISTORIC   45

Summary

The art of the Paleolithic Age is the art of a roaming hunter culture in which men first gave expression to their emotions as artists in the objects they fashioned for the hunt, for daily use, and for personal adornment. In their cave paintings they proved themselves men of sure eye, able to grasp essentials and express them with an economical and forceful naturalism.

Western Europe at this time gives us the best picture of prehistoric art; it is there that excavation and research have been most intensively pursued. In other geographical areas, however, as in China, Africa, and America, evidences of Paleolithic and especially of Neolithic, Bronze, and Iron Age culture are coming to light. We can now see spread over large areas of the world in prehistoric times a culture in which are evident many of the characteristics seen in Europe. Neolithic culture, varying widely in duration in different areas, seems to have been a world-wide base from which evolved the great cultures of antiquity, each conditioned by all the varying geographical, social, economic, and religious forces peculiar to itself.

Bibliography

Avebury, John Lubbock, Baron, *Prehistoric Times*, 7th ed., Holt, 1913.

Breuil, Abbé H., *Quatre Cents Siècles d'Art Pariétal*, Centre d'Etudes et de Documentation Prehistoriques, Montignac, Dordogne, 1952.

Brown, Gerard B., *The Art of the Cave Dweller*, Murray, London, 1928.

Burkitt, Miles C., *The Old Stone Age*, 3rd ed., Bowes & Bowes, London, 1955.

Childe, V. Gordon, *The Dawn of European Civilization*, 4th ed. rev., Kegan Paul, Trench, Trubner, London, 1947.

——, *New Light on the Most Ancient East*, 4th ed. rev., Routledge & Kegan Paul, London, 1952.

Clark, John G. D., *Prehistoric Europe: The Economic Basis*, Methuen, London, 1952.

Coates, Adrian, *Prelude to History: A Study of Human Origins and Paleolithic Savagery*, Philosophical Library, New York, 1952.

Frankfort, Henri, *The Birth of Civilization in the Near East*, Williams & Norgate, London, 1951.

Leakey, Louis S. B., *Adam's Ancestors*, 3rd ed. rev., Longmans, Green, New York, 1935.

MacCurdy, George G., *Human Origins*, 2 vols., D. Appleton, 1924.

Parkyn, Ernest A., *An Introduction to the Study of Prehistoric Art*, Longmans, Green, New York, 1915.

Peake, Harold J. E., and Fleure, Herbert J., *Hunters and Artists* (The Corridors of Time, Vol. 2), Yale University Press, 1927.

Probenius, Leo, and Fox, D. C., *Prehistoric Rock Pictures in Europe and Africa*, Museum of Modern Art, New York, *ca.* 1937.

Raphael, Max, *Prehistoric Cave Paintings*, tr. by Norbert Guterman, Pantheon Books, New York, 1945.

Spearing, Herbert G., *The Childhood of Art; or, The Ascent of Man*, rev. ed., Benn, London, 1930.

Swindler, Mary H., *Ancient Painting*, Yale University Press, 1929.

Wallis, Mrs. Ruth O. (Sawtell), and Treat, Ida, *Primitive Hearths in the Pyrenees*, D. Appleton, 1927.

Windels, F., *Lascaux Cave Paintings*, Faber & Faber, London, 1949.

CHAPTER 2

EGYPTIAN

The Old Kingdom[1]

(ABOUT 4000–2280 B.C.)

The blazing sun, the Nile River, and the great contrasts of the land – the barren desert and the valley fertile with trees, grains, flowers, and birds – completely dominated the early Egyptian. The sun was to him a mighty god, Ra (Re), or Amen-Ra, sailing across the sky each day in his boat, and returning to the east by night along a river of the nether world. Each spring melting snows in the mountains of central Africa caused the Nile to overflow its banks, adding to the fields a deposit of rich soil. This rise became for the Egyptian the symbol of the resurrection of a god he called Osiris, who after a tragic earthly life and death became god of the dead. Just as nature with the rise of the Nile burst into new life and just as Osiris entered upon a new existence in another world, so might every Egyptian experience life after death.

The cyclical rhythm of the Nile and of nature instilled in the Egyptian a deep sense of order, of tradition, of justice engendered by natural forces. This concept, known as Ma'at,[2] constituted one of the most powerful influences in Egyptian civilization and art.

The very early history of Egypt is difficult to reconstruct. This early emer-

[1] Egyptian history is divided into a number of major periods such as the Old Kingdom, the Middle Kingdom, the Empire. The succession of rulers of the same line or family are identified as Dynasties, which are given numbers in sequence beginning with the 1st Dynasty, 3200–2980 B.C. The chronology and spelling of proper names in this chapter are those of William Stevenson Smith of the Museum of Fine Arts, Boston.

ILLUSTRATION ABOVE. 2–1 QUEEN NOFRETETE, wife of Akhenaten (1370–1352 B.C.). Limestone, painted, with eyes of rock crystal. Life-size. Staatliche Museen, Berlin. (Staatliche Museen)

[2] H. Frankfort, *Ancient Egyptian Religion: An Interpretation*, Columbia University Press, 1948, pp. 53 ff.

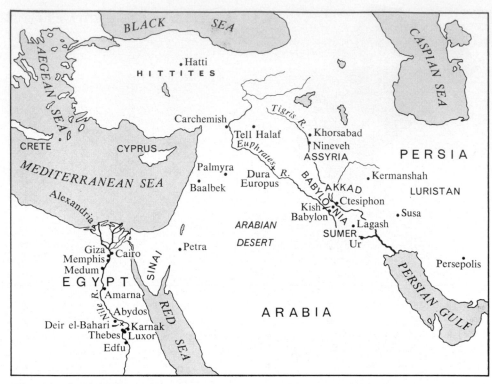

2–2　EGYPT AND THE NEAR EAST IN ANCIENT TIMES.

gence of man from the prehistoric into a civilized condition must have been gradual. Recent discoveries confirm the existence of prehistoric communities adjacent to the Nile valley, but little is really known about the different stages of this development. We do know that before 3000 B.C. the Egyptian evolved his characteristic picture writing, known as hieroglyphs; he invented a calendar, worked out a system of irrigation, and discovered the use of basic metals. The tiny states which emerged along the river slowly coalesced into two kingdoms, Upper and Lower Egypt, which were finally united about 3200 B.C. by a king, or pharaoh, called Menes. The supreme pharaoh owned all the land and appointed the nobles, while the mass of the people were laborers and slaves. The economy was based on agriculture, though there was commerce with the Bedouin tribes of Sinai and

with other Mediterranean peoples.

Our most vivid picture of Egyptian life exists in the art to be found in the tombs, which were carefully built, since one of the major concerns of life in this world was the proper provisioning for life hereafter. An example of this was the concern for the *ka*, which the Egyptians believed was in all features like the body, came into being with the body, and continued through life with it. At death the *ka* went with the body into the next world. Since the *ka* and the body were coexistent, the body after death had to be carefully preserved as a habitation for the *ka* through mummification or by its reproduction in sculpture. Offerings of all kinds nourished the *ka*. In order to secure these necessities and luxuries for the spirit land, which was but a reflection of this world, the Egyptian carved or painted the activities of the deceased upon the tomb walls, or placed in the burial chambers objects or small models, each of which, with the proper incantation, would function normally in the hereafter.

ARCHITECTURE AND SCULPTURE

During the period of the Old Kingdom the desire to create a permanent, safe home for the dead led the Egyptians to erect tombs for their nobles and kings, who could command the necessary resources for such structures. The development of these tombs reached its most imposing form in the Pyramids. The Pyramids are to be found in an area stretching for about fifty miles south from the delta, on the western bank of the Nile, near the Old Kingdom capital of Memphis and the modern city of Giza. The simple geometric form of the pyramid had evolved slowly. The earliest known Egyptians buried their dead in a pit over which they heaped sand, anchored with stones and twigs. Gradually the form of this pit and sand heap evolved into the *mastaba*. The actual chamber below the ground became rectangular and was faced with wood, brick, or stone, and the mound above was also covered with brick or stone. In later constructions one mastaba was piled upon another, forming a step pyramid; then, finally, by filling in the steps, the pure pyramidal form was achieved.[3]

The mastaba was a solid mass except for the chapel — a reception room for the *ka* where offerings were made — and the *serdab* or cellar, a tiny secret chamber in the heart of the structure containing a statue of the deceased, to represent him in the spirit world should anything happen to his actual body. As time went on, the chapel became com-

[3] For a graphic illustration of this development, see James H. Breasted, *Ancient Times*, Ginn, 1935, p. 74.

plex, with additional rooms and corridors whose walls were covered with reliefs vividly picturing everyday life.

These reliefs depict the cultivation of the fields; the raising of cattle; the making of jewelry, vases, and pottery; hunting on the desert or in the papyrus swamp; processions of offering bearers; and banquet scenes. Thus they provide representations of both the necessities and the pleasures of life for the dead in his life hereafter. The scenes are arranged in horizontal zones; the figures are carved in low relief and painted in flat colors which are partly naturalistic and partly governed by an arbitrary color scheme, creating a vigorous wall decoration.

Human figures are shown according to an Egyptian formula: the head and legs in profile, the shoulders and the eye in front view. This was not because the Egyptian was ignorant or unskilled. The artist knew that a man has two arms, although in profile only one can be seen. A complete image, however, was important to the Egyptian, and by twisting the torso to a front view he was able to present the complete body, rather than merely to record an exact visual image. Usually the distortion is not even disconcerting, so skillfully has the artist united the parts in a decorative whole.

This conventional method of treating the figure, which persists in both reliefs and painting throughout the entire course of Egyptian art, is clearly seen in a wooden panel from an early mastaba, that of *Hesi-ra* (Fig. 2-3). Here the figure is not placed in the center of the panel, and yet balance is maintained by the staff and the writing utensils which Hesi-ra holds in his left hand; the horizontals of feet, baton, girdle, and shoulders balance the otherwise insistent verticals. Note the individualized face with its firm mouth and high cheekbones; the careful modeling of neck, shoulders, and knees; the

2–3 PANEL OF HESI-RA. Wood. H. *ca.* 4 ft. Early III dynasty (2780–2680 B.C.). Cairo Museum.

contrast of the broken texture of kilt and wig with the relatively smooth surfaces of the rest of the figure.

Another fine example of Old Kingdom sculpture is the relief of cranes from the *tomb of Ranofer* (Fig. 2–4). Here the Egyptian insistence on order may be seen in the clear relationship of figure to ground. Note how the spaces between the necks of the cranes are an integral part of the design, and how the legs of the cranes form a pattern

which would have been confused if the fifth crane's legs had not been completely omitted. Yet few people notice this omission until it is called to their attention, because the figures are so closely interrelated and the over-all design so compelling.

Uncompleted works show us how these reliefs were carved and painted. The decoration was planned with the help of guidelines to regulate the spaces and the figures; then the figures were sketched in and the background cut away, leaving the design in relief. If the stone was too uneven to offer a good foundation for painting, a thin coating of fine plaster was applied to the surface. The pigments were mixed, probably, with gum and applied to the dry stone or plaster with brushes made of reeds, in flat even tones with no light or shade.

Egyptian skill in painting during the Old Kingdom is illustrated by a rare example, the *Geese from Medum* (Fig. 2–5). The birds fill the panel in a balanced composition which is both naturalistic and abstract — naturalistic in that the painter has closely observed the birds and their characteristic movements, abstract in that he has reduced these observations to a decorative pattern.

Although the mastabas with their lively decorations give us a vivid picture of life during the Old Kingdom, it is the great Pyramids (Fig. 2–6) which have always been the symbol of this early civilization. Of the three Pyramids at Giza, that of *Khufuw*, or *Cheops*, is the oldest and largest. Except for the galleries and burial chamber (Fig. 2–7), it is a solid masonry of limestone which was quarried in the eastern Nile cliffs and floated across the river during the seasonal floods. After the masons finished cutting the stones they marked them with red ink to indicate the place of each in the structure. Then great gangs of laborers

2–4 CRANES. Relief from the tomb of Ranofer. V dynasty (2565–2420 B.C.). Staatliche Museen, Berlin. (Staatliche Museen)

dragged them (the wheel was not yet known) up temporary ramps and laid them course upon course. Finally the Pyramid was surfaced with a casing [4] of pearly-white limestone, cut with such nicety that the eye could scarcely detect the joints.

So accurate was the planning of Khufuw's Pyramid that the most delicate modern instrument shows only about one-half inch of error in the measurement of one side. Yet it is not alone huge size [5] and successful engineering that constitute the art of this

[4] A few casing stones can still be seen, all that remain after many centuries when the pyramids served as stone quarries for the Moslem builders of Cairo.
[5] The size of the *Pyramid of Khufuw* is indicated by some dimensions (in round numbers): length of base, 775 feet, covering 13 acres; height, 450 feet (originally 480 feet). According to Petrie the structure contains about 2,300,000 blocks of stone, each of which averages in weight 2½ tons.

structure, but its formal design – the proportions and simple dignity so consistent with its function and so adapted to its geographical setting.

From the remains around the middle Pyramid at Giza, that of *Khafra* (which is somewhat smaller than that of *Khufuw*, indicating a waning in the economic and political power of the Pharaoh), we can reconstruct an entire Pyramid complex (Fig. 2–8). This consisted of: (1) the Pyramid itself, within or below which was the burial chamber; (2) the chapel, adjoining the Pyramid on the east side, where the offerings were made and ceremonies performed, and where were stored the linen, grain, honey, oil, and other gifts of food and drink, together with rich ceremonial vessels for use in the daily rites; (3) a covered causeway leading down to the valley; and (4) the valley temple, or vestibule of the causeway. Beside the causeway and dominating

2–5 GEESE. Tomb painting near Medum. IV dynasty (2680–2565 B.C.) Cairo Museum.

the temple rose the great Sphinx, carved from a spur of rock to commemorate the Pharaoh. The head is often referred to as a portrait of Khafra, although the features are so generalized that little individuality can be discerned. In size and location it is unique in Egyptian sculpture.

The valley temple of the Pyramid of *Khafra* was built on the post and lintel system: upright supports, or posts, with horizontal beams, or lintels, connecting them. Both supports and lintels were huge rectangular red granite monoliths, finely proportioned, skillfully cut and polished, and entirely devoid of decoration. Alabaster slabs covered the floor, and seated statues, the only em-

2–6 PYRAMIDS OF KHAFRA AND KHUFUW, Giza. IV dynasty (2680–2565 B.C.). (Hoyningen-Huene from Steindorff's *Egypt*, Augustin, New York)

bellishment of the temple, were ranged along the wall. The interior was lighted by a few slanting rays filtering in from above. The pillars of the central aisle were higher than the side walls, and the roof over the central area was therefore higher than that over the sides. In the vertical space between these two levels were slits in the stone forming an embryonic clerestory through which light came. This structural feature is to be found in later Egyptian temples, in Christian churches, and in many modern buildings.

Relief sculpture and painting served to represent activities and belongings which would be useful in the world of the dead, but sculpture in the round served the even more important function of creating an image of the deceased, which could serve as an abode for the *ka*. Should a carefully mummified body by any chance perish, a statue could personify the body in the world to come. For this reason an interest in portraiture developed early in Egypt. Hence, too, permanence of style and material were essential. Though wood, clay, and bronze were used, stone was the primary material — limestone and sandstone from the Nile cliffs, granite from the cataracts of the Upper Nile, and diorite from the desert.

An excellent example of the dignity and serenity, as well as of the sculptur-

al quality, to be found in the statues of the Old Kingdom may be seen in the seated figure of *Khafra* (Fig. 2–9). It was one of a series of similar statues carved for the valley temple of Khafra's Pyramid, which, it will be remembered, was built of massive rectilinear posts and lintels. Since these statues were the only forms to relieve the abstract severity of the temple structure, they must have created a most imposing atmosphere, carved, as they are, from the cubic mass of the stone. This mass is emphasized not only by the retention of the outlines of the original great block of stone, but also by the accent on planes within the figure and the firm modeling of all details. Khafra is seated on a throne, on which is carved the in-

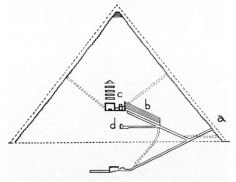

2–7 SECTION OF THE PYRAMID OF KHU-FUW. *a.* Entrance. *b.* Grand gallery. *c.* King's chamber. *d.* Queen's chamber (so-called). (After Hoelscher)

2-8 PYRAMIDS OF KHUFUW AND KHAFRA, Giza. IV dynasty (2680–2565 B.C.) Restored. 1. Pyramid of Khafra. 2. Chapel. 3. Covered causeway. 4. Valley temple. 5. Great Sphinx. 6. Pyramid of Khufuw. 7. Pyramids of members of the royal family and mastabas of nobles. 8. Solar boat (discovered in 1954) to carry the king to the realm of his father, Ra. (After Hoelscher)

2-9 KHAFRA. Diorite. Life-size. IV dynasty (2680–2565 B.C.). Cairo Museum.

2-10 RANOFER. Limestone. H. *ca.* 62 in. V dynasty (2565–2420 B.C.). Cairo Museum.

2-11 HEAD OF A PRINCE. Limestone. Giza. IV dynasty (2680–2565 B.C.) Museum of
Fine Arts, Boston. (Courtesy, Museum of Fine Arts, Boston)

2–12 (Left, above) KA-APER, CALLED SHEIKH EL-BELED. Wood, with eyes of rock crystal. H. 43 in. V dynasty (2565–2420 B.C.) Cairo Museum.

2–13 (Right, above) SEATED SCRIBE. Limestone, painted, with eyes of rock crystal. H. 21 in. From Sakkara. V dynasty (2565–2420 B.C.). Louvre, Paris.

tertwined lotus and papyrus, symbol of united Egypt. Sheltering his head are the protecting wings of the hawk, symbol of the sun, indicating Khafra's divine station as son of Ra. He wears the simple kilt of the Old Kingdom and a linen headdress which covers his forehead and falls in pleated folds over his shoulders. The false ceremonial beard is partly broken off. As a portrait the statue has individuality, yet it is permeated with an imperturbable calm which conveys the enduring power of the pharaoh as well as the abstract concept of kingship.

In the statue of a noble, *Ranofer* (Fig. 2–10), the same sculptural qualities are present, as well as other features characteristic of Egyptian monumental sculpture throughout its long history. Immediately observable, for instance, is the erect stance, with the left foot thrust forward and with arms held rigidly against the body. Although the body is still firmly attached to the block of stone from which it was carved, the clear planes of the broad shoulders, of the torso, and sturdy legs give it vigor and dignity. The entire statue was painted, with details such as the hair, brows and jewelry outlined in color. In general the bodies of the men were painted red, whereas women were colored white or yellow, possibly because Egyptian women were paler due to a more secluded life.

The head of *Ranofer* is in every respect a portrait, but the extraordinary sensitivity of such Old Kingdom portraits is even more striking in the bust of a prince of the family of Cheops (Fig. 2–11). Seldom in the history of sculpture has the elusive spirit of man been so delicately interpreted.

In the *Sheikh el-Beled* (Fig. 2–12) [6] and the *Seated Scribe* (Fig. 2–13) we find lively examples of men whose function was to serve the king in the spirit world as they had in life. Both are more highly individualized than the kings and nobles; both have eyes of rock crystal enhancing their vivacity. The *Sheikh* stands erect in frontal pose, one arm raised to hold his staff. Here the sculptor worked in wood and, by making the arms of separate pieces, which he apparently did not dare to do in stone, he could use a freer pose. Again, the cylindrical character of wood influences the form. The figure was originally covered with linen, glued on to furnish a surface for painting.

The *Scribe*, on the other hand, is carved in limestone. He sits cross-legged, pen in hand ready to take down his master's dictation. Legs, back, and arms are blocked out in large masses; chest, shoulders, and head are individualized. The expression of momentary expectancy in the entire figure has been admirably caught.

The dignity and vitality of Old Kingdom art is also evident in the creations of its other craftsmen. Vessels were usually simple in shape, varying in size from tiny jars for unguents to great

[6] When natives helping in the excavations saw this statue, so impressed were they by its resemblance to their own village chief that they called "Sheikh el-Beled!" or "Chief of the Village," a name it has borne ever since.

2–14 HEAD OF A HAWK. Gold. H. 4 in. VI dynasty (2420–2258 B.C.). Cairo Museum. (Fechheimer)

storage jars, bowls, and plates a foot in diameter. Ornament was rare, for the craftsman depended for his effects upon shape and proportion and upon the intrinsic weight, color, and texture of his material.

The goldsmith cast, chased, soldered, hammered, or plaited his metal with amazing skill. The hawk's head (Fig. 2 14) was originally attached to a bronze body by rivets still left just below the neck. The goldsmith has hammered the metal into shape, probably over a mold, soldered the parts together, and inserted eyes cut from red jasper. Like the painter of the *Geese of Medum* (Fig. 2–5), he has observed the hawk scrupulously and has given expression to its essential form and character with an amazing economy of modeling.

The Middle Kingdom

(2065–1785 B.C.)

The Old Kingdom ended when the highly efficient government of the pharaohs weakened and the landed no-bles, gaining power, plunged the country into a period of struggle and disorder. Out of this conflict arose a feudal state. The pharaoh still stood at its head but he maintained his power only

2–15 AMENEMHAT III (or SESOSTRIS III). (*ca.* 1850–1800 B.C.). Obsidian. H. *ca.* 5 in. Gulbenkian Collection, National Gallery of Art, Washington, D. C. (*Journal of Egyptian Archeology*)

by balancing the nobles one against another. A succession of long reigns testifies to the political stability thus achieved, but scenes of battle and models of weapons found in the tombs reflect wars between north and south Egypt, against the Bedouins of the eastern desert and the Nubians of the south, as well as the final subjugation of Egypt by the Hyksos from Syria.

Economically the Middle Kingdom began with a period of prosperity. Agriculture was furthered by building canals and reclaiming land. Expanding trade led to the conquest of Ethiopia and to the building of forts between the first and second cataracts of the Nile to control the route to the gold mines of the south. Mining operations were also carried on in the Sinai peninsula. And at the end of this period, about 1700 B.C., the horse, which originated in the grasslands of central Asia, appeared in the Nile valley.

Scholars today realize that this Middle Kingdom was an important moment in the evolution of Egyptian culture. Internal troubles, early threats of invasion, as well as the broadening horizons of the Egyptian economy, necessarily changed the Egyptian's outlook on the world and his religion. The still scattered and relatively scanty vestiges of this period make it difficult to interpret fully, but both literary and visual evidence bespeaks a loss of the assurance of the Old Kingdom. The appearance of doubts or worries is shown in the brooding portrait of *Amenemhat III* (Fig. 2–15).

ARCHITECTURE AND SCULPTURE

Since most of the buildings of the Middle Kingdom were of brick, they have crumbled and disappeared. Yet traces remain which indicate that there were pyramid complexes, similar to those of the Old Kingdom, though smaller. There is a Middle Kingdom terraced temple with colonnades at Deir el-Bahari, which may well have been a prototype for *Queen Hatshepsut's temple* at the beginning of the Empire (Fig. 2–16).

We have already noted a change in the character of portrait sculpture. The partially damaged head of *Amenemhat III* (or possibly Sesostris III) (Fig. 2–15) is diminutive; it can be held in the palm of one's hand, and yet it has the effect of a fully life-size representation. It is carved in obsidian, a stone so hard that it required the most accomplished skill in cutting, grinding, and polishing. The stylized headdress, the strong modeling, and the accent on clearly defined planes identify it as Egyptian, while the strong mouth, the drooping lines about the nose and eyes, and the shadowy brows show us a determined ruler who had also shared in the cares of the world.

The Empire

(1580–1085 B.C.)

During the XVIIth Dynasty the Hyksos were overthrown and the way was prepared for the XVIIIth Dynasty, which ushered in the Empire, the most brilliant period of Egypt's long history. At this time Egypt extended her borders by conquest from the Euphrates in the east deep into Nubia to the south. Wider foreign contact brought visiting embassies and new and profitable trade with Asia and with the Aegean islands. The booty taken in wars and the tribute exacted from the subjected peoples made possible the development of a new capital, Thebes, which became a great and luxurious metropolis with magnificent palaces, tombs, and temples along both banks of the river.

Thuthmose III, who died in the fifty-fourth year of his reign, in the first half of the fifteenth century B.C., was the greatest pharaoh in the New Empire, if not in all Egyptian history; and his successors continued the grand traditions he established. Amenhotep IV (1370–1352 B.C.), though, broke with all Egyptian traditions in an attempt to establish a monotheistic religion, centered on the worship of Aten, an old name for the sun god, Ra. In so doing he opposed both politically and religiously the corrupt priesthood at Thebes. He adopted the name of Akhenaten, which means "It is well with Aten," and set up a new capital, Akhetaten, meaning "Horizon of Aten" (now known as Amarna).

Egypt, however, was too crystallized in the traditions of thousands of years, too controlled by its nobles, military leaders, and particularly by the powerful priesthood of Amen, to accept so revolutionary an idea. Upheavals at home and invasions from without caused the empire to dwindle, while Akhenaten, a philosopher rather than a practical man, became entirely absorbed in the new religion. After his death, Amarna was destroyed and the power of Thebes restored.

Some reflection of Akhenaten's period lingers in the decoration of the objects found in the tomb of his son-in-law, Tut-ankh-amen, whose unrifled grave,[7] found in 1922, revealed the extraordinary richness of royal burial. The enormous wealth of the pharaoh enabled him to erect a palace[8] whose decorations reproduced the outdoor world in which he delighted. On the painted or tiled floors and walls were swimming ducks and the animal life of the marshes; across the deep blue background of the ceiling flew flocks of birds and butterflies. The furniture was superbly designed and skillfully constructed (Fig. 2–28). Magnificent gold and silver vessels, blue faïence lotus cups, and rich jewelry all tell of magnificence in contrast to the sterner dignity of the Age of the Pyramids.

As the Empire declined, attempts at reorganization were made by Sety I (1318–1298 B.C.) and by Ramesses II, the Great (1298–1232 B.C.), but the earlier glories were never recaptured.

[7] See Howard Carter and A. C. Mace, *The Tomb of Tut-ankh-amen*, Vols. 1–3, Cassell and Co., London, 1923–33.

[8] For domestic architecture see N. de G. Davies, "The Town House in Ancient Egypt," *Metropolitan Museum Studies*, Vol. 1, Pt. 2, 1928–29; Henri Frankfort on private houses in Amarna, *Journal of Egyptian Archeology*, November, 1922, pp. 144–49; and the *Medinet Habu* publications of the Oriental Institute of the University of Chicago relating to the palace of Ramesses III.

2–16 TEMPLE OF QUEEN HATSHEPSUT (1504–1483 B.C.) at Deir el-Bahari, Thebes. (Hoyningen-Huene from Steindorff's *Egypt*, Augustin, New York)

ARCHITECTURE AND SCULPTURE

The Old Kingdom had been pre-eminently the period of the Pyramid-builder, but the Empire was the period of grandiose temples. Burial still demanded the elaborate care shown earlier, but robberies and neglect had also shown the futility of the pyramid as a place for safe preservation. Nobles and kings now hollowed their burial chambers deep in the cliffs west of the Nile. In the Valley of the Kings, the tombs are rock-cut, approached by long corridors, sometimes extending as deep as 500 feet into the hillside. The entrances to these burial chambers were carefully concealed and the mortuary temples were built along the banks of the river at some distance from the tombs. The temple provided the king during his lifetime with a place for worshiping his patron god and then served as a mortuary chapel after his death. Hence the temples became elaborate and sumptu-

ous, befitting both the kings and the gods.

The noblest of these royal mortuary temples, at Deir el-Bahari, was the *temple of Queen Hatshepsut*, built about 1500 B.C. (Fig. 2–16). Even in its fragmentary condition it rises from the valley floor in three colonnaded terraces, connected by ramps, to the cliffs in which were cut the sanctuary and the shrines. Notice how effectively the long horizontals and verticals of the colonnades and their rhythm of light and dark repeat the pattern of the cliffs above. The pillars of the colonnades, which are either simply rectangular or chamfered off into sixteen sides, are sensitively proportioned and spaced. Sculpture was also an integral part of the entire design. Statues in the round, perhaps two hundred in number, were intimately associated with the architecture. So also were the brightly painted low reliefs covering the walls, remnants of which may still be seen. In Hatshepsut's day the terraces were not

2–17 TEMPLE OF KHONSU. Horizontal and vertical section showing the general arrangements of the temple. (After Perrot and Chipiez)

the barren places they are now, but luxuriant gardens filled with frankincense trees and rare plants brought by the queen from the faraway "land of Punt." [9]

Distinct from the mortuary temples were the great edifices built in honor of one or more of the gods and often added to by successive kings until they reached the gigantic size of the temples at Karnak and Luxor. These temples all followed a similar plan, which may be best studied in a small but well-preserved example such as the *temple of Khonsu,* also at Karnak (Fig. 2–17). The plan is bilaterally symmetrical along a single axis, which progresses from the approaching avenue through different courts and halls to the dimly lit sanctuary. The dominating feature of the approach, along an

[9] This expedition to Punt, the land of incense on the Somali coast, and the rare treasures brought back are pictured in low relief on the walls of the second terrace.

2–18 COLUMNS OF FIRST HYPOSTYLE HALL. Temple of Horus, Edfu. *ca.* 237–57 B.C.

2–19 TEMPLE OF AMEN. Karnak. Hypostyle hall, central part. XIX dynasty (1349–1197 B.C.). From a model. The original columns are 66 ft. high, the capitals 22 ft. wide at the top. Metropolitan Museum of Art, New York.

avenue lined with statuary, is the façade, or pylon, simple and massive, with sloping walls. The broad surface is broken by the doorway with its overshadowing cornice, by four grooves to hold great flagstaffs, and by low reliefs. A curved molding finishes both the top and the sides. Within is an open court surrounded on three sides by a colonnade. Next is a hall — the hypostyle hall — crowded with massive columns and roofed by stone slabs carried on

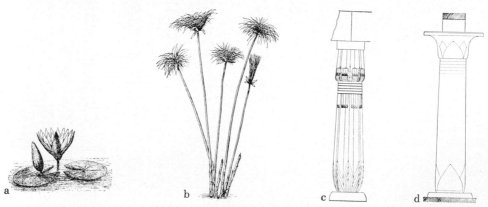

2–20 Columns and capitals derived from natural forms. *a*. Lotus. *b*. Papyrus. *c*. Bud column and capital. *d*. Papyrus flower column and capital. (Borchardt)

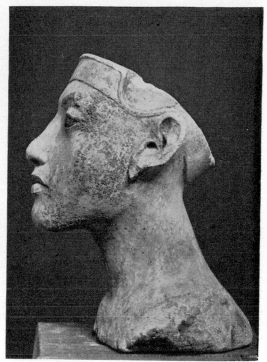

2–21 MASK OF A MAN by the sculptor
Thutmose from Amarna. *ca.* 1380–1363
B.C. Staatliche Museen, Berlin. (Staatliche
Museen)

2–22 AKHENATEN (1380–1363 B.C.).
Sandstone. H. *ca.* 8 in. Staatliche Museen, Berlin. (Grantz)

lintels which rested in turn on impost
blocks supported by the great capitals.
Since these blocks could not be seen
from below, the stone roof must have
appeared to be suspended in air (Fig.
2–18). In most instances the central
rows of columns were higher [10] than
the side ones, providing space for a
clerestory through which light filtered
into the interior (Fig. 2–19). The contrast between the bright sunshine of

[10] In the hypostyle hall of the temple of
Amen at Karnak the columns are 66 feet
high, and the capitals 22 feet in diameter at
the top, large enough to hold 100 men. The
Egyptian did not use cement but depended
upon the weight of the huge stones to hold
the columns in place. For technical methods
of lifting these stones to such heights, see
Somers Clarke and Reginald Engelbach, *Ancient Egyptian Masonry,* Oxford University
Press, New York, 1930.

the open court and the cool dimness of
the hypostyle hall was dramatic and
awe-inspiring. Farther on was the sanctuary — low, dark, mysterious, and secluded. A girdle wall, beginning at the
pylon, surrounded the whole structure.

This plan evolved from ritualistic requirements. Only the pharaoh and the
priest could enter the sanctuary; a chosen few were admitted to the hypostyle
hall; the masses penetrated only into
the open court, while the girdle wall
shut off the entire site from the outside
world. From this basic plan the conservative Egyptian did not deviate for
hundreds of years, even after the
Greeks and Romans brought other
ideas into the Nile valley.

The post and lintel structure of the
temples appears to have had its origin
in early building in which the reeds

and plants of the swamps were firmly bound into sheaves that served as supports and covering. Evidence of this may be seen in the form of the columns and capitals, which resemble sheaves of papyrus or lotus reeds with capitals either in the shape of a cluster of buds or of an open flower; the painted decorations on the surface emphasized these natural details (Fig. 2–20). In fact, the flora of the Nile valley supplied the basic decorative motifs in all Egyptian art.

Equally impressive and a perfect

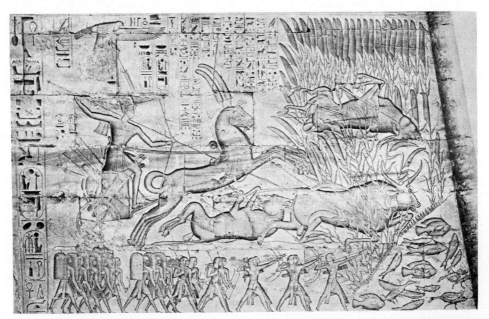

2–24 WILD BULL HUNT. On a pylon of the temple of Ramesses III (1195–1164 B.C.) at Medinet Habu, Thebes. (Oriental Institute, University of Chicago)

2-25 OSIRIS AND GODDESSES. Temple of Sety I (1318–1298 B.C.), Abydos.

complement to the architecture were the colossal statues used at the entrance and in other parts of the temple — figures which closely followed the conventions of the Old Kingdom and retained the grandeur of those earlier statues.

Both temples and tombs were decorated as well with reliefs relating to religious ceremonies or to the life of the deceased. The zonal arrangement characteristic of the Old Kingdom continues, but the grouping of the figures becomes more complex. During the reign of Akhenaten there was a revolution against the strict artistic traditions, just as there had been in the realms of politics and religion. Included in worship of the sun Aten was a deep respect for the forces and forms of nature. An obvious result in art was a tendency toward a relaxation of the conventions and toward an imitation, or representation, of natural forms and actions. It is certainly true that a mask found in a sculptor's studio at Amarna is such a faithful reproduction of the

human face (Fig. 2–21) that one wonders whether it was not molded as a life mask rather than carved as a piece of sculpture. Yet some of the portraits of *Akhenaten* (Fig. 2–22), and certainly the magnificent portrait bust of his queen, *Nofretete* (Fig. 2–1), combine naturalism with sensitive interpretation and the fine modeling to be found in great portrait sculpture. The interest in naturalism led at times to awkward forms such as the curiously elongated heads and torsos to be seen in a number of reliefs and statues. It is believed that these distortions may actually have been physical deformities which were the result either of binding the head or of a disease still current in central Africa. The new informality appears in such scenes as Figure 2–23, where the king and queen are playfully caressing their young princesses. It must be admitted, though, that the artist who painted the floor in the palace of Akhenaten at Amarna was so informal and so preoccupied with representing all the various flora and fauna of the

2–26 TOMB OF NAKHT. Thebes. XVIII dynasty (1570–1349 B.C.).

swamps that there is little order or coherence in the designs of the different zones.

As might be expected, the priests of Amen and the old traditional hierarchy made an attempt immediately after Akhenaten's death to eradicate the new heresy and restore the older forms of worship and government. Amarna was destroyed; other remnants of the art were defaced; and all references to the hated king and queen were removed. Yet the innovations of Amarna are still manifest in reliefs of the XIXth and XXth Dynasties under the Ramessides. In the agitated scene of a *Wild Bull Hunt* (Fig. 2–24), the spearmen and archers of the bottom zone move with a vigorous rhythmic swing; and, although the figure in the central panel of Ramesses III in his chariot is still rendered in terms of the old conven-

tion, the dying bulls are shown with extraordinary visual reality.

The wall decorations in the *temple of Sety I* at Abydos (Fig. 2–25) illustrate how crystallized the old conventions became. The figures are highly stylized, with no interior modeling and no feeling for structure (note that both hands and both feet are the same); they are affected, stilted, and lacking in the vivacity of the Old Kingdom or of the Empire. Yet the related shapes, the ivory-like fineness of the carving, and the simple flat color result in effective mural decoration. This tradition continued in Egypt for more than another thousand years, as may be seen in a relief from the time of Cleopatra.

PAINTING

In the Old Kingdom painting had functioned more as an accessory to relief than as an independent art. Beginning in the Middle Kingdom and increasingly during the Empire, painters alone were called on to decorate walls of rock-cut tombs, partly because the walls were too coarse and rough for carving and partly because of the greater ease and freedom of the brush compared with that of the chisel. The rough walls were first covered with stucco and plaster on which the figures were drawn in firm outline with the help of an over-all grid of squares to assure symmetry and proper proportions. The flat colors were mixed with some binding medium, such as gum, and applied to a dry surface.

Figure 2–26 shows us the interior of the tomb of a noble.[11] The decorative scheme is based on a system of dado, four zones, and border, with a zigzag ceiling pattern which copies that of an Egyptian house. The zones are ordered

[11] For fine color reproductions of this tomb see N. de G. Davies, *The Tomb of Nakht at Thebes*, Metropolitan Museum of Art, New York, 1917.

2-27   FOWLING SCENE. From a Theban tomb. XVIII dynasty (1570–1349 B.C.). British Museum, London. (Oriental Institute, University of Chicago)

in symmetrical balance around the false door painted on the end wall. This door was painted as an entrance for the spirit who received the offerings which we see painted in the lower zone below the door.

On the left wall are the figures of the noble and his wife in large scale to indicate their importance, standing among lively scenes of agriculture and stock raising. On the opposite wall is a *Banquet Scene* with six guests seated upon mats near a blind harper. There is greater freedom of pose and variety of movement here than in Old Kingdom work, and a suavely flowing line of great beauty, though the drawing of

objects and people is still based on traditional conventions of profile rendering.

This is also true in a *Fowling Scene* (Fig. 2-27) in which the noble is standing in his boat and driving the birds from a papyrus swamp with his boomerang. In his right hand he holds three birds he has caught; his hunting cat, on a papyrus stem just in front of him, has caught two more in her claws and is holding the wings of a third with her teeth. His two companions, perhaps his wife and little daughter, are enjoying the lotus they have gathered. The water and the figures are represented by the usual conventions,

2–28 CHAIR. Cedarwood, decorated with embossed gold, claws of ivory. From the tomb of Tut-ankh-amen (between 1362–1353 B.C.). Cairo Museum. (H. Carter)

but cat, fish, and birds show a trend toward a naturalism based upon visual perception.

WOODWORK, METALWORK, GLASS, CERAMICS

The furnishings of the palace and the adornment of kings and nobles reflected the magnificence and ostentation of the Empire. A relatively simple

cedarwood chair (Fig. 2–28) illustrates this functional, structural, and esthetic excellence. Ornamented with open relief carving with gold inlay, it combines inscriptions and symbols into a design of architectonic quality.

Quantities of smaller articles for household equipment and personal use were produced in stone, wood, ivory, glazed terra cotta, glass, metal, and semiprecious stones. Elegant alabaster vases from Tut-ankh-amen's tomb, each cut from a single stone and worked to a translucent thinness, show that the stoneworker was a technical virtuoso. Wood was particularly valued for carving small toilet articles, such as the cosmetic receptacle in Figure 2–29, with designs based upon familiar human, plant, and animal forms.

Glazing, which had been known from prehistoric times, had early been used on tiles for wall decoration. Under the Empire this technique achieved a high technical development and a wide variety of uses — beads, pendants, scarabs, amulets, vases, figurines, and architectural decorations. An especially popular rich blue was obtained from copper by a long process requiring great skill and patience.

Glass was widely used even though the blowpipe was not invented until about the first century B.C. The artist molded the hot glass over a copper and paste core that could later be removed — a slow, laborious procedure. The vase in Figure 2–30 was made in this way.

2–29 PERFUME SPOON. The duck forms the receptacle, the swimming girl the handle. Wood. XVIII dynasty (1570–1349 B.C.). Louvre, Paris.

2–30 VASE. Dark blue glass with dragged pattern in light blue, yellow, and white. H. 3¼ in. Metropolitan Museum of Art, New York.

The body is deep blue and the design is of threads of light blue, yellow, and white glass which were wound about the still hot neck and body of the vessel by a hooked instrument.

Metalworkers and lapidaries were in great demand because of the use of gold on furniture and particularly because of the importance of jewelry in Egyptian costume — crowns, collar-necklaces, necklaces with pendants, armlets, bracelets, ornaments, and clasps for clothing (Fig. 2–31). The lavish gold *coffins of Tut-ankh-amen* (Fig. 2–32), which fitted one within the other, are magnificent examples of the goldsmith's craft.

Summary

Egyptian art has a fascination quite its own. From the decoration of tombs we can reconstruct in great detail the daily life of one of the first peoples to emerge from the twilight of prehistory.

In sculpture in the round, and in relief sculpture, especially of the Old Kingdom, there are numerous examples of the highest quality in terms of technical skill and in the sensitive order of the compositions. Egypt affords an unparalleled opportunity to observe how a tradition, once firmly established, may continue as an official "language" over thousands of years.

During the Old Kingdom those conventions were established which, with but one important break, controlled the long course of Egyptian art. The builders of the Old Kingdom were primarily tomb-builders, and their stone mastabas and pyramids are massive, static, and enduring, thoroughly in harmony with site and function. In these tombs was placed the imposing portrait sculpture which was required by religious belief — conventional in form but filled with an intense vitality. Painting and painted reliefs, chiefly in the chapels of the tombs, employed conventions which, although they presented a dis-

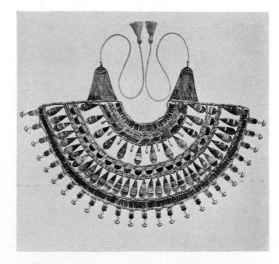

2–31 JEWELRY. Gold, carnelian, green feldspar, and glass. Reign of Thutmose III (1504–1450 B.C.) Metropolitan Museum of Art, New York. (Fletcher Fund, 1919–1922)

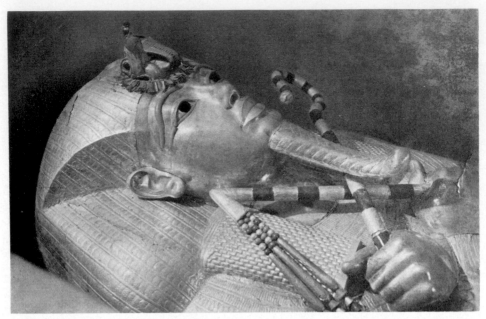

2–32   EFFIGY OF TUT-ANKH-AMEN (1362–1353 B.C.) upon the outermost of the three coffins. Gold over wood inlaid with glass, faïence, and lapis lazuli. Cairo Museum. (Howard Carter)

torted profile view of the human figure, give a vivid picture of Egyptian life. Stonecutters and goldsmiths were also sensitive to materials and effective design. The objects they created for daily use and personal adornment share the sobriety and dignity of the other arts.

During the Middle Kingdom important changes occurred in the social and economic structure of Egypt. A feudal system held sway, and for a time the Hyksos from Syria controlled the Nile valley. Our evidence for this period is scanty, since most of the architecture was of brick, although there are remains to indicate that temples were built which may well have been prototypes for the great structures of the Empire. Sculpture of high quality continued to be carved, and the portraits show the psychological tensions of the time.

The Empire, which lasted for almost five hundred years, saw Egypt's power and influence at its greatest. Her ar-

mies were successful in Mesopotamia as well as in Nubia; and her trade established contacts with the Aegean islands as well. It was the period of great temple building, of Karnak and Luxor. The rock-cut tombs were decorated with mural paintings, often of great vivacity. Sculpture in every category flourished, from colossal statues for the temples to dainty figures as decoration for objects of everyday use. Perhaps the most interesting phenomenon of the period, indeed of all Egyptian history, was the revolt led by Amenhotep IV, known as Akhenaten. His desire to establish a monotheistic religion threatened the authority of the powerful priesthood. He moved the capital from Thebes to Amarna; and sculpture and painting, for a brief moment, seemed to be freed of the conventions imposed by tradition. After Akhenaten's death, however, the priesthood reasserted its authority. The Empire continued to be vigorous and prosperous for more than two centuries, but the forms of art tended to become more and more stereotyped until other influences, such as the Greek and Roman, introduced concepts which were ultimately to replace the traditions of Egypt.

Bibliography

Aldred, Cyril, *Development of Ancient Egyptian Art from 3200–1315 B.C.*, Tiranti, London, 1952.

Badawy, Alexander, *A History of Egyptian Architecture*, Vol. 1, Sh. Studio Misr, Giza, 1954.

Breasted, James Henry, *A History of Egypt*, 2nd rev. ed., Scribner's, 1924.

——, *Egyptian Servant Statues*, Pantheon Books, New York, 1948.

Davies, Nina M., and Gardiner, Alan H., *Ancient Egyptian Paintings*, University of Chicago Press, 1936.

Dimick, Marion T., *Memphis, The City of the White Wall*, University Museum, Philadelphia, 1956.

Drioton, Etienne, *Egyptian Art*, 2nd ed., Arts, Inc., New York, 1951.

Edwards, Iorwerth E. S., *The Pyramids of Egypt*, Penguin Books, New York, 1954 (first published in 1947).

Fechheimer, Hedwig, *Kleinplastik der Agypter*, B. Cassirer, Berlin, 1921.

——, *Die Plastik der Agypter*, B. Cassirer, Berlin, 1923.

Fox, Penelope, *Tutankhamun's Treasure*, Oxford University Press, New York, 1952.

Frankfort, Henri, ed., *The Mural Painting of El-'Amarneh*, Egyptian Exploration Society, London, 1929.

Hassia, *Temples et Tresors de l'Egypte*, Art et Style, Paris, 1954.

Hayes, William C., *The Scepter of Egypt*, Metropolitan Museum of Art, New York, 1953.

Lange, Kurt, and Hirmer, M., *Egypt*, Phaidon Press, London, 1956.

Mekhitarian, Arpag, *Egyptian Painting*, tr. by Stuart Gilbert, Skira, New York, 1954.

Petrie, Sir W. M. Flinders, *Arts and Crafts of Ancient Egypt*, T. N. Foulis, Chicago, 1910.

——, *Social Life in Ancient Egypt*, Constable, London, 1923.

Ranke, Hermann, *The Art of Ancient Egypt*, Phaidon Press, Vienna, 1936; also Allen and Unwin, London, 1936.

——, *Masterpieces of Egyptian Art*, Beechhurst Press, New York, 1951.

Smith, Earl Baldwin, *Egyptian Architecture as Cultural Expression*, D. Appleton-Century, 1938.

Smith, William Stevenson, *Ancient Egypt as Represented in the Museum of Fine Arts*, Boston, 1942.

——, *The Art and Architecture of Ancient Egypt*, History of Art Series, Pelican Books, Baltimore, 1958.

——, *A History of Egyptian Sculpture and Painting in the Old Kingdom*, Oxford University Press, New York, 1946.

Steindorff, George, and Hoyningen Huene, George, *Egypt*, J. J. Augustin, New York, 1943.

Swindler, Mary H., *Ancient Painting*, Yale University Press, 1929.

Vandier, Jacques, *Egypt: Paintings from Tombs and Temples*, New York Graphic Society and UNESCO, New York, 1954.

Wilson, John A., *The Culture of Ancient Egypt*, Phoenix Books (University of Chicago Press), 1956.

Woolley, Sir Charles Leonard, *Digging Up the Past*, Penguin Books, Baltimore, 1954.

Worringer, Wilhelm, *Egyptian Art*, tr. by Bernard Rackham, Putnam, London, 1928.

CHAPTER 3

MIDDLE EASTERN[1]

Babylonian

(ABOUT 3000–1550 B.C.)

In Mesopotamia, the valley between the Tigris and Euphrates rivers (Fig. 2–2), a civilization developed contem-

[1] Recent excavations in Asia Minor, Syria, and Palestine have enormously extended our knowledge of the cultures of these regions during the third, second, and first millennia B.C. The history of the Hittites, the Hurrians, the Mitanni, the Aramaeans, and the Phoenicians is gradually being brought to light, and the historical and stylistic interrelations among these peoples of the Middle East revealed. The complexity of the material, the new discoveries being made each year, and the controversial state of scholarship in the field make it impossible to treat the problems adequately in this necessarily limited survey. A more detailed account can be found in *The Art and Architecture of the Ancient Orient* by Henri Frankfort. Mesopotamian chronology is much disputed among scholars. The dates used in this chapter are based on the chronology of W. F. Albright.

ILLUSTRATION ABOVE. 3–1 CAPITAL FROM PERSEPOLIS. 522–331 B.C. (Oriental Institute, University of Chicago)

poraneously with that of Egypt. The Euphrates to the west, although a quiet river, is almost unnavigable throughout most of its length because of cataracts in the north and sand bars in the south; but the eastern river, the Tigris, is more rapid and forms a highway for the commerce of the valley. Like the Nile, both rivers flood during the rainy season, bringing down vast quantities of rich soil to spread over the fields. But these floods are also destructive and soon convert the mud-brick buildings common to this region into formless mounds.

The Mesopotamian valley divides into two parts, the lower of which, Babylonia, is extraordinarily fertile, and the upper, Assyria, relatively barren. The valley's history is largely an account of struggle among various peoples for control of the sources of food supply. Unlike isolated Egypt, the valley is accessible from the west via the Arabian desert, and from the north, northwest, and east via highland plateaus. Throughout history different racial groups have infiltrated, conquered, and finally been absorbed here.

The very early history of the Mesopotamian people is no clearer than are the prehistoric times in Egypt. It is possible that prehistoric man in both areas discovered the use of metals and devised their systems of writing about the same time, although the cuneiform writing of Babylonia is quite distinct from the hieroglyphs of Egypt. At the dawn of recorded history the lower Mesopotamian valley was occupied by the Sumerians, who may have migrated from the eastern plateaus. They were an agricultural people who learned to control the floods through irrigation and built strong walled towns, such as Ur and Lagash. Then from the western desert came Semitic nomad shepherds who adopted agriculture, absorbed much from Sumerian culture, and built their own cities farther north — Kish, Akkad, and Babylon. Though Sumerian culture prevailed, the ruling power oscillated between the two peoples, the Semites producing two of the mightiest

kings, Sargon (fl. 2340 B.C.) and Hammurabi (ca. 1728–1686 B.C.), under whom Babylon became the capital of the first Babylonian empire.

Religious beliefs, as in all early cultures, centered around nature gods: Anu, god of the sky; En-lil, creator and ruler of earth and "lord of the storm"; Ea, lord of the waters — a healing, benevolent god; Nannar, or Sin, the moon god; Shamash, the sun god; and Ishtar, goddess of love and fertility. The city of Babylon had a patron deity, Marduk, who, as Babylon extended her power over the valley, became the head of the Babylonian pantheon, assuming, in time, even the attributes of the older but powerful Bel of Nippur.

In contrast to the Egyptians, the Sumerians and Semites gave relatively little attention to their burials. Sumptuous objects have been found in royal graves, but the tomb and its decoration had neither impressive architecture nor fine wall painting. Life on this earth was far more important than making provision for the hereafter, and builders were chiefly concerned with the construction of palaces and of temples

3–2 ZIGGURAT AT UR. Reconstructed. H. 92 ft. 2300–2180 B.C. (Joint Expedition of the British Museum and the University Museum, University of Pennsylvania)

to propitiate the gods. Divination was an important part of religion and omens were sought in the conduct of state as well as of daily affairs. In addition to their religious functions the priests were literate and could therefore keep accounts. For this reason they became an important factor in the business life of the country, renting land, bartering wool, cattle, fruits, perfume, and the products of the craftsmen.

ARCHITECTURE

Since the country provided neither stone nor adequate timber, Sumerian architecture was exclusively of brick,

3–3 VICTORY STELE OF NARAM-SIN. H. *ca.* 78 in. Akkadian period (2340–2080 B.C.). Louvre, Paris. (Archives Photographiques)

usually unbaked. Consequently, the post and lintel system of construction was rarely used; but the arch, built of small brick or stone units, and the barrel vault were known early and commonly used.

The characteristic building of the valley was the *ziggurat,* a massive tower of several stories, which formed the most prominent part of a temple complex. Its origins are uncertain. Perhaps this tower with an altar on its summit is evidence that the Sumerians migrated from hilly country and wished to recreate the "mountain of the god" – the "high places" where they had been accustomed to worship.

The *Ziggurat* at Ur, part of a temple of Nannar, of which enough has been excavated to allow a conjectural reconstruction (Fig. 3–2), had a massive base fifty feet high. On this great platform two more successively smaller stages were built, with the uppermost one serving presumably as a temple. On the front three ramplike stairways of one hundred steps each converged upon a landing from which another flight of steps probably led to the shrine, the focal point for the pageantry of ceremonial rites. The striking effect of the different cubic masses and of intersecting planes is in sharp contrast to the simple unity of the Egyptian pyramid. The Babylonian structure is a solid mass of mud brick with a thick facing of baked brick laid in bitumen, designed to withstand floods. The walls have a decided inward slope and all the surfaces and edges are slightly curved, giving the mass compactness and relieving it of the illusion of sag found in long rigid lines. The stages may have been of different colors, used symbolically, and trees and gardens may have been planted on the terraces. The ziggurat occupied one side of a sacred area; about it were irregularly grouped temples to the moon goddess and to minor related deities,

3–4 FRAGMENT OF THE STELE OF UR-NAMMU. III dynasty at Ur (2079–1960 B.C.). University Museum, Philadelphia. (Joint Expedition of the British Museum and the University Museum, University of Pennsylvania)

together with various secular structures belonging to the cult of the god.

SCULPTURE

Lack of stone hampered any substantial development of Sumerian sculpture. There are, however, a few stelae with narrative reliefs, of which the *Victory Stele of Naram-Sin* (grandson of Sargon) (Fig. 3–3), is the finest. Above and larger than his followers is the king wearing the horned headdress of divinity. He is mounting a hill toward the symbols of the great gods, and carries bow and arrow and, under his left elbow, his battle-axe.

A fragment of another such stele (Fig. 3–4) shows King Ur-Nammu pouring a libation into a vase of plants.

The god, Nannar, seated on the right, holds a pickaxe, a measuring rod, and a builder's line, symbolizing his order to the king to build him a temple. In the zone below, the king and a servant, both bearing builders' tools, follow the god to carry out the divine orders. The figures are clothed in the heavy woolen garments characteristic of the valley. It is interesting to note how many of the conventions used in the depiction of human figures are similar to those developed in Egypt, and yet how distinct the two styles are. The head in profile with full-face eye, the twisted torso, the feet, one rigidly before the other — these are also found in Egyptian figures. But the quality of the relief, which accents a pattern of highlights and shadows, and the treatment of the

surfaces which seem unctuous as the light flows across them, contrast with the order and precision of Egyptian reliefs.

These same features may be seen in sculpture in the round. A statue from Tello (Lagash) (Fig. 3-5), carved from diorite which must have been imported from a considerable distance, represents *Gudea,* ruler of Lagash. He is standing with hands tightly clasped, and wears a long woolen mantle which falls away from the right shoulder, leaving the arm exposed. The figure is compact and massive, but it seems as though it had been carved from a cylinder rather than from a cubic mass of stone as in Egyptian sculpture. Details are cut with sharp precision, as in eyebrows, eyes, mouth, and fingers, introducing a broken texture to contrast with the subtly modeled surfaces in the face and the exposed arm.

Great skill in stone carving in miniature is seen in the cylinder seals, usually about an inch and a half high and pierced for a cord (Fig. 3-6). They were made of various stones, both hard and soft, such as agate, jasper, lapis lazuli, carnelian, and alabaster, and were carved in intaglio so that when the seal was rolled over soft clay a raised impression was made. With this impression the Sumerian sealed, signed, and identified his letters and docu-

3–5   STATUE OF GUDEA OF LAGASH (modern Tello). H. 29 in. *ca.* 2125–2025 B.C. British Museum, London. (British Museum)

3–6   CYLINDER SEAL and impression made from it. H. *ca.* 1 in. Reign of Sargon of Akkad (2341–2300 B.C.). The impression shows a hero fighting a bull, and a being — half man, half bull — fighting a lion. The inscription names the owner, the scribe Lugal-Lam. Oriental Institute, University of Chicago. (Oriental Institute)

3-7 INLAID PANEL FROM UR. H. *ca.* 8 in. *ca.* 3000–2700 B.C. Iraq Museum of Antiquities, Baghdad. (Trustees of the British Museum)

ments, which were written on clay tablets. The extraordinary control and sensitivity displayed by the artist working on such a limited surface is especially remarkable when the monumental quality and vigor of the figures are considered.

Another popular technique, allied to sculpture, was the inlay with shell or stone. This is illustrated by a triangular box originally carried on a pole, probably as a standard for ceremonial use. Here the background is lapis lazuli with an occasional dash of red. One of the panels pictures the celebration after a victory (Fig. 3–7). In the upper zone the king, larger than his viceroys, sits facing them, while attendants and captives appear before him with goods and domestic animals, probably the spoils of war. At the far right of the top register a man plays a harp of the type shown in Figure 3–11.

METALWORK

High technical skill was also attained by metalworkers and other craftsmen.

3-8 COPPER RELIEF FROM THE TEMPLE OF NINHURSAG, Al 'Ubaid. H. 42 in. *ca.* 3000–2340 B.C. British Museum, London. (Trustees of the British Museum)

3–9 (Left, above)   GOLD CUP FROM UR. *ca*. 3000–2700 B.C. University Museum, Philadelphia.

3–10 (Right, above)   GOLD HELMET FROM UR. *ca*. 3000–2700 B.C. Baghdad Museum. (Joint Expedition of the British Museum and the University Museum, University of Pennsylvania)

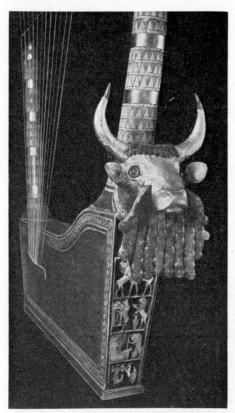

Among the sumptuous royal burial equipment found at Ur are gorgeous ornaments and jewelry, and rich furniture, implements, and utensils.

In metals, bronze was used, but copper was most common, worked by casting, *repoussé,* and engraving. Such reliefs as those in Figure 3–8 were made by building a wooden core, covering it with bitumen, in which the modeling was done, and then hammering thin plates of copper over it. This relief is also significant because of its heraldic design, for which the people in these valleys seem to have had a particular predilection throughout their history. This heraldic ordering of animals or human figures into rigidly symmetrical patterns creates a highly decorative de-

◀ **3–11**   HARP FROM UR. H. 42 in. 3000–2700 B.C. Bull's head of gold foil and lapis lazuli with inlaid eyes. Reconstructed. University Museum, Philadelphia. (Joint Expedition of the British Museum and the University Museum, University of Pennsylvania)

sign, particularly well suited, as well, to the technique of weaving.

The Sumerians were also lavish with gold. A cup (Fig. 3–9) shows masterly proportions and strong contour, its surface hammered into simple flutings with a delicately engraved herringbone pattern and double zigzag finishing both lip and base. Again on a gold helmet (Fig. 3–10) may be seen qualities seldom surpassed either in excellence of technique or beauty of design. Here

the conventionalized hair makes a varied pattern of wave lines, spirals, and sharply angular braiding.

The combining of varied materials is illustrated by a wooden harp (Fig. 3–11) inlaid with shell, lapis lazuli, and red stone. The sounding box terminates in a bull's head of gold with eyes, beard, and horn tips of lapis. The sloping end of the box has four zones of figures in engraved shell set in a dark ground.

Assyrian

(ABOUT 1200–612 B.C.)

The early history of the upper Euphrates valley is still unclear. The early Semite settlements of Ashur were dominated by the kings of Sumer and Akkad who were constantly harassed by the tribes from the surrounding highlands. Among these were the Kassites, a pre–Indo-European people from the

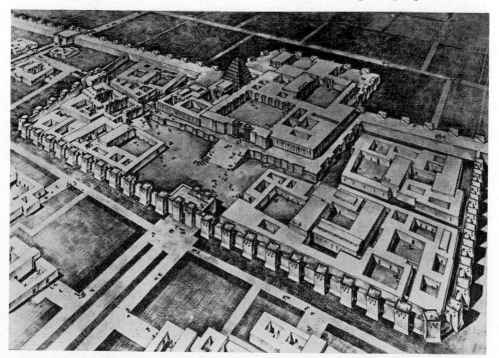

3–12 THE CITADEL OF SARGON II at Khorsabad (modern Dur-Shar-rukin). 722–706 B.C. View from the east. Reconstruction. (Oriental Institute, University of Chicago)

3–13 PALACE OF SARGON II at Khorsabad. Main façade. Reconstructed. Detail of Figure 3–12. (Place)

northeastern plateaus, who were drifting into the valley, bringing with them the horse (about 2000 B.C.). But more important were the Hittites of Anatolia, who invaded the valley about 1925 B.C.

The Hittites, who comprised a loosely united federation of mountaineers of whom little was known until recently, achieved their greatest imperial control over Syria and adjacent lands during the fourteenth and thirteenth centuries B.C. At their capital Hatti (the modern Boghaz Keui), at Carchemish, Tell Halaf, and other sites, they built massive fortress-palaces with bold architectural sculpture at the entrances. We see gigantic, ponderous basalt statues of deities standing on the backs of animals; the "Great Mother" seated on a pedestal adorned with monsters as elemental as the rock itself; reliefs of ceremonial processions and hunting scenes filled with movement. Perhaps the most impressive of all are the great reliefs of gods and ceremonial scenes which are carved in the rock of the Yazilikaya gorges. Here the king, protected by his guardian deity, is led into the presence of the sword god, a lion-shouldered, human-headed deity whose body is a great sword blade thrust into the rock. This is the sword which only the king can draw. It is the prototype of the sword of Arthur and the beginning of the European concept of the epic hero.

About 1200 B.C. the Semitic-speaking Assyrians set up a state which became one of the world's great empires, eventually stretching from the Persian mountains to the Mediterranean, including Egypt and much of Asia Minor as well. Too large for effective organization and administration, it was the prey of numerous attackers, and in 612

3–14 GUARDIAN MONSTER FROM THE PALACE OF ASSUR-NASIRPAL II at Nimrud (modern Calah). 883–859 B.C. Metropolitan Museum of Art, New York.

B.C. it fell to a combination of Babylonians, Medes, and Persians.

The Assyrian state[2] is best known for its military achievements, which were celebrated in its writings and in the relief sculptures that adorned its palaces. Its energy is symbolized in the typically Assyrian sun god from whom it took its name — Ashur, a savage, aloof deity rather than a royal city dweller, as were the nature gods of Sumeria. There was a tingling energy about the Assyrian and a grim cruelty, whether he was fighting, hunting, or indulging in luxurious indolence. This tense, forceful movement is in marked contrast to the calm, refined monumentality of Egyptian art.

[2] The following are the most important Assyrian kings, with their capitals:

> Assurnasirpal II (883–859 B.C.), Nimrud
> Sargon II (722–705), Khorsabad
> Sennacherib (705–681), Nineveh
> Assurbanipal (669–626), Nineveh

ARCHITECTURE AND SCULPTURE

Sumerian forms underlay Assyrian art, but were adapted to meet the demands of an imperial state. Stone, not available along the lower river valleys, could be found in the cliffs to the north. But because the stone was not of good quality its architectural use was limited mainly to foundations and substructures, though it was extensively employed for relief sculpture. Brick was used for superstructures. Temples, as in Sumerian times, were usually built on platforms and dominated by an associated ziggurat.

Palaces were large and complex. The best-known example, *Sargon's palace and temple* at Dur-Shar-rukin (Khorsabad) (Fig. 3–12), is a vast rambling structure covering about twenty-five acres. There were two entrances, one

3–15 FRAGMENT OF PAVEMENT FROM THE PALACE at Nineveh (modern Kuyunjik). Alabaster. *ca.* 700 B.C. British Museum, London. (Mansell)

by a ramp for vehicles, the other by a monumental stairway leading directly to the main entrance. Many small rooms were grouped around open courts: a large one, in the rear, was a center for the affairs of state and the royal living quarters; another, toward the front, was for domestic service. Axial symmetry, which was such a dominant principle in Egyptian architecture, seems to have been of little interest here. The courts with their adjacent rooms, combined with a temple and a ziggurat, present the appearance of an agglomeration of units, added one to the other, impressive in their size and in the dramatic use of oblique and diagonal vistas.

The palace façade (Fig. 3–13) was a massive crenelated wall interrupted by rectangular towers flanking an arched doorway, on each side of which stood winged bulls with human heads.

Around the arch and on the towers were friezes of brilliantly colored glazed tiles. The colossal bulls, or lions, at the entrance (Fig. 3–14) served both to ward off enemies, visible and invisible, and to provide an impressive and fitting architectural decoration. They are partly in the round, partly in high relief, and combine a front view of the creature at rest with a side view of it in motion, contriving the latter by the addition of a fifth leg. The gigantic size, the bold, vigorous carving, the fine sweeping wings, and the patterning of the surface by the conventional treatment of details, all contribute to the creatures' impressiveness and architectural fitness. This is also true of the basically heraldic design of the two monsters, placed back to back, with a human, or divine, figure set as a vertical accent in the center.

The *palaces of Assurnasirpal and Assurbanipal* were partly paved with stone slabs (Fig. 3–15) carved with various motifs, both Mesopotamian and foreign. The brick walls of some of the rooms were sheathed with limestone and alabaster reliefs — thousands of feet of ceremonial, military, and hunting scenes, which were arranged in zones. The reliefs (Fig. 3–16) contain large, firmly planted figures which fill the space and are endlessly repeated, often without defined relationships, though sometimes balanced on either side of a tree of life. As in Sumerian reliefs, there are conventions in the figure style similar to those used in Egypt. But these Assyrian figures are distinctive in their accent on individual prowess indicated by the stylized rendering of the muscles of arms and legs. Such details, combined with incised designs of the costumes and of divine attributes, often produce vigorous surface patterns. The desire, however, to recount the exploits of the ruler at length led to the placing of inscriptions, which run across both fig-

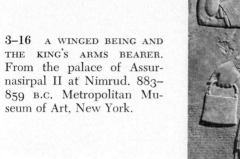

3-16 A WINGED BEING AND THE KING'S ARMS BEARER. From the palace of Assurnasirpal II at Nimrud. 883–859 B.C. Metropolitan Museum of Art, New York.

ures and background with a subsequent visual confusion.

Scenes of banquet, war, and the hunt are expressive of a vigorous society. Hunting was the chief pastime of the Assyrian. On horseback, in chariots, and with dogs, he sought wild asses or, most prized, the lion. In Figure 3 17 the king, mounted, is spearing one lion, while another, wounded, furiously attacks a riderless horse. The desire of

the artist to capture the violence of this moment, which involved many complicated movements, led him to place a number of details in unnatural positions (such as the right leg of the first lion, which seems joined to its back) or to superimpose them in impossible spatial relations. In Figure 3-18 a wounded lioness, her hind quarters paralyzed by an arrow, rears up for a last attack. Seldom has low relief

3-17 THE KING HUNTING LIONS. From the palace of Assurbanipal at Nineveh. 669–626 B.C. British Museum, London.

3–18 DYING LIONESS from palace of Assurbanipal, Nineveh. H. *ca.* 24 in. 669–626 B.C. British Museum, London. (Trustees of the British Museum)

been treated with such delicate sensibility. Natural forms have been recorded with the same keenness of observation we noted in prehistoric cave paintings. But these Assyrian reliefs, instead of being placed in a seemingly haphazard manner, are coherently organized as an integral part of an overall wall decoration, accented by the highlights and shadows of the carving.

Chaldean

(612–539 B.C.)

At the fall of Nineveh in 612 B.C. two kingdoms were established, the Chaldean in the south and the Medo-Persian on the eastern plateaus. Nebuchadnezzar, the Chaldean, rebuilt Babylon so that it surpassed Nineveh in the splendor of its palaces, temples, and famous "hanging gardens." This was the Babylon of which the Greek traveler Herodotus wrote, and the city of the Hebrew captivity. It was fabulously rich, with flourishing markets and trade. Learning was encouraged, particularly in such sciences as astronomy. But Babylon's power was short-lived, for in 539 B.C. it opened its gates to Cyrus the Persian.

Among the buildings excavated in Chaldean Babylon the *Ishtar Gate* (Fig. 3–19) best illustrates the most important Chaldean contribution to the arts — the architectural use of ceramic

3–19   ISHTAR GATE. Babylon, 612–539 B.C. Restored. (Koldewey)

decoration. The design of this double gate conforms to the types found in earlier Babylonia and Assyria. Glazed tiles also had been used much earlier, but the surface of the bricks, even when figures appeared, was flat. The Chaldean artists raised their figures from the background in delicately modeled relief. On the Ishtar Gate were rows of exotic animals, and on the

3–20   LION FROM PROCESSION STREET. Babylon. Glazed tile. L. 7 ft. 612–539 B.C. Restored. (Stoedtner)

walls of the processional street which led from the gate to the *temple of Marduk* were sixty life-size lions (sacred to Ishtar). These animals were molded in relief and glazed[3] in yellow, brown, and red against a ground of turquoise or dark blue with a rosette motif in the border (Fig. 3–20). Possibly as a result of the technique, these animals, whose vigor is suggested by snarling mouths, long nervous tails and carefully depicted muscles, are more stylized than those of the Assyrian

[3] The glazes used by the Chaldeans are opaque and hard and indicate the skill of the craftsmen in keeping the unfired colors from flowing into each other. Probably each brick was molded and enameled separately.

hunting reliefs. Yet few styles in the history of architecture have developed a more colorful and durable surface decoration.

Near the *Ishtar Gate* rose the huge *palace of Nebuchadnezzar* with its terraced gardens, and at no great distance the great ziggurat of the *temple of Marduk* (the "Tower of Babel") with its hanging gardens. Indeed this main gateway of Chaldean Babylon, together with the adjacent palaces and temples with their brilliant gleaming surfaces and rich tropical gardens flashing in the sunshine, must have been an impressive sight, combining a love of rich color with a sense of monumental grandeur.

Achaemenian Persian

(550–331 B.C.)

The end of the Assyrian power had been brought about by the combined effort of the Chaldeans, who were Semitic, and of the Indo-European Medo-Persians, who had migrated from the northern grasslands and had gradually built up an empire on the eastern mountainous plateaus.

About 550 B.C. Cyrus, a Persian vassal of the Median empire, revolted and swept over western Asia with powerful archers and daring horsemen. Babylon fell to him in 539 B.C., Egypt in 525. By 480 B.C. the Persian empire extended from the Indus to the Danube, and only the successful resistance of the Greeks in the fifth century prevented the inclusion of the northern Mediterranean. The Persian empire was thoroughly organized and enjoyed a remarkable period of prosperity under Darius (523–485 B.C.) and his son Xerxes (485–465 B.C.). Theirs was an intelligent rule, but weaker successors

were unable to hold to their high standards. Decline set in, and the decadent state fell before the armies of Alexander the Great in 331 B.C.

The Persian religion, formulated by the great prophet Zoroaster (Zarathustra), recognized the conflict of Good (Ahura-Mazda, Ormazd) and Evil (Ahriman), the ethical value of right conduct, and the final triumph of Good. Fire, the purest of things, was a symbol of Ahura-Mazda and was reverenced in worship.

ARCHITECTURE AND SCULPTURE

The most important source of our knowledge of Achaemenian building is the *palace of Persepolis* (Fig. 3–21), built for the most part by Darius and Xerxes. Upon a huge platform stood a group of audience halls and chambers. The dramatic approach passed through a special entrance, or *propylon,* flanked by colossal human-headed bulls, and

3–21 STAIRWAY TO THE ROYAL AUDIENCE HALL at Persepolis. 522–465 B.C. (Oriental Institute, University of Chicago)

thence at right angles toward the great platform, which was reached by a ceremonial double stairway. Stone is plentiful in this mountainous country. Hence the platform, the monumental stairways, the gateways, and the great columns of the audience halls were of stone, though brick was used for walls, and wood for smaller columns and for roofing. The most noticeable factor — not previously found in Mesopotamia and sharply differentiating Persepolis from Khorsabad — is the use of the column on a grand scale. The vast *Audience Hall* (*Apadana*) contained thirty-six 40-foot columns supporting a wooden roof. When the king, surrounded by his bodyguard and court, received both local subjects and representatives from the vast Persian empire in this hall the general effect must have been one of magnificent, stately ceremonial. The slender fluted columns are peculiarly Achaemenian. In their capitals as decorative motifs are animal figures which consist of the foreparts of bulls, lions, or eagles placed back to back above a leaf design (Fig. 3–1). The wooden beams which rested between the heads were probably covered with pigments and gold leaf, and some of the walls with paintings or enameled tiles.

Many of these decorative motifs must have been part of the Achaemenian inheritance from the earlier civilizations of the Tigris-Euphrates valley. Yet the Persian unquestionably was also sensitive to the cultures of the people whom he conquered and whose motifs and techniques he adapted to his own uses. Thus, though he may have learned of the column in Egypt, his *Audience Hall* at Persepolis is entirely different in effect from the *Hypostyle Hall* at Karnak.

The sculptured friezes at Persepolis are imposing in their monumental serenity. The walls of spacious double staircases, of which at least ten have

3-22 SUBJECTS BRINGING GIFTS of animals, weapons, and vessels to the king. Detail from the stairway to the Royal Audience Hall, Persepolis. 522–465 B.C. (Oriental Institute, University of Chicago)

been found, were ornamented with low reliefs showing processions of royal guards or representatives of various parts of the empire, bringing tribute and gifts to the king (Fig. 3–22). The evenly spaced human figures, broken into groups by conventionalized trees and interspersed by occasional animals, are highly decorative. The cutting of the stone, both in the modeled surfaces and the crisply chiseled details, is technically superb. These figures gave scale to the great columned halls on the platforms above. Their decorative surfaces created striking staccato contrasts in light and shade against the massive stone masonry.

METALWORK

The Achaemenians excelled in gold work. The decoration of an armlet (Fig. 3–23) consists of two winged monsters, the bodies and hind legs of which are indicated in relief, while the wings, breasts, and necks are covered with cloisons that were once filled with colored stones cut to fit the depressions. The animal forms are highly conventionalized, and their simplified outline makes a bold, vigorous design well fitted to the medium. It is possible that this Persian art was influenced by two earlier cultures, which also produced fine metal adornments. Among the scanty vestiges of pre-Achaemenian cultures in Iran are small bronzes found in the province of Luristan. They include objects for religious and personal use, such as long pins, weapons, and ornaments for harnesses and chariots. The motifs are largely animals, real or fantastic, in heraldic relationships, rendered with great technical skill and with a remarkable grasp of the relationships between solids and voids — of the essentials of design, which make positive use of the spaces between the figures. In Figure 3-24 the rhythmic movement is carried by a circle motif. The small circles of the tails expand into those of the wings, and then into the slightly elliptical shape made by the long necks terminating in serpent heads.

Mention must also be made of the significant art of such nomadic peoples as the Scythians and the Sarmatians, who roamed the steppes of central Eurasia and who established contact with Mediterranean and Mesopotamian cultures before the sixth century B.C. There is an affinity, in particular, between the forms of Persian ornament and the jewelry of these "barbarian" tribes which may denote a common origin. What remains of the art of these nomadic warriors and hunters is a wealth of personal adornment — buckles, brooches, great fastening pins known as *fibulae*, and decorative gear for arms and horse trappings — which found its way into western Europe with the migrations of similar tribes and nations at the collapse of the Roman empire. These objects, mostly in gold and bronze, often with insets of garnets, other stones, and sometimes enamel, exhibit great technical skill. Their design, based on animal forms, combines an observation of nature with completely abstract, geometric decoration, and intricately interweaving forms, as may be seen in Figure 3-25. This is called the "animal style" because the basic forms are those of animals, observed with the same sensitivity and keenness of eye as the early Paleolithic cave paintings. In the "animal style," though, the natural forms have become stylized and certain areas, such as the ears, hoofs, or tail, are covered with geometric ornament. It is almost as though the natural forms of the Paleolithic Stone Age had reappeared, in the manner of a geological fault, and pushed through the overlaying cultures of the Bronze and Iron Ages

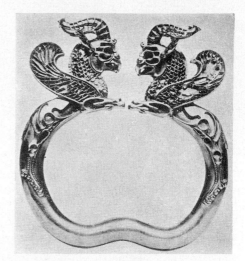

3-23 ARMLET. Gold. H. 5 in. *ca.* 400 B.C. British Museum, London. (Dalton)

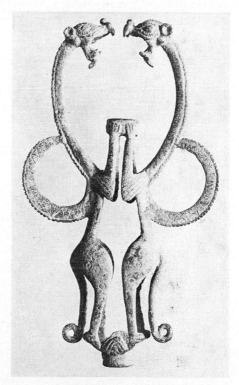

3-24 BRONZE POLE TOP from Luristan. H. *ca.* 6¼ in. *ca.* 650 B.C. Museum of Fine Arts, Boston. (Courtesy, Museum of Fine Arts, Boston)

3–25 BRONZE BELT BUCKLE, found in Ordos Desert. Scythian-Sarmatian animal style. L. 6 in. Royal Ontario Museum, Toronto. (Royal Ontario Museum)

when abstract geometric patterns decorated tools and pots (Figs. 1–8 and 1–12). Although the origin of this art seems to have been in central Asia, it is interesting to note that the "animal style" was also known to, and successfully employed by, the artists of the Han dynasty in distant China to whom it had evidently been communicated by the Huns when they invaded the Far East in the fourth century B.C. The "animal style" appears, as well, in "treasures" found in Siberia. It was also a primary design element in the art of the La Tène civilization, an early Celtic culture which flourished from the fourth through the second centuries B.C. in what is now western Switzerland and adjoining areas. In other words, the highly decorative, essentially abstract style known as the "animal style" was used by people all the way from western Europe to China, and north to Siberia — an area much larger than that included by the so-called civilized world around the Mediterranean Sea.

Sassanian Persian

(A.D. 226–641)

For five and a half centuries following Alexander's conquest, Mesopotamia was dominated first by Hellenistic and then by Roman culture. In the third century A.D. a new power arose in Persia, the Sassanian, so called from a priestly Iranian family who lived in a secluded part of southern Persia and there maintained the old traditions and religion of their race. Having conquered the Parthians, the Sassanians, notwithstanding the welter of Hellenistic, Roman, Parthian, and early Christian influences in the valley of the two rivers, brought about a revival of Iranian culture, especially of the ancestral faith of Zoroaster. This Sassanian empire, with capitals at Istakhr (near Persepolis) and at Ctesiphon (near Baghdad), reached its height under Chosroes (Khosrau) I (A.D. 531–579) and Chosroes II (590–628), when Ctesiphon became a fabulously rich city and one of the most influential centers of the Near East. The Sassanian rulers were great patrons of the arts and encouraged the crafts, particularly the weaving of fine silk textiles, which were in demand by the luxurious Byzantine court and which, in the West, became a strong influence in the evolution of European ornament. When Justinian, in his zeal to propagate the Christian faith, closed the pagan schools of Athens, the artists and scholars fled to the court of Chosroes I, carrying with them the classical traditions and learning, with the result that the Sassanian court was one of the most enlightened of the Near East.

3–26   PALACE AT CTESIPHON. Sassanian. 6th century A.D. (Sarre and Herzfeld)

But, notwithstanding its power and vigor, this empire was short-lived, being one of the first to fall before the fanatical invincibility of the Moslem invaders (A.D. 641).

ARCHITECTURE

Sassanian art shows the great assimilative capacity of the Iranian. Whatever he took he translated into his own idiom and infused with his own dynamic vitality. As with the Achaemenids, the palace was the focus of building; the *palace at Ctesiphon* (Fig. 3–26) is the outstanding example. What little is left of this great structure is eloquent of monumental grandeur, and when one recalls the stucco decorations and — upon reading of the booty taken by the Moslems — the marvelous carpets and furnishings, one can easily believe in its fabled magnificence. An imposing catenary barrel vault of brick which roofs the throne room dwarfs human beings by its magnitude. This great audience hall was closed by a solid façade which was decorated with engaged columns and blind arcades. These do not follow the superimposed system of the Roman style but show a striking variety of arrangement in the stories which reveals an unhampered versatility.[4]

SCULPTURE

Sassanian sculpture is best exemplified in the colossal equestrian reliefs of Ardashir I and Shapur I at Naksh-i-Rustum near Persepolis, and of Chosroes II at Tak-i-Bostan, a villa near the modern Kermanshah which was a famous park in Sassanian times. Here, in an arched recess cut into the rock at the base of a cliff bordering a small lake, is the statue of Chosroes II. His charger Shabdiz (meaning "Black Night") is heavily caparisoned, and the rider is clothed in armor. Though the statue was badly mutilated by the Moslems, it is still impressive in its monumentality and its feeling. The entire figure has an intense vitality and the surface decoration has a quality which recalls the reliefs of Persepolis.

[4] Excavations at Ctesiphon have brought to light a large number of fragments of stone and stucco ornament and other objects. See the *Metropolitan Museum of Art Bulletin*, August, 1932.

3–27 CHOSROES I HUNTING IBEXES. Silver plate, partially gilt. D. 8⅝ in. 6th century A.D. Metropolitan Museum of Art, New York.

SILVERWORK AND TEXTILES

This same pulsating vitality, combined with a sensitive relationship of forms, is evident in the work of silversmiths and weavers. Behind the Sassanian metalworker lay a long tradition of extraordinary quality. As in Assyria, hunting was a favorite pastime. In Figure 3–27 six figures are composed into a unit determined by a circular space. Dynamic curves and countercurves, now flowing together, now meeting at sharp angles, create a forceful pattern through which conventional motifs for drapery, muscles, and manes carry rapid minor rhythms.

Textiles were executed with great skill. Silk weaving had made its way westward from China and became a flourishing industry in Persia, where the craftsmen wove fabrics not only for home use but for Byzantium and western Europe as well. An all-over pattern based upon large medallions connected by small ones is a distinctive feature of these stuffs. In Figure 3–28 the hunter motif again appears. Two kings on winged horses, arranged with

perfect bilateral symmetry are, as in the heraldic designs of Sumeria, holding aloft the cubs of the lioness they have been hunting. The forms of all the figures are so highly generalized that they have become decorative patterns splendidly adapted to the circular space. The astounding vigor of the forms and the highly simplified drawing necessary for a successful textile pattern are harmonized with extraordinary skill in Sassanian fabrics.

Summary

Civilization in the Tigris-Euphrates valley almost paralleled that of Egypt, but the two cultures were quite different and their art forms equally distinct. Open to invasion and conquest, Mesopotamia was ruled by successive, powerful peoples, each of whom established their own culture, in contrast to the long, unbroken traditions of Egypt. They built their palaces and temples of brick, the only plentiful material, and

3–28 SILK TEXTILE WITH THE HUNTER MOTIF. Sassanian. *ca.* 600 A.D. Kunstgewerbe Museum, Berlin. (Lessing)

raised massive ziggurats to dominate these ensembles. Both statues in the round and carved cylinder seals show a combination of naturalism and convention which has considerable vitality. The Sumerians were lavish and expert in their use of gold, as well as of copper, lapis lazuli, and shell. Early in their history they developed heraldic, symmetrical designs which were imitated in many later styles and regions.

Under the Assyrians, particularly from the ninth through the seventh centuries B.C., there was an architecture of worldly magnificence – huge palaces of many rooms around open courts. These were built of brick with surfaces of brilliantly colored tile and with colossal sculpture at the doorways. On the interior walls were reliefs picturing incidents of war, the hunt, and a luxurious life, which are delicately executed and rich as surface decoration.

The brief Chaldean kingdom rebuilt Babylon in an even more sumptuous manner than the conquered Nineveh. The molded and glazed tile reliefs of lions and exotic animals on the Ishtar Gate seem more stylized than do the lively hunting scenes of the Assyrians.

Achaemenian Persian art was a royal art of large scale, fine materials, and rich color. Its most important buildings at Persepolis, of stone, brick, and tile, housed an absolute monarch. Forests of stone columns, approached by spacious stone stairways, with friezes carved in relief, gave a regal impression. The Iranians were also skillful with gold, silver, and bronze, in which they rendered animals at times naturalistically and at times, especially in the Luristan bronzes, in highly decorative forms.

A revival of these first truly Persian forms and of even older Mesopotamian customs took place between the third and seventh centuries of the Christian era under the Sassanian empire. The great vault of the palace at Ctesiphon is evidence of Iranian ability to assimilate and to transform outside influences. The sculpture, and particularly the metalwork and textiles, with their heraldic designs, which were exported to Byzantium and western Europe, show the vitality of the culture of the valley of the two rivers.

Bibliography

Albright, W. F., *The Archaeology of Palestine*, Penguin Books, Harmondsworth, England, 1949.

Champdor, Albert, *Babylone et Mésopotamie*, A. Guillot, Paris, 1953.

Encyclopédie Photographique de l'Art, Vols. 1–3, Editions "Tel," Paris, 1935–38.

Frankfort, Henri, *The Art and Architecture of the Ancient Orient*, Pelican Books, Baltimore, 1955.

——, *The Birth of Civilization in the Near East*, Williams & Norgate, London, 1951.

——, *Cylinder Seals*, Macmillan, New York, 1939.

Ghirshman, Roman, *Iran, from Earliest Times to the Islamic Conquest*, Penguin Books, Harmondsworth, England, 1954.

Grousset, René, *The Civilizations of the East*, tr. by C. A. Phillips, 4 vols., Knopf; Vol. 1, 1931–34.

Gurney, O. R., *The Hittites*, Penguin Books, Baltimore, 1952.

Herzfeld, Ernst E., *Iran in the Ancient East*, Oxford University Press, New York, 1941.

Marek, Kurt W., *The Secret of the Hittites* by C. W. Ceram (pseud.), Knopf, 1955.

Pope, Arthur Upham, *A Survey of Persian Art*, 7 vols., Oxford University Press, New York, 1938–39.

Rostovtsev, Mikhail I., *The Animal Style in South Russia and China*, Princeton University Press, 1929.

Schäfer, Heinrich, and Andrae, Walter, *Die Kunst des Alten Orients*, Propyläen-Verlag, Berlin, 1925.

Schmidt, Erich F., *Persepolis*, Vol. 1, University of Chicago Press, 1953.

Woolley, Sir Charles L., *Dead Towns and Living Men*, rev. ed., Oxford University Press, New York, 1929.

——, *The Development of Sumerian Art*, Faber & Faber, London, 1935.

——, *Ur of the Chaldees*, Benn, London, 1929; Pelican Books, Baltimore, 1954.

Zervos, Christian, *L'Art de la Mésopotamie*, Editions "Cahier d'Art," Paris, 1935.

CHAPTER 4

AEGEAN

ABOUT 3000–1100 B.C.

In 1870 at Hissarlik in Asia Minor the German, Heinrich Schliemann, proved by startling archeological discoveries that the stories of the Trojan War were not groundless myth. His knowledge of the *Iliad* had led him to believe that this site was the location of Troy, and here he found a number of cities and fortresses built one upon the remains of another, together with the evidence of their destruction by fire. Schliemann continued his excavations at Mycenae, from whence Agamemnon and Achilles sailed to avenge the capture of Helen, and here his finds were even more startling.[1] Massive fortress-palaces, elaborate tombs, quantities of gold jewelry and ornaments, cups, and inlaid weapons revealed a magnificent preclassical civilization.

[1] Although Troy is associated with Mycenae in legend, its link with the Aegean world is chronological rather than cultural. Troy was an Anatolian city with a different culture from that of the Greek mainland or of Crete.

ILLUSTRATION ABOVE. **4–1** OCTOPUS JAR from Gournia. H. *ca.* 8 in. 1600–1500 B.C. Herakleion Museum.

But further discoveries were to prove that Mycenae had not been its center. An important Greek legend told of Minos, king of Crete, who had exacted from Athens tribute of youths and maidens to be fed to a Minotaur, half-bull, half-man, which was housed in a vast labyrinth. Might this legend, too, be based on historical fact? An Englishman, Sir Arthur Evans, had long considered Crete a potentially fertile field for investigation. Soon after the end of Turkish rule in 1898 he began work there and a short time later uncovered extensive unfortified palaces of the old sea kings, the plans of which did, indeed, resemble labyrinths (Fig. 4–2). Such findings, primarily at Knossos, have been greatly increased by recent excavations there and also at Phaistos, another important site on the southern coast of Crete.

The origins of the Cretan people remain obscure. Settlement had begun in the Neolithic Age, and from time to time new immigration added to the population. By about 1900 B.C. they had developed a system of writing.

Only recently has this been deciphered and proved to be Greek in form, although its origins seem to have been in Mesopotamia. Crete's soil is quite fertile, but her people were primarily seafarers and traders, bartering their own wares, notably pottery and metalwork, around the Aegean, in Asia Minor, and in Egypt. Their religion was a nature worship centering around a mother goddess whose rites were performed before shrines in the palaces or in caves or groves on the mountaintops.

The Cretans were a proud people. If we judge from the alert, athletic figures painted on their palace walls, they were also a gay people, fond of festivals. Their art is permeated with a movement and a freedom quite distinct from the sobriety of the Egyptians.

At its peak, about 1500 B.C., Cretan

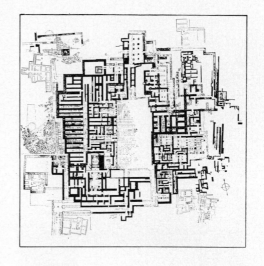

4–2 PALACE OF KNOSSOS, Crete. Plan. *ca.* 1600–1400 B.C. (From Dinsmoor, *Architecture of Ancient Greece*, Batsford, Ltd., 1950)

4–3 GRAND STAIRCASE IN THE PALACE OF MINOS, KNOSSOS. *ca.* 1600–1400 B.C. Restored. (Evans)

4-4 LION GATE. Mycenae. 1350–1300 B.C.

civilization[2] spread to neighboring islands and to the mainland of Greece: to Mycenae and Tiryns. But there tribes from the north were already filtering in, necessitating fortifications and introducing new ideas. By 1100 B.C., a great wave of invaders swept across the mainland and to Crete, where they burned the palace at Knossos and took possession of the Aegean world. Cretan civilization was doomed, but its influence survived in the valuable contributions it made to later Greek culture.

ARCHITECTURE AND PAINTING

Building in Crete emphasized neither tombs, temples, nor fortresses but, instead, palaces for the king and his retainers — large, comfortable, and handsome with ample staircases and courtyards for pageants and ceremonies. Such was the *palace at Knossos* (Fig. 4–2), a rambling structure built around open courts — so large and bewildering that it may well have suggested to the Greeks the labyrinth of the ancient tale. There were gaily decorated living rooms, bathrooms with a drainage system, audience halls with finely paved floors, workshops, and long corridors where wine, grain, oil, and honey were stored in huge jars. Surviving gold cups and ornaments, pottery vessels of eggshell thinness, a gaming board of gold, silver, ivory, and blue enamel, all indicate luxury and wealth.

Several broad stairways in this palace (Fig. 4–3) led to the upper floors of the building, which, set on a hillside, was in some places several stories high. The foundations and the lower parts were of huge, finely cut blocks of stone; but the columns, made of wood, supported lintels and, by opening up the walls, allowed light and air to penetrate the stair wells and the many upper rooms. Distinguishing features of these Aegean columns are their bulbous, cushionlike capitals and the manner in which the column shafts taper

[2] Several names are used for this civilization. "Aegean" is the most inclusive; "Cretan" or "Minoan" may be applied to that aspect which definitely belongs to Crete, "Helladic" to that of the mainland, and "Cycladic" to that of the other islands. "Mycenaean" culture is included in Late Helladic (*ca.* 1550–1100 B.C.).

Cretan history is divided as follows: Early Minoan (3000 to about 2000 B.C.), Middle Minoan (2000–1600 B.C.), and Late Minoan (1600–1100 B.C.).

The Homeric Age described in the *Iliad* and the *Odyssey* (which were not written down until much later) reflects the period of migration and conflict after 1200 B.C.

from top to bottom. Strong evidence that the column had religious significance for the Cretans is its central position in the Temple fresco, in the *Lion Gate* at Mycenae (Fig. 4–4), and in the fact that a column in one of the lower stories of the palace at Knossos is surrounded by a trough for libations.

Painting on columns and on walls was the chief decoration of the palace. The frescoes depicted many aspects of Cretan life: bullfights, processions, and ceremonies as well as scenes from nature: birds, animals, flowers, and fish. In one of these frescoes a tall slender *Cupbearer* (Fig. 4–5), one of a procession of youths, shows the typical Cretan figure style and costume. He has long curly hair, wears an elaborately embroidered loincloth with a silver mounted girdle, and has ornaments on his arms, neck, ankles, and wrist. Although the profile view with the full-view eye is a familiar convention found in Egypt and Mesopotamia, the elegance of these Cretan figures with their pinched waists, their proud, self-confident bearing, and the freedom of their movements distinguishes them from all other early figure styles. As in Egypt, the men were painted red and women yellow, and their rhythmical order against the flat ground broken into wavy bands was highly decorative.

Vivacity and spontaneity characterize the *Toreador Scene* (Fig. 4–6). Although only fragments of it have been recovered, they are extraordinary in their depiction of vigorous movements of different youths, one of whom is shown in the air. We do not know whether they are engaged in a game or in some ritual which involved vaulting over the back of a charging bull, but in either instance great skill and courage must have been demanded. These may be the legendary youths and maidens exacted as tribute from Athens, risking death in conflict with the bull.

4–5 CUPBEARER. Fresco from Knossos. H. *ca.* 5 ft. *ca.* 1500 B.C. Restored. Herakleion Museum.

In scenes of nature we also find observation, imagination, and spontaneity. The *Flying Fish* fresco (Fig. 4–7) is composed in an easy swinging motion and countermotion combined with a short quick rhythm in the rocks and edges of the fins. The bright blues, yellows, and browns add to the decorative quality as well as to the gay atmosphere.

When Cretan culture spread to mainland Greece differing conditions brought fresh developments. The Mycenaean palace was more somber, com-

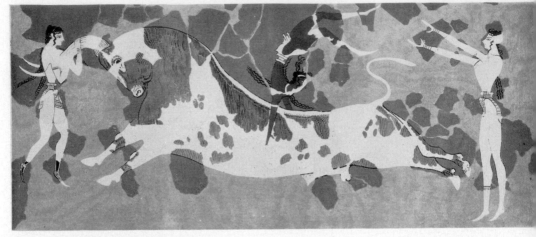

4–6   TOREADOR SCENE. Fresco from Knossos. *ca.* 1500 B.C. Restored. Herakleion Museum.

pact, and fortresslike than its Cretan predecessors and was often built on an easily defended hilltop. At Tiryns, walls twenty feet thick, of unhewn or roughly dressed stone, were called "Cyclopean" by the later Greeks, who imagined them to have been built by that mythical race of giants. Through the walls at intervals run corbeled galleries (Fig. 4–8), which may have been used as part of the defensive structure or as part of a complicated and dramatic ceremonial path leading to the chief room of the palace through a porch and vestibule. This hall of state, known as a *megaron* (Fig. 4–9), was rectangular in form with a central hearth and four columns supporting the roof. An important audience chamber, it may reflect very early customs; it is also significant as the prototype of later Greek temples.

The sternness of these fortress-palaces was enlivened by frescoes, by carvings, and at Mycenae, at least, by an example of monumental architectural sculpture, the *Lion Gate* (Fig. 4–4). This outer doorway of the stronghold is formed of two great monoliths capped with a huge lintel above which

4–7   FLYING FISH FRESCO from Island of Melos. 1700–1550 B.C. Restored. National Museum, Athens.

4 8 CORBELED GALLERY. Citadel at Tiryns. 1400–1000 B.C.

the layers of stone form a corbeled arch leaving a triangular opening to lighten the weight. The arched space is filled with a slab on which two lions, carved in high relief, confront each other on either side of a sacred column of Aegean type, resting their forepaws on its base. Holes near the top of the animals indicate that the heads, now lost, were made of separate pieces of stone or metal. The lions are carved with breadth and vigor and the whole design admirably fills its triangular space, harmonizing in dignity, strength, and scale with the massive stones which form the walls and gate. We find similar groups in miniature on Cretan seals.

Another type of building found at Mycenae is the *tholos*, or so-called beehive tomb. When first discovered, these structures were thought to be store-houses for treasure, hence the most important is still known as the *Treasury of Atreus* (Fig. 4–10). (We now believe that they were important tombs.) Built into a hill and approached by a long passage, the beehive shape is achieved by corbeled courses of stone laid on a circular base. A small rectangular chamber at the side served as a burial place. Frequent holes in the interior surface of the vault seem to indicate that decorations, such as bronze rosettes, were affixed. In the tombs' monumental entrance we find the same combination of lintel and corbeled arch construction as in the *Lion Gate*.

SCULPTURE

Sculpture in the round and in relief, although small in scale, has the same

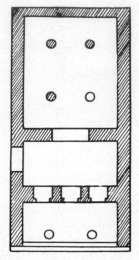

4–9 PLAN OF A MEGARON.

characteristic vigor and distinction that we have seen in Aegean paintings. The small ivory figure, identified as a *Girl Toreador* (Fig. 4–11), is typical of a number of such statuettes, which also include crowned women grasping snakes and therefore identified as snake goddesses. The applied gold bands and ornaments of the costume create, with the ivory, a striking combination of materials, known as *chryselephantine* work, which appealed as well to the Greeks of the Age of Pericles. The delicacy with which these ivory figures are carved accents their feminine grace, yet the girl with her uplifted arms seems poised and tense as though she were participating in an athletic contest, or possibly in one of the games with the bull.

Even more spontaneous in the treatment of the material and in the light-hearted, gay effects achieved are a number of clay figurines, such as the *Girl in a Swing* (Fig. 4–12). The bright colors of the glazed surfaces, the ability to capture the moment of

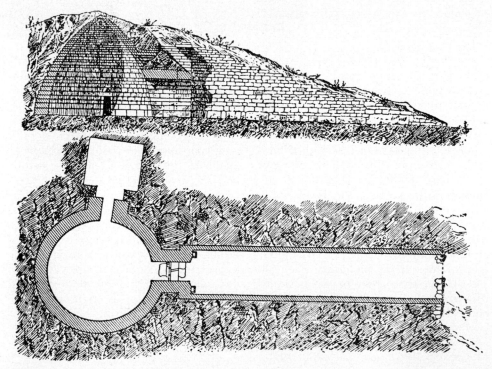

4–10 BEEHIVE TOMB, called the "Treasury of Atreus." Mycenae, *ca.* 1330 B.C. (Perrot and Chipiez)

POTTERY AND METALWORK

Among Cretan craftsmen the potter was of special consequence, his wares being important articles of commerce. Recent discoveries, especially at Phaistos, show a wide variety of shapes and decorations. A large wine krater, for instance (Fig. 4-14), has a varied series of abstract patterns in black, white, and red, with free-standing white lily blossoms applied to the base and upper portions and with white ceramic chains suspended from the rim. Such unexpected combinations of forms appear, at first glance, rather garish and lacking in taste, but they reflect an interesting moment when civilization was emerging from the prehistoric conditions of the Neolithic Age. Somewhat later in date is the famous *Kamares Ware* (Fig. 4-15) (so-called from the cave on Mount Ida where a large number of examples have been found) which is robust in shape with a lustrous black ground setting off the patterns of

4-11 GIRL TOREADOR. Crete. Ivory ornamented with gold. H. 7 in *ca* 1550 B.C. Right arm is restored, but right hand is ancient. Royal Ontario Museum, Toronto. (Royal Ontario Museum)

balance as well as the movement of a figure in space seem part of the spirit of Mediterranean peoples in every age.

This same gaiety is equally evident in the scenes in relief on the surface of a small steatite vase, the *Harvester Vase* (Fig. 4-13). It shows a riotous crowd of harvesters, singing and shouting, following a figure carrying a rattle. Their forward movement and lusty exuberance are vigorously expressed. The pattern of pitchforks fills the upper part of the band, while the figures below, in higher relief, create a variation in surface. The entire design hugs the shape so tightly that it seems to be an integral part of the wall of the vase.

4-12 GIRL IN A SWING. Painted clay. H. 5½ in. 1550-1400(?) B.C. Herakleion Museum.

creamy white interspersed with yellow and red. As time went on, the tendency toward naturalism in decoration increased. Motifs were derived from sea life such as dolphins, seaweed, or the octopus. The tentacles reaching out over the curving surfaces of the *Octopus Jar* (Fig. 4–1) emphasize the volume of the vase. Botanical and animal forms also provided the artist with patterns which he adapted to the jar's surface. The fully developed style appears in what is often referred to as the Palace, or palatial, style, because so many examples have been found at Knossos. Figure 4–16 is an example. The double-ax motif plays through the design — in the shape of the handles, in the spaces between the handles and between the horns of the ox, on the rim, and on the foot. The motif probably has some religious significance, and the vase may have been used for ceremonial pur-

poses. Note the naturalistic sprays of olive in the midst of an otherwise conventional design.

Also of great importance both in Crete and on the mainland was the goldsmith. Among his charming creations were ornamental disks decorated with spirals and butterfly and octopus patterns sensitively adapted to the circular surface and charged with the energy of curvilinear rhythms. This skill is particularly evident in a variety of cups, decorated with scenes in *repoussé*, among which the *Vaphio Cups* (Fig. 4–17), found in a grave at Vaphio in Laconia, are notable. They are a pair, each made of two plates of gold, one of which was worked in *repoussé* for the outside, the other left plain to make a smooth surface for the inside. The plates were then fastened together, the handles riveted on, and some of the details then engraved. One cup shows a bull caught in a net. A second bull, charging furiously, impales with his horns a man whose companion falls

4–13 HARVESTER VASE. Black steatite. Restored. W. *ca.* 4 in. *ca.* 1500 B.C. Herakleion Museum.

4–14 WINE KRATER. Phaistos. H. *ca.* 28 in. *ca.* 2000 B.C. Herakleion Museum. (Prof. Doro Levi, Scuola Archeologica Italiana, Athens)

4-15 KAMARES VASE from Knossos. H. *ca.* 9 in. 2000–1800 B.C. Herakleion Museum.

to one side. A third bull dashes madly from the fracas. The other cup presents a quiet scene. At the right the bull moves toward a cow; in the center he stands beside her; at the left, captured and hobbled, he is bellowing. The three scenes are well united by the trees and the man, and the whole design is admirably composed to fit the space. In both cups, areas not filled by the animal and human figures contain landscape motifs of trees, rocks, and clouds, similar to those in the paintings. The lowness of the relief and the conventional treatment of the trees produce a rich play of light and shade together with varying areas of smooth and rough textures.

4-16 PALACE STYLE VASE. H. *ca.* 30 in. 1600–1500 B.C. National Museum, Athens. (Seager)

Skill in another kind of metalworking is seen in damascened daggers, the bronze blades of which are inlaid with gold, electrum, and a black substance. On one blade, on which a lion hunt is represented, the bodies of the fleeing animals, elongated as if to accentuate their rapid movement, fit admirably into the tapering shape.

One final technique should be men-

4-17 VAPHIO CUPS. Gold. H. 3½ in. 1600–1500 B.C. National Museum, Athens.

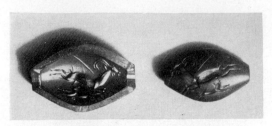

4–18 GEM. Red jasper. 1600–1350 B.C.
Metropolitan Museum of Art, New York.
(Purchase, funds from various donors)

tioned before the end of this brief discussion of the art of a people about
whom we know so little. It is the carving of gems for seals. These miniature
designs (Fig. 4–18) in intaglio show
the same sensitivity for natural forms
which we have noted in other media,
and an instinct for the adaptation of
the design to the available space. It is
interesting to observe that this art of
painstaking skill was not only highly
developed in Mesopotamia but was also continued by the Greeks, who executed, as we shall see, some superb designs.

Summary

Aegean art is directly expressive of
an active people intimate with nature.
It is a refreshing, sprightly art, imaginative and naturalistic, its restless
movement reflecting an exuberance of
body and mind. As excavations bring
to light new evidence about these people, we realize that they lived in communities around the great palaces of
their rulers. The houses as well as the
palaces were richly furnished, and the
walls were gay with frescoes. The variety in Aegean pottery and paintings,
their vivacity and originality, reflect
the eagerness, restlessness, and adven-

turousness of the Cretan seafarers. On
the Greek mainland fortified palaces
give evidence of a war-consciousness
which is reflected in the Homeric tales,
and magnificent metalwork lends au-
thenticity to the descriptions in Homer
of the shield of Achilles and the House
of Alcinous.

Bibliography

Bell, Edward, *Prehellenic Architecture in the
    Aegean*, Bell, London, 1926.
Bossert, Helmuth T., *Altkreta*, 3rd ed. enl.,
    E. Wasmuth, Berlin, 1937.
Evans, Sir Arthur J., *The Palace of Minos*,
    4 vols., Macmillan, New York, 1921–35.
Fowler, Harold N., Wheeler, James R., and
    Stevens, Gorham P., *A Handbook of
    Greek Archaeology*, American Book,
    New York, 1909.
Hawes, Charles H., and Hawes, Harriet A.,
    Crete, the Forerunner of Greece, Harper,
    New York, 1911.
Kantor, Helene J., *The Aegean and the Ori-
    ent in the Second Millennium B.C.*,
    Principia Press, Bloomington, Ind., 1947.
Lorimer, Hilda L., *Homer and the Monu-
    ments*, Macmillan, New York, 1951.
Mackenzie, Donald A., *Myths of Crete and
    Pre-Hellenic Europe*, Gresham, London,
    1917.
Nilsson, Martin P., *Minoan-Mycenaean Reli-
    gion and Its Survival in Greek Religion*,
    2nd rev. ed., C. W. K. Gleerup, Lund,
    Sweden, 1950.
Pendlebury, John D. S., *The Archaeology of
    Crete*, Methuen, London, 1939.
——, *A Handbook to the Palace of Minos at
    Knossos*, Macmillan, New York, 1933.
Persson, Axel W., *Religion of Greece in Pre-
    historic Times*, University of California
    Press, Berkeley, 1942.
Rodenwaldt, Gerhart, *Die Kunst der Antike*,
    2nd ed., Propyläen-Verlag, Berlin, 1927.
Tsountas, Chrestos, and Manatta, J. Irving,
    The Mycenaean Age, Houghton Mifflin,
    1897.
Wace, Alan J. B., *Mycenae, an Archaeo-
    logical History and Guide*, Princeton
    University Press, 1949.

CHAPTER 5

GREEK

Greek art is the expression of a turning point in the history of Western civilization. The conventions and rituals which gave rise to the art of Egypt and Mesopotamia did not disappear, but they were transformed by rational thought and by individual will. The work of art, whether a temple or a statue, was, as in earlier cultures, real as an object of worship. But this work of art also now expressed man's individual observations of the natural world and his desire to understand reality in this different context. Greek art is as a result a compact synthesis of opposites, a harmony between profound passion and rational order. Its clarity and symmetry are not cold but blazing. Its forms are rigorous and mathematical, yet full of life.

In marked contrast to Egypt, with its long horizontals of alluvial plain between desert plateaus under invariable sunshine, Greece is a country of diversified geography and climate (Fig.

ILLUSTRATION ABOVE. 5-1. KYLIX PAINTED BY DOURIS. *ca.* 470 B.C. Metropolitan Museum of Art, New York.

5-2). The deeply indented bays of its rugged coastline make the country half land and half sea; mountain ridges divide it into many small units. The climate is vigorous — cold in the winter, dry and hot in the summer. There is almost always a breeze from the sea. The unusually crystalline atmosphere is often softened by a haze. Both sky and sea are brilliant in color. It is little wonder that the Greeks, who were sensitive to beauty and gifted with imagination, in their joy in nature should people mountains, woods, streams, sky, and sea with divinities; that they should picture Zeus, the king of this realm of gods, as reigning from their loftiest peak, Olympus; the Muses, as dwelling in the deep, cool groves on the long slopes of Parnassus and Cithaeron; and Apollo, the god of wisdom, as speaking from the awe-inspiring rocky clefts of Delphi.

Nature worship evolved into nature personification. The gods assumed human forms whose grandeur and nobility were not free from human frailty. Man became "the measure of all

5-2 GREECE AND THE AEGEAN WORLD IN ANCIENT TIMES.

things"; to create the perfect individual became the Greek ideal.

The Greeks, or Hellenes as they called themselves, appear to have been the product of an intermingling of Aegean peoples and of Indo-European invaders. The first of these invaders began to drift into the area about 2000 B.C., and after 1600 B.C. formed the Mycenaean civilization on the Peloponnesos. Perhaps they were the Achaeans of whom Homer was to write, and who were known to the Hittites of Asia Minor as the Ahhiyava, whose war bands attacked both Egypt and Troy. About 1100 B.C. the Achaeans (or Mycenaeans) were apparently overwhelmed in turn by new invaders from the north, the Ionians and Dorians. The Dorians made the Peloponnesos the center of their power and evidently forced the Ionians eastward across the Aegean to the coast of Asia Minor. As men whose tribal pattern was broken by forced emigration, the Ionians seem to have become more individualistic than the tribally ordered Dorians, whose most characteristic city became conservative Sparta. In Ionia, at least by the eighth century B.C., were developed the epics of individual greatness which cluster around the name of Homer. There too, by the seventh century, the rational philosophers of Miletus had begun to interpret the world in terms of reason rather than of ritual. Between Ionia and the Peloponnesos lay Attica, and there, in Athens, tribal conservatism and individualistic striving combined to produce the most fruitful of all the city-states. Here too memories of the old Minoan civilization remained as myths to give form and dimension to new activities.

By the eighth century B.C. the separate Greek-speaking states had held their first ceremonial games in common: the Olympiad of 756 B.C. From then on, despite their rivalries, they regarded themselves all as Hellenes, distinct from the surrounding "barbarians" who did not speak Greek. The enterprising Hellenes became a trading and colonizing people who enlarged the geographic and cultural boundaries of Hellas. From their contacts with the older civilizations — Egypt, Babylonia-Assyria, Phoenicia — they acquired ideas, motifs, conventions, skills. Tribal organizations had evolved into city-states, each an individual unit. Political development differed from state to state, but a kind of pattern emerged in which rule was first by kings, then by nobles, then by "tyrants" who seized personal power. At last, in Athens, appeared the dynamic balance which was called democracy.

Athens has in many ways become the symbol of Greek culture. Had one visited Athens at the time of its brief flowering after the Persian wars, one would have seen an enterprising business city of about a hundred thousand people, situated on a fertile plain surrounding a lone hill some five miles inland from a bustling harbor. One would have seen an unplanned mass of small sun-dried brick houses set along winding lanelike streets. There were no sidewalks and no drainage system. The chief open space was the *agora,* or market place, with its plane trees for shade; it was surrounded by public offices and covered colonnades called stoas. Though the market always served its primary purpose as a central place for the sale of vegetables, cheese, honey, and flowers, its use was much wider, for here the citizens congregated to lounge in the cool of the stoa, to discuss the latest political development or a new philosophical idea. Such discussion in the agora was the key to the intense political and intellectual life which developed in the Greek city-state, the *polis.* Outside the city walls were olive groves and the gymnasiums where the men went, primarily for the bodily exercise that played so large a part in education and daily life, but also, again, for discussion. And above both the olive groves and the roof tops towered the *Acropolis,* or higher city, formerly a fortress but in this age crowned with temples rising in bright colors against an intensely blue sky (Fig. 5–3).

The Athenian through his religion recognized moral obligations to his city-state and concentrated his thoughts and energies toward the enhancement of its glory. That glory, and the popular basis for it, manifested itself in the great religious festivals, such as the Panathenaic procession, in which all citizens, men and women, old and young, took part. The tragedies of Aeschylus

5-3   VIEW OF THE ACROPOLIS OF ATHENS. (Photo Viollet)

and Sophocles also treated the individual as a member of a group owing moral obligations to the gods.

The remains of Greek civilization enable us to reconstruct the development of Greek style. That this style should in fact have "developed" is in itself significant. Development in the art of Egypt, for example, was minimal; the pattern of ritual and of form was not to be broken. Change in Egypt occurred, when it did, despite the pattern of the culture as a whole. But from the beginning the Greek embraced experiment, even while holding on to the older forms. Development and change were inherent in Greek culture, and certain phases can be noted.

Geometric, Archaic, and 5th-Century

(ABOUT 1100–400 B.C.)

From about 1100 to 400 B.C. four important stages in the development of Greek art may be identified. The first, the *Geometric,* which endured from about 1100 to 700 B.C., is evident in pottery and small bronze sculpture. This was followed by the *Archaic* style, from which architecture may first be studied but which is best seen in sculpture and in vase painting. It lasted until 500 B.C. During the fifth century two phases of Greek *Classic* art flourished. The first, the *Early Classic*, or *Severe*, style, is exemplified in the architecture and sculpture at Olympia, dating from about 470–460 B.C. The second phase of Classic art is also known as the *Age of Pericles*, when the Acropolis at Athens

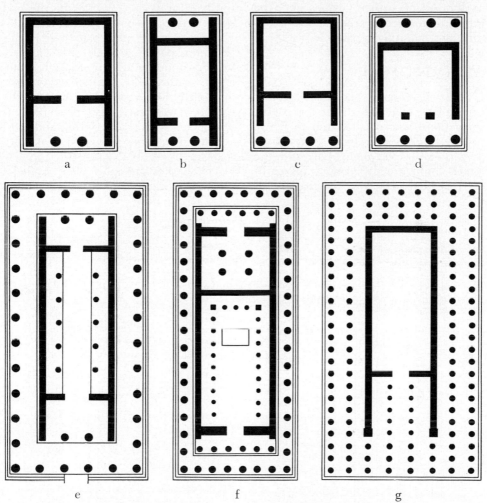

a b c d

e f g

5–4 PLANS OF GREEK TEMPLES. *a*. Treasury of the Athenians at Delphi, a temple *in antis*, so called because the portico is formed by the projecting side walls (*antae*) and two columns set between them. *b*. Temple of Artemis at Eleusis, a temple *in antis* at both ends. *c*. Temple B at Selinus, Sicily, a *prostyle* temple, so called because the columns stand in front of the cella and extend the width of it. Sometimes an additional colonnade is placed at the back of the temple, and it is then called *amphiprostyle*, as in *d*. *d*. Temple of Nike Apteros (Wingless Victory) on the Acropolis at Athens. *e*. Temple of Aphaia at Aegina, a *peripteral* temple, so called because a colonnade completely surrounds the cella, which in this case is *in antis* at both ends. *f*. Parthenon, a peripteral temple; to the prostyle cella an additional room for treasure has been added. *g*. Temple of Hera at Samos. The peripteral plan in such Ionic temples is embellished by doubling the surrounding colonnade, creating a *dipteral* plan. This plan is also characteristically Ionic in the deep pronaos and closed cella.

was rebuilt, but as Athens waned toward the end of the century the style was also transformed. In order to trace the major developments in the different categories of artistic expression, the following text treats architecture, sculpture, and painting separately.

ARCHITECTURE

Since his home was an unpretentious place in which to eat and sleep, since there was no monarch to house royally, and since religious rites were performed in the open, why did the Greek build greatly? Among his earliest recorded acts was the practice of carving statues to his gods. The need to protect these statues led to the building of simple shrines, on which more and more attention was lavished until possibly the qualities of the god were personified in the structure itself. Figure sculpture played its part in this program, partly to embellish the protective building, partly to tell something of the deity symbolized within, and partly as a votive offering. But the building was itself also conceived as sculpture, abstract in form, and possessing sculpture's power to evoke human qualities.

The earliest temples were built of wood, and these wooden forms were in

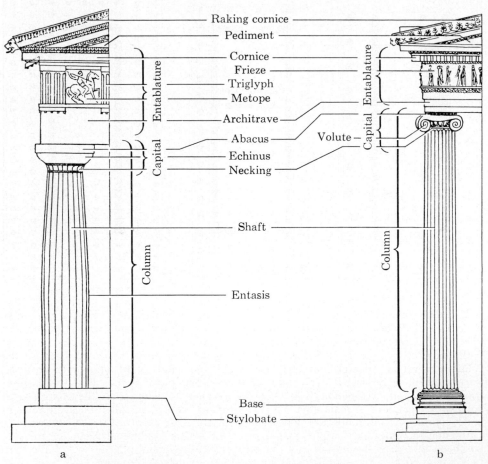

Raking cornice
Pediment
Cornice
Frieze
Triglyph
Metope
Architrave
Abacus — Volute
Echinus
Necking
Shaft
Entasis
Base
Stylobate
Entablature
Capital
Column
Capital Entablature
Column
a
b

5–5 A COMPARISON OF GREEK ORDERS. *a.* The Doric order. *b.* The Ionic order.

time translated into the more permanent and sculptural materials of limestone and marble. Marble was expensive, but mountains of it were available: Hymettos, just east of Athens, with its bluish-white stone; Pentelikon, north of the city, its glittering white peculiarly adapted for carving. The islands of the Aegean, Paros in particular, supplied varying quantities and qualities. It is characteristic of the Greek search for perfection that the masonry of the temples should have been constructed without mortar, the joints being "live": stone was placed directly on stone, and metal dowels or cramps provided stability, or assurance against movement.

In its plan the Greek temple discloses a close affinity with the Mycenaean megaron, and even in its most elaborate form retains basic simplicity: a single or double room (the cella) with no windows and one door (or two for a double cella), and with either (1) a portico with two columns, between the extended walls, or (2) a colonnade across the entire front, or (3) a colonnade across both front and back, or (4) any of these plans surrounded by a single or a double colonnade (Fig. 5-4). The interior space was kept in balance with the solids of the structure, so that the unity of the building was never vitiated.

In elevation the temple had three parts: a base, columnar supports, and a superstructure of lintels and sloping roof with gable ends. Such an elevation is known as an order. Three orders evolved in the course of the Greek style and are differentiated partly by details but chiefly by the relative proportions of the parts. Each served different purposes and embodied different meanings.

The earliest of the Greek architectural orders to be formulated were the *Doric* of mainland Greece and the *Ionic* of Asia Minor and the islands (Fig.

5-5). The Doric order was massive and solid, resembling a well-integrated, sturdy body; the Ionic was high and slender, suggesting a tree or a jet of water. The *Corinthian* order, even more treelike, was not developed until the fifth century B.C., when it appeared inside the temple, as a natural force growing in the darkness of the interior. It was, however, not widely used until Roman times.

Ornament played an important part in the design of the temple and was concentrated on the upper part of the building — in the metopes, the frieze, and the pediments. This ornament was basically sculpture gaily painted in red and blue, with touches of green, yellow, black, and perhaps a little gold. The unpainted parts may have been rubbed with wax. Sometimes they were stuccoed white. By this use of color the artist could bring out more clearly the relationships of the parts, could soften the glitter of the stone at specific points, and could provide a background to set off the figures.

Unlike Egyptian temples, Greek temples faced outward. Rites were performed at altars in front of the temple, and the building itself served only to house the cult statue. It was on the exterior and its surfaces that the architect concentrated his attention in order to make the temple a suitable monument to the deity. The studied relationships of solids and voids, of light and shade in the colonnades, and the lighter accents of the entablature make a sculptural form out of the rectangular cube of the temple.

Having created his architectural vocabulary the Greek set about extracting the maximum expression from it. He did not add words, as it were, but intensified their usage. Earlier Doric temples, like the very ancient Heraion at Olympia, were apparently long and low. These proportions slowly became less extreme and the temple grew wid-

5–6 TEMPLE OF HERA (formerly known as temple of Poseidon) at Paestum. *ca.* 460–450 B.C. (Alinari)

er in relation to its length. As time went on other elements were brought into more balanced relationships. The entablature became lighter, the column slimmer. But there was also, perhaps, a variation between temples according to their site and the deity whom they honored.

At *Paestum* in south Italy, for example, the first temple — to Hera (the so-called Basilica) of *ca.* 540 B.C. — is wide and low under the hill line beyond. The next temple — to Demeter, *ca.* 500 B.C. — stands high and narrow against the highest hill. The last — again to Hera, 450 B.C. (Fig. 5–6) — is a massive complement to the mountain chain. At *Olympia* (Fig. 5–7), where by 460 B.C. a temple to Zeus had been built to the south of the old Heraion under the hill of Kronos, one can note further the meaningful relationships of temple masses to each other. From the entrance gate one viewed the temples as they converged around the shrine to

Pelops which lay between them. The eye of the observer then moved beyond the temples to the hill of Kronos the father, under which nestled the temple of Hera the daughter, while out in space stood the gleaming bulk of the temple of Zeus. Thus the man-made temple and the natural features of the site were used by the early Greek architect to complement each other.

The culmination of this dynamic site planning and of Greek temple construction occurred in the buildings begun by Pericles for the *Acropolis* in Athens (Fig. 5–8). This massive outcropping of solid rock had been fortified in Mycenaean times, and a temple to Athena Polias had been erected there in the sixth century. This and an early Parthenon had been destroyed by the Persians in 480 B.C. Pericles, a generation later, after Athens had become supreme in the Aegean, appropriated the treasury of the Delian league for the rebuilding of the great monuments

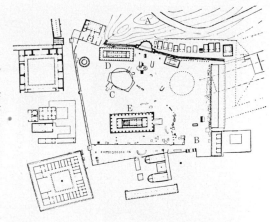

5–7 PLAN OF THE PRECINCT OF ZEUS AT
OLYMPIA. 5th century B.C. *A*. Hill of
Kronos. *B*. Entrance gate. *C*. Shrine of
Pelops. *D*. Temple of Hera. *E*. Temple of
Zeus. (After W. B. Dinsmoor, *Architecture
of Ancient Greece*, Batsford, Ltd., 1950)

of Athens. These have remained the glory of Greece. On the Acropolis the principal buildings are: the *Parthenon*, dedicated to Athena as Wisdom, built by Iktinos and Kallikrates between 447 and 432 B.C.; the *Erectheum*, a complex shrine to Athena, Poseidon, and the city's founders, upon which work ceased in 405 B.C.; and the *Propylaea* (437–432 B.C.), by the architect Mnesicles, a subtly arranged entrance gate which prepared the observer for the sacred world of the Acropolis height. Crowning a bastion, just to the right of the Propylaea, is the jewel-like *Nike Apteros*, a prostyle temple to Athena as Victory, designed by Kallikrates and built probably between 427 and 424 B.C. This looked out toward Salamis

and reminded the Athenian, as he turned to enter into the presence of his city goddess, that her glory had been preserved by the courage of his fathers.

The Propylaea, roughly T-shaped in plan, combined the Doric and Ionic orders and was so placed that the observer as he passed beneath the interior Ionic capitals would have seen directly ahead the colossal statue, now irretrievably lost, of *Athena Promachos* by Phidias. Behind her and to her left rose the Doric Parthenon, and across from it the smaller and delicate Ionic Erechtheum with its porch of Korai as caryatids. These still give scale to the mighty Parthenon columns and seem to advance toward them across the bare rocky summit of the hill. From

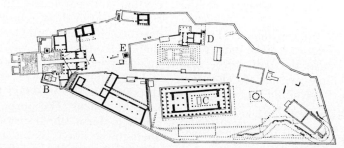

5–8 PLAN OF THE ACROPOLIS AT ATHENS. *ca.* 447–405 B.C. Restored. *A*. Propylaea.
B. Temple of Nike Apteros. *C*. Parthenon. *D*. Erechtheum. *E*. Original site of colossal
statue of Athena Promachos. (From W. B. Dinsmoor, *Architecture of Ancient Greece*,
Batsford, Ltd., 1950)

5–9 PARTHENON. Athens. Of Pentelic marble. Iktinos and Kallikrates, architects. 447–432 B.C.

the Propylaea, the Erechtheum and the Parthenon complement each other across this summit, behind which appears only the empty blue of the blazing sky. Under this sky the bare surface of the hill itself, and the temple surfaces, are blinding white at noonday. The Parthenon, with the upward curve of its stylobate and entablature and the inward slanting of its columns [1] (Fig. 5–9) is the culmination of the hill.

The plan of the *Parthenon* (Fig. 5–4*f*) shows a double cella, one room serving to house the cult statue, the other, the temple treasure. In elevation the Parthenon exemplifies the Doric or-

[1] These deviations from the horizontal and vertical have long been interpreted as a means of correcting optical illusions, but there is general agreement today that they serve primarily not as corrections but as positive distortions to adjust the structure to the site and to give it a greater sense of organic unity and vitality.

der. The columns rise directly, without individual bases, from the *stylobate*, the upper step of the base of a temple which forms a platform for the columns. The shaft diminishes in diameter as it rises, and its contour is a very subtle but lively curve, the *entasis*. The grooves, or *flutings*, of the shafts with their curved shadows and repeated vertical lines both strengthen the rhythm and emphasize the feeling of support in the shaft. The grooves thus enhance the columns by contrasting them with the plain wall of the cella against which they are seen.

The capital consists of the usual three parts: the *necking*, the *echinus*, and the *abacus*. The purpose of a capital is to form the transition from the shaft to the lintel, that is, from the vertical member, the load-carrying element, to the horizontal member, the load. In the Doric capital the first suggestion of the horizontal is in the neck-

5-10 ERECHTHEUM. Athens. *ca.* 420–409 B.C. View from the south. (Clarence Kennedy)

ing; yet the vertical flutings continue up into the capital to the row of concentric ridges which separate the fluting from the echinus The simple vigorous curve of the echinus then carries the line up to the square abacus — not directly, however, for it turns inward as it meets the block, thus indicating the separateness of the parts. From the rectangular abacus the eye is carried easily into the horizontal architrave. Thus by a carefully thought-out design, based upon skillful interplay of direction, the transition from vertical to horizontal, from supporting to supported elements is achieved.

The *architrave* is severely plain and the frieze is composed of alternating *triglyphs* and *metopes*, the triglyphs repeating the verticals of the columns in a more rapid tempo. The architrave and the *frieze* are separated by a simple *stringcourse* and united by the molding of beadlike ornaments beneath

5-11 CARVING FROM THE ERECHTHEUM, with honeysuckle, bead and reel, egg and dart, and leaf and dart motifs. Acropolis Museum, Athens. (Alinari)

each triglyph. The deeply projecting *cornice* finishes the design and protects the frieze from rain. Unity of design between the frieze and the cornice is obtained by undercutting the cornice to correspond with the triglyphs and the metopes, and originally also by the use of harmonious colors. A second cornice, known as the *raking cornice*, completes the *pediment* in a decisive gable shape.

The *Erechtheum*, named after Erechtheus to whom it was in part dedicated (Fig. 5–10), has many unusual features, partly due to the irregular character of the ground on which the temple stands and partly to the number of shrines included within it.[2] The assymmetrical massing, which may possibly not have been intended in the original program for the building, is nevertheless extremely effective as a complement to the symmetrical unity of the Parthenon, just as the Korai of the Porch of the Maidens complement the Parthenon's Doric columns. Later ages have also equated the Ionic columns of the east and north porches of the Erectheum with female elegance. These columns are distinct from the Doric order in many details. They are separated from the stylobate by individual bases, of which the upper *torus* is delicately carved; the fluting of the shaft is more heavily accented; on the necking is a honeysuckle band; and the echinus is decorated with bead and reel, egg and dart, and the double guilloche. The double scroll, or *volutes*, of the capital, which always distinguish the Ionic order, are treated almost as separate accents between the narrow echinus and the thin abacus. The archi-

[2] According to Pausanias, the Greek geographer and historian of the second century B.C., the Erechtheum stood on the traditional site of the contest between Poseidon and Athena for dominion over Athens. The site included a mark in the rock which was the mark of Poseidon's trident, a spring of salt water, and Athena's olive tree.

5–12 HERA OF SAMOS. Marble. H. 6 ft. *ca.* 550 B.C. Louvre, Paris. (Alinari)

trave is divided into three horizontal faces and above it is a frieze of continuous low-relief sculpture, in place of the Doric triglyphs and metopes. Stringcourses and cornices, doorway, and wall bands are delicately carved with dentils, egg and dart, bead and reel, honeysuckle, and braid patterns (Fig. 5–11). The value of such moldings to the Greek may be judged from the fact that he paid, according to the building inscriptions of the Erechtheum, the same price for carving one foot of egg and dart as for one human figure.

And who discovered the combinations of these elements? An inventor of genius. These stones lay inert in the quarries of Pentelicus, unshaped. To group them thus needed not an engineer, but a great sculptor.[3]

SCULPTURE

Greek sculpture was the expression of a vigorously growing people with a strong sense of life, but with a profoundly conservative religious feeling. Its forms were intensely geometric and structural. The basic attitude of the early Greeks toward sculpture may be understood by studying the Geometric period. The images of animals and men were subjected to a structural reordering and geometric intensification. The form of the object itself was intended as an equivalent for, rather than as a representation of, natural form.

Many of these same qualities may be recognized in Archaic monumental sculpture in stone, as in the *Hera of Samos* of *ca.* 550 B.C. (Fig. 5–12). The Hera is basically a cylinder, possibly reflecting a wooden prototype translated into stone and relating to the cylindrical forms of Mesopotamia and the Near East. The goddess stands in a

[3] Le Corbusier, *Towards a New Architecture*, Payson and Clarke, New York, 1927, p. 211.

frontal pose, feet together, the right arm held tightly to the side, the left bent to the breast, probably originally holding some attribute. She is the goddess as a sheathed column, as were the deities of Crete and Mycenae; but here the Greek artist displays his extraordinary sensitivity for surface ornamentation. The stability and order of the lower portions, where the vertical striations of the linen chiton are juxtaposed against the plain surface of the heavy woolen himation, is given movement and life in the upper portion by the curves of the rest of the himation drawn in graceful drapery round the delicate modeling of the human form.

5–13 SEATED FIGURE. From the Sacred Way of the Temple of Apollo near Miletus. 550–530 B.C. British Museum, London. (Trustees of the British Museum)

5-14 KOUROS FROM SOUNION in the National Museum, Athens. *ca.* 615–590 B.C. (Alison Frantz)

A similar sense of repose and majesty permeates the seated figures from a temple near Miletus (Fig. 5–13). An impression of power arises from the sheer massiveness and weight of the stone, and one of dignity from the simple four-sided organization, as in the *Khafra* (Fig. 2–9). Here, too, conventional devices, representing different kinds of cloth, break up the surfaces and create varying textures.

We are again reminded of Egyptian statues by the early *Kouroi* figures (Figs. 5–14 and 5–15). These are youths, some of them victors in games, who are dedicated to a god and are apparently advancing into his presence. Thus they are men, not gods (not "Apollos"). They recall Egypt in the pose with left foot advanced, in the broad square shoulders, and in the rigidly symmetrical organization (Fig. 2–10). The Egyptian and Mesopotamian thought of the human body as a smooth envelope, but the Greek was interested in the separate parts, how they fitted together, and how they worked. On the broad planes of the figure which are related to the original block of stone, anatomical details, such as the knees, are boldly carved. The head also conforms to deliberate geometric laws (Fig. 5–14). The large, bulging eyes and the huge, highly stylized ears accent the sensitive modeling of the nose and mouth and act as unifying elements with the rigid planes of the conventionalized wig. Above the temples, under the wig, the waving lines of the hair recall, as in the Ionic capital, the movement of the sea. Each Kouros differs from the next (Fig. 5–15). In the Kouros from Tenea of about 550 B.C. the young athlete is poised, narrow-hipped, slope-shouldered — a young elegant. He is alert as a hawk, while the Sounion Kouros is solid as a noble mountain.

By the early fifth century a startling transformation occurred in the Kouroi statues. They forsook the frontality which monumental, free-standing sculpture had exhibited since early Egyptian and Sumerian times. The artist was now concerned with the visual reproduction of natural forms, which, although they were less generalized, were still controlled by a geometric order. The weight is shifted to one leg. The figure turns, and the features have an expression of severity, melancholy, and thought. The direct joy in life and triumph of the earlier Archaic period seems clouded by the responsibility of moral decisions. Man seems to have realized that he is involved in specific actions, and as a result the tragic sense of human choice is reflected in Early Classic art.

A similar development may be observed in the development of the *Kore* type (Fig. 5–16). These figures of maidens, *Korai*, dedicated to a goddess, abounded on the Archaic Acropolis of Athens, and many of them have typically Ionian qualities. They bring an exotic Lydian breath into mainland Greece, like maidens drifting west from Sardis, richly clothed, perfumed, and painted blue under the eyes. All of them stand in the same frontal position, left foot advanced, left hand holding up the mantle, right arm bent at the elbow and extended as if holding an offering. The Korai wear the Ionian costume of linen chitons, indicated by ripple marks, with a woolen mantle (the himation) that falls in broad conventional folds from the right shoulder. The marble is undercut along the edge of the folds, giving a feeling of depth, and is painted to represent the decorative border and the pattern of the material. The elaborately dressed hair falls down behind in conventional waves, and a few locks, separating, fall over the breast. Under the sheath of rich clothing the body bursts with life. By the early fifth century these Korai, too, reflect sadness, nobility, and thought. To the joy of the body is joined the tragic depth of the soul; the secluded world of women now was capable of producing an Antigone.

The bronze *Charioteer of Delphi*, from the same Early Classic period (p. 31), exhibits a similar tension between the breath and passions of life and a strictly geometric and linear organization of form. The dark color with reflections and sharp contours, the crisp edges of the details necessitated by the darkness of the material, are characteristic of work in bronze. The statue belonged to a group with chariot and horses, probably erected to commemorate a victory at the races. It represents a youthful aristocrat who stands firmly on both feet, holding the reins in his

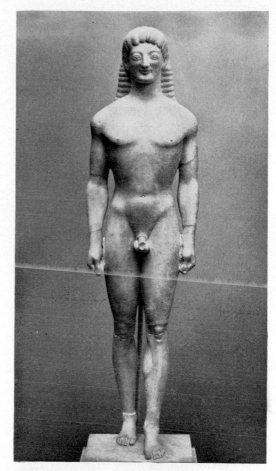

5–15 KOUROS FROM TENEA. *ca.* 570 B.C. Glyptothek, Munich. (Kaufmann)

outstretched hand. He is dressed in the customary garment of a driver, girdled high and held in at the shoulders and the back to keep it from flapping. The hair is confined by a band tied behind. The eyes are made of glass paste and shaded by lashes of hairlike strips of bronze. We feel the sharp clarity of Archaic work in the figure, especially in the lower part, where the folds of the dress have almost the architectural quality of a fluted column; in the sharp lines of the brow; and in the conventional way in which the hair is worked above the band. But we notice, also, the soft curls below the band; the mas-

5–16 (Left) Kore found on the Acropolis. Marble, painted. H. *ca.* 4 ft. *ca.* 530 B.C. Acropolis Museum, Athens. (Right) Kore found on the Acropolis. Marble, painted. H. *ca.* 3 ft. *ca.* 530 B.C. Acropolis Museum, Athens. (Both photos Alinari)

terly modeling in the hand and in the feet, the toes of which cling to the chariot floor; the slight twist of the torso, giving the feeling of an organic structure beneath the dress. The statue is probably a portrait, and yet there are but few individualistic traits about it. It is the quality of triumph as such which concerned the sculptor. The sculptures at Olympia, to be discussed later, show a similar monumental conception combined with directness and dignity of expression.

Another bronze of this age, the *Dis-* *cobolos* (Discus Thrower)[4] of Myron (Fig. 5–17), was revolutionary because of its vigorous movement. This movement, however, was still kept clearly to one plane. The motion represented has been arrested between the backward and the forward thrust of the arm in hurling the discus and, by means of

[4] The original of this statue is lost. A considerable number of copies exist, from which Figure 5–17 is constructed. For the question of copies in Greek sculpture see Richter, *Sculpture and Sculptors of the Greeks*, pp. 133–43.

5–18 STATUETTE OF A HORSE. Bronze
H. *ca.* 14 in. *ca.* 470 B.C. Metropolitan
Museum of Art, New York.

5–17 DISCOBOLOS. Myron. Reconstruct
ed copy of the bronze original. Terme
(National) Museum, Rome.

formal qualities, it becomes an abstract
expression of concentrated force. The
face, contrary to what we should expect at such an intense moment, is im-
passive and broadly generalized. Such
a free pose, suitable for bronze, shows
the artist's complete understanding of
the capacity of his material. This same
sensitivity to bronze as a material and
to its use in rendering natural forms
controlled by abstract order may be
seen in a superb small horse of about
470 B.C. (Fig. 5–18).

The full grandeur of this Early Classic moment is manifest in the great
bronze *Zeus or Poseidon,* found in the
sea off Cape Artemision. The pose is
full of movement but, like that of the
Discobolos, is kept within one plane, so
that the figure still retains the Archaic

clarity of profile. The mighty chest
muscles seem to raise the cantilevered
arms, spread in space, and the powerful torso is richly modeled. Head and
body are alike awesome. The sculptor
makes us feel that this could only be a
god (Fig. 5–19).

Early Greek reliefs have the same
characteristics as the early sculpture in
the round, and in addition solve one of
the problems peculiar to relief: the
suggestion of a greater depth than is
measurably present. Unlike Egyptian
reliefs, in which the figure and the
ground are balanced in an elegant flat
pattern, Greek relief tends to concentrate upon the figure. As in free-standing sculpture the concern is with action
and life. This vitality can be seen in
even such comparatively low reliefs as
those of chariots from the friezes on
the *Siphnian Treasury* (Fig. 5–20),
where the horses give at once a sense
of vivid life, a feeling of the solid in
space, and a clear delineation of figures
against other figures and against the
background. Space is indicated by a
series of shallow parallel planes whose
sharp edges emphasize the contours of

5–19 BRONZE STATUE OF POSEIDON OR ZEUS from Cape Artemision. *ca.* 470 B.C. National Museum, Athens. (Alison Frantz)

5-20 HORSES from a frieze on the Treasury of the Siphnians, Delphi. *ca.* 525 B.C. (Clarence Kennedy)

the horses' necks, bodies, and tails. The broad carving of the bodies seems to insist upon the principal planes, while the conventions for the manes and the tails break these planes in certain areas to add movement and texture to the design.

The Greek artist concentrated in this way upon the figure because he had a story to tell, one which involved the action of gods and heroes as they subdued the monsters of earth and brought order into the world. The earliest pedimental sculpture, such as the *Gorgon pediment* from Corfu, is concerned with this theme (Fig. 5-21). The Gorgon in the center flies to the right, looking out frontally at the ob-

server. Geometrically conceived, in a way typically Greek, she represents an Hellenic reassessment of Near Eastern demonology and a speculation upon the destructive powers of the early female goddess. Note the heraldic panthers flanking her. At the corner of the pediment Zeus kills a giant, a son of earth. The figures are almost in the full round; they dominate the voids between and behind them and are arbitrarily varied in size in order to fit the pediment shape. As time progressed the Greek artist attempted to fill the space more organically with figures so grouped that they appear to be of the same size, participating in a single unified event.

5-21 WESTERN PEDIMENT OF THE TEMPLE OF ARTEMIS at Corfu. *ca.* 600–580 B.C. (Courtesy Verlag Gebr. Mann, Berlin)

5–22 HERAKLES from the temple of Aphaia at Aegina. *ca.* 480 B.C. Glyptothek, Munich. (Clarence Kennedy)

The pedimental figures of the *temple of Aphaia at Aegina* though heavily cleaned and overrestored in the nineteenth century, illustrate this change. The scene probably represents some episode of the Trojan War. Athena, with aegis and spear, stands in the center, with fighting groups balanced on either side. The most noticeable characteristics of the pediment are the freedom of movement and variety of pose. The figures are modeled with vigor and an understanding of the human physique which reflect a careful observation of nature. The figure of *Herakles* as an archer (Fig. 5–22), for example, is complicated in pose in comparison with the free-standing statues of the period, but the form is compact and simple. It is the contrasting direction of line seen in the vertical of

the back, the horizontal of the arm, and the diagonal of the firmly braced leg that gives such a strong impression of the powerful draw upon the bow, and at the same time a feeling of the perfect equilibrium of the whole figure. Many of the earlier stylizations are still present; the angular motifs in the cuirass, for example, strike an harmonious note in the total angularity of the figure.

With the "Severe," Early Classic period, however, more complicated meanings are embodied, as in the pedimental sculpture from the *temple of Zeus* at Olympia. On the west pediment, facing away from the *altars of the Altis*, is the *combat of centaurs and Lapiths* at the wedding feast of Peirithous (Fig. 5–23). The centaurs, half beast, were invited to the celebration

5-23 WESTERN PEDIMENT OF THE TEMPLE OF ZEUS at Olympia. *ca.* 470–460 B.C. Restored by Treu.

but became drunk and attempted to carry off the bride and her maidens. They were prevented by Peirithous and Theseus; and Apollo, appearing above the combat, approved the heroes' chastisement of this breach of hospitality. The scene symbolizes the meaning of the sacred truce of Olympia, which outlawed strife within the consecrated precinct or on the way to it, and the responsibility of men, who, unlike animals, recognize law.

In the center *Apollo*, calm and majestic, thrusts out his arm amid the tumult (Fig. 5-24). He reminds us of the Apollo of Aeschylus in the *Choephoroi*, in which the single protagonist defied the chorus of Furies; and the influence of the drama seems apparent here. On each side are the combatants, in twisted groupings like olive trees, with reclining figures of women in the corners. There is simple modeling without detail in the figures and draperies, which are arranged in broad linear folds to enhance the majestic effect. These figures, as in all early Greek sculpture, were originally waxed and painted so

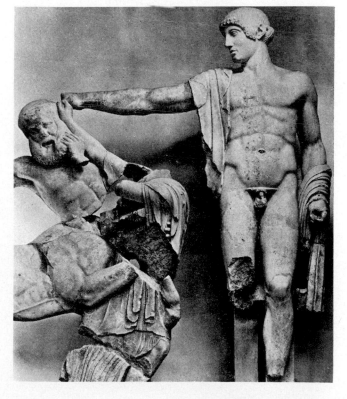

5-24 APOLLO. From the western pediment of the temple of Zeus, Olympia. *ca.* 470–460 B.C. Olympia Museum.

5–26 PARTHENON, METOPE. *Lapith and Centaur.* 447–432 B.C. British Museum, London. (Mansell)

5–25 HERAKLES AND ATLAS. Metope from the temple of Zeus at Olympia. *ca.* 470 B.C. (© Deutsches Archäologisches Institut, Athens)

that the clear outlines were luminous against the darker background.

On the east pediment one saw not a single protagonist and a chorus but instead a rank of men and women. These were like a cast of characters who, as in some scenes from Aeschylus' *Agamemnon,* for example, plot evil against each other. The inevitable tragedy is known to the observer, though unknown to the characters themselves. Only the seer in their midst is aware of the impending catastrophe, but he is powerless to avert it. Pelops and Oenomaus, in the presence of Zeus, await the beginning of their chariot race in which Oenomaus, the killer of thirteen suitors for the hand of his daughter, Hippodameia, will himself fall to the treachery of Pelops. The seer to the right raises his hand in horror as he watches the chariot being damaged, but the river god beyond him coldly and dispassionately observes the crimes of men. Crime and countercrime are

held up now for the judgment of men. There is a terrible stillness in the relief. The forms are clear and spare. The old Archaic joy in strife is being balanced by a sense of tragedy, choice, and alternatives; each man has a new depth of soul. Thus the visual arts moved into the realm of philosophy and drama. It was in the presence of this relief that the Greek athletes took their oath at the altar of Zeus before the Olympic games.

On the metopes of the temple's pronaos *Herakles* carried on his labors (Fig. 5–25). Mighty forces oppose each other in balanced tension. Clear, rounded, solid forms are poised in an architectural order. The body of man, upon whose strength of arm and will depends the moral order of the world, personifies the same qualities as the temple itself.

It was about twenty years later, in honor of Athena and her meaning for the men of the city-state, that the sculptures of the *Parthenon* in Athens were carved. These were done under the direction of Phidias, whose own great works in ivory and gold — the Zeus for Olympia and the Athena Parthenos for

5–27 PARTHENON, EASTERN PEDIMENT. Three female figures, called the "Three Fates." 447–432 B.C. British Museum, London. (Trustees of the British Museum)

the interior of the Parthenon — have disappeared, as have his other original works.

The sculptural decorations of the *Parthenon* are found at three points: in the pediments, on the metopes, and on a continuous frieze [5] which ran around the top of the cella wall, inside the colonnade. The metopes provide an accent of movement by successive compositions of two struggling interlocking figures in high relief — centaurs and Lapiths, gods and giants, Greeks and Amazons. Here is the perfect exemplification of "the inner concord of opposites," as unity was defined by Herakleitos (Fig. 5–26).

The subject of the eastern pediment, the ancient writers tell us, was the birth of Athena, who sprang full-armed from the head of Zeus. The remains are fragmentary, but from a drawing made by a Frenchman traveling in Athens in 1674 we may glimpse part of the composition. In the left corner, the sun god Helios in his chariot is rising out of the sea. Only the head, the shoulders, and the arms of Helios and the heads of the horses are shown. The horses rise to-

ward a seated male figure which may personify Mount Olympus, though it is usually identified as *Dionysos* (Fig. o–17). Next are two seated figures, probably Demeter and Persephone, approached by a standing figure. The central figures have entirely disappeared. To the right are three seated female figures closely grouped, one turned toward the center. In the corner, projecting over the cornice, is seen the head of one of the horses of Selene, the moon goddess, who is sinking into the west as Helios rises in the east. In the *Three Fates*, as the group of three seated female figures has been called (although it may represent Ocean and her daughters) (Fig. 5–27), there is a quiet majesty and a movement as of swirling water. The figures, unlike those of Olympia, occupy space in depth by their projections and recessions. Their rhythms led the eye toward the central group, where order, in the person of Athena, was being born into the world.

The frieze along the top of the cella wall, in very low relief, was seen from below in reflected light against a colored ground. It enriched the plain wall and directed attention toward the entrance to the temple. It represents the

[5] Not to be confused with the regular Doric frieze of triglyphs and metopes. This continuous frieze, an Ionic feature, is unusual.

5–28 PARTHENON FRIEZE, NORTHERN SIDE. *Cavalcade of Mounted Youths.*
Accessories, such as the bridles and reins, were painted on or made of metal
and affixed by rivets (see the holes in the horses' heads). Marble. H. 40 in.
447–432 B.C. British Museum, London. (Mansell)

Panathenaic procession, which took place every four years when the citizens of Athens gathered in the market place and carried to the *Parthenon* the peplos or robe for the statue of Athena. This is the first time that a representation of a nonmythological subject appeared in Greek temple reliefs. Now the citizens of Athens themselves are depicted upon their temple and identify themselves as responsible for its honor. In the part of the frieze which decorated the western side of the building the procession is forming: youths are lacing their sandals, holding their horses or mounting, guided by marshals who stand at intervals, and particularly at the corners, to slow down the movement and guide the horsemen at the turn. In the friezes of the two long sides the procession moves in parallel lines, a cavalcade of spirited youths, chariots, elders, jar-carriers, and animals for sacrifice. Throughout the procession is to be seen that balance of tactile and optical, of the permanent and the instantaneous, which again is characteristically Greek. The eye follows the movements of light and shade in the drapery, but pauses at any point by shifting focus to the broad

areas of planes with their sharply linear outlines. The movement of the procession becomes slower and more solemn as it nears the eastern side, when after turning the corner it approaches the seated divinities, who appear to be guests of Athena at her great festival.[6]

The Cavalcade of Mounted Youths on the north side (Fig. 5–28) is filled with rhythmic movement and spirited action. The backward glance of some of the youths gives a further balance to the general forward movement of the procession; and the infinite variety in the poses of the youths and the horses frees it from any feeling of monotony. The background is flat, with no distance and no unnecessary details. Notice how the figures just fill the space; how the heads, whether the figures are standing or mounted, are on a level;[7] how the flanks of the horses form a

[6] A convenient and inexpensive reproduction of the entire frieze, which is necessary for a realization of the unity of composition and the rhythmic flow of line, is published by University Prints, Cambridge, Massachusetts.

[7] This particular practice of distorting natural proportions for decorative purpose is known as *isocephaly* (heads equal, or on a level). It is a practice by no means limited to Greece.

central band of largely unbroken surface, and how their legs beat a rapid
rhythm in the lower third of the panel.
Originally details and accents were
stressed by color and even by the addition of bronze for reins.

In the portion representing the Jar-
Carriers (Fig. 5–29) the motif of a
youth carrying a jar upon his right
shoulder is repeated, making a design
of decorative quality, ease, and grace
of rhythm which is readily felt but
only fully understood when one observes the subtle variations that occur
in the pose of the head, the arms, and
the hands, and in the arrangement of
the drapery. The figures are no longer

in strong contrast to their background.
As in contemporary Greek painting,
they seem to emerge from it. Such union of sculptural techniques with the
pictorial qualities of painting was an
innovation. It had not occurred at
Olympia, where the figures were clearly tactile and linear.

The unity and equilibrium which
pervade the sculpture of the Parthenon
are also present in the work of Polykleitos, a young contemporary of Phidias. A difference, however, should be
noted: whereas the artists at work on
the Parthenon seemingly achieved their
results spontaneously, Polykleitos formulated into a canon of proportions

5–29   PARTHENON
FRIEZE, NORTHERN SIDE.
Jar-Carriers.   447–432
B.C. Acropolis Museum,
Athens. (Mansell)

5–30 DORYPHOROS. Roman copy after a bronze by Polykleitos. Original *ca.* 450–440 B.C. Museo Nazionale, Naples. (Alinari)

the principles that give rise to unity.[8]

Polykleitos' *Doryphoros* (the Spear Bearer), though known to us only in

[8] Although the written treatise setting forth the "Polykleitan canon" is lost, Galen in his *Placita Hippocratis at Platonis,* Vol. 3, refers to it in this manner: ". . . [beauty consists] in the proportions, not of the elements, but of the parts, that is to say, of finger to finger, and of all the fingers to the palm and the wrist, and of these to the forearm, and of the forearm to the upper arm, and of all the parts to each other, as they are set forth in the Canon of Polykleitos." (H. S. Jones, *Select Passages from Ancient Writers,* Macmillan, London, 1895, pp. 128–29.)

5–31 NIKE FIXING HER SANDAL. From the temple of Athena Nike or Nike Apteros. 421–415 B.C. Acropolis Museum, Athens.

Roman copies, is an excellent example of this attempt (Fig. 5–30). The movement which began to be expressed in early fifth-century sculpture is now disciplined by Polykleitos through the equilibrium of imposed proportions. A native of Argos, he attempted to combine in sculpture the opposites of freedom and order, exactly the task which the democracy of Athens had set itself in politics and at which, under Pericles, it had for a brief and glorious period succeeded.

The style of Phidias and of Polykleitos dominated Greek sculpture during the late fifth century B.C., but the dynamic equilibrium of their work could not long be sustained, and sculpture tended to become more elegant, slighter, and refined. A fragment from the parapet of the *temple of Athena Nike* (Fig. 5–31) has the flavor of virtuosity in the extraordinary skill shown in revealing the figure beneath the drapery. At the same time there is a masterly expression of movement, quite abstract, in the folds which hang between the arm and the leg, through a rhythmic flow of concentric curves. Thus we see that, as the city-state began to disintegrate, sculpture began to emphasize individual traits and elegance.

PAINTING

We know from literary evidence that schools of painting existed in Archaic and Classic Greece. But the actual paintings are entirely gone — the mural paintings in the stoas and other public buildings and the panel pictures as well. Shadowy as ghosts are the famous painters, and yet painting apparently paralleled the development of sculpture and, by the later fifth century, began to take the lead, challenging the sculptor, as already noted in the Parthenon reliefs, to attempt some of the pictorial devices of light and shade which the painters had created. Polygnotus, who was a contemporary of Phidias and a painter as well as a sculptor, attempted, by placing figures one above another, to suggest depth. He used a very limited range of color and appears to have created, together with others, as grandly monumental a style in painting as the sculptors attained in the temple at Olympia and in the Parthenon. Apollodorus the "Shadow-Maker" was also extolled as a fifth-century painter. He seems to have experimented with the use of shadow and light to make his figures appear round, moving thus toward those "appearances" of bodies bathed in atmosphere which the sculptures of the Parthenon also suggest. Since, however, all these paintings have disappeared, we must turn to paintings on vases for some insight into the development of pictorial art during the Archaic and Classic periods.

5–32 GEOMETRIC AMPHORA. Dipylon style. Athenian. 8th century B.C. Metropolitan Museum of Art, New York. (Rogers Fund, 1910)

POTTERY, VASE PAINTING, METALWORK, INTAGLIO, ENGRAVING

Among the elements of the Aegean culture which the Greeks appear to have adopted and expanded was the pottery trade. In the course of time, as increasing exports created a demand for containers for such substances as oil and honey in addition to articles for general household use, the potters' quarters at Athens, known as the Ce-

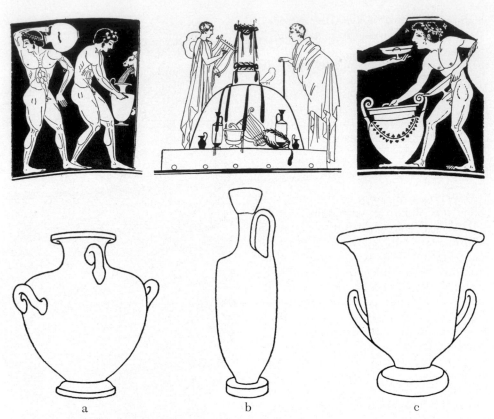

5–33 *a.* The *hydria* (from the Greek word for "water") was the water jar, used chiefly to bring water from the spring. It has three handles, two for lifting and one for carrying. Vase painting showing two youths filling their hydriae at a fountain. *b.* The *lekythos* (oil flask) has a long, narrow neck adapted to pouring oil slowly. It was used chiefly in funeral rites. Vase painting showing two men at a tomb; on the plinth are lekytho, oenochoai, a krater, a lyre, and a wreath. *c.* The *krater* (coming from the Greek verb "to mix") was the bowl for mixing the wine and water, the usual beverage of the Greek. *d.* The *amphora* (meaning "to carry on both sides," referring to the two

ramicus,[9] came to be no inconsiderable part of the city.

The first truly Greek pottery style is called the Geometric because of the nature of the forms which were painted upon it. Cretan decoration had been fluid and organic, but the early Greek forms were abstract and intellectually ordered. This intellectual rigor and geometric order also formed, as we have

seen, the basis for Greek architecture and sculpture. *Geometric* pottery, made from about 1100 to 700 B.C., culminated in the Dipylon ware,[10] of which a large funerary amphora (Fig. 5–32) is an example. Its vigorous shape and small handles are decorated, in a rich brown glaze on light clay, with bands containing geometric motifs and human figures.

Decoration on Greek pottery of this early date only rarely included the fig-

[9] Situated both inside and outside the Dipylon Gate. The name is derived from the Greek word for "potter," whence our "ceramics."

[10] So called because these vases have been found in the cemetery near the Dipylon Gate.

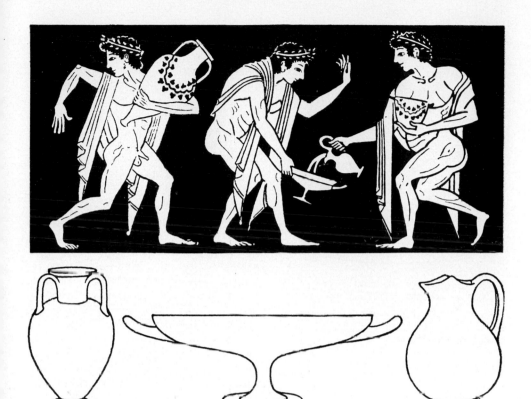

handles) was a vessel for storing provisions: wine, corn, oil, honey. It had an opening large enough to admit a ladle, and usually had a cover to protect the contents. *e.* The *kylix* (from the Greek root "to roll," referring to the vases' being turned on the potter's wheel) was the chief form of the drinking cup. *f.* The *oenochoë* (from the Greek verb "to pour out wine") was the wine jug. The lip is pinched into a trefoil shape, which facilitates pouring. Vase painting showing a youth pouring wine from a slender, high-handled oenochoë into a kylix held by his companion while another youth approaches, carrying an amphora.

ure of man, but it is significant that such figures did appear in what otherwise would have been a purely abstract decoration. This was the period of Homer, and the epic quality of man's experience, recounted in the *Iliad* and the *Odyssey,* was also bound to occur in visual expression. One might well study the spare, rugged quality of these Geometric figures and speculate on the original style of Homer's epics. On the large Dipylon amphora, the scene is a funeral procession, appropriately enough, since in actual usage the amphora stood above the grave and through holes in the bottom slowly dripped a libation of oil into the soft earth covering the corpse below. Horizontal bands of ornament cover the entire surface of the amphora and emphasize the portions they encircle. Each motif is an obsessive study of the relation of the figure to the ground, of the basic structure of a system of ornament in which the space, or ground, between and around the painted decoration or figure is as ordered as the ornament itself. This may be seen partic-

5–34 CORINTHIAN OENOCHOË. Black and purple figures on a yellowish brown clay base. H. 8⅝ in. First quarter 6th century B.C. Metropolitan Museum of Art, New York. (Rogers Fund, 1906)

5–35 FRANÇOIS VASE. H. *ca*. 2 ft. First half 6th century B.C. Named after the man who found it in a grave in Italy. Museo Archeologico, Florence. (Furtwängler-Reichhold)

ularly in the scene on the neck of the amphora, where a warrior stands between two horses. The procession of chariots, placed on the widest part of the vase below the handles, is sharply accented against the clearest ground. As we stand by these huge Dipylon jars we feel something of the majesty of the *Hera of Samos* (Fig. 5–12), whose prototypes were probably being carved in wood when the Dipylon period was at its height.

Considering the quantity of his pottery-making, the number of shapes which the Greek used is small. Once the basic forms were developed, each according to its functional requirements, he devoted himself to refining proportions, contours, placement of the handles, and decoration. Here is the same interest in the refinement and intensification of form within narrow limitations apparent in the development of both architecture and sculpture. The shapes most frequently found may be seen in Figure 5–33. In determining the uses of these vases [11] we are guided by paintings on the pottery; for in these paintings the Greeks have given us an amazing revelation of their everyday life.

As the Greek expanded his trade and colonization, we see evidences in this pottery of closer contact with the older civilizations of the Near East: rows of animals, winged beasts, and rosettes recall Assyria; the lotus, Egypt (Fig. 5–34). The term "Orientalizing" is often given to this style of the eighth and seventh centuries B.C. which appeared on vases produced in Corinth and on the Aegean islands. With the passing of the seventh century B.C. the Greek concentrated his chief concern upon

[11] The common, though misleading, term generally used in speaking of Greek pottery. One needs to remember that these "vases" were largely the pots and pans of everyday life and the containers used by the trader, though some were used for religious and funeral purposes.

5–36 AMPHORA. *Ajax and Achilles Playing Draughts.* By Exekias. Black-figured. 550–525 B.C. Vatican, Rome. (Furtwängler-Reichhold)

himself and his immediate interests, secular and religious. The animal friezes and geometric motifs, often so decorative and suitable as motifs on a curving surface, disappeared before his frankly humanistic preoccupation.

Perhaps the most perfect example of an early Archaic vase is the *François Vase* (Fig. 5–35), which with its volute handles has an extraordinarily vigorous shape. It is a krater and is decorated with concentric bands filled with human and animal figures. These are painted in a brownish-black glaze with touches of white or purple on the natural reddish clay of the background. On the foot is an animated battle between cranes and pygmies, above which rays happily suggest the spreading movement of the surface of the krater. In the horizontal bands above are pictured various mythological scenes of the story of the House of Peleus from which Achilles sprang. These include the Calydonian hunt, the funeral games for Patroclus, and the procession of the gods to the wedding of Peleus and Thetis; and upon the handle may be seen the dead Achilles.

As vase painting developed, the touches of white and purple were used more sparingly, with the result that the black figure stood in even stronger contrast against the reddish clay. This is known as the "black-figure" style. The glaze had now, after centuries of experiment, become a velvety jet-black. The figures were painted in this glaze on the natural red clay and the details in-

5–37 INSIDE OF A KYLIX PAINTED BY EXEKIAS. *Dionysos Sailing over the Sea.* Black-figured. D. 14½ in. 550–525 B.C. Antikensammlungen, Munich. (Furtwängler-Reichhold)

cised with some hard pointed instrument to expose the red beneath. It is almost an engraver's technique, linear and sharp. The zonal arrangement disappeared, and in its place a few larger figures provided the decoration, sometimes grouped in a panel, as on an amphora of Exekias (Fig. 5–36). In this strong, compact shape the handles not only harmonize with the curve as an integral part of the design, but they are attached in such a way that they manifestly fulfill their function of lifting weight. The surface is painted solid black, except for the band with rays just above the base, the decorated panel on the body, and the handles. In the large panel we see Ajax and Achilles seated on stools, bending intently over their game of draughts. Ajax, on the right, as the inscription tells us, calls out "three"; Achilles, on the left, "four." It is a close game. Much greater naturalism than formerly is evident in the pose and in the proportion of the figures, and there is greater freedom in drawing. One hero is helmeted, the

other not; slight differences occur in the position of the limbs and the spears and the decoration of the shields, but there is a strong sense of order and the spaces between the figures are as important to the design as are the figures themselves. The skill and precision seen in the profusion and delicacy of the incised lines of the hair, and in the very elaborate cloaks, are a delight in themselves. We recognize a kinship, stylistically, between this work and Archaic sculpture. A kylix of Exekias (Fig. 5–37), with a representation of Dionysos sailing over the sea carrying his gifts to mankind, is even more decorative in its adaptation of the figures to the circular shape. Here the pirates have turned into dolphins and the vine of Dionysos grows over the mast.

In Figure 5–38 we notice a change from black figures on red to red figures on black. This "red-figure" style is a shift in technique which occurred in the later sixth century. The natural reddish clay was first covered with a red slip and polished. The artist then

5–38 KYLIX PAINTED BY EUPHRONIOS. *Cattle of Geryon.* Red-figured. D. 17 in. *ca.* 500 B.C. Antikensammlungen, Munich. (Furtwängler-Reichhold)

painted, with a fine brush, the details of his design in black and finally covered the background with black glaze. The figures of men and animals no longer are dark and earthy, massive against a light ground, but instead are luminous, like light and air, shining forth from the black background. The school of painting which rapidly developed in Athens at this time unquestionably influenced the style of pottery decoration in general, for the style is freer and more facile than the earlier black-figure style. As this new mode of painting developed, the potter also concentrated, as did the builders and the carvers, upon the niceties of form, which for the potter were proportion,

a   b

5–39 SILVER COINS OF SYRACUSE. *a.* Demareteion. *ca.* 479 B.C. *b.* "Medallion" signed by Euaenetus. Late 5th century B.C. British Museum, London. (Trustees of the British Museum)

thinness of walls, character of profile, and the integration of the handle with the body of the vase. He felt no need to enlarge his limited color scheme, for the polished coppery red against a velvety black created an effect of reserved elegance. On the kylix of Euphronios, for example, the artist has shown scenes from one of the labors of Herakles, the seizing of the cattle of Geryon — on one side the fight over the cattle, on the other the animals being driven away by four youths. Though the narrative element is lively, the effect is still strongly decorative. In the herd of cattle the painted contour lines of the bodies give a sense of roundness, and the animals seem to move in space. In the central disk the figures of the youth and the horse form a compact pattern which seems to partake of the rotary motion of the enclosing circle and at the same time to counter that movement by the severely angular lines of the cloak. Yet one feels creeping into the craft a conflict between ceramics — the art of clay shapes with suitable decoration — and painting in its own right; between the limitation of a given medium and the broad horizons of the painter. In the potter's drawing of the human figure, for example, there is a constant progression toward visual likeness, a preoccupation of the Greek from the time of the Dipylon ware. As the potter neared his objective he seemed to lose his feeling for ceramic decoration, to allow the painter's objectives to triumph over ceramic requirements, even though he drew and modeled with line alone, and included no details of background except a few hints in abstract form. The climax of red-figure vase painting came in the first half of the fifth century, as did the Early Classic "Severe" style in sculpture. The decorative forms were still clear figures against the ground of the vase, as were the sculptures in the pediments and metopes at Olympia (Fig. 5–21). When the figures began to turn in space, as do the figures in the lost paintings which are mentioned in contemporary texts, the character of the red-figure style inevitably lost its vitality, until the style eventually ceased. The white-ground lekythoi from the later fifth and fourth centuries show the last phases of Greek vase painting. The figures scarcely emerge from the ground, defined from it only by line. Across the figures and the ground are placed large areas of more varied and softer colors, reds, yellows, and purples.

Another important Greek technique may be seen in Greek coins. The finest of these coins, curiously enough, were struck not at Athens nor even anywhere in continental Greece, but in Magna Graecia, particularly at Syracuse in Sicily. On the obverse of the

Demareteion [12] (Fig. 5–39*a*) is a four-horse chariot with a Victory flying above; in the segment below, a running lion; and about the edge, a row of dots. On the reverse a profile head, perhaps of the nymph Arethusa, in a faint circle, is surrounded by four dolphins with a Greek inscription which reads in translation "of the Syracusans." The coin is thicker and less even in shape than modern coins, and the metal runs up around the edge on one side of the reverse. This is because Greek coins were struck by hand on an anvil that held the die, without a circular frame to keep the metal from running over the edge. The relief, too, is higher than in modern coins, for the Greek was not hampered by the modern necessity for "stacking." Though the object is small, there is a feeling of amplitude and of quiet orderliness. The circle of the disk is repeated by the dolphins and the inner ring, until the eye is inevitably led to the head in the center. The design is clear and effective, particularly when it is compared with that of later coins decorated with the same motif, in which the naturalistic tendency has entailed decorative loss, as in the *Medallion* (Fig. 5–39*b*).

The carving of gems which were

[12] These coins are named after Demarete, wife of the tyrant Gelon. According to one story, after their defeat at Himera the Carthaginians obtained very favorable terms from Gelon through the influence of Demarete, to whom they gave a large amount of silver from which these coins were struck.

5–40 GEM. *Stag.* Intaglio. Rock crystal. W. 15⁄16 in. 5th century B.C. Museum of Fine Arts, Boston. (Courtesy, Museum of Fine Arts, Boston)

mounted in rings and used as seals was also widely practiced by Greek artists. Perhaps an inheritance from Crete was the love of animal and bird forms and their frequent use on these seals. In Figure 5–40 we see a sympathetic observation of nature and a design admirably adapted to the shape of the gem. Like the coins, the gems are relief sculpture in miniature. In carving them the craftsman probably used a metal drill with powdered emery and oil, so that the process required not only keen eyesight but a very sensitively trained touch and a patience which considered neither time nor money. The "fineness" of Greek art as a whole certainly owed much to that tradition of careful craftsmanship in precious materials of small scale which can be traced back to the gem cutters of Crete.

4th-Century and Hellenistic

(ABOUT 400–1ST CENTURY B.C.)

The disastrous Peloponnesian War, which ended in 404 B.C. with the complete defeat of Athens, left Greece drained of its strength. Sparta and then Thebes took the leadership, both unsuccessfully, until Philip of Macedon, shrewdly playing upon mutual jealousies, brought the whole country after 338 B.C. into subjection and a semblance of unity. His son Alexander the Great (356–323 B.C.) by his conquests spread Hellenic culture over large areas of the East. This last phase of ancient Greek culture, called the Hellenistic, extended from Sicily east to the Indus River in northwest India. It flourished until the first century B.C., when Rome became ascendant. Athens was no longer the focus of this civilization but only a provincial city-state in comparison with the magnificent cosmopolitan centers of Asia Minor and Egypt — Ephesus, Rhodes, Pergamon, and Alexandria (Fig. 5–2).

Another result of the Peloponnesian War was the loss of the classic balance between the city-state and the individual. The serene idealism of the fifth century, born of a simple robust concept of mind and matter, of man and the state, gave way to unrest and skepticism. The "know thyself" of Socrates, taught as he went about among the people in the streets, the agora, and the gymnasium, led inevitably to a more purely individualistic point of view. By questioning, Socrates had endeavored to help men gain "wisdom" empirically, to weigh and to judge out of their own experience rather than to consult the oracles. Euripides, too, seems to have regarded the individual as paramount, and both he and Socrates are mercilessly lampooned by Aristophanes on this point. During the fourth century B.C. man's intellectual independence was firmly established by Plato — however much he himself regretted the passing of the old ways — and finally by Aristotle. Having lost much of his confidence in the group and its gods, the Greek carried on his search to know himself and to achieve tangible personal rewards rather than work out his destiny only in conjunction with the state.

While Greece was enacting her daring drama of human discovery, Rome, in the Italian peninsula, though always partly Hellenized, was slowly developing in careful and typically Roman ways. Gradually it had conquered Italy, Sicily, and Carthage, and then, partly through circumstance and partly through desire for expansion, it came eastward, defeated the Macedonian power, and made Greece a Roman province. While this was a political victory, it was not a cultural one. Hellenic ideas continued to dominate both in the eastern Mediterranean and in the western, even though deeply modified by the taste of the victors. The world of later antiquity, both Greek and Roman, was essentially Hellenistic.

ARCHITECTURE

The inevitable result of the Peloponnesian War was a cessation of building in the countries immediately affected. But in Asia Minor there was great activity, and there the Ionic temple reached an apex of grandeur. Old Archaic prototypes were rebuilt, such as the *temple of Artemis* (Diana) at Ephesus, which had been damaged by fire. The principal development in building, though, was toward increased interior space. Such a temple as that of *Apollo* at Dydyma (Fig. 5–41) enclosed a large area and placed the sanctuary in a shrine within it. Architecture began to be concerned with interior volumes. It was this interest in interior space which culminated in Roman architecture and created the tradition out of which the Christian church developed.

The more varied, complex, and cosmopolitan culture of the Hellenistic Age demanded a great variety of buildings. Characteristic of such new civic structures was the basilica, or enclosed meeting place, at Delos, of about 200 B.C. The many columns supporting the trabeated structure of the roof formed a large pavilion. The building was en-

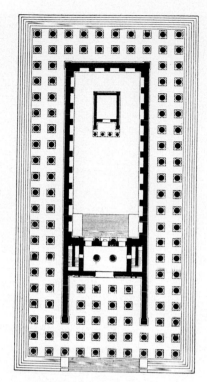

5-41 TEMPLE OF APOLLO at Dydyma, Miletus. (Restored by Wiegand.) Designed by Paeonius of Ephesus and Daphnis of Miletus. Begun 313 B.C., left unfinished *ca.* A.D. 41; deliberately left unroofed. (From W. B. Dinsmoor, *Architecture of Ancient Greece*, Batsford, Ltd., 1950)

tered along the side, and the central portion was lighted by clerestory windows, recalling the hypostyle halls of Egyptian temples. Domestic architecture also became more complicated as the individual began to value private life, but it never attained the elaboration achieved by the family-conscious Roman.

One of the most significant developments in architecture during this period was the rise of a new type of city planning, to be seen, for instance, at Miletus and Priene. In the plans of these two cities is to be found the triumph of abstract reasoning and of mathematics. They are laid out on a

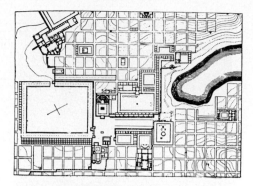

5-42 PLAN OF THE AGORA and surrounding areas. Miletus, Asia Minor. Restored by Gerkan. (From W. B. Dinsmoor, *Architecture of Ancient Greece*, Batsford, Ltd., 1950)

rectangular grid system, traditionally invented in the fifth century by Hippodamos of Miletus (Fig. 5-42). Such planning was superbly urban, insisting as it did on man-made order. The rigid organization of streets, intersecting at right angles, was, however, not allowed to become static. At Priene, for instance, public and private areas are beautifully balanced, and the site was so developed that the surrounding landscape might be enjoyed even from the heart of the city.

Pergamon, situated on a dramatic site, typifies in many ways Hellenistic architecture. The noble acropolis, with a splendid view, dominated the surrounding areas, which were defined by decisive stoas and by a series of strategically placed public buildings on the sloping hillsides. Among the most famous of these was the great *altar of Zeus*, which enclosed a mighty staircase between the wings of an Ionic colonnade. The simple altar of earlier times was transformed into a temple which seemed to reach out to include the impressive vista before it. The great frieze of vigorous sculpture, which will be described in the following pages, contributed to the emotional intensity of the theatrical environment.

5-44 DEMETER. From the temple of Demeter at Cnidos. Marble. *ca.* 350 B.C. British Museum, London. (Clarence Kennedy)

5-43 PRAXITELES. *Hermes with the Infant Dionysos.* Marble. H. 7 ft. *ca.* 350 B.C. Museum, Olympia.

SCULPTURE

Changing ideals also made themselves manifest in sculpture. In the *Hermes of Praxiteles* (*ca.* 350 B.C.) (Fig. 5-43), there is, for example, a refined personal charm which is more insistent than is the integrity of the marble. There is a languid ease and refined grace throughout the figure. The god is represented standing, with a shift in weight from the left arm, supporting the upper body, to the right leg, so that the pose with its fluid axis has a mannered curve. On his arm he holds the infant Dionysos, who reaches for something (probably a bunch of grapes) which the god held in his right hand. Hermes is looking not at the child, but off into space, with a dreamy expression in his eyes and a half-smile playing about his mouth. The whole figure, particularly the head, seems in a deep reverie — the god seems withdrawn in self-admiration. The modeling is exquisite. Soft shadows follow the planes as they flow imperceptibly one into another. The delicacy of the features is enhanced by the rough way in which the hair is indicated, and the deep folds of the realistic drapery are an effective contrast to surfaces of the figure.

The refined elegance of Praxitelean

5-45 FRIEZE OF THE MAUSOLEUM OF HALICARNASSUS. *ca.* 350 B.C. British Museum, London. (Trustees of the British Museum)

sculpture was altered in the work of Scopas — to judge from a few badly damaged heads — to show sharp intensity of feeling, conveyed especially by means of upturned head and deep-set eyes shadowed by heavy brows. The capacity of individuals for intense personal emotion is investigated and projected. These tendencies are also to be seen in the *Demeter of Cnidos* (Fig. 5-44). The goddess is heavily draped in her cloak, one corner of which is drawn up over the back of her head, throwing into relief her quietly tragic face with its deep-set eyes, which give the illusion of a real glance. Another example of mid-fourth century sculpture is the frieze on the *Mausoleum of Halicarnassus* (Fig. 5-45), depicting a fight between Greeks and Amazons. The figures are thin and lithe, somewhat strained in pose; their faces and bodies express human passion, and the restless drapery intensifies the impetuosity which sweeps through the group. Long spatial rhythms move across the surface of the relief and are accented by rich pictorial use of shadow.

An important sculptor of the generation following Praxiteles and Scopas was Lysippos, court artist to Alexander the Great. No work of his is known to be extant except in copies, but two im-

portant innovations of this time may possibly be credited to him. One was the change in taste (noticeable in all the arts) in the matter of proportions. The new canon of taste required a more slender, supple figure. This may, indeed, have been influenced by the second innovation (foreshadowed, to be sure, in earlier work) — the full realization of the figure in space (Fig. 5-46). The earliest Greek figures had been in a stiff frontal position, with the planes closely related to the stone block from which they had been carved; they could be best seen from only one or two positions. The form was enclosed in space — space was its limit. Even when the figure was treated less rigidly so that the torso as well as arms and legs moved in a curve, it was still seen satisfactorily only from one or two points of view. In this respect an Archaic *Kouros* (Fig. 5-14) and the *Hermes of Praxiteles* (Fig. 5-43) are more nearly alike than are the *Hermes* and the *Apoxyomenos* of Lysippos (Fig. 5-46). In the *Apoxyomenos* the arms curve forward. The figure encloses space and twists in it, and the small head is thrown into stronger perspective by the large hand.

Such movement, in a space which now acts as an environment rather than

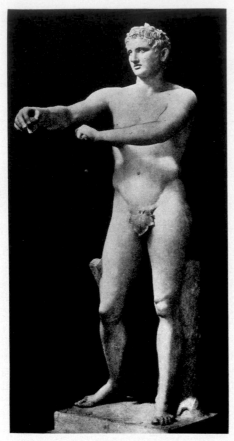

5-46 APOXYOMENOS (Roman copy). Lysippos. Marble. Original late 4th century B.C. Vatican, Rome.

5-47 NIKE OF SAMOTHRACE. To commemorate a naval victory in 306 B.C. Louvre, Paris.

as a limit for the form, is found in the great *Nike of Samothrace* (Fig. 5-47). Here the turn in the torso produces a feeling of motion which is strongly supplemented by the clinging, windswept drapery. This drapery, richly shadowed by deep undercutting, as if by broad brush strokes, shows how Hellenistic artists favored pictorial means of expression.

The tendency toward pictorial shadows and the expression of intense feeling is epitomized in the *altar at Pergamon*, on the frieze representing the battle between the gods and the giants (Fig. 5-48). Athena, moving rapidly toward the right, clutches one of the

winged giants by the hair, forcing him to the ground; on the right Earth, mother of the giants, a half-length figure, looks to Athena appealingly; above her, Victory approaches to crown the goddess. Force is powerfully conveyed by the use of violent contrasts of direction organized on sharp diagonals, by rich modeling, and by deep undercutting. The Greek vision of the climactic instant is still seen against a neutral background. Now, however, the background is almost obscured by shadows. The figures explode from it as shafts of light. All these devices are baroque characteristics, closely similar to those

5–48 FRIEZE FROM THE ALTAR OF ZEUS at Pergamon. *ca.* 175 B.C. Formerly in Pergamon Museum, Berlin.

developed in seventeenth-century Europe. Unity is achieved by over-all organization in which the parts flow one into the other, rather than by the carefully studied relationships of separate parts as in the Early Classic period. In such pictorial unity, produced by the movement of light, we must again recognize the strong influence of painting.

Although the Archaic and Classic sculptors always presented the female figure clothed, Hellenistic artists carved their goddesses, or Aphrodites, nude. The famous *Venus of Milo* in the Louvre is an example, as is the *Aphrodite of Cyrene* (Fig. 5–49). Here the feeling for stone as stone has quite surrendered to the ambition of making stone look as though it were soft, warm flesh. Such effects as these can be obtained only by brilliant technical skill and by an almost erotic concentration upon the softness of the body.

Realism of appearances was a concern of this late age, exactly as it has since always seemed to be when man becomes primarily interested in the self and material things. It reveals itself in the modeling of the *Pergamon reliefs,* or in such famous groups as the *Laocoön,* which belongs to this period, but is best seen in the many Hellenistic genre figures and reliefs. In all these, aspects of human and animal appearance were investigated. An example may be seen in the *Old Market Woman* (Fig. 5–50).

In contrast to the depiction of old age may be set the elegance of fashion and youth, as in the *Tanagra figurines,* perhaps the most charming examples of Hellenistic genre (Fig. 5–51). Thousands have been found, chiefly in graves, and yet their purpose is unknown. They show all kinds of everyday attitudes trivial in subject but dainty in execution and bright in color. They reflect a late period's taste for ownership by an individual, that is, for the *objet d'art.*

5–49 APHRODITE. Found at Cyrene in North Africa. Marble. *ca.* 100 B.C. after 4th-century type. Terme (National) Museum, Rome.

5–50 OLD MARKET WOMAN. Marble. 2nd century B.C. Metropolitan Museum of Art, New York.

As the individual and his taste became objects of primary consideration portraiture, as such, developed. Busts of individuals were being carved by the middle of the fifth century. By the Hellenistic period portrait sculpture was in full bloom. The individual was represented realistically. Yet, with the typical and unchanging Greek desire to seize the essential meaning of any subject, this realism was tempered by focusing attention upon what the man was, upon the nature of his soul (Fig. 5-52). Thus Greek portraits did not

record, as early Roman portraits tended to do, only the play of fugitive emotions across the human face. Instead they presented the subject's typical aspect as his will and actions had made him. A tendency towards generalization may also be seen in the use of certain prototypes for different categories of people: the bearded philosopher type, for instance, or Lysippos' portraits of Alexander, which became the ideal type for the ruler.

It is interesting to note that the Hellenistic individual, avid as he was for personal experience and served as he

5-52 DEMOSTHENES. Copy of original by Polyeuktos of Athens, *ca.* 280 B.C. Ny Carlsberg Glyptotek, Copenhagen.

5-51 LADY WITH A FAN. Tanagra figurine. Terra cotta, painted. H. 8 in. Museum of Fine Arts, Boston. (Courtesy, Museum of Fine Arts, Boston)

was by technically skilled artists, apparently often exhibited a revulsion against precisely this virtuosity. Thus many Hellenistic works also exist which attempted to recapture the simplicity and directness of Archaic or Classic prototypes. Such "archaizing" tendencies appeared also in Roman art for apparently similar reasons.

PAINTING

In the fourth century and in the Hellenistic Age, the problem of studying painting is much the same as it was in the fifth century. Although texts relate that flourishing schools of painting existed, almost none of their paintings are extant. Zeuxis and Parrhasius (fifth and fourth centuries), Apelles and Protogenes (of the time of Alexander the Great) are described in famous stories which stress their technical skill and realism — the same characteristics we have found in sculpture. But a basis for actual knowledge or judgment of these paintings is lacking.

The Greek painters, we are told, experimented in perspective, light and shade, and color in order to model figures and to create the illusion of forms in actual space. In later vase painting, exemplified by the *Kertch vases*, made in Athens in the fourth century and

5–53 KERTCH VASE. Mid-4th century B.C. British Museum, London. (Percy Gardner, *The Principles of Greek Art*, Macmillan, 1914)

followed in the vases of south Italy, line is used as an instrument of baroque movement and the surfaces are enriched coloristically by drops of white paint (Fig. 5–53). In the *Alexander Mosaic* (Fig. 5–54) from Pompeii, regarded as having been inspired by a Greek painting of the late fourth century, we perhaps may catch a glimpse of a large Greek composition, though allowances should be made for the mosaic technique. It is a battle scene, set in space as upon a shallow stage and thought to represent the Battle of Issus, where Alexander defeated Darius. Alexander is seen to the left as

5–54 BATTLE SCENE BETWEEN ALEXANDER AND DARIUS. Mosaic. From the floor of the House of the Faun, Pompeii. L. 17 ft. *ca.* 100 B.C. Museo Nazionale, Naples. (Alinari)

a young, haggard, and possessed warrior. He plunges into the midst of the
Persians and transfixes one of Darius'
guards with his lance. But his eyes are
riveted on Darius himself, toward
whom the spectator's attention is also
directed by the foreshortened horse in
the center of the picture. Darius, borne
backward out of the battle by his companions, whose lances are beginning to
toss in the counter movement of retreat, still reaches out his hand toward
his dying companion as the great king
he is meant to be. He is aware of the
threat of Alexander but his thought, in
the midst of the tumult, is for his men.
The whole composition of the painting
resounds with these countermovements,
which are both physical and psychological, created by the shock of bodies
in space and the anguished glances of
human beings. Thus there is movement
in depth and powerful lateral movement as well. The upper part of the
panel is unbroken except for a gnarled
tree and the shafts of spears, which
complement each other above the nature of the forces that agitate the lower
part. The modeling with light and
shade may well be compared with that
of the Pergamon frieze, which was unquestionably influenced by paintings
of this kind.

Summary

Greek art from its earliest days to
the late fifth century B.C. passed through
four stages of evolution in style: the
Geometric, the Archaic, the Early Classic, and the Classic.

The first style, identified as Geometric, may be studied in small bronze
sculpture and especially in pottery
produced between approximately 1100
B.C. and 700 B.C. Its forms were abstract, highly ordered and spare. A
freer, curvilinear decoration with animals and monsters, not unlike those of
Mesopotamian art, appeared, particu-

larly on pottery made in the eighth
and seventh centuries B.C. It is usually
known as the Orientalizing style because of its affinities with the East.
These early styles provide a basic vocabulary of forms essential for an understanding of Greek art.

During the sixth century B.C. Archaic
art developed, and we may study the
first temples and the powerful free-
standing marble statues known as the
Kouroi and the Korai, as well as black-
figure vase painting. It was a moment
of energetic growth, in which the artist, striving to give substance to his
concepts, was daring in experimentation with his materials. In his struggle
for expression he used simple forms,
mostly massive and monumental, in
which each part was a conventional
device, conceived in visual terms and
controlled by geometric order. The different parts of a figure were built into
an organic structure, in which the image lived an intense life of its own,
personifying the special qualities of
men and of women and of natural
forces. Greek form became "tactile." It
must be experienced basically by the
sense of touch. It was also constantly
in search of a unity, which, as Herakleitos wrote in the sixth century B.C.,
"is an inner concord of opposites, a
harmony of tensions; as of the bow and
lyre." [13]

By about 475 B.C., directly after the
Persian wars, a sense of detachment
and reflection, a concern with human
fate, will, and the soul, entered the
plastic arts. Out of a unique balance
between geometric order and the ac-
knowledgment of visual appearances
arose the "Classic" art of the fifth century B.C. This art had two distinct
phases. The first, called "Early Classic"
or "Severe," is best seen at Olympia on
the Peleponnesos shortly after 470 B.C.,
where its subject matter is the moral

[13] Herakleitos, *On the Universe*, Vol. 4, tr.
by W. H. S. Jones, Heinemann, London, 1931.

consequences of human thought and action. It reflects a philosophy built upon newly perceived depths of the human soul and upon man's duty to bring moral order into the world. Its mood was tragic, or Aeschylean. Its forms were luminous, solid, still "tactile," and spare.

The second phase of Classic art moved away from the concepts of Olympia. It may best be seen in the architecture and sculpture of the Periclean and post-Periclean work on the Acropolis in Athens. Whereas Olympia had concentrated upon a statement of human destiny in direct and vigorous terms, the new forms of Periclean Athens reached out toward life as a whole. The noble discipline of the generation which had fought at Salamis and Plataea brought forth the splendid optimism of Athena's chosen city. The movement was toward experiment and release from older patterns, but the old ways were still present, exerting their control. Out of this dynamic tension between old and new arose the "balance" of Classic Greek art. It was not a calculated balance, imposed upon sensation, as later "classicizing" arts were to be, but a living balance. Thus "tactile" experience was now supplemented by "optical" experience, in which forms revealed themselves in the movement of light and shadow. To the solid, generalized form of the Archaic was joined a desire for the fleeting and the changing. The timeless and the instantaneous were synthesized. It was the mood of Sophocles. The Athena of Athens was its ideal deity, balancing in herself both intellect and feeling, the ideal courage of the male and the comfort of the female presence. She embodied an Athenian democracy which was daring and triumphant in all things until the Peloponnesian Wars. The individual, though newly made aware of the self, still gave himself wholeheartedly to the city-state and was valued in balance with it. So arose one of the splendid moments in the history of mankind.

After the fifth century Greek building activity centered beyond the Greek mainland, particularly in Asia Minor. The more cosmopolitan character of late Greek civilization led to a broader architectural scope, which included more secular structures. Interior space began to be developed. City plans were organized on geometrical lines. In sculpture, grace and elegance and a desire to express human emotions gradually replaced the rugged generalizations of the preceding fifth century. This type of mannered refinement was dominated in the later fourth century by a desire to express powerful emotions and to bring the spectator into closer relationship with the image by projecting the forms into space. As sculptural form became truly three-dimensional, a baroque use was also made of the rich modelings of light and shade which seem to have been developed by the painters of the period. Thus the trend as a whole was in the direction of an imitation of the visual perception of appearances and of a manipulation of emotional states.

This last expression of ancient Greek civilization affected the entire Mediterranean world, forming an international culture which was to be inherited by Rome.

Bibliography

Alexander, Christine, *Jewelry, the Art of the Goldsmith in Classical Times*, Metropolitan Museum of Art, New York, 1928.

Beazley, John D., *Attic Black-Figure*, Humphrey Milford, London, 1928.

——, *The Development of Attic Black-Figure*, University of California Press, Berkeley, 1951.

——, and Ashmole, Bernard, *Greek Sculpture and Painting to the End of the Hellenistic Period*, Cambridge University Press, 1932.

Bell, Edward, *Hellenic Architecture*, Bell, London, 1920.

Bieber, Margarete, *The Sculpture of the Hellenistic Age*, Columbia University Press, 1955.

Boas, George, ed., *The Greek Tradition*, Johns Hopkins Press, Baltimore, 1939.

Borovka, Gregory, *Scythian Art*, tr. by V. G. Childe, Benn, London, 1928.

Budde, Erich G., "Helladic Greece," *Bulletin of the Museum of Art*, Rhode Island School of Design, December, 1939, pp. 1–17.

Buschor, Ernst, *Greek Vase-Painting*, tr. by G. C. Richards, Dutton, 1922.

Carpenter, Rhys, *The Esthetic Basis of Greek Art of the Fifth and Fourth Centuries B.C.*, Longmans, Green, New York, 1921.

Casson, Stanley, *The Technique of Early Greek Sculpture*, Oxford University Press, 1933.

A Catalogue of Sculpture in the Department of Greek and Roman Antiquities, Pts. 1–2, British Museum, London, 1928–31.

Charbonneaux, Jean, *La sculpture grecque archaïque*, Editions de Cluny, Paris, 1938.

——, *La sculpture grecque classique*, Editions de Cluny, Paris, 1943.

Collignon, Maxime, ed., *Le Parthénon*, 8 pts., Librairie Centrale d'Art et d'Architecture, Paris, 1910–12.

Cossío, Manuel Bartolomé, and Pijoán, José, *Summa Artis*, Vols. 1–10, Espasa-Calpe, Madrid, 1931–46; esp. Vol. 4.

Dinsmoor, William B., *The Architecture of Ancient Greece* (rev. and enl. ed. based on the first part of *The Architecture of Greece and Rome* by William J. Anderson and R. P. Spiers), Batsford, London, 1950.

Encyclopédie photographique de l'art, Vols. 1–3, Edition "Tel," Paris, 1935–38; esp. Vols. 2–3.

Fowler, Harold N., Wheeler, J. R., and Stevens, G. P., *A Handbook of Greek Archaeology*, American Book Company, New York, 1909.

Fyfe, David Theodore, *Hellenistic Architecture*, Cambridge University Press, 1936.

Gardiner, Edward N., *Olympia: Its History and Remains*, Oxford University Press, 1925.

Gardner, Ernest A., *Ancient Athens*, Macmillan, New York, 1907.

——, *The Art of Greece*, The Studio, London, 1925.

——, *Greece and the Aegean*, Harrap, London, 1933.

——, *A Handbook of Greek Sculpture*, 2nd ed., Macmillan, London, 1915; reprinted 1929.

Gardner, Percy, *The Principles of Greek Art*, Macmillan, New York, 1914.

——, and Blomfield, Sir Reginald, *Greek Art and Architecture*, Oxford University Press, New York, 1922.

Goodyear, William H., *Greek Refinements, Studies in Temperamental Architecture*, Yale University Press, 1912.

Greek Painting, Metropolitan Museum of Art, New York, 1944.

Grinnell, Isabel H., *Greek Temples*, Metropolitan Museum of Art, New York, 1943.

A Guide to the Principal Coins of the Greeks from about 700 B.C. to A.D. 270, British Museum, London, 1932.

Hege, Walter, and Rodenwaldt, Gerhart, *Olympia*, Sidgwick & Jackson, London, 1936.

Hoyningen-Huené, George, and Chisholm, H. J., eds., *Hellas*, J. J. Augustin, New York, 1944.

Johansen, Peter, *Phidias and the Parthenon Sculptures*, tr. by Ingeborg Andersen, Copenhagen, 1925.

Lamb, Winifred, *Greek and Roman Bronzes*, Dial Press, New York, 1929.

Laurie, Arthur P., *Greek and Roman Methods of Painting*, Cambridge University Press, 1910.

Lawrence, Arnold W., *Classical Sculpture*, Jonathan Cape, London, 1929.

——, *Later Greek Sculpture*, Harcourt, Brace, 1927.

Livingstone, Sir Richard Winn, *The Greek Genius and Its Meaning to Us*, 2nd ed., Oxford University Press, New York, 1923.

——, ed., *The Legacy of Greece*, Oxford University Press, 1921.

Loewy, Emanuel, *The Rendering of Nature in Early Greek Art*, tr. by John Fothergill, Duckworth, London, 1907.

Marquand, Allan, *Greek Architecture*, Macmillan, New York, 1909.

Minns, Ellis H., *Scythians and Greeks*, Cambridge University Press, 1913.

Paton, James M., ed., *The Erechtheum*, restored by G. P. Stevens, text by L. D. Caskey and others, Harvard University Press, 1927.

Payne, Humfry, and Young, G. M., *Archaic Marble Sculpture from the Acropolis*, Cresset Press, London, 1936.

Pfuhl, Ernst, *Masterpieces of Greek Drawing and Painting*, tr. by J. D. Beazley; latest ed., Macmillan, New York, 1955.

Pottier, Edmond, *Douris and the Painters of Greek Vases*, tr. by Bettina Kahnweiler, 2nd ed., Dutton, 1917.

Poulsen, Frederik, *Delphi*, tr. by G. C. Richards, Gyldendal, London, 1920.

Richter, Gisela M. A., *Ancient Furniture: A History of Greek, Etruscan and Roman Furniture*, Oxford University Press, New York, 1926.

——, *Animals in Greek Sculpture*, Oxford University Press, New York, 1930.

——, *Archaic Greek Art Against Its Historical Background*, Oxford University Press, New York, 1949.

——, *Attic Red-Figured Vases*, Yale University Press, 1946.

——, *The Craft of Athenian Pottery*, Yale University Press, 1923.

——, *Handbook of the Classical Collection*, 6th ed., Metropolitan Museum of Art, New York, 1930.

——, *The Sculpture and Sculptors of the Greeks*, new rev. ed., Yale University Press, 1950.

Ridder, André H. P. de, and Deonna, Waldemar, *Art in Greece*, tr. by V. C. C. Collum, Knopf, 1927.

Robertson, Donald S., *A Handbook of Greek and Roman Architecture*, Cambridge University Press, 1954.

Rodenwaldt, Gerhart, *Die Kunst der Antike*, Propyläen-Verlag, Berlin, 1927.

——, and Hege, Walter, *Akropolis*, Deutscherkunstverlag, Berlin, 1937.

Roes, Anna, *Greek Geometric Art: Its Symbolism and Its Origin*, Oxford University Press, London, 1933.

Rostovtsev, Mikhail I., *The Animal Style in South Russia and China*, Princeton University Press, 1929.

——, *Iranians and Greeks in South Russia*, Oxford University Press, 1922.

——, *Out of the Past of Greece and Rome*, Yale University Press, 1932.

Schrader, Hans, *Die Archaischen Marmorbildwerke der Akropolis*, V. Klostermann, Frankfurt am Main, 1939.

Seltman, Charles T., *Approach to Greek Art*, Studio Publications, New York, 1948.

Smith, A. H., *The Sculptures of the Parthenon*, British Museum, London, 1910.

Swindler, Mary H., *Ancient Painting*, Yale University Press, 1929.

Warren, Herbert L., *The Foundations of Classic Architecture*, Macmillan, New York, 1919.

Zervos, Christian, *L'art en Grèce*, Editions "Cahiers d' Art," Paris, 1934.

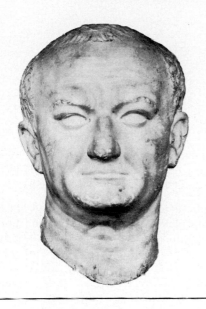

CHAPTER 6

ETRUSCAN
AND
ROMAN

The peoples of Italy were touched at an early date by the radiance which emanated from Greece, but they had deep and tenacious qualities of their own. Etruscan and Roman art must be recognized as a synthesis of influences from outside sources and of elements indigenous to Italy. It is important that we understand the quality of this art, for Rome as a world power was the immediate heir of all earlier Mediterranean cultures. Its art was in many ways the synthesis of the art of antiq-

ILLUSTRATION ABOVE. 6–1 VESPASIAN. Marble. A.D. 69–79. Terme (National) Museum, Rome. (Terme Museum)

uity in a manner quite distinct from Greek art. Rome was also deeply involved in bringing civilization to western Europe. The art of Rome was, therefore, in later times often regarded as the symbol of the art of antiquity.

The early histories of Greece and Italy are roughly parallel. But the vigorous development in Greece after the Persian wars of the fifth century B.C., culminating in the Age of Pericles, found no counterpart in Italy, where culture was retarded by the bitter struggles among competing Italic peoples and between these peoples and the Etruscans.

Etruscan

(ABOUT 1000–2ND CENTURY B.C.)

Legend and archeology both now indicate that there was at least a settlement of Italic peoples among the

hills along the Tiber River as early as the eighth century B.C. To these settlements the name of Rome was eventually given. From the very beginning the Etruscans were Rome's chief rivals.

6 / ETRUSCAN AND ROMAN 153

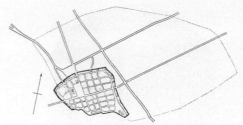

6–2 ITALY IN ROMAN AND ETRUSCAN TIMES.

The Etruscans had come to Italy during the eighth century B.C. — probably from Asia Minor — and had many cultural affinities with the Ionian Greeks. In the sixth century B.C. they controlled most of northern and central Italy from their heavily fortified cities — Tarquinia, Veii, Perugia, Orvieto, Praeneste, and other sites in what are now Tuscany and Umbria.

The Etruscans were apparently warrior overlords to the Italic population, and their wealth was based on farming, commerce, and — according to the Greeks — piracy. At home they seem to have lived luxuriously in gaily decorated houses and to have feasted and danced with a suppleness and verve

6–3 PLAN OF EARLY POMPEII. *ca.* 6th century B.C. (From Riis, *An Introduction to Etruscan Art*, Munksgaard, 1953)

which seem partly Ionian, partly Barbarian. Their reputation for cruel and unrestrained behavior is based largely upon the testimony of the ancient Greeks and Romans, who were their enemies. Nevertheless, the scenes painted in Etruscan tombs tend to indicate that their society had many aspects which were in fact violent and extravagant. Indeed, these qualities may have played a decisive role in the formation of an energetic and creative culture in Italy. Etruscan art clearly shows a mixture of tenaciously retained early types and vigorous innovations, which was to contribute to the art of Rome.

Such an Etruscan innovation, according to classical literature, was the kind of regular town plan later used by the Romans. This plan may have been based upon that of the military camp and derived from the fortified

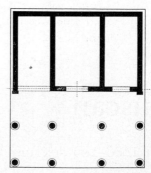

6–4 VITRUVIUS' PLAN OF AN ETRUSCAN TEMPLE. (Wiegand's reconstruction. After Robertson)

settlements of the late Bronze Age. Certainly it differed from the Greek grid system as developed by Hippodamos of Miletus in the fifth century B.C. (Fig. 5–42). In the Etruscan town the area was divided into four approximately equal quarters by two intersecting roads, the *cardo* and the *decumanus*. The decumanus ran east and west, crossing the cardo at right angles. The other, subordinate streets were smaller and ran parallel to these two main thoroughfares. At the center of the town, near the intersection of the cardo and decumanus, was the site of the more important public buildings and civic activities (Fig. 6–3). Here was the origin of the *Roman Forum*.

The origins of the Etruscan temple, on the other hand, may very possibly have been in Greece. Its plan, for example, closely resembles the Greek prostyle plan (Fig. 5–4). Yet the Etruscan adaptation, in typical fashion, developed its own characteristics. It

6–5 ETRUSCAN TUMULUS AT CERVETERI. 5th–4th century B.C. (From M. Pallottino, *The Necropolis of Cerveteri*, Libreria Dello Stato, Rome, 1957)

rested on a high base (podium) with steps at one end only, and was constructed mostly of wood and sun-dried brick in a post and lintel system, with a heavy wooden superstructure above an entablature of brightly painted terra cotta. The Etruscan emphasis on

6–6 TOMB OF THE LEOPARDS. Tarquinia. Fresco decoration. *ca.* 480–470 B.C.

6–7 CANOPIC CINERARY URN from Dolciano. 6th century B.C. The head, of terra cotta, is placed in a bronze model of a chair as found in the tombs. Museo Etrusco, Chiusi.

cal tombs of the sixth century B.C., such as those at *Cerveteri* (Fig. 6–5). These *tumuli,* partially cut from the rock and covered with earth, carry on an ancient Mediterranean tradition with their domical shapes, related perhaps to the *tholoi* at Mycenae.

In the Italic house, developed partly by the Etruscans, old traditions were also retained but given important new characteristics, which were to find their climax in Roman times. The early Etruscan house was a rectangular dwelling with a sloping roof, as may be seen in the *Tomb of the Leopards* (Fig. 6–6). It is known to us today chiefly through clay models. Invention showed itself in the development of the atrium, a high, square central hall lighted through a large opening in the roof. Around this impressive interior space the other rooms of the house were symmetrically arranged. Thus the oldest houses at Pompeii, which date from the early third century B.C., consist of various rooms grouped axially and symmetrically around their central atrium. This atrium was the focus of family life and the shrine for the *lares* and *penates,* the family gods. The ancient sacred hearth of Mediterranean religion found in this way an appropriate architectural expression, and the noble atrium gave to Italic domestic architecture an importance and dignity beyond that developed by the Greeks.

The Etruscans, at least during their later history, made considerable use of the masonry arch, another structural device which was to become of profound importance for Roman building. Etruscan gates and aqueducts, constructed on the arch principle, show a set of forms very different from those favored by the Greeks.

In sculpture the Etruscans showed a preference for work in clay and bronze. In both of these materials the forms are modeled rather than carved; they

a highly ornate façade and the relatively spare treatment of the sides and rear concentrated attention upon the entrance porch. There was thus an axial organization quite different from that of the Greek temple. Behind the entrance porch was the shrine, divided into three equal cellae (Fig. 6–4). These formed dark caves behind the pavilion of the porch. The temple was thus not meant to be seen as a sculptural mass from the outside, like the Greek temple, but was instead intended to create interior space. It was a place of shelter; and over it all, according to Vitruvius, was spread its widely overhanging roof. A similar interest in the interior, enclosed spaces of architecture is evident in the Etruscan coni-

6–8 SARCOPHAGUS from Cerveteri. Terra cotta, painted. 6th–5th century B.C. Villa
Papa Giulio, Rome. (Anderson)

were thus suitable to the impetuous
Etruscan temperament with its love of
quick movement and fluid expression.
Etruscan bronze vessels and mirrors
with incised mythological scenes were
famous and were highly prized objects
in Greece itself. Funerary urns and
sarcophagi with recumbent portrait figures present some of the best examples
of Etruscan sculpture. A canopic urn
from Dolciano, near Chiusi (Fig. 6–7),
has a full, rounded hollow shape and
crude vitality, which is particularly apparent in the terra-cotta head with its
strong features and massive neck. On
the rugged Italic forms has been superimposed a supple smoothness which
may also be seen in Ionic Greek examples. But the accent on the individuality of the man and his wife (Fig. 6–8),
who recline on the lid of a sarcophagus
as though on a couch, is specifically

Etruscan. They are clearly described
effigies intended to satisfy the demands
of a pervasive cult of the dead.

In the *Apollo of Veii* (Fig. 6–9) the
Greek Archaic elements, though immediately evident, are superficial; the
awkward lurching vigor of the powerful figure is primarily a forceful expression of clay modeling techniques. This
Apollo moves like a dangerous animal.
His physical presence embodies small
concern for the Greek preoccupation
with harmonious proportions or idealized humanity. The treatment of surface ornamentation as independent of
the vigorous natural forms recalls similar attitudes shown in the early "animal style," Barbarian in its antecedents
(see pp. 89–90), which may thus be
considered an important component of
Etruscan art. A fluid undulation of
plane and line expressed through sub-

6–9 APOLLO OF VEII. Terra cotta, painted. *ca.* 500 B.C. From ridgepole of Etruscan temple. Villa Papa Giulio, Rome.

6–10 DETAIL OF BRONZE RELIEF from the Perugia chariot. *ca.* 500 B.C. Antikensammlungen, Munich. (Photo Wehrheim)

The modeled surfaces and shifting points of interest, characteristic of Etruscan sculpture, may also be seen in later Etruscan portraits done under the influence of the Hellenistic portrait of personality. In the famous *Capitoline Brutus* (Fig. 6–11), for example, the modeling of the features creates a sense of shifting expression. This is not the Greek essence of personality, intellectually grasped and carved in its most characteristic elements. Instead it is the chance image of a human being as he reacts to the changing pressures of life.

Vigor and variety also impress one in the paintings in Etruscan tombs. Since Greek painting is known to us only from paintings on vases and through a few Roman copies, we must turn to these Etruscan wall decorations for examples of large-scale painting in the Greco-Roman world from the sixth through the second centuries B.C. Done usually in fresco, although a few examples are painted directly on the stone, these impressive decorations covered the interiors of the rock-cut tombs. On the roof, or ceiling, the designs were chiefly conventional, geometric patterns, but on the walls were scenes of

tle modeling is also evident in a bronze relief on a chariot from Perugia (Fig. 6–10). The heraldic design, again closely related to the Barbarian "animal style," exhibits the volatile emotional character of the Italic mind and is little concerned with the structural balance and rationalized geometry to be found in comparable Greek reliefs, such as that of a Gorgon from the temple of Corfu (Fig. 5–21).

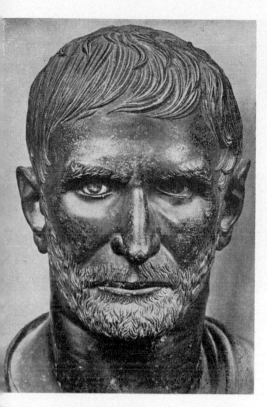

funeral banquets, dancing, athletic contests, or hunting.

Typical of some of the first-known Etruscan paintings are those of the *Tomb of the Baron* (Fig. 6–12). As in Greek Archaic compositions there is a clear relationship between figure and ground, with the contours of the figures sharply defined. The bright colors are used conventionally as flat tones within the bounding contours, although a rudimentary suggestion of atmosphere, or depth of space, may have been intended by the curious blue areas around the horses' legs and manes. An awesome rhythm gives the entire scene a stately quality.

Somewhat later in date are the decorations of the *Tomb of the Leopards* (so called because of the two hunting leopards in heraldic composition in the gable) (Fig. 6–6). Below the animals is a lively banquet scene, in which the turning figures are filled with action. The rhythmic pattern and the clarity of the composition and of the contours may be likened to the sculptures of Aegina (Fig. 5–22), in the Early Classic, Severe style. A final example, from

6–11 CAPITOLINE BRUTUS. *ca.* 1st century B.C. Museo dei Conservatori, Rome. (Musei Capitolini)

6–12 TOMB OF THE BARON. Tarquinia. Fresco decoration. *ca.* 510 B.C. (Alinari)

6–13 TOMB OF THE SHIELDS.
Tarquinia. *Banquet Scene.*
3rd century B.C. (Alinari)

the *Tomb of the Shields* (Fig. 6–13), shows how strongly Etruscan art must have been influenced by Hellenistic developments of the third and second centuries B.C. The interest in specific details and in the anecdotal aspects of reality foreshadows the art of late Republican and Imperial Rome.

Roman

(ABOUT 2ND CENTURY B.C.–A.D. ABOUT 400)[1]

As Rome asserted itself, and by conquest and alliance gradually extended its control over the Italian peninsula

[1] The important divisions of Roman history are as follows:
  Regal period: 753–509 B.C.
  Early Republican period: 509–282 B.C.
  Later Republican period: 282–60 B.C.
  Julius Caesar: 60–44 B.C.
  Augustan Age: 44 B.C.–A.D. 14
  Julio-Claudian emperors: A.D. 14–68.
  Flavian emperors: A.D. 68–96
  Antonine emperors: A.D. 96–180, including
      the reign of Hadrian (A.D. 117–138).
  Severan emperors: A.D. 193–235.
  The military emperors: A.D. 235–284.
  The Tetrarchy: A.D. 284–323.

and ultimately over the entire Mediterranean basin and most of western Europe, it began to develop its own distinctive characteristics. In its early days Rome had employed Etruscan builders and ceramic workers. Indeed, Etruscan masonry structure, the form of its temples, and an interest in realistic portraiture became very much a part of the Roman artistic tradition. Rome had also come into contact with Greece at an early date and was fully

  Constantine I, the Great: A.D. 306–337.
  So-called "Edict of Milan" or "Peace of
      the Church": A.D. 313.
  Dedication of the new capital of the Roman
      empire, Constantinople: A.D. 330.

aware of Greek art. But only in the later Republican and the Augustan ages did Hellenism become a conscious fashion. "Conquered Greece led the conqueror captive," proclaimed Horace, who was a poet of the Augustan Age. Shiploads of Greek marbles and bronzes were brought to Rome by generals and provincial governors to adorn their palaces, and, when the supply was exhausted, copies were made or Greek artists employed to create new ones. Fashionable art for a time became to a large extent mere copying of Greek works. Finally a deeper assimilation took place, and the art of Imperial Rome emerged as a product both of its richly varied heritage and of its own unique genius.

The main energy of Rome was devoted to conquest and administration, while conquest, in turn, opened the way for the spread of Roman civilization. Roman cities sprang up not only all around the Mediterranean basin but also as far north as the Danube, the Rhine, and the Clyde. Each city was a center for the propagation of Roman government, language, and customs and was closely connected with Rome itself by a well-planned system of roads and harbors. Both by force of circumstance and by temperament the Roman was at once warlike and cautious, disciplined, implacable, and conservative. He emphasized the careful observation of tradition as a primary principle of order. His concern was for the decency of life as guaranteed by law and by the state. The life of a Roman of the Imperial period, in contrast with the relative simplicity of that of the fifth-century Athenian, was extraordinarily complex. Rome about A.D. 200 was the capital of the greatest empire the world had yet known, an empire that was efficiently organized, with fifty thousand miles of magnificent highways and sea routes safe for travel and commerce. Rome itself was both

cosmopolitan and splendid. The size, power, and complexity of the empire called for an impressive capital. And while the practical demands arising from the administration of a great empire required the building of roads, bridges, sewers, and aqueducts, the Imperial ideal called also for public buildings which would adequately express the dignity and diversification of the state. To build practically and grandly required skill in engineering.

Rome also administered the Late Antique world wherein the old Hellenistic values were dying and new concepts were being born. By the third century A.D. a number of pressures not only destroyed political stability but also gave to Roman art a variety of expression probably unparalleled until modern times. A weariness with the world fostered renewed growth of mystery cults and salvation religions. Attention turned toward a possible order beyond that of the visible world. Chris-

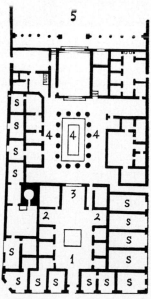

6–14 HOUSE OF PANSA. Pompeii. Plan. 1. Atrium. 2. Alae. 3. Tablinum. 4. Peristyle. 5. Garden. S. Shops.

6–15 ODYSSEY LANDSCAPE. *Ulysses in the Land of the Lestrigonians.* Fresco. 1st century B.C. Vatican Library. (Foto Sansaini)

tianity eventually answered those desires for salvation and promised that order, and it was around the symbol of the Cross that the Roman empire of the West made its last stand. Before A.D. 500 Rome itself had succumbed to the mounting pressures of the Barbarian nations. But Christianity and the forms which late Rome had developed were ultimately to conquer the Barbarians in their turn.

DOMESTIC ARCHITECTURE AND PAINTING

The Romans continued to exhibit the traditional Italic concern for home and family. The prominence of domes-

tic architecture as a characteristic of Roman civilization left its imprint on the entire empire. Roman dwellings were of three types: the *domus* or private house, the *villa* or country house, and the urban *insula* with an apartment to each story. These *insulae* had windows and loggias facing the street as well as a courtyard, about which several such structures were sometimes grouped.[2] Much of the life of the poor classes was spent away from their dwellings, around the public buildings, in the places of amusement, and in the porticoes and parks. Imperial Rome was magnificent in its

[2] Donald S. Robertson, *A Handbook of Greek and Roman Architecture*, pp. 307–09.

system of parks, gardens, and fountains, all made possible by the generous supply of water brought to the city by a system of aqueducts.

The town houses of the well-to-do were of the atrium type found at Pompeii and Herculaneum, many of which, protected by the volcanic ash and lava in which they were buried, are extraordinarily well preserved, with their mural decorations still fresh and sometimes with their equipment and household utensils undisturbed. Such a house stood flush with the sidewalk. Through a narrow door one entered a vestibule (Fig. 6–14), which led into the (1) *atrium*. This had an opening in the center of the roof and a corresponding sunken place in the floor to collect rain water. Along the sides were

small rooms; at the end, where the atrium extended the full width of the building, were two wings, (2) *alae*. Behind the atrium was the (3) *tablinum*, in which the family archives and statues were kept. The *tablinum* could be shut off or could afford a passage to the (4) *peristyle,* a large colonnaded court of Hellenistic origin. This court contained fountains and a garden, about which were grouped the private apartments of the family. At the back there was sometimes another (5) garden. Small rooms along the outer sides of the house, opening on the street, were used as shops (S). It is clear that the house faced inward, depending upon its courts for light and air. When opened through its entire length it afforded a charming vista of open court,

6–16 THE TROJAN HORSE, from Pompeii. Fresco. Museo Nazionale, Naples. 1st century A.D. (From *Roman Painting* by Amedeo Mauri, courtesy of Skira, Inc.)

gardens, fountains, statues, colored marbles, mosaics, and brightly painted walls. An interpenetration of closed and open vistas was created by the dynamic but harmonious play of columns, walls, and courts. Yet underlying these diverse effects lay a strict axial symmetry.

This type of house, with its small number of doors and windows, offered considerable stretches of wall space for decoration. The decoration commonly used varied between types which emphasized the wall as a barrier and others which opened the wall and enhanced the space of the room. Such murals have been found chiefly at Pompeii and Herculaneum. The colors were sometimes delicate (greens and tans), sometimes striking (red and black) to throw the panels or figures into relief, and there was a rich creamy white in the borders. The Roman obtained a certain brilliance of surface by

a careful preparation of the wall. The plaster, which was specially compounded with a mixture of marble dust, was laid on layer after layer. It was beaten with a smooth trowel till it became very dense, and then was polished to an almost marble-like finish.

The change from flat to spatial wall decoration in Pompeii and Herculaneum has been divided, perhaps rather arbitrarily, into four styles.[3] The first, or "Incrustation" style (*ca.* 175 B.C. to 80 B.C.) divided up the closed wall surface by using polychrome panels in bright areas of solid color with occasional textural contrasts schematically rendered. Greek prototypes for this style exist in Hellenistic houses on the

[3] This is described in the writings of Pollio Vitruvius, a Roman architect under Augustus. His fame rests chiefly on his treatise *De Architectura*, which was compiled partly from previous sources but also to a great extent from his own experience.

6–17 FRESCOES OF VILLA ITEM (Villa of the Mysteries). Near Pompeii. Augustan Age. (Alinari)

island of Delos. In the second, or "Architectural" style (*ca.* 80 B.C. to 1 A.D.), which may have been a Roman invention, the decoration of the wall surface was no longer restricted to a single plane. Space was apparently extended beyond the wall by the definition of forms in a visually convincing but not geometrically rationalized system of multipoint perspective. Columns and windows were painted on the surface in perspective, to give them an appearance of relief, and such a framework often enclosed a large painted scene. Architectural details were so portrayed, through skillful use of color and shadow, that they produced an additional illusion of depth and distant landscape. Roman inventiveness coupled with the Roman desire to present many aspects of reality found in this second style an appropriate pictorial expression.

In the famous *Odyssey landscapes* (Fig. 6–15) a colonnaded foreground

divides the otherwise continuous stretch of landscape into eight compartments, in which are represented scenes from the Homeric epic. Although the outdoors is brought into the room, the landscape is represented as though in a vision, even somewhat fantastically with a certain superstitious reverence. The human figure is subordinated to the shimmering land and, rapidly sketched, is almost lost within it. The flickering play of color and light creates an emotionally potent world of pictorial illusion. The technique of quick brush strokes with alternation of highlights and shadows is developed even further in another and somewhat later narrative scene at Pompeii. In this painting, called the *Trojan Horse* (Fig. 6–16), the Roman artist totally abandoned the tactile interest of earlier painting for the pursuit of purely optical values and effects. This is called *illusionism,* since the forms themselves

6–18 THIRD-STYLE DECORATION. From Pompeii. 1st century A.D. Museo Nazionale, Naples. (From *Roman Painting* by Amedeo Mauri, courtesy of Skira, Inc.)

are not delineated, but an optical illusion of them is achieved by a free treatment of broad areas of color and by sharp contrasts of light and dark. At first glance the effects are not unlike those created by the Impressionist painters of the nineteenth century (see pp. 661–63), but closer examination reveals how different the two styles are both in technique and point of view. The nineteenth century sought the impression of natural light as it was momentarily reflected by forms in nature. The Roman artist wished to create the illusion of forms in space — forms which seem to have their own inner source of light. The Impressionists were interested in the scientific analysis of light and color; and their technique consisted in the juxtaposition of small areas of pure color. Roman *illusionism* was much freer in its interpretation of natural forms; the light can hardly be said to be that of nature. The technique is also very free, with much

of the spontaneous effect of water color.

The complexity and diversity of Rome made it natural for a variety of painting styles to be carried on at the same time. In the painting of *Herakles Strangling the Serpents* (Fig. 6–19), the adherence to the Hellenistic prototype on which the scene is based persists in the substantial definition of the figures as material forms rather than as patches of light or color. In the remarkable frescoes of the *Villa Item* (*Villa of the Mysteries*) near Pompeii (Fig. 6–17), however, the figures are linear and sculptural rather than optical, and the feeling of the wall is definitely retained. The figures move within a very shallow space, as in a relief. They are constructed in light against a darker ground, with an extraordinary grasp of the structure of the figure and its relation to adjoining figures. The sculptural quality of the murals is further enhanced by enabling the spectator to see the whole story at once.

The third, or "Ornate," style (*ca.* 1 A.D. to 50 A.D.) is refined, mannered, and linear. It tends to beautify the wall surface and reduces the painted columns, architraves, and façades to ornamental adjuncts. The wall is often divided by painted slender, twisted columns covered with plant forms, and the areas between are filled with monochromatic landscapes. These scenes are in panels rather like pictures hung on a wall, framed and placed with exquisite delicacy (Fig. 6–18).

The last or fourth style of Pompeii (*ca.* 50 to 79 A.D.) is called the "Intricate" style. The painters, apparently under the influence of the contemporary Roman theater, returned to the use of architectural frames and open vistas (Fig. 6–19). An airy perspective, rather than a linear one, is created by areas of color flooded with light and atmosphere. The aerial prospect unites the whole wall in a complex baroque

6–19 FOURTH- or INTRICATE-STYLE DECORATION. From the Casa dei Vettii, Pompeii. 1st century A.D. (Alinari)

way incorporating all the lessons of previous experiments in optical illusion.

Sometimes, however, purely coloristic methods were also used to create the illusion of tactile reality (Fig. 6–20). The similarities between the convincing masses and textures of such a still life and one by Cézanne (Fig. 20–18) are striking indeed.

Besides mural painting, the Romans practiced panel painting for a variety of purposes, such as votive pictures for temples and portraits for libraries and private houses. Great quantities of Greek paintings were also taken to Rome. Yet none of these remain, and the development of Roman painting after the fourth style may be seen only in the narrative mosaics of the second and third centuries A.D. These continue the principles demonstrated in the *Villa of the Mysteries* (Fig. 6–17). The forms are more solid and linear than

6–20 STILL LIFE from Pompeii. 1st century A.D. Museo Nazionale, Naples. (From Pfuhl, *Masterpieces of Greek Drawing and Painting*, Macmillan, 1926)

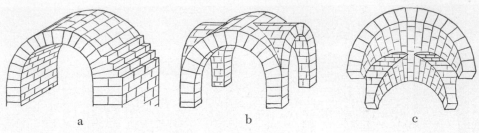

6–21 ROMAN VAULTING SYSTEMS. *a.* Barrel vault. *b.* Cross vault seen from above. *c.* Cross vault seen from below.

in fourth-style painting, with a strong accent on the clear exposition of the narrative.

At this time another and very distinct mode of painting developed in the lands of the Near East along the shores of the eastern Mediterranean. In this new style illusionism and physical substance were both discarded. Human figures were presented frontally with clear outlines separating them from their background. Lacking body they became ethereal and otherworldly (Fig. 7–3). Facing frontally and looking out with staring eyes, they projected themselves with inescapable intensity into the spectator's world. They were no longer illusions of reality in a deep picture space. Instead they were strict psychological injunctions aimed directly at capturing the spectator's attention, overwhelming his inertia or his unbelief, and forcing him finally to accept revelation upon their own terms. Their flat colors and rhythmic patterns were wonderfully decorative.

ARCHITECTURE

Heir to the techniques and aesthetics of the rich Etruscan and Hellenistic past, Roman architecture during the Empire solved, for the first time in Western history, the problem of enclosing large volumes of space and of organizing complex combinations of varying types of structures. The Roman architect availed himself of the column, the wall, the vault, and the dome in designs which were controlled by axial planning and the careful use of sources of light. In Rome, the capital of a complex world empire, practical as well as aesthetic needs led to the erection of many kinds of buildings. Secular as well as religious, the structures were frequently on a scale hitherto untried. Ample material was at hand: abundant wood and stone (travertine, tufa), good clays for brick, and lava and pozzuolana (sandy earth) for concrete. Those materials not at hand, such as the nearly fifty varieties of colored marbles used for their color and texture, could be imported easily by the Roman fleets. Brick and concrete masonry covered with stucco or faced with stone or marble veneer eventually, in Rome itself, supplanted solid stone construction. The arch rather than the post and lintel became the basic structural method, although for many reasons the post and lintel system was retained for a long time as a structural or decorative adjunct.

The chief engineering problem for Roman architecture was how to enclose and roof over a vast space, to give this space proper illumination while still keeping it open and free of the supports necessary under a flat roof (compare with, for instance, the hypostyle halls of Egypt, Fig. 2–19). The simplest vault used by the Romans was the "barrel" vault (Fig. 6–21). This is, in essence, a succession of arches

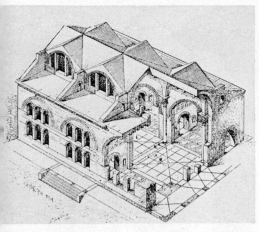

6-22 BASILICA OF MAXENTIUS or CONSTAN-
TINE. Rome. A.D. 306–312. Plan and section.
(From J. Durm, *Handbuch der Architektur*,
J. M. Gebhardts Verlag, Leipzig)

joined together, resting directly upon
the side walls, which must either be
thick enough to support the weight or
be reinforced by buttresses. This vault
can be made of concrete by building
up a temporary wooden framework
(known as centering) of the exact size
and shape of the finished vault, to hold
the fluid mass until it is set. The vaulting we see in Figure 6–29 has been
made by cutting the barrel vault at
right angles at regular intervals by
other barrel vaults, thus securing what
is known as the "crossbarrel" vault. If
the height of the crossing barrel vaults
is the same, the result is a "groin"
vault, the line of intersection being
called the groin. A barrel vault over a
large area not only would have been
heavy in appearance but would have
allowed no space for high windows.
The advantage of the cross or groin
vault is not only that it is lighter in appearance because of its intersecting
planes but also that it admits "clerestory" windows. The use of such vaults
has another advantage. In the barrel
vault the thrust — that is, the downward and outward forces exerted by
the vault — is along the entire length

6-23 PONT DU GARD. Nîmes. Augustan Age.
(Ewing Galloway)

of the wall; in the groin vault it is exerted only at the points at which the
groins converge. Hence it is at these
points only that heavy buttressing is
needed, and the interior can thus be
kept free of load-carrying walls. Proper
support is secured by heavy walls built
at right angles, which are pierced by
arches and thus form side aisles to the
main hall (Fig. 6–22).

The Romans, like the Etruscans,
built solidly and well. Their public
buildings, their roads, bridges, and
aqueducts, combine utilitarian requirements with a fine sweep of line. The
aqueducts, which still swing across the
Campagna to bring mountain water to
Rome or to span streams in several
tiers as in the *Pont du Gard* (Fig. 6–
23), have the stark beauty of function
expressed by the rhythmic movement
of well-spaced arches. Contemporary
with this extensive utilitarian architecture the Romans also built temples,

6–24　MAISON CARRÉE. Nîmes. 1st century B.C. (Hershel Levitt)

such as the *Maison Carrée* at Nîmes (Fig. 6–24). Here the traditional post and lintel system continued to be used. The *Maison Carrée* is derived from the Etruscan podium type with its axially placed stair and wide porch. These elements were modified by the use of Greek masonry construction and Corinthian columns, which are placed peripterally, but are engaged in the cella wall. The Roman temple is thus a synthesis of Etruscan and Greek prototypes. The pavilion of the porch and the cave of the cella are drawn together by the columns which serve to define the façade, to screen the space before the cella, and to force the eye of the observer to follow their rhythmical placement along the side walls.

Similarly, the Roman forum combined the traditional functions of the central market and civic center of the Etruscan towns with the ornamental aspect of the Hellenistic Greek agora. The forum offered an opportunity to develop further the effects of repetitive patterns of columniation. Originally the *Forum Romanum* was the market place; booths and shops ran along the sides. But at an early date religious and civic activities began to encroach; the shops were crowded out to the side streets and the Forum became primarily the center of the city's civic life. In the open space were commemorative statues of emperors and generals, and the great platform from which public speeches were made. Entirely surrounding it and crowning the surrounding hills were imposing buildings. The Imperial Fora, built by various emperors from Augustus on, reached a culmination in the *Forum of Trajan* (Fig. 6–25), where all the units of the vast group were definitely related to one another and to a unified design, instead of being merely set down wherever space and topography permitted, as in the old Roman Fora. A strict axial symmetry organized the series of courts

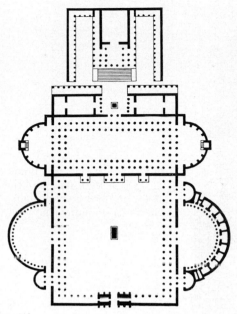

6–25 THE FORUM OF TRAJAN. Rome. Plan. A.D. *ca.* 113.

and buildings which in plan were treated as an ornamental pattern in two dimensions. Through a monumental archway one passed into a great open court flanked by semicircular wings

with shops. One then entered the basilica, which was covered, passed through the library and around the famous Trajan's column, and finally arrived at the temple of the deified emperor — the climax of the ensemble. So strong was the requirement for order in the Roman mind that nothing, not even the accidents of topography, could interfere with it. The planning was abstract and decidedly urban. It made its own geometric world and was little concerned with the relationship between that world and nature. It was thus purely metropolitan in its intentions and stood in contrast to the man-nature balance created by Archaic and Classic Greek planning. A similar geometric rigidity of thought and execution may be observed in the standard formula for the Roman imperial towns scattered all over the Empire, as exemplified in the town plan of Timgad in North Africa.

One of the most important types of civic buildings was the basilica, a covered pavilion used for various purposes, particularly for law courts. As in

6–26   COLOSSEUM OR FLAVIAN AMPHITHEATER. Rome. A.D. 70–82. (Anderson)

6 /   ETRUSCAN AND ROMAN   171

6–27 ARCH OF TITUS. Rome. A.D. 81. Restored on the sides. A bronze four-horse chariot surmounted the arch. (Alinari)

the *Basilica Ulpia* in Trajan's Forum, it was a rectangular structure with semicircular tribunals (or apses) at both ends where the courts sat. The central portion was divided by rows of columns or piers into a hall with side aisles. The roof of the central hall was higher than that of the side aisles, thus permitting clerestory lighting. Many of these elements were, as we shall see, incorporated into the early Christian churches.

The *Colosseum* (Fig. 6–26) and the *Arch of Titus* (Fig. 6–27) illustrate another principle in Roman architecture. In both of them there is a combination of arched construction and of the post and lintel system, in which the column or pilaster with an entablature serve as a decorative design, imparting to the buildings the traditional classic scale. In the *Colosseum* a series of arches, as

in the aqueducts, are applied to a three-dimensional program, but their continuous thrusts, nonclassic in feeling, are masked and contained by the rectangular bay system of engaged columns and entablatures. The interior construction is concrete faced with brick, with hard stone at points of stress. The exterior is of travertine masonry set without mortar but clamped by iron dowels. The rhythm of the engaged columns and the entablature not only unifies the arched openings but also forms a fine single sweep of curve which, repeated on each story, accents the basic cylindrical form.

Places of amusement, the circuses, the theaters, the amphitheaters, and the great baths (*thermae*), which were so essential to Imperial Rome, challenged the engineering ability of her builders.

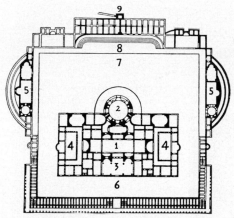

6–28 BATHS OF CARACALLA. Rome. Plan.
A.D. 211–217. The central buildign is 750
by 380 ft 1, *Tepidarium*, or warm lounge.
2. *Calidarium*, or hot room. 3. *Frigida-
rium*, or cooling room, with a swimming
pool open to the air. 4. Open peristyles.
5. Lecture rooms and libraries. 6. Prome-
nade. 7. Garden. 8. Stadium. 9. Aqueduct
and reservoirs.

6–29 BATHS OF CARACALLA. Rome. A.D.
211–217. Tepidarium, restored by Spiers.
(Anderson and Spiers)

Huge crowds had to be accommodat-
ed, both indoors and out, and had to
be given, through great scale and opulence, a sense of release from the facts
of everyday existence. The *thermae*
were a center for diversified social life.
They provided the Roman not only
with his daily bath, hot, warm, or cold,
but also with his library and lounging
place. A plan (Fig. 6–28) gives us some
conception of the great extent of these
baths and also of the orderly cross-
axial planning which organized the
different parts into a single whole. Figure 6–29 reconstructs one hall, the
tepidarium, of the *Baths of Caracalla*.
The impression is of vast spaciousness
and, in the rich marble facings, carvings, and coffered ceilings, of magnificence and splendor. By the use of the
crossbarrel vault the Roman builder
conquered space. Even today the ruins
of the huge vaults are impressive.

The *Pantheon*, probably designed by
the Emperor Hadrian himself (*ca.* A.D.
118–26), is the clearest statement of

the principles through which Roman
architecture enclosed space and created its own interior universe. It was
designed as a planetarium, a temple to
the whole universe. The Pantheon consists of a cylinder with but one entrance, the doorway. On the cylinder
rests a dome, low and rather incon-
spicuous on the exterior, gently
mounded like Etruscan tombs (Fig.
6–30). Domes had been built before,
but never on such a scale. The Roman's
ideal of great scale made him daring,
while his practical nature and his engineering skill kept him within the
bounds of structural possibilities. The
walls, twenty feet thick, of brick and
concrete, are solid except for the
niches, over which are imbedded in the
masonry brick relieving arches as thick
as the entire wall. These arches carry
the thrust of the dome down to the
solid masonry. The dome is constructed of horizontal layers of brick
laid in thick cement, strengthened by
a series of ribs converging in the

6–30 PANTHEON. Rome. A.D. 118–126. Originally the outer walls were faced with marble and stucco and the dome was covered with bronze plates.

6–31 INTERIOR OF THE PANTHEON. Rome. A.D. 118–26. Painting by Paninni (18th century). National Gallery of Art, Washington, D. C. (Samuel H. Kress Collection, National Gallery)

crown. Between these ribs are the typical Roman coffers, which both diminish the weight by being adapted to the wedge shape and add to the perspective of the dome. At the entrance to the Pantheon is a colonnaded portico of Hellenistic design which masks the domed cylinder behind so that, upon entrance, the great space of the interior bursts upon the spectator (Fig. 6–31). This awesome impression results from the simplicity of a design carried out on a very large scale – a dome set on a circular wall and illuminated by an oculus in the crown from which light in a shaft models the interior and admits the heavens above.

In the Pantheon in Rome, Hadrian formulated an impressive, finite definition of the Roman universe. In his imperial villa, at nearby Tivoli, Hadrian invoked all available architectural experience to create a dramatic, picturesque environment (Fig. 6–32). Varying axes, conforming with topographical situations, gave coherence to curvilinear patterns of great diversity. The interrelations of mass and volume, of interior and exterior spaces were explored with the talent of a virtuoso. In many ways Hadrian's villa was the logical conclusion to Roman experiments in creating the illusion of space. Grottoes, pools, pavilions, domed and open spaces evoked the archetypes of traditional forms, and the sounds of flowing water complemented the presence of abundant light.

Whereas the vistas of Hadrian's villa explored the possibilities of perception in depth, the façades of buildings such as the library at Ephesus or the rock-cut sanctuary at Petra are illusionistic screens, modulating light in much the same manner as did painting of the fourth, "Intricate" style of Pompeii.

By the end of the second century A.D. a slow dissolution of the central authority of Rome began; it continued, with increasing anarchy, during the third century. As the Pax Romana became a distant memory, lack of confidence in the material world turned men's minds inward to more spiritual values. The Emperor Diocletian, at the end of the century, established a fixed, social hierarchy. When the new order of the Empire and the new order of the spirit in Christianity coalesced under Diocletian's successor, the Emperor Constantine, another era had begun. Just as Roman architecture had mirrored the worldly strength of the Empire, so now a new style – the Late Antique – evolved to meet the new demands. The *palace of Diocletian* at Spalato, in reality a fortress protected by its walls from the Barbarian invaders, was a closed, rigidly symmetrical, cubical block, in contrast to the open plan of *Hadrian's Villa* at Tivoli. At Spalato the complete exclusion of the world of nature made a tense atmosphere, in which the Emperor sought security as a divine potentate. Similarly in the *Basilica of Maxentius* in Rome (Fig. 6–22) the interior spaces were clearly defined and compartmentalized by the barrel vaults over the aisles and the groin vaults over the nave. These massive vaults, with the forceful

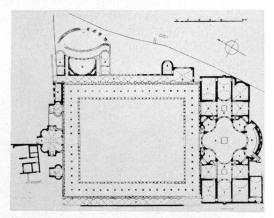

6–32 THE "PIAZZA D'ORO." Hadrian's Villa, Tivoli. Plan. A.D. *ca.* 123–124. (From J. Durm, *Handbuch der Architektur*, J. M. Gebhardts Verlag, Leipzig)

6–33 ARA PACIS (Altar of Peace). Erected 13-9 B.C. to commemorate the victories of Augustus in Spain and Gaul. Detail of decoration. Terme (National) Museum, Rome.

geometry of their repetitive curves swept from support to support, buttressed each other and allowed the nonsupporting walls beneath them to be opened up into windows.

In the nymphaeum which has been called the *temple of Minerva Medica* the relationship of interior spaces became more complex, and their definition by light was greatly enriched. The exterior of the structure was simple and geometrical. In the interior the rhythms were entirely those of the arched and vaulted structural system. The space was rich in color and light. Here Late Antique experiments in optical effects were fully developed. The interior space was lit, not from above by a single oculus, which would clearly model

it, as in the Pantheon, but instead by many windows under the dome. These set up a dazzle of light, making the space definitions shimmering and unclear while the shadowed dome floated magically above.

A discussion of Roman architecture is incomplete without mention of its use of architectural ornament. This was not merely an addendum to the architectural mass. Ornament served to modify the structure, often to conceal it. The restraint of the Greek in the use of moldings and decoration was too severe to suit the Roman's taste and purpose. He preferred the Corinthian capital to the more austere Doric and Ionic, not only for its increased surface richness but also for its organic plant forms.

A medium used most effectively by the Romans was stucco applied as a finish to the rough concrete vaults and walls. The surface was divided by moldings into geometric patterns which frequently enclosed figures, or was filled with naturalistic spirals or other motifs and dainty figures. The stucco was made of marble dust, both durable and fine in texture. The moldings and the figures were worked in the wet stucco partly by stamps, noticeably in the moldings, and partly freehand. As in the fresco technique, the rapidity with which plaster dries requires rapid workmanship, and consequently the figures depend for their effect not so

6–34 Roman rinceau. Decorative relief. A.D. 2nd century. Lateran Museum, Rome.

much upon careful modeling as upon spontaneity, ease of workmanship, and freely flowing line.

Qualities deriving from such techniques can be seen even in marble cutting, as in a section of the *Ara Pacis* (Fig. 6–33). From a central group of acanthus rises a vertical foliate form with curving stems which branch off to cover the surface with spiral forms terminating now in a leaf, now in a flower or rosette; near the top a swan with outspread wings has alighted. While naturalistic representation has formed the basis of the decoration, the ultimate effect is dependent partly upon the delicacy and precision of the carving and partly upon the carver's restraint in keeping his design within a clear decorative pattern.

The ornamental design composed of undulating foliate vine motifs, known as the *rinceau* (Fig. 6–34), became one of the most popular in Roman decorative art, especially as applied to pilasters and borders. Later it formed the basis of much Renaissance ornament. With the Flavian emperors, this naturalistic ornament sacrificed decorative quality to a greater illusion of actual appearance. Details of plant and bird forms were copied from nature, and this natural effect was enhanced by the way in which the marble was cut. An almost atmospheric effect was produced, as in the rose columns of the *tomb of the Haterii* (Lateran). By the time of the reliefs on the *Arch of Septimius Severus* at Leptis Magna in Africa, the floral forms were abstracted into sharp, repetitive patterns of light and shade. We shall note a similar development in Roman sculpture.

SCULPTURE

Free-standing statues in great profusion stood in the Roman fora and in both public and private buildings. Villas and baths were museums of Greek

6–35 UNKNOWN ROMAN. Marble, Republican period. Albertinum, Munich. (Kaufmann)

sculpture,[4] whether originals, copies, or adaptations to suit Roman taste. These copies, however, are not truly Roman sculpture, which emerges most convincingly in portraiture and in relief. During the Hellenistic period the generalization which had distinguished earlier portraits had given way to individualistic work. The Roman's desire for literalness, together with his custom of keeping in his house, always before his eyes, the *imagines* (wax masks) of his ancestors, influenced the sculptor to accentuate still further individual traits. And not to be disregarded is the Etruscan influence which, with its expressionistic realism, persisted in late Republican portraiture. In the head of a Roman (Fig. 6–35), for

[4] We read of 285 bronze and 30 marble statues brought from Corinth in 145 B.C.; of 500 bronzes brought from Delphi by Nero — two illustrations only of the ransacking of Greece to deck Rome.

6–36 THE EMPEROR AUGUSTUS ADDRESSING HIS ARMY. Marble, originally painted. *ca.* 10 B.C. Found in the Villa of Livia, wife of Augustus, at Prima Porta. Vatican, Rome. (Alinari)

now faced the cataclysmic first century B.C. with unbending disapproval.

But when we turn to the statue of *Augustus* (Fig. 6–36), the feeling is different: an idealized generalization has taken the place of the old Republican particularity. The emperor stands easily. He wears an elaborately decorated metal cuirass with leather fringe over his linen tunic and carries his military cloak thrown over his left arm. In every part of the costume is seen skill in the rendering of texture: the soft and heavy quality of the cloths, the rigidity of the metal, and the tough nature of the leather. In his left hand Augustus holds the scepter; his right is lifted in the direction of his glance as if he, *imperator,* were addressing his troops. But the face does not characterize Augustus in detail. There are no individual lines to indicate personal idiosyncrasies. It is rather a generalized type distinctly reminiscent of Greek work. The Augustan Age was indeed a period when the acquisition of Greek statues and the influence of Greek art and thought were at their height. Yet the controlled, idealized features, together with the allegorical scenes depicted on the breastplate, are a new juxtaposition of forms. They represent a new kind of balance between varying tensions, similar to the new balance which Augustus brought to the Roman world after its century of chaos. Augustus, in the *Prima Porta* statue, no longer represents the person of the man but is instead the embodiment of an order idealized and given form in the Roman empire. The new balance is not the instinctive, dynamic one of the Periclean Age, for example, and hence it is not classic in the true sense of the word. It is "classicizing," consciously attempting to be classic. Hence it is calculated and rather dry, and should be defined as "neoclassic."

The generalizing tendency of the Augustan Age did not maintain itself

example, one is struck by its character, at once alive and masklike. One should also note how the technique seems to derive from a sensitivity to scored clay. An active personality is revealed through the externals of a physiognomy which is set like a modeled mask upon the solid structure beneath. The bony structure of the head, the keen eye, the sparse hair, the lines and wrinkles which are the peculiar characteristics of an individual, all combine to give us an expressive portrait of one of the rugged men of stubborn will who had helped, in the earlier days of the Republic, to lay the foundations of Rome's greatness and who

long against the Roman love for literalness. Thus the spirited portrait of *Vespasian* (Fig. 6–1) is an individualistic expression of the rugged soldier that we know Vespasian to have been, an expression not so detailed as the Republican portraits, nor so trenchant. The incisiveness and the linear quality of the latter have been softened by a gradual blending of detail. The head has a fine stoic air of physical and moral strength. By Hadrianic times there began a withdrawal from the customary activist philosophy of the Roman to an investigation of the self and a reassessment of the traditional virtues (Fig. 6–37), a movement expressed most explicitly in the writings of the philosopher emperor, Marcus Aurelius.

When we come to such a portrait as that of *Caracalla* (Fig. 6–38), certain elements have been added to achieve a greater illusion of life. The turn in the head that greatly heightens the impression of vivacity; the rough mass of hair that contrasts with the smoothly finished face; the naturalistic treatment of the eyes, with drilled pupils, deepset in the shadow of heavy brows — all these means have been combined to create an illusion of natural appearance in conjunction with penetrating characterization. The brutalization of power which affected those who held the beleaguered role of emperor is implicit in the lowering glance of this baroque figure. The embattled will of Caracalla was defeated, as was Rome in the third century, by internal weakness in the face of great pressure.

But the Roman world was able to transcend its defeat in the physical world by a transference of its values to the spiritual plane. This, perhaps beyond all else, was the mightiest achievement of Late Antiquity. Roman temporal order was thus succeeded by the spiritual order which was realized in Christianity. The hierarchic and

6–37   HADRIAN. Marble. A.D. 117–138. National Museum, Athens. (Alinari)

6–38   CARACALLA. Marble. A.D. 211–217. Berlin. (Berlin Museum)

6-39 CONSTANTINE. Colossal marble head. A.D. 306–337. Museo dei Conservatori, Rome. (Anderson)

fixed withdrawal from the mundane in favor of otherworldly experience and power is expressed in the frozen-faced *Constantine* (Fig. 6–39). The geometry of this head is like that of the exterior of the contemporary *Minerva Medica:* strict, closed, and severe. As in *Minerva Medica* the experience seems concentrated within, a deep and transcendent exaltation, expressed by the

staring eyes. Later the traditional Antique insistence upon the substantiality of the physical form was to be fully dissolved and the flesh was to become irrelevant.

In Roman figural reliefs a somewhat similar and very important development can be discerned. In the procession of men, women, and children on the *Ara Pacis* (Fig. 6–40) Rome for the first time presented its ruling classes without the gloss of idealizing mythology used in the Hellenic world. Nor are the people of the city themselves shown here, as on the great and unique Parthenon frieze. Instead the imperial family and groups of senators are balanced in ritual procession. The relief is higher in the foreground figures and lower in the background, creating a distinct sense of depth. Details of clothing and figures are carefully depicted and the faces are portraits of men and women from childhood to old age. The purpose of the composition has been to give an illusion rather than an organized expression of a procession. In fact, the illusion has a transitory aspect, as the figures are shown in the relaxed postures that preceded the beginning of the ceremony. The latent realistic tendency is carried further in the reliefs on the inner side of the *Arch of Titus* (Fig. 6–41), in which a full pictorial illusionism, created by light and shade and comparable to fourth-style painting, is achieved. The triumphal parade emerges from space, comes forward in an arc of movement, and disappears back into depth through a triumphal arch. In the reliefs on the *Column of Trajan* (Fig. 6–42) a different kind of space is developed in order to make possible a continuous narrative style. Figures are shown above and behind each other in scenes which successfully bring together Hellenic types in typically Roman landscape settings. Each scene is bound to the next by the constantly repeated figure

6–40 ARA PACIS. Detail of Procession. 13–9 B.C. Uffizi, Florence.

6–41 RELIEF from Arch of Titus. *Triumphal Parade with the Spoils from Jerusalem.* A.D. 81. Rome. (Anderson)

6–42 TRAJAN'S COLUMN. Detail of reliefs. A.D. 117. Rome. (Alinari)

of the emperor. Trajan in his person is the protagonist of the dramatic life of the Roman empire and people at their apogee. A detailed record of his military campaigns is depicted on the reliefs which spiral around the shaft from base to summit. Trajan is the repeated focus of attention.

As time went on, such focus upon the emperor became more insistent and prepared the way for the moment in art when all attention was in turn to be directed to the Christ.

By the time of the *Severan reliefs* at Leptis Magna (Fig. 6–43), a rigid frontality has been imposed on the figures. The imperial group is now defined sharply by the vibrating alternations of unmodulated light and shadow. All illusions of depth of space is destroyed by the insistent pattern which functions on the two remaining parallel planes of the relief and projects the forms forward toward the spectator, not backward into space. Some aspects of this style may have come from Near Eastern sources, where, as in Dura Europus and Palmy-

6–43 ARCH OF SEPTIMIUS SEVERUS at Leptis Magna, North Africa. *Triumph of the Emperor.* A.D. 203–204. (Fototeca Berenson)

6–44 RELIEF from the Arch of Constantine. Rome. A.D. 315. (Fototeca Unione Roma)

ra, important experiments toward these new ends had already taken place. The way was thus prepared for the minute, depersonalized forms of the band of reliefs on the *Arch of Constantine* (Fig. 6–44), with Constantine firmly placed in the center as the focus of all interest. The Hellenistic and earlier Roman concern for earthly "appearances" has largely disappeared in favor of a more abstract, rigorous symbol. The Greek love for the living body has been transformed into a preoccupation with a transcendent image — an image which strongly influenced the Christian art of the Middle Ages.

METALWORK, POTTERY, GLASS

The skill of the Romans in the use of metal may be seen in the casting of large sculpture but also in such small bronzes as the candelabra, furniture supports, and household utensils found in great variety at Pompeii. The wealth and splendor of life made demands upon both the goldsmith and the silversmith, requiring them to furnish fine plate for luxurious tables. A few finds

of treasure[5] give us a glimpse of the lavishness displayed at the famous Roman feasts. The silver krater from Hildesheim (Fig. 6–45) is finely shaped, with handles so adjusted that one feels their unity with the structural lines of the vase. Low reliefs, done in *repoussé* and similar to the *Ara Pacis* floral decorations, give a play of delicate light, shade, and line over the surface. At the base the relief is higher, more elaborate, and more compact, thus strengthening the support. The design here consists of two griffins back to back in a heraldic position, from which rises a conventional plant form. From this and from the sweeping wings of the griffins delicate spirals rise and spread over the surface, terminating in naturalistic forms. Clinging to the stems and tendrils are tiny children attacking with tridents the sea animals which twine among the spirals. Here is the playful imagery of a sophisticated Hellenistic and Roman world.

[5] One of the rich finds of silverware was at Hildesheim, Germany, and is known as the Hildesheim Treasure. Another, the Boscoreale Treasure, most of which is in the Louvre, was discovered at Boscoreale near Pompeii.

6–45 SILVER KRATER from the Hildesheim Treasure. Probably Augustan Age. Berlin. (Giraudon)

6–47 PORTLAND VASE. 1st century A.D. Blue and white glass. H. *ca*. 10 in. British Museum, London. (Mansell)

Similar motifs are found in the Augustan *Arrentine bowls*. These were made of a fine reddish clay, with the decoration stamped in relief on the outside by means of molds in which the design had been cut in *intaglio*. The Roman lapidaries of the Augustan Age were also skilled in cameo cutting,

6–46 THE "GEMMA AUGUSTEA." Cameo showing Augustus and Roma at the Triumph of Tiberius. A.D. *ca*. 12. Kunsthistoriches Museum, Vienna.

which consists in carving a design in relief in a striated stone, such as sardonyx, in such a way that each layer — the layers usually are alternately light and dark, and number from two to nine — will be utilized in working out the design (Fig. 6–46).

The cameo technique was carried over by the Roman into the craft of the glassworker, as we see in the *Portland Vase* (Fig. 6–47). Up to the second or first century B.C. glass had been molded, a laborious process. About that time the blowpipe was invented, causing a rapid growth of the glass industry, and glass supplanted, to a large extent, the more usual pottery for everyday use. In making such a vase as the *Portland*, the glassworker shaped the deep-blue vase with his blowpipe and then dipped it into opaque white liquid glass. The handles were molded separately and added. When thoroughly hard, the white layer was cut away, leaving the raised white in relief against the deep-blue ground. The rather dry, neoclassic forms were to exert a considerable influence on Western art in the late eighteenth and early nineteenth centuries.

The Roman preoccupation with fine work in semiprecious materials continued a tradition as old as Mediterranean antiquity itself. This tradition late Rome was to transmit to the Middle Ages, where the dazzling brilliance of work in jewels, metals, glass, enamels, and mosaics was to be taken as a material expression of divine radiance.

Summary

Rome, in a sense, inherited all the older traditions of Mediterranean antiquity. The effect of Etruscan art persisted notwithstanding the Hellenization of Roman culture. In the hands of Roman engineers the bold vigor of Etruscan stone construction on the arch principle produced structures of large conception and solid engineering. Engineering was in fact only another manifestation of that Roman impulse toward order which found expression in law and governmental organization.

Roman architecture was preoccupied with enclosing vast spaces. The great material and technical resources at her command made this possible. At the same time, Imperial architecture was profoundly influenced by the illusionistic effects which had been developed in painting. Complexes of buildings were organized with pictorially conceived screens of columns and disciplined by an axial symmetry of space recession. The psychic necessities of a sophisticated age produced a marvelous complexity of rhythmic variation upon basic architectural types. But by the third century A.D. the architectural forms began to be stiffened and simplified into the basically curvilinear rhythm of their structural system.

The Etruscan heritage combined with the Roman passion for fact rather than for abstraction led to a portraiture of great vitality during the Republic.

The idealism of Augustan times and the materialistic realism of the Flavians were transformed into baroque expressionism in the early third century. This was succeeded in the end by the spiritual intensity and geometric clarity of the Late Antique. Relief sculpture, also, partook of a similar progression (1) from surface order (2) to a full spatial illusionism (3) to a continuous narrative style, and finally (4) to a sharp, hieratic frontality. The spiritual experience which Late Antiquity desired was ultimately satisfied in Christian art.

Bibliography

Alexander, Christine, *Jewelry: The Art of the Goldsmith in Classical Times*, Metropolitan Museum of Art, New York, 1928.

Anderson, William J., and Spiers, R. P., *The Architecture of Ancient Rome*, rev. by Thomas Ashby, Vol. 2 of *The Architecture of Greece and Rome*, 2 vols., Scribner's, 1927.

Bailey, Cyril, ed., *The Legacy of Rome*, Oxford University Press, New York, 1923.

Barrow, R. H., *The Romans*, Penguin Books, Harmondsworth, England, 1949.

Beazley, Sir John D., *Etruscan Vase-Painting*, Oxford University Press, New York, 1948.

Breasted, James H., *Ancient Times*, 2nd ed. rev., Ginn, Boston, 1935.

Brendel, Otto, "Prolegomena to a Book on Roman Art," *Memoirs of the American Academy in Rome*, 21:7, 1953.

Carcopino, J., *Daily Life in Ancient Rome*, Yale University Press, 1940.

Chase, George H., *Greek and Roman Sculpture in American Collections*, Harvard University Press, 1924.

Dawson, Christopher M., *Romano-Campanian Mythological Landscape Painting*, Yale University Press, 1944.

Goldscheider, Ludwig, *Etruscan Sculpture*, Oxford University Press, New York, 1941.

——, *Roman Portraits*, Oxford University Press, New York, 1940.

Grenier, Albert, *The Roman Spirit in Religion, Thought, and Art*. tr. by M. R. Dobie, Knopf, 1926.

Gusman, Pierre, *L'art décoratif de Rome*, 3 vols., Librairie Centrale d'Art et d'architecture, Paris, 1908–14.

Hamberg, P. G., *Studies in Roman Imperial Art*, Almquist & Wicksells, Uppsala, Sweden, 1945.

Hanfmann, George M. A., *The Etruscans and Their Art* (reprint of the *Bulletin of the Museum of Art*, Rhode Island School of Design, Providence, July, 1940).

——, *The Season Sarcophagus in Dumbarton Oaks*, 2 vols., Harvard University Press, 1952.

Lamb, Winifred, *Greek and Roman Bronzes*, Dial Press, New York, 1929.

Lehmann, Phyllis L., *Roman Wall Paintings from the Boscoreale in the Metropolitan Museum of Art*, Archaeological Institute of America, Cambridge, Mass, 1953.

Lehmann-Hartleben, Karl, *Die Trajans-saule*, Walter de Gruyter, Berlin, 1926.

——, and Olsen, Etling C., *Dionysiac Sarcophagi in Baltimore*, Institute of Fine Arts, New York University, 1942.

Lukomskii, Georgii K. *L'art étrusque*, Editions Duchartre, Paris, 1930.

McClees, Helen, *The Daily Life of the Greeks and Romans*, 6th ed., Metropolitan Museum of Art, New York, 1941.

Maiuri, Amedeo, *Roman Painting*, Skira, New York, 1953.

Mau, August, *Pompeii: Its Life and Art*, tr. by F. W. Kelsey, Macmillan, New York, 1902.

Pallottino, Massimo, *Etruscan Painting*, Skira, New York, 1953.

——, *The Etruscans*, Pelican Books, Harmondsworth, England, 1955.

——, and Hurliman, M., *Art of the Etruscans*, Vanguard, New York, 1955.

Platner, Samuel B., *A Topographical Dictionary of Ancient Rome*, completed and rev. by Thomas Ashby, Oxford University Press, New York, 1929.

Poulsen, Fredrik, *Etruscan Tomb Paintings: Their Subjects and Significance*, tr. by Ingeborg Andersen, Oxford University Press, New York, 1922.

Richter, Gisela M. A., *Handbook of the Classical Collection*, 6th ed., Metropolitan Museum of Art, New York, 1930.

Riis, P. J., *An Introduction to Etruscan Art*, E. Munsgaadd, Copenhagen, 1953.

——, *Tyrrhenica*, E. Munsgaadd, Copenhagen, 1941.

Rivoira, Giovanni T., *Roman Architecture*, tr. by G. McN. Rushforth, Oxford University Press, New York, 1925.

Robertson, Donald S., *A Handbook of Greek and Roman Architecture*, Cambridge University Press, 1954.

Rodenwaldt, Gerhart, *Die Kunst der Antike*, Propyläen-Verlag, Berlin, 1927.

Rostovtsev, Mikhail I., *The Social and Economic History of the Roman Empire*, Oxford University Press, New York, 1926.

Ryberg, I. S., "Rites of the State Religion in Roman Art," *Memoirs of the American Academy in Rome*, Vol. 22, 1955.

Showermann, Grant, *Eternal Rome*, Yale University Press, 1925.

——, *Rome and the Romans*, Macmillan, New York, 1931.

Strong, Eugénie S., *Art in Ancient Rome*, 2 vols., Scribner's, 1928.

——, *Roman Sculpture from Augustus to Constantine*, Scribner's, 1907.

——, *La scultura romana da Augusto a Constantino*, 2 vols., Fratelli Alinari, Florence, 1923–26.

Swindler, Mary H., *Ancient Painting*, Yale University Press, 1929.

Toynbee, J. M. C., *The Hadrianic School*, Cambridge University Press, 1934.

Weege, Fritz, *Etruskische Malerei*, M. Niemeyer, Halle, Germany, 1921.

Wickhoff, Franz, *Roman Art*, tr. by Mrs. S. A. Strong, Macmillan, New York, 1900.

EUROPEAN
ART

THE development of western European civilization from the decay of Rome to the dawn of the modern age (the third through the eighteenth century) may be studied in a series of coherent artistic styles, which succeeded one another and were universally adopted, though in varying degrees, by the emerging national entities.

Early Christian art was the art of Late Antiquity endowed with Christian meaning. It was succeeded by Byzantine art, which dominated the Eastern Christian world, including Russia, long after the fall of Constantinople in 1453, and influenced the development of Western art as well.

The Middle Ages in western Europe were not, as their title suggests, an historical hiatus. Early Christian and Barbarian forms appear side by side in the art of the Carolingian Revival of the eighth and ninth centuries; and these diametrically opposed concepts finally combined in the original art of the Romanesque monasteries during the eleventh and twelfth centuries. The rural environment of Romanesque art contrasts sharply with the urban surroundings of the succeeding Gothic style, which appeared in the twelfth century and endured through the fifteenth, just as the Romanesque visionary and fantastic themes contrast with the Gothic presentation of the Christian encyclopedia. The Gothic cathedral was not only a symbol but also an image of the Christian universe, and as such has never been surpassed.

With the Renaissance, art presented a new interpretation of man and his world. The new humanism found inspiration in the writings and art of Classical Antiquity, from which it created a rational order for the Christian world. The governing principles of Renaissance art were defined during the fifteenth century in Italy, and there the style received its fullest expression early in the sixteenth. It was during the sixteenth century that Renaissance art spread throughout Europe and Russia, being also transported across the Atlantic by the early colonists.

In sixteenth-century Italy certain transformations of style became evident, which we recognize today as revealing the characteristics of Mannerism. Mannerism was primarily the expression of the artist's state of mind in a world in crisis — an expression in which he forced the classic Renaissance forms into willful exaggerations. As new scientific and philosophical concepts challenged the Church and it in turn reaffirmed its tenets through the Counter Reformation, artists developed the Baroque style — a powerful, often sensational art. In Baroque art the participant is presented with elements of great complexity organized into a tightly integrated whole. In the eighteenth century these elements were refined on a more delicate scale, in the Rococo style. Yet by the middle of the century an archeological and antiquarian interest in a variety of past styles marked the beginning of the revivals and eclecticism which were so evident as the modern world came into being.

◄   NOTRE DAME, CHARTRES. Statue column from central west portal (detail). 1145–1150. (Art Historical Seminar, Marburg)

CHAPTER 7

EARLY CHRISTIAN AND BYZANTINE

(A.D. ABOUT 200–1453)

The history of the early centuries of the Christian era is as disordered and complex as the simultaneous disintegration of the Roman empire and the world of antiquity. In the eastern Mediterranean, Rome was succeeded by the Byzantine empire, which indeed

ILLUSTRATION ABOVE. **7–1** CHALICE OF ANTIOCH. 5th–6th centuries A.D. Silver gilt. H. 7½ in. Metropolitan Museum of Art, The Cloisters, New York. (Cloisters Fund, 1950)

called itself the Eastern Roman empire. In western Europe, though, the dismemberment was more complete as the leaders of the various Barbarian nations tried to assume power in the different regions where they had settled. Finally, control of the Mediterranean Sea itself was seized by the forces of Islam, which also overran the lands from Syria west across North Africa and into Spain (see pp. 491–92). Each of these cultures developed its own distinctive style of art.

Early Christian

(A.D. ABOUT 200–700)

Early Christian art is the art of Late Antiquity when it has Christian connotations. Its general geographical limits are those of the Mediterranean basin,

and its time limits extend from the third into the eighth century (Fig. 7–2). Since Christianity appeared in a world vigorously dominated by Rome, and since the new Christian order was only gradually defined, it was to be

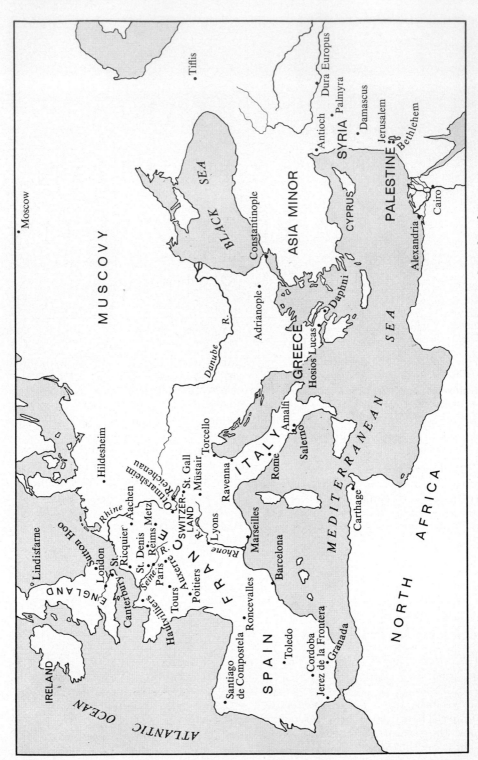

7–2 THE MEDITERRANEAN WORLD in Early Christian and Medieval times.

7–3   MOSES LEADING THE TWELVE TRIBES THROUGH THE RED SEA. Mural from the Synagogue, Dura Europus. A.D. *ca.* 240. National Museum, Damascus. (Yale University)

expected that the first forms of Christian art should have been directly borrowed from the Late Antique world. It also follows that, since the art of the Roman empire was itself in process of transformation during the third and fourth centuries (see p. 168), Early Christian art should be difficult to define in terms of a coherent homogeneous style.

Early in the fourth century, during the reign of Constantine I (306–337), two major events affected the development of Western civilization: the so-called Edict of Milan (313), which recognized Christianity as one of the official religions of the Roman state; and in 330, the move of the capital of the empire from Rome to Constantinople (Istanbul), a move which very shortly divided the empire into two parts. During the reign of Justinian (527–565), a final attempt

was made to reunite the empire; and his general Belisarius almost succeeded in bringing the entire Mediterranean basin once more under the control of a single ruler. This was a moment of great prosperity; and Justinian not only rebuilt Constantinople after the Nike riots of 532 had set fire to the city, but also embellished such cities as Ravenna, the seat of his viceroy in the West.

As early as the third century, it became apparent that two distinct ways of looking at man and his universe were struggling for supremacy. One, predominantly Hellenic in origin, sought to represent the visual appearance of natural forms in space and the actuality of man's experience. The other, basically Semitic in origin, sought the abstract representation of ideas, through symbols and the direct, simple narration of events, which were given artistic form by rhythmic orna-

7-4 PARTING OF LOT AND ABRAHAM. Nave mosaic. Santa Maria Maggiore, Rome. 5th century. (Alinari)

mental, surface designs. If the history of Western thought consists in the attempted fusion of these two different concepts of reality,[1] such a fusion could not have been expected to occur while the ancient world was disintegrating and the new Christian order was seeking its own definition.

The contrast between the Semitic and Hellenic manner of depicting an event may easily be seen by comparing a wall painting from the synagogue at Dura Europus on the Euphrates River (Fig. 7-3) with a detail of a mural from *Santa Maria Maggiore* in Rome (Fig. 7-4). The scene from Dura, showing Moses and the twelve tribes crossing the Red Sea, is presented with a minimum of detail. The major interest is in the concept of the event, which needed only to be evoked in

[1] See Alfred North Whitehead, *Adventures in Ideas,* Mentor Books, New York, 1955, p. 125.

order to be a source of inspiration. No attempt was made to create natural forms in space, and the design is linear, flat, and decorative. The artist in Rome, however, was more interested in the actual event itself. A descendent of such painters as those who decorated the walls at Pompeii (see Fig. 6-19), he strove for pictorial illusionism. His forms are modeled so that they appear to exist in three dimensions. The figures of Lot and Abraham move with natural motion and gestures, and other pictorial details are included in order to convince the observer that the scene actually happened.

This Early Christian art was primarily an art of symbols. Many of the images were simple, familiar objects or animals, which had Christian connotations only to the members of the Christian communities. The fish, for example, was represented again and again

7–5 THE TRANSFIGURATION, WITH ST. APOLLINARIUS. Mosaic of the apse of Sant' Apollinare in Classe, Ravenna. 6th century. (Alinari)

because its Greek letters ιχθυσ were also the Greek initials for Jesus Christ, Son of God, Saviour. Other prominent symbols were: the ship (Latin *navis*, whence "nave" in the early churches), symbol of the Church itself, in which the faithful were carried over the sea of life, and its mast with a crosstree representing the Cross. Pagan symbols were often infused with new meanings: the peacock, the bird of Juno, emblem of immortality, symbolized for Christians the Resurrection; Orpheus with his lyre, surrounded by birds and beasts, became the symbol of Christ, summoning all the faithful. Such symbols, then as now, constitute a language. Since they tend to isolate or to emphasize some dominant element of the person or thing symbolized, their meanings are naturally expressed in generalized or abstract forms.

Biblical stories were also favored,

such as those of Jonah and the whale, Daniel in the lion's den, and the three Hebrews in the furnace, all of which were an assurance of the resurrection of the faithful.

An illustration of a symbolic and narrative representation may be seen in the apse of *Sant' Apollinare in Classe*, just outside Ravenna (Fig. 7–5), where the *Transfiguration* is depicted in a mosaic (now partially restored). Against a gold ground is a large blue medallion with a jeweled cross, symbol of the Christ. Just above, the hand of God and the dove issue from the clouds on an axis with the cross (the three together symbolizing the Trinity). On each side in the clouds appear the figures of Moses and Elijah; below are three sheep, the three disciples who accompanied Christ to the foot of the Mount of the Transfiguration. Beneath, in the midst of green

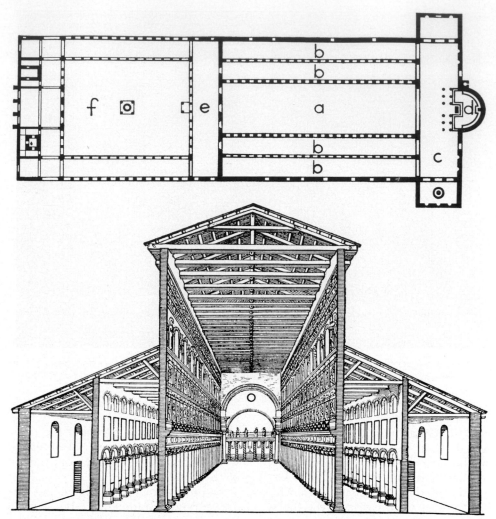

7–6 OLD ST. PETER'S. Rome. 4th century A.D. Reconstruction of plan and section. W. *ca.* 215 ft. Destroyed to make way for the present cathedral. *a.* Nave. *b.* Aisles. *c.* Transept. *d.* Apse. *e.* Narthex. *f.* Atrium.

fields with trees, flowers, and birds, stands St. Apollinarius with uplifted arms, accompanied by twelve sheep symbolizing the twelve Apostles and forming, as they march in regular file across the apse, a wonderfully decorative base. In a language that was understood by all Christians the story is told; and the saint to whom the church is dedicated is made manifest. At the same time the essentially abstract design intensifies the splendor of the half-dome and enhances the emotional reaction to the scene.

ARCHITECTURE

Early Christian meetings were held wherever convenience dictated. The "Christian house" in Dura Europus with vestibule, atrium, meeting room, and baptistery, is an example of such a meeting place, dating from about A.D. 240. It differed in no way from

7–7 SANTA MARIA IN COSMEDIN. Rome. Late 8th century. Remodeled and restored.
(Anderson)

other domestic structures of the period,
and only its decorations identify it as
specifically Christian.

After the Church was officially recognized in A.D. 313, it became possible
to erect Christian places of worship,
and almost immediately there was a
great demand for them. It was not long
before rectangular structures of varying dimensions were being built
throughout the empire. These buildings, called basilicas, were so perfectly
adapted to the demands of the Christian liturgy that the arrangement of
the several parts provided a basic formula for the subsequent development
of Christian architecture. Although the
origin of the basilican church has been
a favorite subject for scholarly debate,
it is generally agreed that the Roman
civil basilica, such as the *Basilica of
Ulpia* in Trajan's Forum (Fig. 6–25),
was the most important prototype.
These classical basilicas, however,
were entered on the long sides rather
than from one end, so that they lacked

the powerful orientation and emphasis
of the Christian church.

A typical Early Christian basilica,
and one of the most important, was
Old St. Peter's in Rome, originally built
in the fourth century, but destroyed in
the fifteenth century to make way for
the present St. Peter's. Its plan (Fig.
7–6) shows: a rectangular building entered through an open colonnaded
court, the atrium (*f*), one side of which
forms the narthex or vestibule (*e*); the
body of the church with a nave (*a*),
low side aisles (*b*), an apse (*d*), and
a transverse aisle or transept (*c*), placed
between the nave and apse and projecting slightly beyond the walls of the
nave and aisles. This T-shaped plan
has often been compared to the form
of the Cross, but there is no evidence
that the Early Christian builders desired to create such a symbol in the
plan, especially since the transept
is lacking in many of the early basilicas.

A more modest basilica, *Santa Maria*

7–8 SAN VITALE. Ravenna. Mosaics and marble veneer. The apse. A.D. 526. (Anderson)

7–9 SANT' APOLLINARE IN CLASSE. Ravenna. Exterior. A.D. 534–538. (Alinari)

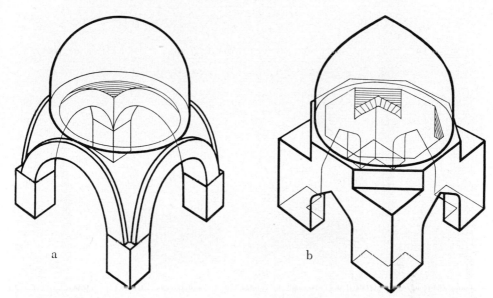

a   b

7–10   *a.* Dome on pendentives. *b.* Dome on squinches. In pendentive construction, the
Byzantine solution, the dome rests upon what is in effect a second and larger dome from
which segments have been sliced, to form the four arches bounding the square. By
transferring the weight to piers rather than to the wall itself, pendentive construction
made possible a lofty, unobstructed interior space (Fig. 7–12). In squinch construction,
favored by Mohammedan builders, the dome rests upon an octagon formed by building
arches (or corbeling or lintels) across the four corners of the square.

in Cosmedin[2] in Rome (Fig. 7–7),
shows this same axial arrangement
without a transept, but with a choir for
the use of the clergy, surrounded by
a marble screen, which occupies almost half the nave. A quick glance at
the columns of this nave reveals how
the Early Christian builders often took
capitals, column shafts, and bases, as

[2] Built in the sixth century; enlarged in the
eighth century; restored in the twelfth. The
church has frequently been remodeled, notably in the late Renaissance, when a façade
was added, and in 1894–99, when it was restored to its eighth- and twelfth-century form.
This continuous remodeling of churches, especially in Rome, makes them a confusing com-
posite of Early Christian, Romanesque, Renaissance, and Baroque styles and leaves but
few in their original style.
   For a sensitive understanding of the formal
relationships in *Santa Maria in Cosmedin*, see
Le Corbusier, *Towards a New Architecture*,
tr. by Frederick Etchells, Payson & Clarke,
New York, 1927, pp. 160 ff.

well as other building materials and
decorations, from pagan buildings and
reused them in a rather haphazard
manner. The nave walls, resting on
columns, rise higher than the outer
walls, providing space for clerestory
windows which directly light the nave
and leave an uninterrupted wall space
below the windows for mosaic or
painted decorations. Both the central
nave and the side aisles of these early
basilicas were roofed in wood and
brightly painted while the apse was
usually vaulted in masonry. The remarkable richness of the interior decoration of many of these early churches
may be seen in *San Vitale*, in Ravenna
(Fig. 7–8), where thin slabs of marble
veneer and marble columns with carved
and painted marble capitals vie with
resplendent mosaics which cover all
the upper portions of the church. This
elaborate and colorful treatment of the

7–11 HAGIA SOPHIA. Istanbul. A.D. 532–537. Exterior. Minarets added later.

interiors contrasted with the simple, undecorated exteriors, as at *Sant' Appollinare in Classe,* in Ravenna (Fig. 7–9). Here the geometry of the major masses, with the free-standing cylinder of the campanile, provided the prototypes for Italian medieval building for many centuries.

Another form of building was also widely used in Early Christian times; and, although it found particular favor in the Near East and Russia, it frequently appeared in the West also. This was the central-plan church, of varying types: circular, as in the ancient *tholos;* square; cruciform, with the arms of the cross of equal dimensions, as in a Greek cross; or polygonal. The dominant structural device was always the dome covering the central portion. In Figure 7–10 two of the principal methods for supporting a dome over a square area are shown. The ingenious system known as the *pendentive* was developed apparently after many years of experiment by builders in the Near East. The spherical triangles and the arches concentrate the load of the dome on the four corner piers, so that a *dome on pendentives* seems almost to float like a great billowing canopy over the unobstructed space beneath. The dome was also a symbol of the heavens. This reference to the cosmic universe added greatly to the mystic, contemplative atmosphere particularly desired in the Near Eastern churches, where the celebration of the Mass was a mystery hidden from the people behind a screen, known as the *iconostasis* (Fig. 12–7).

The central plan was normally used, in western Europe as well, for baptistries and for certain royal chapels.

7-12 HAGIA SOPHIA. Istanbul. A.D. 532–537. Interior.

The fact that the *Anastasis*, or shrine over the Holy Sepulchre [3] in Jerusalem, was a circular, domed construction also gave this form an especial significance.

The supreme achievement of domical construction is the vast *Santa Sophia*, or more properly *Hagia Sophia, Church of the Holy Wisdom*, built for Justinian by Anthemius of Tralles and Isidorus of Miletus in Constantinople

[3] The church of the Holy Sepulchre in Jerusalem was first built by St. Helena, the mother of Constantine, early in the fourth century. It was a complex structure with an atrium, a basilican church with a nave and double side aisles, behind or beyond which was a courtyard, with a monument for the Calvary and with the circular *Anastasis* over the Holy Sepulchre itself. The original buildings were entirely rebuilt by the Crusaders in the twelfth and thirteenth centuries, but only a few portions of this Medieval construction have survived the subsequent rebuildings and transformations.

between 532 and 537 (Fig. 7–11).[4] Indeed *Hagia Sophia* still stands as one of the greatest architectural triumphs of all times in any part of the world (Fig. 7–12). Here are some of the phrases of the poet Paulus, an usher at the court of Justinian, written to commemorate the dedication of the church:

About the center of the church, by the eastern and western half-circles, stand four mighty piers of stone, and from them spring great arches like the bow of Iris, four in all; and, as they rise slowly in the air, each separates from the other to which it was at first joined, and the spaces between them are filled with wondrous skill, for curved walls touch the arches on either side and spread over until they all unite

[4] The vastness of *Hagia Sophia* may be read in its dimensions: the plan is about 240 by 270 feet; the dome is 108 feet in diameter, and its crown is 165 feet above the pavement.

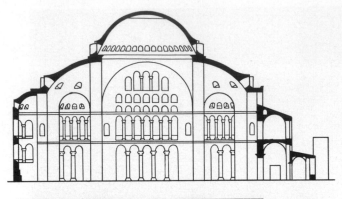

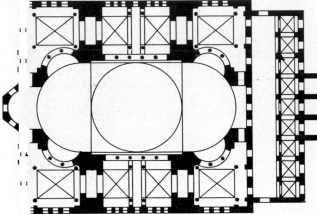

7-13 HAGIA SOPHIA. Istanbul. Diagrammatic section and plan. The atrium, originally built in front of the church, no longer exists and is not shown in this drawing.

above them. . . . The base of the dome is strongly fixed upon the great arches . . . while above, the dome covers the church like the radiant heavens. . . .

The mason also has fitted together thin pieces of marble figuring intertwining tendrils bearing fruit and flowers, with here and there a bird sitting on the twigs. Such ornament as this surrounds the church above the columns. The capitals are carved with the barbed points of graceful acanthus all gilt; but the vaulting is covered over with many a little square of gold, from which the rays stream down and strike the eyes so that men can scarcely bear to look.[5]

The great dome does, indeed, dominate both the exterior and the interior of *Hagia Sophia*. In plan, though, and in structure (Fig. 7–13) there is a lon-

[5] W. R. Lethaby, "Santa Sophia, Constantinople," *Architectural Review*, April, 1905, p. 12.

gitudinal emphasis which classifies the building as a domed basilica rather than as a central-plan church. The dome on pendentives rests on four massive piers. Along the east-west axis are two great half-domes, each of which is penetrated by two smaller half-domes, and to the east is the vault of the apse. In a lateral, or north-south, direction, the two massive arches are filled by screening walls pierced by tiers of windows. The aisles, which flank the central area, are surmounted by galleries, which were reserved for Justinian and his court when they attended Mass or special ceremonies. Both aisles and galleries were vaulted with domed groin vaults. It is estimated that the structure is composed of about 40 per cent brick and 60 per cent mortar, with the exception of the four great piers, which are stone.

7-14 EMPEROR JUSTINIAN AND FOLLOWERS. Mosaic. San Vitale, Ravenna. 6th century. (Alinari)

This masonry was admirably suited to the construction of intricate series of arches and vaulted surfaces.

In structure and in the combination of complicated, curvilinear masonry surfaces, the builders of *Hagia Sophia* were following the great tradition of Roman architecture (pp. 168–77).

Yet *Hagia Sophia* stands unique. It is not the rich ornamentation of the interior, so beautifully described by Paulus, that confounds the spectator but rather the awesome space, enclosed by man in an ever-ascending series of domical vaults, themselves pierced by shafts of light. Procopius, Justinian's official historian, tells how he stood "transfixed, not knowing where to look."

Here light is the mystic element. Light that glitters in the mosaics, that shines forth from the marbles, that pervades and defines spaces which in themselves seem to escape definition.

We shall see later how light was also a preoccupation of Western Medieval builders, but we shall also see how different were the results they achieved. At *Hagia Sophia*, clarity as the heritage of Greece, power and assurance from Rome, and transcendental mysticism of Eastern Christianity are combined to create a monument which is at once a summation of Antiquity and a positive expression of Christian belief.

PAINTING

Early Christian painting appears in two very distinct techniques: mosaic decoration of large wall areas, and tempera or pen and ink illustrations, known usually as *miniatures*, executed for the early religious manuscripts. The painter was also called upon to decorate walls with murals, a less expensive medium than mosaics, and to produce panel paintings; but few mu-

7–15 DETAIL FROM THE JOSHUA ROLL. *Joshua Before the Walls of Jericho.* Copy of an original executed in the 5th–6th century. Vatican, Rome. (Muñoz)

rals, outside of the catacombs, or panels of this early period have survived.

Since mosaic is such a special medium, and since it was so favored by the Early Christian and Byzantine artists, a brief analysis of its technique is necessary. By *mosaic* is meant a design worked out by means of small cubes of colored glass or stone, called *tesserae*, set in plaster (Plate 2). Light is reflected from the surface of the tesserae, and, since they are often of different textures and since the wall surfaces are usually uneven, the effect is of a shimmering, radiant surface. Gold leaf was used under transparent cubes or applied to the surfaces of reddish cubes and secured by a thin layer of transparent glass to create a neutral, almost indefinable atmosphere in the backgrounds, which glow as though they generated their own light.

Mosaic was employed by many early civilizations, as in Mesopotamia, and highly developed especially by the

Hellenistic Greeks and by the Romans, who used it constantly with tesserae of marble as a sumptuous floor decoration. Although the medium naturally develops generalized, simple forms, many Roman artists and their Early Christian followers were capable of rendering the illusion of three-dimensional forms in space almost as effectively as in mural painting. The progressive flattening of the forms and heightening of the decorative, rather than of the pictorial, effect are admirably demonstrated in a series of mosaics excavated in Antioch, dating from the second into the sixth centuries.[6] Yet one has only to compare the mosaic representing Justinian and his court (Fig. 7–14) with a slightly earlier one from Santa Maria Maggiore (Fig. 7–4) to realize that there is no question of a declining technical skill, but rather

[6] See C. R. Morey, *The Mosaics of Antioch*, Longmans, Green, 1938, which has good colored reproductions.

7–16 VIENNA GENESIS.
*Joseph Recognizes His
Brothers.* 5th–6th century. Österreichische
Nationalbibliothek, Vienna. (Aus dem Bildarchiv d. Öst. Nationalbibliothek)

of a changing attitude, of a demand for forms different from those of the old Latin West. The figure of Justinian, in the splendid Roman imperial robes, is more a symbol than an image of the emperor. The rhythmic pattern of the design formed by the figures of Justinian with his followers, outlined against the gold tesserae of the background, has an abstract quality well suited to the decoration of architecture.

Miniatures, illustrating early Biblical texts, exhibit the same stylistic variations. A detail from the *Joshua Roll* (Fig. 7–15) [7] shows the figures modeled and moving freely in a space which includes the image, as well as

[7] This manuscript was originally a continuous roll 32 feet long and 1 foot wide, with pen-and-ink and color illustrations of the Hebrew conquest of the Promised Land, occupying most of the space, interspersed with the text in Greek. It has now been cut into sections and mounted for preservation. The manuscript belongs to the period when the long roll used by Egyptians, Greeks, and Romans was being superseded by the *codex*, a book made of separate pages bound together, the usual modern method. The existing example of the *Joshua Roll* is a copy, probably done in the ninth or tenth century, of an original executed in the fifth or sixth century.

the Antique symbol (the crowned, seated lady to the right), of a town, Jericho, with trees and roads included as pictorial elements. Here is the lingering Hellenistic tradition, which certain great metropolitan centers, such as Alexandria and Antioch, as well as Rome, clung to as long as possible. In the *Vienna Genesis* (Fig. 7–16), executed about the same time, probably in Asia Minor, the essential elements of the narrative have been selected for representation in an empty, or neutral, space. There is little interest in the modeling or movement of the figures, which by their gestures or positions relate enough of the event to enable the spectator to recognize what is taking place. The vivid colors against the rich purple background produce a striking effect, undulled by the passage of time. Many other illustrated manuscripts were produced by the Early Christian artists. These manuscripts were easily transported and numbers of them survived to reach Medieval courts and monasteries as royal gifts or as the treasured acquisition of some pious traveler. They served as copybooks or sources of inspiration for artists throughout the Middle Ages, so that, in addition to their own intrinsic

7–17 SARCOPHAGUS OF THEODORE. 7th century. Sant' Apollinare in Classe, Ravenna. (Alinari)

quality, they are of continuing historic significance.

SCULPTURE

The most important existing examples of Early Christian sculpture are stone, marble, and ivory reliefs.[8] The sculptor had an active part in the decoration of the early churches, carving capitals, screens, and other architectural ornaments. He was also called on to decorate the surfaces of large sarcophagi and of small ivory plaques, which were used as writing tablets or book bindings, or in reliquaries and other liturgical vessels and furnishings. The ivories, as well as the illustrated manuscripts, were easily portable, and

their dissemination transmitted Early Christian images and forms to succeeding generations. The subject matter and the style of this relief sculpture are analagous to those of painting, with a similar growing emphasis on flat, decorative designs.

In some of the early sarcophagi the surface is covered with scenes from the Old and New Testaments, crowded together one upon the other for purposes of narration, with little regard for the design, as in Roman third-century sculpture. Quite a different style is represented by the low-relief decoration of the *Sarcophagus of Theodore* (Fig. 7–17). Here the decoration is composed of symbols, each of which by itself and in conjunction with the others conveys a clear, definite message. In the center of the side in a circle is the sacred monogram.[9] Facing it

[8] Sculpture in the round exists, as in the Good Shepherd statue in the Lateran Museum (Rome), but, perhaps because such figures were closely akin to the graven images of the pagan, they were not often produced. Sculpture in wood was also done, as in the doors of Santa Sabina (Rome), but again only rare examples of such work have come down to us.

[9] This monogram consists of the first two letters in the Greek name of Christ, chi and rho; in the side angles formed by the chi are the Greek letters alpha and omega, frequently used to symbolize the divinity of Christ.

7–18 BISHOP'S CHAIR, called the *Throne of Maximianus*. Wood, inlaid with ivory panels and borders. 6th century. Archiepiscopal Palace, Ravenna. (Anderson)

7–19 CAPITAL. 6th century. San Vitale, Ravenna. (Alinari)

are two peacocks, symbols of eternity. Flanking them are scrolls with birds and fruiting vines, while on the lid are an inscription and three wreaths enclosing sacred monograms; the different panels are framed with decorative moldings derived from Classical ornament.

The major stylistic trends of Early Christian art may be clearly seen in the famous ivory *Throne of Maximianus* (Fig. 7–18). The figures of St. John the Baptist and four Apostles retain much of the freedom of pose and fluid modeling of Antique sculpture; but the other narrative scenes are flat and decorative, as in the Semitic tradition, with little attempt to reproduce the image of natural forms in space.

We have already mentioned that in many of the early basilicas the capitals and other decorative features had originally been part of the structure of neighboring pagan buildings. As this supply dwindled, particularly in western Europe, sculptors carved imitations of Corinthian and other Roman forms of the orders. By the sixth century new capital forms appeared, simpler in profile and better suited to the over-all surface pattern of the ornament. Such capitals may be seen in *Hagia Sophia* as well as in the churches of Ravenna (Fig. 7–19), where an original device, the impost block, was also used. This block of stone, in the shape of an inverted truncated pyramid, was inserted between the capital and the arches above, presumably to concentrate the thrust and load of the arches directly onto the column shafts. The lacy designs, based on floral motifs, which cover the capitals, impost blocks, and sometimes the spandrels and arches above them, differ sharply from the richly molded, high-relief garlands and rinceaux which ornamented such typically Roman structures as *Trajan's Forum* (see Fig. 6–34). Here the patterns, often picked out by drilling rather than by modeling, lie on a frontal plane against the deep shadows of the background, like lace on velvet. In most instances the effect of these designs was heightened by the use of colors applied to the backgrounds and to parts of the surfaces.

METALWORK AND TEXTILES

Early texts describe rich decorations for the altars, precious liturgical vessels, and splendid vestments for the clergy. Of the vast number of such items created for the rapidly expanding church, most have disappeared.

An outstanding example is the *Antioch Chalice* (Fig. 7–1), an openwork silver goblet,[10] cast in an intricate design, with finely executed details. It displays the survival into the fifth or sixth centuries of the highly developed skills of Antiquity and shows the degree to which Near Eastern influences affected the surviving Hellenistic forms, for naturalism in the flora and fauna is combined with highly decorative pattern of the over-all ornament. Its iconography is still perplexing, for there are two figures which seem to represent the Christ, but there are only ten Apostles. There is an eagle, not unlike the imperial Roman eagle, which may signify the triumph of Christianity over the empire; but it is difficult to know whether the other birds and animals, almost hidden in the vines, were included as additional symbols or as purely decorative details. They certainly add greatly to its charm and fascination.

[10] Since the outer frame or shell is openwork in the shape of a vessel to contain liquids, it must originally have served to hold a metal liner or glass bowl. The rumor that it was made to protect the goblet used at the Last Supper is unfounded.

Weaving was also an important art in Early Christian times, important both in its quality and in the influence of its designs on the other arts of the Middle Ages. During the early centuries of the Christian era, the Coptic[11] textiles of Egypt supply us with patterns woven in wool upon linen, sometimes directly in the garment or hanging and sometimes on borders or medallions to be appliquéd. But silk fabrics, rather than linen, were the most important textile product of the East and were used for garments, hangings, and vestments, and as shrouds for the dead or as wrappings for the bones and other relics of numerous saints, which demanded the finest material. For several centuries before the time of Justinian, Persia held a monopoly of the silk industry, controlling not only the manufacture of these fabrics but their sale as well. To circumvent this monopoly of an article much desired by the wealthy Byzantines, legends state that Justinian introduced the silk industry into the empire with the help of two monks, who smuggled eggs of the silkworm out of China in hollow staves. Typical of the designs of such textiles is a hunting scene, frequently found on these stuffs and evidently of Persian origin (Fig. 7–20). The design is a medallion repeat pattern within which hunters and game offer forms for a symmetrical composition of flat decorative units.

Summary

The complex world of the later Roman empire was the environment in which Early Christian art developed. Its forms were those of Late Antiquity. Its imagery and symbolism were Christian.

Among the many regional, or pro-

[11] "Coptic" refers to the Christian communities of the Nile valley, which flourished until the seventh century.

7–20 SILK TEXTILE. Detail showing one of a series of circular medallions, interspersed with floral motifs, which covered the fabric. Diam. 9½ in. Syria, 7th century. Metropolitan Museum of Art, New York.

vincial, variations of Late Antique art, two major, and seemingly opposite, ways of depicting reality may be identified. The typically Western approach, which had its origins in Greek, or Hellenic, art, particularly in the forms developed during the Hellenistic Age, sought to represent the illusion of forms in space. The actuality of an event, the observation of the world of nature, were of primary significance, and artists sought to create the illusion of this reality in their paintings and carvings. But there was another concept of reality, which emphasized the significance of an event rather than its appearance. This was essentially an Eastern, or Near Eastern, approach, identifiably Semitic as distinct from Hellenic. Since the event itself was accepted as the reality, its evocation was all that was necessary. These Near Eastern forms, therefore, evolved as decorative symbols in a flat, two-dimensional space. As Christian dogma developed, the symbolic interpretation of reality was more and more favored so that Near Eastern flat, decorative art also seemed to be favored; but the world of Hellenic Antiquity was never completely lost sight of; and it was revived again and again during the Middle Ages.

Christian architecture also received its first definition at this time. The Early Christian basilica, emphasizing axial symmetry with a dynamic focus on the high altar at one end of the building, established a basic formula for most Medieval churches. In the Eastern Roman empire a central plan with a dome, or domes, as covering was developed, culminating in the resplendent Hagia Sophia in Istanbul.

Byzantine

(A.D. 726–1453)

In the Eastern Roman, or Byzantine, empire, during the eighth and part of the ninth centuries (726–843), a controversy raged over the worship of images. It is known as the Iconoclastic Controversy, and, although its effects were minor in western Europe, it had significant results in the Eastern empire. In the year 726 artistic representations of all sacred personages were outlawed by the emperor so that artists were forced either to flee or to express their talents in secular terms. For those who remained, this led to a re-examination of their Hellenic past with the result that, when religious painting was again encouraged, a subtle blending of the pictorial (Hellenic) and decorative (Semitic) styles appeared. This new style reached its fullest expression during the Second Golden Age of Byzantine history under the Macedonian dynasty in the tenth and eleventh centuries. Another brilliant period, often known as the Byzantine Renaissance, occurred under the Palaeologi, who came to power in the thirteenth century (1261) and remained until Constantinople finally fell to the Turks in 1453. These two periods, roughly spanning six centuries, saw the development of a distinct culture and of special forms in architecture, painting, and sculpture. In general, Byzantine art may be identified as an imperial art, a court art, which adopted certain strict conventions and which was distinguished by its regal splendor.

ARCHITECTURE

Byzantine architecture of the Second Golden Age is not noted for such grandiose achievements as *Hagia Sophia*. Following the example of the New Church, or *Nea*, built for Basil I in Constantinople,[12] the typical Byzantine church was relatively modest in size, while sumptuous in ornamentation. The central plan was almost exclusively used, with variations on the Greek cross form most favored. In St. Mark's in Venice, for instance, begun in the eleventh century, the great arms of the cross are covered by domes, as is the crossing. More typically, though, the cross, still enclosed in a square, had a principal dome over the crossing and four subsidiary domes over the four corners, with barrel vaults covering the arms of the cross (Fig. 7–21). Apses, or chapels, were usually present to the east, and a narthex, sometimes two of them, covered with a series of domes, provided entrance vestibules from the west. The domes on pendentives were raised on drums, which were vertical cylinders of masonry, pierced by windows to light the interior and which augmented the effect of the domes in the exterior massing of the building (Fig. 7–22). Their interiors, covered by mosaics or frescoes placed in accordance with strictly observed customs, were in many ways the greatest achievements of Byzantine art (Fig. 7–23). The exterior, in contrast to the plain surfaces of Early Christian buildings, was richly decorated with designs in the masonry. These churches, surrounded by special chapels or by the complex structures of a monastery, were startling notes in the usually dramatic landscape.

[12] The *Nea Ekklesia* ("New Church"), in the Great Palace of the Byzantine emperors at Constantinople, was dedicated on May 1, A.D. 880 (R. H. J. Jenkins and C. Mango, *Dumbarton Oaks Papers*, Vols. 9 and 10, Harvard University Press, 1956, pp. 123–40).

PAINTING

Byzantine painting both in its iconographic program and in its distinctive style produced a mystic atmosphere as well as a Christian cosmology quite different from anything in the West. The Eastern Orthodox liturgy symbolized so explicitly the events and teachings of the New Testament, and the Byzantine painter was so successful in his representation of Christian ideals and of the Christian universe on the walls of the churches that the Eastern Christian seldom felt the need of visiting the Holy Land or of embarking on pilgrimages to sacred shrines as did his fellow Christians in western Europe.[13]

After the Iconoclastic Controversy had been settled in 843, in favor of allowing sacred images to be painted, the Eastern clergy adopted a rigid system for the decoration of their churches. This system specified exactly

[13] See Otto Demus, *Byzantine Mosaic Decoration*, pp. 14–29.

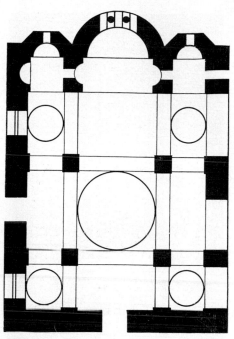

7–21　PLAN OF BYZANTINE CHURCH OF THE SECOND GOLDEN AGE. North Church, St. Saviour Pantocrator, Istanbul. Early 12th century.

7–22　THE CHURCH OF THE THEOTOKOS PAMMAKARISTOS (the All-Blessed Virgin). Istanbul. 12th century. (William MacDonald)

7-23 CHURCH OF THE MONASTERY OF XENOPHONTOS, Mt. Athos, showing frescoes. 11th century. (Millet, *Monuments de l'Athos*, 3rd ed.)

what scenes or images were to be placed on which wall or vault. On the upper portions of the building were placed the celestial hierarchy — the Pantocrator (Ruler of All) represented by an awesome bust of Christ dominating everything from his position in the central dome. In the pendentives were the four evangelists; in the eastern apse the Virgin Mary; and so on until all the vaults, arches, and other surfaces had a scene or saintly personage assigned to them. The lower portions of the walls were devoted to terrestrial events and people, including local or especially venerated saints, martyrs, and church dignitaries. The Last Judgment in dramatic detail occupied the back wall, so that the faithful faced it as they left the church. This immutable order imposed a sense of completeness, of serenity and confidence — a

composure seldom found in the more restless, inquisitive West.

The Byzantine artist of the Second Golden Age also developed a new style, capable of depicting metaphysical reality, of revealing otherworldly concepts through the representation of the substance of nature. He did this by fusing the two opposing traditions — the Hellenic and the Semitic — which he had inherited from the Late Antique, Early Christian world (see p. 191). This achievement was not, of course, a rapid process, nor did it suddenly come to light in any given locality. Manuscripts of the late ninth and tenth centuries show evidence of this blending, as do the recently uncovered mosaics of *Hagia Sophia*,[14] which date from this period.

The fully developed style may be seen in such mosaics as those of the monastery at *Daphni*, in Greece, executed in the eleventh century (Fig. 7-24). Here in the Crucifixion the gold background provides a radiant measureless space, which, however, is given a certain stability by indications of ground and of naturalistic flowers at the foot of the cross. The figures of Mary and of St. John are neither the flat, frontal symbols of Justinian's time (Fig. 7-14), nor are they fully modeled, corporeal beings. In their poses and their gestures they turn toward the cross, as though participating in the anguish of the Saviour, but remain apart, respectful of the event itself and of its significance. The Christ on the cross is depicted in a similar manner.

[14] The work of removing the plaster, which was added by the Turks to cover the original mosaics, and of consolidating the mosaics throughout *Hagia Sophia* was begun by the late Thomas Whittemore and is being continued under the auspices of the Byzantine Institute. Four preliminary reports of this work have been published to date: *The Mosaics of St. Sophia at Istanbul*, Oxford University Press, Paris, for the Byzantine Institute, 1933–1952.

7-25 BUST OF CHRIST. Catholicon Hosios Lucas. 11th century. (Otto Demus, *Byzantine Mosaic Decoration*, Kegan Paul, Trench, Trubner, 1948)

7-24 CRUCIFIXION. Mosaic. Daphni, Greece. 11th century. (Alinari)

The delicate rhythms of the body suspend it between the sufferings of mankind and the assurance of salvation. The entire scene is clothed with dignity, with compassion, with absolute faith. The complications and distractions of many Early Christian scenes have been eliminated, so that an almost Hellenic clarity dominates the composition.

The proportions of these figures at *Daphni* are abnormal in their elongation. This adds to their elegance and suggests that the images refer to more than mere humanity. Such distortions were, of course, deliberate and constitute one of the most distinctive characteristics of the Byzantine style. Another type of distortion may be seen in the bust of Christ at *Hosios Lucas* (Fig. 7–25). At first glance one does not realize that the areas of the face which in normal light would be rendered as deep shadows appear here as bright highlights. This might be called reverse, or negative, modeling (as in photographic negatives). These mosaics were lit by reflected light or by torches or candles from below, heightening this negative modeling so that the figures seem to glow from within.

The colors of Byzantine mosaics were brilliant, and, since the tesserae were often irregularly set, light shimmers across the surfaces. Arbitrary handling of the colors also enhances the dramatic effect of many scenes, but it is the freshness of the stone and glass surfaces and their perfect suitability as wall decorations which place them among the major achievements in the history of art. The Holy Virgin in the apse of *Torcello*, for example (Fig. 7–26), is ineffable, majestic, and serene. Her blue gown against the glowing gold background, her towering stature, her omnipresence, captivate, humble, and inspire whoever stands before her.

During the thirteenth and fourteenth centuries, when the Byzantine empire was revived under the Palaeologi, the art of mosaic and mural painting again flourished. Some of the

7–26 VIRGIN WITH APOSTLES. Apse mosaic, Torcello cathedral. 11th century. (Alinari)

best preserved and most striking examples of Byzantine style have recently been uncovered in the *Mosque of the Ka'riye* [15] (originally the Church of the Blessed Saviour of the Chora) in Constantinople. The fresco in the half-dome of the apse of a side, probably a mortuary chapel, shows the Christ, in brilliant white raiment, raising Adam and Eve from the dead (Fig. 7–27). The delicacy of line and extraordinary sense of color values add to the intensity of this scene.

While the characteristics of Byzantine painting were developed in the mural decorations of the churches, it was through miniatures in manuscripts

[15] The first publication of these mosaics was prepared by Russian archeologists in the early 1900's. It was not until 1947, though, that their systematic recovery was undertaken by the Byzantine Institute, first under the direction of Thomas Whittemore and more recently of Professor Paul Underwood. For preliminary reports see the *Dumbarton Oaks Papers,* Nos. 9–10, 1956; and No. 11, 1957.

and especially through the panel paintings, more popularly known as icons, that the elements of the style were spread abroad. Such an icon is the famous *Vladimir Madonna,* probably executed by an artist in Byzantium in the eleventh century, exported to Vladimir, and then taken to Moscow in 1395 to protect that city from the Mongols (Fig. 12–8). The figures of Mother and Child are compactly united into a majestic group which fills the panel with its decorative pattern. The pensive, almost sorrowful expression of the Virgin and the configuration of the eyes, nose, and mouth are characteristic Byzantine conventions.

SCULPTURE

Although carved ornament continued to be used in Byzantine churches, monumental stone sculpture was never encouraged to the degree that it was in western Europe. Life-size figures in

7-27 THE HARROWING OF HELL. Fresco. Ka'riye Djami, Istanbul. *ca.* 1310–1320. (Byzantine Institute, Inc.)

the round apparently offended the East Christians, who associated them with pagan idols, whereas painted images, particularly with the stylistic conventions which developed, could create forms less directly identifiable as natural ones. The Byzantine sculptor was called on, though, to carve small statues and reliefs, particularly in ivory, which were used to adorn books and caskets or to function as venerated images in much the same manner as the painted icon. The *Virgin and Child* between St. John the Baptist and a bishop saint (Fig. 7–28) is such a group in low relief, originally flanked by two other plaques, to form what is known as a triptych. This group has many of the same qualities as the mosaics in *Daphni.* Even though the

sculpture is small, the dignity of the Virgin and of the two saints who respectfully touch her garment or turn to support her arm, the unity of the composition, the elongation of the figures, and the controlled patterns of the draperies give the group grandeur and monumentality.

METALWORK AND TEXTILES

The lavish splendor of the Byzantine court astounded all who saw it. Costumes were heavy with embroidery of metal thread and hung with metal adornments. Banquets and ceremonies were served with costly utensils, and the furniture was covered with metal, ivory, and enamel plaques. This splen-

7–29 ST. PETER. Enamel and gold plaque. Diam. 4 in. 10th century. Metropolitan Museum of Art, New York.

7–28 VIRGIN AND CHILD. Ivory. H. 6¾ in. 11th century. Dumbarton Oaks Collection, Washington, D. C. (Byzantine Institute, Inc.)

dor, as well as the clergy's demand for rich vestments and liturgical furnishings called for the best efforts of skillful artisans of every type. Many of these objects found their way to distant lands as royal gifts, as items of trade, or as plunder, so that Byzantine techniques and forms became widely known.

Closely allied to paintings, though the product of metalworkers, were the enamel plaques used to decorate many varieties of religious and secular objects. Most Byzantine enamels are of the *cloisonné* type (see p. 218). Because of the precious materials used and the long, tedious process, the enamels were small and served chiefly to adorn larger objects. To an even greater extent than the mosaic worker, the enameler must reduce his design to simple terms, for the beauty of the finished product is dependent upon the

effect of minute lines (the *cloisons*) and the bold juxtaposition of brilliant colors. In the plaque representing *St. Peter* (Fig. 7–29) a surprising amount of character has been expressed in the face framed by the white hair and beard. The geometric, abstract pattern of the lines in the clothing gives vitality to the solid blues and yellows, and the polished gold background is in perfect harmony with the glazed surfaces of the enamel. Technical devices such as the linear design of the clothing were often imitated in turn by painters, so that these particular conventions also became part of the Byzantine style.

Byzantine artists also excelled in the casting of bronze. An outstanding example of this work may still be seen at the south entrance to the narthex of *Hagia Sophia*, where the "Beautiful Gates" were executed as early as 838. The fame of this work was such that similar doors were ordered from Constantinople for a series of Italian churches in the eleventh century (for example, at Amalfi, St. Paul's Outside the Walls in Rome, Atrani, Montegargano, and Salerno). The technique frequently included ornament in silver or enamel. This is another example of how original works of Byzantine art appeared in western Europe.

Summary

During the Macedonian dynasty in the tenth and eleventh centuries and under the Palaeologi in the fourteenth, Byzantine artists created a distinct style which expressed the ideals of Eastern Orthodox Christianity and answered the needs of a sumptuous court. Closely supervised in its iconographic program by the clergy, the mosaic and fresco decoration of the central-plan churches exhibits a blending of earlier traditions. This new style in its search for forms expressive of otherworldly concepts treated the human figure and natural phenomena in a manner which endowed them with monumentality and with an ethereal quality of sublime dignity. The conventions, which include distorted proportions, linear decorative patterns, and unified compositions, are present in all the different artistic media.

Bibliography

Anthony, Edgar W., A History of Mosaics, Sargent, Boston, 1935.

Butler, Howard C., and Smith, E. B., Early Churches in Syria, Princeton University Press, 1929.

Byron, Robert, The Byzantine Achievement, Knopf, 1929.

——, and Talbot Rice, David, The Birth of Western Painting, Knopf, 1931.

Conant, Kenneth J., A Brief Commentary on Early Medieval Church Architecture, Johns Hopkins Press, Baltimore, 1942.

Coptic Egypt, Brooklyn Museum, New York, 1944.

Crowfoot, J. W., Early Churches in Palestine, Oxford University Press, New York, 1941.

Cunynghame, Henry H. S., European Enamels, Methuen, London, 1906.

Dalton, Ormonde M., Byzantine Art and Archaeology, Oxford University Press, New York, 1911.

Demus, Otto, Byzantine Mosaic Decoration, Kegan Paul, Trench, Trubner, London, 1941.

Diehl, Charles, Byzantine Portraits, tr. by Harold Bell, Knopf, 1927.

——, History of the Byzantine Empire, tr. by George B. Ives, Princeton University Press, 1925.

——, Manuel d'art byzantin, 2nd ed. rev., Vols. 1–2, A. Picard, Paris, 1925–26.

——, La peinture byzantine, Paris, 1933 (with l'Académie des Inscriptions et Belles-Lettres [Fondation E. Piot]), Les Editions G. van Oest, Paris.

Diez, Ernest, and Demus, Otto, Byzantine Mosaics in Greece: Hosios Lucas and Daphni, Harvard University Press, 1931.

Early Christian and Byzantine Art, Walters Art Gallery, Baltimore, 1947.

Goodenough, Erwin R., Jewish Symbols in the Greco-Roman Period, Pantheon Books, 1933.

Grabar, André, Byzantine Painting, Skira, New York, 1953.

Hinks, Roger P., Carolingian Art, Sidgwick & Jackson, London, 1935.

Jacobus de Voragine, The Golden Legend, tr. and adapted from the Latin by Granger Ryan and Helmut Ripperger, 2 vols., Longmans, Green, New York, 1941.

Jameson, Anna B. Murphy, Sacred and Legendary Art, 2 vols., Houghton Mifflin, ca. 1911.

Kraeling, Carl H., The Synagogue, Yale University Press, 1956.

Lethaby, William R., Medieval Art, new ed., Scribner's, 1913.

Lowrie, Walter, Monuments of the Early Church, Macmillan, New York, 1901.

Maskell, Alfred O., Ivories, Putnam, 1905.

Morey, Charles R., Christian Art, Longmans, Green, New York, 1935.

——, Early Christian Art, Princeton University Press, 1942.

——, The Mosaics of Antioch, Longmans, Green, New York, 1938.

Natanson, Joseph, Early Christian Ivories, Tiranti, London, 1953.

Pagan and Christian Egypt: Egyptian Art from the First to the Tenth Century A.D., Brooklyn Museum, New York, 1941.

Pierce, H., and Tyler, R., L'Art Byzantin, Librairie de France, Paris, 1932.

Porter, A. Kingsley, Medieval Architecture, 2 vols., Baker and Taylor, New York, 1909.

Rand, Edward R., Founders of the Middle Ages, Harvard University Press, 1929.

Rice, David Talbot, Byzantine Art, Oxford University Press, New York, 1935.

Rostovtsev, Mikhail I., Dura-Europos and Its Art, Oxford University Press, New York, 1938.

Showerman, Grant, *Eternal Rome*, rev. ed., Yale University Press, 1925.

Smith, E. Baldwin, *The Dome*, Princeton University Press, 1950.

Swift, Emerson H., *Hagia Sophia*, Columbia University Press, 1940.

Underwood, Paul A., "First Preliminary Report on the Restoration of the Frescoes in the Kariye Camii at Istanbul by the Byzantine Institute, 1952–1954," *Dumbarton Oaks Papers*, Nos. 9 and 10, 1956.

Van Millingen, Alexander, and Traquair, Ramsey, *Byzantine Churches in Constantinople*, Macmillan, London, 1912.

——, *Byzantine Constantinople*, Murray, London, 1899.

Volbach, Wolfgang F., *Early Christian Mosaics*, Oxford University Press, New York, 1946.

Von Simson, Otto G., *Sacred Fortress*, University of Chicago Press, 1948.

Warner, George F., *Illuminated Manuscripts in the British Museum*, Series 1–3, British Museum, London, 1910.

Whittemore, Thomas, *The Mosaics of St. Sophia at Istanbul*, No. 1, Oxford University Press, Paris, 1933 (Report of the Byzantine Institute).

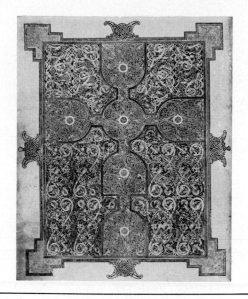

CHAPTER 8

MEDIEVAL

(ABOUT 400–1500)

Early Medieval

The contrast between the Eastern and Western portions of the Roman empire during the six hundred years following the fall of Rome was striking. The wealth and luxury, the sophistication, manners, and learning of the court at Constantinople had no counterpart in the West, except in Spain, where the Caliphate of Cordoba rose to almost equally brilliant heights (see pp. 491–92). In the West some scholars have rather scornfully called the period the Dark Ages, when the light of civilization was all but extinguished. Yet this was the time when the people, the languages, and the geographical divisions of modern Europe were being molded — a crucial period whose arts were not dark but very colorful.

ILLUSTRATION ABOVE. 8–1 LINDISFARNE GOSPELS. *Decorative page at beginning of Gospel of St. Matthew.* ca. 700. British Museum, London. (Trustees of the British Museum)

Barbarian [1]

(ABOUT 400–750)

Relations between Mediterranean peoples and the barbarians from the north or northeast are mentioned very early in the history of Greece. The name "Barbarian" was coined by the Greeks and used later by the Romans to refer to all foreigners who were as yet uncivilized in Greco-Roman terms. These Barbarians included, as we have seen (see pp. 89–90), the Scythians and the Sarmatians, who appeared along the northern shores of the Black Sea as early as the sixth century B.C. The term also referred to those nations from beyond the Rhine and Danube rivers who were called Germans by Tacitus, the Roman historian, and with whom the Romans had begun hostilities by the first century B.C. Even though Rome regarded them as for-

[1] Sites mentioned in this section may be found on the map on p. 190.

eigners, these Germans eventually were accepted as soldiers in the Roman armies and even as emperors. In the fourth century A.D., however, the eruption of the Huns from the east forced all these nations and tribes back against the Roman frontiers, which Rome found more and more difficult to defend. In A.D. 376 the Roman emperor Valens allowed the Visigoths to settle west of the Danube. Two years later they revolted against maltreatment by Roman officials and in a battle near Adrianople killed the emperor and nearly two-thirds of his army. After this, Rome offered little resistance to the different Barbarian nations, who crossed into western Europe almost at will.

These so-called invasions were in reality migrations of ethnic groups seeking, not to overthrow the Roman empire, for which they had a great admiration, but to find a place where they could settle peacefully and consolidate their own forces. When feudalism finally emerged in the ninth century, its elements were a combination of late Roman and Barbarian customs and laws. During this period of dislocation and uncertainty, the Church, benefiting from the prestige of such early leaders as St. Augustine and St. Gregory, constituted the only central authority. It was at this time that the foundations for its later authority were firmly established.

We should bear in mind that almost all the Barbarian nations as they entered the Roman empire were already Christian, although the creed they had been taught was the Arian one, which had been condemned as heretical by the orthodox Catholic church. The leadership of Rome was strengthened when the Frankish king, Clovis, was converted as a Catholic. During his reign (481–511) the Franks gained control over the Burgundians, the Visigoths, and other nations in the area

now known as France, which then recognized the Pope in Rome. With the success, later in the sixth century, of St. Augustine's mission to England, where he became the first archbishop of Canterbury, Catholicism and the authority of Rome were firmly established in western Europe. But before we trace the development of the Christian art of western Europe, we must understand more fully the art of the Barbarian nations, which was based on principles entirely different from those which had dominated the Mediterranean world for so long.

METALWORK

This colorful art, brought by the Barbarians as they moved into western Europe, was an abstract art of simple geometric designs in metalwork, which, with the exception of certain stylized animal forms, ignored the world of nature. In the chapter on Mesopotamian art we described the character and the widespread use of what is called the "animal style," which appeared with the Scythians as early as the sixth century B.C. (see Fig. 3–25). This animal style, or conventions derived from it, are important elements in Barbarian art, which is also characterized by the desire to cover the entire surface of an object with decorative, abstract patterns. The principle of over-all design, also known as the principle of *horror vacui*, occurs as well in the art of some primitive cultures and in the art of Islam. In Barbarian art the designs were executed in what is known as the *cloisonné* technique. This consisted of soldering or fastening small metal ridges, usually of gold (the *cloisons*), to a metal background. In the compartments thus formed was placed an enamel paste, to be subsequently fired, or semiprecious stones, such as garnets, or pieces of colored glass. The *cloisons* remain visible on the surface and are an important part of the design. These personal adornments (Fig. 8–2) were highly prized possessions, handed down from generation to generation. Some of the princely hoards must have been dispersed at an early date if we are to account for identical techniques and designs discovered in widely divergent areas. Other collections or "treasures" must have been accumulated over a period of time, which could explain the different forms present in such a magnificent discovery as the one at *Sutton Hoo* in England.[2]

Often an original piece was reworked and combined with others to form a new object, and this practice was continued late into the Middle Ages, so that portions of Barbarian jewelry are often incorporated in reliquaries and book covers of much later dates.

During these early centuries at the beginning of the Middle Ages, interest in metalwork was so intense that the colorful effects of the jewelry designs were imitated in the painted decorations of manuscripts, in stone sculpture, and even in the masonry of the early churches. Work in metal, it may be said, was the primary technique of the early Middle Ages.

PAINTING AND SCULPTURE

Although we may presume that the walls and ceilings of churches were enlivened with painted decorations and that altars and other liturgical furniture were also painted, since this was

[2] Excavated in 1939, the site of Sutton Hoo in Suffolk is now identified as being associated with the burial of the East Anglian king Anna, who died in 654. The fabulous treasure has been described by Rupert L. S. Bruce-Mitford in "The Sutton Hoo Ship-Burial," *Proceedings of the Suffolk Institute of Archaeology and Natural History,* London, Vol. 25: 1–78, 1952.

8–2 ORNAMENTS AND FIBULAE with glass and paste inlays in cloisonné technique. Possibly of Frankish origin. Western Europe, 5th–6th century. Metropolitan Museum of Art, New York. (Gift of J. Pierpont Morgan, 1917)

the least expensive decoration, the only evidence we have of the beginning of Early Medieval painting is in the decoration of manuscripts.

The most famous of these manuscripts, such as the *Book of Kells* and the *Lindisfarne Gospels,* were written and decorated by Irish monks about the year 700. The distinctive element in these designs is the interlace ornament. The Celts, who moved west to Brittany in France and then north across to Ireland, Wales, and other parts of Britain, had always been particularly fond of spiral and curvilinear designs and the interlace. The decorative page at the beginning of the Gospel of St. Matthew in the *Lindisfarne Gospels* (Fig. 8–1) is an exciting, vastly complicated, yet harmonious pattern. The tense space created by the

8–3 TOMB OF THEODORIC. Ravenna. *ca.* 530. (Alinari)

ARCHITECTURE

Although the Barbarians, as is to be expected of nomadic or semi-nomadic people, did not have a developed architectural tradition,[3] there is increasing evidence that a number of important buildings were constructed during the late fifth and sixth centuries. The reconstruction plan of the church of St. Martin at *Angers* in France [4] shows how the basic elements of the Early Christian basilica were being continued with modifications. Portions of some Anglo-Saxon churches in England and of Visigothic ones in northern Spain still exist, as does the tomb of the Ostrogothic king, Theodoric, in *Ravenna*, built in the sixth century (Fig. 8–3). The solid masonry of Theodoric's central-plan structure, with its interestingly built arches, may reflect an attempt to build in a Roman manner; but the huge single stone, hollowed into the shape of a saucer and used to cover the central portion, recalls the great monoliths of the early dolmen rather than the vaults of Rome.

Carolingian

(750–987)

The Carolingian dynasty was founded in 752 when Pepin the Short was crowned King of the Franks. Although the Carolingians remained in power for less than one hundred and fifty years, they restored the concept of empire in the west, introduced the feudal regime as a means of organizing

interlace patterns must be described in terms similar to those used for the space in Cubist painting of the early twentieth century. Although some of the designs seem capable of proliferation without limit, others are narrowly bound within specific frames, and yet the different areas combine into a vital, tremendously vigorous over-all decoration.

Except for a few isolated workshops in southern France and in Italy, where the Early Christian traditions of Late Antiquity were faithfully preserved until the seventh century, it may be said that sculpture in stone gradually disappeared as a technique. In Ireland and Northumbria there are many stone crosses from this period, some of which closely imitate metalwork, and others which show the image of man; but elsewhere in western Europe, stone sculpture was crude indeed.

[3] There is evidence that some of the nations built important wooden structures in eastern Europe, but no thorough study of the texts and of recent archeological discoveries behind the Iron Curtain is as yet available.

[4] For a thorough and interesting study of this site and the changes which occurred to the older Roman city at Angers, see George H. Forsyth, *The Church of St. Martin at Angers.*

society, and encouraged a revival of learning and of the arts.

A single man, Charles the Great, or Charlemagne (*Carolus Magnus*), is often credited with the major achievements of the Carolingian Revival. On Christmas Day, 800, in Rome, he was crowned emperor by Pope Leo III. He thus became a successor of the Caesars, reaffirming the belief that the Roman empire had continued to exist in the West as it had in the East. A skillful and respected general, a great hunter, rough and in many ways still a barbarian, illiterate beyond learning to sign his name, he was, nevertheless, a great patron of the arts. Alcuin of York, Peter of Pisa, Theodulf a Visigoth, Einhard (his biographer) a Frank, were all summoned to his court. He attended their discussions whenever possible and established schools not only at court but in almost every monastery. He encouraged Alcuin to reform handwriting, and the famous *Caroline minuscule*, which we still imitate today, was developed (see Fig. 8–5).

MANUSCRIPT ILLUMINATION

While Byzantium was involved in the Iconoclastic Controversy (see p. 208), western Europe, following the lead of Carolingian artists, was concerned with the re-introduction of the image of man in the visual arts. We have seen how interest in representing the figure of man dwindled under the influence of Barbarian fascination with abstract ornamental design. Yet the Christian attitude in general favored an art which could instruct as well as inspire the faithful, who throughout Europe were predominantly illiterate. As early as 787 Carolingian artists of the Palace school at Aachen were illustrating manuscripts of the Gospels and other sacred texts with miniatures in which the figures of Christ and the

8–4 MINIATURE FROM THE ADA GOSPELS. *St. Luke. ca.* 800. Stadtbibliothek, Trier, West Germany. (Stadtbibliothek, Trier)

Apostles were once more the centers of interest. The only available prototypes for such images were Early Christian miniatures or such other portable objects as ivory carvings, which consequently were numbered among the most treasured possessions of the monasteries in whose scriptoria (writing rooms) the new manuscripts were produced. Yet the Carolingian artist, as part of his Barbarian heritage, emphasized surface ornamentation, so that these eighth- and ninth-century images are readily distinguishable from earlier ones.

A page from the *Ada Gospels* (Fig. 8–4) clearly illustrates these characteristics. Here St. Luke, identified by the bull above, which is his symbol, sits in a rather elaborate cubicle surrounded

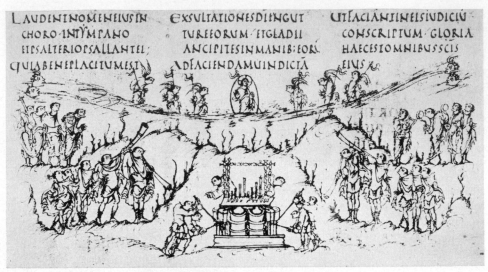

LAUDINTNOMINEIUSIN   EXSULTATIONESDIINGUT   UTFACIANTINEISIUDICIU
CHORO·INTYMPANO   TUREEORUM·ETGLADII   CONSCRIPTUM·GLORIA
ETPSALTERIOPSALLANTEL; ANCIPITESINMANIB:EOR.   HAECESTOMNIBUSSCIS
QUIABENEPLACITUMEST   ADFACIENDAMUINDICTA   EIUS·

8–5 UTRECHT PSALTER. *Psalm 150*. Hautvilliers or Reims, *ca*. 830. University of Utrecht Library. (Universiteitsbibliotheck, Utrecht)

by an architectural frame. Although the artist has tried to imitate the receding lines of the architectural background and the curved back of the chair — which created a sense of depth in Roman painting — and although the Apostle is seen full face with his extended hand holding a writing stylus, the entire page is treated as a flat, two-dimensional design. The same is true of the flowing folds of the classical drapery in the costume, which are treated as nervous linear accents quite independent of the figure beneath. Natural forms are represented, but the pictorial illusionism of Late Antiquity has given way to an over-all decoration.

Carolingian artists also revived narrative illustration, as we see in one of the most extraordinary and enjoyable of all medieval manuscripts, the famous *Utrecht Psalter*, written at Hautvilliers or Reims, France, about 832 (Fig. 8–5). The text, in three columns, is profusely illustrated by pen-and-ink drawings in the margins. The spontaneity of the small figures' actions and the rapid, sketchy technique with which they are rendered have tremendous vitality.

From details of the figure types, their dress and accessories, scholars feel certain that the artist was following one or more manuscripts done some 400

8–6 SACRAMENTARY OF METZ. *Christ in Majesty*. Northern France, mid-9th century. Bibliothèque Nationale, Paris. (Bibliothèque Nationale)

years earlier; but his interest in simple human emotions and actions and the almost naïve emphasis given to natural gestures are Medieval qualities. (Note how the two musicians playing the pipe organ shout at their helpers to pump air more strenuously.) It is this candid observation of man, often in his unguarded moments, which was to lend such charm to the art of the later Middle Ages.

The degree to which the traditions of both Late Antique and Barbarian art survived independently of each other may be seen in a page from the *Sacramentary of Metz* (Fig. 8–6). Here Christ sits in glory surrounded by a *mandorla,* or almond-shaped frame, which is painted in close imitation of metalwork, as is the decorative border of the entire page. Below the mandorla are two reclining figures — the pagan symbols of water and earth — rendered with illusionistic modeling obviously inspired by a late Roman example. Although the juxtaposition of these two contrasting modes of vision may appear rather harsh to our eyes, the Carolingian artist was unconsciously evoking his immediate heritage, which had not, as yet, had time to fuse into a single stylistic unity.

The first steps toward such a fusion may be seen at the end of the Carolingian period in some gold book covers and ivory carvings. One of the most sumptuous of all book covers is the gold and jeweled front cover of the *Four Gospels* (Fig. 0–19), executed about 875 in northern France and now in the Pierpont Morgan Library. The heavy border and the jeweled medallions are a triumph of the goldsmith's technique, with many of the settings rising almost an inch above the surface. Most of these jewels and their settings may well have been handed down from generation to generation before being reused here. The figures in gold *repoussé* stand in clear relief against a

8–7 THE CRUCIFIXION and other scenes, Ivory relief. Northern France, mid-9th century. Staatsbibliothek, Munich. (Bayer. Staatsbibliothek)

background devoid of any decoration. It is the manner, though, in which each figure conforms to the space allotted to it, which indicates a new decorative sensitivity on the part of the artist.

It has been pointed out [5] that Carolingian artists seemed to follow the iconography of their sources quite carefully until about the middle of the ninth century, when they began to combine various prototypes and to invent their own scenes. The ivory book cover (Fig. 8–7) ascribed to the artist Liuthard shows what skillful carvers these artists were and how elaborately they combined scenes — here related to the Crucifixion.

The richly decorated manuscripts,

[5] See Roger P. Hinks, *Carolingian Art,* p. 122.

8–8 FULRAD'S CHURCH. St. Denis. Foundations and wall masonry. 775. (Sumner Crosby)

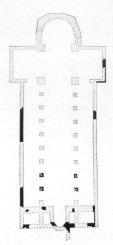

8–9 FULRAD'S CHURCH. St. Denis. Reconstructed plan. 775. (Sumner Crosby)

with their ivory and gold covers, were highly prized by succeeding generations, and large numbers of them still exist in libraries and museums throughout the world. Iconographic details and stylistic peculiarities have enabled scholars to separate them into a number of different groups and to identify, at least in general terms, the workshop or monastic scriptorium which produced them: the Palace group, Reims, Tours, and others. These manuscripts seem to have attracted the best artistic talents and to have inspired work in other media. The relatively few wall paintings of the period which have survived, such as those at Reichenau, Müstair, or Auxerre, look as though they were greatly enlarged miniatures. Scenes from history, as well as allegorical subjects, are mentioned in texts, but no vestiges have survived.

ARCHITECTURE

Until recently, the study of Carolingian art has been limited almost exclusively to miniatures, goldsmith

work, and ivory carvings. Sculpture in the round and stone carving in general almost disappeared as techniques at this time; and architecture could be studied only in the light of a few scattered, heavily restored buildings.

New excavations and careful re-examination of existing structures have proved, however, that many important buildings were erected and that Carolingian architects should be credited with many of the innovations which characterize later Medieval styles. The Roman technique of solid stone masonry was revived; additions and transformations adapted the Early Christian basilica to the needs both of the parish and of the clergy; and plans ideally suited to the demands of monastic communities were also developed. Certain basic Roman principles of construction, such as the mixing of mortar with crushed tile or brick, and methods for maintaining harmonious proportions between the different parts of a building were still available to these Carolingian masons.[6]

[6] It is interesting to recall that the earliest surviving manuscript of Vitruvius, *De Architectura,* is a ninth-century copy, evidently made by a Carolingian scribe in a Swiss monastery.

The abbey church at *St. Denis*, just north of Paris, was dedicated in 775 and was thus one of the earliest Carolingian buildings. A detail of the foundations and three lower courses of masonry of one of its side walls shows the solid construction of these churches (Fig. 8–8). Similar heavy masonry can still be seen, although thoroughly restored, in the piers and walls of the royal chapel at *Aachen*, built about 800.

Many of the more important Carolingian innovations in church building may be seen in Figure 8–9. A choir for the monks was in the nave, and the western portions also had an apse to provide a royal burial place or a royal loge. Even more important was the inclusion of towers as major elements in the massing of the building. These towers, with their slender spires, were

to provide the typical Medieval silhouette for most of western Europe.

Monasteries, as we have mentioned, were important in the revival of learning. Monasticism had developed in the Near East in response to the belief that the most perfect Christian life should be led in seclusion, removed from the evil temptations of ordinary life. In 526 St. Benedict adapted the earlier regulations to the needs of western Europe. This Benedictine Rule, demanding, among other things, vows of poverty, chastity, and obedience, provided the basic organization for most Western monasteries. Daily life was rigidly controlled and each community became self-sufficient. A schematic plan for such a community was prepared in 819, supposedly by Einhard, the biographer of Charlemagne, for the monastery of *St. Gall* in Switzerland (Fig. 8–10).

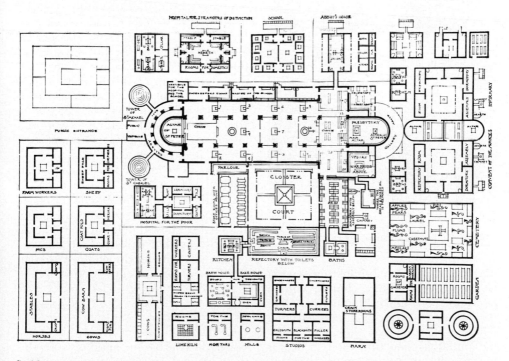

8–10 SCHEMATIC PLAN FOR A MONASTERY. St. Gall, Switzerland. *ca.* 819. The various activities here constitute a complete social unit. (From Porter, *Medieval Architecture*, Yale University Press, 1912)

8–11 BRONZE DOORS OF HILDESHEIM CA-
THEDRAL. *ca.* 1015–1022. (© F. Stoedtner)

Near the center, dominating everything, was the abbey church, with a
cloister (not unlike the early colonnaded atrium) at one side, around
which were grouped the most essential buildings: meeting room (chapter
house), dormitories, refectory, kitchen,
and storage rooms. Other necessary
gardens and buildings, including barns,

bakery, brewery, workshops, school,
hospital, and guest house were grouped
to suit the location or specific needs of
the community. This Carolingian plan
met the major requirements of Western
monasticism throughout the Middle
Ages.

In 887, with the death of Charles'
great-grandson, Charles the Fat, the
power of the Carolingians ceased. For
another century their descendants vied
with the counts of Paris for authority
in France, while another dynasty, the
Ottonians (919–1024) continued the
concept of empire in the West by establishing the so-called Holy Roman
empire in Germany and in Italy. In the
Rhineland and in the recently established monasteries and towns of Germany, the Ottonians were able to keep
alive the concept of a Western empire, and Otto III (983–1002) in
particular was open in his desire to
emulate his illustrious ancestor, Charlemagne. Otto's mother, and regent during much of his reign, was Theophano,
a Byzantine princess; but in spite of
this close connection with the East,
direct imitation of the Byzantine style
in the work of the German artists is
not evident at this time. The degree to
which Carolingian prototypes were followed may be seen at Ottmarsheim,
where an attempt was made to build
a copy of Charlemagne's chapel at
Aachen. The famous bronze doors of
the cathedral of *Hildesheim* (Fig. 8–
11), cast for Bishop Bernward about
1020, also show how the Carolingian
figure styles and narrative scenes were
continued and developed by Ottonian
artists into the eleventh century.

Summary

At the beginning of the Middle Ages,
when the Barbarian nations were settling in western Europe, many of the
skills and artistic sensibilities which
characterized the work of Late Antique

and Early Christian artists were gradually transformed. Even the idea of representing man in his own likeness evoked little interest. Yet there is no denying the decorative quality of the jewelry and of many of the magnificent pages in the Irish manuscripts. The enjoyment of vigorous ornamental patterns and the fascination with fantastic animal designs were a legacy of the Barbarian nations to the development of Medieval art in all its phases.

During the Carolingian Revival of of the late eighth and ninth centuries, a series of richly illuminated manuscripts, as well as ivory carvings and metal reliefs, were produced by artists in the monastic and royal workshops. In these illuminations and reliefs the image of man, which had almost disappeared from the art of the preceding centuries, was once more as important as it had been in Early Christian art. This image, both as a symbol and as a part of narrative scenes illustrating religious texts, combined with an interest in abstract ornamental designs and a desire for an over-all decoration, serves to distinguish these pages and carvings from earlier work and to mark them as outstanding examples of Early Medieval art. In the tenth and early eleventh centuries these same tendencies were further developed by the artists of Ottonian Germany.

The art of building was also revived. Solid masonry construction was used in monastic churches and in royal or private chapels. Important changes were made in the basilican plan of the church, especially in the enlargement of the western portions and in the inclusion of towers as an integral part of the massing. Also, with the growth of Western monasticism, designers took account of the various activities within a monastery in their plans for a new community.

Early Medieval art, which covers a span of time almost as long as that occupied by the development of Greek art, introduced into western Europe the purely ornamental forms of Barbarian art, based on principles directly opposed to the traditions of the art of Antiquity. As these new elements were slowly assimilated and as Christianity gradually assumed its dominant role, the forms of a new — a Medieval — art began to emerge.

8–12 MOISSAC. *Christ in Glory*. Central portion of tympanum of south portal. Early 12th century. (Gudiol)

Romanesque

(11TH–12TH CENTURIES)

Romanesque art [7] developed during the eleventh and twelfth centuries, when the anarchy inherent in feudalism seemed about to disrupt western Europe into small, continually warring communities. In spite of the unsettled times a vast number of stone churches were built, many of which were richly decorated; an analysis of these buildings with their ornament discloses the

existence of a coherent artistic style in most of Europe, arising from a universal attitude toward man and his destiny. The massive stone walls of the churches and of the fortresses express the need for security; and the great stone portals and mural paintings reflect the preoccupation with the end of the world described in the Apocalyptic visions, those "epics of chaos" echoing with the thunder of the Last Judgment (Fig. 8–12). [8]

The social environment from which

[7] For the location of Romanesque sites see the map on p. 244.

[8] The Revelation of St. John the Divine.

8-13 CHATEAU GAILLARD. 1197. Les Andelys, France. (F. W. Nash)

Romanesque sprang was twofold: it was feudal and it was monastic. Feudalism was a complicated series of personal obligations and services based on control of a fief, a piece of land. The lower classes were bound to the land and to the service of their lord, who in principle gave them protection and security. The lords, or nobles, held fiefs in varying ways from each other or from an overlord, such as a king. Inevitably, many of them became large landowners and so powerful that they ignored their obligations and defied their king. Their time was spent in petty wars to protect or to increase the extent of their holdings. The *chateau fort*, or castle, with its dungeon, or keep, surrounded by walls and moats, was the symbol and seat of feudal authority (Fig. 8-13). This feudal world, dominated by men, is perfectly mirrored in such *chansons de geste* as the *Song of Roland*, which relates Charlemagne's invasion of Spain, the treacherous defeat of his rear guard and the death of the paladin Roland in the Pyrenean pass of Roncesvalles. Another heroic undertaking — William the Conqueror's invasion of England in 1066 — is vividly recorded in the *Bayeux Tapestry*. While tradition states that Matilda, William's wife, and her handmaidens embroidered the piece (it is an embroidery, not a tapestry), which was designed to be hung in the cathedral of Bayeux, most scholars believe that it was done at the orders of Odo, bishop of Bayeux, according to designs made in England. While details of the armor and weapons of the time may be studied in this fascinating record of the invasion, feudalism and military exploits should not be regarded as the principal stimuli for Romanesque art. This lay in the monasteries.

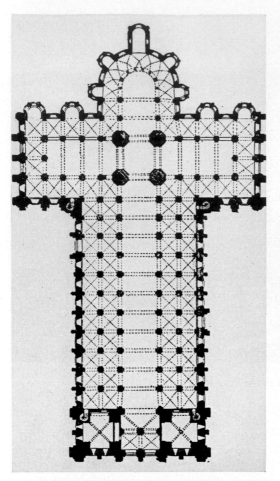

8–14 ST. SERNIN. Toulouse. Plan. *ca.* 1096–1130. (After Viollet-le-Duc)

Monasticism, as well as feudalism, reached its peak at this time. In contrast to feudalism, monasticism provided seclusion from the world, an assurance of salvation and almost the only means of receiving an education. The history of monasticism, which as we have seen began in the early Middle Ages, is essentially a sequence of reform movements. Monasteries grew wealthy, since gifts and bequests to them were potent means of assuring salvation. With wealth came luxury and laxness, in reaction to which recurrent reforms were to be expected.

These reforms often led to the formation of new monastic orders. One of the most famous was the Cluniac order, founded early in the tenth century and centered in the main abbey at Cluny near Mâcon in France. Owing allegiance only to the pope in Rome, it formed, with the vast number of its priories scattered all over Europe, a centrally organized administration in sharp contrast to the centrifugal tendencies of feudalism. The Cluniac reform, based on a liberal interpretation of St. Benedict's original rule, stressed intellectual pursuits, the study of music, and the cultivation of the other arts. Its vast resources, though, soon provoked still another reform, this time based on a strict interpretation of the Benedictine Rule, with emphasis on self-denial and manual labor. This was the Cistercian order, which also grew rapidly, especially under St. Bernard of Clairvaux between 1125 and 1153. These two were the great Romanesque orders, but it was Cluny which especially fostered the arts.

Both feudalism and monasticism were essentially sedentary. Each sought to establish self-sufficient communities and to withdraw from or to ward off contacts with the world at large. It would be a mistake, though, to consider Romanesque culture a static one. Two major impulses led large portions of the population to move about: the cult of relics and the Crusades. Pilgrimages to Santiago de Compostela in northwestern Spain, to Rome, to the Holy Land, and to innumerable other shrines (for almost every church had a relic) meant a constant flow of people over roads which today would be considered all but impassable. Even more dramatic were the Crusades, the first two of which, in 1097 and in 1147, belong to this period. These mass treks of thousands of people from western Europe to Palestine were more than romantic episodes; and their effects were more lasting than the transitory victories, or more often defeats, of the armies which undertook them. They definitely established the supremacy of the Church as a leader of the people. They reopened the Mediterranean to commerce and established closer relations with the great trading centers in the Near East — a powerful stimulus to revival of trade and commercial activity in the West. They show the tremendous energy, as well as the optimism in the face of seemingly insurmountable difficulties, characteristic of the people who built and decorated the Romanesque abbeys and who, as Raoul Glaber, an eleventh-century historian, said, covered the land with "a white robe of churches."

ARCHITECTURE

Romanesque builders of churches faced three major problems: obtaining adequate space and circulation; building solid, fireproof structures; and admitting the light of day to the interiors.

The popularity of pilgrimages and of the cult of relics brought great crowds, even to relatively isolated places. The problem of space could be solved quite easily by increasing the length of the nave, by doubling the side aisles, and by building upper galleries, or tribunes, over the inner aisle, to be used for overflow crowds on special occasions. Circulation was more complicated, though, since the monks' choir often occupied a good portion of the nave. The extension of the aisles around the eastern end — this latter curved passageway is known as an ambulatory — and the opening of chapels for altars off the arms of the transept and off the ambulatory provided space for the free circulation of pilgrims, as well as for liturgical processions. The plan of such a "pilgrimage" church may be seen in Figure 8–14. Not all Romanesque churches, of course, were

as large as this one, nor did every one have an ambulatory with radiating chapels, but the chapels are typical Romanesque features, especially when treated as separate units projecting out from the mass of the building.

Another Romanesque characteristic observable in this plan is the use of thick, continuous walls and of massive, quite closely spaced piers. Romanesque was an architecture of solid masonry, of mural construction. The wooden roofs of earlier churches were prey to fire, and the desire for permanent, fireproof structures led to the building of stone vaults over the entire church. These heavy vaults required solid walls and heavy piers to support them and to meet their powerful diagonal or outward thrusts.

The most common Romanesque vault was the semicircular barrel, or tunnel vault (Fig. 8–15). These continuous vaults put constant pressure along the entire length of the supporting masonry. If, as in most instances, the nave was flanked by side aisles, the main vaults rested on arcades, and their thrust was carried to the thick outer walls by the vaults over the aisles. In larger churches the tribune galleries over the side aisles provided extra room, and their vaults, which often were half-barrel or quarter-circle, were an integral part of the structure, buttressing the high vaults over the nave (Fig. 8–16).

The round, or semicircular, arch is traditionally associated with the Romanesque style. Yet in Burgundy and in Provence in France, Romanesque builders used the broken, or pointed arch, both for the arcades along the nave and for the barrel vaults themselves. The pointed arch or vault brings the diagonal exterior thrusts nearer to the vertical. It thus requires less buttressing.

Intersecting barrel, or groin, vaults were also used in Romanesque church-

8-15 ST. ETIENNE. Nevers. North side of nave. Late 11th–early 12th century. (Yale Photo Collection)

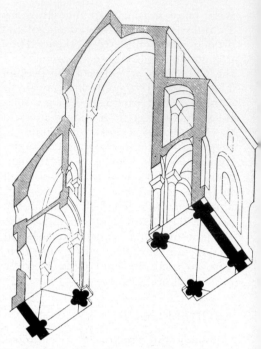

8-16 ST. ETIENNE. Nevers. Isometric view. 11th–12th centuries. (From A. Choisy, *Histoire de l'Architecture*, Gautier-Villars Publ., 1899)

es, especially over the side aisles, although in a few instances, as in *La Madeleine* at Vézelay, they appear over the nave. Groin vaults, of course, were widely used by Roman builders (pp. 168–69), who saw how the concentration of thrusts at four supporting points allowed windows in the side walls. The great Roman vaults were made possible by an intricate system of brick and tile relieving arches, as well as by the use of concrete, which could be poured into forms and which solidified into a homogeneous mass. The technique of mixing concrete did not survive into the Middle Ages, though, and the technical problems of building groin vaults of cut stone and heavy rubble, which had very little cohesive quality, limited their use almost entirely to small areas.

Other masonry vaults were also used.

The dome, supported on either pendentives or squinches, was almost always placed over the crossing in Romanesque churches, and an interesting group of churches in southwestern France used a series of domes to cover the naves as well. Mention should also be made of ribbed vaults (p. 247), which the Romanesque masons – in Lombardy, Normandy, and England – used before they were exploited by the Early Gothic builders of the Île-de-France. But Romanesque builders were not interested in either the technical or aesthetic potentialities which were to develop into Gothic.

The most characteristic feature of the Romanesque vault was that it defined very specifically the volume which it covered. Its massive construction and its precise shape created separate units which combined in an additive manner to establish the whole. The massiveness of the vault, however, made it difficult to open the walls so that daylight might penetrate the interior. It was only the more daring Romanesque mason who devised a structural system, as in the Cluniac churches of Burgundy, which allowed him to pierce clerestory windows in the nave elevation. Even these were small, and a Romanesque interior remains dark, although the assertive strength of the piers, walls, and vaults emphasizes its different parts.

Without light directly illuminating the upper portions of a church, there was little occasion for architectural ornament. But there is a majestic rhythm in the double arcades of a nave, such as that of *St. Sernin*, Toulouse — a rhythm not unlike that of a Roman aqueduct — and the treatment of the piers and arched openings is simple and direct. The openings give the impression of having been cut through the masonry, leaving the angles of the arches and piers abrupt and clean. The same incisive treatment of angles and planes is retained in the Cluniac churches of Burgundy, but the elements are more complicated (Fig. 8–17). The basically cruciform piers have fluted pilasters attached to each face; the arches have one or two added responds; above the arcades is a blind arcade with carved ornament — even the transverse arches under the vaults are double, and the capitals at each different level are intricately carved. The clerestory windows in these elevations, though not large, cast light directly on these surfaces, emphasizing the multiple accents of the sharp angles.

Each interior unit of a Romanesque church is immediately recognizable from the exterior as, for example, in a typical Auvergne church in the center of France (Fig. 8–18). The semicylindrical chapels cluster around the am-

8–17 AUTUN CATHEDRAL. Side aisle and nave. Early 12th century. (Pierre Kill, *Zodiaque*)

bulatory, above which rise the vaults of the sanctuary or choir. These multiple units to the east of the transept, so much more complicated than the simple Early Christian apse, are all included in the single term, chevet. The strong, rectangular cubes of the transept are surmounted by an octagonal tower over the crossing, which provides a necessary single accent and gives unity to the entire eastern portion of the building. In Normandy the western entrance was also given particular emphasis by two solid towers which rise above the mass of the façade, itself pierced by triple doors and by two levels of windows, reflecting the interior disposition of nave and aisles and of the three-story elevation. This symmetrical, two-towered façade, known as the "harmonic" façade, was to receive special attention by Gothic builders.

8–18 NOTRE DAME. Orcival, from southeast.
12th century. (Archives Photographiques)

8–19 PETERBOROUGH CATHEDRAL. Nave,
looking east. *ca.* 1155–1175. (C. N. & Co.)

One of the apparently confusing features of Romanesque architecture is the variety of regional or local types of buildings. Ten or more types may be identified in France alone, each with its distinctive system of vaulting and its varying solutions to the problem of lighting the interior. England followed closely the Norman types — a natural result of William the Conqueror's invasion in 1066. Certain distinctive elements, however, such as the long, low, rectilinear massing; flat eastern ends; a precocious use of the ribbed vault (notably at the cathedral of *Durham,* as early as 1097); and the use of multiple rounded moldings give this country as well its own particular Romanesque style (Fig. 8–19).

In Germany and in Italy are equally distinctive Romanesque types. The German churches of the eleventh and twelfth centuries follow many of the Carolingian-Ottonian traditions, nota-

bly in the retention of the double-apse plan, with towers at both ends of the building. The interiors, which are often quite austere, have a spaciousness not unlike the early basilicas. This influence may well have come from Italy, since the "Roman empire of Germany" established by the Ottonians continued to unite the two countries. Even more noticeable was the German adaptation of the "decorative" or "Lombard" bands, composed of thin pilasters with small blind arcades used extensively as exterior ornamentation. This predilection for decorative forms recurs again and again in the history of German art (Fig. 8–20).

The Italian Romanesque is more difficult to define. As in France there are several local types. In Lombardy the ribbed vault was used in the eleventh century. At *Sant' Ambrogio,* Milan, for instance, the nave is covered by large stone vaults with diagonal arches crossing underneath them. The huge masonry piers are compound, with attached colonnettes and pilasters in accordance with the arches which they support; but galleries over the aisles in place of clerestory windows mean that the interior is very dark indeed. At the other extreme of the peninsula, in Apulia, there is also a group of solidly built stone churches. But the most typically Italian buildings are those of Tuscany, where the plans, massing, and other features closely adhere to the traditions of the Early Christian basilica, and the use of colored marble veneers and inlays and of open arcades as decoration reflects an innate Italian love of surface ornament. The cathedral group at *Pisa*, with its separate baptistery, church, and campanile (the famous Leaning Tower) illustrates all these characteristics (Fig. 8–21). The cathedral of *Lucca* has an even more richly decorated façade; and at *San Miniato* in Florence, the Italian preference for plane geometry, in contrast to the forms of solid geometry preferred in France, may be clearly seen.

In Spain, where the Christian kingdoms of the north were asserting their authority against the weakening Caliphate of Cordoba, many important Romanesque churches were built. In Catalonia experiments in covering the nave with stone barrel vaults were begun in the late tenth century. This series of distinctive small churches, picturesquely placed in the mountains of the Pyrenees, show affiliations with the structures of Lombardy and give early evidence of many similar crosscurrents, revealing unexpected economic or intellectual relationships between separated communities throughout Europe. By the middle of the eleventh century, northern Spain, largely through the influence of the monastic order of Cluny, had turned toward France for moral and financial help in the fight against

8–20 MAINZ CATHEDRAL. West end. 11th–12th centuries, with later additions. (Rudolph Lesch)

Islam. Romanesque churches appeared in many Spanish communities along the great pilgrimage route to *Santiago de Compostela*. There, in the northwest corner of Spain, where the relics of St. James the Great have been venerated since the early Middle Ages, a superb Romanesque church, closely following the "pilgrimage" type we noted at *St. Sernin* of Toulouse, was begun in 1075 and nearly completed by 1122, although some of the sculpture was still being carved in the last quarter of the century.

SCULPTURE

In 1127 St. Bernard of Clairvaux wrote:

O vanity of vanities, yet no more vain than insane. The Church is resplendent in her walls, beggarly in her poor. She

8–21 BAPTISTERY, CATHEDRAL, AND CAMPANILE. Pisa. 11th–12th centuries, with later additions. (Alinari)

clothes her stones in gold and leaves her sons naked . . . in the cloister, under the eyes of the Brethren who read there, what profit is there in those ridiculous monsters, in that marvelous and deformed comeliness, that comely deformity? To what purposes are those unclean apes, those fierce lions, those monstrous centaurs, those half-men, those striped tigers, those fighting knights, those hunters winding their horns? Many bodies are there seen under one head, or again, many heads to a single body. Here is a four-footed beast with a serpent's tail; there a fish with a beast's head. Here again the forepart of a horse trails half a goat behind it, or a horned beast bears the hinder quarters of a horse. In short, so many and so marvelous are the varieties of divers shapes on every hand that we are more tempted to read in the marble than in our books, and to spend the whole day in wondering at these things than in meditating the law of God. For God's sake, if men are not ashamed of these follies, why at least do they not shrink from the expense? . . .[9]

In his anger, St. Bernard has given a superb description of Romanesque sculpture. "That deformed comeliness, that comely deformity," even in translation from the Latin, embodies the spirit as well as the actual forms created by these carvers to decorate their monasteries. To an extent which even the late Roman artists would never have understood, the Romanesque sculptors completely disregarded in their images relationships to nature or to a natural order in terms of scale and normal proportions for the figures. Yet anyone who has studied a Romanesque portal, or a capital inside the building,

[9] *A Documentary History of Art*, sel. and ed. by Elizabeth G. Holt, Anchor Books, Garden City, N. Y., 1957, pp. 20–21.

8–22 MOISSAC ABBEY
CHURCH. South portal.
Early 12th century.
(Gudiol)

must realize that underlying the fantasy there is an order, giving these reliefs great strength, particularly in their function in a massive architectural ensemble.

Stone sculpture, we have already noted, had almost disappeared from the art of western Europe during the eighth and ninth centuries. The revival of the technique is one of the most important Romanesque achievements. As stone buildings began to rise again, the impulse to decorate parts of the structure with relief carving in stone was inevitable. It was to be expected that the artists should turn for inspiration to surviving Roman sculpture and to other sculptural forms such as ivory carving or metalwork. But

these artists had their own unique attitude toward ornamental design and its relation to architecture. The architectural limits of the different parts of a portal [10] or of the specific shape of a capital provided frames which these artists respected rather than ignored. The portal on the south side of the nave of the abbey at *Moissac* in southwestern France (Fig. 8–22) exemplifies such an entrance.

In the interior of the churches carved decoration was limited almost exclusively to the capitals, although

[10] These include: the jambs, the lintel, the semicircular tympanum beneath the round arch(es), or archivolt(s), and in some instances a pier, or *trumeau*, in the middle of the doorway.

8–23 MOISSAC. Cloister. 12th century. (Gudiol)

some altars were richly ornamented. The capital, from its first appearance in the architecture of Egypt and of Mesopotamia, always presented a challenging problem to the architect. Its design should conform to or give emphasis to its function, which is to act not only as an element of support, transmitting the load of upper portions to the shaft of the column, but also as a form to achieve the transition from the rectilinear shapes of the entablature above to the cylindrical shape of the column below. The design should also accent the continuity of the surfaces, which in most instances were to be viewed from several different angles. The Romanesque figured, or historiated, capitals are a continual source of interest and delight. In a cloister, such as that of the abbey of Moissac (Fig. 8–23), where there are over fifty capitals with scenes on them, as well

as some thirty with purely ornamental designs, the skill and ingenuity of the Romanesque artist may be fully appreciated.

While there are many exceptions, it is striking how often the design of a capital or of a tympanum seems to follow an organized pattern based on the curvilinear symmetry of a palmette motif or variants thereof. Notice how this is true of capitals from the Moissac cloister (Fig. 8–24), and how, for instance, the central portion of the Moissac tympanum (Fig. 8–12) is framed by the two elongated angels and how the symbols of the evangelists are symmetrically arranged on each side of the Christ, in repetitive curvilinear patterns. There is some echo of the heraldic designs so familiar throughout the history of Mesopotamian art, but here at Moissac the decorative abstract quality underlying Barbarian art seems to have fused with the ordered logic of Mediterranean forms to produce an entirely new and vigorous style. The tympanum at *Autun* (Fig. 8–25) shows scenes of the Last Judgment arranged in separate panels within the great semicircle of the arch. The elongated angels on each side of the Christ and the fact that the entire area is covered with carved figures unite the different panels. It is this order, imposed again and again on visionary scenes or on monstrous combinations of animal and human forms, which gives Romanesque sculpture both its vitality and its monumentality.

In keeping with the mural character of the architecture this relief sculpture is carved into the stone, and, although figures and details often exist almost in the round within the relief, they do not project beyond the bounding planes of the masonry. The carving is bold and direct; and the treatment of such decorative details as folds of drapery usually follows an ornamental pattern, often with swirling curvilinear rhythms, rather than seeking to imitate natural folds of clothing or to reveal the solid forms of the body beneath.

The development of Romanesque sculpture more or less parallels that of architecture, with early experiments appearing at the beginning of the eleventh century and with the major examples of the fully evolved style being executed during the first quarter of the twelfth. In certain areas of France, notably in the Poitou and Saintonge of the southwest, and in England and Germany the style was still vigorous during much of the second half of the twelfth century. Some of this later sculpture shows how the respect for the architectural frame gradually diminished and how mastery of the technique of stone carving led to ornate decorations.

PAINTING

Often relief sculpture was painted to heighten the effect of the design. A dark background emphasized the ornamental patterns of the figures and color accented the incised folds of the drapery. It is difficult for us to judge the effect of this eleventh- or twelfth-century painted ornament, since very little has survived. Usually a painted interior is a restoration dating from the nineteenth or twentieth century, but there is sufficient evidence to prove that such painted decoration was frequently used in Romanesque buildings; and it is likely that the bright colors might appear rather blatant to our eyes today.

In addition to this colorful decoration of the architecture, figures and religious scenes were often painted on the walls or the vaults. A surprisingly large number of these murals have survived in England, southern Germany, France, and northern Spain.[11] Although

[11] An almost complete inventory of these medieval murals may be found in E. Anthony, *Romanesque Frescoes.*

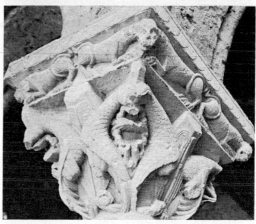

8–24 MOISSAC. Capitals from the cloister. Early 12th century. (Cudiol)

they are not as sumptuous nor as elegant as the Byzantine mosaics of this same period, these Romanesque murals are boldly executed, forming a strong complement to the sturdy architecture they adorn (Fig. 8–26). Some of the figures and the composition of certain scenes seem to be distorted in order to fit into or to accent the architectural frames in which they are placed, such as the semidome of an apse or the spandrel between two arches, while many others are in panels much as though they were enlarged pages from an illustrated Bible.

8–25 AUTUN CATHEDRAL. *The Last Judgment.* Western portal. *ca.* 1120. (Pierre Kill, *Zodiaque*)

Miniature painting in religious manuscripts continued to be an important monastic activity. In northern France and the Rhineland, in England and in Spain, these illuminations provide valuable evidence of the manner in which the Carolingian traditions were transformed into the Romanesque and finally the Gothic style. A number of English manuscripts identified as the Winchester group have full-page illustrations with wide, highly decorative borders and a figure style which, although directly inspired by the Reims Carolingian group, has a distinctively English linear quality. Another interesting series of illuminations are Spanish, beautifully exemplified by the *Beatus of St. Sever* (Fig. 8–27). The brilliant colors used to define the simple architectural borders, and the flat zones, or stripes, of the backgrounds, enhance the literal interpretations of the Apocalyptic scenes, which have seldom been rendered so effectively.

METALWORK AND ENAMELS

In the eleventh and twelfth centuries metalwork was one of the most important artistic media. The head of the Christ from the *Werden Crucifixion* (Fig. 8–28) shows the consummate mastery of bronze casting achieved by Rhenish artists. The sensitive balance between natural and abstract forms, the decorative effect of the stylistic details, and the powerful modeling of the facial planes heighten the expressiveness of this poignant symbol. Artists of the Rhine and Moselle areas also excelled in the art of enameling. The wings of a triptych, possibly made by Godefroid de Claire, and presented to the abbey of Stavelot by Abbot Wibald (*ca.* 1150), show how effective the combination of different metal techniques can be (Plate 3). Here the frame and other details in copper and silver gilt, the embossed silver col-

8–26 CHAPEL OF ST. HUGH, abbot of Cluny. Berzé-la-Ville. 12th century. (Archives Photographiques)

umns, the precious stones and gems, and the *champlevé* enamel medallions, relating the story of the *Finding of the True Cross* and scenes from the life of Constantine, create a sumptuous reliquary. This lavish use of precious materials was considered only right and fitting for the revered relics of the Holy Cross it contained and symbolized.

Summary

The study of Romanesque art discloses that, despite the anarchical tendencies inherent in the feudal regime, western Europe had a common culture, a uniform outlook seeking security and assurances of Christian salvation. In a world dominated by petty warfare and by mass military undertakings, such as the Crusades, it was normal that themes which themselves echoed the miserable cries of the damned or pictured the scourges and pestilences accompanying the end of the world should preoccupy the minds of men. Many of the illustrations for the Apocalypse have the urgency and anguish of the twentieth-century *Guernica* by Picasso (cf. Figs. 8–27 and 20–49).

Romanesque architecture gives evidence of a growing social stability in the countries of western Europe. Yet the many local types of building reflect a feudal accent on multiple, semi-independent, self-sufficient communities.

8–27 COMMENTARY OF BEATUS, *The Apocalypse of St. Sever.* 1028–1072. Bibliothèque Nationale, Paris. (Bibliothèque Nationale)

8–28 HEAD OF CHRIST. Bronze Crucifixion. Late 11th century. Werden. (From Swarzenski, *Monuments of Romanesque Art,* University of Chicago Press, 1954)

The important buildings were the abbey churches, many of which survive today. Thick walls and solid, closely spaced piers created a feeling of security. The volumes of the nave, aisles, transept, choir, ambulatory, and chapels were clearly defined. It was an architecture in which mural character was a positive assertion of strength.

The technique of monumental stone sculpture was revived; and the portals, as well as the capitals of the interior piers and columns, were carved with grotesque creatures and visionary scenes. These fantastic themes were given order by the attention paid to the architectural frames in which the sculpture was placed and by an underlying ornamental structure which related the different parts of the designs.

The illustration and decoration of Biblical texts with colorful paintings was practiced as it had been since Early Christian times. The style of these miniatures, developed from Carolingian and Ottonian sources, was often enlarged to fill the needs of a mural decoration, for the walls and vaults of the churches were frequently covered with paintings. The altars were richly decorated with sumptuous reliquaries and liturgical vessels, which showed how the art of bronze casting, goldsmith work, and enameling flourished, particularly in the valleys of the Rhine and the Moselle.

The changing character of the Medieval world, however, and the achievements of the Early Gothic artists by the middle of the twelfth century meant that Romanesque became rapidly outmoded, even though its principles were adhered to in many regions well into the thirteenth century.

Gothic

"Gothic" was first used as a term of derision by Renaissance critics who scorned its lack of conformity to the standards of classic Greece and Rome. The men of the thirteenth and fourteenth centuries, however, referred to the Gothic cathedrals as *opus modernum* (modern art) or *opus francigenum* (French art). They recognized in these structures, which towered over their towns, a style of building and of decoration which was original. It was with confidence in their own faith that they regarded their cathedrals as the real image of the City of God, the Heavenly Jerusalem, which they were privileged to build on earth. There are strong contrasts between the Gothic and the Romanesque milieu and point of view. By understanding them we may better begin to understand the Gothic world (Fig. 8–29).

Romanesque society was dominated by the uncertainties inherent in the anarchical tendencies of feudalism. Gothic society was also feudal, but it was an ordered feudalism. The monarchy, especially in England and France, asserted itself strongly to limit the independence of the powerful barons and other feudal overlords. Centralized government was established; and law and order instilled confidence in people of all walks of life. As this confidence replaced fear and insecurity, the Gothic world emerged.

Romanesque society had been dominated by men. But in Gothic society women and the qualities they represented took on a new importance. The career of Eleanor of Aquitaine, one of the extraordinary women in Western history, is evidence of the degree to

8–29 CATHEDRAL OF NOTRE DAME. Chartres. Air view of chevet. 13th century, with later additions. (Sumner Crosby)

which the status of women changed during the twelfth century. In addition to being the wife of two kings (Louis VII of France and Henry II, Plantagenet) Eleanor was the mother of two others (Richard the Lion-hearted and John). Her early years in the court of her father, William of Aquitaine, taught her the new songs of the troubadours; and she was one of the first to rule over a "court of love," where respect for the lady was prerequisite and from which was to emanate the code of chivalry of the later Middle Ages.

Another type of love, the compassionate love of a mother for a child or for the erring in general, blossomed in the cult of the Virgin Mary, who as the Mother of Heaven and the guarantor of redemption was constantly represented in Gothic art.

Confidence and security encouraged the revival of trade, a gradual process which began as early as the tenth century but which did not really become

8–30　FRANCE AND THE RHINELAND.

well-established until cities in Italy as well as in northern France and the Lowlands began to be responsible for their own government and economy. The growth of cities in the twelfth century created an urban environment in sharp contrast to the rural monastic communities which had fostered Romanesque art (Fig. 8–30). It was in the cities that Gothic art developed; and it was the urban cathedral, seat of the bishop, the administrative center of a diocese, which became the typical Gothic edifice rather than the rural abbey church with its adjacent monastic buildings.

Cities were also conducive to the rise of the universities. The monastic and cathedral schools of the earlier Middle Ages had sought to keep the learning of the Fathers of the Church alive and to reassess these teachings in the light of developing Christian thought. They were properly called schools, and from them the universities evolved in the twelfth and thirteenth centuries.

A new spirit of inquiry, free discussion, and analysis which flourished in the universities is typified by Abelard, who died in 1142, just as the Gothic style was being defined. His restless mind prepared the way for the dialectic system of Gothic Scholasticism. Abelard, whose love for Héloïse ultimately brought him more renown than his learning, boldly exposed theological contradictions in an attempt to reconcile Christian faith with human reasoning. His disregard for traditional authority emphasized the dignity of the human mind and encouraged a reassessment of man's position in the Christian universe.

It was the new Gothic cathedral which offered the most striking contrast with the Romanesque church. The study of these cathedrals is based today on an evaluation of the relationship of medieval theory to practice — of *scientia* to *ars*. Few, if any, of these scholarly studies have been able to strike a balance between the primary evidence of the structures themselves and the theories derived from the writings of the time. In medieval terms *scientia* was concerned primarily with theory, whereas *ars* was practical skill, technical knowledge. Thus, when a medieval architect spoke of the "art of geometry," he was not considering the abstract qualities of geometrical forms as we might today, but rather the practical uses to which mathematical forms and formulae might be put in designing a piece of sculpture or in erecting a building. When he spoke of the "science of geometry," he was concerned with the different theories, say of proportions, which different mathematical systems create. An understanding of Gothic architecture will not be reached, however, by trying to decide whether

it was predominantly concerned with *ars* or with *scientia*, but rather by realizing that the cathedrals were the result of both technical skill and theory, of *ars et scientia*. It is in the stones themselves, in the extraordinary sensitivity of the Gothic mason for stone as a building material, that the spirit of Gothic architecture is to be discovered.

Early Gothic

(1140–1194)

Gothic art made its appearance in a spectacular way. On the 11th of June, 1144, King Louis VII, Eleanor of Aquitaine, his queen, members of the royal court, and a host of distinguished prelates, including five archbishops and fourteen bishops, as well as a vast crowd, converged on the royal abbey of *St. Denis*, just a few kilometers north of Paris, for the dedication of the new choir. This choir, with its crown of chapels radiant with stained glass windows, set a precedent which the builders in the region around Paris, the Île-de-France, were to follow for the next half-century.

Two personalities were particularly influential in the formation of the Gothic style: St. Bernard of Clairvaux and Suger, abbot of St. Denis. St. Bernard insisted that faith was mystical and intuitive rather than rational. He upheld this with all the persuasiveness of his powerful personality and eloquence and by the example of his own personal holiness.

In spite of St. Bernard's thunderings against lavish decorations and elaborate architecture, the Gothic style was initiated by one of his friends, another abbot who, accepting the saint's admonitions to reform his monastery, built

8–31 ST. DENIS. Rib vaults of ambulatory and radiating chapel. 1144. (Pierre Devinoy)

his new church in a style which surpassed the splendor of Romanesque. This friend was the Abbot Suger, who rose from humble parentage to become the regent of France during the Second Crusade. From his youth, Suger wrote, he had dreamed of the possibility of embellishing the church which had nurtured him. In 1122 he was elected abbot of St. Denis and within fifteen years was at work rebuilding the old monastery, which had been in use for almost three hundred years. As he made his plans for the new building, he must have recalled many of the churches seen during his travels. Workmen and artists were summoned from many regions. St. Denis was one of the last great monastic churches to be built; and it is known as the cradle of Gothic art (Fig. 8–31).

ARCHITECTURE

. . . Moreover, it was cunningly provided that — through the upper columns and central arches which were to be placed upon the lower ones built in the crypt — the central nave of the new addition should be made the same width, by means of geometrical and arithmetical instruments, as the central nave of the old [Carolingian] church; and, likewise, that the dimensions of the new side-aisles should be the same as the dimensions of the old side-aisles, except for that elegant and praiseworthy extension, in [the form of] a circular string of chapels, by virtue of which the whole [church] would shine with the wonderful and uninterrupted light of most luminous windows, pervading the interior beauty.[12]

Abbot Suger's description of the new choir at St. Denis is a key to an understanding of Early Gothic architecture. As he says, the major dimensions of the new structure were dictated by an older church; and he proudly mentions the technical devices, "geometrical and arithmetical instruments," which made this possible. But it was the "elegant and praiseworthy extension," the "string of chapels" with "luminous windows," which proclaimed the new style.

Although the crypt at *St. Denis* was built as a foundation for the choir above it, a comparison of their plans and structure reveals the major differences between Romanesque and Gothic building (Fig. 8–32). The thick walls of the crypt create a series of separate volumes, whereas the absence of walls in the choir above leads to a unified space. The crypt is a mural construction and it is vaulted with groin vaults. The choir is a skeletal construction; its vaults are Gothic rib vaults (Fig. 8–31).

A rib vault is easily identified by the presence of crossed, or diagonal, arches under a groin vault, or vault with pen-

[12] *Abbot Suger on the Abbey Church of St-Denis* . . . , tr. by Erwin Panofsky, p. 101.

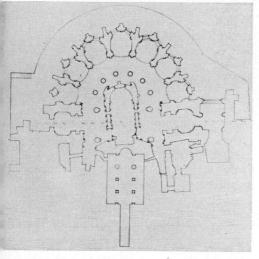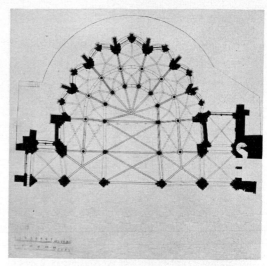

8–32   ST. DENIS. Plans of (a) crypt and (b) choir. 1140–1144. (After Sumner Crosby)

etrations. These arches form the armature which is the basis of Gothic skeletal construction. The Gothic vault may
be distinguished from other rib, or
arched, vaults by (1) the use of the
pointed, or broken, arch as an integral
part of the skeletal armature, and
(2) by the presence of thinly vaulted
webs, or severies, between these arches, all of which have their crowns at
approximately the same level. The diagrams in Figure 8–33 illustrate these
principles. Flexibility was a major ad-

vantage of the Gothic vault, as was the
fact that the armature of arches, although it did not entirely support the
vaulted webs, made it possible to pre-
determine the alignment and concentration of thrusts which had to be buttressed.

Although the Medieval mason unquestionably derived great satisfaction
from his mastery of these technical
problems and at times must have been
preoccupied with them, he did not permit them to be an end in themselves.

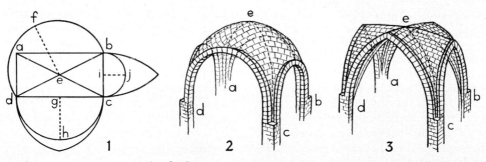

8–33   THE RIB VAULT. (1) abcd is an oblong bay to be vaulted; ac and bd are the
diagonal ribs; dc, the transverse; and bc, the wall arches. If semicircular arches are used
their radii and therefore their heights will be different: ef, gh, and ij. The result will be
a domical vault (2) irregular in shape and difficult to light. The Gothic rib vault
(3) used pointed arches for the ribs, so that the crowns of all the ribs reach the same
height. The result is a lighter, more flexible system, affording ample space for large
clerestory windows.

8–34 ST. DENIS. Ambulatories and radiating chapels. 1144. (Pierre Devinoy)

The ambulatories and chapels at St. Denis are proof that the rib vault was exploited, as Suger wrote, so that the whole church "would shine with the wonderful and uninterrupted light" (Fig. 8–34). This was the *scientia* — the theory — which motivated the creation of the Gothic style; and it was technical daring, or *ars*, which made it possible. It was only natural, as new churches in the Île-de-France were begun, that they be built in the new style.

When the cathedral of *Noyon* was begun between 1145 and 1150, the general arrangement of the St. Denis choir was followed, but the separation of the radiating chapels by solid masonry walls was a reversion to the compartmented spaces of the Romanesque (Fig. 8–401). At Noyon, though, and in the cathedral of *Laon*, begun a few

years later, the distinctive Early Gothic four-story interior elevation was used (Fig. 8–35). The four-story elevation consisted of the main arcade between the nave and side aisle, a large gallery or tribune as wide as the side aisle, a triforium passage in the thickness of the wall and the clerestory windows under the nave vaults. This system permitted the raising of the exterior walls high enough to buttress the thrust of the nave vaults, which were stabilized as well by the thickness of the masonry in the upper portions of the nave. Another invention of the Early Gothic builder was the flying buttress, which reached over the lower vaults of aisle and tribune with an arch to buttress directly the major points of thrust of the nave vaults.[13] With the mastery of this structural form, the technical vocabulary of Gothic architecture was complete (Fig. 8–29).

Important advances in the design of the exterior were also part of the Early Gothic experience. At *Laon,* although it is an early example, the doorways under protective porches and the towers above have been treated as an integral part of the mass of the building (Fig. 8–36). The different stories of the interior elevation are reflected in the levels accented on the façade, although a discontinuity, which was later to be regulated, between the central portion and the two flanking ones under the towers, is still noticeably present. Typically Gothic are the deep embrasures of the doorways and windows and the open structure of the towers, as well as the sculptural decoration

[13] The first such buttresses appeared at the collegial church at Mantes and at Notre Dame, Paris, *ca.* 1180–1185. The first buttress in Paris was in the corner between the choir and transept. Those along the nave date shortly after; but the great arches around the eastern part of the choir were added in the thirteenth century, as were all the flying buttresses which may be seen today as part of the structure of most Early Gothic buildings.

8-35 NOTRE DAME. Laon. Nave. 1160–1205. (Archives Photographiques)

8-36 NOTRE DAME. Laon. West façade. 1160–1205. (Archives Photographiques)

which provides accents to the design of the entire façade.

Laon also has towers flanking each of the transept arms and a lantern tower over the crossing, which with the two western towers gives a total of seven, the perfect mystic number composed of four and three, the evangelists or the gospels and the Trinity. This complement of towers was the ideal Gothic solution for the massing of a cathedral, although in most instances only the bases for the towers were built, as funds for their completion were seldom available after the rest of the structure and its decoration had been finished.

SCULPTURE

The sculpture decorating the twelfth-century buildings of the Île-de-France was as expressive of the new Gothic spirit as was the architecture. It is true that the Last Judgment remained, as in Romanesque, a central theme, but it became a symbol of salvation rather than one of damnation. It was also combined with other scenes and symbolic figures so that it was treated as part of a larger theme rather than as the symbol of the dogma itself. Sculpture emerged completely from the interior of the church and dominated the western entrances, which were regarded as the "gateways to the Heavenly Jerusalem" and as the "royal portals."

These *royal portals,* so called because of the statues of kings and queens on the embrasures flanking the doorways, are typified by the west portals of *Chartres* cathedral (Fig. 8–37) carved about 1145–1150.[14] At Chartres

[14] The portals of St. Denis, dedicated on June 9, 1140, may rightly be regarded the first Gothic portals, but they have been so badly mutilated that their study is long and

8–37   NOTRE DAME. Chartres. Western, or royal, portals. *ca.* 1145–50. (Pierre Devinoy)

the three portals are treated as a single unit proclaiming the majesty and omnipotence of Christ. His birth, the Presentation at the Temple, and Christ in Majesty with his Virgin Mother are shown on the right portal, and his Ascension into Heaven on the left portal. Scenes from his life and from the Pas-

complicated. Other early "royal portals" exist on the cathedrals of Bourges and Le Mans, and on such churches as Étampes and St. Loup de Naud.

sion are vividly carved on the capitals, which continue as a frieze from one portal to the next. On the central doorway is shown Christ's Second Coming, surrounded by the symbols of the four Evangelists, with the Apostles below, seated as representing the corporate body of the Christian Church. In the archivolts of the right portal are the seven liberal arts, the core of Medieval learning, and therefore symbolic of man's knowledge which will lead him

ment, the royal ancestors of Christ. It is almost certain that the Medieval observer also regarded them as figures of the kings and queens of France, symbols of secular as well as of Biblical authority.

These statue columns are among the few original forms of architectural sculpture to have appeared in any age (Fig. 8–38). At first glance they seem to follow many of the precepts of Romanesque sculpture: disregard for normal proportions; rigid adherence to an architectural frame (the column); and decorative surface treatment of drapery folds. Yet the differences are striking and important. The statues stand out from the plane of the wall. They move into the space of the observer and participate in it with him. The reality of the symbolism of these statues is heightened by the naturalism of their features and of details in the clothing, which show the Gothic interest and confidence in man. As the Gothic style developed, this realism was transformed first into the idealization of the perfect Christian and finally into portraiture of the specific individual.

STAINED GLASS

Stained-glass windows are the Holy Scriptures because they shut out wind and rain; and since their brilliance lets the splendor of the True Light pass into the church, they enlighten those inside.[15]

This emphasis on light is also found in the opening verses of the Gospel According to St. John, which were read at the close of every Mass:

. . . In him was life; and the life was the light of men. And the light shineth in the darkness. . . . *That* was the true Light, which lighteth every man that cometh into the world.[16]

[15] Adapted from Hugues de St. Victor, *Speculum de mysteriis ecclesiae*, Sermo II.
[16] John 1:4, 5, and 9.

to the true Faith. The signs of the zodiac and scenes representing the various labors of the twelve months are carved in the left portal archivolts as symbols of the cosmic and of the terrestrial worlds; and around the central tympanum are the twenty-four elders of the Apocalyptic vision, accompanying the Second Coming of Christ. The most striking figures are the great statue columns flanking each doorway — the kings and queens of the Old Testa-

How different from the sonorous verses of Revelations (p. 228). And how different are these shining walls of colored light, which change with every passing hour or cloud, from the painted walls of Romanesque or from shimmering Byzantine mosaics.

Colored glass was used as early as the fourth century to decorate the windows of churches. The technique must have been gradually perfected during the tenth and eleventh centuries, since the first accurately dated windows, those of the choir of St. Denis in 1144, show a high degree of skill; and Suger states that they were "painted by the exquisite hands of many masters from different regions," [17] proving that the art was widely known at that time. Yet the stained glass window may be said to be the hallmark of the Gothic style, for at no other time were they so perfectly executed or so perfectly employed.

Imperfections, or unexpected results, in making this colored pot glass were frequent, as we learn from Theophilus' *Schedula diversarum articum,* in which he also advises the artist to profit by these errors in making his window. Yet this was not an art left entirely to chance. The different properties of colors were well understood and carefully controlled.[18] The glass was blown and either "spun" into a round plate of varying thickness or shaped into a cylindrical "muff" which was cut and rolled out into square pieces. These pieces were then broken or cut into smaller fragments and assembled on a flat table, covered with chalk dust, according to the design of the painter. Many of the pieces were actually "painted" with a dark pigment so that details of a face, of clothing, or of any part of the design could be rendered. The fragments were then "leaded," or joined together by strips of lead which were expertly used to separate colors or to heighten the effect of the design as a whole (Plate

8–38 NOTRE DAME. Chartres. Statue columns. West façade. *ca.* 1145–1150. (Sumner Crosby)

[17] *Abbot Suger on the Abbey Church of St-Denis . . . ,* tr. by Erwin Panofsky, p. 73.
[18] See L. Grodecki, *The Stained Glass of French Churches.*

8–39 NOTRE DAME. Chartres. Stained glass windows. (Left) *Notre Dame de la Belle Verrière*, 12th century. (Right) *Story of Charlemagne and Roland*, 13th century. (Pierre Devinoy)

4). The window was finally strengthened by an armature of iron bands, which in the twelfth century was placed as a grid of vertical and horizontal strips over the design, but in the thirteenth century was curved to follow the different patterns of the medallions and surrounding areas (Fig. 8–39).

The effect of these glowing, translucent paintings, which often seem to be held suspended in space by the stone armature of the structure itself, can hardly be described in words. In fact, their presence is so compelling that the development of Gothic architectural forms may well have been influenced by the desire to have more and more stained glass both at a level near the pavement and high under the vaults. By the middle of the thirteenth cen-

tury, as we shall see, architectural techniques were so perfected that the space of cathedrals, such as *Beauvais*, or of chapels, such as the *Sainte-Chapelle* (Fig. 8–46), is defined by the burning intensity of the "painted windows" rather than by the stone structure.

MINIATURES, ENAMELS, AND METALWORK

Throughout the twelfth century the monastic scriptoria and workshops of England, northern France, and the Rhineland continued to produce richly decorated manuscripts, bronze crucifixes, fonts, candlesticks, and lavishly ornamented liturgical vessels and reliquaries of precious metals, jewels, and enamelwork. Perhaps because the mon-

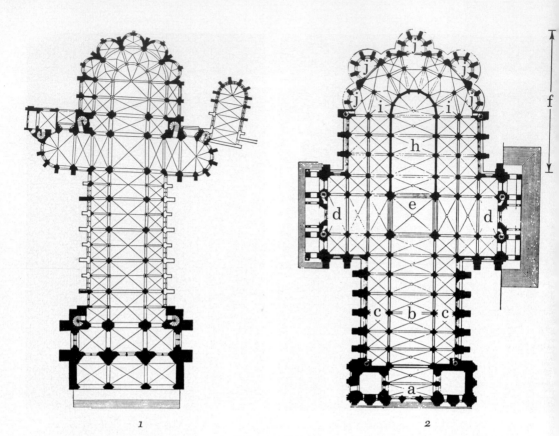

8–40 GOTHIC PLANS. Terms: *a.* West façade. *b.* Nave. *c.* Aisles. *d.* Transept. *e.* Crossing. *f.* Chevet, composed of: (*h*) choir; (*i*) ambulatory; (*j*) radiating chapels; (*k*) lady chapel. *1.* Cathedral of Noyon: note long nave, unusual rounded transept, and choir plan. Cf. St. Denis (Fig. 8–9.) *2.* Notre Dame, Chartres; note harmonious proportions

asteries were the native environment of Romanesque ideas and forms and because the influence of the Île-de-France only gradually penetrated these centers, the introduction of strikingly new concepts in these arts is hardly perceptible until late in the twelfth century. Mention has already been made of such an outstanding artist as Godefroid de Claire, and to his should be added the names of Ranier de Huy, Roger of Helmarshausen, and Nicolas of Verdun, all of them metalworkers. Of Nicolas of Verdun and his followers at the end of the twelfth century it has been said that:

The chasm between the physical and the spiritual worlds which pervaded the

thought and art of the Romanesque period is bridged, and their differences are reconciled. The Gothic era had started.[19]

High Gothic

(1194–1248)

On October 3, 1187, Jerusalem fell to Saladin. Western Christendom was shocked and the Pope immediately appealed to the three major kings, Henry II of England, Philip Augustus of

[19] H. Swarzenski, *Monuments of Romanesque Art*, University of Chicago Press, 1954, p. 35.

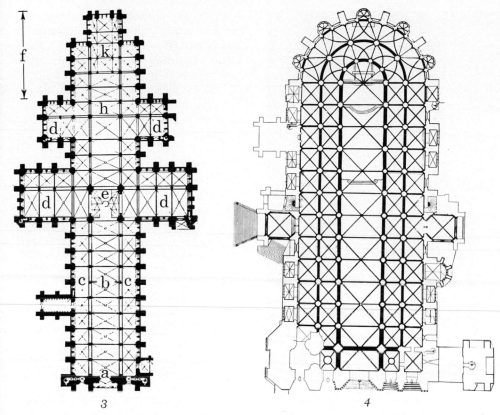

of nave, transept, and choir. *3*. Cathedral of Salisbury: note double transept and flat chevet. *4*. Cathedral of Bourges: note absence of transept, resulting in unified, continuous plan. (*1* from Seymour, *Notre Dame of Noyon*, Yale University Press, 1939; *4*, R. Branner)

France, and Frederick Barbarossa of Germany, to lead a Third Crusade to liberate the Holy City. In 1191, with the capture of Acre in Palestine, the Crusade ground to a stop. Frederick had been drowned in a small river in Asia Minor. Philip Augustus returned to care for his kingdom, and Richard I, the Lionhearted, Henry's son and successor, remained, assuring himself a place in romantic literature but able to achieve only a truce with Saladin the following year. It was the last of the great Crusades — the last time the Papacy was able to summon the forces of Christendom. Within the next twenty-five years other momentous events were to shape the destiny of Europe.

In 1212 at Navas de Tolosa the Christian forces in Spain defeated the Almohades, and the fate of the Moors was sealed. In 1214 Philip Augustus won the battle of Bouvines against the combined forces of England and Germany. Modern France began to emerge as an entity; and Germany, torn by feudal strife, soon lost its leadership of the Holy Roman empire, which itself disappeared. In England John was forced by his barons, in June 1215, to sign the *Magna Charta*, and the principle of a limited monarchy was established.

A recital of these events may seem a curious introduction to what has been called the Age of the Cathedrals, or the Age of Faith. Emphasis should be

8–41 BOURGES CATHEDRAL. Nave and aisles. 1190–1220. (Archives Photographiques)

ately, to be completed for the most part by 1220.[20] This new cathedral is usually considered the first of the High Gothic buildings — the first to have been planned from the beginning for the use of flying buttresses. At almost the same moment, canons of the chapter at *Bourges* were beginning an ambitious campaign to rebuild their cathedral. With these two — Chartres and Bourges — Gothic architecture found two different, completely satisfactory solutions.

At *Chartres*, after the fire, the overall dimensions of the new structure were determined by the towers left standing at the west and by the masonry of the crypt to the east which for reasons of economy were to be used as foundations. The new plan (Fig. 8-40-2), however, was not restricted by earlier forms and shows an unusual equilibrium between the choir, transept, and nave, which are of almost equal dimensions.

The site at *Bourges* was different. To the west the town crowded in and the chapter's lands were limited. The decision was taken to build the entire new choir outside the old city walls, compensating for the difference in levels by first building a vast crypt. At Bourges[21] the plan is a continuous one (Fig. 8-40-4), eliminating the transept entirely, so that the double side aisles flanking the nave continue without interruption from the western façade around the choir to the east. The sense of unity established by this plan was furthered by the unusual elevation. The inclusion of a triforium passage

given, though, to the remarkable vitality of Western civilization at this time and to the fact that the forces which had been at work since the Early Middle Ages were culminating in the creation of the nations of modern Europe. Other "Gothic" traits (mentioned at the beginning of this section) also emerged as positive social forces. And these years, the last decade of the twelfth and the first four of the thirteenth century, were those of the great cathedrals.

At *Chartres* a great fire consumed the town on June 10, 1194, and the cathedral, which had only recently been rebuilt, was again destroyed except for the crypt, the western towers, and the "portail royal" between them. A new cathedral was begun almost immedi-

[20] The richly decorated transept portals and porches date from the second third of the century, and the spire of the north tower was built by Jean Texier in 1506.

[21] Only the choir was finished by 1220, and the nave not before 1270; the great western window was the work of Guy de Dammartin about 1390; and the north tower was rebuilt early in the sixteenth century after it had collapsed in 1506.

8–42 NOTRE DAME. Chartres. Nave, looking east. 1197–1220. L. 236 ft.; with choir, 367 ft. W. 54 ft.; with aisles, 107 ft. H. 112 ft. (Pierre Devinoy)

and clerestory lighting between the side aisles, and the heightening of the main arcade, with the same triforium and clerestory design above it, produces a rhythmic harmony while providing windows at three different levels so that light saturates the interior volumes (Fig. 8–41). The close relationship between the volumes of the aisles and nave is enhanced by the light which thus pervades the entire space.

The elevation of *Chartres* is different (Fig. 8–42). As at Bourges, the use of flying buttresses made it possible to eliminate the tribune gallery over the side aisle (a familiar feature of Early Gothic), but the proportions of the elevation are different, as are the spatial relationships. The three-story elevation of Chartres emphasizes the large clerestory windows, which are of almost exactly the same height as the main arcade. The triforium provides a dark accent between the two major zones of light, but the volumes of the side aisle remain distinctly separate from the primary volumes of nave, transept, and choir. At Bourges the relationships are elusive, almost indefinable. The unity of Chartres is logical and coherent. It is, perhaps, for this reason that the Chartres elevation became the favored one, providing the Gothic system used throughout most of Europe. The au-

8–43 AMIENS CATHEDRAL. Nave, looking east. 1220–1236. L. 240 ft; with choir 370 ft. W. 49 ft.; with aisles, 108 ft. H. 140 ft. (Clarence Ward)

dacity, the inimitability, of Bourges meant that it was not adaptable to other proportions or conditions, and only a few architects attempted to reinterpret its system. Yet its solution for the creation of a Christian universe in Gothic terms has seldom if ever been equaled.

The cathedrals of *Reims* and *Amiens* perfected the Chartres program.[22] A

[22] *Reims*, the cathedral of the consecration of French kings, was begun after a fire, in 1210, had destroyed the old Carolingian building. Jean d'Orbais and his successor, Jean le Loup, built the choir and transept, finished in 1241; but the nave was not completed for many years, although work on the sculpture of the western portals was begun toward the middle of the century. *Amiens* was begun in 1220, according to the design of Robert de Luzarches. The nave was finished in 1236 and the radiating chapels in 1247, but work on the choir continued until almost 1270 and the towers remained incomplete until early in the fifteenth century.

8–44 NOTRE DAME. Chartres. South transept, detail. *ca.* 1210–1250.

view of the nave at Amiens shows how the structural system and the proportions of Chartres matured during the High Gothic period. Even a photograph conveys an impression of the majesty of this interior (Fig. 8–43). The scale is established by the height of the bases and capitals of the piers; and, although our eyes cannot measure exactly the height of the elevation (the crown of the vaults is 140 feet above the pavement), we sense immediately the vast size and extraordinary achievement of this stable, skeletal construction.

SCULPTURE

The sculpture adorning the portals of these cathedrals also shows Gothic art at its height. The extent of its iconography is as vast and complicated as the encyclopedic *Summae* of the time. Most of the figures are symbolic, but many of them, particularly the grotesque gargoyles, or rainspouts, and other details of the upper portions, are purely decorative and show the vivacity and charm inherent in the Medieval spirit at this moment, when it was confident in the assurance of its faith.

M. Emile Mâle [23] discovered in Vincent of Beauvais' *Speculum majus* the categories which mirror Medieval thought. The Mirror of Nature, which includes all natural phenomena, was not an objective or scientific analysis of nature, but rather the recording of the appearance of things as the reflection

[23] M. Mâle's extensive study of Medieval iconography has been published in several volumes covering Gothic art from the twelfth century until after the Council of Trent. One of these volumes has been translated into English: *Religious Art in France in the Thirteenth Century;* and a small collection of other passages from the different volumes exists in English in *Religious Art, from the Twelfth to the Eighteenth Century.*

of God's beneficence. The Mirror of Morals emphasized the virtues and vices as symbols of the proper life and the way to knowledge. The Mirror of Instruction, or Science, symbolized with the Fall and Redemption man's ability to redeem himself if he so wills, and the manner in which the Seven Liberal Arts as well as other branches of learning may aid him in this endeavor. The fourth, and last, Mirror was that of History, which, through scenes illustrating the Old and the New Testament, the Apocrypha, the lives of saints, and other religious themes, provided man with inspiration for a Christian life.

The flowering of the Gothic style in sculpture may be studied in the sucessive, if rather complicated, sequence of statues and reliefs on the transept portals of *Chartres* (Fig. 8–44).[24] Also, the great western portals of *Amiens*, carved during the 1220's and 1230's, seem to create their own perspective, drawing us into the City of God. The Last Judgment is shown on the central portal at Amiens, whereas the right portal is dedicated to the Virgin Mary and the left, or north, one to St. Firmin, the patron saint of Amiens. The north, or dark, side of the cathedral stresses scenes of the Old Testament, whereas the south side, bathed in light, emphasizes the teachings of the New Testament.

The *Beau Dieu,* or Teaching Christ, on the *trumeau* of the western central portal, epitomizes High Gothic sculpture (Fig. 8–45). Here Christ is no longer the stern judge. He has come down from the tympanum closer to

[24] This decoration began about 1205 on the central portal of the north side and continued without pause for the next decades roughly in this order: central portal, south; side portals, south; side portals, north; and finally the addition of the porches in the 1230's.

◄ 8–45   BEAU DIEU. Central portal, west façade, Amiens cathedral. 1220–1238. (Archives Photographiques)

mankind, and, instead of maintaining an attitude of threatening aloofness, evinces a kindly interest, prepared to instruct, even assist, humanity in its salvation. The statue has lost none of the monumentality of the Early Gothic statue columns, but it is now of normal human proportions and exists almost as a statue in the round, though still closely related to the architecture of which it is a part. The details of the drapery are carefully executed and the rhythmic folds of the lower portions contrast with the simplicity of the upper torso, which in turn enhances the dignity of the massive head. Here the generalized planes create features which, though human, are idealized and present the Christian Divinity in a timeless, mature serenity.

STAINED GLASS

Although little stained glass remains in the windows of *Amiens* and *Reims*, *Chartres* retains most, and *Bourges* much, of its original glass, showing the splendor of this art at its height. The fame of the Chartrain artists spread throughout Europe, and they were hired, when possible, to execute windows elsewhere. As the areas of these windows increased, the tonality of the colors also changed. In the twelfth century the blues, for instance, were light and blazing. In the thirteenth, the blues became darker, as though to control the total amount of light entering the interior.

In most of the *Chartres* windows are small figures or scenes, usually at the bottom, identifying the guild or corporation which contributed the funds for the glass (Plate 4). This has often been cited in support of a theory that the cathedrals were the result of a vast communal endeavor. There is ample evidence that donations, often of royal or noble origin, as well as from individual penitents or corporate groups,

swelled the coffers of the clergy and made possible the cathedrals themselves. It is equally certain that trained artisans, highly skilled masons, sculptors, and glass painters were responsible for the actual work, which was beyond the talent of the ordinary craftsman or worker, then as now.

One need only compare the west windows of Chartres with those in, say, the south transept to understand the extent to which this art matured. In the twelfth century the windows pierced the walls, where they remain suspended like jewels. In the thirteenth, the vast rose window fills the entire wall area, and below it are more windows, more light, where the large figures of the prophets of the Old Testament are shown with smaller ones, from the New Testament, on their shoulders.

MINIATURES, ENAMELS, AND IVORY CARVING

In the figure styles found in illuminated manuscripts and in enamel and goldwork Romanesque forms remained dominant until by gradual change a new style emerged. In miniatures the new tendencies may be seen in the gold backgrounds, which assume more importance as a positive element against which the figures are clearly defined. The figures themselves are more carefully articulated and begin to move in space. As secular artists began to replace monastic ones, the miniatures became less and less didactic symbols and more objects of delight in their own right.

While the great Mosan and Rhenish workshops continued to be active, centers such as *Limoges* in France began to produce reliquaries, book covers, and other objects in copper gilt and enamel. Later in the century this production was organized and "Limoges enamels" became known all over Eu-

8–46 SAINTE-CHAPELLE. Paris. Interior. 1248. (Archives Photographiques)

rope, although the style and craftsmanship gradually declined. Ivory carvings also became more and more popular as lay patrons began to seek decorations for their private chapels or homes. In general, though, this sculpture remained under the influence of the monumental forms being executed for the cathedrals. It was only in the succeeding age that as *objets d'art* they assumed elegant, sophisticated forms.

Refined Gothic

(MID-13TH–14TH CENTURIES)

The mid-thirteenth century in both England and France is generally considered one of prosperity and progress in the development of the national state and culture. With this prosperity came refinement and sophistication. Courtly love, as recounted in the *Roman de la Rose*, was codified, and courtship between lover and mistress

rigorously defined. It was the Age of Chivalry, marked by a nostalgia for the past and by elegant manners and fanciful costumes.

Early evidence of these refinements may also be seen in the arts. The great rose windows, with tracery radiating from the center like spokes of a wheel, have provided the name *Rayonnant* or "radiating" for the architecture of the time. These new tendencies are perfectly exemplified in the *Sainte-Chapelle*, built in 1248 to house relics of the Crown of Thorns, brought to Paris by Louis IX after the ill-fated Sixth Crusade.[25] This royal chapel (it was part of the palace on the Île de la Cité) is virtually a glass reliquary. The stone supports have been reduced to slender buttresses, which from the interior are hardly noticeable between the immense windows, which still retain most of their mid-thirteenth–century glass (Fig. 8–46). Although the chapel was heavily restored in the nineteenth century, it is interesting to examine the polychrome decoration of the arcades below the windows, which includes inlaid glass mosaics, so that the interior is covered with shimmering color. Statues of the apostles also decorate the interior. They stand on soffits quite independent of the architecture, and their relaxed poses, with multiple axes, foreshadow the graceful rhythms of later thirteenth- and fourteenth-century sculpture. Here are technical and aesthetic refinements which would have disturbed the grave harmonies of art earlier in the century.

Even more daring in its technical exuberance was the cathedral of *Beauvais*, begun in 1247. The choir, whose vaults soar 157 feet above the pave-

[25] The architect of the *Sainte-Chapelle* is believed to have been Pierre de Montreuil, who also was responsible for rebuilding the nave, transepts, and choir of St. Denis and for completing the remodeling of the transepts of Notre Dame in Paris.

8-47 BEAUVAIS CATHEDRAL. Choir. 1247-
ca. 1290. (Archives Photographiques)

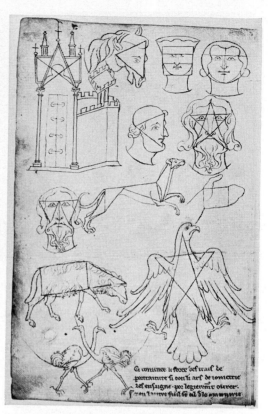

8-48 PAGE FROM NOTEBOOK OF VILLARD
D'HONNECOURT, French architect, mid-13th
century. Bibliothèque Nationale. (Bibliothèque Nationale)

ment (Fig. 8-47), was finished in 1272,
but the project was overambitious and
the vaults collapsed in 1284, because
the piers of the main arcade were too
widely spaced and the major buttresses
too slim. The piers were then doubled,
the buttresses reinforced, and the
vaults rebuilt, but work on the transept lagged so that it was not finished
until the sixteenth century. At this time
Jean Vaast erected a stone spire 501
feet high over the new crossing of the
transept. It, too, was overambitious
and it crashed to the ground in 1573.
Thus Beauvais was never finished; it is
evident that by the mid-thirteenth
century refinements too audacious to
be successful were changing the equilibrium and order of the earlier cathedrals.

A unique record of Medieval architecture from this same period exists in
the notebook of Villard d'Honnecourt,
an architect from northern France who
visited many of the great cathedrals
while they were still under construction. Many of his sketches show methods of construction and mason's tools
which are still being studied by scholars. Of unusual interest, also, are drawings which represent the results of a
disputatio as to the most perfect plan
for a choir or how the *ars de geometrie*
may be useful in designing figures (Fig.
8-48). The search for an ideal solution
for a building and the codification of
artistic procedures are essentially academic in spirit, conscious evaluations
of a style which has already reached
and passed its complete definition.

The degree of refinement in Gothic

8–49 REIMS CATHEDRAL. *Annunciation and Visitation.* Central portal, west façade. Mid-13th century. (Archives Photographiques)

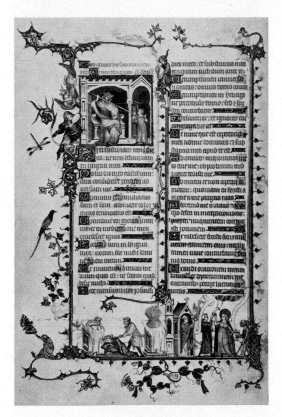

8–50 PAGE FROM THE BELLEVILLE BREVIARY by Jean Pucelle. 1343. Bibliothèque Nationale. (Bibliothèque Nationale)

sculpture at this time may be seen in the figures of the west façade of the cathedral of *Reims* (Fig. 8–49). These four statues, representing the Annunciation and the Visitation, reveal markedly different stylistic characteristics. We shall comment later on the two figures of the Annunciation on the right, with their surprising resemblance to the forms of late Roman sculpture. For the moment, let us look at the other two. The demure Virgin stands quietly, the simplicity of the rendering of her gown and of her features accenting her humility in a manner characteristic of the serenity and equilibrium of High Gothic forms. The Angel, in comparison, stands with graceful, curving contours. The vertical axis of the High Gothic has given way to multiple axes, which give movement to the figure; and the proportions have become slender and elegant. A slight smile, "the Reims smile," flickers across the mouth. These are all characteristics of refinement, which became more evident as the thirteenth century advanced. Indeed the famous *Vièrge Dorée,* so-called because her crown was originally gilded, on the south transept of

Amiens, is the embodiment of all these tendencies. The charm of her pose and the technical virtuosity of every detail are the summation of elegant sophistication.

Identical tendencies may be observed in the miniatures of manuscripts. As early as 1256 the superb *Psalter of St. Louis* was filled with active figures of graceful, elongated proportions. Here an architectural frame is an important part of the design, and it is significant that this architecture has the delicate "wheel" windows of the Rayonnant style, as well as slender columns and other details of this refined architecture. During the fourteenth century, under the leadership of Jean Pucelle, the decoration of a manuscript page was regarded in a new light (Fig. 8–50). The entire page became the province of the illuminator, and the borders, which were extended to invade the margins, included not only decorative tendrils

and floral ornaments but also myriads of insects, small animals, and grotesques as well as vignettes of daily life. The lively actions of the figures and their delicate rendering provide the basis for the so-called International Gothic style, which spread over all of Europe in the later fourteenth century.

Although Gothic art was known throughout Europe as *opus francigenum,* or French art, and although its major forms were developed in France, Gothic buildings were erected in every country of western Europe. Because of local traditions and native predilections, each country developed its own Gothic style.

ENGLAND

Throughout the Middle Ages there was great building activity in England (Fig. 8–51). The unusually complete records which have survived in many

8–51 ENGLAND, IRELAND, WALES, AND SCOTLAND.

8–52 SALISBURY CATHEDRAL. 1220–1258. (Aerofilms Ltd., London)

instances also afford us a welcome insight into Medieval techniques and economy, as well as providing the names of numbers of architects, so that in England, after the thirteenth century, Gothic architecture largely escapes the anonymity prevalent elsewhere.

The rebuilding of the eastern end of *Canterbury* was necessitated by a fire in 1174. The work was first directed by a Frenchman, William of Sens, who fell from a scaffolding in 1178 and was succeeded by another William, this time an Englishman. Although the three-story elevation and the proportions of the choir may be likened to the Early Gothic cathedral of *Sens*, a striking use of Purbeck marble in the shafts of the attached colonnettes and in the structure of the clerestory is quite distinct from the presumed French prototype. Particularly English is the emphasis on linear accents achieved by the contrasting colors and textures of the building materials.

Salisbury cathedral, begun in 1220 and finished within forty years, presents an unusually uniform structure as well as most of the typically English Gothic traits. Its location in a park, or close, surrounded by lawns and stately trees (Fig. 8–52) contrasts markedly with the Continental cathedrals, around which the city dwellings nestle closely. Equally distinctive is the long, rectilinear plan with a double transept and with a flat eastern end (Fig. 8–403). Its height, in comparison with that of *Amiens*, built at almost exactly the same time, is modest, and the flying buttress was used sparingly, as a rigid prop rather than as an integral part of the armature of arches. The façade is a stone screen which extends across the western end of the nave without reference to the interior disposition of the building. The crossing tower, with its tall stone spire, was added in the fourteenth century, and provides a necessary focal point for the cubic masses of the rest of the building. The interior has the conventional three-story elevation, but the use of different colored marbles, of clustered piers with multiple attached colonnettes, and of sharply pointed arches with richly molded openings all indicate that this is English. A view of the *Lady Chapel* (Fig. 8–53) shows the incredibly slender piers composed of unattached shafts of Purbeck marble, which seem to tether the billowing vaults to the ground, rather than to act as their supports. Not only is this daring construction, but its linearity and slender forms were forerunners of the Rayonnant style on the Continent.

The term Decorative style is applied to many of the buildings of the later thirteenth and fourteenth centuries. The choir of *Ely* cathedral is a typical example; and one may also see at Ely in the Lady Chapel, built during the third decade of the fourteenth century, how this fascination with curvilinear ornament led to the exuberant forms which characterize the Late Gothic style on the Continent. Equally precocious was the development of a decorative scheme, composed primarily of vertical and horizontal accents. It has been suggested that this design first appeared in the *royal chapel of St. Stephen*, attached to the palace of *Westminster* in London, in the mid-1400's and that it should be identified as a Court style which spread throughout the country and finally produced the famous Perpendicular style of the fifteenth and sixteenth centuries.

Comparatively speaking, English

8–53 SALISBURY CATHEDRAL. *Lady Chapel.* 1220–1225. (National Buildings Record)

Gothic sculpture was less concerned with the monumental ensembles to be found on French cathedral portals and was more interested in decorative details and in the carving of highly ornamental tombs. The screen façade of *Wells* cathedral has a series of figures which show, as does the architecture, the English instinct to emphasize linear design. English carvers were also noted for their work in alabaster, examples of which often found their way across the Channel.

The decoration and illustration of manuscripts continued to be of great interest to English artists, and the production of richly decorated psalters, particularly during the fourteenth century, probably excelled in quantity and quality those of any other country. The *Tickhill Psalter* of the early fourteenth century, which has been in the New York Public Library since 1932, illustrates the exuberance of this art (Fig.

8–54 TICKHILL PSALTER. *Tree of Jesse*. Early 14th century. New York Public Library. (Spencer Collection, New York Public Library)

8–54). The vocabulary of ornamental motifs seems limitless, and, as many of the pages in this manuscript remained unfinished, a student may observe the technique in varying stages of completion. Other famous examples, such as the *Arundel Psalter* (before 1339) and *Queen Mary's Psalter*, have miniatures with figures full of nervous energy. The latter is prodigiously illustrated with hundreds of pen-and-ink drawings, many colored with washes. In fact, there are some six hundred such drawings in the margins of this single manuscript, in addition to twenty-four miniatures. The drawings are vivacious observations of daily activities of the time, which seem to come alive again as one turns the pages. Unfortunately, this art all but ceased about the middle of the fourteenth century, due perhaps to the effects of the Black Death in 1348–49.

GERMANY

During the thirteenth century the concept of the Holy Roman empire gradually faded and disappeared. Germany was finally separated into a series of semi-independent principalities and duchies, which individually, however, were fairly well administered. The kingdom of Bavaria and the newly organized areas of east Germany prospered particularly in the fourteenth century, whereas west Germany remained divided into multiple, essentially antagonistic units until the sixteenth century.

At first glance the most striking characteristic of German building at this time is its respect for tradition. Indeed, Romanesque forms were still predominant in many areas, and these forms, it will be remembered, emulated the Carolingian and Ottonian periods. The cathedral of *Bamberg*, as an example, was begun before 1229. The plan and massing include the familiar Rhenish double-apse system with towers flanking both apses, in this instance influenced by those of *Laon*. Almost the only feature to identify this building as Gothic is the use of rib vaults, which are buttressed only by the heavy masonry of the walls.

Gothic influences increased during the thirteenth century. In some instances, as at *Limburg-an-der-Lahn*, consecrated in 1235, the Early Gothic four-story elevation was still retained. But in others, such as the cathedral of *Cologne*, begun in 1248, the nascent forms of the French Rayonnant were so daringly interpreted that credit for their invention is often given to Gerhardt, the architect of Cologne, who, it

8–55 ST. ELIZABETH. Marburg. 1233–1283. (Franz Stoedtner)

seems probable, was trained in France. The choir of Cologne (the nave was not finished until the nineteenth century) with its impressive dimensions (the vaults are 150 feet high), its carefully controlled proportions and its glazed triforium, must rank with the most significant Gothic achievements of any time or country.

More original even than the choir of Cologne were the *Hallenkirche*, the hall churches, which were particularly well adapted to the preaching needs of the German clergy. The exterior of the *Elizabethkirche* at Marburg (1233–1283), with its double-towered façade, appears conventionally Gothic. Its plan, with what is usually called a trefoil apse — meaning that the transept arms are rounded and have dimensions identical with those of the eastern apse — stems from a tradition extending back to the Early Middle Ages. The interior, though, has side aisles of a height equal to that of the nave,

which is lighted by tall windows in the outer walls. The result is an interior space even more unified than that of other Gothic structures; and this form was to be widely used by later Gothic architects (Fig. 8–55).

German sculpture is equally distinctive in the thirteenth century. Carved on the portals of the cathedral of *Strasbourg* are figures which have an elegance and delicacy closely resembling French Gothic, as well as others which show the German emphasis on emotion. Such exaggerations may be seen in some of the statues of the portals of *Bamberg*, but they are even more evident in the magnificent ensemble of sculptural decorations done for the cathedral of *Naumburg* about 1245. A detail from the richly carved rood screen separating the nave from the choir emphasizes the drama of the moment of the betrayal and arrest of Christ (Fig. 8–56). The participation of each figure in the event is intensely

8–56 NAUMBURG CATHE-
DRAL. *Betrayal and Arrest of
Christ. ca. 1245.* (From E.
Panofsky, *Die Deutsche
Plastik*, Kurt Wolff Verlag,
1924)

portrayed by the depiction of details
and by the contortions of the features
of each face. Such expressionism is
characteristic of German art throughout most of its history.

SPAIN

After the victory of the Christian
forces over those of the Almohades in
1212, the power of the Moors was restricted to the small Emirate of Granada in the extreme south of the peninsula. But it was not until 1474, with
the marriage of Isabella of Castile to
Ferdinand of Aragon, and finally with
the conquest of Granada in 1492, that
Spain was united under a single rule.
During the thirteenth and fourteenth
centuries these relatively small kingdoms prospered and Spanish cities
grew rapidly. Barcelona became one of
the great Mediterranean ports. Some of
the cities, such as Seville, were truly
cosmopolitan centers where Christian,
Jew, and Moslem lived side by side.
Into this culture Gothic art was, as
elsewhere, imported from France.

Among the early rib vaults to appear
in Spain are those of the cathedral of
Ávila, whose plan and general ordering
resemble those of the Early Gothic
choir of Vézelay in Burgundy. Later

the influence of the cathedrals is evident. At *Toledo* and *Burgos* the program of Bourges was modified to suit
the new environment. A comparison
of a section of the cathedral of Toledo,
begun in 1227, with that of Bourges
reveals how the Spanish sought wide,
ample spaces, without concern for the
great heights of the northern examples.
In the cathedrals of *Barcelona* (started
in 1298) and of *Leon,* the Chartres
system was followed, although the
major proportions and even certain
structural forms were greatly changed.

There is no difficulty in recognizing
that the cathedral of *Seville* is a Gothic
structure. The form of the piers, the
pointed arches, the details of the elevation and vaults are unmistakably so.
From the exterior, though, one might
mistake its unbroken massing for that
of a mosque, and the distinctive high-
pitched roofs of northern buildings are,
of course, not present. It is the effect of
light, in the interior, which is so different from the north. And this may be
experienced in an even more dramatic
manner at *Palma* (Fig. 8–57). Here the
beams of sunlight pierce the semidark-
ness, as though searchlights were slowly sweeping the interior, illuminating,
as the sun's position changes, one detail after another. The high arcades

8–57 CATHEDRAL, PALMA DA MAJORCA. 14th century. (Archivo Mas)

and the wide spaces with these dramatic shafts of light create a mystic, dramatic atmosphere.

Gothic techniques persisted for a long time in Spain, and written records tell us many things about the secrets of Gothic construction. Until the revolution in 1934 these cathedrals, as well as most Spanish churches, preserved the wealth of interior decorations inherited from the Middle Ages. Perhaps in no other country could one participate so fully in the spirit and drama of the Medieval environment.

ITALY

Italy's unique position in the Medieval world has already been commented upon. Because of the controversies over the papacy and the rivalries which broke out during the collapse of the Holy Roman empire, conditions in Italy might have been more chaotic than elsewhere had it not been for one important, typically Gothic, element.

The cities of northern Italy, the "Lombard League," were among the first in western Europe to benefit by the revival of trade. The ports of Genoa, Pisa, and Venice prospered, and gradually the manufacturing and financial centers of Tuscany — Siena and Florence — also acquired positions of wealth and power. The flourishing progress of these merchant oligarchies in the early years of the fourteenth century was suddenly curtailed by a series of reverses and tragedies in the 1340's. By 1345 almost every banking house in Florence had failed, as well as many in Siena. But these disasters were followed by an even greater one in 1348 – the Black Death, the bubonic plague, which carried off more than half the population during the summer months. The loss of family and friends, the piles of decaying corpses – these and other horrible memories could not be forgotten. The plague struck again in 1362 and in 1374, but not with such violence. Thus the second half of the fourteenth century presents quite a different scene from the first.

Italian art of this period has been traditionally regarded as distinct from the art of the rest of Medieval Europe. The *dolce stil nuovo*, first used by Dante to describe late thirteenth-century poetry, has been applied to other arts, particularly to that of Giotto, whose work we shall discuss in some detail. The sculpture and painting, even certain aspects of the architecture, are usually treated as an introduction to the art of the Renaissance, as a revolution against, or break from, what are often called the stifling conventions of Medieval art. Yet much of this art is as profoundly of the Middle Ages as are the pages of the *Divine Comedy*. If we have chosen to discuss it as part of the Medieval tradition, it is not to belittle its originality or its significance for the art of later times.

SCULPTURE

Imitation of the art of Antiquity has often been interpreted as a harbinger of Renaissance humanism. Anyone familiar with Medieval art, though, will recall similar imitations during the Carolingian period, in Romanesque art, and in French Gothic as well. The statues of the Visitation on the west façade of *Reims* (Fig. 8–49) show an unmistakable interest in late Roman sculpture, even though the modeling of the faces reveals their Gothic origin. Sketches in a similar style may be found in the notebook of Villard d'Honnecourt (p. 263). The thirteenth-century sculpture of Niccolò Pisano (active 1258–1278) in Italy, however, reveals an interest in the forms of Antiquity unlike that of his predecessors.

This may have been due to the Holy Roman emperor Frederick Barbarossa's great nostalgia for the glory that was Rome, which fostered a revival of Roman sculpture and decoration in southern Italy before the mid-thirteenth century. It was in this environment that Niccolò Pisano received his early training, so that he is more properly called Niccolò d'Apulia. In typically Italian fashion Niccolò's sculpture was not concerned with the decoration of great portals closely in harmony with the architecture of which they were a part. His art, rather, was the carving of marble reliefs and ornament for large pulpits, of which the most famous are in the baptistery of *Pisa* (1260) and the cathedral of *Siena* (begun in 1266). The presence of the Roman sarcophagi in the *Campo Santo* at Pisa may well have supplied him with models. Yet in his figures Niccolò achieved a certain robust grandeur (Fig. 8–58) which recalls Etruscan funeral sculpture even more than that of the later Roman empire. A comparison of Niccolò's work with that of his son Giovanni (*ca.* 1250-*ca.* 1320) shows how deep were the currents of Gothic naturalism and linear rhythms which Giovanni adhered to and which continued to be evident in most sculpture throughout the fourteenth century.

In contrast to Giovanni's agitated figures are the clarity, the calm rhythms, and the architectural fitness in every detail of the tombs and ciboria of Arnolfo di Cambio (died 1302). Gothic

8–58 NATIVITY, from pulpit by Niccolo Pisano. 1260. Baptistery, Pisa. (Alinari)

linearism, again, marks the work of Lorenzo Maitani (*ca.* 1275–1330) in the low reliefs on the façade of the *Orvieto* cathedral.

Sculpture seems to have been more actively pursued in centers other than Florence until an unrelated Pisano, Andrea (*ca.* 1290–1348), was commissioned by Florence to make bronze doors for the baptistery. As frames for each panel Andrea used a geometric motif, found in Gothic sculpture and illuminations. Within these he placed low reliefs of simple composition with smoothly flowing lines, admirably adapted to the spaces. In his reliefs on the campanile of the cathedral one feels the largeness of Niccolò's style and the dynamic force of Giovanni's. However, the amplitude of Andrea's forms, which are based upon a direct observation of nature, their clear placement in shallow space, and their highly sensitive relation to the hexagonal shape seem to point to the influence upon Andrea of his contemporary Giotto.

ARCHITECTURE

The citizens of *Siena* began the rebuilding of their cathedral in 1245,

those of *Florence* about 1296.[26] In both structures the simple cubic massing of nave and side aisles, the free-standing campanile, and the separate baptistery all recall features of Early Christian architecture. The alternating light and dark colors of the masonry at Siena emphasize the Italian love of bright effects. At Florence the exterior decoration of different colored marble veneer in bold rectilinear patterns continued a tradition of Romanesque times which endured during the Renaissance. Such formal abstract relationships are typical elements of Italian design. The interior of the Florence nave, which is covered by Gothic rib vaults, shows the Italian treatment of space in the wide arcades, minimizing the separation of nave from aisle.

It is difficult to describe in terms of a Gothic vocabulary such churches as *St. Francis of Assisi* (1228–1253) or particularly the *Arena Chapel* in Padua, built for the Scrovegni family (1303–1305), on whose walls are the

[26] Work on the cathedral continued at Siena until about the end of the fourteenth century. At Florence the nave was finished about 1350; the great dome over the crossing, by Brunelleschi (1425), is one of the monuments inaugurating the Renaissance.

8–59   CA D'ORO. Venice. 15th century. (Alinari)

great frescoes of Giotto and his followers.

One more variant of the Italian
Gothic style should be noted — that of
Venice, where the colorful surroundings seem to be the ideal environment
for the decorative qualities of later
Medieval forms, as exemplified in the
Ca d'Oro (Fig. 8–59) or in the *Ducal
Palace*. The presence of these buildings
also accents the fact that in many Italian cities secular Gothic buildings still
survive, particularly the city halls, as in
the case of the *Palazzo Vecchio* in
Florence.

PAINTING

Two major, and quite different,
trends existed in Italian painting of the
thirteenth century. One, the Sienese,
was distinctly Medieval and Byzantine, with its accent on abstract patterns and linear design, emphasized by
gold backgrounds and by the tempera

technique, so familiar in the painting
of miniatures. The other, the Florentine
trend, followed traditions of ancient
Rome. It was interested in the depiction of reality, in giving the illusion of
natural forms in three-dimensional
space, and it preferred the large areas
of walls, painted while the plaster was
still damp in a true fresco technique.

Duccio di Buoninsegna (1268–1319)
represents the Sienese tradition at its
best. The great *Maestà*, begun in 1308
and finished in 1311, when it was carried in a triumphal procession to
the cathedral, would alone establish
his reputation among the outstanding painters of western Europe. The
lyrical quality of his line and the
delicacy of his detail may be seen in
the figure of the Madonna and Child
seated in majesty on a throne of mar-
ble-inlay cosmati work. Through the
resplendent color gleams the gold of
the ground, of the exquisitely tooled
halos, and of small details — a beauti-

8-60 DUCCIO. *Three Marys at the Tomb*. A panel from the back of the Maestà. 1308–1311. Siena Cathedral Museum. (Alinari)

ful example of tempera painting. Set in its original elaborate Gothic frame, with its liberal use of gold in the background and details, with the clear massing of large areas of color, it must have given the glowing effect of a gold-ground mosaic.

On the reverse of this altarpiece was a series of small panels illustrating scenes from the life of Christ which show Duccio's power of narration — for these little pictures were meant to be read, as were the windows of Chartres. While the composition of the *Three Marys* (Fig. 8–60), for example, as a whole and in detail is traditional in Byzantine art, using elements of a widely known pictorial language, the three figures produce an effect of solidity and the sculptured hills give a considerable feeling of space. The sharply defined areas of color, often of contrasting hues, and the flat gold background and halos leave one with the impression of a sumptuously decorative panel.

The Florentine tradition, exemplified by the extraordinary frescoes of Giotto di Bondone (1266–1337), is more obscure in its origins. A primary interest in the modeling of form in light and shadow to give the illusion of weight and of material existence in space recalls similar qualities in the mosaics and frescoes attributed to Pietro Cavallini, who was born about 1250 and was

8–61   GIOTTO. *Lamentation*. Fresco. 1305. Arena Chapel, Padua. (Alinari)

active in Rome during the latter part of the thirteenth century. Giotto's other important predecessor, who is commonly believed to have been also his teacher, was Cenno di Pepi, known as Cimabue. Cimabue's style, originally much closer to Byzantine traditions than that of Cavallini, may be seen in his Madonnas in the Uffizi Gallery in Florence and in the Louvre, and in the fresco of the *Madonna with St. Francis* in the lower church of *St. Francis of Assisi*. In this last painting we may see how freely his figures move and the impression of their reality, especially in the St. Francis.

When we turn to the frescoes by Giotto, we realize how different they are from the work of Cavallini or Cima-

bue, and how original his genius was. While his figures are defined by a heavy line, as well as by the modeling of their features and clothing, the line defines a contour, not an edge or a decorative portion of some design. This contour is sculptural, as is the monumentality of his compositions; and it is in this way that he belongs to the Middle Ages, for, as scholars have remarked, many of his figures would be quite at home with those of the cathedral portals.

Giotto's style [27] may be examined in

[27] In recent years a number of scholars have questioned the attribution of many frescoes to Giotto's hand, noting not only a certain inferiority in the execution of the figures and other details, but also a crowding or com-

8–62 SIMONE MARTINI (assisted by Lippo Memmi). *Annunciation.* 1333. Uffizi, Florence. (Alinari)

frescoes such as the *Lamentation* in the Arena Chapel (Fig. 8–61) and the *Death and Apotheosis of St. Francis* in *Santa Croce*, Florence. In both of them the space in which the figures are placed is limited. One does not question the weight, the corporeal existence, of these bodies, which indeed at times seems to be exaggerated; but one

is also aware of their relationship to the frontal plane of the fresco — the wall — and to each other as carefully integrated units in the design as a whole. Each group has its own definition and each contributes to the rhythmic order of the composition. In the *Lamentation* the strong diagonal of the rocky ledge, with its single dead tree,

plexity in the compositions which denies the lucidity and monumentality of his other paintings. All are agreed about his work at the Arena Chapel in Padua, which must date from about 1305, and about his frescoes in the chapels of Santa Croce in Florence, done about 1320, and about the Madonna in the Uffizi. The most serious controversy revolves around the great cycle of frescoes depicting the life of St. Francis in the upper church at Assisi, traditionally attributed to Giotto and

dated about 1300. Since written evidence is lacking, opinions are based on stylistic analysis and these, it may be expected, will continue to vary. Current scholarship suggests that the St. Francis cycle must have been completed about 1307. It does not deny the influence of the Florentine's style, which it believes, however, is better exemplified by other works. The Assisi frescoes, it states, must have been done by Florentine artists influenced by Giotto, or with a similar background.

8–63 AMBROGIO LORENZETTI. *Good Government* (detail). Fresco. 1338–1340. Palazzo Pubblico, Siena. (Yale Photo Collection)

concentrates our attention on the group around the head of Christ in the lower left. All movement beyond this group is contained, or arrested, by the massive bulk of the seated figure in the corner of the painting. The seated figure to the right establishes a relationship with the center group, whose gazes and gestures draw us back to the head of Christ. In the *Death* scene the organization of space and of the groups is based on the horizontal figure of St. Francis, and the space is precisely defined by the scenery-like architectural screen which contains the group of figures. The three closely knit groups consist of five figures each, and the rhythmic beat of three is emphasized by the kneeling figures around the body of St. Francis. As our gaze is led from group to group and back to the focal point of the head of St. Fran-

cis, we discover more and more rhythmic accents which unify and establish the solemn harmony of the scene. Giotto's art may properly be interpreted as part of Medieval art, but its implications were not to be exploited fully for at least another century, when the artists of the Renaissance began their exploration of methods of depicting the world of visual reality in humanistic terms.

The artistic successors of Duccio and of Giotto, some of whom were their contemporaries, if they did not reach the same heights of attainment, often created paintings of extraordinary charm and vivacity.

Simone Martini (1284–1344) was steeped in the traditions of Siena. His *Annunciation* (1333) (Fig. 8–62), painted to be seen in the dim light of a chapel of Siena cathedral, has a lyric quality of line and an attention to delicate detail which is heightened by the brilliance of the expansive gold background and the decorative effect of the gilt frame. The angel, with fluttering draperies, appears to have just alighted with an olive branch, whereas the Virgin, surprised while reading, draws back in modest humility and awe as the angel's words, embossed on the background, reach her. Medieval symbolism and decorative qualities supplement the grace of this exquisite tempera panel. Simone also painted the impressive fresco of *Guido Ricci* in the Palazzo Pubblico in Siena and toward the end of his life traveled to Avignon, in southern France. There he helped to decorate the palace for the popes and contributed to the formation of the International Gothic style, which was to spread throughout Europe in the later years of the fourteenth century.

Ambrogio Lorenzetti painted the great frescoes of the *Good* and *Bad Government* (1337–1340) in the Palazzo Pubblico of Siena. For the *Good Government* (Fig. 8–63) he created a vast panorama, which looks down as from a peak on a city and its adjacent countryside. The figures, both within and without the walls, move in a convincing three-dimensional space, which, however, is treated as though it were a vast tapestry, covered with a never-ending series of engaging scenes and details of fourteenth-century life. The colors of the fresco, though now faded, add to the gay, exciting atmosphere. In Ambrogio's work the different points of view of Siena and Florence seem to have combined to present an impressive style for the future.

Late Gothic

(14TH–16TH CENTURIES)

While it is difficult to identify an historic moment for the disappearance of the Middle Ages, the late fourteenth and the fifteenth century in general present points of view which may be called Late Medieval, with a number of stylistic manifestations which may rightly be identified as Late Gothic.

Although the fourteenth century began with promising prosperity throughout most of Europe, famines and wars broke out which seemed capable not only of wrecking any economy but even of decimating the population. The Black Death of 1348 (p. 272) erupted in Italy and rapidly spread northward, crossing the Channel into England, where its ravages went on for another year. In 1340 the naval victory at Sluys gave the English control of the Channel and opened the One Hundred Years' War. This depleted England and despoiled France until the Maid of Orleans, Jeanne d'Arc, reversed the tide of English victories and conquests so that by 1453 only Calais remained in English hands and the war finally ended. During this period of disruption

8–64 HEAD OF CRUCIFIED CHRIST. Detail of wooden Crucifixion. Perpignan cathedral. 14th century. (From Gid and Jahan, *Le Dévot Christ*, Editions O.E.T., Paris, 1935)

and dismay Late Gothic art was produced.

It is small wonder that pessimism, disillusion, or frantic gaiety seemed to possess the people. A preoccupation with death was to be expected, and with it gruesome scenes of death and desolation. As the plagues struck down peasants and nobles alike, the *Danse Macabre*, or Dance of Death – in which people in all walks of life were depicted accompanied by a skeleton – became a popular theme and appeared painted on the walls of churches or in manuscripts. A change in the attitudes toward religion was also to be expected. The faith of the thirteenth century gave way to pietism, to an accent on mysticism and to dramatic representations, both in liturgical drama and mystery plays, of the sufferings of Christ or of martyrs and saints (Fig. 8–64).

The Virgin mourning over the dead body of her Son — the *Pietà* — became a favorite theme, as did the Entombment of Christ, which was carved in all realism with life-size figures and placed as dramatically as possible within the churches. It also became fashionable for the nobles and royalty to entertain lavishly with feasts, pageants, and festivals of increasing splendor and fantasy. Society assumed more and more sophisticated manners and elegant costumes, which are vividly represented in the miniatures (Fig. 8–70).

ARCHITECTURE AND SCULPTURE

Two major styles distinguish Late Gothic architecture: the Perpendicular in England and the Flamboyant on the Continent. We have already noted how the vertical and horizontal decorative accents from which the name Perpendicular was derived had their origin in the Court style of the earlier fourteenth century in England (p. 267). This basic design, combined with a highly or-namental vaulting system, which included supplementary ribs, liernes, and tiercerons, was influential in the formation of the French Flamboyant. In the full development of the Perpendicular, as in *Henry VII's chapel* at Westminster Abbey, London (1503–1519), the vault construction became so virtuoso that the keystones were suspended from the vaults and the decorative design covered the entire surface, spreading out in patterns similar to the ribs of a fan, giving rise to the term "fan vaulting" (Fig. 8–65).

In France this late style is known as Flamboyant, a term, like the Rayonnant (p. 262), derived from the stone tracery of the windows. This curvilinear tracery resembles tongues of flame, and the same flickering effect of light is achieved in the architecture by an emphasis on the surface ornament, which at times carried the technique of stone carving to its very limits. Few completely new churches were built in this style, although many secular buildings, such as town halls (Fig. 8–66), guild halls, and private homes, show its characteristics. More typical were ad-

8–65 WESTMINSTER ABBEY. London. *Chapel of Henry VII.* Detail of the ceiling.

8–66 TOWN HALL. Brussels. 1401–1455. (Belgian National Tourist Office)

8–67 CHURCH OF NOTRE DAME. Louviers. South porch. 1494.

ditions to, or changes in, existing structures, as seen on the south side of *Louviers* (Fig. 8–67), where all the exuberant details, dramatic effects, and open forms of a baroque style may be seen.

As the fourteenth century progressed, more and more interest in the individual as a specific personality was expressed. This became evident particularly in funerary sculpture, where the carving developed from a mere generalized and idealized recumbent effigy into a portrait with all the details of the individual's features and costume delineated. The progress of this development may be studied in the tombs at St. Denis, where the statue of *Philip IV*, the Fair, done about 1340, is often identified as the first portrait in French Gothic art. By 1380 the tomb of the famous marshal of the French armies, *Bertrand du Guesclin*, shows a complete portrait in every detail (Fig. 8–68).

As technical virtuosity developed and interest in realistic detail increased, there was also a return to the monumental concepts so fundamental to the Gothic sculpture of the cathedrals. These tendencies were given their fullest expression in the work of Claus Sluter, who was the principal artist for the dukes of Burgundy from 1389 until his death about 1406. His work at Dijon, in France, is properly looked upon as one of the last flowerings of Gothic sculpture. The great *Puits de Moïse*, or Well of Moses (Fig. 8–69), designed as a massive base for a Calvary, is not only a summation of the complex symbolism of the Middle Ages, but also a

8–68 TOMB OF BER-
TRAND DU GUESCLIN. St.
Denis. *ca.* 1380. (Pier-
re Devinoy)

8–69 CLAUS SLUTER. *Well of Moses.*
Chartreuse de Champmol, Dijon. Early
15th century. (Archives Photographiques)

monument of grandeur and dramatic emphasis. The complete mastery of stone carving shown and the accent on sharp contrasts of light and shade created by the deep undercarving of the open forms display qualities similar to those of architecture of the time.

PAINTING

The outstanding examples of Late Gothic painting emphasize the elegance of courtly life and manners in contrast to the ebullience and dramatic fervor of sculpture. Evidence of the early tendencies toward refinement in French art have already been examined (p. 262). Such tendencies seem to have combined with the poetic lyricism of Italian painting to produce what has been called the International style of Gothic art. There is justification for such a term in the presence of almost stylistically identical paintings in Spain, Austria, Germany, England, France, and also Italy.

It seems certain that the International style itself was developed by French artists, and perhaps its most typical example was made for a French patron, the Duc de Berry, although the artists, Pol de Limbourg and his brothers or associates were, from their names, probably Flemish. A page from the *Très Riches Heures,* a Book of Hours, made for the Duc de Berry about 1416 (Fig. 8–70), shows the attention to surface pattern, the bright, sharply contrasting colors, and the generally decorative quality which are typically Medieval. There is an interest, as well, in spatial representation which very likely was a contribution from Italy. The "International" characteristics, however, are most clearly seen in the elongated figures and their elegant, somewhat fantastic, costumes. In many other paintings these features are combined with a crowding of the figures and an agitation of linear effects which is often to be seen in mannerist styles of other periods.

Summary

Gothic art was the art of western Europe for more than three centuries. Distinctive in its use of an armature of stone arches to erect vast buildings whose walls were largely of colored glass, it was the culmination of Christianity's search for a style perfectly expressive of its faith and aspirations. Sculpture covered the cathedral portals with an encyclopedic representation of Christian thought, and the interiors were resplendent with the colored light of the windows and the rich decorations of the choirs and altars. This Christian universe, which offered constantly changing vistas as the faithful moved from the western entrance to the eastern chapels, was itself in the process of constant transformation as the Gothic style developed, maintaining a fundamental unity in the vocabulary of its forms while allowing each country or people to interpret the style in its own way.

The Early Gothic, which sought to

8–70 TRÈS RICHES HEURES OF DUC DE BERRY. *Month of April.* Miniature. By the Limbourg brothers. *ca.* 1416. Musée de Condé, Chantilly. (Giraudon)

exploit and perfect the new structural techniques, as well as those of stained glass and of unified ensembles of sculpture, was limited almost exclusively to the Île-de-France, the royal domains around Paris. These experiments occupied the second half of the twelfth century, creating such typical forms as the statue column, the four-story elevation in the nave, and finally the flying buttress. By the end of the century the way was prepared for the building of the great cathedrals.

The first half, roughly, of the thirteenth century may be called the Age of Faith, or the Age of the Cathedrals. It was the period when Gothic artists, working in complete confidence, produced with the same technical devices a wide variety of solutions for the buildings regarded as the City of God on earth. It was an age of dynamic assurance and inventiveness, which, however, soon gave way to refinements and attempts to carry the Gothic formulas to their very limits.

This Age of Refinement was of longer duration than the preceding ones, lasting from the mid-thirteenth century through most of the fourteenth. In France the Rayonnant style, in England the Decorative and Court style, sought technical perfection and elegant decorative surfaces. This was the period as well when the miniatures in richly decorated manuscripts became truly Gothic. Gothic forms were exploited in all the European countries, among which Italy was, perhaps, the most original, creating forms in sculpture and painting which were to be the basis for the art of the Renaissance.

Late Gothic art was produced in a period of turmoil, anguish, and uncertainty. During the latter part of the fourteenth and most of the fifteenth century, while the Renaissance style was being defined in Italy, Gothic forms were elaborated and given an emotional emphasis with intentionally dramatic results. As the Medieval world drew to its close, Gothic art sought a realistic representation of the world, which, however, was still considered a symbol and was treated as part of a decorative pattern rather than as a representation of the actual world.

Bibliography

EARLY MEDIEVAL

Beseler, Hartwig, *Die Michaeliskirche in Hildesheim*, Mann, Berlin, 1954.
Brehier, Louis, *L'art en France*, La Renaissance du Livre, Paris, 1930.
Brown, Baldwin, *The Arts in Early England*, Murray, London, 1926.
Clapham, A. W., *English Romanesque Architecture Before the Conquest*, Oxford University Press, New York, 1930.

Connant, Kenneth, *Carolingian and Romanesque Architecture* (800–1200), Pelican Books, Baltimore, 1959.
Crosby, Sumner, *The Abbey of St. Denis*, Yale University Press, 1942.
Dewald, Ernest T., *The Illustrations of the Utrecht Psalter*, Princeton University Press, 1932.
Forsyth, George H., *The Church of St. Martin at Angers*, Princeton University Press, 1953.
Goldschmidt, Adolf, *Die Elfenbein Skulpturen*, Vol. 1, B. Cassirer, Berlin, 1914–26.
——, *German Illumination*, Pegasus Press, Paris, *ca.* 1928.
Henry, Françoise, *Irish Art in the Early Christian Period*, Methuen, London, 1940.
Hinks, Roger P., *Carolingian Art*, Sidgwick & Jackson, London, 1935.
Hubert, Jean, *L'Architecture Religieuse du Haut Moyen Age en France*, Imprimerie Nationale, Paris, 1952.
——, *L'Art Pre-Roman*, Les Editions d'Art et d'Histoire, Paris, 1938.
Kendrick, Thomas D., *Codex Lindisfarnensis* (facsimile), Oltun, Urs Graf, 1956.
Leeds, E. T., *Early Anglo-Saxon Art and Archaeology*, Oxford University Press, New York, 1936.
Lehmann, Edgar, *Der Frühe Deutsche Kirchenbau*, Deutscher Verein für Kunstwissenschaft, Berlin, 1938.
Morey, Charles R., *Christian Art*, Longmans, Green, New York, 1935.
Porter, A. Kingsley, *The Crosses and Culture of Ireland*, Yale University Press, 1931.
Rey, Raymond, *L'Art Roman et ses Origines*, E. Privat, Toulouse; H. Didier, Paris, 1945.
Rivoira, G. T., *Lombardic Architecture*, Heinemann, London, 1910.
Schlunk, Helmut, *Ars Hispaniae*, Vol. 2, Editorial Plus Ultra, Madrid, 1953.
Sexton, Eric H. L., *Irish Figure Sculptures*, Southworth-Anthoensen Press, Portland, Me., 1946.
Sullivan, Edward, *The Book of Kells*, Studio Publications, New York, 1952.
Swarzenski, Hanns, *Monuments of Romanesque Art*, University of Chicago Press, 1954.

ROMANESQUE

Adams, Henry, *Mont-Saint-Michel and Chartres*, Houghton Mifflin, 1913.
Anthony, Edgar, *Romanesque Frescoes*, Princeton University Press, 1951.
Aubert, Marcel, *L'Architecture Cistercienne en France*, Editions d'Art et d'Histoire, Paris, 1953.

Boase, Thomas S. R., *English Art, 1100–1216,* Oxford University Press, New York, 1953.

Clapham, Alfred W., *English Romanesque Architecture after the Conquest,* Oxford University Press, New York, 1934.

Connant, Kenneth J., *Carolingian and Romanesque Architecture (800–1200),* Pelican Books, Baltimore, 1959.

Cook, Walter W. S., *Ars Hispaniae,* Vol. 6, Editorial Plus Ultra, Madrid, 1950.

Crichton, George H., *Romanesque Sculpture in Italy,* Routledge & Kegan Paul, London, 1954.

Cunynghame, Henry H. S., *European Enamels, Methuen,* London, 1906.

Foçillon, Henri, *Art d'Occident,* A. Colin, Paris, 1948.

——, *L'Art des Sculpteurs romans,* E. Leroux, Paris, 1931.

——, *Peintures Romanes,* Hartmann, Paris, 1938.

Forsythe, George H., *The Church of St. Martin at Angers,* Princeton University Press, 1953.

Gardner, Arthur, *English Medieval Sculpture,* Cambridge University Press, 1951.

——, *An Introduction to French Church Architecture,* Cambridge University Press, 1938.

——, *Medieval Sculpture in France,* Cambridge University Press, 1931.

Jameson, Anna B. Murphy, *Sacred and Legendary Art,* 2 vols., Houghton Mifflin, ca. 1911.

Maskell, Alfred O., *Ivories,* Putnam, 1905.

Michel, Paul H., *Romanesque Wall Paintings in France,* Editions du Chêne, Paris, 1949.

Millar, Eric G., *English Illuminated Manuscripts from the Xth to the XIIIth Century,* Les Editions G. van Oest, Paris, 1926.

Porter, A. Kingsley, *Lombard Architecture,* Yale University Press, 1915–17.

——, *Medieval Architecture,* 2 vols., Yale University Press, 1915.

——, *Romanesque Sculpture of the Pilgrimage Roads,* 10 vols., Marshall Jones, Boston, 1923.

Ricci, Corrado, *Romanesque Architecture in Italy,* Brentano, New York, 1925.

Rickert, Margaret, *Painting in Britain in the Middle Ages,* Pelican Books, Baltimore, 1954.

Saxl, Fritz, *English Sculptures of the Twelfth Century,* H. Swarzenski, ed., Faber & Faber, London, 1954.

Stenton, Sir Frank W., *The Bayeux Tapestry,* Phaidon, New York, 1957.

Stone, Lawrence, *Sculpture in Britain in the Middle Ages,* Pelican Books, Baltimore, 1955.

Swartwout, Robert E., *The Monastic Craftsman,* Heffer, Cambridge, England, 1932.

Swarzenski, Hanns, *Monuments of Romanesque Art,* University of Chicago Press, 1954.

Webb, Geoffrey, *Architecture in Britain: The Middle Ages,* Pelican Books, Baltimore, 1956.

Whitehill, Walter M., *Spanish Romanesque Architecture of the Eleventh Century,* Oxford University Press, New York, 1941.

Zarnecki, Jerzy, *Later English Romanesque Sculpture, 1140–1210,* Tiranti, London, 1953.

——, *English Romanesque Sculpture, 1066–1140,* Tiranti, London, 1951.

GOTHIC

Abbot Suger on the Abbey Church of St-Denis and Its Art Treasures, tr. by Erwin Panofsky, Princeton University Press, 1946.

Adams, Henry, *Mont-Saint-Michel and Chartres,* Houghton Mifflin, 1913.

Ackerman, J. S., "Ars sine scientia nihil est," *Art Bulletin* 31:84–111, June, 1949.

Arnold, Hugh, *Stained Glass of the Middle Ages in England and France,* new ed., Macmillan, New York, 1940.

Boase, Thomas S. R., *English Art, 1100–1216,* Oxford University Press, New York, 1953.

Bond, Francis, *The Cathedrals of England and Wales,* Scribner's, 1912.

Bony, J., *French Cathedrals,* Thames & Hudson, London, 1951.

Colombier, Pierre, du, *Les Chantiers des Cathedrales,* Picard, Paris, 1953.

Conant, Kenneth J., *Benedictine Contributions to Church Architecture,* Archabbey Press, Latrobe, Pa., 1949.

Crosby, Sumner McK., *L'Abbaye royale de Saint-Denis,* Hartmann, Paris, 1953.

Cunyghame, Henry H. S., *European Enamels, Methuen,* London, 1906.

Dupont, J., and Gnudi, C., *Gothic Painting,* Skira, New York, 1954.

Evans, Joan, *Art in Medieval France,* Oxford University Press, New York, 1948.

Foçillon, Henri, *Art d'Occident,* A. Colin, Paris, 1938.

Forsythe, George H., *The Church of St. Martin at Angers,* Princeton University Press, 1953.

Frankl, P., "The Secret of Medieval Masons," *Art Bulletin,* 27:46–60, March, 1945.

Gardner, Arthur, *French Sculpture of the Thirteenth Century*, Medici Society, London, 1915.

Grodecki, Louis, *The Stained Glass of French Churches*, Editions du Chêne, Paris, 1947.

Gudiol, J., *Spanish Painting*, Toledo Museum of Art, Ohio, 1941.

Hahnloser, Hans R., *Villard de Honnecourt*, A. Schroll, Vienna, 1935.

Harvey, J., *The Gothic World*, Batsford, London, 1950.

Haskins, Charles H., *The Renaissance of the Twelfth Century*, Harvard University Press, 1927.

Herbert, John A., *Illuminated Manuscripts*, Putnam, 1911.

Houvet, Etienne, *Cathédrale de Chartres*, 7 vols., A. Faucheux, Chelles, France, 1919.

Jameson, Anna B. Murphy, *Sacred and Legendary Art*, 2 vols., Houghton Mifflin, *ca.* 1911.

Karlinger, Hans, *Die Kunst der Gotik*, Propyläen-Verlag, Berlin, 1927.

Kubler, George, "A Late Gothic Computation of Rib Vault Thrusts," *Gazette des Beaux Arts*, Paris, Vol. 26, Series 6, December, 1944.

Lambert, Elie, *L'Art Gothique en Espagne*, H. Laurens, Paris, 1931.

Lasteyrie, R. de, *L'Architecture religieuse en France à l'époque gothique*, A. Picard, Paris, 1926–27.

Mâle, Emile, *L'art religieux du XIIIème siècle en France*, A. Colin, Paris, 1922.

——, *Notre-Dame de Chartres*, Hartmann, Paris, 1948.

——, *Religious Art from the Twelfth to the Eighteenth Century*, Pantheon Books, New York, 1949.

——, *Religious Art in France in the Thirteenth Century*, Dutton, 1913.

Maskell, Alfred O., *Ivories*, Putnam, 1905.

——, *Wood Sculpture*, Putnam, 1912.

Meiss, Millard, *Painting in Florence and Siena after the Black Death*, Princeton University Press, 1951.

Moore, Charles H., *Development and Character of Gothic Architecture*, 2nd ed., Macmillan, New York, 1899.

Natanson, Joseph, *Gothic Ivories of the 13th and 14th Centuries*, Tiranti, London, 1951.

Panofsky, Erwin, *Early Netherlandish Painting*, Harvard University Press, 1953.

——, *Gothic Architecture and Scholasticism*, Archabbey Press, Latrobe, Pa., 1951.

A Picture Book of English Medieval Wall Paintings, Victoria and Albert Museum, London, 1932.

Pirenne, Henri, *Medieval Cities*, Princeton University Press, 1925.

Pope-Hennessy, John, *Italian Gothic Sculpture*, Phaidon Publishers, New York, 1955.

Read, Herbert E., *English Stained Glass*, Putnam, 1926.

Salzman, Louis F., *Building in England Down to 1540*, Oxford University Press, New York, 1952.

——, *English Life in the Middle Ages*, Oxford University Press, New York, 1926.

Seymour, Charles, Jr., *Notre-Dame of Noyon in the Twelfth Century*, Yale University Press, 1939.

Simson, O. von, *The Gothic Cathedral*, Pantheon Books, New York, 1956.

Street, George E., *Some Account of Gothic Architecture in Spain*, 2 vols., Dutton, 1914; new ed., G. G. King, London, 1914.

Taylor, Henry O., *The Mediaeval Mind*, 4th ed., 2 vols., Macmillan, New York, 1925.

Venturi, L., and Skira-Venturi, R., *Italian Painting*, Skira, New York, 1950.

Ward, Clarence, *Mediaeval Church Vaulting*, Princeton University Press, 1915.

CHAPTER 9

RENAISSANCE[1]

(15TH–16TH CENTURIES)

During the Renaissance (literally translated "Rebirth") forms in art were again, as in Antiquity, based on the perception and imitation of forms in nature. Although there had been revivals of Antiquity in Medieval times, the Renaissance marks a profound break from the Middle Ages because this revival coincided with a new spirit in man: a new subjective, psychological self-awareness as well as an objective interest in the world. The men of the Renaissance were acutely conscious of the modernity, as well as the historical importance, of their age. They used

[1] The division of this chapter into fifteenth century (Early Renaissance) and High Renaissance (first quarter of the sixteenth century) does not imply a gradual rise toward the attainment of an ideal of art or a subsequent decline in the period of Mannerism (the rest of the sixteenth century). It reflects growth and change arising out of different traditions and aspirations in different countries.

ILLUSTRATION ABOVE 9–1 MICHELAN-GELO. *Bruges Madonna. ca.* 1500. Notre Dame, Bruges. (Soprintendenza alle Gallerie, Florence)

the term *rennovatio,* which has essentially the same meaning as our term Renaissance, in referring to it. The basic aim of Renaissance art was to clarify and find meaning in man's experience of himself and of the natural world by means of a rationally constructed ordering of physical reality.

One of the outstanding characteristics of the Renaissance was the interest in and the importance placed on the individual. There was a pride in personal achievement and a desire for lasting fame rarely known in the Middle Ages. Everywhere the individual stood out from the crowd. The biographies of famous men no longer dealt with the heroes of Antiquity (as in Boccaccio), but with men of the writer's own century (such as Vespasiano da Bisiticci's *Vite di uomini illustri del XV*). The artist, too, was accorded greater individual recognition, once he had completed the long traditional apprenticeship in his craft and had established himself as a master. Class distinctions and social hierarchies became less rigid, and social distinction began to be assessed on the basis of merit.[2] The cult of the individual reached such a point that, for example, the town of Spoleto requested to be allowed to keep the remains of the painter Fra Filippo Lippi (d. 1469) because Florence, his native city, already had so many famous men buried within her walls while Spoleto had so few. As man and his life on earth became more important, curiosity about man and the physical aspects of the world increased, giving impetus not only to the new art of the Renaissance but also to the beginnings of present-day science.

One of the most significant phenomena of the Renaissance was the admiration and emulation of Antiquity. Artists devoted themselves passionately to the study of ancient (primarily Roman) art, which, in its lifelike representation of the human body and nature, seemed to them to have perfected what they themselves were striving to achieve. As their understanding of the Antique grew, their interpretations of it became increasingly free and in some cases approached in their own terms Hellenic ideals of beauty. The humanists of the fifteenth century rediscovered many of the writings by Roman and Greek authors which had been lost during the Middle Ages. While their greatest literary contribution was, perhaps, the translation of these works (Marsilio Ficino finished his translation of the complete works of Plato into Latin, commissioned by Cosimo de' Medici in 1484), they also wrote commentaries on them and used them as models for their own historical, rhetorical, poetic, and philosophical writings.

These writings, as well as the translations of the texts of Antiquity, were made widely and inexpensively available for the first time through an invention which must rank as one of the most important contributions of the Renaissance — the printed book. Printing was not the invention of one man or of one place but the growth of centuries. Various reproductive devices, such as a stamp for initial letters, had been known for some time. In the fourteenth century paper became more and more common, though vellum and parchment continued to be used for fine books. But it was not until the decade from about 1450 to 1460 that printing with movable type became established at Mainz in Germany. This was such a significant invention that by the end of the fifteenth century printing was being practiced in all the countries of western Europe.

Early printed books (incunabula) closely resembled handmade books (manuscripts) of the period in composition, form of letters, and decoration. Only the small-lettered text was printed; initials and decorations in the margins were added by hand after the printing had been completed. For nearly a century printed books followed the tradition of manuscripts, for they had no title page, chapter headings, running titles or pagination. The unity in the design of early printed books in Italy appears in small pamphlets issued at Florence, known as *rappresentazioni* because they reproduced the plays given on saints' days. In the place of a title page the pamphlets had a woodcut with the representation of an angel as a herald to announce the play, and perhaps a characteristic scene from the life of the saint who was being celebrated. The illustrations in these books were intended to elucidate the text through visualization; they were harmonized with the letterpress through the balanced spacing of the composition of the whole page and their linear technique. The unity of letterpress, margins, type, and illustrations marks the printing of this period as one of the

[2] This aspect of the Renaissance was particularly stressed by J. Burckhardt, *The Civilization of the Renaissance in Italy,* tr. by S. G. C. Middlemoore.

POLIPHILO QVIVI NARRA,CHE GLI PAR VE AN‑
CORA DI DORMIRE,ET ALTRONDE IN SOMNO
RITROVARSE IN VNA CONVALLE,LAQVALE NEL
FINEE RA SER ATA DE VNA MIR ABILE CLA VSVR A
CVM VNA PORTENTOSA PYRAMIDE,DE ADMI‑
RATIONE DIGNA,ET VNO EXCELSO OBELISCO DE
SOPR A.LAQVALE CVM DILIGENTIA ET PIACERE
SVBTILMENTE LA CONSIDEROE.

A SPA VENTEVOLE SILVA,ET CONSTI‑
pato Nomere euaso,&gli primi altri sochi per al dolce
somno che se haura per le fesse & prosternate mebre dif‑
fuso relicti,me ritrouai di riouo in uno piu delectabile
sito assai piu che el praecedente.Elquale non era de mon
ti horridi,& crepidinose rupe intorniato, ne falcato di
strumosi iugi. Ma compositamente de grate montagniole di non tro‑
po alteria. Siluose di giouani quaerculi, di robur, fraxini & Carpi‑
ni, & di frondosi Esculi, & Ilice, & di teneri Coryli,&di Alni, & di Ti‑
lie, & di Opio, & de infructuosi Oleastri, dispositi secondo laspecto de
gli arboriferi Colli. Et giu al piano erano grate siluule di altri siluatici

9–2 PAGE FROM THE HYPNEROTOMACHIA
POLIPHILI (*Strife of Love in a Dream*).
Printed by Aldus Manutius at the Aldine
Press in Venice (1499).

high points in the art of bookmaking.
The most important Italian printer at
the time was the Venetian, Aldus Ma‑
nutius, whose edition of the *Hypnero‑
tomachia Poliphili* (Fig. 9–2) admira‑
bly demonstrates these qualities.

In addition to being a work of art,
the book's primary function was the
communication of ideas which, origi‑
nating in Italy, gradually captured the
minds of western Europe. The ideas
themselves concerned man and human‑
istic studies.

The term "humanism" originally re‑
ferred to the study of Greek and Ro‑
man authors. However, it has come
to denote the general concern for hu‑
man values which had been the essen‑
tial content of Antique literature. The
most important aspect of Renaissance
humanism was the belief in man's free‑
dom, through his reason, to determine

those human values for himself. In his
Discourse on Human Dignity the hu‑
manist Pico della Mirandola (1463–
1494) has God address man thus:

The nature of all other beings is limited
and constrained within the bounds of laws
prescribed by Us. Thou, constrained by
no limits, in accordance with thine own
free will, in whose hand We have placed
thee, shalt ordain for thyself the limits of
thy nature. We have set thee at the world's
center that thou mayest from thence more
easily observe whatever is in the world.
We have made thee neither of heaven nor
of earth, neither mortal nor immortal, so
that with freedom of choice and with hon‑
or, as though the maker and molder of
thyself, thou mayest fashion thyself in
whatever shape thou shalt prefer.[3]

The humanists, nevertheless, did not
look upon themselves as pagans. It was
possible, for instance, for a scholar to
prove the forgery of the Donation of
Constantine without feeling that he
had compromised his Christian faith.
The two great religious orders founded
in the thirteenth century, the Domini‑
cans and Franciscans, were as domi‑
nant in setting the tone of fifteenth‑
century Christian thought as they had
been earlier, and they continued as
patrons of the arts. Within the estab‑
lished religious orders humanist clerics
strengthened rather than weakened
the reputation of the Church. Human‑
ists, sometimes in orders, were ap‑
pointed to important posts in the city
government. The Florentine office of
chancellor, for example, was held by
such distinguished men of letters as
Poggio Bracciolini, Leonardo Bruni,
and Carlo Marsuppini.

In the political sphere government
by the guilds was gradually replaced
by individual rule. During the thir‑
teenth century the wealth and power

[3] Pico della Mirandola, *Oratio de hominis
dignitate* (1485), tr. by E. L. Forbes in *The
Renaissance Philosophy of Man,* University
of Chicago Press, 1956, pp. 224–25.

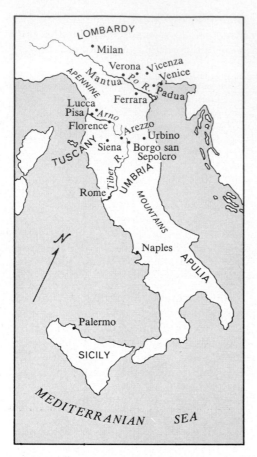

9–3 ITALY IN MEDIEVAL AND RENAISSANCE TIMES.

Florence the major guilds seized the power of government in 1282; in 1293 a more democratic rule was instituted, to include all the craft guilds, with the issuance of the Ordinances of Justice, which were also aimed at curbing the influence of the remaining feudal aristocracy. In 1342 the failure of the Florentine banking houses led to the appointment of a tyrant, the Duke of Athens, to stabilize the government. Another dramatic eruption was the Ciompi revolt of 1378, when the workmen attempted to wrest the government from the guilds and take it into their own hands.[4]

Although the factions had their acknowledged leaders, these were merely spokesmen for a group and did not occupy the unique position which was finally acquired in the fifteenth century by the Medici family. Cosimo de' Medici, the first of the family to rule, held, by his own choice, no rank higher than that of citizen; yet he maintained virtual control of the city and passed this on to his sons. In name Florence was still a republic, and held to republican ideals; but the city under the Medici became, in fact, a principality. The same phenomenon could be observed throughout Italy, for the fifteenth century saw everywhere the disappearance of the guild oligarchy and the emergence of the princely ruler. With some exceptions, the princes were well educated, benevolent, and patrons of the arts. The encouragement and commissions given to artists by Lorenzo the Magnificent and Federigo da Montefeltro are well known. Even Sigismondo Malatesta, an almost pathologically vicious tyrant, recognized and fostered the talents of leading artists.

Under both commune and princes the artist fulfilled an important function in the life of the city, since the Church, the nobles, and wealthy mer-

of many Italian cities grew with the rise of a thriving wool trade (Fig. 9–3). Florence in particular was noted for her finished cloth, which was sold to all parts of Europe. As their wealth increased, the guilds, including the powerful wool guild, commanded ever greater political influence until the city, and with it much of the patronage of art, was in their hands. The guild government, called the commune, was essentially a republic controlled by the merchant classes. Commercial setbacks or jealousies within the guild coalitions created a highly unstable government in which the control of power frequently changed hands overnight. In

[4] For a full account, see F. Schevill, *History of Florence*, Harcourt, Brace, 1936.

chants were in constant need of his works. He could satisfy all these different demands since, because of the apprentice system, he was a versatile craftsman.[5] Each well-known artist had a shop (*bottega*) — forty-one of these are recorded in Florence (total population about 150,000) between 1409 and 1444 — which a boy could enter at the age of ten or twelve as an apprentice.[6] There he learned how to grind colors, prepare a panel of seasoned wood for painting, use gold leaf, and transfer cartoons (the master's preliminary drawing) to the panel or wall. After some years spent in mastering these and other fundamentals of his craft, an apprentice was entrusted with the execution of minor parts of an altarpiece, usually following the design of the master. Eventually he left the master's shop and was admitted to the painters' guild as a master, with the right to set up a *bottega* of his own. As an outgrowth of the individualistic and rationalistic spirit of the Renaissance, the traditions and standards of the shop system were gradually relaxed during the fifteenth century and virtually disappeared by the latter part of the sixteenth in favor of instruction in the academies of art.[7]

For public and officials, art was a matter of intense civic interest and enthusiasm. The archives of fifteenth-century Florence reveal that the city council spent an astonishing amount of time and money upon art projects, such as the competition for the design of the cathedral dome or the location of Michelangelo's *David*. When Leonardo had made his cartoon of the *Madonna and Child with Saint Anne* (now in the Louvre), "the chamber wherein it stood was crowded for two days by men and women, old and young — a concourse, in short, such as one sees flocking to the most solemn festivals, all hastening to behold the wonders produced by Leonardo and which awakened amazement in the whole people."[8]

In this environment man awakened to his own nature and importance as an individual and to the possibilities of individual growth and development in a relatively fluid society. The emergence of an historical sense (fostered particularly by the early humanists, beginning with Petrarch) made the individual more keenly aware of Antiquity and of its pertinence to his own life than would have been possible in the Middle Ages. Personal observation of the physical world replaced authoritarian and purely deductive reasoning in viewing the world. Florentine art of the fifteenth century is strongly colored by these tendencies. Individualistic in expression and ordered according to observation of the external world, this art strove to make man aware of his own position and significance.

[5] Versatility in many arts rather than specialization in one characterized the artists of the Renaissance. All were trained in several crafts and all joined in making the furnishings for churches and palaces, and the costumes and equipment for pageants which were a feature of Renaissance life.

[6] For a detailed account of the craft learned by painters *ca.* 1400, see Cennino Cennini, *Il libro dell'arte,* tr. and ed. by D. V. Thompson, Jr.

[7] The art academy, however, is not so much a Renaissance as it is a Mannerist phenomenon. See Nikolaus Pevsner, *Academies of Art,* Macmillan, New York, 1940.

[8] Giorgio Vasari, *Lives of Seventy of the Most Eminent Painters, Sculptors, and Architects,* ed. by E. H. and E. W. Blashfield and A. A. Hopkins, Vol. 2, Scribner's, 1913, p. 393. (For another, more readily available edition, see the bibliography.)

15th-Century Italy

The Foundations — First Third of the Century [9]

The transition from the Middle Ages to the Renaissance can be seen especially well in the sculptors, Jacopo della Quercia (1375–1438) and Nanni di Banco (*ca.* 1390–1421), the one a Sienese by birth, the other a Florentine. Both adopted the broad, naturalistic style of the late fourteenth century as their starting point. They infused this tradition, however, with new vitality through their typically Renaissance preoccupation with monumental, three-dimensional form; in addition, Jacopo brought to it an individual, robust energy, and Nanni a hardness and clarity derived from Roman Republican sculpture.

Jacopo della Quercia's earliest major work, the *tomb of Ilaria del Caretto*, is related to French fourteenth-century sculpture in its scheme — the figure lying on the bier with a dog, symbol of fidelity, at her feet — as well as in the highly refined, soft texture given to the marble. The unbroken, gliding horizontal folds of the drapery suggest a mood of passivity and stillness above the quicker rhythms and stronger contrasts of light and shade in the putti with garlands — a motif taken from Roman sarcophagi which became popular in

[9] Renaissance art, particularly in the fifteenth century, was an organic development reflecting the restless energy of strong personalities and the interaction of new ideas and forms in the different artistic media. For this reason the discussion here has been organized in terms of thirds of a century, which approximate successive generations, even though certain individuals were often forceful influences in more than one of these periods. The categories of architecture, sculpture, and painting are treated in varying order in an attempt to emphasize the unity of the arts at this time.

the Renaissance. Between 1409 and 1419, Jacopo worked on a fountain, called the *Fonte Gaia*, in the principal square of Siena, for which he provided the design and, aided by workshop assistants, the sculptural decoration of reliefs and free-standing statues. Jacopo's robust energy is most impassioned in his late works, as in the relief of the *Expulsion* (Fig. 9–4). Carved in shallow relief and set into the frame in a closely knit pattern of curves and diagonals, the figures are constructed so that they seem capable of breaking out of the confines of the relief, thus dramatizing the rebellion of man against a fate which binds him, outcast and alone, to shape his life on earth. This is a characteristically Renaissance interpretation of the theme of the Expulsion, which we find again, though ex-

9–4 JACOPO DELLA QUERCIA. *Expulsion* Marble relief panel from the portal of San Petronio, Bologna. 1425–1429. (Brogi)

pressed in somewhat different terms, in Masaccio's fresco in the Brancacci Chapel (Fig. 9–10).

Although the swaying, curvilinear rhythms of the pose, the drapery, and the scroll in Nanni di Banco's early figure of the prophet *Isaiah*, executed for the cathedral of Florence, again recall French Gothic sculpture, the massiveness and cubic definition of the body, particularly of the firmly implanted head and the great torso, create a truly Roman effect of power. Nanni's later group of *Quattro Santi Coronati* (Fig. 9–5) [10] shows the same qualities (cf. Fig. 6–37). The group as a whole is an early solution to the Renaissance problem of integrating figures and space on a monumental scale. By placing the figures in a semicircle within their deep niche and relating them to each other by their postures and gestures as well as by the arrangement of draperies, Nanni has achieved a wonderfully unified spatial composition. But these implacable figures, whose noble bearing expresses — as in Roman art — the self-willed restraint through which men of great emotional vehemence may attain order and reason, are also joined in a no less remarkable psychological unity. While the figure on the right speaks, pointing to his right, the two men opposite him listen and the one next to him looks out into space, meditating on the meaning of the words. This scheme of unifying a group of figures by conversation was later adopted by Renaissance painters in representations of the Madonna and Child surrounded by saints, when it is known as the *sacra conversazione* (see Fig. 9–16).

The search for new forms capable of expressing new ideas was carried forward most dramatically in the early years of the century by the sculptor

[10] The Four Crowned Saints, martyred at the time of the Roman emperor Diocletian, were the patron saints of the Guild of Sculptors, Architects, and Masons.

9–5   NANNI DI BANCO. *Quattro Santi Coronati.* Marble. *ca.* 1408–1413. Or San Michele, Florence. (Alinari)

Donatello (1386–1466). His statue of *St. George*, done in 1416 (Fig. 9–6), shows a youthful knight clad in armor, standing firmly on both feet and glancing left under a slightly furrowed brow. The folds of the naturalistically tied cloak contrast with the rigid armor, while the shield simplifies the contour and renders the mass more compact. But, though the figure is firmly rooted to the ground, there is a turn in the torso as well as in the head; and an upward rhythm is stressed by the sweep of the cloak, which follows the turn in the pose. This movement is by no means the same as the sweeping surface rhythms of Gothic sculpture but is rather, as in Jacopo della Quercia's *Allegorical Figure*, a movement in space around a vertical axis producing a dynamic, living quality. The mystic

glance reveal a self-assurance and a reliance on his own intellectual powers which are also characteristic of his creator, Donatello.

Shortly after the completion of the St. George, Donatello was called on to supply figures for the niches on the campanile of the cathedral of Florence, a project which, like the figures for Or San Michele, had originated in the preceding century. Donatello's *Habakkuk* shows a meditative and ascetic character. The heavy mantle, falling in massive folds from the shoulder, for the most part conceals and represses the body, though the modeling of the right arm, shoulder, and throat indicates an intimate study of anatomy, not as an end in itself but as a means of expressing character.

In contrast to the *Habakkuk*, whose intensity is cloaked by passivity, the *Jeremiah* (Fig. 9–7) assumes a restless, defiant pose, with tense articulations and abrupt meetings of verticals and horizontals in the arms and drapery. The compressed lips, the eyes peering from under the dark overhang of the brows, and the sharp angle of the wrist as the right hand clenches the leg express the righteous anger of the fiery prophet and at the same time indicate tensions which are to become more dominant in Donatello's later work.

Donatello made excursions into the field of relief sculpture as well. The influence of painting, perhaps that of his friend Masaccio, is strongly felt in the *Feast of Herod* (Fig. 9–8), executed for the baptismal font of the Siena cathedral. Here Donatello organized the narrative, involving many figures, into a dramatic composition which creates the illusion of deep space. This apparent space is achieved in a relatively shallow relief by the use of a rational one-point perspective and the overlapping of receding planes in the architecture. The *Cantoria* of slightly later date, on the other hand, is more sculp-

9–6 DONATELLO. *St. George.* Marble. 1416. St. George was the patron saint of the Guild of Armorers, who commissioned the statue for a niche on the exterior of Or San Michele. The original statue has been removed from the church to the Bargello (the National Museum) and a reproduction placed in the niche. National Museum, Florence. (Alinari)

and chivalrous nature of the ideal Gothic warrior-saint, such as the St. Theodore from Chartres, is here subordinated to the self-contained and stoic expression of individual will. The firmness of St. George's pose and

9–7 DONATELLO. (Left) *Habakkuk. ca.* 1423–1426. Popularly called Lo Zuccone, meaning "Pumpkin-Head," by the Florentines. (Right) *Jeremiah.* 1427–1436. Both marble, *ca.* 6½ ft. Campanile, Florence. Now in the Cathedral Museum, Florence. (Alinari)

turally conceived. Here one is conscious only of surging rhythms playing through a static framework. In the narrow space between the mosaic colonnettes and the gold mosaic ground, putti swing from side to side with all the spontaneity and exuberance of children at play.

During the early part of the fifteenth century, however, the sculptor Ghiberti gained, if anything, greater influence and a more sympathetic audience than Donatello by following less extreme measures. He adapted the linear grace of the early fifteenth-century "Gothic"

style in Florence to the monumental and expressive power of the new style. Lorenzo Ghiberti (1378–1455), although trained as a painter, is best known as a worker in metal. He first comes to our attention in 1403 as victor in a competition for the design of bronze doors for the baptistery of Florence.[11] In the layout of the second

[11] There are three sets of doors on the baptistery at Florence: the first, made by Andrea Pisano for the eastern doorway (1334–1336), which faces the cathedral, were moved to the south door to make way for those made by Ghiberti in 1403–1424; these in turn were moved to the north door

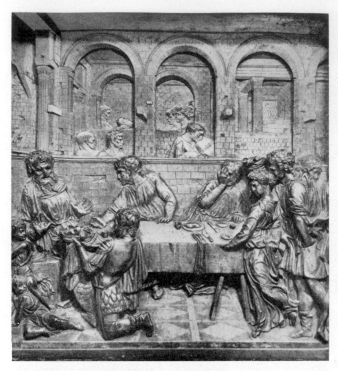

9–8 DONATELLO. *Feast of Herod*. Bronze relief on the baptismal font, Siena cathedral. 1425–1427.

doors of the baptistery, Ghiberti followed the pattern of Andrea Pisano. The *Temptation* panel indicates that the sculptor was concerned chiefly with the swing of the line and the graceful movement his figures could weave within the quatrefoil frame. He created a pattern built on arcs of circles which approach but do not meet.

Ghiberti, however, was not untouched by the work of his contemporaries. Tendencies that we have already seen in Donatello's work make themselves felt in Ghiberti's bronze *St. Matthew* (1418–1420) for Or San Michele. But Ghiberti is best known for the third doors of the baptistery, the so-called *Gates of Paradise* (1425–1452). Here, after 1425, he abandoned the pattern

in order that the second pair by Ghiberti, the famous "Gates of Paradise" (1425–1452), might be placed in the eastern doorway, the most important entrance. Seven artists submitted designs in 1401, among them Jacopo della Quercia and Filippo Brunelleschi, whose work is discussed in the following pages.

of the earlier doors and divided the space into rectangular panels, each containing a relief set in plain moldings. When gilded, the reliefs produced with their glittering movement an effect of unrivaled splendor and elegance.[12]

The individual panels, such as the *Meeting of Solomon and the Queen of Sheba* (Fig. 9–9), clearly recall painting in the depiction of space as well as in the treatment of the narrative, and some exemplify more fully than painting many of the principles Alberti was later to formulate in his *Della pittura* (see pp. 300n., 302). In his relief Ghiberti created the illusion of space partly by pictorial and partly by sculptural means. In the architecture he used the painter's one-point perspective construction to heighten the illusion of

[12] It may have been this that called forth from the grim stonecutter Michelangelo the remark, "They are so fine that they might fittingly stand at the Gates of Paradise."

9–9 LORENZO GHIBERTI. *Meeting of Solomon and the Queen of Sheba* from the "Gates of Paradise." Panel from eastern doors. 1425–1452. Baptistery, Florence. (Brogi)

depth. At the same time the figures themselves reinforce this illusion. The lower section of the relief actually bends out slightly toward the viewer. On this inclined plane the figures appear almost as full round, some of the heads standing completely free. As the eye progresses upward, the relief becomes flatter and flatter until the architecture of the background is represented by barely raised lines. By means of this "sculptor's aerial perspective," which gives the illusion of forms becoming less distinct as they appear deeper in space, Ghiberti attained a greater sense of depth than had heretofore been possible in a relief. It should be noted, however, that Ghiberti's figures do not occupy the architectural space he has created for them. Rather they are arranged along two parallel planes in front of the grandiose architecture which, in accordance with views expressed by Alberti in his *Ten Books on Architecture*, reflects in its forms the dignity of events shown in the foreground. The festive pomp and processional opulence of the scene, including horsemen, soldiers, and Orientals, enables us to visualize events such as the great Church councils of the fifteenth century, in particular the Council of Florence of 1439, which sought to bring together the Byzantine (Orthodox) and Western (Catholic) churches. From Ghiberti's biography we also know that he admired and collected classical marbles, bronzes, and coins. Their influence is clearly seen in some of the figures of soldiers and in certain profile heads reminiscent of Roman cameos.

Although the study of sculpture enables us to recognize the innovations of many of the new Renaissance concepts, we must turn to painting if we are to understand their true significance. Vasari [13] tells us that the frescoes by Ma-

[13] Giorgio Vasari, author of *The Lives of the Painters, Sculptors, and Architects*, which was first published between 1550 and 1568, is a major source for our knowledge of artists

ciate the importance of Masaccio's innovations one has only to compare his *Expulsion* (Fig. 9–10) in the Brancacci Chapel with the fresco opposite it, the *Temptation*, by his teacher, Masolino.[14] Where Masolino's figures are elegant within linear contours which suggest only a shallow relief, Masaccio's are typified by an almost peasantlike coarseness and fully sculptural forms which generate a deep implied space. He heightens the illusion of space, as did Jacopo della Quercia in his almost contemporaneous relief (Fig. 9–4), by the overlapping of planes. In the *Expulsion* the modeling of the two figures more than anything else indicates the deep landscape in which they move. The beat of Adam's feet on the ground marks man's presence on the earth, while the cry that issues from the mouth of Eve gives voice to the anguish felt by men deprived of God. Adam and Eve do not resist; there is no physical contact with the angel. Nor are the figures crowded against the frame. Rather they move on inexorably, driven by the will of the angel and by their own deep grief. It is a simple scene treated with a power we are not

[14] Masolino da Panicale (1383–1447) began to paint in the Brancacci Chapel in Santa Maria del Carmine, Florence, in 1425, but completed only the two lunettes (now destroyed) before he left to work elsewhere. In August 1427 he and Masaccio, teacher and student, continued the frescoes, working side by side, until toward the end of the year Masolino once more departed, leaving Masaccio to continue alone until the fall of 1428, when he also left (for Rome) without finishing the painted decoration. This was completed later in the century by Filippino Lippi. In his art Masolino continued Gothic and International style traditions, though he imbued them with a new, Renaissance sense of lucid, geometric order and a rational control of space, as in his *Banquet of Herod* at Castiglione d'Olona (*ca.* 1435). He taught Masaccio little except the craft of painting, but he himself was considerably influenced by his pupil's monumental and revolutionary style, particularly in the *Raising of Tabitha* in the Brancacci Chapel.

9–10 MASACCIO. *Expulsion.* Fresco. 1427. Brancacci Chapel, Santa Maria del Carmine, Florence. (Brogi)

saccio (1401–1428) in the Brancacci Chapel were studied by successive generations of Florentine artists. To appre-

from Giotto to Michelangelo. His biographies of artists were the first to attempt to trace the historical development of art.

9–11 MASACCIO. *Tribute Money*. Fresco. 1427. Brancacci Chapel, Santa Maria del Carmine, Florence. (Brogi)

to meet again until the same subject is treated by Michelangelo.

In the *Tribute Money* (Fig. 9–11) Masaccio grouped together three episodes: in the center Christ, surrounded by his disciples, tells St. Peter that in the mouth of a fish he will find a coin to pay the imperial tax demanded by the tax collector who stands in the foreground, his back to the spectator. At the left, in the middle distance, we see St. Peter struggling to extract the coin from the fish's mouth, while at the right, with a gesture of great finality, he thrusts the coin into the tax collector's hand. Masaccio's figures recall Giotto's in their simple grandeur, but they stand before us with a psychological and moral self-realization that is entirely new. The bulk of the figures is not realized through generalized modeling, as in Giotto, but by means of the light which strikes them, illuminating only those parts of the solids that obstruct its path and leaving the rest in deep shadow. Between these two extremes the light is a constantly active, fluctuating force, which we feel as a tangible substance. In the creation of space filled with atmosphere Masaccio anticipated the achievements of the

High Renaissance; no painter between Masaccio and Leonardo da Vinci created with this degree of actuality the illusion of space as a substance of light and air existing between our eyes and what we see.

The individual figures in the *Tribute Money* are massive, as in Giotto's frescoes, but they also express bodily structure and function as do Donatello's statues. We feel bones, muscles, and the pressures and tensions of joints; each figure conveys a maximum of contained energy. Vasari said: "Masaccio made his figures stand upon their feet." The main group is shown in a spacious landscape, rather than in the confined stage space of Giotto's frescoes. The foreground space is generated by the group itself, in which all the heads are on one level, as well as by the architecture on the right, shown in a one-point perspective construction in which the location of the vanishing point coincides with the head of Christ. The foreground is united with the distance by aerial perspective — a consistent diminution in the intensity of light and color. Through his monumental formal presentation Masaccio not only enhances but also transcends the signifi-

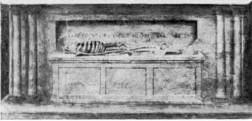

9-12 MASACCIO. *Trinity with the Virgin, St. John, and Donors.* Fresco. 1427. Santa Maria Novella, Florence. (Soprintendenza alle Gallerie, Florence)

cance of the specific theme of the *Tribute Money.* His figures, in a barren world, appear as the patriarchal archetypes of the Renaissance concept of man.

In the fresco of the *Trinity* (Fig. 9-12), executed in the spring of 1427, only a year before his premature death,

Masaccio painted a square chapel covered with a coffered barrel vault derived from Antique Roman tomb chapels. He placed the vanishing point of the perspective construction at a low eye level, thus creating the illusion of an actual structure whose interior volume is an extension of the space in which the spectator is standing. He also achieved a rational, metrical coherence in the spatial arrangement of the architecture and figures which, by maintaining the mathematical proportions — based on squares and rectangles — of the surface design, is responsible for the unity and harmony of this monumental composition.

The most imposing and daring architectural embodiment of this new Renaissance spirit is Brunelleschi's dome for the cathedral of *Florence* (Fig. 9-13), which was begun in 1420.[15] In contrast to the spherical domes of the Pantheon (Fig. 6-30) and Hagia Sophia (Fig. 7-11) which are, when seen from the exterior, shallow and partly concealed shells whose principal function is the enclosing of interior volume, Brunelleschi's octagonal ribbed dome was designed to dominate the cathedral and the city of Florence with its exterior mass. In asserting itself as a sculptural mass, the *duomo,* like the architecture of Antiquity, is a stable, powerful, self-contained form, "rising above the skies, ample to cover with its shadow all the Tuscan people." [16]

[15] Construction of the cathedral itself was started in 1296 and was completed during the fourteenth century, save for the immense undertaking of the dome over the crossing. After decades of debate and controversy, the city council finally entrusted the construction of the dome to Brunelleschi.

[16] It was described and praised in these words by Leon Battista Alberti in his *Della pittura,* written in 1435 (tr. by J. R. Spencer). The dome was finished in 1436, although the lantern — the small structure as its apex — was not added until 1446-1461. Brunelleschi, who was a sculptor until comparatively late in life, is known primarily as an architect. He lived from 1377 to 1446.

9–13 CATHEDRAL OF FLORENCE, or Santa Maria del Fiore (St. Mary of the Flower). So called because of the lily in the coat of arms of the city. 1296–1462. The present façade was added 1875–1887. The design of the detached campanile is ascribed to Giotto. The dome was begun by Brunelleschi in 1420.

Among Brunelleschi's first patrons were the Medici, for whom he designed the church of San Lorenzo. Its *Old Sacristy* (Fig. 9–14), probably completed by 1429, reveals a rigorous intellectual order and clarity, typical of the Early Renaissance, in the definition and articulation of interior volume by walls which are treated as thin, clean planes. Just as the ribs of the Duomo, which converge and intersect in its lantern, organize and give direction to interior space, so the pilasters, the entablature, and the moldings in the Old Sacristy establish the network for a rationally proportional, geometric ordering of interior space. These members, made of a brownish-gray stone called *pietra serena,* were applied to the wall after it had been erected, and have, therefore, no structural function.

Their purpose, in other words, is a purely aesthetic one, involving nothing but the organization or construction of space. Another factor in this organization of space is the attention given to lucid proportions. The sacristy is essentially a cube surmounted by a hemispherical dome. The entablature divides the cube into two halves, so that both the lower and upper sections of the wall are twice as wide as they are high. This proportion of 1 to 2 pervades the whole building (the height of the dome is in a proportion of 1 to 2 to the height of the cube beneath it, for instance) and is characteristic of the effort of Early Renaissance architects to express simple, mathematical relationships in their buildings.

In this way the first generation of Renaissance artists established a new

9–14 SAGRESTIA VECCHIA. San Lorenzo, Florence. *ca.* 1419–1429. The frames for the doors, with their projecting pediments, the bronze doors themselves, decorated with relief panels, the large reliefs over the doors, and the terra-cotta roundels in the second story are by Donatello, *ca.* 1434–1443. Brunelleschi is said to have objected to them because they impaired the purity and harmony of his design. (Alinari)

style. Humanism, with its interest in man and the world of nature, found inspiration in the literature and art of ancient Greece and Rome. The dignity of man was proclaimed and artists strove to depict him in a space which could be rationally organized. Equally rational proportions gave an order of abstract harmonies to the new architecture.

Enrichment and Consolidation — Second Third of the Century

The artistic achievements of Brunelleschi, Donatello, Masaccio, and others inspired the humanist Leon Battista Alberti (1404–1472) to formulate the first modern treatise on the theory of painting. In his *Della pittura,* written in 1435, he wished to persuade both artists and patrons to accept the new order of art. He saw the aim of painting (or pictorial relief) in what he called the *istoria* — a dramatic representation of an event, employing one-point perspective for the visual, temporal, and spatial unity of the composition in which the figures were to portray and project their emotions, as well as the moral significance of their actions, through their bodily postures and gestures. Although many of the theories expounded by Alberti had been explored by the artists of the early fifteenth century, it was during the middle decades that these theories became explicit in the work of certain artists and were enriched by the efforts of others.

PAINTING

The painter Fra Angelico (*ca.* 1400/05–1455), for example, was a personality comparable to Ghiberti and one enjoying a similar popularity, although his work was not as original in formal or compositional inventiveness.[17] Like Ghiberti he began his career in the tradition of the Gothic International style. His earliest activity was as an illuminator of manuscripts, perhaps in the shop directed by Lorenzo Monaco; hence his works always retained a particular precision and coloristic refinement. But he also came into contact with the new ideas of Brunelleschi and Masaccio, and in his *Visitation* of about 1435 (Fig. 9–15) he painted one of the pur-

[17] The artist's given name was Guido di Pietro, which he retained until he became a Dominican monk about 1425. It has recently been shown that Fra Angelico was born not in 1387, as had been thought, but shortly after 1400. Thus he received his training as a painter while the Early Renaissance was already in full swing.

9–15 FRA ANGELICO. *Visitation*. Predella panel of Altarpiece of the Annunciation in the museum at Cortona. *ca.* 1435. (Soprintendenza alle Gallerie, Florence)

est visions of landscape of the Early Renaissance. The definition of the foreground by the perspective rendering of the building, the clear three-dimensional construction of the figures, and the planes of the landscape — submerged in light — which carry the eye backward, show the degree to which Fra Angelico had absorbed the new style. We see this also in the lucidity with which the action is represented.

In 1438 Cosimo de' Medici commissioned Fra Angelico to paint a new altarpiece for the high altar in the recently reconstructed church of San Marco (Fig. 9–16), which was attached to the Dominican convent where Fra Angelico was then residing as a friar. An early example of the *sacra conversazione* (p. 293), the painting bears a close relationship, in its spatial composition and arrangement of figures, to theories in Alberti's *Della pittura*. The angels in symmetrical groups flanking the Renaissance throne of the Madonna turn to

speak to one another or to look out at the spectator. The saints grouped in the foreground speak and gesture with the same freedom, leading our eye toward the central point of interest, the Madonna. In the foreground the patron saints of the Medici, Cosmas and Damian, form the base of an equilateral triangle whose apex is the Madonna. The balance and harmony, the air of quiet dignity which the painting projects emerge with the same conviction in Fra Angelico's frescoes in the upper corridor of San Marco and in his late frescoes in the Chapel of Nicholas V (1450–1455) in the Vatican.

In the *Last Supper* (Fig. 9–17) by Andrea del Castagno (*ca.* 1423–1457), painted in the late 1440's and covering one entire wall of the refectory of the convent of Sant' Apollonia in Florence, we see a severity and clarity of form also characteristic of this phase of Florentine painting. Christ and the disciples, with Judas isolated at the front

of the table, according to Medieval tradition, are painted as immovable, sculptural solids. The style of Castagno's contemporary, Domenico Veneziano (*ca.* 1410–1461) is less imposing but shows great psychological and formal flexibility and a more refined sensitivity to light and color. Though born in Venice, where his first artistic train-

ing may have been in a shop of mosaic workers, Domenico was active in Florence and assimilated Florentine forms. His *sacra conversazione* (Fig. 9–18) from Santa Lucia de' Magnoli recalls both Nanni di Banco's *Crowned Saints* (Fig. 9–5) and Fra Angelico's *San Marco Altarpiece* (Fig. 9–16). Here, however, the saints not only are

9–17 ANDREA DEL CASTAGNO. *Last Supper.* Fresco. 1445–1450. Sant' Apollonia, Florence. (Brogi)

9–18 DOMENICO VENEZI-
ANO. *Madonna and Child
with Saints.* Church of Santa
Lucia de' Magnoli. 1442–
1448. Uffizi, Florence. (Alinari)

related to each other by their postures
and gestures, but also seem to move toward each other across the marble
floor. Each has an individual expression
and character, yet all participate in a
common, psychologically explicit mood
of contemplation. The integration of
figures, space, and architecture is
brought about chiefly by light which
casts a bold diagonal shadow across
the niches in the background, and saturates the colors with an harmonious
luminosity. Because the eye level of
the architectural setting is low, the figures seem to tower over the observer
with monumental aloofness. Domenico's colorism as well as his fluid line
were adopted and stylized by his pupil, Alleso Baldovinetti (1425–1499).

The most famous artistic heir of Domenico Veneziano, Piero della Francesca (*ca.* 1420–1492), assisted him in

► 9–19 PIERO DELLA FRANCESCA. *Baptism of Christ. ca.* 1445. National Gallery,
London. (Courtesy of the National Gallery, London)

9-20 PIERO DELLA FRANCESCA. *Visit of the Queen of Sheba to Solomon*. Detail of fresco. 1452–1466. San Francesco, Arezzo. (Alinari)

Florence during the early 1440's but never returned there as an independent painter. One of the greatest masters of perspective, on which he wrote a theoretical treatise, Piero developed Domenico's sophistication in the handling of light and color so that color became the very matrix of his three-dimensional forms, lending them a new density as well as fusing them with the surrounding space. His early *Baptism of Christ* (Fig. 9–19), painted for a church in his native town of Borgo San Sepolcro in Umbria, shows Piero's geometric purity of design, his architecturally simplified figures, and his clear, limpid light in an expansive landscape. Piero's major work was a cycle of frescoes in San Francesco, Arezzo, on the Legend of the True Cross, painted in-

termittently between 1452 and 1466. In the left portion of the scene of the *Visit of the Queen of Sheba to Solomon* (Fig. 9–20), the queen kneels before a bridge made from the tree, planted over the grave of Adam, which was destined to be used for the Cross. The figures of the compact group behind her are precisely localized and related to each other by the shapes and the sequence of contrasted color masses in the ample space defined by the colonnade on the right. They communicate a profoundly convincing sense of actuality, infused with a self-contained calm which sustains them in their processional gravity.

The *Resurrection* in the town hall of Borgo San Sepolcro (Fig. 9–21), painted while the Arezzo frescoes were ap-

9–21 PIERO DELLA FRAN-
CESCA. *Resurrection of
Christ.* Fresco. *ca.* 1465.
Town Hall, Borgo San Sepol-
cro. (Soprintendenza alle
Gallerie, Florence)

proaching completion, not only presents the religious event itself but is
also an allusion to the regeneration of
the fertile powers of the earth. This is
indicated by the contrast between the
barren and fertile aspects of the landscape on the left and right. It is also
emphasized by the prominence of the
sleeping soldiers in the foreground,
whose lethargy is in marked contrast to
the figure of the risen Christ. The
Christ stands, one foot on the sepulchre, with the fixed, hypnotic presence
of a Byzantine Pantocrator, but the figure is also imbued with the radiance
and splendor of such pagan gods as
those from the pediment of the temple
of Zeus at Olympia. As the luminous
pink of Christ's mantle contrasts with
the somber, dark tonalities of the sol-

diers' costumes, so his erect frontality is
opposed to the spatially complex diagonals in the group below. The risen
figure is stabilized in a composition
consisting of two interpenetrating triangles, while the whole of his body below the shoulders is contained within
the rolling, tapestrylike mass of the
hills. Piero has fused aspects of Christianity and Antiquity in this image of
Christ.

The influence of Piero della Francesca, who was in Ferrara in 1449–1450,
was important in the redirecting of the
energies of painting in northern Italy
which took place under the leadership
of Andrea Mantegna (1431–1506).
North Italian painting of the early fifteenth century had been chiefly preoccupied with decorative and coloristic

9–22 (Above) ANTONIO PISANELLO. *The Vision of St. Eustace. ca.* 1435. National Gallery, London. (Courtesy of the Trustees of the National Gallery, London)

◄ 9–23 ANDREA MANTEGNA. *St. James Led to Martyrdom.* Fresco. *ca.* 1454. Destroyed in World War II, formerly in the Church of the Eremitani, Padua. (Anderson)

elaboration of surface patterns and naturalistic detail. A highly refined sensitivity and subtlety in adjusting those values to one another had been developed by the Veronese painter and medalist Antonio Pisanello (*ca.* 1395–1450). In his small panel of the *Vision of St. Eustace* (Fig. 9–22) painted about 1435, Pisanello created a fairy-tale world of poetic intimacy, weaving with miraculous delicacy of touch the naturalistic representation of animals, flora, and figures into a luminous tapestry-like composition. In this picture we recognize qualities of the International style, which was the dominant artistic language of northern Italy until about 1450; but with Mantegna's frescoes in the Eremitani Church in Padua, painted from 1448–1455, north Italian painting fell in line with the humanistic art of Florence. The perspective in *St. James Led to Martyrdom* (Fig. 9–23), with its boldness of foreshortening, imparts to the figures a dramatic monumentality reminiscent of Donatello. The compactness of the figures is defined with a hardness as indestructible as stone or metal. In this way Mantegna imposed a sense of permanence on his ideal vision of Antiquity, in which he was much more archeologically exact than his Florentine contemporaries. The Triumphal Arch and the armor of the Roman soldiers are copied directly from Roman remains in and around Padua. The typical north Italian richness of his color is handled not primarily as a decorative element, but as de-

fining solids in a space organized by a clearly established perspective. It is in this respect that Mantegna is greatly indebted to Piero della Francesca.[18]

Since the beginning of the fifteenth century there had been an exchange of artistic ideas between Florence and northern Italy. Besides the examples of Domenico Veneziano, who came to Florence from Venice, and of Piero della Francesca, whose importance in the development of north Italian art we have seen, the Florentine painters, Paolo Uccello (*ca.* 1396–1475) and Fra Filippo Lippi (*ca.* 1406–1469) had also crossed the Apennines to work respectively in Venice and Padua. Uccello's visit left him with a lasting impression. In one of his large panel paintings of the *Battle of San Romano* (Fig.

[18] The three great *quattrocento* painters of Ferrara, Cosimo Tura (1430–1495), Francesco Cossa (*ca.* 1436–1478), and Ercole Roberti (1456–1496), adopted the exaggerated sculptural modeling of Mantegna but tended to transform it into patterns which became so emotional that they were at times even grotesque.

9–24 PAOLO UCCELLO. *The Battle of San Romano. ca.* 1456. National Gallery, London. (Courtesy of the Trustees of the National Gallery)

9–25 FRA FILIPPO LIPPI. *Madonna and Child*. 1437. Galleria Nazionale d'Arte Antica, Rome. (Anderson)

9–24), for the Medici Palace, he created a fantasy which recalls the processional splendor of Gentile da Fabriano's *Adoration of the Magi* of 1423 or the tapestrylike luminosity of Pisanello's *Vision of St. Eustace* (Fig. 9–22). But the imaginary world of Paolo Uccello, in contrast to the surface decoration of the International style, is constructed of immobilized solid forms, foreshortened (as in the fallen soldier in the left foreground) according to a rigid application of perspective. The rendering of three-dimensional form, used by other painters for representa-

tional or expressive purposes, became for Uccello an end in itself, with a magic of its own which he exploited to satisfy his amazingly inventive and original imagination. His fascination with perspective had little in common with the rationality of Piero della Francesca's or Masaccio's concern for defining the metric proportionality of space. Rather, Uccello's was an irrational, consuming passion for arranging the forms of solid geometry in space.

The features reminiscent of the International style in Uccello's *Battle of San Romano* were a common property of Florentine painting shortly after the middle of the century. Perhaps the most famous and typical instance of this sumptuous, romantic style are Benozzo Gozzoli's frescoes representing the *Journey of the Magi* (1459) in the chapel of the Medici Palace.[19] These are also splendid examples of a decorative tendency in Florentine painting which came to the fore particularly in the same period.

Side by side with the decorative and monumental strains in Florentine painting there existed a linear tendency reaching back to the Sienese, Simone Martini. This linearism was given significant redirection by Fra Filippo Lippi, who was to be Botticelli's teacher. Strongly influenced by Donatello, particularly in his early works, such as the *Madonna and Child* of 1437 (Fig. 9–25), Fra Filippo was the first Renaissance painter to use line in a sculptural rather than in a two-dimensional sense. Here the line itself has plastic power in defining the bulk of heavy, compact figures and an almost explosive vehemence in its movement through space.

A good deal later, in a quieter, more

[19] Benozzo Gozzoli (1420–1495) was a pupil of Fra Angelico; the most important among the projects in which he assisted his master was the fresco decoration of the Chapel of Pope Nicholas V in the Vatican (1447–1449).

9–26 FRA FILIPPO LIPPI. *Adoration of the Christ Child. ca.* 1460. Ehemalige Staatliche Museen, Berlin. (Walter Steinkopf)

9–27 LUCCA DELLA ROBBIA. *Cantoria* (Singing Gallery). 1431–1438. Museo dell'Opera del Duomo, Florence. (Alinari)

9–28 DONATELLO. *David*. Bronze. *ca.* 1435. Bargello, Florence. (Brogi)

gentle style influenced by Fra Angelico, Fra Filippo painted an *Adoration of the Christ Child* (Fig. 9–26) for the Medici. Its lyric, religious character reflected a revival of Medieval pietism and asceticism which occurred in Florence toward 1450.

SCULPTURE

Rhythmic grace and lucidity of action are typical, as we have just seen, of one aspect of Italian painting of the second third of the fifteenth century. These same characteristics may be seen in the sculpture of Luca della Robbia (1399–1482). He is best known as the head of a family workshop which produced glazed terra cotta objects — images of the Madonna and Child, altarpieces, escutcheons, and architectural decorations. His marble *Cantoria* (Fig. 9–27) for the cathedral of Florence (1431–1438), the companion of Donatello's "Singing Gallery," approaches closely in spirit as well as in form such Antique reliefs as those of the *Ara Pacis* in Rome (Fig. 6–33).[20] In contrast to Ghiberti's pictorial relief, Luca's figures fill the whole area of their panels; the further figures, carved in a lower relief than those in front, are aligned in symmetrical groups in a narrow space. Their rounded forms are animated by quiet, composed rhythms in contrast to the rush of movement in Donatello's *Cantoria* and are carved with a smooth hardness quite different from Donatello's rich textural effects. This more idealized and classical treatment of form is also found in the works of the sculptors Michelozzo (1396–1472), Bernardo Rossellino (1409–1482), and Agostino di Duccio (1418–1481).

The work of Donatello best exemplifies, as it did in the earlier decades, the vitality and intensity of the new style. It is likely that one of the first important private commissions for sculpture was given at this time to Donatello by Cosimo de' Medici, for a bronze statue of *David* (Fig. 9–28) which stood, by the 1460's, in the courtyard of the Medici Palace, together with Donatello's group of *Judith and Holofernes* (1455), symbols of the Florentine love of liberty and hatred of tyrants. In the *David*, Donatello presents a classically proportioned nude with a balance of opposing axes, of tension and relaxation, which

[20] The similarity is the more remarkable since the first fragments of the *Ara Pacis* were not excavated until the sixteenth century.

9–29 DONATELLO. *Erasmo da Narni*, called *Gattamelata*. Bronze. 1446–1447. Padua. (Alinari)

recalls, and is perhaps derived from, Roman copies of Polykleitan statues. Although the body has an Hellenic, almost Praxitelean radiance, the figure is involved in a complex psychological drama unknown to Antique sculpture.

The glance of this youthful, still adolescent hero is not directed primarily toward the severed head of Goliath, but toward his own graceful, sinuous body, as though, in consequence of his heroic deed, he were becoming con-

9–30 DONATELLO. *The Miracle of the Penitent Son*. Bronze relief. High altar, San Antonio, Padua. 1446–1447. (Brogi)

Donatello's equestrian statue (1446–1447) in Padua of the Venetian *condóttiere* Erasmo da Narni, called *Gattamelata* (Fig. 9–29). As a commemorative monument of personal glorification the *Gattamelata* recalls such Roman equestrian statues as the *Marcus Aurelius* on the Campidoglio. The closely knit mass of man and horse, implanted on a lofty elliptical base, has a powerful, stable unity. In Donatello's reliefs in San Antonio in Padua, particularly the *Miracle of the Penitent Son* (Fig. 9–30), he moved away from the austere, intellectual control of the *David*, the *Gattamelata*, or his earlier reliefs toward an impassioned rendering of violent emotional expression and movement. The figures are sketchily indicated in low relief and the crowd is not treated as a group of individuals but as a galvanized mass. Donatello was perhaps the first artist who imbued a group of figures with a single, predominant emotion which transcended and yet possessed each of its members. The most extraordinary examples of Donatello's intense emotional expression are to be seen in his late works, such as his wooden statue of *Mary Magdalene* (Fig. 9–31) in the baptistery of Florence or his *St. John the Baptist* (1457) in the cathedral of Siena. An expressionistic pathos emerges from the nervous, uncompromisingly harsh treatment of the emaciated bodies which is matched in emotional intensity only by the ascetic extremism of certain phases of German and Spanish art.

9–31   DONATELLO. *Mary Magdalene.* Wood. *ca.* 1454. Baptistery, Florence. (Alinari)

ARCHITECTURE

In architecture as in sculpture new directions were sought after the opening decades of the century. In Donatello's work we have seen an intensification of psychological and dramatic tensions. Similarly Brunelleschi imbued his architectural forms with dramatic power by treating them in a more

scious, for the first time, of its beauty, its vitality, and its strength. Man's self-awareness, as we have already seen, this discovery of the self, was a dominant theme in Renaissance art. Mastery and control over the self are shown in sculptural manner, as may be seen in the interior of *Santo Spirito*, begun in 1434 (Fig. 9–32). While these tendencies indicate one of the future directions of Florentine art, another side of Brunelleschi's style, seen most clearly in the *Pazzi Chapel*,[21] is important for understanding the art of the middle of the fifteenth century.

The façade of this building shows an extraordinarily subtle treatment of solid and void, of crystalline lights, cool grays, and shadows interspersed with deft accents of delicate color. The interior shows a far greater complexity and subtlety in the proportions and the articulation of volume marked by the pilasters and moldings in *pietra serena* than does the sacristy that Brunelleschi built at *San Lorenzo* (Fig. 9–14). In this way Brunelleschi intensified the intellectual effect of the building: one may "read" it almost as a geometrical theorem in that it places greater demands on the reason than on the emotions of the observer. There is a sense of physical coolness in the restrained play of *pietra serena* moldings against the white plaster of the wall and in the pure geometry that determines their location. The chapel has an air of austerity, of aloofness, which heightens its grandeur despite its reduced and rather familiar scale.

Similar tendencies can be seen in the architecture of Michelozzo (1396–1472) and of Leon Battista Alberti (1404–1472).[22] These architects were

9–32 BRUNELLESCHI. *Santo Spirito*, Florence. Begun 1434. (Brogi)

among the first to execute private buildings designed to rival the magnificence of ecclesiastical and civic structures. The early Renaissance *palazzi*, made possible by the large private fortunes of the leading Florentine families, express a magnificent confidence in the present. Because almost all the major public architectural projects in Florence were either completed or well on their way to completion before 1440, citizens could further adorn the city only by concentrating on private dwellings. The *Medici-Riccardi Palace* (Fig. 9–33), built by Michelozzo for Cosimo de' Medici beginning in 1444, served such an end. As the home of the ruling family of Florence and as the center of their banking interests, it was used both as palace and fortress,

---

[21] The Pazzi were one of the major rival families of the Medici, remembered particularly for the Pazzi conspiracy of 1478, when Giuliano de' Medici was assassinated at High Mass in front of the altar of San Lorenzo, though Lorenzo the Magnificent, his brother, escaped.

[22] Michelozzo, who has already been mentioned as a sculptor, was also the favorite architect of the Medici. Alberti, although renowned as a humanist who wrote treatises not only on painting and architecture but also on sociology and ethics, was also, among other things, a practicing architect. With Leonardo

da Vinci he exemplifies most completely the Renaissance ideal of the universal man.

9–33 MICHELOZZO. *Medici-Riccardi Palace*. Florence. Begun in 1444 for Cosimo de' Medici and acquired by the Riccardi family in 1659. (Alinari)

expressing at once the strength of the family and a bourgeois reluctance to display wealth ostentatiously.[23] It is a simple, massive structure whose strength is accentuated by the use of rusticated stone on the ground story. Originally there were few openings on this level except for a loggia on the corner to accommodate the family's banking business. For defense the palace turned its back on the street, relying as did the Antique Roman house on an inner court and garden for light and air. In the upper stories of the façade the severity of the ground floor is modified by dressed stone which presents a smoother, less imposing surface with each successive story. The building is essentially a geometric block divided into stories by long, unbroken

[23] Cosimo had rejected Brunelleschi's design for a palace because it seemed to him to be more appropriate for a prince than for his role of first among citizens of the republic.

horizontal stringcourses which give direction, articulation, and coherence to the exterior space of the street. The façade is capped by a great cornice decorated with dentils, egg and dart moldings, and acanthus derived from Classical architecture.

Contemporary with the rise of the Florentine *palazzi* the rich merchant class of Venice expressed similar ambitions in their private dwellings. Venice at this time was unique among Italian city-states for, because of its lucrative trade with the East, it was as much Eastern as Western. Its geographical position — on a group of islands originally chosen as a place of refuge from the Huns — isolated it from other Italian cities, enabled it to develop more individualistically, to cling longer to Medieval styles and delay the coming of the Renaissance. Since the city was free from internal feuds because of its remarkably stable government and free from external foes because of its geographic location, Venetian architects did not, as did the Florentines, give a fortresslike character to their palaces. The Gothic *Ducal Palace* and *Ca d'Oro* (Fig. 8–59), with their light, open tracery, warm color, and rapid movement of light and dark reflected in the water of the canals, are typical of the Venetian love of opulent, pictorial effects. Only much later in the *Vendramin Palace* (1460–1475) (Fig. 9–34) do we see influences similar to those in Florence: the ordering of elements into a classically balanced symmetrical design and a substitution of Classical for Medieval detail. The ground story, with the entrance in the center, serves as a base for the lighter construction above; each story is terminated by a unifying entablature. The façade consists of a central portion of three groups of framed windows separated by single columns on either side and by a single window with double columns at either end. Thus the building

9–34 PIETRO LOMBARDO. *Vendramin Palace*. Venice. 1481.

attains a clear articulation of symmetrical proportion and rhythmic coherence.

In the *Rucellai Palace* in Florence (Fig. 9–35), designed by Alberti, Antique architectural motifs are more fully assimilated. Classic entablatures separate each story, and pilasters between the windows follow the classic superposition of orders seen in the Colosseum (Fig. 6–26). Here these elements create the effect of a tense skeletal framework stretched tightly over the plane of the façade and integrated with it by means of the pattern of carefully calculated breaks between the stones in each of the framed fields. Alberti applied elements of Antique Roman architecture in his buildings with greater enthusiasm and understanding than any other architect of the Early Renaissance. If his projected design for *San Francesco* in Rimini had been completed, he would have converted a Gothic church into a grandiose Renaissance structure culminating in a dome derived in form and meaning from that of the Pantheon. As the building stands, only the façade, incorporating the forms of a Roman triumphal arch, and the sides, with niches recalling Roman tomb structures, were executed according to Alberti's directions. They show qualities of monumental grandeur and intellectual coolness for which we have seen parallels in Brunelleschi and which can similarly be found in the *Rucellai Palace*, where, in the smooth, unified pattern of the façade, Alberti eliminated the textural contrasts of the Medici Palace. He emphasized subtle geometric relationships between the parts and the whole.[24] As

[24] Alberti defined beauty as the adjustment of all parts in proportions, so that one cannot add or subtract or change anything without impairing the harmony of the whole.

9–35 LEON BATTISTA ALBERTI. *Rucellai Palace,* Florence. 1446–1451. (Brogi)

a result the building acquired an aloofness not unlike that of the Pazzi Chapel.

In Alberti's last design, the church of *Sant' Andrea* in Mantua — begun in 1472 — the eastern end, with the choir and transepts forming arms of equal length around the domed crossing, is planned as if it were a self-sufficient, centralized building. This tendency, which we also find in Brunelleschi's plan for *Santo Spirito* (Fig. 9–36), in which the aisles are led uninterruptedly around the transepts and choir, shows the Renaissance preoccupation with the centrally planned building type common in Antique Roman architecture, particularly in temples and other pagan religious structures. The aesthetic, geometric harmony as well as the religious symbolism [25] of the centralized plan made it, according

[25] The basic shape around which a centrally planned building is developed, and which is given architectural expression in the

to Alberti, the ideal form for Christian churches, to which he never referred except by the Antique term of "temples." Although in Santo Spirito and Sant' Andrea the central type has been combined with the Medieval basilical plan, many uncompromisingly centralized churches were built or projected during the Renaissance,[26] culminating in Bramante's and Michelangelo's projects for *St. Peter's* in Rome (Fig. 9–70). In the long run, however, it was Alberti's Sant' Andrea, with its Latin cross plan as well as its treatment of volume, which determined the essential form of most sixteenth- and seventeenth-century Christian churches. Instead of the flat roof and the segmentation of interior space by columnar arcades separating nave and aisles, as in Santo Spirito — a tradition rooted to some extent in Early Christian architecture — Alberti unified interior volumes by covering the nave with a massive coffered barrel vault and by replacing the side aisles with small, subordinate chapels framed by molded arches. Clearly Alberti was emphasizing the Roman principle of vast enclosed volumes in contrast to Brunelleschi's principle of space as defined by the organization of wall surfaces through the careful ordering of decorative members. These two successive phases of Early Renaissance architecture were, in a sense, resolved and integrated during the High Renaissance, particularly in the work of Bramante. Yet before we can approach the definition of Renaissance art in the early years of the sixteenth century,

dome, is the circle. According to Renaissance Neo-Platonic philosophy the circle, most perfect geometric shape, was a symbol for and expressed the divine perfection of God.

[26] The first of these was Brunelleschi's *Santa Maria degli Angeli* in Florence, begun in 1434 but never completed. The purest embodiment of Alberti's ideal church is Giuliano da Sangallo's *Santa Maria delle Carceri* in Prato (1485–1491).

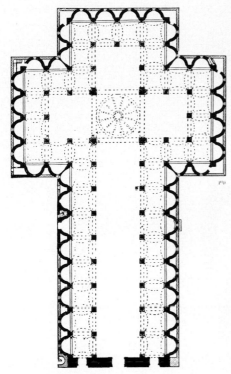

9–36 BRUNELLESCHI. *Plan for Santo Spirito*, Florence. Begun 1434. (Stegmann and Geymuller, *Architecture of the Renaissance in Tuscany,* Architectural Book Publishing Company)

we must complete our investigation of fifteenth-century painting and sculpture.

The Personal Interpretations — Last Third of the Century

SCULPTURE AND PAINTING

Florentine sculpture of the last third of the fifteenth century is an art of personal interpretation of the achievements of preceding generations. One of its new categories was the portrait bust, commissioned by private individuals. The personages recorded by the most subtle carver of the age, Desi-

9–37 ANDREA DEL VERROCCHIO. *Putto Holding a Dolphin.* Marble. *ca.* 1470–1475. Courtyard, Palazzo Vecchio, Florence. (Brogi)

derio da Settignano (1428–1464), lived in a world of exquisite nuances, embodied in marble surfaces of an incredibly delicate translucence and almost liquid softness. As we see in Desiderio's bust of *Marietta Strozzi*, this technique is capable not only of conveying sentiment but also of capturing, with a new intimacy and psychological insight, the fleeting expression through which character may reveal itself. In contrast to Donatello's late work, individualism is here tempered and balanced by a sensibility for classic, ideal beauty, grace, and elegance. Desiderio's values were, in general, shared by Antonio Rossellino (1427–1478), Mino da Fiesole (1430–1484), and Benedetto da Maiano (1442–1497), even though these sculptors, in contrast to Desiderio, tended more and more to empha-

9–38 ANDREA DEL VERRO-
CCHIO. *Colleoni,* a condottiere,
or military leader. Bronze.
1481–1488. Piazza di Santi
Giovanni e Paolo, Venice.
(Anderson)

size the structure and clearly defined massiveness of their figures, thus revealing that they were also the artistic heirs of Luca della Robbia and of Antonio Rossellino's father, Bernardo.

The most important artist to emerge from the milieu of Desiderio was the painter and sculptor Andrea del Verrocchio (1435–1488).[27] Among his sculptures the elegantly poised, graceful bronze *David* (*ca.* 1465) betrays Desiderio's legacy in its refinement and subtle modeling of planes. The form of the later *Putto Holding a Dolphin* (Fig. 9–37), carved in the early 1470's as the centerpiece of a fountain in the courtyard of the Palazzo Vecchio, is conceived with the freedom and daring of a new moment in fifteenth-cen-

tury sculpture. Verrocchio has represented the running and turning action as a spiraling movement reaching out into space in all directions. And since the buoyant little figure is meant to be looked at not from a single, frontal point of view, but from all sides, Verrocchio is here heralding one of the achievements of High Renaissance sculpture.[28]

In Verrocchio's last work, the equestrian statue of *Colleoni* in Venice (Fig. 9–38), which was not erected on its high pedestal until after the artist's

[27] The nickname "Verrocchio," by which he became universally known, means literally "True Eye."

[28] The *putto* type was a typical Renaissance fusion of Antique and Christian motifs, for through the addition of a pair of wings the Hellenistic Amor, or Cupid, could now also be thought of as an angel. Thus he appeared not only in the context of mythological scenes like Titian's *Rape of Europa* but also in profoundly religious pictures, such as Raphael's *Sistine Madonna.*

death, all traces of the gentle and graceful style of Desiderio have disappeared. The commander seems suddenly to shift his whole weight to the stirrups and, in a fit of impassioned anger, to rise from the saddle with a violent twist of his body. Every detail of the form is charged with an exaggerated, brittle tautness, while the diagonal, angular tensions in the composition enhance the impetuous movement and power. Fulfilling the artistic demands of a new generation, the *Colleoni* is a dramatic contrast to the calm monumentality of Donatello's *Gattamelata* (Fig. 9–29).

The changes in Verrocchio's style from the *David* to the *Colleoni* cannot be understood without taking into account the influence of the sculpture of Antonio Pollaiuolo (*ca.* 1431–1498). Also important as a painter and engraver, Pollaiuolo infused the nervous movement and emotional expressiveness of Donatello's late style with a new linear mobility, spatial complexity, and dramatic immediacy. His small-scale group of *Hercules and Antaeus*, not quite eighteen inches high, is a thrilling embodiment of the splendid ferocity and vitality of elemental, physical conflict. The figures are interlocked in a tightly wound coil, and the flickering reflections of light on the dark gouged surface of the bronze contribute to the effect of movement and fluidity.

The panel representing the *Apollo and Daphne* (Fig. 9–39), contemporary with the group of *Hercules and Antaeus*, shows Pollaiuolo not only as a master of anatomy and line, but also of landscape and light. The mythological subject has been imagined so vividly that it has been made part of fifteenth-century life and located in the Arno river valley not far from Florence, whose towers appear in the distance. Instead of relating figures and space in a rationally clear, abstract perspec-

9–39 ANTONIO POLLAIUOLO. *Apollo and •Daphne. ca.* 1475. National Gallery, London. (Courtesy of the Trustees of the National Gallery, London)

tive construction, Pollaiuolo observed man and nature more naturalistically and tended to merge them in a hovering, incandescent atmosphere. This image of the world, not fixed and stable like Masaccio's or Piero della Francesca's, but fluid and changing, may also be seen in the great engraving called the *Battle of the Nudes*. Pollaiuolo here shows the typical Renaissance mastery of several techniques, for, although the engraving is composed only of lines, the figures are sculptural and the plate as a whole has the extraordinary order and vitality of a painting.

Sandro Botticelli (1444–1510) shared Antonio Pollaiuolo's mastery of line and movement, though the more poetic, romantic, and imaginary world

9–40 SANDRO BOTTICELLI. *Dante and Beatrice Leaving Purgatory.* Drawing, illustrating Dante's *Divine Comedy*, Paradise, I. 1492–1497. Kupferstichkabinett, Berlin. (From Lippmann, *Drawings of Sandro Botticelli*, Lawrence and Bullen, 1896)

of his paintings has little in common with the fleeting naturalistic visions of Pollaiuolo. Botticelli's feeling for line finds its purest expression in his drawings for the *Divine Comedy*. His illustrations, particularly of the *Paradiso*, are a mystic, disembodied interpretation of Dante's majestic poem. The opening canto of the *Paradiso* is illustrated (Fig. 9–40) by a delicate silverpoint and pen drawing in which the wraithlike figures of Dante and Beatrice rise effortlessly from the Mount of Purgatory. With the greatest economy Botticelli indicates growth habits of trees swayed by the wind, the far reach of the horizon, and the illimitable space above. He is not concerned with naturalistic representation nor with modeling by light and shade. Here all is movement; the trees bend in a direction opposite to the movement of Dante and Beatrice to heighten the upward surge; the circular

sweep of the trees and the water suggests the rotation of the earth and a path of movement with the figures at its vortex. Botticelli's line flickers, indicating the forms of figures without giving them weight. All is ordered toward an emotional, mystic identification with Dante and Beatrice, who rise as pure soul and pure movement to the empyrean.

Botticelli's interpretation of the *Divine Comedy* shows the influence of Neo-Platonic thought, whose chief exponent, the humanist Marsilio Ficino (1433–1499), was, like Botticelli, a member of the intimate circle around Lorenzo de' Medici (Lorenzo the Magnificent). Ficino believed that the soul could ascend toward a union with God through contemplation of beauty which reveals and manifests the two supreme principles of the Divine: love and light. This approach, so different from the earnest search of the early fifteenth century to comprehend man and the natural world through a rational order, was also expressed in the allegorical pageants which were staged as chivalric tournaments but which revolved completely around allusions to classical mythology. A similar trend is to be found in the poetry of the 1470's and 1480's.

Botticelli's mythological paintings of the *Birth of Venus* (ca. 1485) and the *Garden of Venus*, called the *Primavera* (ca. 1478), were based on a poem by Angelo Poliziano (1453–1494), another humanist of the Medici circle, describing a tournament held in 1475 celebrating Lorenzo the Magnificent's younger brother Giuliano and his mistress Simonetta Vespucci. In the *Birth of Venus*, which in Neo-Platonic terms was the appearance of love in the form of pure, idealized beauty, the goddess, whose features are those of Simonetta, is blown ashore by two wind gods; on the right the nymph Pomona, descended from the ancient Italian goddess of fruit trees, runs to meet her with a white, diaphanous mantle. It is a composition of animation, grace, and movement, conveyed by patterns of musically undulating and fluttering lines in a substanceless, ethereally lighted space.

At this time of crisis in Florentine history, when the iconoclastic reform of Savonarola's protests was about to erupt, Botticelli felt compelled to return, at times, to a formalism which would combine freedom of movement with the rationalism and monumentality of the earlier part of the century — a tradition which had been continued and naturalistically embellished by his more prosaic, pragmatic contemporary Domenico Ghirlandajo (1440–1494). This preoccupation of Botticelli's is already apparent in the clear spatial construction of his early *Adoration of the Magi* (National Gallery of Art, Washington), but its most impressive product was the *"Calumny" of Apelles* (Fig. 9–41), painted about 1495. The small panel is an attempted reconstruction, on the basis of a description in Alberti's *Della pittura*, of a famous lost composition by the Greek painter Apelles. Calumny and Envy, accompanied by Treachery and Deceit, drag an innocent victim before a judge, while Ignorance and Suspicion whisper into the judge's ears, which are those of an ass. At the left naked Truth points toward heaven in protest, thereby implying the futility of man's endeavors to be just except through the contemplation of divine justice — a typically Neo-Platonic conception. She (Truth) is seen by ominous, shrouded Remorse, but remains invisible to the others, who are caught up in the headlong vehemence of their fury. The *istoria* is set in an Antique hall of justice, which signifies Roman dignity and virtue and whose cubically clear architectural masses, together with the calm expanse of sea and sky beyond, stabilize the graceful, undulating movement of the figural group. In its formal properties of movement and stability as well as in its expressive qualities of grace and dignity the *"Calumny" of Apelles* presents significant elements which the fifteenth century bequeathed to the High Renaissance. In its specific content it also reflects the impact of Savonarola, who was demanding that men turn their eyes to God, threatening that, because their self-indulgence and vanity prevented them from seeing divine truth, they could be saved from eternal damnation only by self-denial and repentance. But Botticelli's most remarkable achievement in this painting is the reconciliation of the two conflicting movements, Humanism and Neo-Platonism on one hand with Christian reform on the other — a conflict which constituted one of the major crises of the waning fifteenth century.

9–41 SANDRO BOTTICELLI. *"Calumny"* of Apelles. *ca.* 1485–1490. Uffizi, Florence. (Alinari)

Before this storm broke in 1494, coinciding with the invasion of Italy by the French under Charles VIII and the beginning of the eighteen-year exile of the Medici, Botticelli had been called to Rome by Pope Sixtus IV (1471–1484) to participate in the fresco decoration of the walls of a new building which bore the pope's name, the *Sistine Chapel*. Botticelli was one among several of the most gifted painters of that time who were engaged, between 1481 and 1483, on this project, which consisted of scenes from the life of Moses on one wall and from the life of Christ on the wall opposite. The other artists were the Florentines Domenico Ghirlandajo and Cosimo Rosselli (1439–1507); the Umbrians, Luca Signorelli (1450–1523), Bernardino Pinturicchio (1454–1513), and Pietro Vannuci, called Perugino (1450–1523), the teacher of Raphael. The scenes are composed of compact groups of figures, including portraits of contemporary personages, occupy-

ing a relatively shallow foreground which leads, often rather abruptly, to the large, clear masses of naturalistically rendered architectural or landscape backgrounds. The religious subjects have been represented as dignified, keenly observed contemporary events following each other as an impressive frieze below Michelangelo's majestic ceiling. All the compositions convey a common grandiose air of actuality, summing up many tendencies and achievements of the fifteenth century: its formal monumentality and vigor, its vivacity of movement and psychological expression, and its rare equilibrium between sober, clear-headed realism and splendid decorative opulence.

One artist of the generation of those who decorated the walls of the Sistine Chapel has been remembered above all others. Although his incredible wealth of interests and skills made him the epitome of the universal man of the Renaissance, we are concerned with

Leonardo da Vinci (1452–1519) primarily as an artist. His unquenchable curiosity is best revealed in his voluminous notes, liberally interspersed with sketches on botany, geology, zoology, optics, hydraulic and military engineering, varieties of physical and mechanical science, animal lore, anatomy, perspective, light, and color.[29] Leonardo's great ambition in his painting, as well as in his scientific endeavors, was to discover the laws underlying the flux and processes of nature. With this end in view he also studied man and contributed immeasurably to our physiological and psychological knowledge of ourselves. Leonardo believed that reality in an absolute sense is inaccessible to man, but that we can know reality only through its changing image. Thus he considered the eyes to be our most vital organs and sight our most essential function, since through these man can grasp the image of reality most directly and profoundly. Thus it is possible to understand Leonardo's insistence, stated many times in the course of his notes, that all his scientific investigations were merely directed toward making himself a better painter.

In Leonardo's work, including his (for the most part) unrealized sculptural and architectural projects, we already begin to approach the High Renaissance, for he often anticipated formal solutions of Raphael, Michelangelo, Bramante, and Titian. His concern with human values led him to a study of those gestures and movements which betray the passions of the soul, and finally to a study of movement itself as the most fundamental, concentrated manifestation of life. At the same time

9–42 LEONARDO DA VINCI. Drawing of a *star-of-Bethlehem* and other plants. Red chalk finished in pen and ink. *ca.* 1506. Collection of Her Majesty the Queen, Windsor. (Crown copyright reserved. Royal Library, Windsor)

he searched for a means of clearly organizing his compositions in two dimensions as well as in space. He found this control in the rational organization of space as proposed by the artists of the early fifteenth century. One of his innumerable drawings epitomizes these two tendencies, which he welded into a new synthesis in his art. His *Star-of-Bethlehem* (Fig. 9–42) is more than just the recording of a careful observation of nature. Although the plant is easily recognizable from Leonardo's careful description of it, he has, at the same time, altered its growth habits in order to create a greater impression of movement. This serves both to indicate the growth and development of the plant through time and to satisfy Leonardo's predilection for swirling involuted movement. The leaves on the right side of the plant rise from the central mass and swoop down in the

[29] Leonardo lists these as well as other more specific interests and accomplishments in a letter of self-recommendation which he wrote to Lodovice il Moro, Duke of Milan, in 1481 (see E. Holt, *Literary Sources of Art History*, pp. 169–70).

9–43 LEONARDO DA VINCI. *Madonna of the Rocks*. Begun 1483. Louvre, Paris. (Alinari)

shape of a spiral; those on the left curl down and meet others curling up. The entire plant emerges as a small maelstrom of spiraling movement. These explosive convolutions appear again, engulfing the earth in the cloudbursts of Leonardo's drawings of the *End of the World*, done toward the close of his life. These same characteristics, embodying the archetypal savagery of war, may also be seen in the copies of his lost fresco of the *Battle of Anghiari* (*ca.* 1503–1506).

The antithesis of this love of movement can be found in Leonardo's studies of proportion and particularly in his *Man of Perfect Proportions*. The textual origin of this drawing can be found in Vitruvius' *De architectura*, in which the Roman architect states that a man

of perfect proportions standing erect with his arms outspread can be inscribed in a square, or with his arms raised and legs spread he can be inscribed in a circle. Antiquity exerts its influence here, and yet it is Antiquity modified by the early Renaissance. The proportions utilized by Leonardo and the means for discovering them are drawn essentially from Leon Battista Alberti's *De statua*, just as the perspective studies which fill so many pages of his notebooks are derived from Alberti's *Della pittura*. In order to control the freedom and movement of the latter part of the fifteenth century, Leonardo returned to its earlier achievements of geometry and order.

This mingling of order and movement finds its first expression in Leonardo's unfinished *Adoration of the Magi*.[30] Studies for the painting show him wrestling with the problem of whether to use a relatively shallow space with great freedom in postures and movement or whether to employ the more static poses that the one-point perspective system of the earlier fifteenth century demanded. It is an index of Leonardo's genius that he discovered a solution by which he could combine the positive elements of both systems: freedom of movement within a controlled and ordered space. In the painting as he has left it, the Madonna is in the center, somewhat back from the frontal plane — a position emphasized by the inward movement of the kneeling king on the right. She is encircled by a group of figures who seem to wheel around her in space. In the

[30] The underpainting, in browns, has been laid in; a few of the heads and the Child's figure are quite completely modeled in light and shadow, but the Virgin's and the kings' are only sketched. The painting would have been completed by continuing the modeling and then adding the local color, either in tempera or in the newer oil medium which Leonardo used in his later works.

background horsemen, ruined architecture drawn in perspective, trees, and landscape indicate a deep space and act as foils to the galaxy around the Virgin. Leonardo had set himself both a formal and a psychological problem in this painting: how to express the spatial unity of a dramatic group all of whose movements focus on the more quiet, somewhat isolated central figure, and how to express the emotional unity that binds the dramatic figures together in their adoration of the Christ Child. It is characteristic of the intensity of Leonardo's artistic preoccupations that as soon as he saw that his solutions to these problems had breathed life into the composition he did not feel the craftsman's obligation to finish the painting. This reveals a principle of great interest for an understanding of the creative process, for it means that execution is important only insofar as it reveals the artist's idea.[31]

Various reasons, among them the mounting critical climate of Florence, made Leonardo decide to offer his services, most particularly as a pageant designer, military engineer, and sculptor, to the more prosperous, cosmopolitan Duke of Milan, and, accordingly, he left Florence in 1481. His first painting of the Milanese period, the *Madonna of the Rocks*, in the Louvre (Fig. 9–43), begun in 1483,[32] embodied some of Leonardo's statements concerning the purpose of painting:

[31] This was to lead to the notion that the artist's inspiration can be more directly and spontaneously apprehended in an unfinished than in a finished work. Michelangelo, for instance, deliberately left many of his late sculptures unfinished. As an aesthetic attitude it became one of the important criteria of artistic value in the period of Romanticism, notably in the works of the French painter Eugène Delacroix (1798–1863).

[32] A second version of this painting, executed between about 1495 and 1508, mostly by Leonardo's Milanese pupil Ambrogio de Predis, is in the National Gallery in London.

9–44 LEONARDO DA VINCI. *Mona Lisa.* Portrait of the wife of Zanobi del Giocondo. *ca.* 1503–1506. Louvre, Paris. (Alinari)

A good painter has two chief objects to paint — man and the intention of his soul. The former is easy, the latter hard, for it must be expressed by gestures and the movement of the limbs. . . . A painting will only be wonderful for the beholder by making that which is not so appear raised and detached from the wall.

In other words, modeling with light and shadow and the expression of emotional states were, for Leonardo, the heart of painting. He felt that a somewhat diffused light was particularly useful to attain these ends, a light in which "toward evening or in bad weather I have noticed the features of men and women in the streets and marked what grace and softness can be seen thereon." [33] The figures in the *Madonna of the Rocks* are knit together

[33] *The Notebooks of Leonardo da Vinci,* ed. by Edward MacCurdy, Empire State Book Co., 1935.

9-45 LEONARDO DA VINCI. *Last Supper*. 1495–1497. Refectory of Santa Maria delle Grazie, Milan. The doorway was cut through at a later date. (Pinacoteca di Brera)

into a pyramidal group — an early example of a form typical of the unified spatial ordering in High Renaissance compositions — which emerges by subtle gradations and nuances from the half-light of the cavernous, visionary landscape. Light simultaneously veils and reveals the form of all things. Thus they are immersed in a layer of atmosphere which exists between them and our eyes. Through their modeling they seem to be within our immediate grasp, yet their atmospheric envelope makes them inaccessible to us. We cannot see except what optical vision enables us to see: not a fixed, absolute reality, but only the fluid optical image of reality. What is true of Leonardo's presentation of external form also applies to his interpretation of the inner content of his figures. We are able to penetrate deeply into their character, yet we feel that the essence of their personalities eludes us, that we can never absolutely know them. The most profound and moving embodiment of Leonardo's conception of vision — of

the eye as well as of the mind — and therefore justifiably one of the world's most famous paintings, is the portrait of *Mona Lisa* in the Louvre, painted (*ca.* 1503–1506) after Leonardo had returned to Florence (Fig. 9–44).

While still in Milan Leonardo painted the *Last Supper* (Fig. 9–45). In spite of its ruined state, it is, both formally and emotionally, his most impressive work. Christ and the twelve Disciples are seated in a simple, spacious room, at a long table set parallel to the picture plane. The highly dramatic action of the painting is made still more emphatic by the placement of the group in a quiet setting. The Christ, with outstretched hands, has just said, "One of you will betray me." At this statement a wave of intense excitement passes through the group as each Disciple asks himself, "Is it I?" The force and lucidity with which this dramatic moment is expressed are due to the abstract organization of the composition. In the center the Christ is in perfect repose; isolated from the Disciples, his figure, which is framed by the central window at the back and emphasized by the curved line over the opening (the only curved line in the architectural framework), is the focal point of all lines in the composition. The agitated Disciples are fitted into this framework in four groups, united within themselves and also to one another by the movements of their gestures and postures. The two figures at the ends are more quiet, as if to enclose the over-all movement, which grows more intense as it approaches the figure of Christ, whose calm at the same time halts and intensifies it. Heinrich Wölfflin saw that the classic element in this painting is found in the Christ's silence, for in the silence following his words "the original impulse and the emotional excitement continue to echo and the action is at once momentary, eternal and complete." [34]

Summary

The life, the works, and the artistic reputation of Leonardo da Vinci express both fifteenth- and sixteenth-century ideals. He is at once the paradigm of the universal man exalted by the fifteenth century and the courtly gentleman of the sixteenth, best defined by Baldassare Castiglione in his famous *Il Cortegiano*.

More than any other artist of his time Leonardo brought together the divergent artistic tendencies of the fifteenth century in Italy. His researches into natural phenomena exhibit all the curiosity and wonder of the fifteenth century together with that century's optimistic belief in the power of man's mind to comprehend the world around him. Like Alberti, Leonardo's spiritual predecessor, he seems to have felt that mathematics and logical deductions based on observation of the material world would lead ultimately to the discovery of the principles underlying appearance. This side of Leonardo's artistic personality is most closely allied with the first half of the fifteenth century in Florence, with the problems faced by Masaccio, Brunelleschi, Donatello, and by their artistic heirs Piero della Francesca and Domenico Veneziano. The modes of spatial representation, particularly the one-point perspective construction, and the means of creating monumentality in figures and compositions discovered by these earlier artists reappear in Leonardo's notebooks and early paintings, as the drawings for the *Adoration of the Magi* and the chapter on perspective in his projected treatise on painting clearly show. At the same time Leonardo's own immediate past and his early artistic training made him fully aware of the limitations of these early discoveries. He was concerned not only with spatial construction but also with problems of movement, and in this respect he drew heavily on the art of Pollaiuolo and Botticelli and on his own master, Verrocchio. These two major trends of the fifteenth century — monumentality and mathematically ordered space at the expense of movement on the one hand, and freedom of movement at the expense of monumentality and controlled space on the other — are harmonized and brought into balance in Leonardo's *Last Supper*. This work and Leonardo's career leading up to it are at once a synthesis of the artistic developments of the fifteenth century and a prefiguration of the High Renaissance style of the early sixteenth century in Italy.

[34] Heinrich Wölfflin, *Classic Art*, Phaidon Publishers, New York, 1952, p. 27.

15th Century in the North

During the fifteenth century the differences in artistic style between Italy and the rest of western Europe became strongly marked. Whether the art of France and the Low Countries was a continuation of the Gothic tradition or whether it was a phenomenon similar to the Renaissance in Italy has been debated at considerable length but without any satisfactory conclusion. In architecture, and to a lesser extent in sculpture, there was no clear break with the Gothic tradition as there was in Italy. In fact, throughout western Europe the construction of churches and civic buildings in the Gothic style continued well into the sixteenth century. Examples of architecture and sculpture which may be distinguished from Medieval forms occurred sporadically toward the end of the fifteenth century, but the break became definitive only with the importation of Italianate forms in the sixteenth century. The development of painting presents a more complex problem.

Low Countries

Because Gothic architecture aimed at the elimination of the wall, the northern European painter had no tradition of monumental decoration such as the Italians had produced in their mosaics and frescoes. Like his Medieval predecessor, the painter of the fifteenth century in the north was most often trained in the making of manuscript illuminations and in the naturalistic coloring of sculpture. Herein lies one of the essential differences between the painting of the Low Countries and that of Italy in the fifteenth century. Because of the tradition of fresco painting, the Italian artist tended to conceive his compositions in broad and general terms. He was less interested in detail than was his northern counterpart. Italian panel paintings tend to give the impression of reduced, and portable, frescoes, while many northern panels of the same period seem to be enlarged manuscript illuminations executed on wood instead of parchment.

The northern artist's concern with detail, frequently categorized as "Late Gothic realism," was encouraged and made possible by the development of an oil technique. Traditionally Jan van Eyck is credited with this invention, although the true facts surrounding its early history still remain mysterious. As far as we know, Flemish painters built up their pictures by superimposing a translucent paint layer, called a glaze, on a layer of opaque paint. The binding medium for both pigments had a fast-drying oil as a base. This oil had been known and used by certain painters in the late Middle Ages. The secret of the new technique seems to have been an as yet unidentified supplementary substance which went into the composition of the glazes. Thus painters were able to create colors seemingly lit from within and richer than had previously been possible. As a result, northern painting of the fifteenth century is characterized by a deep, intense tonality, glowing light, and hard, enamel-like surfaces quite unlike the high-keyed color, sharp light, and rather matte surfaces of Italian tempera.

The differences between the painting of Italy and northern Europe are emphasized by the fact that, when oil painting spread to Italy after the mid-century, it did not radically affect Italian sensibility to form. Although the color of Italian painting became richer, particularly in Venice, the new medium, which in time completely replaced tempera, was exploited toward typically Italian ends — the creation of an atmospheric landscape space and of figures that blend with the landscape. On the whole, artistic communication between the north and south of Europe seems to have been limited to a few individuals throughout the fifteenth century. Both areas tended to develop independently of each other. By the beginning of the sixteenth century, however, the forms of Italian art had moved north and were beginning to transform the local Late Medieval traditions.

The political background against which the development of northern fifteenth-century art unfolded was not unlike that of Italy. In the beginning of the century the commercial free cities dominated the scene. Slowly they fell under the rule of princes until the beginning of the sixteenth century saw the emergence of France as a nation, under the centralized government of her king, and the growth of the Hapsburg empire.

As in Italy the wealth and leisure necessary to encourage the growth of the arts was based on commerce. Among the commercial cities of the north, Bruges was the most important and, like Florence, derived her wealth from the wool trade and from banking. Until late in the fifteenth century an arm of the North Sea, now silted up, reached inland to Bruges. Here ships brought raw wool from England and carried away with them the fine manufactured woolen cloth famous throughout Europe. The wool trade brought bankers, and Bruges became the financial clearinghouse for all of northern Europe. In her streets merchants from Italy and the Near East rubbed shoulders with traders from Russia and Spain. Despite the prominence of her sister cities — Ghent, Louvain, and Ypres — Bruges so dominated Flanders that the Duke of Burgundy chose to make the city his capital and moved his court there from Dijon.

Coexistent with a development of commerce and wealth almost modern in tone, the social structure of the north adhered to the hierarchies of the Middle Ages. The nobles and clergy continued to rule, even though the true source of wealth and power was the bourgeoisie. This large middle class, in turn, was still organized and controlled by the guild system which had taken form in the early Middle Ages. In the north the guild dominated the life of the average man to an even greater extent than in Italy. To pursue a craft, a man had to belong to the guild controlling that craft — the painter, for example, to the Guild of St. Luke, which included the saddlers, glassworkers, and mirror-workers as well. To secure membership in the guild the aspiring painter was apprenticed in boyhood to a master, with whom he lived as a son, and who taught him the fundamentals of his craft: how to make implements, how to prepare panels with gesso, and how to mix colors, oils, and varnishes. When the youth had mastered these problems and had learned to work in the traditional manner of his master, he usually spent several years as a journeyman, working in various cities, observing and gaining ideas from other masters. He was then eligible to become a master and was admitted to the guild. Through the guild he obtained commissions; the guild inspected his painting for honest materials and workmanship, and the guild secured him adequate payment. The result of such a system was the solid craftsmanship which characterizes the best work of Flanders as well as Italy.

Like their Italian contemporaries, northern European painters explored the visible world and rejected many of the schematic forms of the Middle Ages.

9–46 JAN AND HUBERT VAN EYCK. *Adoration of the Mystic Lamb.* Ghent Altarpiece. St. Bavon, Ghent. 1426–1432. (Copyright A.C.L., Brussels)

But while the Italian reconstructed the visible through a rational order based on mathematically determinable relationships of solids and voids, the northerner's interest in reality expressed itself in a passionate desire to translate into form the minutiae of appearance. The firm linear design and deep, resonant color, however, create a unity in these works which transcends the mere reproduction of objects in nature.

Jan van Eyck (*ca.* 1390–1441) was essentially a product of the late Middle Ages, but through his contributions to the art of painting he went beyond the older traditions to found new traditions of his own. His *Ghent Altarpiece* (Fig. 9–46) [35] was painted at

about the same time as Masaccio's frescoes in the Brancacci Chapel. Some of the essential differences between Flemish and Italian painting of the fifteenth century can best be seen by contrasting Van Eyck's *Adam and Eve* (Fig. 9–47) with Masaccio's *Expulsion* (Fig.

older brother, Hubert, whose role in beginning the altarpiece is given by an inscription later repainted. The large size of the altarpiece, approximately 14½ × 11 feet, would seem to indicate collaboration of some sort and perhaps successive changes in the design of the whole. For a fascinating account of recent discoveries in the structure of the *Ghent Altarpiece,* see Paul Coremans and others, *L'Agneau Mystique au Laboratoire,* De Sikkel, Antwerp, 1953; a summary in English was published as "Studies in Conservation" in the *Journal of the International Institute for the Conservation of Museum Objects,* Vol. 1, 4, 1954, pp. 160–61.

[35] Scholars are still unable definitively to disentangle what part was executed by Jan's

9–10). Despite the greater subtlety and completeness of modeling possible through the use of oil glazes, the Flemish figures carry strong Medieval overtones. The nude is considered not only as a faithful record of human "being" but as a symbol of the sin redeemed by the Lamb of the central panel. The tragedy of man's fate so prominent in Masaccio does not emerge.

As a whole, this work is an outstanding example of the large folding altarpiece typical of the north, with shifting meanings for the observer as the unfolding of the panels reveals new subjects in sequence. The very form of the folding altarpiece expresses the Medieval tendency to uncover truth behind natural appearances, to clothe thought in allegory, to find "essential" meaning hidden beneath layers of secondary meanings. When closed, the Ghent altarpiece shows the Annunciation — the moment of the incarnation of redemption — and below it portraits of the donor of the altarpiece and his wife, as well as simulated statues of St. John the Baptist and St. John the Evangelist. When opened, it reveals a sumptuous, colorful representation of the Medieval conception of the redemption of man. In the central panel of the lower register, the community of saints comes from the four corners of the earth, through an opulent landscape, toward the altar with the Lamb, from whose heart blood flows into a chalice, and toward the octagonal fountain of life into which flows the "pure river of water of life, clear as crystal, proceeding out of the throne of God and of the Lamb" (Rev. 22:1). In the upper register God the Father, in a resplendent red mantle, is flanked by the Virgin, represented as the Queen of Heaven with a "crown of twelve stars upon her head," and by St. John the Baptist, who is pointing to the figure of God, thus acting as a mediator between man and the divinity. The soft texture of

9–47   JAN VAN EYCK. *Adam* and *Eve*, from the Ghent Altarpiece. 1426–1432. (Copyright, A.C.L., Brussels)

hair, the luster of pearls, the gleam of other jewels, in fact all the details in these figures, are indicated with extraordinary realism and a love of rich display. Equally sumptuous in detail, the Adoration scene is also organized as a symmetrical composition with the Lamb as its focal point. Two concentric arcs, composed of the angels kneeling at the altar and the prophets and apostles surrounding the fountain, swing about the axis on which the altar is centered, while, from the outer circle, the groups of saints radiate toward the four corners.

The organization of realistic detail into a transcendent whole is perhaps most clearly seen in Jan van Eyck's *Madonna of the Canon van der Paele*. Here we find united the pious aura of his *Annunciation* (National Gallery, Washington), the genre detail of the *Arnolfini Wedding* (National Gallery, London), and the exactness of his portraiture. The figures are grouped in a manner somewhat reminiscent of the many *sacra conversazione* which appeared in Florence at about the same time. The architecture, the richly decorated rug, and the figures all lead the eye to the Madonna and Child, who sit in the apse of a church. The rich texture of her red robes makes a strong contrast with the white surplice of the kneeling Canon van der Paele. A similar contrast plays across the space between the dull glint from the armor of St. George and the rich brocades of St. Donatus. Despite the apparently uncontrolled exuberance of color, Van Eyck sagaciously disposed it in a manner which isolates each form from its neighbor. He thus unified the composition through harmonies which relate the forms to each other and to the whole. The judicious use of detail enabled the artist to convey even more elaborate symbols than had his Medieval predecessors; thus the arms of the Virgin's throne and the historiated capitals of the pilasters behind her make reference to the Old Testament prefigurations of the coming of Christ that were so well known throughout the Middle Ages. This same love of detail gives us a greater insight into the character of the donor. The eyeglasses and wrinkled face indicate his age, the open missal his piety. On his face we read the contented look of a man so sure of himself and his position that he can regard divinity with neither fear nor wild exultation. As an individual and as an artist Van Eyck indicated his pride of creation by including his own portrait, seen as a reflection in the shield of St. George.

Rogier van der Weyden (*ca.* 1400–1464) continued the traditions begun by Jan van Eyck with important modifications of his own. His early training under the Master of Flémalle [36] at Tournai gave his art a more emotional and rhythmic direction than that of Van Eyck. Throughout his career Rogier invented new motifs and compositions that not only had a lasting effect on the art of the Low Countries but also influenced German artists such as Martin Schöngauer (d. 1491) and Michael Wohlgemuth, Albrecht Dürer's master.

In Rogier's *Descent from the Cross* (Fig. 9–48) the emphasis is on emotional content. He made no attempt to create a deep landscape space, as did Jan van Eyck, but compressed the figures and the action onto a shallow stage to concentrate our attention. Detail is subordinated to a careful balancing of masses and a formal organization based on curvilinear rhythms. A common emotion runs through the group, uniting it psychologically. The figures are reminiscent of those in carved wooden altarpieces of the period, such as Veit Stoss's altar for the Church of Our Lady in Cracow, Poland (1477–1489).

While Rogier was primarily an emo-

[36] Although the works of this painter constitute a well-defined artistic personality, he is difficult to identify by name, though it has been suggested that he was Robert Campin.

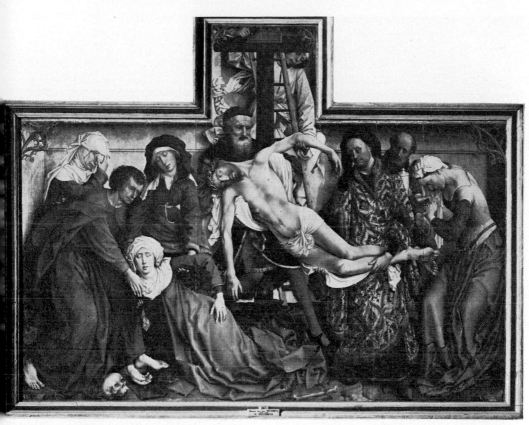

9–48 ROGIER VAN DER WEYDEN. *Descent from the Cross. ca.* 1435. Prado, Madrid. (Museo del Prado)

tional painter, he was capable not only of the intense, unrelenting pathos of the *Descent from the Cross* but also of the gentle restraint and serene intimacy which we feel in the central panel of his *Bladelin Altarpiece* (Fig. 9–49). Here our eyes find release from the hushed concentration of the foreground in the typically Flemish detailed perfection of the landscape (where, on the left, an angel announces the birth to the shepherds) and the stately town in the background. In contrast to the *Descent* Rogier's altarpiece deliberately emphasizes spatial recession by setting the architecture into space at a slant, so that we are immediately led into the distance. An atmosphere of stillness and equilibrium is maintained by the quiet composition of the figures of the Virgin, Joseph, and Peter Bladelin, the donor, who form a lucidly spaced triangular pattern around the Infant Child.

In the words of Erwin Panofsky,

Roger's world is at once physically barer and spiritually richer than Jan van Eyck's. Where Jan observed things that no painter has ever observed, Roger felt and expressed emotions and sensations — mostly of a bitter or bittersweet nature — that no painter had ever recaptured. The smile of his Madonnas is at once evocative of motherly affection and full of sad foreboding. The expression of his donors is not merely collected but deeply pious.[37]

Among the works of the ensuing generation of Flemish painters, those

[37] E. Panofsky, *Early Netherlandish Painting,* p. 249.

of Hugo van der Goes (*ca.* 1440–1482) are characterized by a personal transformation and distortion of rationalism similar to that of Botticelli and Pollaiuolo in Florence. In the central panel of his large *Portinari Altarpiece* (Fig. 9–50),[38] a new use of color characterized by silvery-gray tonality is added to the emotional expressiveness of Rogier and the sumptuous detail of Van Eyck. The triangle of Rogier's *Bladelin Altarpiece* appears again in the Virgin and angels surrounding Christ, but the organization becomes more complex with the introduction of diagonal movements initiated by St.

[38] This deeply moving altarpiece was commissioned by Tommaso Portinari, the representative of the Medici bank in Bruges. The donor appears with his wife and children on the flanking wings of the altarpiece. Shortly after its completion in 1476, the panel was sent by him to adorn the high altar in the chapel of the Hospital of Santa Maria Nuova in Florence. Its detailed naturalism, particularly in the heads of the shepherds, had a considerable influence on Florentine painters, as is shown most clearly in Domenico Ghirlandajo's *Adoration of the Magi* of 1485.

Joseph and the group of shepherds. In the manner of Jan van Eyck, the symbolism is enriched by the inclusion of a sheaf of wheat to indicate Bethlehem, a harp in the tympanum of the building at the rear signifying the palace of David, and bouquets of iris and columbine symbolic of the sorrows of Mary. But the rational spatial organization of Van Eyck is distorted for expressive ends; the floor of the stable seems to be tipped up in relation to the plane of the ground behind it. Nor are the figures controlled by a rational scale. The shepherds who appear to be farther back in space than the Virgin are represented as the same size or larger. These apparent inconsistencies indicate an intensely subjective, visionary conception of the event.

The pietistic fervor of a Hugo van der Goes, great as it may be, is often characteristic of the end of a period. Such was the case in the Low Countries. The innovations of Jan van Eyck and Rogier van der Weyden were beginning to lose their force under the

9–50 HUGO VAN DER GOES. *Adoration of the Shepherds.* Central panel of the Portinari Altarpiece. *ca.* 1476. Uffizi, Florence. (Alinari)

pressure of the Italian Renaissance. The spread of literary humanism had brought with it the artistic humanism of Italy. By the end of the century Italianate elements were introduced into the paintings of the Low Countries, resulting in a strange mixture which persisted on into the sixteenth century until the local traditions were finally overcome by Italian forms.

Along with Hans Memling (*ca.* 1435–1494) and Joos van Ghent (active 1460–1480), who tended, however, toward elongated, slightly archaizing forms, Gerard David (*ca.* 1460–1523) clearly indicates the transitional style of the end of the fifteenth century. A native of Oudewater, he spent most of

his life in Bruges, where he absorbed some of the more superficial aspects of Jan van Eyck's work. His *Judgment of Cambyses* shows a corrupt judge seated on the bench listening to the king who confronts him with an enumeration of his crimes. The subject was a popular one in the Low Countries; both Rogier van der Weyden and Dirck Bouts had executed similar panels for the cities of Brussels and Louvain. However, in the midst of this Medieval setting with the gorgeous northern robes of the king and his courtiers we find discordant elements introduced from the Italian Renaissance and from Roman Antiquity. The genre detail of the scratching dog contrasts strangely

9–51　JEAN FOUQUET. *Marriage of the Virgin*, from the Book of Hours of Etienne Chevalier. 1452–1460. Musée Condé, Chantilly. (Giraudon)

with the Italianate *putti* holding garlands of fruit and with the two roundels derived from Roman cameos. The comparatively austere style of the Italian Renaissance could be assimilated only with difficulty by an artist saturated with the richness of northern painting. A fusion of the two styles became possible only in the period of Mannerism, later in the sixteenth century.

France

In France there was no wealthy bourgeoisie, comparable to that in the Low Countries, localized in strong towns and interested in fostering the arts. For France the Hundred Years' War had been a deterrent to economic enterprise or stability. During the fifteenth century the anarchy of the wars and the weakness of the kings resulted in a group of rival duchies. The strongest of these, the duchy of Burgundy, spread into the Low Countries by marriage and political alliance until it became essentially Flemish, particularly in the art commissioned by the court. In France artists joined the retinues of the wealthier nobility — the dukes of Berry, Bourbon, and Nemours — and sometimes the royal court, where they were able to continue to develop an art which is typically French despite its regional variations. The French painter, though naturalistic, was not so insistent upon detail as the Flemish and German artist. He had a larger, more selective way of seeing his world and a greater facility in schematic organization. His predilection for poise and gravity, for an easy flow of line, and for suave rhythms lent an air of graciousness to his paintings. Behind French painting of the fifteenth century we sense the great architectural sculpture of the twelfth and thirteenth centuries; at times we can even discern a deliberate revival of this monumental tradition.

Jean Fouquet (*ca.* 1420–1481) is the outstanding French artist of the fifteenth century. During his career he worked for Charles VII, for the duke of Nemours, and for Etienne Chevalier, the king's minister of finance and a member of the rising bourgeoisie. Between 1445 and 1447 Fouquet was in Italy, where he painted a portrait (now lost) of Pope Eugene IV and became acquainted with Italian art. His *Marriage of the Virgin* (Fig. 9–51), from the Book of Hours of Etienne Chevalier, immediately suggests Ghiberti (cf. Fig. 9–9), Fra Angelico's frescoes in the Chapel of Nicholas V, and Piero della Francesca, whose influence is even more clearly seen in the *Visitation* from the same manuscript. The architectural background is An-

9–52　PIETÀ. *ca.* 1460. School of Avignon. Louvre, Paris. (Alinari)

tique in inspiration, obviously derived from a Roman triumphal arch. The twisted columns also recall Fouquet's visit to Rome, where a similar column was displayed in Old St. Peter's as a relic from the temple of Solomon. Although the perspective construction is not completely consistent, its inspiration is Italian, as is the figure of the disappointed suitor breaking a rod over his knee. But the vivid, amusing contrast between him and the phlegmatic, rotund suitor on the left, which served as a kind of staged prologue or accompaniment to the ceremony, has been painted with a typically northern predilection for specific detail. Similarly, the drapery of the Virgin has the long, sweeping folds of French fourteenth-century sculpture. One of Fouquet's great achievements was that, on the basis of the great French tradition of

Gothic sculpture and illumination, he arrived at a personal and undeniably monumental synthesis between the Flemish sensitivity for recording the world of nature and the Italian gift for ordering it.[39]

A strong Gothic, Late Medieval tendency still dominated much of French fifteenth-century painting. In Fouquet's own work it informs the hieratic, immobile compositions of his *Ma-*

[39] Such a synthesis is, however, also a typical and, one might even say, unique characteristic of French, most particularly of Parisian, culture. Arthur Koestler recognized this when he had Monsieur Anatole, in *The Age of Longing,* say that "in the exact spot [where Paris now stands] the ancient road from Rome pierced the waterway of the Seine. Here the North was fertilized by the Mediterranean, and everything that has happened [in Paris] since is a continuation of that event."

9–53 STEPHAN LOCHNER. *Madonna in the Rose Garden.* ca. 1430–1435. Wallraf-Richarts Museum, Cologne. (Bildarchiv, Rh. Museum, Cologne)

Holy Jerusalem are silhouetted against the luminous, golden background. The simplified, harsh shapes of the main group have been arranged in powerfully expressive, blocklike patterns. The figures are bathed in glowing light that emanates from the gold background. The emotional intensity of their grief is expressed so that it transcends the limits of time and place and attains a symbolic grandeur. As in the Low Countries, native French traditions were to be replaced, beginning in the early sixteenth century, by those of the Italian Renaissance. As a result of the French invasions of Italy and the consequent importation of Italian artists to execute royal commissions, French art became the most Italianate in northern Europe.

Germany

To an even greater extent than in France, the development of German painting of the fifteenth century was strongly colored by the achievements of Flemish painting. In northern Germany the influence of Jan van Eyck joined forces with the tradition of the International style to produce the gentle, pictorially ornate world of delicacy and charm which characterizes the works of Stephan Lochner (*ca.* 1405–1451), the leading master of the school of Cologne. He was noted for his many compositions of the idyllic theme of the *Madonna in the Rose Garden* (Fig. 9–53), which seems particularly suited to his sophisticated and refined sensibilities. Sometimes referred to as the "Soft" style because of its feminine suavity and curvilinear rhythm, Lochner's manner was very different from the sculptural, blocky "Hard" style of southern Germany as we find it in the work of Conrad Witz (*ca.* 1400–1447). Although the *Miraculous Draught of Fish* (Fig. 9–54) by this remarkable painter also shows Flemish tendencies in the meticulous, naturalistic study of

donna and Child with Angels in the museum at Antwerp (*ca.* 1450) and of the late *Pietà* in the parochial church at Nouans (*ca.* 1470–1475). Untouched by the humanism of the Italian Renaissance, this tradition was preserved with tenacious reverence in the south of France. Among its outstanding examples are the huge, colorful *Coronation of the Virgin* (1453–1454) by Enguerrand Charonton and the famous *Pietà* (*ca.* 1460) of the school of Avignon in the Louvre (Fig. 9–52). The *Coronation* is as encyclopedic in its program as the carved tympana of the French cathedrals and as resplendent in its execution as Van Eyck's Ghent Altarpiece, though the character of its forms is more flat, angular, and abstract. In the great *Pietà* the donor, with his gnarled, oaken face, kneels at the left; behind him the towers of the

9–54 CONRAD WITZ. *The Miraculous Draught of Fish.* 1444. Musée d'Art et d'Histoire, Geneva. (Musée d'Art et d'Histoire)

the landscape, houses, and reflections in the water, there is an Italianate simplification and monumentality in the design and spatial organization of the composition. It is one of the first pictures of the Renaissance in which the landscape not only predominates over the figures but is also the representation of a specific place — the shores of Lake Geneva, with the town of Geneva on the right and the white ranges of the Alps in the far distance. In the latter part of the fifteenth century the "Hard" style became the vehicle for complex, spiky patterns, related to Gothic lineality, in the engravings and paintings of Martin Schöngauer

(d. 1491). While this artist looked mainly to Flemish art, particularly to the expressive manner of Rogier van der Weyden, the Italian element in German painting received an intensely personal interpretation in the expressionistic use of sculptural figures and perspective foreshortening in Michael Pacher's paintings (*ca.* 1435–1498).

Spain and Portugal

The elaborately ornamental Gothic tradition persisted in fifteenth-century painting in Spain. The foremost masters of this rich, glittering style were Jaime Huguet (d. 1492) and Bartolomé

Bermejo (active 1470–1498), although in the spatial compositions of his later work Bermejo showed a clear awareness of the principles of Italian art. But despite a considerable influx of Italian artists during the fourteenth and fifteenth centuries, Spanish painting remained closer to that of northern Europe than to that of Italy. As in Germany, the predominant and increasingly significant influence toward the end of the century was that of Flanders. This is especially apparent in the works of Fernando Gallego (active 1467–1507). One of the painters of greatest individual expressive power and temperament in the Iberian peninsula was the Portuguese Nuño Gonçalves (d. 1471). His mastery in composing broad, simplified shapes and in the creation of a timeless, abstract emotional grandeur make him comparable only to the painter of the Avignon *Pietà*.

Summary

During the fifteenth century the humanistic values of the Renaissance had been developed predominantly, though not exclusively, in Italy, and they did not become the commonly accepted property of all of Europe until the following century. In the Low Countries and France, as well as in Germany and the Iberian peninsula, the fifteenth century was still dominated by the institutions and attitudes — political, social, and cultural — of the Middle Ages. The art of these countries continued under the shadow of the Gothic cathedral, and only with the formation of the Hapsburg empire, the spread of humanistic learning, and the imminence of the Reformation was this shadow dispelled sufficiently to permit a general assimilation of the new principles of Italian art.

The High Renaissance in Italy

Before the end of the fifteenth century Florence lost her unique position of leadership in the arts, for the innovations of her artists had become the property of Italian artists regardless of political boundaries. This is not to suggest that Florence no longer produced the giants of an earlier age. Leonardo and Michelangelo called themselves Florentines even though they spent a great part of their lives outside the city, and the turning point in Raphael's artistic education occurred as a result of his experience of Florentine art. Moreover, Florence shared with Rome the beginnings and growth of Mannerism, a style which was to dominate western Europe throughout the sixteenth century.

But now it was Rome which began to claim the artistic pre-eminence formerly enjoyed by Florence. A series of powerful and ambitious popes who wished to embellish the Eternal City drew many artists to Rome and provided them with challenging tasks. At the same time Venice, restricted in her trade with the East as a result of the fall of Constantinople in 1453, began to expand on the Italian peninsula. Contact with her neighbors had opened the door to the Renaissance, which, already highly developed on the mainland, now rapidly took root and quickly flourished along her canals. Therefore our discussion of the High Renaissance must move from the confines of Tuscany to include almost all of Italy north of Rome. And with the advent of Mannerism, a truly international style, our scope must be broadened to include most of western Europe.

The High Renaissance in Italy held sway for no longer than twenty years — from the turn of the sixteenth century to the death of Raphael. Yet its limits must be moved back to include Leonardo's *Madonna of the Rocks* (Louvre, 1483–1485; National Gallery of London, 1495–1506) and *Last Supper* (1495–1497) and must be extended well toward the middle of the sixteenth century to include Titian (1477–1576).

The art of this period can generally be characterized by a calm grandeur, order, and balance. In painting, figures move with stately grace and measured gestures through large and airy spaces. In groups of figures, the same slow and simplified movement binds them together. Every part is ordered by an intellectual, formal logic in an indissoluble unity. Sculpture and architecture as well were influenced by this desire for unity; the style of the period demanded that each work of art be an harmoniously self-sufficient entity. At the same time, this calm and order did not lead to monotony, for the artist was concerned with a rich variety that had neither the naïveté of the Early Renaissance nor the capriciousness of Mannerism. High Renaissance style is one of active equilibrium, balancing complex and manifold contrasts. It possessed a vitality and richness which embodied or implied elements of the later Mannerist as well as of the Baroque styles. Because of this all-embracing scope and the nobility of its statement, the High Renaissance style has been called classic; it is stable without being static, varied without

being confused, and dignified without being dull.[40] As in Greece, this classic moment, which for a brief span unified and balanced the conflicting experiences of a people, was difficult to maintain. In a changing world the artist might either repeat the compositions and forms of the moment in a sterile academic manner, or revolt from it by denying or exaggerating its principles. For these reasons the High Renaissance was of short duration.

PAINTING AND SCULPTURE

The artist most typical of the High Renaissance is Raphael (1483–1520). His growth retraced the tendencies of the fifteenth century, stated most clearly a High Renaissance style, and prepared the way for Mannerism. Born in a small town in Umbria near Urbino, Raphael probably learned the first rudiments of his art from his father, Giovanni Sanzio, a provincial painter connected with the court of Federigo da Montefeltro. While still a child he was apprenticed to Perugino, who had been trained in Verrocchio's shop with Leonardo. In Umbria, Perugino had developed a personal style quite different from that of his more gifted contemporary. In his paintings gently swaying, cylindrically simplified figures of restrained bearing and softly eloquent sentiment, and quiet, dignified architectural settings are shown against the undulating slopes, broad valleys, and tree-softened skylines of the landscape around Perugia. The most significant formal quality of these works is the harmony of their spatial composition. Perugino's lingering influence on the young Raphael can be clearly seen in the *Madonna and Child with a Goldfinch*, painted shortly before 1504, in

[40] The most sympathetic and illuminating discussion of the High Renaissance style in Italian art is Heinrich Wölfflin's *Classic Art*.

9–55 RAPHAEL SANZIO. *The Marriage of the Virgin.* 1504. Brera, Milan. (Alinari)

which we find the same subdued coloring, circular forms, and gentle landscapes as in Perugino's Madonnas. The graceful gesture of the hand holding the book, the pious glance of the Christ Child, and the modish high brow and small mouth of the Virgin are reflections of the suave charm of Perugino which Raphael soon discarded as he moved more and more away from his master's influence.

Raphael's greater debt to his master was the means of controlling and harmonizing the construction of space. Raphael's *Marriage of the Virgin* (Fig. 9–55) is closely modeled on Perugino's fresco of *Christ Delivering the Keys to St. Peter,* painted in the Sistine Chapel in 1481. Raphael used the perspective grid of the pavement, certain architectural elements, and the arrangement of

figures of his master, therewith acquiring some of Perugino's awkwardness in the integration of figures with the space around them. Both figure groups occupy the front of the composition, where they inhabit a narrow strip directly behind the picture plane. Yet, despite the difficulties caused by his obvious borrowings, Raphael was already beginning to show signs of his future greatness. Although scarcely twenty-one, he was able to recognize and remedy some of the weaknesses of Perugino's composition. By reducing the number of figures and their architectural accompaniment, he was able to concentrate their action. He replaced the spidery, agitated figures with which Perugino attempted to fill the empty space behind the major figures by fewer and calmer ones which, through their color and silhouette, more effectively link foreground and background.

Four years in Florence, 1504 to 1508, gave Raphael a new stimulus. Here in the home of the Renaissance he discovered that the style of painting he had so painstakingly learned from Perugino was already outmoded. The two arch-rivals and titans of the period, Leonardo and Michelangelo, were engaged in an artistic battle whose repercussions were to last for centuries. Crowds flocked to Santissima Annunziata to see the recently unveiled cartoon for Leonardo's *St. Anne, Madonna, and Christ Child.* Michelangelo replied with his *Doni Tondo* (Fig. 9–59).[41] Both artists were commissioned to decorate the walls of the Sala del Consiglio in the Palazzo Vecchio, Leonardo with the *Battle of Anghiari* and Michelangelo with the *Battle of the Cascina.* Although neither artist completed his

[41] The *tondo,* or circular composition, became popular, especially for representations of the Madonna and Child, about the middle of the fifteenth century. It was used in painting and sculpture mainly by Florentine artists, though it also occurs in the work of Raphael and the Mannerists.

task and although nothing is left of their labors today, the effect on artists in Florence, and especially on one as gifted as Raphael, must have been considerable.

Under the influence of Leonardo, Raphael began to modify the Madonna compositions he had learned in Umbria. The small *Cowper Madonna* (Fig. 9–56) shows how he began to place the Madonna within rather than in front of the landscape. Raphael altered Perugino's circular compositions by relating the figures to each other in a more unified fashion through the use of the right angles of a square complicated by diagonal movements of pose and glance. The somber modeling of the flesh tones in the *Madonna with a Goldfinch* is replaced by a more subtle Leonardesque modeling. The whole tonality of the panel is lighter and brighter, enhancing the airy effect and feeling of spaciousness.[42]

The *Deposition of Christ* (Fig. 9–67), painted in 1507, demonstrates most clearly the impact of Florentine painting on Raphael's art and, at the same time, underscores the rapidity with which he absorbed these new influences. When Atalanta Baglioni, the wife of the tyrant of Perugia, commissioned this painting, she probably had in mind a *Deposition* similar to one (now in the Pitti) completed by Perugino in 1495 while Raphael was still in his shop. Raphael, however, was no longer interested in the rather obvious sentiment with which Perugino had

[42] Further indication of Florentine influences on Raphael can be seen in the *Madonna del Cardellino* (*ca.* 1505) in the Uffizi and the *Belle Jardinière* (*ca.* 1507–1508) in the Louvre. In both, Raphael has used the pyramidal composition of Leonardo's *Madonna of the Rocks*. The figure of the Christ Child in both paintings is, on the other hand, strongly reminiscent of Michelangelo's *Bruges Madonna* (Fig. 9–1). We may also note the influence of the *Mona Lisa* on Raphael's portrait of *Maddalena Doni* (*ca.* 1506–1507) in the Uffizi.

9–56 RAPHAEL SANZIO. *Small Cowper Madonna.* After 1504. Widener Collection, National Gallery of Art, Washington, D. C. (National Gallery)

transposed a sculptural theme into painting. In Raphael's composition the crosses are starkly outlined against a distant hill, their harshness contrasting with the soft silhouettes of the trees. Instead of the flaccid, gentle Christ of Perugino — a kneeling attendant seems to be expecting him to speak — Raphael's Christ is completely without life. He weighs heavily on the men who bear his body with straining muscles. His face still bears the marks of recent pain. The softness of Raphael's Umbrian period has been replaced by an interest in muscular figures and great exertion; the sweetness of his earlier compositions by an almost harsh virility emphasized by his strong use of color. The heritage of Masaccio and Pollaiuolo as well as the Florentine love of Antiquity — the Magdalene rushes forward like an officiant from a Roman sarcophagus — bear new fruit in this panel. Raphael's debt to Florentine painting is even more obvious in the seated figure who receives the falling Virgin. Here he has reversed the pose of the Madonna in Michelangelo's *Doni Tondo*, completed some three or four years earlier.

By 1508 Raphael had accepted the elements of Florentine painting most suited to his own inclinations, although he had not as yet wholly assimilated them. At no time did he copy the compositions of his elders (with the possible exception of rapid sketches in his notebooks), but rather chose ideas, forms, and motifs to create the personal monumental style which he was to develop further in Rome.

We must interrupt our account of Raphael's career at this point to follow briefly the course that Florentine painting took upon his departure in 1508.

The High Renaissance style in Florence was carried on by a group of painters headed by Andrea del Sarto (1486–1531) and Fra Bartolommeo (1475–1517). These painters belonged to the generation following those who had worked on the walls of the Sistine Chapel. Working along the lines of the monumental tendency of Florentine painting, these artists sought to achieve animation as well as solemnity by enriching and varying the postures of figures in space while at the same time balancing their opposing movements in clear, stable masses. Through their modeling by light and shade, based on Leonardo's, they created figures in fully rounded relief emerging out of a containing atmosphere. Deep, full-bodied colors enhance the measured, vital rhythm of their compositions. After an early preoccupation with the grouping of figures, usually in a space clearly defined by architectural settings, both Andrea del Sarto and Fra Bartolommeo began to explore, toward the end of

their careers, expressive possibilities which were often curiously willful and personal. In this way they were instrumental in preparing the ground for the Mannerist style.

We may now return to Raphael, who was called to Rome by Pope Julius II in 1509, and there achieved the most complete embodiment of the classic style of the High Renaissance in his paintings for the *Stanza della Segnatura* [43] in the Vatican. The young painter, whose work hitherto had been largely confined to panels, was commissioned to decorate the Pope's personal library in fresco. The themes of Raphael's compositions are the ways of attaining human knowledge and wisdom while epitomizing the virtues and learning suited to a pope. The four walls illustrate Theology, Jurisprudence, Poetry, and Philosophy, while smaller compositions on the ceiling unite the whole according to a complex iconographical scheme. Raphael has enlarged the space of the room and peopled it with a race of demigods. On one wall the so-called *Disputà*, representative of Theology, swings back into space like the apse which Raphael's countryman, Bramante, was then planning for St. Peter's. Opposite it the *School of Athens* (Fig. 9–57), whose subject is Philosophy, moves directly back into space, recalling the nave of St. Peter's.

In the *Disputà* two arcs approach each other at the central axis, around which all parts are balanced symmetrically. The upper arc encloses the scene in Heaven, where the Christ is seated between the Virgin and Saint John, surrounded by saints, angels, and cherubim, with God the Father above, and the dove below. The lower arc contains a more varied group, in which each figure contributes by its pose or gesture and its color to the

[43] The room in the papal apartments where the pope signed official documents.

9–57 RAPHAEL SANZIO. *School of Athens.* 1509–1511. Stanza della Segnatura, Vatican, Rome. (Anderson)

movement in the direction of the four Fathers of the Church gathered about the altar. Here stands the monstrance, symbol of the mystery of the faith; silhouetted against the highest light and on the vertical axis, it is the focal point of the design. A serene Umbrian landscape unites the two groups. The *Disputà*, or Disputation on the Mystery of the Sacrament, is a magnificent and grandiose presentation of the theme of the *sacra conversazione,* which we first saw in Nanni di Banco's *Quattro Santi Coronati.*

The monumental architectural setting, recalling Roman imperial architecture (and probably reflecting the projected interior of the recently begun rebuilding of St. Peter's), makes the *School of Athens* an even more impressive work. Within this majestically

enclosed, colossal volume the figures of the philosophers of Antiquity, brought together in groups, move easily and clearly, with eloquent postures and gestures, splendid self-assurance, and instinctive dignity. The composition is organized, as in the *Disputà*, along a series of great arcs. From the center, where Plato and Aristotle stand, silhouetted against the clear blue of the sky within the framing arch in the distance, the groups of figures are rhythmically arranged in an elliptical movement which swings forward and then back again to the center (Fig. 0–7). By moving through the wide opening in the foreground along the perspective pattern of the floor, we are made to penetrate the assembly of philosophers and are led, by way of the reclining Diogenes, up to

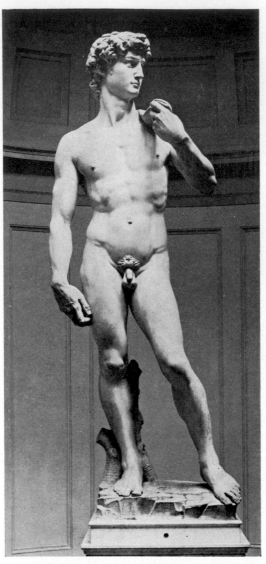

9–58 MICHELANGELO. *David.* 1504. Accademia, Florence. (Alinari)

form had also been attempted philosophically by the humanist Pico della Mirandola (1436–94), whose *Oration on the Dignity of Man* (1486) is reflected in the program of the Stanza della Segnatura.

In the work of Michelangelo Buonarroti (1475–1564) we meet a less tractable personality than Raphael's. Frequently irascible, he was as impatient with the shortcomings of others as with his own. His jealousy of Raphael, his dislike of Leonardo, and his almost continual difficulties with his patrons are all well known. Perhaps these personal problems arose out of his strong and stern devotion to his art, for he was always totally absorbed in the work at hand. He identified himself with the task of artistic creation so completely that his reactions to his rivals were often impulsive and antagonistic.[44]

As a youth Michelangelo was apprenticed to the painter Domenico Ghirlandajo. Later he came under the protection of Lorenzo the Magnificent and studied sculpture under one of Lorenzo's favorite artists, Giovanni Bertoldo (*ca.* 1440–1491), a former collaborator of Donatello who specialized in small-scale bronzes. When the Medici fell in 1494, Michelangelo fled to Bologna, where he executed a work for the Church of San Petronio and studied the sculpture of Jacopo della Quercia. These early influences had a definite impact on the work of the mature Michelangelo, even though his major source of inspiration lay always within himself.

One of the earliest indications of this strong originality occurs in the marble *Madonna and Child* (Fig. 9–

the leaders of the two great opposing camps of Renaissance philosophy, who, surrounded by their adherents, have here been reconciled. The accord between Aristotelianism and Platonism — indeed, if we take the *Disputà* and the *School of Athens* together, between Christianity and paganism — which Raphael achieved through

[44] Michelangelo's character has, in this respect, often been compared to Beethoven's. The personal letters of both, however, reveal a deep sympathy and concern for those close to them, and the same profound understanding of humanity which informs their works.

9–59 MICHELANGELO. *Holy Family,* called the *Doni Tondo. ca.* 1503. Uffizi, Florence. (Alinari)

1), which he carved about 1500 and which was soon after given to the church of Notre Dame in Bruges. The High Renaissance desire for unity led Michelangelo to reject the conventional composition of the *quattrocento* in which the Child either stands or sits on the Madonna's knees. By placing the Child between her knees he brings the figures into a more unified whole. The Child's torso twists as his right hand reaches around to grasp her left, creating an upward spiraling motion that continues through the left shoulder and head of the Virgin to return down her right arm to its point of origin. The whole composition is characterized by a rising and descending spiral of movement which never breaks outside the outline but always turns back on itself. As a result both pose and movement bind the two figures into a new unity typical of the Classic moment. At the same time, both Mother and Child take on an introspective aspect more in keeping with the dignity required by the new age than

with the gay lightheartedness of similar *quattrocento* compositions. In the marble *David* (1504) Michelangelo achieved a new heroic monumentality in the representation of the nude as well as of the psychology of the figure (Fig. 9–58). Moreover, he intensified these two aspects and integrated them more completely than do the works of Antiquity or of Donatello, which were his models.

Throughout his life Michelangelo thought of himself as a sculptor, even though he was famous then as now for his work in painting and architecture. The sculptor's approach dominates in all his work, as we see in the *tondo* painted for the Florentine Doni family (Fig. 9–59). This painting has been called Michelangelo's answer to Leonardo's extremely popular cartoon for *St. Anne, the Virgin, and Christ Child.* The reply is typically Michelangelesque. Where Leonardo's forms were soft and melting, Michelangelo's are hard and clear. To Leonardo's ambiguity and imbalance he opposes clarity and

9–60 MICHELANGELO. *Sistine Chapel ceiling.* 1508–1512. Vatican, Rome. (Alinari)

a solidly balanced group. The muscular forms of the Holy Family, the ascending and descending compositional spiral similar to that of his *Bruges Madonna,* and the clear light playing over the extremely sculptural forms demonstrate Michelangelo's adherence to the ideals of the High Renaissance.

As has been noted, Michelangelo considered himself a sculptor; when Pope Julius II ordered him to decorate in fresco the ceiling of the *Sistine Chapel* he rebelled. But the pope was adamant and bent Michelangelo to his will. The result was a colossal scheme of decoration, a penance alike to the artist while he painted it and to the spectator who wishes to look at it (Fig. 9–60). The first impression of a vast complex of humanity thundering above us gradually reveals, however, a great pattern, the motifs of which are rhythmically repeated and inextricably coordinated. Old Testament prophets and sibyls sit in niches flanked by pilasters on which *putti,* caryatid-like, hold up the painted cornice running the length of the vault. This forms a framework for the central panels and links them formally with the monumental seated figures, whose repeating pattern leads the eye from the larger to the smaller panels, unifying and accentuating the rhythmic pulse of the composition. Within the strongly marked, unifying architectural framework, which neither articulates nor illusionistically breaks through the ac-

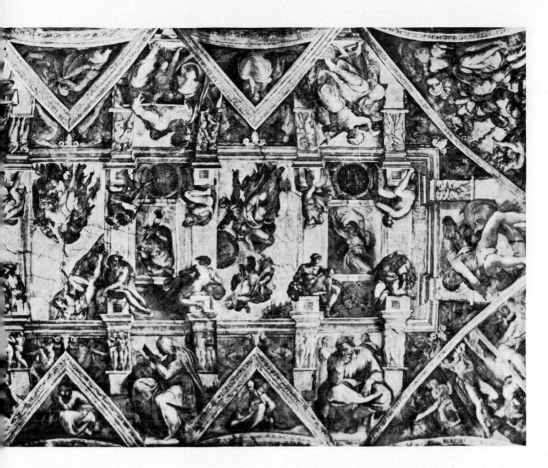

tual vault of the ceiling but imposes on it an entirely new constructive character, our eyes seize upon figure after figure, each sharply outlined against the neutral tone of the architectural setting or the plain background of the panels. Why did Michelangelo relentlessly concentrate on the human figure in decorating this ceiling? Although a complete answer can probably never be given, we know that to Michelangelo the human body was beautiful not only because of its form but because of its spiritual and ethical significance, the state of mind or soul its form could so successfully express. He represented it, as the Greeks had, in its most simple, elemental aspect; in the nude, or simply draped, with no background, no ornamental embellishment,

and with an idealized physiognomy.

The *Temptation and Expulsion of Adam and Eve* (Fig. 9–61) illustrates his effective use of the human figure and, in comparison with Jacopo della Quercia and Masaccio, indicates not only the extent of his debt to the *quattrocento* but also the ways in which the ideals of his age differed from those of his predecessors. In this fresco Michelangelo returned to a Medieval device of including two episodes of a narrative within one frame, a device dictated by the desire to enlarge the emotional and symbolic meaning of his subject. The two incidents are shown separated by the tree which is encircled by the serpent, yet bound together by a long arc sweeping upward on the left through Adam's body and

9–61 MICHELANGELO. *Temptation and Expulsion of Adam and Eve*. Sistine Chapel ceiling. 1508–1512. Vatican, Rome. (Anderson)

along his arm, and down through the arm of the angel and the body of Eve on the right. The forms of her arms reaching for the fruit are repeated in Adam's feeble gesture warding off the sword of the avenging angel. As Adam and Eve are drawn together in desire as they reach for the fruit, so they are drawn together in suffering when driven from the Garden of Eden. On the one hand are the foliage and rough rocks of a new world, on the other the barren and desolate plain in which they must now live. Throughout his life Michelangelo was a deeply religious man greatly affected by the Protestant Reformation, the preaching of Savonarola, and the irregularities of the papal court. In the ceiling of the *Sistine Chapel* he expressed his profound moral convictions in the powerfully sculptural forms of an ideal humanity.

In the spandrels of the arches he portrayed the Old Testament ancestors of Christ, while along the sides he placed, as we have noted, the prophets and sibyls who had predicted his coming. In this group of ideal creatures Michelangelo expressed his own introspective nature and preoccupation

with man's spiritual problems. Thus the figure of the prophet *Jeremiah* (Fig. 9–62) — with the drooping right shoulder, the weight of the head on the right hand, the limp left hand, and the ponderous weight of the great body — conveys total absorption in deep thought. There are no details to individualize this prophet; the forms and the emotion have been so generalized that we feel this is not only Jeremiah brooding over Israel, or Michelangelo himself pondering in isolation and melancholy, but also the archetype of every human being who loses himself in contemplation of the problems and mysteries of life. Such introspection passes the bounds of classic ideals. It suggests the turmoil and uncertainty characteristic of Mannerist art, and it was in this new vocabulary that Michelangelo next expressed himself.

The development of Venetian painting in the closing years of the fifteenth century is similar in its broadest terms to the tendencies already exhibited during this period in Florence. Giovanni Bellini moved away from the austerely sculptural effects of his earlier *Pietà* toward softer and broader forms conceived to an even greater extent in terms of color and chiaroscuro. This change in Bellini's style, which occurred in the later 1470's, was largely due to the influence of Antonello da Messina (*ca.* 1430–1479), who painted an altarpiece in Venice in 1476. Antonello also introduced the technique of oil painting into Venice.

Giovanni Bellini's altarpiece, painted for the church of *San Giobbe* in Venice (Fig. 9–63), is still a work of the Early Renaissance. The figures of this composition tend to exist more as individuals than as rhythmic articulations of an integrated whole. Nevertheless, Bellini had already begun to express the classic concepts of order, balance, and clarity. The space is large, airy, and nobly defined by architecture and the golden mosaic in the dome of the apse, and the figures are arranged in the pyramidal grouping preferred by the High Renaissance. The light subtly reveals the forms without creating strong outlines. Ve-

9–63 GIOVANNI BELLINI. *San Giobbe Altarpiece. ca.* 1487. Accademia Bella Arti, Venice. (Alinari)

netian love of color touched by a diffused light becomes so dominant in the work of Bellini that his *San Zaccaria Altarpiece* of 1505 (Church of San Zaccaria, Venice), although based on the same organization, is completely altered by the quality of the light. In this later work Bellini created a more fully developed High Renaissance composition which added simplicity to the order, balance, and clarity of the earlier altarpiece. This coloristic approach to painting, initiated in Venice by Giovanni Bellini, was enriched by the influence of Giovanni's young and gifted pupil, Giorgione.

Giorgione (*ca.* 1475–1510), who, like the seventeenth-century Dutch painter Vermeer, was one of the greatest masters in the handling of light, left but

9–62 MICHELANGELO. *Jeremiah.* Sistine Chapel ceiling. 1508–1512. Vatican, Rome. (Anderson)

9–64 GIORGIONE. *Castelfranco Madonna. ca.* 1500. Cathedral, Castelfranco Veneto. (Alinari)

few paintings, for he died young. His early *Castelfranco Madonna* (Fig. 9–64) reflects a tranquil, lyrical mood characteristic of his luminous visions. The Madonna and the Child on a lofty throne, together with the flanking saints, form a pyramidal group set in a rectangular framework of floor, wall, and throne; behind them stretches a landscape flooded in light. Depth is expressed by parallel planes which recede quietly from the foreground to the horizon. A symmetrical surface pattern of triangles and rectangles, given force by the dynamic diagonal of the banner, is frequently repeated throughout the composition and connects foreground and background. Color, too, contributes to the mood, for warm, rich reds are set off by large areas of cool greens and blues.

In Giorgione's *Fête Champêtre* (Fig. 9–65) the basic organization is much less obvious, less symmetrical, and more subtle; the organizing lines are intuitively felt rather than clearly visible, for most of the edges are blurred by atmosphere or lost in shadows. Color rather than line dominates and harmonizes the organization of this painting. A warm red in the cloak of the lute player marks the center of interest. As we have seen, this coloristic innovation was only partly Giorgione's invention, for it had been inherent in Venetian painting almost from its origins. It derived also from the oil technique introduced by Antonello da Messina. However, the subtle and knowing use of color was given its most refined expression during Giorgione's brief career. In this he set the direction for the future development of Venetian painting as well as for one of the major streams of western European painting as a whole.

An important change at about this time was the almost universal adoption of canvas, with its rough-textured surface, in place of panel as the support for paintings. The great technical importance of Venetian painting was based on the innovation of a mode of painting in which the white canvas was darkened with a brownish wash. On this the artist painted the forms of the picture fairly completely in monochrome, and then applied colors in several layers of oil glazes.

Another element in the *Fête Champêtre* is both Giorgionesque and Venetian — a profound sensitivity to an idyllic charm and a tranquil, brooding mood. Vasari reports that Giorgione was an accomplished lutist and singer; adjectives from poetry and music seem best suited to describe the pastoral air and muted chords of his painting. Among the Italians it was the Venetians who first expressed a love of nature and a realization of its potentiali-

9–65 GIORGONE. *Fête Champêtre. ca.* 1505. Louvre, Paris. (Archives Photographiques)

ties for the painter, though they never represented it except as inhabited by man.

The most prodigious and prolific of the great Venetian painters was Titian (1485/88–1576), who was trained by both Giovanni Bellini and Giorgione. Titian learned so well from them that there is still no general agreement as to the degree of his participation in their late works. Soon, however, his robust and exuberant nature found release in bolder interpretations of traditional subjects and more striking designs, which set his works apart from those of his masters. In the *Assumption of the Virgin* (Fig. 9–66), his first major work, Titian was, like his contemporaries in Rome and Florence, striving to create a sense of ordered movement within a deep and clearly defined space. But he was also, to a greater ex-

tent than they, concerned with the immediate sensuous impact of this movement on the beholder. His Apostles are earthbound, separated from the ascending Virgin by a serene sky broken only by their straining arms. In contrast to their ponderous gestures, airy *putti* effortlessly sweep the sumptuous, coloristic mass of the Virgin upward. Above, the figure of God the Father, surrounded by attendant angels, stops this movement and, by his downward glance, sets up a countermovement by which the dynamic forces of the composition are held within the frame. The outermost *putti* and the apostles below perform the same function, conforming to one of the unstated ideals of the High Renaissance that the composition be self-contained and obey the restrictions of the frame. A comparison of Titian's slightly later *Deposition* (Fig. 9-

9–66 TITIAN. *Assumption of the Virgin.* 1516–1518. Santa Maria dei Frari, Venice. (Alinari)

67) with the same subject by Raphael (Fig. 9–67) indicates the differences between a fully classic work and one which, painted at an early stage of Raphael's career, only approaches the classic. Whereas Raphael's composition is broken into two groups, Titian's is united into one. The division of interest in Raphael's *Deposition* between the groups around the figures of the Virgin and of the Christ has been replaced by a unity of interest focused on the body of Christ. The two figures

bearing the body become two arcs of a semicircle enclosing him — arcs which are repeated in the figures of the Virgin and St. John. Every gesture and every glance leads the eye of the spectator back along an elliptical path to the center of interest. The uncertainties of the young Raphael, who was just beginning to master new forms, may be contrasted with the mature knowledge of Titian, who knew how to reduce the number of figures so as to heighten the impact of his drama without losing a sense of variety while he subdued the landscape elements so that only the most general indication of place is given.

In his treatment of the nude, Titian combined with his Venetian sensitivity to color the High Renaissance preoccupation with the nude as the most perfect means of expressing its ideal of man. Because he realized the full capabilities of the oil medium as a means for rendering the most subtle nuances of flesh tones, Titian's art was a vital experience in the education of Rubens and Renoir. Titian's *Venus of Urbino* (Fig. 9–68) is a glorious study in textures such as one would expect from a Venetian; there is a sensuous yet thoughtful differentiation between the warm, melting flesh of Venus and the cold, hard stone of the column behind her, and between the smoothness of the sheet and the rough fabric of her couch. Color and light are used primarily to define textures, but at the same time the red of the divan in the foreground is repeated in a higher key by the red robe of the servant in the background, thus providing a means of gauging the extent of space represented in the painting.

ARCHITECTURE

The rhythmically ordered stability characteristic of the painting of the Classic moment can also be found in

9–67 (Right) RAPH-
AEL SANZIO. *Deposi-
tion of Christ.* 1507.
Borghese Gallery,
Rome. (Below) TI-
TIAN. *Deposition. ca.*
1525. Louvre, Paris.
(Both photos Ali-
nari)

9–68 TITIAN. *Venus of Urbino. ca.* 1538. Uffizi, Florence. (Alinari)

the architecture of the period. Here, too, leadership in the field passed from Florence to Rome, in the person of Donato Bramante (1444–1514). Early in his youth Bramante left his native Urbino, where he had been trained as a painter, for the court of Milan. There he abandoned painting and, under the influence of the works and the writings of Brunelleschi, Alberti, and perhaps of Filarete [45] and Leonardo — all of whom had been influenced by the Antique — he developed the High Renaissance

[45] Antonio Averlino (*ca.* 1400–after 1465), called Filarete, was a Florentine goldsmith, sculptor, and architect. He is known chiefly for the bronze doors of St. Peter's in Rome (*ca.* 1433–1445), the Ospedale Maggiore in Milan (begun on Filarete's plan in 1456, altered somewhat during construction and greatly after his departure in 1465), and his treatise on architecture (1461–1462, with additions in 1465).

form of the centrally planned church. In Milan his churches of San Satiro and Santa Maria della Grazie retain the northern Italian love of exuberant architectural decoration, which he put aside soon after he arrived in Rome in 1499. His *Tempietto* (Fig. 9–69) is all but devoid of ornament, relying instead on the sculptural treatment of the exterior to create a sense of mass and movement. This small building, designed to mark the spot of St. Peter's crucifixion, indeed gives the appearance of a solid sculptural reliquary; in fact, it was originally planned to stand, somewhat like a reliquary, under the protection of a colonnaded circular court. At first glance the building seems unnecessarily strict and rational, with its clean, cold Tuscan Doric order and abstract circular plan repeated in the portico and steps of the stylobate.

At the same time Bramante achieved a wonderful harmony betwen the parts and the whole through the proportions of the dome, drum, and base. The balustrade accents in shorter beats the rhythm of the portico and breaks up a too rapid ascent to the drum, while the pilasters on the drum itself repeat the ascending motif and lead the eye past the cornice to the ribs of the dome. The regulated play of light and shade around the columns and balustrade and in the deep-set rectangular windows alternated with shallow shell-capped niches enhances the experience of the building as an articulated sculptural mass.

The same architectural concept guided Bramante's plans for the new St. Peter's, commissioned by Pope Julius II in 1505. The traditional basilican form of the old church was to be discarded in favor of a Greek cross plan (Fig. 9–70). As originally designed by Bramante the church was to have consisted of a cross with arms of equal length, each terminated by an apse. The crossing would have been covered by a large dome, and, on the diagonal axes, smaller domes over subsidiary chapels would have enclosed the whole in a square. Bramante's ambitious plan called for a boldly sculptural treatment of the walls and piers under the dome. Thus he wished to create a large enclosure by the same means with which he had achieved the visual effect of mass in the *Tempietto*. The wish to unify interior volume and exterior mass motivated Michelangelo as well as Bramante in their plans for *St. Peter's*. During Bramante's lifetime the actual construction had not advanced beyond the building of the piers of the crossing and the lower walls of the choir. With the death of Bramante the work passed from one architect to another, none of whom advanced it to any great degree until Michelangelo was appointed by Pope Paul III in 1546

9–69   BRAMANTE. *Tempietto*. 1502. San Pietro in Montorio, Rome. (Anderson)

to complete the building.[46] The modifications that he brought to Bramante's design increased the sculptural effect of both interior and exterior and cre-

[46] The first director in charge of *St. Peter's* after Bramante was Raphael, who held the post until his death in 1520. He, as well as his successors, Giuliano and Antonio da Sangallo and Baldassare Peruzzi, reverted to a longitudinal, Latin cross plan. All of these plans, however, were destined to remain on paper. Under the papacy of Clement VII (1523–1534) building activity had practically come to a halt, and only under Paul III (1534–1549) was the actual construction resumed on the crossarms surrounding the piers of the dome. Michelangelo supervised the work from 1546 until his death (1564); he was followed by Piero Ligorio, Giacomo da Vignola, and Giacomo della Porta, who completed the dome. The façade was built by Carlo Maderna (1606–1626), and the great court with double colonnades by Giovanni Bernini (1656–1663) (see p. 398).

ated a greater unification of space, thus anticipating the Baroque. The compactness and effectiveness of the building as conceived by Bramante and Michelangelo was somewhat diminished later by the lengthening of the nave and by the addition of a wide façade which cuts off the view of the dome. Thus only the back view of the cathedral gives some conception of the complete unity of masses which underlay Michelangelo's sculptural design (Fig. 9–71).

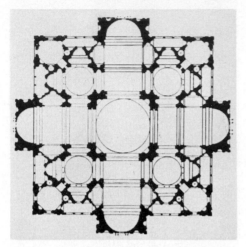

9–70　BRAMANTE'S PLAN FOR ST. PETER'S. Rome. *ca.* 1505. (After Geymüller)

The building consists of a closely knit unit of cube and half-cylinders, which in their volumes, surfaces, and contours form an harmonious base for the great dome, which rises like a symbol of universal authority. The exterior cornices are not continuous, but are broken. By advancing and receding they create a movement in depth as well as laterally. The movement in depth, a three-dimensional quality, becomes stronger in the drum of the dome, where deeply projecting pairs of colonnettes crowned with a sharply broken

9–71　ST. PETER'S. Rome. View from the west, as designed by Michelangelo. 1546–1564. (Alinari)

9-72 FARNESE PALACE. Rome. Architects: Antonio da Sangallo, 1530–1534; Michelangelo, 1546, who designed the cornice, and Giacomo della Porta, who completed the palace *ca.* 1580. (Anderson)

cornice not only serve as bases for the great ribs of the dome but also carry the eye inward and outward as it sweeps around the drum. The emphasis on unity through movement, internally and externally, transcends the High Renaissance principles of self-containment and stability, and anticipates the Baroque style.

In the field of secular architecture, the palaces designed by Bramante have been preserved only in his drawings. From these it is apparent that the *Farnese Palace* (Fig. 9–72), designed by Antonio da Sangallo the Younger and Michelangelo, represents a similar design of classical balance and symmetry calculated to attain an effect of princely dignity. Facing a spacious paved square, the rectangle of the smooth façade is framed and firmly anchored by the quoins and the cornice, while long lines of windows mark a majestic beat across it. The window casements are no longer flush with the wall, as in the

Medici Palace (Fig. 9–33), but project out from its surface, so that, instead of being a flat, thin plane, the façade becomes a spatially active, three-dimensionally felt mass. Each casement is a complete architectural unit, consisting of a socket, engaged columns, entablature, and pediment. The variations in the treatment of these units in each of the three stories, as well as the alternation of triangular and curved pediments in the *piano nobile*, prevent the symmetrical scheme from being rigid or monotonous. The rusticated doorway and second-story balcony surmounted by the Farnese coat of arms, by emphasizing the central axis, bring the horizontal and vertical forces of the design into harmony.

Summary

All the artists of the brief years identified as the High Renaissance were governed by a desire to achieve calm, ordered, and balanced compositions that would not be lacking in movement or variety. The monumentality and dramatic grandeur of their works were almost too imposing for their successors, for they invited emulation but defied imitation. The ideals they expressed were as difficult to maintain as to achieve. Shortly after the completion of the *Stanza della Segnatura* and of the *Sistine Ceiling*, both Raphael and Michelangelo moved away from the balance of their mature work to the style which was to be called Mannerism. With the death of Leonardo and of Raphael, each of the younger artists trained by them began to pursue his own separate ideals. Michelangelo, who outlived Raphael by forty-four years, was, before the middle of the sixteenth century, to discard Mannerist tendencies and, in his architectural designs of *St. Peter's* and the *Campidoglio*, to foreshadow the Baroque.

Sixteenth-Century Mannerism

Italy

Mannerism, as a term descriptive of an artistic style, was first used, in the sixteenth century, in a derogatory sense. Only since the early decades of the twentieth century has the term, as well as the art to which it refers, been accepted in a more dispassionate sense. Mannerism is now regarded essentially as a conscious revolt against the ideals of the High Renaissance. The Protestant Reformation, the moral corruption of the papacy, the French invasions of Italy, and the sack of Rome in 1527 were all external forces creating an unsettled environment in which Mannerism could develop. Mannerism was primarily the expression of the artist's state of mind in a world of crisis.

Artists turned away from the observation of nature or the Antique to seek inspiration in the Platonic *Idea* — referred to by them as the *disegno interno* — which fired their creative fervor. Where the art of the High Renaissance strove for balance, Mannerism sought imbalance. The calm stability of classic art was replaced by a restlessness which led either to expressionistic distortion or to emotionless, masklike rigidity. This exaggeration of classic ideals, in either a positive or a negative direction, applies to the Mannerist treatment both of space and of the human figure. The space of late sixteenth-century painting and architecture is frequently enigmatic. At times it seems compressed so as to move rigidly into depth; it may, on the other hand, be so flat that objects in it appear almost two-dimensional. The human figure lost the gravity and the fullness given it by Raphael, Titian, or Michelangelo and became elongated, stiff, or sinuously graceful. The work of art tended to become more and more spiritualized.

Leonardo, in his painting of the *Virgin, St. Anne, and Child,* and Raphael, as well, showed dissatisfaction with the calm stability of their earlier works. One year after the completion of the *School of Athens* (Fig. 9–57), in the room adjoining the Stanza della Segnatura. Raphael's fresco, the *Expulsion of Heliodorus* (Fig. 9–73), indicated one of the directions Mannerism was to follow. The architecture of the *School of Athens* creates an expanding space in which the figures move calmly, while that of the *Expulsion of Heliodorus* seems to restrict the space and accel-

9-73 RAPHAEL SANZIO. *The Expulsion of Heliodorus.* 1511–1512. Stanza d'Eliodoro, Vatican, Rome. (Anderson)

erate or arrest the movements of the figures. The walls on either side of the vaults in the *School of Athens* set definite limits to the space and give it direction; in the *Heliodorus* the walls are replaced by half-concealed side aisles which, with the receding series of domes over the nave, create a complicated and enigmatic background. Our eyes are not led along a path of restful movement and back to a central point of interest; they are attracted, instead, to the emptiness of the central area, denying in this manner the stability created by the figures of Plato and Aristotle in the *School of Athens*. The continuous movement throughout the fresco, charged with abrupt changes of direction, fails to be resolved at a point of rest. There are sudden contrasts between the gigantic scale of the fallen Heliodorus on the right, or the kneeling woman on the left, with the figures around them; or between the immobility of Pope Julius II and his bearers with the violent action on the opposite

side. This willful ambiguity of space, scale, and action has been created with a full knowledge of its effects of unresolved tension and imbalance.

At about this time Michelangelo also began to intensify the expression of tensions which had been only latent in the Sistine Ceiling. The conflicts and ambiguities which became the ideals of Mannerist art are reflected in his sculpture (*Medici Tombs*, 1520–1534), architecture (*Laurentian Library*, ca. 1524–1526, finished by Vasari and Ammanati in 1559), and painting (*Last Judgment*, Sistine Chapel, 1536–1541).

For the *Medici tombs* Michelangelo erected the New Sacristy, off the right transept of the Florentine church of *San Lorenzo*, where the Medici, who had returned from exile in 1512, were to be buried, as their forebears had been buried in Brunelleschi's Old Sacristy. On opposite sides of the chapel stand the tombs of Giuliano de' Medici (Fig. 9–74) and of Lorenzo de' Medici, nephews of Lorenzo the Magnificent.

9–74   MICHELANGELO. *Tomb of Giuliano de' Medici.* 1524–1533. New Sacristy, San
Lorenzo, Florence. (Brogi)

9–75 MICHELANGELO. *Vestibule of the Laurentian Library*, Florence. 1524–1526. (Brogi)

These tombs have been integrated into a complicated architectural-sculptural scheme. At first glance it seems as though Michelangelo were following the ideals of the High Renaissance, for the composition of the tombs is basically that of a pyramid. Since the two figures are symbolic of the active and contemplative life, they represent two conflicting facets of human personality harmonized in a perfect individual. On closer examination, however, this apparent stability and harmony is disturbed by the recumbent figures. They seem to be sliding down the sloping sides of the sarcophagi and create the same sense of instability which we have already encountered in Leonardo's *St. Anne, Virgin, and Christ.* The figure of Giuliano, represented as the active man, is actually as incapable of action as is his more contemplative brother. His pose is not that of one who is about to spring into action; his right hand in particular hangs listlessly over his marshall's baton in a relaxed and supine manner. The figure of *Day* below does not suggest the period of activity of the active man, but peers fearfully over its powerful, drawn-up shoulder. *Night,* the symbol of rest, lies tense and unrelaxed. The artist has surrounded her with an owl, poppies, and a mask symbolic of the dreams which trouble her sleep. In these sculptural groups Michelangelo has suggested powerful psychological forces incapable of being translated into action. Everywhere there is a feeling of instability. There is no conviction, as in the High Renaissance, that the action implicit in the figures will continue unchanged through time, but rather there is a sense of tension and imminent change.

In the vestibule of the *Laurentian*

Library (Fig. 9–75) the tensions and ambiguities which contribute to the *malaise* so characteristic of Mannerist art are strongly felt. Here Michelangelo has made the vestibule itself much taller than it is wide or long, giving the impression of a vertically compressed, shaftlike space. In the walls stone seems to have been deprived of its natural properties of weight and stability. The columns, imprisoned within the wall, do not exercise their normal supporting function — a feature which has been intensified by the stringcourse and cornice which break and recede from the plane of the wall with them. Their weightlessness is further enhanced by the fact that they look as though they were supported by small brackets. The staircase flows out into the vestibule, crowding the already constricted space. As the visitor turns to mount the stairs, he is faced with a puzzle, for the wings of the staircase seem to have more steps than the center. At the same time, the steps of the

center appear to move out, forcing him back against the wall.

As the principal figures of the High Renaissance either died or came to accept Mannerism, a new generation of painters appeared in Florence. These artists had not participated in the classic style to the same degree as their elders, but moved directly into Mannerism. Chief among these was Jacopo Carucci (1494–1557), called Il Pontormo. The Mannerist ambiguities only suggested in the painting of the preceding generation are clearly stated in his *Joseph in Egypt* (Fig. 9–76). Here in his treatment of space the near and the far approach each other so as to create doubt in the observer's mind. The figures on the left seem to give the clue to the scale of the painting, and yet their spatial relation to the statue on the column and to the group of people immediately to the right is most ambiguous. The greatly reduced scale of this second group seems to suggest that they are farther back in space, but there is no indication along the ground that this is actually so. The steps leading to the upper room appear to carry the eye into the background as well. The group of figures huddled behind a large boulder are also ambiguous in their spatial location. The rapid shift in scale, the exaggeration of proportion and pose are knowingly used by the artist to create insecurity. In addition, Pontormo here illustrates another side of the Mannerist artist, his acceptance of eclecticism as a virtue. The statue in the middle distance seems to be an imitation of Michelangelo's *Bacchus*, while Vasari's statement that Pontormo and many others of his generation borrowed heavily from German prints is apparently borne out by the buildings in the distance, which could have come from Dürer's 1498 engraving of the *Prodigal Son*.

Another facet of fully developed Mannerist art is illustrated by Pontormo's *Deposition*, done as the altarpiece for the Capponi Chapel in Santa Felicita, Florence, in 1562–1568. Here he tends to negate the ample space of the High Renaissance by forcing his figures against the picture plane in a two-dimensional pattern. He creates a rising and descending circular movement which rotates around a void. To intensify this sense of instability, torsos are lengthened out of proportion to the rest of the body. The delicate coloring of the painting, which tends toward light blues and pinks, also enhances the exaggerated and effeminate grace of the figures.

Il Rosso Fiorentino (1494–1540), like Pontormo a pupil of Andrea del Sarto, used means similar to Pontormo's to compress space but filled it with turbulent action. His painting of *Moses Defending the Daughters of Jethro* (Fig. 9–77) recalls the titanic struggles and powerful musculature of Michelangelo's figures in the Sistine

9–77 IL ROSSO FIORENTINO. *Moses Defending the Daughters of Jethro.* 1523. Uffizi, Florence. (Alinari)

Ceiling, and yet any attempt at a sculptural definition of the human body is frustrated by the hard, cold light. The quality of the light and the equally cold color tend to emphasize the two-dimensionality of the composition, for Rosso seemed to be striving to render an extremely complex and violent action within a compressed, limited space, so that surface is emphasized as a two-dimensional pattern. Later in his career he was to develop a more elegant and sensual style. When Francis I called him in 1530 to decorate the palace at Fontainebleau, he had all but forsaken this earlier violence for more elongated and graceful forms.

In architecture the Mannerist concepts expressed by Michelangelo in his work for the Medici were grafted onto the Mannerist tendencies in Rome and carried from there to northern Italy.

9–78 GIULIO ROMANO. *Palazzo del Te*, Mantua. 1525–1535. Detail of court. (Frederick Hartt)

The most noteworthy among the architects involved in this development was Giulio Romano (1494–1546), who began his career as a painter, assisting Raphael in the Stanze of the Vatican. In 1523–24 Giulio transferred his activities from Rome to Mantua, where he found a patron in the ruling Gonzaga family. His construction of their pleasure villa outside the walls of the city, the *Palazzo del Te*, created a type of Mannerism in architecture more obvious than that of Michelangelo. The courtyard (Fig. 9–78) is heavily rusticated, and, although this use of rustication goes back to the *Medici Palace* (Fig. 9–33), the treatment of the stone in the two structures is entirely different. In the lower story of Michelozzo's building the rustication seems to be a part of the stones which make up the

structure. In the *Palazzo del Te* the rusticated stones appear to be only applied, for the large joints around them suggest that the true plane of the wall lies somewhere behind them. The heavy Doric columns are unnecessarily powerful for the light architrave they support, and they seem, at the same time, to be part of and yet independent of the wall. The most shocking feature of the building — and it was clearly intended to shock the beholder — is the dropping of every third triglyph in the entablature of the court façade. This desire to startle and to create ambiguities and tensions is as typical of Mannerist architecture as it is of Mannerist painting.

In Rome, Baldassare Peruzzi (1481–1536) was no less Mannerist than Giulio Romano in his approach to the urban structure of the *Palazzo Massimo*

9-79 BALDASSARO PERUZZI. *Façade of Palazzo Massimo alle Colonne*, Rome. Begun 1535. (Anderson)

alle Colonne (Fig. 9-79). Compared with a building such as the *Farnese Palace* (Fig. 9-72), there is a strange relation of void to solid: the great expanse of wall in the upper stories creates an unusual clash with the small but deep void of the entrance. One experiences little sense of mass or of weight in the curved façade which is crisply cut by the windows; it is almost a two-dimensional theatrical prop, particularly in the upper levels. The small windows of the intermediate story are enclosed in ornate leathery frames, a style of ornament which was later elaborated with the greatest exaggeration in the strapwork details of France, the Low Countries, and England. On the ground floor the pilasters set up a regular rhythm abruptly broken by the columns of the entrance. The façade

of a High Renaissance building can be scanned like a line of verse, but here the columns are separated by unequal spaces which make such scansion impossible. We see again how a Mannerist architect exploited irregularity and imbalance in deliberate contradiction of High Renaissance principles.

With the artists of what may be called the second generation of Italian Mannerism the characteristics we have noted became even more intensified. The visual arts were invaded by complexities of literary content. Many paintings could not be understood without the artist's detailed explanation of his iconography.[47]

The first academies were founded to

[47] See Vasari's letter to Duke Alessandro de' Medici in E. Holt, *Literary Sources of Art History*, pp. 203-04.

9–80   ANGELO BRONZINO. *Portrait of a Young Man. ca.* 1535–1540. Metropolitan Museum of Art, New York. (Bequest of Mrs. H. O. Havemeyer, 1929; H. O. Havemeyer Collection)

provide a sense of security in an insecure time by establishing artistic rules based on the ideals of the High Renaissance. Nostalgia for the achievements of the "great masters"and a conscious search for formulas as a means of attaining perfection provided academic criticism and rules to plague the painter. Vasari's *Lives* appeared, in which he praised and criticized quite dogmatically according to the taste of his time and attempted to place Florentine art above all others. The architectural theories of Serlio, Vignola, and Palladio were printed and disseminated throughout Europe along with translations of Vitruvius. The artistic fragmentation that had begun before the death of Raphael, the desire for uniqueness at any cost, became even more pronounced during the last half of the sixteenth century in Italy.

One of the most eloquent spokesmen of this age was the Florentine painter Angelo Bronzino (1503–1572). As a student of Pontormo he participated in the very beginnings of Mannerism, and yet his style is so individual that there is little danger of confusing him with his master. In his *Allegory of Time and Love,* Bronzino compressed space to an even greater extent than Pontormo or Rosso had done. The forms of the composition are as complex, entangled, and ambiguous as the meaning. Amid the erotic overtones of the central figures, Venus and Chronos, and heightened by the light colors surrounding them, a mask (symbol of deceit) and an anguished gripping hand create the psychological tensions Mannerist art demanded. The elongated proportions of the Venus embody the most stylish canon of the period, and contribute to the air of sensuality and modishness of the painting.

Sometimes the tenor of a period can be most clearly seen in its portraits, for in the interpretation of a particular individual, an artist frequently, with acute psychological precision, projects the preoccupations of his time. Such seems to be the case with Bronzino's *Portrait of a Young Man* (Fig. 9–80). The subject is an elegant and mannered youth, a man of books and society rather than a man of action or a merchant. His somewhat effeminate and introspective air is far removed from the self-assured portraits of the merchants who made fifteenth-century Florence a financial center for western Europe and the cradle of the Renaissance. The old ways have been replaced by the somber etiquette and clothing of the Spanish conquerors. The carefree, lyrical spirit of the age of Lorenzo the Magnificent was giving way to gloomy Spanish pietism and the Inquisition. The olive green walls of the room in which this young man stands, the deep purplish color of the

9–81 GIOVANNI DA BOLOGNA. *Mercury.*
ca. 1572. Bargello, Florence. (Alinari)

9–82 IL PARMIGIANINO. *Madonna del Collo Lungo. ca.* 1535. Uffizi, Florence. (Alinari)

table, and his own black clothing serve to intensify his "black humor." On the arm of the chair and on the table appear the ever-present Mannerist masks, for at this time appearances are only deceitful; nothing is certain any more.

With Bronzino Florentine Mannerism virtually came to an end. The continuation of Mannerism depended in large measure on several outstanding non-Florentines, among whom the French sculptor Giovanni da Bologna (*ca.* 1524–1608), as he was called in Italy, stands out as a leading example. In Florence he competed successfully with Benvenuto Cellini and Ammanati for the patronage of the Medici. He is perhaps best known for his bronze statue of *Mercury* (Fig. 9–81), although it is not as typically Mannerist as are the sea nymphs which he cast in bronze to accompany Ammanati's *Fountain of Neptune* in Florence. In the *Mercury* there is again the same elongation of form which we have come to recognize in Mannerist art, along with the stagy and exaggerated pose and gestures. Mannerist ideals as well led Bologna to his technical virtuosity in the use of the material. The

9–83 TINTORETTO. *Finding of the Body of St. Mark. ca.* 1562. Brera, Milan. (Alinari)

whole weight and torsion of the bronze figure is concentrated in the left foot and its support, heightening the feeling of instability and tension. Like Benvenuto Cellini (see his *Perseus* and the account of its casting in Benvenuto's *Autobiography*), Giovanni da Bologna was a consummate technician who controlled the materials of his art so well that he was free to obtain whatever visual effects he desired.

The gracefulness which began to invade Mannerist art reached its apogee in Italy in the work of Francesco Mazzola (1503–1540), called Il Parmigianino. His *Madonna del Collo Lungo* (Fig. 9–82), painted near the end of his short life, contains a great many of the tendencies which recur throughout Mannerist painting. The foreground space which the Madonna and attendant figures occupy is greatly compressed, yet suddenly and without

transition we are plunged into a deep and rapidly receding background occupied by tall slender columns and the equally elongated figure of a prophet. The contrast between a tightly compressed space which is then suddenly released in depth has been set up willfully to create a sense of instability and shock in the observer. The same tensions are met in the intense crowding of figures between the Madonna and the left edge of the composition. Here there is constriction; on the other side of the composition, release. The figures on the left break the frame and the composition in width just as the row of columns on the right break it in depth. The elongated figure of the Child is placed in a thoroughly unstable position. These features, together with the exaggerated proportions of the Madonna and her small head set on a columnlike neck, were what most

9–84 GIORGIO VASARI. *Uffizi Courtyard*, Florence. Begun *ca.* 1560. (Alinari)

impressed the non-Italians of the sixteenth century who knew this work.

In Venice Mannerism reached new levels in the paintings of Tintoretto (*ca.* 1518–1594), for he combined the Mannerist tendency toward dematerialization with a Venetian sense of color learned from his master Titian. This unique development in Venetian painting paralleled in many respects the late sculpture of Michelangelo and led on, as well, to El Greco. Like Michelangelo, Tintoretto was early interested in sculptural plastic form. With this he combined the typically rich Venetian palette, but as his work progressed he reduced the sensuousness of color in order to dematerialize his forms. The earlier aspect of his work can be clearly seen in the *Presentation of the Virgin*. The figures are all sculpturally conceived, particularly the brightly lighted man and woman of the foreground. The space is somewhat restricted in depth, but we feel little of the crowding and compression of Florentine Mannerism. Like Pontormo in his *Deposition*, Tintoretto created Mannerist tensions and ambiguities by placing the important figure on the fringes of the action and by making it as difficult as possible for the eye to arrive there.

The *Finding of the Body of St. Mark* (Fig. 9–83) has an even more complex composition than the *Presentation*. In this painting there is the same Mannerist compression of space and rapid flight into depth without resolution of the movement as in the contemporary courtyard of the *Uffizi* by Vasari (Fig. 9–84). In both the painting and the architecture there is no point of climax and no means of return. Although the space is partially enclosed at the end, a small opening is left allowing the observer to look beyond and wonder. The powerful individual figures of the

9–85 TINTORETTO. *Ascension of Christ.*
1576–1581. Scuola di San Rocco, Venice.
(Anderson)

heightened by the dark shadows along
the vaults and by the deep reds of the
figures that emerge from the gloom.
Already Tintoretto's new color sense is
making itself felt. Although the standing and recumbent figures in the foreground give a sculptural impression,
Tintoretto has rendered them primarily
as patches of color which suggest the
forms without modeling them.

This tendency toward dematerialization reached its peak in Tintoretto's
late works (as in the *Last Supper* of
ca. 1592–1594 in San Giorgio Maggiore,
Venice), yet it was already quite apparent about fifteen years earlier in his
Ascension in the Scuola di San Rocco
(Fig. 9–85). Here the figure of Christ
spirals upward out of a turbulent welter of clouds and angels. Color, form,
and movement intensify his upward
surge, but below, all the figures are
earth-bound. In the center Tintoretto
has created a void in which two figures
only intensify the contrast between the
inaction of the lower section and the
violent movement of the upper. These
two figures are brushed in lightly with
rapid nervous strokes, suggesting form
without defining it. Color seems to flick-
er across these figures, dissolving them
into flamelike spirits — an effect we
shall also observe in El Greco's art.

Opposed to the intense visual excitement of Tintoretto's painting, Venice and its surrounding territory also
saw the quieter, more stable art of Veronese's painting and Palladio's architecture. If these two artists exaggerated
in any way it was in an overemphasis
on classic symmetry and balance.
Theirs is almost an academic insistence on logic and on a complex system of mathematical proportions derived from the simple proportions of
the High Renaissance. Of these two, the
architect Andrea Palladio (1508–1580)
is the more important for the development of western Euopean art.
Throughout his life he was mainly oc-

painting are related in a design which
is based essentially on an X shape, but
individual elements of the composition
tend to deny this simple basis. On the
left the figure of St. Mark, who has
miraculously appeared to point out the
sarcophagus containing his body, initi-
ates a diagonal movement leading to
the sarcophagus from which the body
is being removed, but this is countered
by the nude corpse and the kneeling
old man. The counterdiagonal initiated
in the kneeling figure leads to a clump
of three figures in the right foreground
which threaten to fall out of the frame.
The air of mystery and tension is

cupied in building country or city homes for the wealthier classes of the Venetian territory, and thus was concerned with problems similar to those which later faced the architects for the gentry of England and the American colonies. His buildings, and more particularly the ideas and drawings of his architectural treatise, *I quattro libri dell' architettura*, dominated the architecture of England and her American colonies in the eighteenth century.

While no single building is in itself typical of Palladio's style, some notion of his range can be gained by comparing the *Palazzo Valmarano* (Fig. 9–86) with the *Villa Rotonda* (Fig. 9–87). In plan the *Palazzo Valmarano* is rigidly symmetrical, with each side repeating the other, and the rear half of the building much like the front half. On the façade Palladio shows the degree to which he was aware of Mannerist tendencies. His use of a giant order evokes Michelangelo's buildings on the *Campidoglio* in Rome, but here the columns and pilasters have been complicated. In the two windows flanking the door Palladio created ambiguities which make it difficult to locate the plane of the wall. The giant Ionic pilasters overlap the smaller Corinthian order, while the rustication of the window strips are given Tuscan capitals, making the plane of the wall appear to lie somewhere behind. At the same time reliefs are placed above the windows on a plane forward of that of the window casements. The plane of the wall has been virtually eliminated by the proliferation of spatially shifting motifs which have been spread over it. In the upper story the window frames crowd the cornice and are in turn compressed by the capitals of the giant order. The tension of the façade is further increased by the weakening of the corners where one would expect to find the greatest strength. In the *piano nobile* the end windows have been reduced in

9–86 ANDREA PALLADIO. *Palazzo Valmarano*, Vicenza. Begun *ca.* 1566. (Alinari)

size, while the rhythm of the pilasters is broken by the introduction of a caryatid on the upper story and by small Corinthian pilasters on the ground floor. On the lower level an equal complication is the omission of relief ornament and the lowering of the windows.

Although Mannerist tensions exist in many works of Palladio, he could also be rigidly logical. Such logic characterizes the *Villa Rotonda* (Fig. 9–87). Essentially the building is a cube surrounding a cylinder, topped by a hemispherical dome. The four porches are smaller squares repeating the form of

9-87   ANDREA PALLADIO. *Villa Rotonda,* near Vicenza. Begun 1567. (Alinari)

the major square along its primary axes. The tendencies toward mathematically exact proportions and precise, simple geometric forms that we first met in Brunelleschi have here been carried to a point of almost static regularity. The dwelling is at once a temple and a piece of garden sculpture, abstract, noble, and totally aloof. The rather dry quality of the building is far removed from the extravagances of Giulio Romano or of Michelangelo, for it already indicates the fixing of Mannerist exuberance in the Vitruvian rules and logic of the ensuing academies. The low basement, high *piano nobile,* and small attic, as well as the tall columned porticoes, exerted a great influence on academically minded architects of succeeding generations.

Summary

Mannerist art of sixteenth-century Italy does not readily lend itself to summary or synthesis. Broad movements within the period can be indicated, yet these are frequently contradicted to some extent by the work of individual artists. The period as a whole seems to have been characterized by a multitude of aims. Each artist sought to express himself in an intensely personal style which frequently had little relation to the work of his contemporaries. Not infrequently, moreover, one artist altered his personal style quite radically within the period of a few years.

In most general terms, Italian Mannerism shows broad progression from its earliest tentative statements, in the work of Raphael after the *Stanze della Segnatura* and of Michelangelo after the *Sistine Ceiling,* until it finally merged with and was overwhelmed by the Baroque. What could perhaps be called the first Mannerist style found its clearest expression around 1525 in the works of Pontormo, Il Rosso, and Michelangelo in Florence and in the works of Peruzzi and Giulio Romano in Rome. Political upheavals before 1530 scattered these artists throughout Italy and western Europe, so that each tended to continue his artistic development in essentially personal terms without reference to his contemporaries. About the middle of the century Bronzino in Florence and Tintoretto in Venice represented a second generation of Mannerist artists.

Throughout this whole period, however, there were artists who escaped any attempts at stylistic classification. The academies and their frequently stifling influence on art became stronger as the century progressed. The art of Palladio, Veronese, and Vasari, although it sometimes exhibited academic tendencies, was too individualistic to be adequately described by such a generalization. Michelangelo, as well, frequently exhibited in his work a highly personal development. At one time he was in harmony with the work of his contemporaries; at another time he ran counter to them or, more often, anticipated the general development of sixteenth-century art by as much as twenty years. Baroque tendencies are perhaps more clearly prefigured in his work than in that of any other artist of the sixteenth century in Italy.

Mannerist art on the whole, however, seems to have been primarily concerned with the expression of unresolved tensions, ambiguities, and complication for their own sake. More than a mere transitional phase between the High Renaissance and the Baroque, it was rather a richly varied period during which serious artists struggled to find a new syntax for the formal vocabulary they had inherited from the fifteenth century and the High Renaissance.

Western Europe

The art of western Europe during the sixteenth century is characterized by a sudden awareness of the advances made by the Italian Renaissance and by a desire to assimilate this new style as rapidly as possible. Many artists traveled to Italy to study the new art at first hand; others were brought into contact with it either directly through imported artists or indirectly through the numerous Italian engravings which circulated throughout western Europe.[48] Near the beginning of the century there are some examples of naïve imitations of Italian buildings and paintings; toward the end of the century the Italian style had been fully assimilated and new local traditions established. Naturally the impact of Italian art varied widely according to the artist, the time, and the place. Many artists never abandoned existing local traditions, whereas others were frequently content to borrow only motifs or the general form of a composition. In Germany the wealthy merchant class maintained close commercial relations with Venice, and the humanists were in contact with the Neo-Platonic academy of Florence. As a result, Albrecht Dürer's art frequently illustrates Florentine thought clothed in Venetian and German forms. In France the series of invasions of Italy brought an acquaintance with the Renaissance in Milan. Francis I persuaded Leonardo da Vinci to spend his last years in France, and he also engaged Benvenuto Cellini, Il Rosso, Primaticcio, and others to decorate his palaces. As a result Florentine Mannerism strongly colors the art of the "school of Fontainebleau." In Spain, because of her holdings and wars in Naples, Genoa, and Milan, the provincial variants of sixteenth-century Italian Mannerism were best known. Spanish architecture of the sixteenth century was influenced primarily by these provincial styles and by the theoretical works of such men as Vignola and Serlio. Many architects, however,

[48] One of the most prolific Italian engravers was Marcantonio Raimondi; he rarely invented his own compositions, but copied those of other artists, particularly of Raphael. In this way, many of the panel paintings and frescoes by the artists of the Italian Renaissance became the common property of all of Europe.

9–88 MATTHIAS GRÜNEWALD. *Crucifixion.* Detail of Isenheim Altarpiece. *ca.* 1513–1515. Unterlinden Museum, Colmar. (Unterlinden Museum)

still clung to the traditions of Spanish Gothic, and Spanish painting was still strongly under the influence of fifteenth-century Flanders. The foreigner, El Greco, dominated the period, although his effect on the development of Spanish painting was rather slight. None of these countries had a Classic moment comparable to that of Italy. In each there was a period of transition between native Late Gothic styles and the acceptance of Italian Mannerism.

Germany

During the fifteenth century, German painting, as we have seen, developed along its own expressionistic lines

with some influences from Italy and the Low Countries. The *Isenheim Altarpiece* in the museum of Colmar (Fig. 9–88), executed between 1513 and 1515 by Matthias Grünewald (1485–1530), epitomizes several important traits of early sixteenth-century German art: mystical pietism; brutally realistic portrayal of the agony of Christ's passion; a visionary, pantheistic concept of nature in landscape; and an intricate expressionistic linearism in the rendering of form. Meanwhile, Dürer, Holbein, and Cranach [49] were

[49] Lucas Cranach (1472–1553) was court painter to the Elector of Saxony. In his art he is representative of the South German tradition of landscape painting, but is more fa-

9–89 ALBRECHT DÜRER. *Adam* and *Eve*. 1507. Prado, Madrid. (Museo del Prado)

also setting out to soften the crassness of the native style without sacrificing its vigor, to infuse a feeling of structure into its forms, and to eliminate much of its detail in favor of greater generalization, while still retaining the restless, intricate Gothic line.

It was Albrecht Dürer (1472–1528) who first effected this reconciliation. On his trips to Italy he was much impressed by the painters and by the "secrets" of their art which he endeavored to learn. He studied perspective and the theory of proportions in order to capture the logic and order which characterized the High Renaissance in Italy. Dürer's paintings of *Adam* and *Eve*

mous for his portraits. He was also in touch with humanist circles and painted many mythological subjects.

(Fig. 9–89) exemplify this attempt to express Italian ideals with essentially German forms. Adam has the proportions and pose of a Roman statue or a nude by Raphael, yet there is a Northern attention to detail in the figure; also, the apple he holds and the ground on which he stands would have been more generalized in a contemporary Italian work. In contrast to the somewhat Italianate Adam, the figure of Eve is clearly related to the Germanic types that appear in Dürer's Madonnas and portraits. Although Eve's pose goes far back in Mediterranean art, the self-conscious treatment of the nude and the enamel-like surfaces underscore the northern origins of the work.

While Dürer was still a young man, the printing press was beginning to

9–90 ALBRECHT DÜRER. *St. Jerome in His Study.* Copper engraving. 1514. Metropolitan Museum of Art, New York. (Fletcher Fund, 1919)

which the severely geometric order of the composition thus attains is enhanced by the warm, softening light. We feel deeply touched by the contemplative mood in the room at the same time that we are made to sense that it is part of a greater world which extends beyond the windows as well as outward from the picture toward us.

In 1510, the same year as his *St. Jerome,* Dürer engraved on copper an entirely different subject, his well-known *Melancholia I* (Fig. 9–91). Where the religious life of St. Jerome seems calm and relaxed, the life of the creative artist, as indicated in this print, is full of unresolved tensions and frustrations. The complex symbolism of the engraving is based primarily on concepts derived from the Florentine Neo-Platonic academy; the willful ambiguities and the brutal crowding of the composition reflect the ideals of nascent Italian Mannerism. About the seated winged figure of Melancholy the instruments of the creative arts lie strewn in idle confusion; she is the personification of knowledge without the ability to act. Beside her a winged *putto* scribbles industriously on a slate — signifying action without knowledge. Everywhere we find the frustration of powerful forces, one of the themes so widely exploited by Italian Mannerists. According to the astrological theories of the time, the artist, or any man of creative activity, is a subject of Saturn. As such he is characterized by a melancholic humor bordering on madness which plunges him into despondency or raises him to the heights of creative fury. Like the Mannerists to the south, Dürer conceived of the artist (and thus of himself) as a genius who struggles to translate the pure *Idea* in his mind into gross but visible matter. In a sense this engraving illustrates the personal frustrations of Dürer, but in a larger context the frustrations are those of European Mannerism as well.

make books available. Illustrations began to be used commonly in printed books as early as about 1475. The extraordinary technical ability of German artists in woodcarving and their feeling for line as the chief means of creating form, as well as for its intrinsic calligraphic possibilities, were pre-eminent qualifications for successful illustration. In this field lies Dürer's greatest contribution to Western art. He used both the woodcut and the copper engraving to create an *œuvre* that has seldom been rivaled for quantity and quality in the field of graphic arts. In one of Dürer's best-known prints, *St. Jerome in His Study* (Fig. 9–90), perspective is used with a mastery matching that of the Italian High Renaissance but with a different, typically northern European aim. Dürer has constructed the space so that the spectator feels himself included in it. The quality of intimacy

Like Dürer, Hans Holbein the Younger (1497–1543) belonged to Renaissance Germany with all its internal turmoil and difficult transitions into sixteenth-century life. In his portraits, however, he had the selective ability to extract from the total visual impression a definite linear motif to which he subordinated whatever detail he used. His lines are clear-cut and sustained, not broken, indefinite, and restless like those of many northern painters. Technically, Holbein belongs to the fifteenth-century Flemish tradition, for the color surfaces of his paintings are as lustrous as enamel, the tones rather flat with slight use of shadow, and highly decorative.

Holbein's *Ambassadors* (Fig. 9–92) contains much of the esoteric symbolism of Dürer's *Melancholia I* and of the sixteenth century in general. Ostensibly it is the double portrait of two ambassadors from the court of Francis I to that of Henry VIII, and can be appreciated on this level alone. One feels here, as in Van Eyck's work, that paint has been transmuted into the very materials it represents. The objects in the "still life" are rendered with the same meticulous care as are the figures. A string is broken on the lute; not a figure is missing from the astronomical instruments. The stable and quiet composition is interrupted only by a long gray shape which rises diagonally from the floor. When viewed from the proper angle, this shape is recognized as a death's head, for like Dürer, Holbein was interested in symbolism as well as in radical perspectives. The objects of the still life, like those in the *Melancholia I*, indicate the active life, yet this painting is not so much an illustration of Renaissance melancholy as it is of the Medieval preoccupation with death. An open hymnbook with Luther's translation of *Veni, Creator Spiritus* and of the Ten Commandments may be intended to stress the reforming spirit of

9–91   ALBRECHT DURER. *Melancholia I*. Copper engraving. 1514. Metropolitan Museum of Art, New York. (Dick Fund, 1943)

the Protestant church and the salvation it offered.

In Holbein it is difficult to distinguish between the emotional and formal exaggerations of Italian Mannerism and the same tendencies of Late German Gothic. The forty-one woodcuts known as the *Dance of Death* disclose a dramatic power and an exuberant inventiveness scarcely known in the Medieval treatment of the same subject, although the subject itself had its origins during the plagues and wars of the Middle Ages. To a certain extent the macabre aspects of these prints are an inheritance from the Middle Ages designed to appeal to the northern pietistic audiences for whom this book was published. At the same time, the theme of the imminence of death applied equally well to Holbein's own time and was frequently exploited by Mannerists throughout Western Europe. Whatever the intentions behind the work,

Holbein's figure of Death, a skeleton imbued with life and alert movement, always plays his part with grim irony as he mockingly enters into the activity of each individual depicted.

The German artist in the graphic arts and painting found the exploitation of line most suited to his temperament. In his hand, line always preserved qualities of its own — abstract, intricate, and interweaving — quite apart from its use in demarking areas and defining planes. Line produced for him effects of vivid, never-ending movement and texture. Superb technical ability combined with love of decoration often led artists to load with ornament not only buildings but also altars, grilles, and even the pages of their early printed books. Technical virtuosity and aesthetic effectiveness seem to have been synonymous in their mind, though such masters as Dürer, Holbein, and Cranach, through their contacts with Italian art, infused northern linear realism with compositional organization.

Low Countries

The great century of Flemish painting was the fifteenth. During this century communication between Flanders and Italy increased, for not only did the two have a common interest in the manufacturing and trade of cloths, but Flemish artists began to journey more frequently to Venice and Florence. We see evidences of this contact creeping into Flemish art — in the interest in the figure as expressed in the nude; in the depiction of Renaissance instead of Gothic architecture and architectural details, and in Italian figure types and landscape. During the sixteenth century two main currents existed simultaneously in the Low Countries. One was a native tradition, which continued the

9–93 HIERONYMUS BOSCH. *Temptation of St. Anthony*. Middle panel of a triptych. *ca.* 1495. National Museum, Lisbon.

work of the fifteenth century, with minor variations or direct copying, leading to a type of genre painting that was
sometimes charming, sometimes satirical or fantastic. The other trend was
the elements of Italian art which began to blend with the Mannerist tendencies of Late Gothic in the work of
the "Antwerp Mannerists" [50] and their

contemporaries in Bruges and elsewhere — such as Gossart, Blondeel, Jan
van Scorel, and Van Orley (characteristically represented by *Virgin and
Child*, Metropolitan Museum, New
York).

A unique painter in the Flemish tradition was Hieronymus Bosch (*ca.*

[50] The school of painters known as the
Antwerp Mannerists was among the earliest
that attempted to fuse the formal principles

of the Italian High Renaissance with northern
naturalism. Joachim Patinir (d. *ca.* 1524) was
one of the first painters for whom landscape
could be the dominant subject of a picture.

9–94   PIETER BREUGHEL THE ELDER. *The Wedding Dance.* 1566. Detroit Institute of Arts. (Detroit Institute)

1450–1516). His visions of Hell and Paradise are a mingling of Medieval and Renaissance fantasy, of Medieval pietism and Renaissance Platonism. Usually a landscape or an architectural framework, receding into space, provided the setting which Bosch peopled with a multitude of real and imaginary figures all treated with meticulously rendered detail. In this dream world, prefiguring the nightmare landscapes of modern Surrealists, real and unreal are equally believable. The enamel-like colors with their crisp edges are juxtaposed to create a decorative pattern with strong emotive content. Bosch's esoteric works (Fig. 9–93) stand outside the development of northern painting; he had no precursors, except in terms of technique, and his successors borrowed only his imaginative concepts without their emotional and psychological content.

Pieter Breughel the Elder (1525/30–1569) had his roots in native traditions, and yet he was able to use for his own purposes elements from other traditions without subscribing wholly to their ideals. Influences from the landscapes of Joachim Patinir and the Antwerp Mannerists, from the fantasies of Bosch as well as compositional motifs from the Italians all came together in his work. His strong core of peasant robustness seemed to preclude the intellectuality or affected elegance of the Mannerism practiced by his contemporaries in the north.

Breughel's power and originality in ordering the teeming, full-blooded peasant life of his day into grandiose compositions is best seen in his handling of a large crowd, as in the *Wedding Dance* (Fig. 9–94). The individuals in the foreground, while retaining their particularity of type, costume,

9–95 CHATEAU OF CHAMBORD. 1526–1544. (N.D. Photo)

and environment, are drawn with such economy and emphasis at vital points that each becomes an embodiment of the rhythm of the dance. The group as a whole is firmly knit into interlocking curves in depth — movements which are carried partly by line and partly by shapes and color areas — united and accented by the static trees and standing figures.

With Breughel an era in the Low Countries came to an end. The wars which resulted in the separate entities of Catholic Belgium and Protestant Holland created societies with a new artistic climate and new tastes in art. With the coming of the Baroque both countries joined the main stream of European art and, in the persons of Rubens and Rembrandt, became leaders rather than followers. The old Flemish taste for detail lived on in the innumerable paintings of Dutch interiors, but was transformed according to the ideals of a new style.

France

Until the sixteenth century France remained largely Gothic. Each local community was a relatively independent civic and religious unit. In the sixteenth century, however, a greater national unity and a more cosmopolitan outlook now began to replace the Medieval tradition of local solidarity. With the exchange of commodities and of ideas a broader attitude toward life was established. The warmth and splendor of Italy captivated the northerners, even those who came primarily on political missions, like Charles VIII, who during his expedition to Italy in 1494 lived for some time in the Medici Palace in Florence. Even more influential than Charles was Francis I (1515–1547), a great patron of all the arts, who not only brought ideas from Italy but induced Italian artists, such as Leonardo da Vinci and Benvenuto Cellini, to come to France to execute commissions for him. The attempt to glorify the state and the monarch meant that the religious art of the Middle Ages was superseded, for it was the king and not the Church who now held power.

The tendency in France away from religious toward secular interests created a greater demand for chateaux and civic buildings. Many of the features of the old castles, such as the towers and battlements, had become so traditional that they persisted, even though the protective function of the

9–96 LOUVRE COURT, Paris. Façade by Pierre Lescot and Jean Goujon. 1546–1576. (Archives Photographiques)

castle had ceased with the advent of gunpowder. Climatic conditions also determined several features character-istic of northern buildings: steep roofs and a large number of windows, chim-neys, and fireplaces.

We see the Italian influence emerg-ing in the wing built by Francis I at Blois. The steep roof with its dormers and chimneys, the large windows with mullions, the niches containing statues, the gargoyles are all French, but the Italian elements reveal themselves in the regularity of the design, the repose that comes from the balance of vertical and horizontal directions, and the Clas-sical pilasters and carvings. Traditional love for the Gothic verticalism, howev-er, made the builder break his entabla-tures with pilasters.

Typical of the Early Renaissance chateaux is *Chambord* (Fig. 9–95). These chateaux were great country

places, usually built near enough to a forest to serve as hunting lodges. The plan of Chambord shows regularity and symmetry — a central square mass with four rounded towers at the cor-ners, set in a court surrounded on three sides by an outer line of rooms, and the whole surrounded by a moat. In the building, as it stands, horizontality dominates and ornament is sparse. As a mass, the chateau consists of interplay-ing rectangular and cylindrical vol-umes; in its fenestration it combines curving and angular motifs. Compensa-ting for the restraint below, the roof presents a fantastic group of steep sur-faces, with dormers and chimneys crowding around a central lantern.

The architecture of *Blois* and *Cham-bord* was still French at heart. During the reign of Henry II (1547–1559), however, treatises by Italian architects were translated and Italian architects

9–97 JEAN GOUJON. *Nymphs.* 1548–1549. Fontaine des Innocents, Paris. (Archives Photographiques)

came to work in France, while at the same time the French turned to Italy for study and travel. This interchange brought about a more thoroughgoing revolution in style, though it never eliminated certain French elements. In the *Louvre*, which now replaced the old royal palace on the Ile de la Cité, the projecting central and corner pavilions are descendants of the tower pavilions and the central gate of the early fortresslike chateaux. That part of the Louvre (Fig. 9–96) which was built by the architect Pierre Lescot (1510?–1578) and the sculptor Jean Goujon (d. before 1568) is one of the finest illustrations of French Renaissance style. The typically French details of this façade are somewhat lost in the large court which it now faces, for the projections, the shadows, and the detail are too delicate to carry a great distance. Each story forms a complete order; the pilasters no longer break through the entablature as at Blois; the cornices project enough to furnish a balancing horizontal accent. The arcading on the ground story reflects the Antique Roman combination of the arch and lintel, and is recessed enough to produce more shadow than the upper stories, thus strengthening the base of the design. On the second story the pilasters rising from bases, and the alternating curved and angular pediments supported by consoles, have direct antecedents in the Roman High Renaissance palace; but the decreased height of the stories, the larger size of the windows, and the sloping roof are northern. In this façade we see the best of French Renaissance architecture: masterly design both in the balance and in the proportions of the large elements, as well as delicacy, charm, and taste in details and ornamentation.

Sculpture in France, like architecture, slowly shifted away from its Gothic traditions to a style strongly influenced by the Italian Renaissance. Both Gothic and Renaissance elements can be seen, side by side, in the relief by Michel Colombe representing *St. George and the Dragon* (1508–1509, Louvre). The figures are still attached to the relatively flat ground in an essentially two-dimensional, curvilinear design in Medieval fashion; yet the introduction of spatial recession in the

9–98 IL ROSSO FIORENTINO. *Venus Reproving Love.* 1530–1540. Gallery of Francis I, Fontainebleau. (Archives Photographiques)

valley landscape and the clarity in the rendering of the action show the sculptor using Renaissance elements derived from fifteenth-century Florence. It was Cellini, in his work in France, who gave a more Mannerist direction to French sculpture (in the *Diana of Fontainebleau* attributed to him, for example), as did Il Rosso and Primaticcio in their stucco reliefs at Fontainebleau. Influenced by these artists, Jean Goujon, in his *Caryatids* (1550–1551, Louvre) and in his famous *Nymphs* (Fig. 9–97), exhibited tendencies toward academic classicism which we have noted in his co-worker Lescot.

Painting in France, however, was another matter. Under the leadership of the Italians, Il Rosso, Primaticcio, and Niccolo dell' Abate, installed at Fontainebleau by Francis I, Mannerism soon replaced the fading remnants of the earlier style. A group of still unidentified painters, known as the school of Fontainebleau, grew up under the influence of these Italians. They wholeheartedly adopted the courtly elegance fostered by Francis I, and created a typically French interpretation of Mannerism which spread throughout France and into neighboring countries.

Il Rosso Fiorentino, whose work in Italy we have mentioned earlier, became the court painter of Francis I shortly after 1530. In France his style no longer betrayed the turbulent harshness of the *Daughters of Jethro* (Fig. 9–77) but instead revealed a manner in which elegance and grace played a more and more important role. His assistant at Fontainebleau was Francesco Primaticcio (1504/05–1570), who had worked with Giulio Romano in Mantua. In all probability the younger painter was influential in hastening Il Rosso's evolution toward mannered grace. Il Rosso's decoration of the *Galerie François I* is purely Mannerist in concept. Here he combined for the first time painting, fresco, imitation mosaic, and stucco sculpture in low to very high relief. The abrupt transitions from one texture to another and the equally abrupt transitions in scale are typically Mannerist. In *Venus Reproving Love* (Fig. 9–98) Mannerist com-

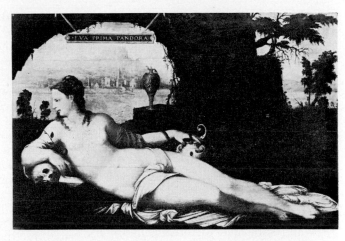

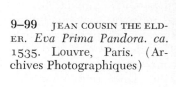

9–99   JEAN COUSIN THE ELD-
ER. *Eva Prima Pandora. ca.*
1535.   Louvre,   Paris.   (Archives Photographiques)

pression of space and elongated grace
are again dominant. The same grace
appears in the large flanking caryatids,
but one is jarred by the shift in scale
between the painted and the stucco
figures. There is an equally abrupt
transition between the caryatids, the
reliefs below them, and the figures
above the painting. The use of strapwork — the plaster elements above and
below the caryatids which look like cut
and rolled leather decorations — is also
characteristic. This motif is repeated
throughout the decoration at Fontainebleau, and soon became so popular that
it formed a standard part of all Mannerist decoration, particularly in the
north. Together with Primaticcio and
Cellini, Il Rosso influenced much of
French painting of the sixteenth century toward mannered elegance, continued after his death by Primaticcio
at Fontainebleau. Although his paintings at Fontainebleau are lost, the few
remaining stucco groups by Primaticcio indicate continued emphasis on elements introduced by Il Rosso.

Jean Cousin the Elder (d. 1560/61)
worked in the provinces without close
contact with the royal enterprises at
Fontainebleau. Nevertheless, his *Eva
Prima Pandora* (Fig. 9–99) betrays the
same Mannerist tendencies as the art
of the court. There is the elegance we

have noted elsewhere and an air of
gloom and foreboding which the northern Mannerist loved to exploit. Motifs
such as the grotto, dripping foliage,
and the death's head were more
strongly emphasized in German Mannerism than here, but their use to
heighten the sense of depression is the
same. The subject itself is indicative of
sixteenth-century taste, for throughout
western Europe there was a similar
commingling of pagan mythology and
Christianity.[51]

During the sixteenth century Italian
art was predominant in France. Its influence was direct and overpowering
in architecture, sculpture, and painting. Only portraiture offered any resistance to the imported style. As the
century progressed native artists assimilated the new elements and created
a distinctively French expression. As
their own understanding and command
of the new style increased, they began
to replace the foreign artists. The wars
of religion toward the end of the century halted the great progress of the
first half of the century, but did not
wholly stifle the arts. With the return

[51] Félix Chrétien's, *Moses and Aaron* (1537,
Metropolitan Museum, New York) is a
provincial example of the French Mannerist
type. This panel was commissioned as a
pendant to Holbein's *Ambassadors.*

of peace France was again oriented toward Italy by the Medici queens and by the literary men of her court, but now French artists traveled to Italy to study instead of learning from imported artists.

Spain

Its geographical position and mountainous terrain tended to isolate Spain from most of the other countries of Europe. Yet it was the prey of foreign conquerors — Roman, Goth, and Moor — and subjected to foreign influences, from Flanders, Italy, France, and the Near East. The advent of the Moors and their long residence in the peninsula were a provocation to the Christians, whose long struggle against the infidels, combined with native conserv-

9–100 Portal, University of Salamanca. *ca.* 1530.

atism, made them grim fighters for the Faith and severe opponents of all forms of heresy. The Church, with a conservative and overzealous priesthood, was always a dominant power. Hence it was in Spain that the Inquisition flourished as in no other country of Europe. Constant struggle and religious fervor made the Spaniard fanatical on the one hand and emotional and mystical on the other.

It was not until after the fall of Granada in 1492, when the Moors were expelled, that any semblance of political unity in the peninsula was possible. By the sixteenth century, largely through royal marriage and inheritance, Spain had become a first-rate power, holding large sections of Europe and acquiring wealth through its newly discovered possessions in the Americas.

Spain, like other European countries, accepted the Renaissance in its architecture, adapting it to local conditions and fusing it ingeniously with the native formal vocabulary, especially in ornament. This amalgam, known as the Plateresque style,[52] is well illustrated by the *town hall of Seville* and by the entrance of the *University of Salamanca* (Fig. 9–100). Plateresque ornament, with its extraordinary accent on highlights and shadows, heightened by the brilliant sunlight, was usually concentrated around the doors and windows; its decorative value was enhanced by the plain surfaces surrounding it. On the *Salamanca* entrance a richly decorated panel rises above the double portal. The ornament is arranged in three zones separated by double stringcourses and crowned by an elaborate cresting. Engaged clustered shafts frame the panel and furnish a needed vertical direction. The higher they are placed on

[52] A name derived from *platero*, a silversmith, and applied to the style because of the delicate execution of its ornament.

9–101 ESCORIAL, near Madrid. Juan Bautista de Toledo and Juan de Herrera, architects. 1563–1584.

the façade, the more the carvings increase in depth and boldness; they are broken by portrait medallions, heraldic emblems, and a sculptured group. The motifs, Italian in derivation, include *putti*, masks, grotesques, and the rinceau.

Plateresque was the most original accomplishment of the first half of the sixteenth century, and the brevity of its existence — only about half a century — was due to external causes. It was still vigorous when Philip II came to the throne in 1556. But it was too imaginative, too exuberant, and too emphatic in its ornament to please that austere and morose monarch. So, by royal order, a cold, unadorned classic ideal was imposed on Spain, and the warm Spanish style gave way to grim and solemn majesty, exemplified by the *Escorial* (Fig. 9–101), a huge, somber structure comprising church, monastery, and buildings of state, the work of the architect Juan de Herrera (1530–1597).

Spanish sculpture of the sixteenth century was largely made of wood, which was plentiful and cheap. Wood

also offered a good surface for painting, which was considered as important in a finished statue as the carving.

The advent of Italian influence is seen in the work of Alonso Berruguete (*ca.* 1486–1561). In Rome he had studied not only sculpture but also architecture and painting, and was alleged to have been a pupil of Michelangelo. On his return to Spain he worked in a melodramatic style in which the controlled movements of Italian art were transformed into the uncontrolled contortions which suited the Spanish love of realism and intense emotionalism. In his statue of *St. Peter* there is a brittle tenseness in the expressive face and in the lean, almost skeletonlike hands and feet. The drapery sweeps about the figure in massive folds, with a broad simplicity which accentuates the emaciation of the body.

A very close interrelationship and unity of style existed between the builders, sculptors, and other craftsmen of Spain. But painting produced sporadic outbursts from the hands of strong individuals, who often worked

9–102 EL GRECO. *Virgin with Sts. Ines and Tecla.* 1597–1599. Widener Collection, National Gallery of Art, Washington, D. C. (National Gallery)

in alien traditions rather than in a normally evolving national expression. Before the sixteenth century locally differentiated groups of painters produced mainly religious miniatures, frescoes (Spanish churches, like Italian, provided large wall areas), and panels in a Medieval style. Foreign influence, however, infiltrated, now from Siena, now from Flanders, now from France; and in the late fourteenth and

fifteenth centuries there evolved in Spain a Late Gothic style which is often difficult to distinguish from that of Flanders, France, or Italy.

In the sixteenth century one of the sporadic outbursts in Spanish painting occurred in the work of Domenico Theotocopoulos (*ca.* 1547–1614), called El Greco, who had been born on Crete but came to Italy as a young man. In his youth he was trained in the traditions of Late Byzantine frescoes and mosaics of the "Second Golden Age." While still young he went to Venice, where he was connected with the shop of Titian, although Tintoretto's painting seems to have made a stronger impression on him. A brief trip to Rome explains the influences of Roman and Florentine Mannerism on his work. By 1577 he left, for some unknown reason, for Spain, and he spent the rest of his life in Toledo. El Greco's art is a strong personal blending of Late Byzantine and Late Italian Mannerist elements. The intense emotionalism of his paintings — which appealed to the pious fervor of the Spanish — and the dematerialization of form, relying heavily on color, bind him to the sixteenth century and to Venetian Mannerism. His strong sense of movement and use of light, however, prefigure the Baroque. El Greco's art is not strictly Spanish, even though it appealed to certain segments of that society, for it had no Spanish antecedents and had but small effect on subsequent Spanish painting.

These almost irreconcilable elements — late Italian and Byzantine — are evident in his early *Assumption of the Virgin*. The composition is based on Titian's painting of the same subject, though the organization is close to Tintoretto. The panel is divided into two parts. Below, the apostles are grouped about the empty tomb in a circle from which the Virgin rises in a floating, spiral movement. The sharp point of the sarcophagus lid, the break in the circle of apostles, the uplifted hands, the horns of the crescent moon, the long slashes of light on the Virgin's robe, all accentuate this movement. In her ascent she is surrounded by a group of angels whose lightness and agitation contrast with the solidity of the firmly rooted figures below. As surface pattern, sharp triangles furnish the dominant motif, marked chiefly by edges where color areas meet. Everywhere the eye is guided by abrupt transitions from color to color, from light to dark. This sharp cutting of areas and planes, often by the juxtaposition of complementary colors, was boldly at variance with the Venetian practice of soft transitions. El Greco's Byzantine and Mannerist training is evident in his building forms out of color and light and integrating them into a design which by its own abstract power makes forceful the inner significance of the incident.[53]

The stylistic direction indicated in the *Assumption* becomes even more evident in the *Virgin with Sts. Ines and Tecla* (Fig. 9–102). Here the verticality of the earlier work becomes more pronounced. The elongation of the two female saints begins the movement seen in the Virgin's vertical ascent, which is carried out by the attenuation of her figure and that of the Christ Child. The angular void between the saints has been so compressed that the Virgin's buoyancy is heightened. Brilliant slashes of light play across the draperies with electric vitality. The same unearthly light touches the delicate faces, throwing the eyes into brooding shadow. Light and color are used not so much to

[53] The development of El Greco from a strong reliance on Venetian models to a style in which the forms are completely etherealized by an ecstatic swirl of unearthly light and color can be most effectively traced in his series on the subject of *The Expulsion of the Money Changers.*

9–103   EL GRECO. *Portrait of Cardinal Guevara. ca.* 1596–1600. Metropolitan Museum of Art, New York. (Bequest of Mrs. H. O. Havemeyer, 1929, H. O. Havemeyer Collection)

model form as to create a rapid and nervous movement across the surface. There is little concern with creating a space or movement within that space. Color helps create the illusion that the saint on the right is slightly in front of the one on the left, and yet this movement in depth remains shallow. El Greco was concerned primarily with emotion; this he created by vibrant color and by the exaggeration of his weightless, upward-reaching figures.

In two portraits, *Cardinal Guevara* (Fig. 9–103) and *Fray Palavicino* (Museum of Fine Arts, Boston), executed toward the turn of the century,

El Greco seems to reach the freest expression of his highly personal style. Light, which moved rapidly across the surface in earlier paintings, now becomes even more nervous and agitated. In the portrait of the Cardinal, El Greco's brush almost attacks the canvas with quick excited strokes. In the highlights and in the lace we can follow the artist's hand as he laid on the pigment now in short flicks, now with long jagged strokes which create the impression of tortuously agitated surface movement. Tensions are created by the ambiguity of the cardinal's pose. One hand is tense, the other relaxed; the upper torso seems to rest against the chair back, the lower seems to start forward as the draperies rush backward. At the same time the head is neither framed nor free of the door, but partially overlaps it. It is difficult to know whether El Greco wished to make a personal comment on the character of the Cardinal-Inquisitor. He did, however, make a comment on his own times, in which individual insecurities and tensions existed in the midst of external pomp and religious certitude.

The people of western Europe sought solutions for their insecurities during the Baroque period by turning either to the absolute power of the State or to pietistic sects and visionary saints. In his late work El Greco moved into the world of pure spirit where matter no longer hinders the flight of the soul. Earth and sky are of the same stuff and are equally unreal in his brooding *View of Toledo* (Metropolitan Museum, New York) (Fig. 0–20). In El Greco Mannerist ideals are intensified to a final point. His emotionalism, form-dissolving color, and abstract design can neither be imitated nor carried farther. The last word in Mannerism had been spoken in Spain; in Italy the new Baroque style was already beginning to appear.

Summary

Mannerist art as it spread from Italy across western Europe continually encountered varying degrees of opposition from local styles. In Spain and France it easily influenced native art forms. In Germany and the Low Countries Italian Mannerism blended with lingering northern Medievalism to emphasize national styles. Because the sixteenth century marked the definition of the modern national states of western Europe, it is not surprising to find at this time the emphasis on national styles in art. Each of these, however, drew its inspiration first from Italy, assimilating this inspiration into a national expression to a greater or lesser degree. All these styles participate in the common and larger uniting style which we have identified as Mannerism.

Bibliography

Alberti, Leon Battista, *On Painting*, tr. by J. R. Spencer, Yale University Press, 1956.

Anderson, W. J., *The Architecture of the Renaissance in Italy*, 5th ed., Scribner's, 1927.

Antal, F., *Florentine Painting and Its Social Background*, Kegan Paul, Trench, Trubner, London, 1948.

Argan, G. C., *Fra Angelico*, Skira, New York, 1955.

——, *Botticelli*, Skira, New York, 1957.

——, and Lassaigne, J., *The Fifteenth Century*, Skira, Geneva, 1955.

Berenson, Bernhard, *The Drawings of the Florentine Painters*, 3 vols., University of Chicago, 1938.

——, *Italian Painters of the Renaissance*, Phaidon Publishers, New York, 1953.

——, *Italian Pictures of the Renaissance*, Oxford University Press, New York, 1932.

Biagi, Luigi, *Jacopo della Quercia*, Arnaud, Florence, 1946.

Blunt, Anthony, *Art and Architecture in France, 1500–1700*, Pelican Books, Baltimore, 1953.

——, *Artistic Theory in Italy*, Oxford University Press, New York, 1941.

Bode, Wilhelm von, *Die Kunst der Frühre-naissance in Italien,* 2nd ed., Propyläen-Verlag, Berlin, 1926.

Brown, A., and Rankin, W., *A Short History of Italian Painting,* Dutton, 1914.

Burckhardt, J. C., *The Civilization of the Renaissance in Italy,* tr. by S. G. C. Middlemoore, Oxford University Press, New York, 1945.

Byron, Robert, and Talbot Rice, David, *The Birth of Western Painting,* Knopf, 1931.

Cairns, Huntington, and Walker, John, eds., *Masterpieces of Painting from the National Gallery of Art,* Random House, 1944.

Castiglione, Baldassare, *The Book of the Courtier,* tr. by L. E. Opdycke, Scribner's, 1903.

Cellini, Benvenuto, *Autobiography,* tr. by J. A. Symonds, Modern Library, New York, 1927.

Cennini, Cennino, *Il Libro dell'Arte,* tr. and ed. by D. V. Thompson, Jr., Yale University Press, 1932-33.

Chastel, André, *L'art italien,* 2 vols., Larousse, Paris, 1956.

Clapp, Frederick M., *Jacopo Carucci de Pontormo,* Yale University Press, 1916.

Clark, Kenneth, *Leonardo da Vinci,* Macmillan, New York, 1939.

——, *Piero della Francesca,* Phaidon Press, London, 1951.

Conway, Sir W. M., *The Van Eycks and Their Followers,* Murray, London, 1921.

Crowe, Sir J. A., and Cavalcasselle, G. B., *History of Painting in North Italy,* ed. by Tancred Borenius, 3 vols., Scribner's, 1912.

——, *New History of Painting in Italy,* ed. by L. Douglas, Groes, London, 1912.

DeTolnay, Charles, *Michelangelo,* Vol. 1, "The Youth of Michelangelo," 1943; Vol. 2, "The Sistine Ceiling," 1945; Vol. 3, "The Medici Chapel," 1948; Vol. 4, "The Tomb of Julius II," 1954; Princeton University Press.

Dimier, Louis, *French Painting in the 16th Century,* Scribner's, 1911.

Dussler, Luitpold, *Giovanni Bellini,* A. Schroll, Vienna, 1949.

Dvorak, M., *Geschichte der Italienischen Kunst,* 2 vols., R. Piper, Munich, 1927.

Edgell, George H., *A History of Sienese Painting,* Dial Press, New York, 1932.

Freedberg, Sydney, *Parmigianino,* Harvard University Press, 1950.

Friedlander, Max J., *Die altniederländische Malerei,* 14 vols., B. Cassirer, Berlin, 1924-37.

——, *Early Netherlandish Painting from Van Eyck to Breugel,* Phaidon Press, London, 1956.

Friedlander, W., *Mannerism and Anti-Mannerism in Italian Painting,* Columbia University Press, 1957.

Ganz, Paul, *Hans Holbein, the Younger,* Phaidon Publishers, New York, 1950.

Geck, F. J., *Bibliography of Italian Early Renaissance Art,* University of Colorado, 1932.

——, *Bibliography of Italian High Renaissance Art,* University of Colorado, 1933.

——, *Bibliography of Italian Late Renaissance Art,* University of Colorado, 1934.

Glaser, Curt, *Les Peintres Primitifs Allemands,* Les Editions G. van Oest, Paris, 1931.

Glück, Gustav, *Die Kunst der Renaissance in Deutschland, den Niederlanden, Frankreich, . . . ,* Propyläen-Verlag, Berlin, 1928.

Goldscheider, Ludwig, *El Greco,* Phaidon Publishers, New York, 1938.

——, ed., *The Painting, Sculpture and Architecture of Michelangelo,* Phaidon Publishers, New York, 1953.

Gould, C., *An Introduction to Italian Renaissance Painting,* Phaidon Publishers, New York, 1957.

Grossmann, F., ed., *Brueghel, the Paintings: Complete Edition,* Phaidon Press, London, 1956.

Hartt, Frederick, *Giulio Romano,* Yale University Press, 1958.

Heydenreich, L. H., *Leonardo da Vinci,* Macmillan, New York, 1954.

Hind, Arthur, M., ed., *Albrecht Dürer, His Engravings and Woodcuts,* Stokes, New York, 1911.

Holt, E. G., *Literary Sources of Art History,* Princeton University Press, 1947.

Horst, Carl, *Die Architektur der Deutschen Renaissance,* Propyläen-Verlag, Berlin, 1928.

Huizinga, J. *The Waning of The Middle Ages,* Longmans, Green, New York, 1924.

Jameson, Anna B. M., *Sacred and Legendary Art,* 2 vols., Longmans, Green, New York, 1905.

Janson, H. W., *The Sculpture of Donatello,* Princeton University Press, 1957.

Krautheimer, R. and T., *Lorenzo Ghiberti,* Princeton University Press, 1956.

Lassaigne, J., *Flemish Painting,* Skira, New York, 1957.

Leonardo da Vinci, *The Notebooks of Leonardo da Vinci,* tr. by Edward MacCurdy, 2 vols., Harcourt, Brace, 1938.

MacLagen, Eric, *Italian Sculpture of the Renaissance*, Harvard University Press, 1935.

McComb, Arthur, *Bronzino*, Harvard University Press, 1928.

Marle, Raimond van, *The Development of the Italian Schools of Painting*, 19 vols., M. Nijhoff, The Hague, 1923–39.

Mather, Frank J., Jr., *A History of Italian Painting*, Holt, 1923.

Mayer, August L., *El Greco*, Delphin-Verlag, Munich, 1916.

Mesnil, J., *Masaccio et les debuts de la Renaissance*, M Nijhoff, The Hague, 1927.

Middledorf, Ulrich A., *Raphael's Drawings*, H. Bittner, New York, 1945.

Offner, Richard, *Italian Primitives at Yale University*, Yale University Press, 1927.

Ortolani, Sergio, *Il Pollaiuolo*, U. Hoepli, Milan, 1948.

Paatz, W., *Die Kunst der Renaissance in Italien*, W. Kohlhammer, Stuttgart, 1953.

Panofsky, Erwin, *Albrecht Dürer*, 3rd ed., 2 vols., Princeton University Press, 1948.

——, *Early Netherlandish Painting*, Harvard University Press, 1954.

Paintings and Sculpture from the Kress Collection, National Gallery of Art, Washington D. C., 1945.

Pater, W., *The Renaissance*, Modern Library, New York, no date.

Pevsner, Nikolaus, "The Architecture of Mannerism," *The Mint*, Routledge & Sons, London, 1946.

——, *An Outline of European Architecture*, Scribner's, 1948.

Pittaluga, Mary, *Fra Filippo Lippi*, Del Turco, Florence, 1949.

Pope-Hennessy, John, *The Complete Work of Paolo Uccello*, Phaidon Publishers, New York, 1950.

——, *The Paintings of Fra Angelico*, Phaidon Publishers, New York, 1952.

——, *Sienese Quattrocento Painting*, Phaidon Press, London, 1947.

Post, C. R., *History of Spanish Painting*, 3 vols., Harvard University Press, 1943.

Ricci, Corrado, *Architecture and Decorative Sculpture of the High and Late Renaissance in Italy*, Brentano, New York, 1923.

Richter, George M., *Giorgio da Castelfranco*, University of Chicago Press, 1937.

Ring, Grete, *A Century of French Painting*, Phaidon Publishers, New York, 1949.

Salmi, Mario, *Paolo Uccello, Andrea del Castagno, Domenico Veneziano*, U. Hoepli, Milan, 1938.

Sandberg-Vavala, E., *Uffizi Studies*, L. S. Olschki, Florence, 1948.

Schubring, Paul, *Die Kunst der Hochrenaissance in Italien*, Propyläen-Verlag, Berlin, 1926.

Scott, Geoffrey, *The Architecture of Humanism*, 2nd ed., Scribner's, 1924.

Seymour, C., Jr., *Masterpieces of Sculpture from the National Gallery of Art*, Coward-McCann, New York, 1949.

Sterling, Charles, *La Peinture Française: Les peintres du moyen âge*, P. Tisné, Paris, 1942.

Suida, W., and Goldscheider, Ludwig, *Raphael*, Phaidon, New York, 1941.

Symonds, J. A., *A Short History of the Renaissance in Italy*, ed. by A. Pearson, Holt, 1894.

Tietze, Hans, *Tintoretto*, Phaidon Publishers, New York, 1948.

——, and Tietze-Conrat, Erica, *The Drawings of the Venetian Painters in the 15th and 16th Centuries*, J. J. Augustin, New York, 1944.

Tietze-Conrat, Erica, *Mantegna*, Phaidon Press, London, 1955.

Vaccarino, Paolo, *Nanni di Banco*, Sansoni, Florence, 1950.

Vasari, Giorgio, *The Lives of the Painters, Sculptors, and Architects*, tr. by A. B. Hinds, 4 vols., Dutton, 1927.

Venturi, Adolfo, *A Short History of Italian Art*, tr. by E. Hutton, Macmillan, New York, 1926.

Voss, Hermann G. A., *Die Malerei der Spätrenaissance in Rom und Florenz*, 2 vols., G. Grote, Berlin, 1920.

Wescher, P., *Jean Fouquet and His Time*, Reynal & Hitchcock (Harcourt, Brace), 1947.

Wittkower, Rudolf, *Architectural Principles in the Age of Humanism*, Warburg Institute, University of London, 1952.

Wölfflin, Heinrich, *Classic Art*, Phaidon Publishers, New York, 1952.

——, *Principles of Art History*, tr. by M. D. Hottinger, Holt, 1932.

CHAPTER 10

BAROQUE

AND ROCOCO

(1600–1750)

Late in the sixteenth and early in the seventeenth century a more confident, self-assured attitude reasserted itself after the doubts and uncertainties characteristic of the mid-sixteenth century. Pessimism was replaced by a more positive outlook; tensions were eased. But the differences between the two periods can easily be exaggerated. The transition from one to the other was not abrupt. Furthermore, seventeenth-century artists continued to use, although for a new purpose, many of the novel and exciting forms developed by the Mannerists.

The term "Baroque" is often applied to the art of the seventeenth century. The origin of the word is not clear. Possibly it comes from the Portuguese *barroco,* meaning an irregularly shaped pearl. Certainly the term was originally used in a disparaging sense, referring to an opulent extravagance in the art of the period, and this connotation still persists. The term "Baroque" is

ILLUSTRATION ABOVE. **10–1** FRANÇOIS BOUCHER. *The Toilet of Venus, ca.* 1750. Metropolitan Museum of Art, New York.

satisfactory only if we consider it as connoting the underlying common interests of the artists of the period.

All this implies complexity, even apparent contradictions, in the nature of the art itself. Indeed there is a rich, at times almost bewildering, variety in the forms employed. The situation is by no means confined to the visual arts. For instance, at the time when the Church, roused to reform through the Counter Reformation, reasserted the mystery of the Christian faith with almost Medieval intensity, Descartes in his *Cogito, ergo sum* was well on the way to displacing this Medieval faith with reason. It was the century of Francis Bacon, Galileo, and Isaac Newton; of the invention of the telescope, the microscope, and the thermometer; of the discovery of the circulation of the blood. But it was also the century which saw the major developments in such a complex and emotionally exuberant art form as the opera, and which (on its darker side) countenanced a veritable orgy of witch hunts.

In spite of this complexity we now

realize that the seventeenth century had a number of common objectives which give the period unity. These canons were first observed in the form of architecture, painting, and sculpture — in the art of Bernini and Borromini in Italy, of Rubens, Vermeer, and Rembrandt in the Lowlands, of Velázquez in Spain, and of the court of Louis XIV at Versailles; and in a magnificent series of eighteenth-century German churches. This, the Baroque period, was one of the most dynamic and powerful in the history of Western culture.

Italy

ARCHITECTURE

Rome was the fountainhead of that more lavish and opulent aspect of seventeenth-century art to which the term "Baroque" was originally applied. The seeds of the style, sown in the sixteenth century, particularly by Michelangelo, grew quickly in his native Italian soil. Furthermore, the Church, and in particular the recently established militant Jesuit order, welcomed those elements in the style which were in harmony with the strongly emotional tenor of Counter-Reformation Catholicism.

The Roman Baroque architects sought, often with great ingenuity and subtlety, to supply the spectator with a rich variety of sensations. Suggestions of movement and change, of a fluid or organic relationship between the parts of the building, are characteristic. The architect called on every resource at his disposal to obtain these effects; planning and spatial organization reached unprecedented complexity; surfaces were treated sculpturally; color and (above all) light were consciously brought into play. And yet, in the hands of the major architects of the period, this lavish array was marshaled with marvelous control and precision. An infallible feeling for climax

10–2 ST. PETER'S. Rome. View, showing the façade (1612) of Maderna and the great piazza (after 1656) by Bernini. (Anderson)

and focus ordered the various elements so that the total effect was never merely sensational. At its best the emotional impact produced by a Roman Baroque building is akin to that of a fugue, another of the great Baroque art forms. Each is an organism of great complexity which in the end reveals itself as a tightly integrated whole.

With its powerful religious motivation the seventeenth century was a great age of church building and remodeling. One of the major tasks of the period was the completion of *St. Peter's*, which had been left unfinished by Michelangelo's successors. The final extended form of the nave and the façade were the work of Carlo Maderna from 1606 to 1612, while the major interior decorations and the great piazza before the church were added by Giovanni Lorenzo Bernini in the middle part of the century (Fig. 10–2). The choice of an oval shape for the main piazza rather than the inherently more stable form of a circle or square is characteristic of the period. So also are the great colonnades which enclose the space in a fascinating way, presenting the spectator, as he crosses the area, with a fluid boundary, partly open, partly closed, ever changing with his position. Within the piazza an obelisk and a pair of splashing fountains provide minor foci for the spectator's attention. But Bernini, with a typical Baroque feeling for climax, never forgot that the piazza was only a prelude to the church, and the great sweep of entablature above the colonnade brings the spectator's eye inevitably around to the façade of the building. Such a concern with the dynamic organization of large exterior spaces as Bernini exhibited in Rome is typical of the Baroque period.

Bernini sought to supply a comparable sense of climax inside St. Peter's by the construction of a huge bronze baldachino placed over the high altar

10–3 GIOVANNI BERNINI. *Baldachino Over the High Altar in St. Peter's*, Rome. 1624–1633. (Alinari)

(Fig. 10–3) under Michelangelo's great dome, and by the elaborate decoration of the eastern apse. Here, with a wide variety of materials and with the swirling forms of spiral columns and curving ornament, he established a focus for the vast interior.

When the Roman Baroque architects were free to design their own buildings without limitations imposed by their predecessors, their freedom of invention was amazing. One of the most ingenious was Francesco Borromini (1599–1667), whose tiny church, *San Carlo alle Quattro Fontane*, is an excellent example of a Baroque treatment of the central-type building so dear to the High Renaissance. The plan (Fig. 10–4) at first glance appears

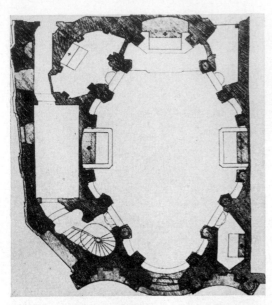

10–4 FRANCESCO BORROMINI. *San Carlo alle Quattro Fontane*, Rome. Plan. *ca.* 1638. (After Fokker, *Roman Baroque Art*, Oxford University Press, 1938)

10–5 FRANCESCO BORROMINI. *San Carlo alle Quattro Fontane*. Interior of the dome. *ca.* 1638. (Alinari)

to depend on a complicated series of interlocking ovals yielding an irregular interior space enclosed by an undulating surface. However, when the viewer looks upward into the dome of the little building (Fig. 10–5), it seems that Borromini may have intended him to sense a relationship between San Carlo and a Renaissance church. The same central dome and the four flanking semidomes are there, but now they are constructed in such a way that they appear to have yielded to pressure from two sides. The result spatially is a sense of flow and fusion between the compartments instead of the emphasis on the clearly defined units which was characteristic of High Renaissance building.

The longitudinal or axial church plan, however, outweighed the central plan in popularity during the seventeenth century. It was more satisfactory for the performance of church ritual, newly emphasized by the Counter Reformation, and it was also more satisfactory for preaching. With this axial form the Baroque architect was also inventive, as one can see in Carlo Rainaldi's *Santa Maria in Campitelli* (Fig. 10–6), the interior of which was done between 1656 and 1675. The spectator's impression, when he steps inside the door of this church, is of a complicated sequence of spaces stretching off before him toward the altar. He cannot sense the precise size of these spaces; indeed, he is misled by the architect into supposing some of them larger than they are. The flood of light, admitted by the dome beyond the second arch, for instance, would lead one to expect a lateral extension of space, a transept, where none in fact exists (Fig. 10–7). The deliberate breaking up of the space with arches and columns, further accented by the different light sources, is typical of the Baroque love of complexity. But see also how this intricate array is ordered by the

10-6 CARLO RAINALDI. *Santa Maria in Campitelli*, Rome. (Vatican Museum, Rome)

rhythmic repetition of paired columns leading toward the altar, which with its mass of gilded rays, brightly lighted by concealed windows at either side of the apse, becomes the clear focus of attention.

SCULPTURE

In sculpture the dominating personality was also Bernini (1598–1680), who was even more distinguished in this field than in architecture, though to his way of thinking the two fields were closely related and interdependent. His *baldachino* in St. Peter's, for instance, is as much sculpture as architecture, as is the great shrine in the apse which he devised to hold the chair of St. Peter.

The *altar of St. Teresa* in Santa Maria della Vittoria (Fig. 10–8) demonstrates even more clearly Bernini's skill in integrating sculptural, architectural, and pictorial concepts. The group of

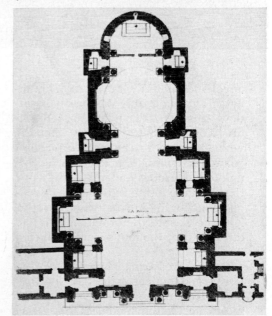

10-7 CARLO RAINALDI. *Santa Maria in Campitelli*, Rome. Plan. 1656–1675. (After Fokker, *Roman Baroque Art*, Oxford University Press, 1938)

10–8 GIOVANNI BERNINI. *The Ecstasy of St. Teresa.* Cornaro Chapel in Santa Maria della Vittoria. Rome. 1644–1652. (Anderson)

angel and saint in white marble, illuminated from above by a concealed window, appears to float against a background of darting gold rays; and the whole is set in a richly carved niche of colored marbles. The effect, which is palpably sensuous and yet at the same time ecstatic in the intensity of its religious feeling, is an epitome of the spirit of the Counter Reformation as it had developed by the mid-seventeenth century.

Bernini was equally successful in a less grandiloquent vein. His portrait busts, for instance, are among the most direct and immediately appealing works in the whole range of seventeenth-century art. That of Bernini's patron, *Cardinal Scipione Borghese* (Fig. 10–9), with its subtle understanding of the mobility of the human face, captures a characteristic momentary expression, conveying a vivid impression of personality.

PAINTING

The development of Baroque painting in Italy is more complicated than that of architecture or sculpture. Differing points of view appeared at the beginning of the century, and these were never fully reconciled. The two artists who did most to establish these divergent trends were Michelangelo Merisi da Caravaggio (1573–1610) and Annibale Carracci (1560–1609). Both artists reacted against Mannerist painting in their desire to understand reality, not in terms of a rational "idea"

10–9 GIOVANNI BERNINI. *Cardinal Scipione Borghese.* 1632. Borghese Gallery, Rome. (Anderson)

but rather by careful observation of the natural world. Whereas Caravaggio turned with startling directness to an empirical observation of the objects about him, Annibale Carracci preferred to approach the physical world more indirectly through forms devised by his predecessors. The *Youthful Bacchus* (Fig. 10–10) is an excellent example of Caravaggio's earlier work. The artist has conveyed with uncanny precision a wide range of sensations of texture. The surfaces of the glass, the leaves, the flesh, the fruit are clearly differentiated from one another through careful observation of the different ways in which light plays over the various surfaces. Caravaggio's study of the way in which light creates highlights and shadows also enabled him to suggest the roundness and solidity of forms. All this creates a sensuous and physically immediate impact quite different from that evoked by Mannerist pictures.

10–10 CARAVAGGIO. *The Youthful Bacchus. ca.* 1595. Uffizi, Florence. (Soprintendenza alle Gallerie, Florence)

10–11 ANNIBALE CARRACCI. *Polyphemus Hurling Rocks at Acis. ca.* 1600. Gallery of the Farnese Palace, Rome. (Alinari)

10–12 GIOVANNI GAULLI (BACICCIO). *The Triumph of the Name of Jesus. ca.* 1670. Church of Gesù, Rome. (Alinari)

Annibale Carracci paid more attention than Caravaggio to the accomplishments of his predecessors, though when he utilized devices employed by earlier painters he transformed them to emphasize a Baroque sense of unity. The *Polyphemus Hurling Rocks at Acis* (Fig. 10–11), from a series of frescoes which he executed for the gallery of the Farnese Palace in Rome, is a fine example of this creative metamorphosis. The basic compositional device, the opposition of a large foreground object on one side against a small distant object on the other, was popular with many sixteenth-century artists, especially Tintoretto. Yet if one compares this work with the *Finding of the Body of St. Mark* (Fig. 9–83) Carracci's new spirit is immediately apparent. Instead of emphasizing the tension be-

tween the foreground and the background, Carracci used the diagonal to focus attention on the action of Polyphemus, dominating the foreground.

Both Caravaggio and Carracci attracted followers among Italian seventeenth-century painters. As time went on an exaggerated sense of the opposition between the two artists developed; the differences in outlook were accentuated by critics, while the underlying common qualities were ignored. Carracci, with his fuller acceptance of tradition, appealed to the intellectuals and critics so that his reputation, and the reputations of artists sympathetic to his point of view, for a time eclipsed that of Caravaggio. Yet Caravaggio's exciting observation of natural forms ultimately proved more popular, with the result that his influence spread through-

10–13 GIOVANNI BATTISTA TIEPOLO. *Apotheosis of the Pisani Family.* Fresco. 1761–1762. Villa Pisani, Stra. (Alinari)

out Europe, especially in the Low Countries and in Spain.

The synthesizing tendency of Baroque art — the combining of qualities from the various visual arts into one grand ensemble — had a powerful effect on the development of ceiling painting in seventeenth-century Italy. Starting with the work of Carracci in the *Farnese Gallery,* which in turn owed much to the *Sistine ceiling,* decorative schemes of increasing complexity and magnificence were evolved throughout the century. In a ceiling such as that painted for the *Gesù* by Giovanni Battista Gaulli (known as "Baciccio") (1639–1709), sculpture and painting are played against the vaulted surface of the nave in a deliberate desire to mislead the spectator as to the physical dimensions of the space in the building, and to create the illusion of a boundless vista opening toward Heaven (Fig. 10–12). Yet here, too, in the dazzling brilliance of the central Jesuit emblem to which everything is related, one finds the characteristic Baroque concern for coherence and unity.

The final chapter in the long story of ceiling painting in Italy came in the eighteenth century with the work of the Venetian, Giovanni Battista Tiepolo (1696–1770). In the painting of Tiepolo and his contemporaries the illusionistic tendencies of the seventeenth century were relaxed; the emphasis was rather on the creation of gay, brightly colored schemes of great elegance and grace which, for sheer effectiveness as décor are unsurpassed (Fig. 10–13).

10–14   PETER PAUL RUBENS. *Rape of the Daughters of Leucippus. ca. 1617.* Munich.

Low Countries

The attitudes characteristic of seventeenth-century art in Italy quickly found sympathetic echoes elsewhere in Europe. Sometimes these developments were stimulated by direct contact with Italian art, but sometimes they appear to have been independent and indigenous. Frequently the results, at least in painting, equaled and even surpassed anything the Italians produced. Thus of all the European artists active in the seventeenth century, it was a Fleming, Peter Paul Rubens (1577–1640), who most completely realized in painting the rich, exuberant Baroque effects which Bernini, Borromini, and others achieved in sculpture and architecture.

Rubens lived in Italy for eight years (1600–1608) as court painter to the duke of Mantua. Before he returned to

10–15 PETER PAUL RUBENS. *Kermess* (Village Carnival). *ca.* 1635–1636. Louvre, Paris. (Girandon)

his native Antwerp he had assimilated the whole range of Italian sixteenth-century painting and also studied the work of Caravaggio and Carracci. Indeed, he was able to synthesize the points of view of these two artists with a success which none of their Italian followers achieved, combining Caravaggio's sensuous appeal with Carracci's dynamic compositions and heroic forms. With an energy like that of Tintoretto, Rubens usually chose dramatic themes, whether the subject was religious or mythological, landscape, portrait, or genre. In the *Rape of the Daughters of Leucippus* (Fig. 10–14) the surface pattern, organized by intersecting diagonals and verticals, consists of areas of extraordinarily rich contrasting textures — the soft luminous flesh of the women, the bronzed muscular flesh of the men, lustrous satins, glinting armor, and the taut skin of horses. Yet the picture is not organized simply as surface pattern, but as a tightly knit group of solid masses in space. Each unit of this design is built up of solid forms defined by color and light, as in Titian's late works, rather

than drawn in the Florentine sense of draftsmanship.

In many paintings from Rubens' later career, such as the *Kermess* (Fig. 10–15), organization and suggestions of movement in depth are developed even further. The exuberant movement of the dancers is offset by the quiet spaciousness of the distance and by the solidity and repeated verticals of the trees and the house.

Anthony van Dyck (1599–1641), a younger Flemish painter, moved from an initial style closely related to the dazzling exuberance, impetuosity, and frank sensuality of Rubens toward one of comparative sobriety and elegant refinement. These qualities were particularly felicitous in the many portraits of the English and Continental nobility which constitute the major part of Van Dyck's work. Van Dyck was able to capture subtle nuances of character and temperament so that his portraits often reflect with great sensitivity not only the individual personality but also the general environment of the sitter. Thus his portraits of Genoese aristocrats, with their rich, somber costumes

10–16 SIR ANTHONY VAN DYCK. *James Stuart,* Duke of Richmond and Lenox. 1632–1640. Metropolitan Museum of Art, New York. (Gift of Henry G. Marquand, 1889)

these adjoining countries: ethnically the Dutch were closer to the Germans, whereas the Flemings were related to the French. In the Flanders of Rubens the Catholic Church of the Counter Reformation was strong. Protestantism was dominant among the Dutch, and the consequent puritanical attitude toward art did much to limit the production of sculpture, religious pictures, or anything recalling pagan myths or even historical subjects. As we think back over the art of the Middle Ages and of the Renaissance, we realize that, if religious subjects had been prohibited, one of the major stimuli for artistic activity would have disappeared. What then remained to enrich the lives of wealthy Hollanders? For they were wealthy, since during the early part of the Spanish rule the Dutch, like the Flemish, had flourished. The East India Company had been formed and the discovery of the New World had opened up further opportunities for trade and colonization. The great Dutch commercial cities, such as Haarlem and Amsterdam, had been stimulated and enriched, and civic pride was strong.

Under these circumstances

Dutch painting . . . was and could be only the portrait of Holland, its exterior image, faithful, exact, complete, with no embellishments. Portraits of men and places, citizen habits, squares, streets, countryplaces, the sea and the sky — such was to be . . . the programme followed by the Dutch school, and such it was from its first day to the day of its decline.[1]

Thus it came about that the Dutch painters pried into the pictorial possibilities of everyday life. They kept an eye on their patrons, the middle-class burghers, who were acquiring wealth and position and wanted paintings to hang on the walls of their houses as evidence of their prosperity. The paint-

[1] Eugène Fromentin, *The Masters of Past Time,* Phaidon Publications, New York, p. 130.

and proud bearing are never to be confused with those he painted of the English gentry of the court of Charles I, pictures which in their ineffable languid elegance tinged with melancholy have done so much to determine, even to the present day, opinion concerning the ill-fated king and his courtiers on the eve of the Civil War (Fig. 10–16).

By the Peace of Westphalia (1648) the northern part of the Low Countries, or Netherlands, became independent of Spain, while Flanders in the south remained Spanish territory. There are marked differences between

ers also instinctively realized that a copy of the actual appearance of things would best suit the Northern appetite for realism.

The portraits by Frans Hals (*ca.* 1580–1666) show us these people in a vigorous and contagiously joyful manner. In the *Laughing Cavalier* (Fig. 10–17) a self-confident soldier with a suggestion of bravado looks out at us with a direct glance while over his face ripples a fleeting expression, reminiscent of the sculptured portraits Bernini was executing in Italy at about the same time. The simple pattern of sweeping curves and sharp angles, the color scheme, and the contrast of cool quiet and warm vivacious areas are in harmony with the nonchalance and bravado of the subject.

Momentary surface expression is characteristic of much of Hals' work, and his technical methods were particularly suitable to his purpose. As his career progressed he became ever more economical in his brushwork,

constructing wonderfully convincing forms with a few vigorous strokes.

Hals also painted many group por-

10–17 FRANS HALS. *Laughing Cavalier.* 1624. Wallace Collection, London. (Anderson)

10–18 FRANS HALS. *The Archers of St. Adrian.* 1623. Frans Hals Museum, Haarlem. (Braun)

10–19 REMBRANDT VAN RIJN. *Portrait of a Man.* 1630's. Kunsthistoriches Museum, Vienna. (Kunstverlag Wolfrum, Vienna)

traits of civic organizations, a type of portrait painting popular in the Netherlands. In those of *The Archers of St. Adrian* at Haarlem (Fig. 10–18) and *The Governors of the St. Elizabeth Hospital,* he has grouped the figures so that each is equally visible and each head is an individualized portrait. But the artist has managed to tie them into a loose pattern and to create a vivacious surface by his vigorous painting of the textures of lace, velvet, satin, and metal.

Dutch Baroque painting would be considered delightful and meticulous but lacking in the essential qualities of a truly great art were it not for the work of Rembrandt van Rijn (1606–1669). His achievements made Dutch painting outstanding in the history of Western art.

In the early part of his career, during the 1630's in Amsterdam, Rem-

brandt's work was in the spirit of the times and in accord with the expectations of his bourgeois patrons. His *Portrait of a Man* (Fig. 10–19) exhibits as much care and precision in describing details of costume and accidents of individual physiognomy as the most punctilious sitter could wish for. But in addition to this verisimilitude the portrait exhibits a remarkable clarity in the three-dimensional definition and spatial placement of the figure which sets the Rembrandt painting apart from the many similar pictures executed by his contemporaries.

When Rembrandt, during this period of his career, turned to a mythological or religious subject he brought to it a turbulent emotional excitement not unlike that of his older neighbor Rubens. In the early *Supper at Emmaus* (Fig. 10–20), for instance, Rembrandt used every pictorial device available to make the scene as startling as possible. The two disciples are depicted thrown into complete confusion by the realization that their supper companion is the Christ. Christ himself is silhouetted against an intense light which immediately focuses attention on him. His position in space, at the forward end of a diagonal leading off into the depth of a further room, also contributes to intense concentration of interest on his figure.

During the decade of the 1640's Rembrandt's artistic personality underwent a profound change. He moved away from the factual, objective portrait and the turbulent, excited subject picture toward a quieter, more psychologically suggestive mode of expression. One can see the nature of this shift immediately if one compares a portrait of the 1630's with a later work such as his *Self-Portrait* (Plate 6). While losing none of the rich suggestions of texture which were present in the earlier picture, Rembrandt has gone beyond external veri-

10–20 REMBRANDT VAN RIJN. *Supper at Emmaus. ca.* 1630. Musée Jacquemart-André, Paris. (Courtesy Wildenstein & Co., Inc.)

similitude and encouraged the spectator to ponder the personality and thoughts of his subject. When one seeks an explanation of how this almost magical effect is obtained, one quickly realizes the importance of Rembrandt's understanding of the expressive function of light. Soft velvety shadows frame the face, especially around the eyes and mouth. It is to these areas of the face that a spectator looks to discover expression and mood. By veiling these parts in shadow Rembrandt calls on us to develop the expression ourselves, a personal involvement with the picture which leads to intensification of our emotional reaction. But the measure of Rembrandt's artistry is the skill with which he is able to direct our musings, knowing at just what point shadow ceases to be suggestive and becomes simply an obstruction.

Rembrandt's later religious pictures show a shift in intention comparable to that in the portraits. It is fascinating to compare the early *Supper at Emmaus* (Fig. 10–20) with another representation of the scene which Rembrandt painted in 1648 (Fig. 10–21). All the overt excitement, physical actions, and turbulence have been eliminated. A simply balanced composition gives stability and at the same time centers attention gently on the Christ, whose head, at the apex of a pyramid of light, becomes the focus of the picture.

10-21   REMBRANDT VAN RIJN.
Supper at Emmaus. 1648.
Louvre, Paris. (Giraudon)

Through a method analogous to that employed in the late portraits, Rembrandt directs the spectator away from the external, physical situation toward speculation about the psychological and spiritual significance of the scene.

That Rembrandt was a master of line as well as light and shadow is amply demonstrated by his many drawings and etchings. Perhaps no other artist has ever been able to convey as much with a few strokes of a pen or scratches of an etching needle. The wonderful small etching, *Six's Bridge* (Fig. 10–22), is a splendid example of the apparent ease and economy with which Rembrandt could suggest a calm, majestic view. Yet a study of this little print quickly reveals that a firm sense of order and structure underlies its seeming spontaneity. The long diagonal from the lower left back into depth is played with keen sensitivity against carefully placed vertical and horizontal accents so that a spacious, calm, and stable effect is obtained.

Rembrandt's drawings exhibit the same almost uncanny command of structure through a few, apparently random strokes. Nowhere is the general control which Baroque artists exerted over their materials more effectively demonstrated than in a drawing such as *Two Women Teaching a Child to Walk* (Fig. 10–23), in which both the figures and the whole character of the incident are set down with brilliant and astonishing brevity.

Contemporary with Hals and Rembrandt was a group of painters [2] who supplied the Dutch with another kind of picture to hang on their walls: small paintings of their homes, their courtyards, their streets, and their everyday activities. Genre, which had been infrequent as subject matter for the painter before the seventeenth century, not only was popularized by these

[2] Important in the group are Pieter de Hooch (1629–1683); Jan Steen (1626–1679); Gerard Terborch (1617–1681); and Jan Vermeer (1632–1675).

"Little Dutch Masters" but was kept on a high level of artistic treatment. In the *Pantry Door* by Pieter de Hooch, we are in a Dutch home where a young woman just outside the pantry is handing a small jug to a little girl. There is the usual beamed ceiling and tiled floor; in the room beyond is a chair, and above it a portrait near the half-open window through which light and air pour in, flooding the room and permeating even the darker corners of the foreground. There is nothing of profound significance about the picture, but much that is quietly human. What interests us is the masterful way in which the artist makes us aware of the interior. The bright outside light coming through the windows emphasizes, by contrast, the dimmer light inside, and the color intensities are so true that we get a convincing impression of the air-filled space and distance. The two figures are placed effectively against the wall and act as foils to the rectilinear pattern of the architecture.

The differing textures of various objects afforded these painters opportunity to create interesting surfaces. Terborch, for instance, shows extraordinary craftsmanship in the painting of lustrous satins and velvets, and heightens their quality by surrounding them with contrasting hues and brush strokes.

10-24 JAN VERMEER. *A Young Woman at a Casement. ca.* 1665. Metropolitan Museum of Art, New York.

With Jan Vermeer of Delft we reach a climax in Dutch genre painting. A complete equilibrium is maintained between two concerns — visual perception and abstract organization — and the fullness with which each is realized gives Vermeer's paintings their great distinction. His *Young Woman at a Casement* (Fig. 10-24) represents an everyday scene. There is perfect poise and serenity in the picture and a feeling of great coolness and restfulness. The informal, asymmetrical design is based upon rectangles, in window, map, table, and still life, countered by the curves of the figure, the pitcher, and the basin; and upon the interplay of various textures and qualities of materials represented: smooth, rigid glass and metal, stiffened linen, a thick rug which weighs down solidly. The light from the window falls upon the wall with the subtlest gradations of tone, unifying all the objects with its blue tonality.

The importance given the objects on the table in this as well as other paintings by the "Little Dutch Masters" directs attention to a subject hitherto given only a small place in the field of painting, but soon to assume a prominent role — still life. Painters saw that objects from everyday life offered great possibilities for the development of simple pictures constructed of related shapes, textures, and colors — pictures which achieved esthetic significance apart from any subject matter.

As landscapists the Dutch also produced pictures of great quality. They recognized in the country they saw about them as many possibilities for pictorial expression as in their homes. In the *Swamp* (Fig. 10-25) of Jacob van Ruisdael (1628–1682) we are looking across a marshy place in the woods, surrounded by great gnarled trees whose trunks are reflected in the open stretch of water. Plants fringe the edge of the swamp; a duck flies off

10–25 JACOB VAN RUISDAEL. *Swamp*. Mid-17th century. Hermitage, Leningrad.

to the left where two others are swimming; the light illumines a great log half in the water, a slender birch sapling, and a great oak; behind the trees the clouds bank up with a suggestion of movement. The calm and stillness tinged with melancholy, the skill with which the humid atmosphere of the swamp is captured, reveal the artist's sympathy and intimacy with nature. Yet here too, as in *Six's Bridge* and the genre paintings, beneath the casual appearance, and also beneath the close empirical observation of the face of nature, lies a firm sense of structure and design.

Spain

The seventeenth century is an imposing period in the history of Spanish art. As in other countries there is evidence of direct artistic influence from Italy. Yet the Spaniards maintained a rather remote attitude toward the subjects they depicted, and this detachment, combined with the typically fervid Spanish temperament, gives the Baroque style in Spain its own particular flavor. In sculpture, for instance, the *St. Francis* (Fig. 10–26) by Pedro de Mena (1628–1688) reflects all the intense interest in close observation of the surfaces of flesh and fabric which one finds in Bernini. Indeed, the illusionism, which included painting surfaces to simulate various textures, exceeds anything the Italians would have done. At the same time there is none of the concern for exuberant and dynamic effects so strong in Italy. The fervid piety of Spain at this time found quiet, intense images more sympathetic than the excited, extroverted saints created by Bernini. In architecture, likewise, the Spaniards generally avoided the spatial complexities which so fascinated the Italians and concentrated instead on a rich sculptured treatment of sur-

10–27   josé de ribera. *St. Jerome. ca.* 1630. Pinacoteca del Museo e Gallerie Nazionale di Capodimonte, Naples. (Soprintendenza alle Gallerie, Naples)

10–26   attributed to pedro de mena. *St. Francis.* Wood. Mid-17th century. Toledo cathedral.

face, a preference which culminated in the late seventeenth and early eighteenth century in the work of José de Churriguera (1650–1723).

But the chief glory of Spanish seventeenth-century art was painting. Early in the century a kinship with certain Italian artists may be observed. Valencia, with its close political connections with Naples, produced painters who worked in that city with Caravaggio's followers. It may be in this way that the abrupt chiaroscuro, strong color, and close observation of surfaces characteristic of Venetian painters was transmitted to Spain. The forceful José

10–28   DIEGO VELÁZQUEZ. *Surrender of Breda. ca.* 1635. Prado, Madrid.

de Ribera (*ca.* 1590–1652), who typifies this group, passed much of his active career in Naples. His emphasis on
dark and light and his realistic physical
types relate his work to that of Caravaggio. His rich but rather dryly applied pigment, however, and his emphasis on fervent religious expression
are typically Spanish (Fig. 10–27).

The early work of Diego Velázquez
(1599–1660), the greatest of the Spanish seventeenth-century painters, is also
closely related to the international Ca-
ravaggesque style. But as Velázquez
matured, his art gained independence.
Though grounded in the achievement
of early seventeenth-century painters,
he became almost unbelievably subtle

in the skill and understanding with
which he was able to convey texture,
mass, space, and atmosphere. His *Surrender of Breda* (Fig. 10–28), painted
about 1635, depicts an event of a decade before. After a long siege, with military distinction on both sides, the town
of Breda surrendered to the Spanish
forces. Velázquez shows Justin of Nas-
sau, the Flemish governor, handing the
keys of the town to the commander of
the Spanish army, Spinola. The artist
has conveyed with restraint and subtlety the idea of victor and vanquished,
crystallized in the gestures of the two
commanders and amplified in the bearing and arms of their attendants. The
pictorial arrangement further enhances

10–29 DIEGO VELÁZQUEZ. *Las Meniñas* (*Maids of Honor*). 1650's. Prado, Madrid. (Anderson)

the theme of the picture. The opposing forces are grouped in two wide complementary arcs circling broadly to enframe the two commanders. It is an arrangement which, in its utilization of depth, is typical of seventeenth-century painting and yet, in its stable balancing of elements, is quite unlike the more exuberant aspect of the period exemplified by Rubens.

Las Meniñas, or the *Maids of Honor* (Fig. 10–29), which was painted near the end of Velázquez's career, summarizes his interests and achievements. It represents an apparently casual interior scene in which the little Infanta Margarita, accompanied by her maids of honor, by dwarfs and a dog for amusement, is standing before a large canvas on which Velázquez himself is painting. The rhythmic, curvilinear organization of this group in the foreground contrasts sharply with the almost rigidly defined geometry of the rest of the painting. The receding perspective lines of the room are arrested by the figure of the grand marshal in the doorway and are strongly opposed by the gaze of the artist as he stares out beyond us as though regarding the king and queen, whose reflected images in the mirror place them behind our position as spectators. The apparent naturalness of this scene is heightened by the artist's rich treatment of the Infanta and the group around her, upon whom the light falls from the window at the right. In many instances the details are rendered by juxtaposition of different pigments in dashing strokes, now thin, now heavy, which seem to foreshadow Impressionist painting of the nineteenth century.

A large portion of Velázquez's work is in the form of portraits of Philip IV and his court. With these figures in their rich state costumes the artist was able to create exquisite harmonies of

10–30 DIEGO VELÁZQUEZ. *Innocent X.* 1650. Doria Gallery, Rome. (Anderson)

silver gray, black, and rose, and of varying textures put on in light, skillfully calculated strokes which blend the tones and suggest rather than depict the forms. But in painting these royal portraits Velázquez kept to himself whatever interpretation he made of the personalities involved or whatever emotional reaction he experienced. Yet in the portrait of *Innocent X* (Fig. 10–30), painted during the second of the artist's visits to Italy, there is not only objective reality in its tersest essentials, an arresting design of curves and angles, a masterly use of pigment in a play upon reds and whites in contrasting textures of satin, lace, velvet, and metals, but also a piercing penetration and forceful presentation of personality.

In the work of Bartolomé Esteban Murillo (1618–1682) the reserved and even austere character of much early seventeenth-century Spanish painting is replaced by a gentler, more lyric note in which sentiment predominates. In his numerous representations of the *Immaculate Conception* these qualities, together with a softening of the forms, an emphasis on rhythmic surface organization, and a use of soft, pastel tints all point toward an outlook more characteristic of the eighteenth than the seventeenth century.

10–31 FRANÇOIS MANSART. *Orleans Wing of the Chateau at Blois.* 1635–1638. (Copyright *Country Life*)

France

During most of the sixteenth century French art still showed many Medieval traits. The acceptance of Italian ideas grew as the century developed, but France never completely abandoned her own artistic personality. The mingling of ideas throughout the century produced much art of great charm, especially in the field of domestic architecture, where the picturesque features of Late Gothic were often sensitively combined with the order and coherence of Renaissance planning.

In the seventeenth century French artists adopted with greater assurance Italian modes of thought, and the traces of Medieval form became more and more difficult to identify. Yet a distinctly French personality was retained

and France's artistic prestige increased as the century progressed. Before the end of the century France had begun to take over from Italy leadership in the world of art.

The reasons for the shift are to a large extent political. Under Louis XIII and Louis XIV France grew to be the dominant power among European nations. French rulers, especially Louis XIV together with his minister Colbert, attached great importance to art as a means of exalting and adorning the monarchy and gave it liberal patronage. To be sure, under Louis XIV the state also dictated the form and character of art, but these restrictions became less stringent in the eighteenth century.

10-32   PERRAULT, LE VAU, and LE BRUN. *East Façade of the Louvre.* Paris. 1665.

ARCHITECTURE

The ideals of French seventeenth-century art are hardly anywhere more clearly stated than in the work of François Mansart (1598–1666). The wing which Mansart added to the chateau at *Blois* (Fig. 10–31) expresses clearly the polished dignity and sobriety which characterize much French art of the period in contrast to the more exuberant and fanciful art forms popular at the same time in Italy and Flanders. The strong rectilinear organization and tendency to design in terms of repeated units reminds one of Italian architecture of a century earlier. Yet the emphasis on a focal point, achieved through the colonnades, the changing planes of the walls, and the concentration of ornament around the portal, is characteristic of Baroque architectural thinking in general.

Mansart, though his designs always appear highly ordered and rational, was no pedant; he adjusted and improvised freely to suit a particular situation. But it is easy to see how the ideals embodied in a building such as *Blois*

10-33   JULES HARDOUIN-MANSART. *Hôtel des Invalides Chapel*, Paris. 1692–1704. (Raymond R. Buckley)

10–34 VERSAILLES. *Galerie des Glaces.* Decorated *ca.* 1680 by Charles Le Brun.

might be transformed into rather rigid academic regulations in the hands of less gifted men. Thus later in the century, under Louis XIV, when the demand for building had greatly increased and a veritable army of architects, decorators, and garden designers was necessary to meet the royal requirements, the designs tended to become stereotyped.

Yet there are occasional buildings which belie this trend. The east façade of the *Louvre* (Fig. 10–32), for instance, designed for Louis XIV by Claude Perrault (1613–1688) working together with Louis Le Vau (1612–1670) and Charles Le Brun (1619–1690), combines the desired qualities of imposing nobility and quiet restraint without recourse to hackneyed formulas. Again at the end of the century, the *Chapel of the Invalides* (Fig. 10–33) by Jules Hardouin-Mansart (1646–1708), a greatnephew of François,

achieves grandeur in a precise and elegant architectural vocabulary. In the *Invalides Chapel* the greater saliency of the parts of the façade, through their organization in several planes, suggests thinking more akin to that of Italian Baroque architecture than that of French. Also Italian in feeling is the treatment of the interior, in which a low shallow dome is opened to reveal a view of an upper dome brightly painted and illuminated by concealed windows.

The French gardens, an integral part of the plan they surrounded, were as formal as the age itself. Those laid out at *Versailles* by André Le Nôtre (1613–1700), Louis XIV's landscape architect, illustrate how magnificent the gardens had become. Water, often brought at great expense over a considerable distance by elaborately contrived hydraulic devices, played an important part. Garden design called for great basins to catch the reflections of the buildings, for fountains large and small, and for cascades and canals. Statues of river gods and of playing children and great ornamental vases of lead served as accents in the fountains or against the tall clipped hedges bordering the gardens. Broad walks and long avenues afforded fine vistas while great masses of trees framed the design.

The interiors of the buildings reflect the same desire for formal grandeur one encounters outside. Careful attention was paid to detail of the interior decoration; each element, from wall paintings to doorknobs, was designed in keeping with the whole. In the royal residences this consistent quality was possible because of the centralization of the arts in the Gobelins' establishment, which was purchased for the crown in 1662. At that time its production was not limited to tapestries but also included furniture, metalwork, jewelry, and textiles. Louis XIV's ideal was dignity and magnificence; and artists were in the service of the state to

please and glorify the monarch. The *Galerie des Glaces*, or Hall of Mirrors (Fig. 10–34), although today empty of its sumptuous furnishings — including bejeweled trees — retains its splendor. The view over the gardens is impressive, but it is the mirrors, which reflected the image not only of the royal court but also of the outside world, which identify the *Galerie* as being Baroque. The furniture of the period is consistently heavy and rich, of massive construction and elaborate veneering with fine woods, usually decorated with metal ornaments of various alloys.

On the death of Louis XIV the nobility threw off this heavy dignity and turned to the sparkling gaiety which characterized the reign of Louis XV. The age found a perfectly harmonious expression in the style known as Rococo.[3] Dainty rooms for conversation or

[3] From the French term *rocaille*, which literally means "pebble" but which refers especially to the small stones and shells used to decorate the interiors of grottoes. Such shells were a part of Rococo ornament.

10–35 HOTEL DE SOUBISE, Paris. *Upper Salon.* 1737–1740. Decorations by Germain Boffrand.

10–36 BALTHASAR NEUMANN. *Vierzehnheiligen*. Interior. 1743–1772. (Bildarchiv Foto Marburg)

card playing are typical of the style (Fig. 10–35). Slender proportions and never-ending movement in easy curves, light colors with lavish gilding, the use of many mirrors to add vivacity with their reflections — these identify this fragile, highly sophisticated style. Its asymmetrical, curvilinear surface patterns contrast with the sumptuous, sculptural qualities of the seventeenth-century Baroque; the change in emphasis is thoroughly characteristic of eighteenth-century art forms in general. Such rooms, with their daintily colored decorations of flowers and garlands, were in complete harmony with the minuets played in them, with the elegant costumes of lustrous satins and brocades, and with the equally elegant manners and sparkling wit of the people who graced them. The furniture

shows the same curved lines and slender proportions as the rooms.

The Rococo in architecture quickly became an international style during the early eighteenth century. The great prestige enjoyed by France gave impetus to this development, but there were indications throughout late seventeenth-century Europe of a general shift toward a lighter, gayer, more decorative type of expression. One of the most distinctive variants of Rococo architecture was in southern Germany, an area which had lain rather dormant artistically during the seventeenth century but which was the scene of a great wave of church building in the eighteenth. The pilgrimage church of *Vierzehnheiligen*, built by Balthazar Neumann, is one of the finest of these buildings. The interior (Fig. 10–36), in the undulating character of its walls and the complexity of the space, reminds us of the work of such seventeenth-century Italians as Borromini. But the light, gay colors, the rhythmic linear patterns, the flood of light throughout the interior, and the conception of the surfaces as screens rather than as sculpture all bespeak the temper of the Rococo rather than of the Baroque.

SCULPTURE

French Baroque sculpture is not as distinguished as either Baroque architecture or painting. Much of it was more dependent on the Italian Baroque than were the other arts. Some of the sculptors, such as Pierre Puget (1620–1694), modeled themselves fairly di-

rectly on Bernini; but others, like François Girardon (1628–1715), followed the French tendency toward sobriety so evident in the architecture. Much of the sculpture was executed as garden ornaments, accents in the vast formal schemes laid out by Le Nôtre and his followers. Within this context the pieces are often admirable, making an important contribution to the effectiveness of such gardens as those at Versailles, but as sculpture alone they seldom reward close study.

In the eighteenth century, French sculpture assumed a more independent and attractive character. The Rococo style, with its emphasis on elegant, intimate interiors, created a demand for sculpture of small dimensions to which the French sculptors responded with great success. Michel Clodion

10–37 JEAN ANTOINE HOUDON. *Voltaire.* 1781. Comédie-Française, Paris.

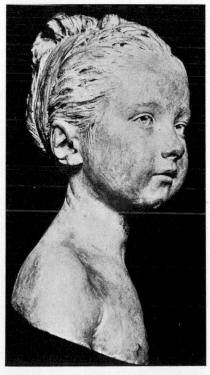

10–38 JEAN ANTOINE HOUDON. *Louise Brogniart.* 1778. Louvre, Paris.

(1738–1814) and Etienne Falconet (1716–1791), two of the most engaging sculptors, produced many dainty, charming figures in clay, marble, and porcelain which admirably complement the other accessories of the Rococo. Gay, witty themes predominate, usually with a lightly veiled erotic note.

Jean Antoine Houdon (1741–1828), one of the outstanding sculptors of the later eighteenth century, was particularly successful with portraits. Fascinated by the leading men of his time, whom he was commissioned to portray, he even traveled to America to model the statue of *George Washington* now in the Virginia state capitol. In the portrait of *Voltaire* (Fig. 10–37) Baroque qualities — restlessness, ephemeral pose, realism, the dependence upon heavy draperies for pictorial effect — are modified by the usual French poise and suave line. In the terra cotta portrait of *Louise Brogniart* (Fig. 10–38), the vivacious turn of the head, the quick glance of the eye, and the mobile expression around the mouth are caught and expressed in clay, a medium essentially suitable for depicting fleeting expressions.

PAINTING

French seventeenth-century painting, as well as architecture, exhibited an awareness of what was going on in Italy without being slavishly imitative. The two major groups of Italian painters — both the followers of Caravaggio, who experimented with exciting light effects and closely observed detail, and the more eclectic and cerebral followers of the Carracci — had French counterparts, though the Frenchmen nearly always retained distinct personalities. Georges de la Tour (1593–1652), for instance, delighted in artificial lighting effects, using strongly illuminated figures merg-

ing into deep shadows, a method akin to that employed by Caravaggio. Yet De la Tour combined these interests with a broad, monumental composition and generalized treatment of solids distinctively his own (Fig. 10–39).

The more academic temper of the Carracci won many adherents in France, especially in the second half of the century. It appealed to the French love of rational order, a strong feature of the other arts in the country during the same period. Also, it was easily adaptable to the rather bureaucratic and mass-produced art demanded by Louis XIV. Louis found an artistic entrepreneur admirably suited to his needs in the painter, Charles Le Brun, who undertook with his staff of assistants the vast decorative schemes in Versailles and other royal residences. Le Brun took as his prototype the Carracci decoration of the gallery of the Farnese Palace, but modified it to

10–39 GEORGES DE LA TOUR. *St. Sebastian, ca.* 1650. Staatliche Museum, Berlin. (Photo-Werkstatt)

10–40   LOUIS LE NAIN. *Peasant Family.* 1642. Louvre, Paris.

achieve greater grandeur and a rhetorical style perfectly in keeping with the architecture and temper of the French court.

French seventeenth-century painting also shows an awareness of the art of the Low Countries, though once again there is no direct imitation. Louis Le Nain (1593–1648), for instance, produced popular genre subjects of peasants and laborers similar to those of the "Little Dutch Masters." Yet he was less inclined to linger over the minutiae of daily life or the transitory aspects of light and atmosphere than were De Hooch or Vermeer. Le Nain concentrated rather on building clear, solid forms related to one another in simple, stable compositions. At the same time he recognized all the human values of the subject, and portrayed both their immediate expression and their wider implications with sincere directness (Fig. 10–40).

The two outstanding French seven-

teenth-century painters, Poussin and Claude, chose to pass the major portions of their active careers as expatriates in Italy. Yet, though both were profoundly affected by what they found in and around Rome, they remained temperamentally close to their own country. Both display the characteristically French delight in quiet, architectonic structure in contrast to the more exuberant and dynamic forms of the Baroque so popular in Italy and Flanders.

Nowhere was the general esteem in which seventeenth-century painters held the artists of the High Renaissance more clearly evident than in the work of Nicolas Poussin (1594–1665). First Titian and then Raphael were the models which Poussin set himself. In the end the rational order and stability of Raphael proved most appealing. In the *Ordination* (Fig. 10–41), for example, one finds the eloquent but controlled gestures and actions,

10–41 NICOLAS POUSSIN. *Ordination.* One of a set of seven pictures illustrating the sacraments, painted in 1647. The Earl of Ellesmere (on loan to the National Gallery of Scotland, Edinburgh). (Courtesy the Earl of Ellesmere)

fitted into a carefully balanced composition, which are characteristic of so much of Raphael's work. But the greater prominence given to the landscape around the figures reflects Poussin's interest in this aspect of the physical world, an interest shared by so many of his contemporaries.

Occasionally in the latter part of his career Poussin's interest in landscape almost submerged the figural subject matter of his painting, and yet he retained the same basic qualities of order and stability. In the *Funeral of Phocion* (Fig. 10–42), for example, each figure, tree, and building is a distinct unit in and of itself, yet each is closely related to the slanting plane which stretches from the foreground to the distant mountains. The emphasis on the solid geometry of the forms and on their relationships to each other in

an abstract pattern gives them an even more formal unity than that achieved in other Baroque paintings. Indeed, Poussin, who was chosen to be the first president of the French Academy in 1648, is difficult to analyze in terms of the Baroque style. His interest in natural forms, in deep, fully developed spatial relationships, and above all in an order willfully created by man, identify his style, though, as typically seventeenth century.

In comparison with the landscapes of Poussin, those of Claude Gellée (1600–1682), also called Claude Lorrain, are suffused with golden light and soft atmosphere, with elements derived from nature arranged in a stable, architectural fashion. In the *Egeria* (Fig. 10–43) Claude has massed his trees and buildings to serve as a framework for the opening through

10–42 NICOLAS POUSSIN. *Funeral of Phocion.* 1648. Louvre, Paris.

10–43 CLAUDE GELLÉE (LORRAIN). *Egeria.* 1669. Museo Nazionale, Naples. (Anderson)

10–44 ANTOINE WATTEAU. *Embarkation for Cythera.* 1717. Berlin. (Braun)

which the spectator sees a vast luminous vista stretching toward the horizon. Claude was fond of adding a pensive note to his pictures with a few Classical ruins nestling in the foreground or silhouetted against the light sky — gentle reminders of the transitory achievements of man. In essence it was the mood of the Italian landscape which Claude sought to capture, and it was this stress on the subjective side of nature which made his work so popular with the early romantics at the end of the eighteenth century.

In painting as in architecture the solemn dignity of the seventeenth century gave way in the early eighteenth to the lighthearted frivolity of the Rococo. Most Rococo painting is in complete harmony with the architecture; it is gay, decorative, and bright-colored and emphasizes curvilinear patterns. Seen in the settings for which they were intended, such paintings as those of François Boucher (1703–1770; Fig. 10–1) add a final note of gaiety and elegance, often tinged with sensu

ality, to the ensemble. This facet of the Rococo appears at its most attractive in the work of a late eighteenth-century painter, Jean-Honoré Fragonard (1732–1806), whose magnificent draftsmanship and infallible decorative sense always tided him over the sentimentality to which Rococo themes exposed the painter.

The greatest of the French painters during the Rococo period was Antoine Watteau (1684–1721). It was he more than any other who laid the foundations of this style in painting, and yet he completely transcended its limitations as formulated by the academies. In his masterpiece, the *Embarkation for Cythera* (Fig. 10–44), all the courtly elegance of the later Rococo is achieved without the rather brittle artificiality so evident in the work of most of his followers. The color is richer, a sense of atmosphere is retained, and the figures (though of the utmost refinement) are always closely observed and solidly constructed. The mood suggested by a Watteau paint

10–45   JEAN-BAPTISTE CHARDIN. *Still Life. ca.* 1760. Louvre, Paris.

ing is also distinctive. Gaiety is always tempered by a somewhat wistful note. One sees it in the indecision and backward glance of the central lady in the *Embarkation for Cythera* and in the slightly melancholic expression which Watteau gave to his numerous portraits of clowns. All these qualities endow Watteau's pictures with a richness of visual and emotional suggestion not shared by those of any other Rococo artist.

Almost equally outstanding was Jean-Baptiste Siméon Chardin (1699–1779), an artist who painted more modest subjects. Not only in theme but in attitude toward form Chardin seemed to continue the tradition of Le Nain and the "Little Dutch Masters" of the seventeenth century. Sometimes it was the interior of the middle-class home which Chardin, like the Dutch

painters, saw as raw material with pictorial possibilities. However, he was always more alive than his predecessors to the subtleties of a domestic situation, often building his pictures around some delightful minor anecdote in a thoroughly eighteenth-century fashion. In other instances, especially his still-life painting, his interest in genre seems to be simply as pictorial material for its own sake. In the composition of the *Still Life* (Fig. 10–45) a large rectangular box is placed diagonally in space — a diagonal emphasized by the pipe-stems and the shadows — and balanced by a number of cylindrical objects. With all the means at the painter's disposal these objects are built into an organization which in their unity and harmony have a power of their own quite separate from the representational content.

England

Though English artistic expression since the Middle Ages has been outstanding in literature and admirable in some of its architecture, it has only infrequently risen to the highest level in painting, and even less often in sculpture. The vigor of Medieval art in England — cathedrals, carvings, illuminated manuscripts, embroideries — had been due to the stimulus and patronage of the Church. But when, in the sixteenth century, Protestantism secured a stronghold and the monasteries were destroyed, this patronage ceased and England was deprived of a large class of skilled craftsmen. Protestantism in general was averse to religious representation, an attitude which was extreme among the Puritans and became even iconoclastic under the Commonwealth (1649–1660). The restoration of the Stuarts, however, changed this trend. The aristocracy, whose wealth and position had greatly increased through the acquisition of large colonial holdings, now commissioned the building of fine mansions on great estates, and fine furnishings and portraits. But, except in architecture, there was such a dearth of native talent that kings and lords were forced to look abroad for artists. This need was most apparent in the field of portrait painting. Not until the eighteenth century did a British school of painting of any real distinction evolve. And this, like the Dutch, was devoted primarily to portraiture and landscape.

ARCHITECTURE

Gothic practices lived on in English building, as in French, long after Renaissance architects in Italy had struck out in new directions. During the sixteenth century the English made mi-

nor concessions to Italian architectural ideas. Classical ornament made frequent appearances in the decoration of buildings and there was a distinct trend toward more regular and symmetrical planning. But not until the early seventeenth century was there a wholehearted acceptance of the principles which governed Italian architectural thinking. The revolution in English building practice was primarily the work of one man, Inigo Jones (1573–1652), who was Surveyor (i.e., architect) to James I and Charles I. Jones was in Italy, on one occasion at least, for over a year. He greatly admired the work of the sixteenth-century architect Palladio, whose book on architecture and buildings in north Italian towns Jones must have studied with much care. From the stately buildings of Palladio, Jones selected certain motifs and systems of proportions which he used as the basis of his own architectural thinking. The nature of his achievement is evident in the *Banqueting Hall at Whitehall* (Fig. 10–46). The façade is a design of dignity and clarity, using two orders superimposed in the form of columns in the center and pilasters near the ends. There is practically nothing here that Palladio would not have recognized and approved, but the building as a whole is no copy. While working within the architectural vocabulary and syntax of the revered sixteenth-century Italian, Jones retained his own independence as a designer, and in choosing to accent the center of his building by making the order project further in this area he exhibited a taste for focus (or climax) more characteristic of seventeenth- than sixteenth-century architecture.

The best-known English seven-

10–46 INIGO JONES. *Banqueting Hall,* Whitehall Palace, London. 1619–1622.

teenth-century architect was Sir Christopher Wren (1632–1723). Wren was strongly influenced by Jones, but he also traveled in France, where he must have been much impressed by the splendid palaces and state buildings which were being created in and around Paris. Although this French contact led Wren to embellish Jones' style somewhat, one can readily see, in a design such as that for *Hampton Court,* that underneath the more opulent surface ornament the younger man was thinking in an idiom closely related to that of his predecessor.

After the Great Fire which almost completely obliterated London in 1666, Wren was called upon to design many new buildings, especially churches, to replace those destroyed. It was not an easy task because the churches often had to be fitted into small irregular areas. However, Wren showed himself an architect of great ingenuity and invention, working out a rich variety of schemes to meet awkward circumstances. In designing the exteriors of the churches he concentrated his attention on the towers, the one element of the structure which would set the building apart from its crowding neighbors. Wren's *St. Mary-le-Bow* (Fig.

10 47) would seem insignificant were it not for the tower which begins at the street level as a strong square structure no more pretentious than its secular neighbors. As it overtops them it takes on a more elegant character, evolves into increasingly slender polygonal and circular forms with encircling colonnades, and finally terminates in a slender spire. The skyline of London as Wren left it was dotted with such towers, which served as prototypes for later buildings both in England and America. Half a century later, when James Gibbs designed *St. Martin's-in-the-Fields* (Fig. 10–48), the general form of the tower was still based clearly on Wren's ideas, though a more ample space around the church led the architect to add a stately Classical portico at the front and a corresponding pilaster order around the sides of the building.

If Wren's London parish churches were probably the most influential of his buildings, the most famous is certainly *St. Paul's cathedral* (Fig. 10–49). Considering its size the cathedral was built with remarkable speed, in little over forty years, and Wren lived to see it completed. The form of the building was constantly modified and

10–47 SIR CHRISTOPHER WREN. *St. Mary-le-Bow*, London. *ca.* 1680. Gutted in World War II.

10–48 JAMES GIBBS. *St. Martin's-in-the-Fields*, London. 1721. (Raymond R. Buckley)

refined as it went up, and the final appearance of the towers was not determined until after 1700. The splendid skyline composition, with the two foreground towers acting so effectively as foils to the great dome, must have been suggested to Wren by similar schemes devised in the mid-seventeenth century by Italian Baroque architects. Wren himself was never in Italy, but he doubtless saw sketches of Italian designs.

The tendency toward a more exuberant type of architectural design, akin to Italian Baroque, had a brief

flowering in the work of a small group of English architects associated with Wren at the end of his career. The best-known of these men, Sir John Vanbrugh (1664–1726), displayed at *Blenheim* (Fig. 10–50) a command of picturesque silhouette, massing, and invention in architectural detail which is thoroughly Baroque. The design has the love of variety and contrast tempered by a desire for focus which one finds so frequently in the architecture of seventeenth-century Italy. Yet Vanbrugh does not appear to have borrowed anything directly from earlier

Italians, but to have evolved his forms primarily in his own imagination.

But Vanbrugh's type of architecture did not please English patrons for long. Even before *Blenheim* was complete a conscious reaction had begun against what were considered the ponderous and bizarre qualities it embodied. The leader of the reaction was a young nobleman, Richard, Earl of Burlington (1694–1753), whose battle cry was "Back to Palladio and Inigo Jones." Burlington gathered around him a group of architects who were able successfully to impose a style based on the work of Palladio. They studied and copied the works of the master in a rather more servile manner than had Inigo Jones, and yet the final result would rarely be confused with Palladio's work. *Burlington House* (Fig. 10–51), though clearly based on Palladian motifs, combines them with emphasis on their decorative value rather than on their structural or functional utility as Palladio would have done.

10–49 SIR CHRISTOPHER WREN. *St. Paul's Cathedral*, London. 1675–1710. Although damaged in World War II, the structure has survived almost intact.

10–50 SIR JOHN VANBRUGH. *Blenheim Palace*. 1705–1724. Engraving after Maurer. British Museum, London. (Trustees of the British Museum)

10–51 RICHARD, EARL OF BURLINGTON. *Burlington House,* London. 1717. (From the plate in *Vitruvius Britannicus*)

PAINTING

British painting of the seventeenth century is marked by an insularity due partly to its separation from the influences current on the Continent and partly to its frequent dependence upon foreign artists, whose influence remained but little assimilated. Not until the mid-eighteenth century did British painting become really distinguished. In painting

the English temperament does not take kindly to the creation of monumental design in terms of three-dimensional form; but prefers a narrative and descriptive art based on close observation of nature, given a whimsical or dramatic turn, and put in terms of color and linear rhythm.[4]

This analysis characterizes one of Britain's highest accomplishments, English and Irish Medieval illumination, as it also does the distinguished school of British painting of the late eighteenth and early nineteenth centuries.

During the period of the Renais-

[4] W. G. Constable in the catalogue of the College Art Association, *International,* 1933, p. 37.

sance and the seventeenth century very little native painting of distinction was produced in the British Isles. To be sure, the miniaturists of the sixteenth century, such as Nicholas Hilliard, showed great promise, and during the seventeenth century there were a few good native painters, such as William Dobson. But generally the work of these men was submerged beneath that of more distinguished foreigners. First Holbein, in England from 1532 to 1543 at the invitation of Henry VIII; then Van Dyck, resident at the court of Charles I from 1632 until his death in 1641; and then Sir Peter Lely, a Dutch painter in England for the last forty years of his life (d. 1680), set the styles in portrait painting accepted by the royalty and aristocracy.

In the second quarter of the eighteenth century a truly English style in painting emerged with William Hogarth (1697–1764). Hogarth waged a lively campaign throughout his career against the English feeling of dependence upon and inferiority to Continental art. Certainly if all English

10–52   WILLIAM HOGARTH. *Breakfast Scene* from "Marriage à la Mode." *ca.* 1745. National Gallery, London. (Courtesy of the Trustees of the National Gallery)

painting had been comparable to his there would have been little justification for such a feeling. Though Hogarth himself would have been the last to admit it, his own painting owes much to the work of his contemporaries across the Channel in France. He used the same bright, opaque colors, applied with dash and virtuosity, which were so popular with the Rococo painters. Yet his subject matter, which was frequently moral and satirical in tone, is distinctively English. It was the great age of English satirical writing, and Hogarth, who knew and admired this tradition and included Henry Fielding among his closest friends, clearly saw himself as embodying this interest in the visual arts. His favorite device was a series of nar-

rative pictures following a character or group of characters in their encounters with some social evil. He was at his best in a picture such as the *Breakfast Scene* (Fig. 10–52) from the *Marriage à la Mode* series, in which the marriage of the young viscount, arranged through the social aspirations of one parent and the need for money of the other, is just beginning to founder. Here the bright, gay character of the Rococo style is admirably suited to the situation. When Hogarth attempted a more dramatic and emotionally tense scene, his rather scattered formal organization prevented him from achieving the strength of a Goya or a Daumier (p. 658). Yet the very fact that Hogarth did attempt to embrace such a range of emotional expression in his work is itself significant, and pointed toward a shift in the intentions of European artists which was one factor at work in undermining the Rococo.

Summary

In a survey of seventeenth-century art the national or regional schools stand out with such apparent clarity that underlying common interests are easily overlooked. Yet, when one considers the art of the century as a whole in contrast to the previous Mannerist art, it becomes apparent that a consistent and widespread shift in point of view took place about 1600. However inventive and genuinely creative the Mannerists were in the forms they devised, they were motivated fundamentally by a rather perverse and negative outlook — an outlook which evinced distrust of the physical world and the normal, rational relationships which operate within it. The seventeenth-century artists generally rejected such an outlook and turned with renewed interest to the study of physical phenomena and to the exploration of the rational order which they assumed underlay the nature of things. The manifestations of this attitude were diverse, but the attitude itself runs as a sort of common denominator through most of the art of the period. It is a point of view which links the seventeenth century to the fifteenth and early sixteenth, and to this extent the Baroque is direct heir of the Renaissance. But to this rationalistic quality is often added a concern for excitement and drama which may be regarded as an inheritance from the Mannerist period.

In the early eighteenth century another shift, this time a minor one, is apparent. It is most noticeable in France, where it took the form of a deliberate reaction against the solemn pomp characteristic of the art of the Louis XIV epoch and led to the formation of the Rococo style. Everywhere in Europe a sparkling gaiety became the quality artists sought to attain. In form the change was toward elegant, curvilinear, decorative patterns rather than the exploration of mass, space, and atmosphere which had interested the seventeenth-century artists. But the change was one in emphasis or degree rather than in kind. Changes of a more fundamental character began to appear in European art about 1750, pointing toward a new period in the history of art.

Mid-18th Century

During the middle decades of the eighteenth century a number of curious things happened in European art. On the surface they seem unrelated and not particularly important, but taken together they suggest a dissatisfaction with the limitations of the gay, decorative Rococo style and a search for means by which to realize a wider range of emotional expression. Evidence of this shift is widespread about 1750 and is particularly noticeable in England, a country which, during the late eighteenth century, suddenly rose to prominence in the visual arts. A brief glance at what was happening in European art about 1750 will set the stage and help to prepare us for the major developments which take place at the end of the eighteenth and the beginning of the nineteenth century.

In architecture evidence of new di-

10–53 SANDERSON MILLER. *Sham Medieval Ruin.* Hagley Park, Worcestershire. 1747. (Copyright *Country Life*)

10–54 JAMES STUART. *Doric Portico.* Hagley Park, Worcestershire. 1758. (Copyright *Country Life*)

10–56 SIR JOSHUA REYNOLDS. *Nelly O'Brien. ca.* 1760. Wallace Collection, London. (Reproduced by permission of the Trustees of the Wallace Collection)

10–55 SIR JOSHUA REYNOLDS. *Duchess of Hamilton. ca.* 1760. Lady Lever Art Gallery, Port Sunlight. (Reproduced by permission of the Trustees)

rections came first in rather trivial garden buildings such as the sham Medieval ruin and the Doric portico at *Hagley Park* (Figs. 10–53 and 10–54). Neither structure is concerned with the basic function we normally assign buildings: that of providing shelter by enclosing a space; both indeed are useless from this point of view. The structures were intended simply to be looked at. Their program was the train of thought which they could arouse in the spectator. The forms were chosen not so much for their intrinsic value as for their rich associations which could

set the spectator musing about civilizations remote in time or place from his own. In the late eighteenth century, as we shall see in subsequent chapters, an ever-widening repertory of forms or period and regional styles was called upon in the building of houses, churches, and public buildings.

A comparable state of affairs is noticeable in European painting after 1750. Sir Joshua Reynolds (1723–1792), for instance, painted in a highly intellectual, self-conscious fashion. He studied the works of the acknowledged European masters with great care and often borrowed extensively from them. But his intention was certainly not to deceive his public by this practice. Quite the contrary, he expected those who saw his pictures to recognize and enjoy these allusions to other works. This eclectic point of view often gave rise to situations which are puzzling to the student accustomed to the consistent practices of Renaissance and Baroque painters. At first glance it is, for instance, startling to find Reynolds producing simultaneously two portraits so completely different in conception and style as the *Duchess of Hamilton* and *Nelly O'Brien* (Figs. 10–55 and 10–56), but such variety is frequent in the work of late eighteenth-century artists.

Reynolds' great rival as a portraitist, Thomas Gainsborough (1727–1788), is more consistent and less sophisticated. Occasionally, as in his famous *Blue Boy*, Gainsborough alluded to the work of earlier painters, especially that of Van Dyck, but generally he sought to evoke a mood directly through fluid, rhythmic brushwork, soft, almost diaphanous forms, and pastel shades (Fig. 10–57). The lyric quality of Gainsborough's late work has often been compared to the painting of Watteau at the beginning of the century, and certainly there is a spiritual kinship between the two. But Gainsborough is not for that reason to be considered a late manifestation of the Rococo. The wistful mood he shares with Watteau is, as we have already noted, a peculiarly personal manifestation rather than a trait of the Rococo style in general.

On the Continent the shift away from the Rococo often took different directions from those in England. The French painter Jean Baptiste Greuze (1725–1805) chose to develop the emotional side of his art through the subjects he selected for his pictures rather than through the character of his forms. He gave special attention to situations involving domestic virtues, particularly in a bourgeois or rustic setting (Fig. 10–58). This was a type of theme, being popularized in French literature at about the same time by Rousseau,

10–57 THOMAS GAINSBOROUGH. *The Morning Walk* (Mr. and Mrs. Hallet). *ca.* 1785. National Gallery, London. (Courtesy of the Trustees of the National Gallery)

which met with enthusiastic approval, especially from critics such as Diderot.

In Italy during the mid-century Giovanni Battista Piranesi (1720–1778) aimed for a quite different type of emotional excitement through his choice of highly imaginative and awesome themes treated with great formal complexity. The deep, intricate space suggested in one of his *Carceri* plates (Fig. 10–59) recalls the spatial constructions of some Baroque painters, but the fantastic quality of the scene belongs to the early Romantic period rather than to the seventeenth century.

These developments in mid-eighteenth century art are so varied that no clear new direction emerges. They seem rather like tentative experiments, a searching for means by which to expand the emotional and expressive po-

10–58 (Above) JEAN BAPTISTE GREUZE. *The Village Betrothal.* Exhibited Salon, 1761. Louvre, Paris. (Archives Photographiques)

10–59 (Right) GIOVANNI BATTISTA PIRANESI. *Carcere* (Interior of a Prison). *ca.* 1750. (From Focillon, *Piranesi*, Librairie Renouard, Paris, 1918)

tentialities of the visual arts. It is not until the very end of the century and the beginning of the nineteenth that the spirit behind these moves found full realization. But it is clear that after the mid-eighteenth century the prevailing attitude is one which, in its highly self-conscious realization and exploitation of a wide range of means for artistic expression, is different from that which motivated Baroque and Rococo artists.

Bibliography

There are no good general books covering the whole of Baroque and Rococo art, but there are many specialized studies concerned with particular geographical areas or individual artists. Most of the books in the very brief list which follows contain in turn more extensive and specialized bibliographies for the topics covered

GENERAL READINGS

Friedrich, C. J., *The Age of the Baroque, 1610–1660*, Harper, 1952.

Scott, Geoffrey, *The Architecture of Humanism*, Scribner's, 1924; Anchor Books, Garden City, 1954.

Sypher, Wylie, *Four Stages of Renaissance Style*, Anchor Books, Garden City, 1955.

Willey, Basil, *The Seventeenth-Century Background*, Columbia University Press, 1950; Chatto & Windus, London, 1934.

Wölfflin, Heinrich, *Principles of Art History*, tr. by M. D. Hottinger, Holt, 1932.

ITALY

Fokker, Timon H., *Roman Baroque Art: The History of a Style*, Oxford University Press, New York, 1938.

Friedlander, W. F., *Caravaggio Studies*, Princeton University Press, 1955.

Hinks, Roger P., *Michelangelo Merisi da Caravaggio: His Life . . . , His Legend . . . , His Works*, Faber & Faber, London, 1953.

McComb, Arthur, *The Baroque Painters of Italy*, Harvard University Press, 1934.

Mahon, Denis, *Studies in Seicento Art and Theory*, Warburg Institute, London, 1947.

Morassi, Antonio, *G. B. Tiepolo: His Life and Work*, 2 vols., Phaidon Publishers, New York, 1955.

Voss, Hermann G. A., *Die Malerei des Barock in Rom*, Propyläen-Verlag, Berlin, 1924.

Wittkower, Rudolf, *Gian Lorenzo Bernini, the Sculptor of the Roman Baroque*, Phaidon Press, London, 1955.

LOW COUNTRIES

Bode, Wilhelm von, *Great Masters of Dutch and Flemish Painting*, tr. by M. L. Clarke, Duckworth, London, 1909.

Burckhardt, Jakob C., *Recollections of Rubens*, tr. by Mary Hottinger, Oxford University Press, New York, 1950.

Fromentin, Eugène, *The Masters of Past Time: Dutch and Flemish Painting from Van Eyck to Rembrandt*, tr. by A. Boyle, Phaidon Press, London, 1948.

Rosenberg, Jakob, *Rembrandt*, Harvard University Press, 1948.

Swillens, P. T. A., *Johannes Vermeer, Painter of Delft, 1632–1675*, tr. by C. M. Breuning-Williamson, Spectrum Publications, Utrecht and New York, 1950.

Trivas, Numa S., *The Paintings of Frans Hals*, Oxford University Press, New York, 1942.

SPAIN

Trapier, Elizabeth, *Ribera*, Hispanic Society of America, New York, 1952.

——, *Velazquez*, Hispanic Society of America, New York, 1948.

FRANCE

Adhémar, Hélène, *Watteau: sa vie, son œuvre*, P. Tisné, Paris, 1950.

Blunt, Anthony, *Art and Architecture in France, 1500 to 1700*, Penguin Books, Baltimore, 1953.

——, *François Mansart*, Warburg Institute, London, 1941.

Dimier, L., *Les peintres français du XVIIIe siècle*, 2 vols., Les Editions G. van Oest, Paris, 1928–30.

Florisoone, Michel, *Le dix-huitième siècle*, P. Tisné, Paris, 1948.

Fontaine, André, *Les Doctrines d'art en France . . . de Poussin à Diderot*, Laurens, Paris, 1909.

Kimball, Sidney, *The Creation of the Rococo*, Philadelphia Museum of Art, 1943.

ENGLAND

Beckett, R. B., *Hogarth*, Routledge & Kegan Paul, London, 1949.

Summerson, John N., *Architecture in Britain, 1530–1830*, Penguin Books, Baltimore, 1953.

Waterhouse, Ellis K., *Painting in Britain, 1530–1790*, Penguin Books, Baltimore, 1953.

CHAPTER 11

COLONIAL

AMERICAN

(16TH–19TH CENTURIES)

Latin America[1]

Gold and the Cross led the Spaniard to attempt to impose upon the Indian the Spanish pattern of civilization, to transform the New World into a New Spain. At its greatest extent the Spanish empire came to include all South America except Portuguese Brazil, all Central America, and much of the southern and western parts of the United States. At the same time, the highest attainments of Latin American art are found in the areas of the highest indigenous American attainment: in Mexico and Guatemala, the home of Maya, Mixtecs, Toltecs, and Aztecs; and in the Andean regions of Ecuador,

[1] Since the arts of Central and South America, beginning with the sixteenth century, owed more and more to the traditions and concepts of western Europe, they are treated in this chapter. The earlier, non-European forms are discussed in Chapter 17.

ILLUSTRATION ABOVE. 11–1 THE MASON LIMNER. *Alice Mason.* 1670. The Adams Memorial Society. (George M. Cushing, Jr.)

Peru, and Bolivia, the site of the pre-Inca and Inca peoples.

Mexico

New Spain, the earliest of the viceroyalties, followed upon the conquest by Cortes, in 1521, of the Aztec capital of Tenochtitlan, on whose ruins he built his own capital, Mexico City. A generation was needed to extend and consolidate the conquest, to plan and lay out the towns and cities according to the new Italian Renaissance conceptions, and to try to bring the Indians into conformity with the new pattern of life.[2] Much of this was the

[2] For the conquest of Mexico and for an account of the work of both the conquistadors and the missionaries, see W. H. Prescott, *History of the Conquest of Mexico*, Modern Library, 1936, and Bernal Diaz del Castillo, *True History of the Conquest of Mexico*, tr. by Maurice Keating, McBride, 1939. It is through the chronicles of the missionaries that we learn much of preconquest Indian life.

11–2 FAÇADE OF THE AUGUSTINIAN CHURCH AND RECTORY AT ACOLMAN, MEXICO.
Completed by 1560. (Dirección de Monumentos Coloniales, Mexico City)

work of missionaries, who always accompanied the conquistadors and who
strove not only to convert the Indians
but frequently to protect them against
the exploitation of the Spanish overlords. In building the churches and convents which rose in great numbers, the
missionaries employed Indians, who
were already skilled in many native
arts, and taught them Spanish styles.
The Indian, with no written language,
possessed a keen memory and a tenacious hold on his own ancient culture.
When not strictly copying Spanish
models he often introduced native motifs and infused the European naturalism with his own conventional and abstract style. Meanwhile in the isolated
villages the indigenous arts survived
and continued.

The characteristic sixteenth-century
building was the fortress-church, such

as the convents [3] of *Huejotzingo, Acolman* (Fig. 11–2), or *Actopan:* massive
stone structures with thick walls, few
windows, low towers flanking the portal, and some carving to accent the
doorway. Gothic vaulting or finely
carved Mudejar ceilings, together with
a lofty retable rich in gold and poly-
chromed wood carvings, embellished
the interior. The churches were set in
large courts surrounded by a strong
stone wall, with chapels at the corners
of the court and another open chapel
near the entrance of the church. This
new arrangement, not found in Spain,
was developed to accommodate the
mass conversions which followed the
efforts of the padres.

Shortly before 1600, growing wealth
led to the building of fine mansions

[3] In Mexico "convent" is used for both
convent and monastery.

11–3 CATHEDRAL OF PUEBLA. Mexico. 1556–1649.

11–4 CATHEDRAL OF PUEBLA. High altar by Manuel Tolsa. 1797–1819.

and, with the arrival of bishops from Spain, of cathedrals. The artists invited from the mother country at first brought the current Renaissance style, the *Plateresque* (see p. 390). As a result, many a mansion or convent bears delicate carvings to accentuate its portal or to add a note of grace to its patio. This style was followed in the early seventeenth century by a brief period of the severe Herreran style,[4] of which the cathedral of *Puebla* is an example (Fig. 11–3). In general, this cathedral follows a basic type almost universal in Hispanic America: cruciform in plan, vaulted, with a dome over the crossing and twin towers to flank the main portal, as at the Escorial in Spain, from

[4] Juan de Herrera was the architect of the Escorial near Madrid (1563–1598). His style recalls that of Vignola, although it is marked by greater severity (see p. 391).

which this design derives. In *Puebla* the towers have clear profiles, unbroken surfaces, and reticent ornament, while the glazed tile covering the dome and the lanterns of the towers set off the gray stone of the rest of the building. This sober exterior contrasts with the sumptuous effect of the interior, with rich marbles on floors and walls, with stone and wood carvings, *rejas*, polychrome and gilded sculpture, and paintings. The high altar in particular (Fig. 11–4) is spectacular in its combined use of many materials, its broken cornices and multiple profiles.

The tile-covered domes which rise in such numbers above the roof levels of Puebla are witnesses to the great ceramic industry of the city. The Indians of the locality were already skilled in the craft when the Spaniards introduced the Talavera ware, a tin-enameled tile chiefly in blue, white, and yellow which was used for wall facings, for fountains in patios and plazas, and for domes of churches all over Mexico. The designs are usually geometric or floral but occasionally include figure work with evidence of influences from such divergent cultures as the Moorish and Chinese, derived from objects brought by traders. The tile-covered dome is a mark of Mexican colonial architecture.

The *cathedral of Mexico* (Mexico City) was begun in the Herreran style, but during the prolonged period of its construction it took on elements of the Baroque — as in the great volutes and the sumptuous façade — and in its sacristy produced a variant of the Baroque, the "Ultrabaroque" or Churrigueresque.[5] This latter style invaded all the arts, the furnishings as well as the buildings themselves. The façades of the churches are lofty panels of stone carved like the wooden altarpieces within. The convent of *Tepotzotlan* illustrates these characteristics, as does the church of *San Sebastian and Santa Prisca* at Taxco (Fig. 11–5).

This spirited, lavish style, so expressive of eighteenth-century Hispanic society, gave way about 1780 to standards of correct neoclassic academic practice.

South America

Farther south in the Andean highlands were other colonial cities which, with Mexico City, were the great art centers of Hispanic America: Quito, Lima, and Cuzco. From Mexico the conquistadors, lured by gold, pushed southward to Peru, where in 1533–

[5] "Churrigueresque" refers to the work of the Churriguera family in Spain during the eighteenth century, and by extension to extravagant ornament throughout the Hispanic world.

11–5 SAN SEBASTIAN AND SANTA PRISCA. Taxco. 1748. (Harold Grossman from Black Star)

1534 Pizarro overthrew the Inca empire. Soon after, the Spaniards laid out the new city of Lima, and upon the ruins of the Inca capitals at Cuzco and Quito they erected Spanish cities.

The evolution of art in Mexico was largely duplicated in the viceroyalty of Peru. Here appeared the same transplantation of Spanish ideology, religion, artists, and works of art; and the same persistence of native traditions.

The city of Lima was the symbol of Spanish power and culture in western South America. Outbound ships laden with gold and silver returned to her harbor with statues, paintings, furniture, tiles, even whole retables in pieces ready to be assembled — the art of Spain literally transported to the New World. This transplanted Spanish art

11–6 EL PALACIO DE TORRE-TAGLE. Lima. 1730–1735. Originally a private mansion, now the Ministry of Foreign Affairs. (Archive of Hispanic Culture, Library of Congress)

showed little influence from the native peoples, for the site of the new city of Lima was not a strong center of Indian culture.

Though ecclesiastical architecture perhaps dominated Hispanic American art, secular building, like the *Torre-Tagle Palace* at Lima (Fig. 11–6), also engaged the attention of architects. Some of their works were municipal buildings; many more were mansions for the upper classes. These mansions were built on the Mediterranean plan, around patios; only a portal, accented by carving, hinted at the magnificence within. The large rooms made an ample setting for the massive carved furniture, the hangings and silver, the Sevillian tiles, or the Mudejar ceiling. In these furnishings, particularly in the carvings, the weaving, and the silver,

we sometimes find pure Spanish designs, but more frequently the same combinations of Spanish and Indian forms as in the stone carvings.

In Cuzco, on the other hand, a different situation affected this transplanted Spanish style. The high valley of Cuzco is fringed by austere mountains and is subject to frequent earthquakes. Though the conquistadors tried to demolish the Inca capital, they did not succeed. The Inca walls were too solid to destroy. Thus the new city arose on the foundations and walls of the old, and the masonry, often re-used from Inca buildings, is as solid and somber as the mountains from which it was cut.

Though most of the buildings in Cuzco date from after the destructive earthquake of 1650, the *cathedral* itself

11–7 CATHEDRAL OF CUZCO. Peru. Of granite taken from Inca structures. Completed 1564; reconstructed after the earthquakes of 1650 and 1950. (Archive of Hispanic Culture, Library of Congress)

(Fig. 11–7) survived the shock; it has, however, been subjected to much rebuilding. It is a low, heavy building with squat towers, high doorways, and reused Inca masonry. The projecting portal introduces a three-dimensional movement into a flat façade of Herreran style, while the low three-aisled interior is spanned by rib vaults borne upon piers of correct Renaissance Tuscan order.

In such churches as *San Sebastian* (Cuzco) and *La Compañía* (Arequipa, Fig. 11–8) Indian traditions survive both in subject matter and in technique. The introduction of Indian motifs — local flora and fauna — occurs even in these religious buildings. The naturalistic Renaissance forms have been flattened out; the crisp carving has a linear quality which sharply defines the light and dark and recalls the pre-Inca carvings from Chavin or Tiahuanaco. It also reminds us that Moorish ornament, which so insistently emphasizes the surface, permeated all

Spanish work. The figures, as in the niches of San Sebastian, are strangely flat and strictly frontal in pose, in strong contrast to the restless three-dimensional quality of Baroque sculpture.

Cuzco was a center of painting, metalwork, and wood carving, both for its own churches, monastic institutions, and mansions and for the entire viceroyalty. Many of these figures approximated the Spanish realistic style; others were more abstract, such as the stone figures on the façade of *San Sebastian*. The canopied pulpits in particular were lavishly carved and, with the paintings and retables, enriched the otherwise sober interiors.

On the still higher, bleaker plateau of Alto Peru in the vicinity of Lake Titicaca (now chiefly in Bolivia), in such cities as La Paz and Potosí, the environment is much more hostile to man than in the green valleys around Cuzco. The thin, clear air sharpens the outlines against a metallic sky; the

11–8 LA COMPAÑÍA. Arequipa, Peru. 1698.

mountains are sheer masses of stone with sparse vegetation. Here the austere Tiahuanaco culture flourished. In this area the influence of the native peoples is strong, as is apparent in the church of *San Francisco* (La Paz), low and massive, its portal composed, as in the much older style of Tiahuanaco, of strong horizontals and insistent angles; and again in the church of *San Lorenzo* at Potosí, once the great silver city of Charles V. Here the richly carved portal, set in a deep niche, contains many elements of Spanish seventeenth-century architectural ornament, but the style has been transformed in two ways. First, colonial motifs are more abundant than elsewhere — angel-like figures playing musical instruments, sirens, and, on the columns, figures of Indian dancers in feather costumes. Second, the manner of carving and of combining elements resembles textile design. The balanced vertical and horizontal lines combined with curves provide a framework for many figures, simplified into abstract, flat forms. This same metamorphosis of Spanish style in Alto Peru is apparent in many of the rich carvings of retables and pulpits, as well as in the figure sculpture in which the pathetic expressions of Spanish theatrical realism are modified into ornamental patterns of geometric character.

As we move southeast along the passes into northwestern Argentina, the carvings and also the paintings become simple representations of passionate feeling expressed through highly con-

11–9 SAN FRANCISCO. Quito, Ecuador. Interior, toward sanctuary. 1564–1574; restored 1755–1770.

ventional forms. Northwestern Argentina was on the periphery of Peru. With Spanish influence weaker in proportion to its distance from Cuzco, the Indian peoples retained much of their own pattern of life, as did the Pueblos on the northern periphery of Hispanic America.

Quito, a late capital of the Inca empire, though high in the Andes, is much farther north than Cuzco and hence enjoys a milder climate. After the conquest numerous monastic schools were set up under the tutelage of the friars or of artists who came from Spain, so that the city became a center for making statues, carvings, and paintings for its own churches, monastic institutions, and mansions, and for export to other Hispanic colonies. Churches and con-

vents, which had followed the usual sixteenth- and seventeenth-century evolution of styles, suffered badly from earthquakes and in the process of repair and rebuilding took on, in the eighteenth century, an opulence unsurpassed in America.

Two churches in Quito illustrate this opulence: the Franciscan church and monastery, *San Francisco,* and the Jesuit church, *La Compañía. San Francisco,* with its cloisters and subsidiary buildings, is typical of the great monastic institutions; it occupies an entire city block. In external appearance it shares with all high Andean structures a low massiveness. Its heavy, severe portal prepares one but little for the richness of the interior decoration, where the work of the carver, the gild-

11–10 LA COMPAÑÍA. Quito, Ecuador. 1722–1765.

chrome sculpture. Large areas which remain quite flat are covered with angular Moorish ornament which sets off the more delicate curvilinear Renaissance carvings.

In creating these rich interiors architects, sculptors, carvers, gilders, and painters worked in close collaboration. Sixteenth-century carvers produced statues of a Late Gothic character. In the seventeenth century a style based on the Spanish Baroque emerged.

Between or fringing the two great art centers in Mexico and the Andean highlands are areas where varying conditions led to differences of style. In Guatemala, earthquakes, a predominantly Indian population, and the tradition of Maya ornament all favored a low, massive type of building, gay with colored plaster walls and ornament. In the Caribbean, as at Santo Domingo, Plateresque and Herreran styles dominate. In the highlands of Colombia, the transplanted Spanish settlers retained the Moorish habit of building fine ceilings of wood in geometric patterns (*artesonados*).

Brazil, settled by the Portuguese, experienced no succession of Medieval and Renaissance styles such as occurred in the Spanish colonies. The earliest extant buildings, which date from the late seventeenth century, as well as those of the eighteenth, follow Portuguese styles closely, with adaptations due to climatic differences, such as the introduction of lattices to protect against the equatorial sun. The coastal cities had a brief period of Herreran building, as in the cathedral of *Salvador* (Bahia).

Later in the century appeared buildings of a very different character, not the Churrigueresque of Mexico and Quito but a style which closely followed Lisbon modes, with a French Rococo flavor. The churches — the parish church of *Pilar* (El Salvador), for example — tend to be small, tall, and

er, and the painter are combined. In the apse (Fig. 11–9) is a framework of richly carved and gilded columns, above which is a broken cornice supporting many free-standing statues.

La Compañía (Fig. 11–10) presents a strong contrast to *San Francisco*. Though low and without towers, it is lighter in effect. The façade is a unified design, with movement in depth — greater in the central section, lesser in the lateral. A delicate play of light and shade over the surfaces comes from low reliefs accented by overshadowing niches and openings and particularly by the twisted columns at the entrance. If the façade of *La Compañía* is reservedly rich, the interior is opulent. The gold shines not with a metallic glitter but with a warm glow, owing to age and to the use of red and white pigment in the carvings and accents of color in the paintings and in the poly-

11–11 SÃO FRANCISCO. Ouro Preto, Brazil. 1765–1794. Planning and decorative sculpture are both attributed to Antônio Francisco Lisbôa ("O Aleijadinho"). (Archive of Hispanic Culture, Library of Congress)

slender, rectangular in plan, with no transepts, no vaulting, no dome. The lightness of the color — for they are usually plastered — the many openings, the delicacy of the Rococo-like ornament, produce an effect of lightness and elegance in strong contrast to the heavy, dark, massive structures of eighteenth-century Andean buildings.

In the late seventeenth century and in the eighteenth the discovery of gold and diamonds a few hundred miles inland in Brazil led to a unique development in a group of isolated mining towns, the chief of which was Ouro Preto.[6] In this heavily wooded moun-

[6] Ouro Preto, in the state of Minas Gerais, has been made a Brazilian national monument to preserve the colonial character of the town, like Taxco in Mexico and Williamsburg in the United States.

tainous plateau, quite out of contact with European sources, a distinctive regional style evolved. The responsibility for building lay with the Third Order of St. Francis (a lay order) and the local churches. A native gray soapstone furnished excellent material for masonry, which was usually stuccoed, and for carving. It was augmented by an orange sandstone, used in bases, pilasters, and cornices, which added a note of contrasting warmth.

Most of the churches follow a style unlike that of the rest of South America. Based upon Portuguese traditions they are rectangular in plan, with round towers and a single doorway with carved ornament flanked by two windows having a circular window directly above, around which the cornice bends. The pediment is finished

11–12 BOM JESUS. Congonhas do Campo, Minas Gerais. Soapstone prophets of 1796–
1805 by Antônio Francisco Lisbôa. (P. L. Goodwin and G. E. Kidder-Smith, *Brazil
Builds*, Museum of Modern Art, New York, 1943. Photo by G. E. Kidder-Smith)

with broken scrolls. Such is *São Francisco* at Ouro Preto (Fig. 11–11). Here
the elegant carving of the portal and
on the disk which takes the place of
the window above is the work of the
mestizo, Antônio Francisco Lisbôa,
known as O Aleijadinho ("The Little
Cripple"). O Aleijadinho, whose hands
and feet were badly crippled, was an
architect as well as a sculptor. His
dominant influence is seen in portals,
pulpits, fonts, altars, and stations of
the cross, both in stone and in wood,
in many churches in the state of Minas
Gerais. These show an independent
use of the Portuguese Rococo practiced
in the coastal cities. Garlands, scrolls,
ribbons, and figures are carved with
strength and boldness; and the more-
than-life-sized stone figures of the
prophets (Fig. 11–12) possess a power
and a vitality seldom met in Hispanic
American art.

North America

Hispanic America north of the Rio
Grande occupies the southwestern and
extreme southern part of the United
States. Florida, the Gulf Coast, and the
entire Southwest as far north, roughly,
as San Francisco were all a part of
New Spain.

In the Gulf area Spanish buildings of
various kinds appeared, most prominently at New Orleans, where in the
Plaza (now Jackson Square) rose the
simple *cathedral* and the *cabildo*, or
municipal building. Both of these
Spanish buildings were later altered
by the French, who in remodeling superimposed their own style. More elaborate, though still provincial in comparison with their Mexican prototypes,
are the churches and convents in
Texas and Arizona. *San Xavier del Bac*
(near Tucson) is the most elaborate

example of the Baroque style in a local idiom. Lack of stone and skilled labor led to the use of adobe brick, the usual building material of the Indians, for the construction of walls, vaults, and domes. The walls were plastered white, and the ornamentation of molded plaster was concentrated in the central part of the façade. The interior, rich in carvings, gilding, and color, though deriving from Spanish sources, shows many evidences of Indian conception and execution.

In California, where the Spanish missionaries penetrated in the late eighteenth century, economic conditions and lack of strong Indian building traditions led to one of the most ingenuous expressions of the Spanish Baroque, a unique and charming simplicity which fitted local requirements and climatic conditions admirably. In the construction of these missions — in their plans, massing of parts, and decorative elements — is the final dilution of Spanish Baroque, a simplification similar to that found in the interior of South America. At times the customary towers are omitted and, as a functional substitute, the gable is pierced to hold the bells, as at *San Gabriel*. This solution for hanging the bells (*espadaña*) is found in Mexico and Spain as well.

When we turn, however, to the Pueblo area of the Rio Grande valley in New Mexico, we immediately find this Spanish style strongly altered. Here the level of indigenous culture was high and the Pueblos were unusually tenacious of their heritage, so that the resulting pattern of life was largely Indian. Their conservatism is seen in the retention of the great communal houses, as at Taos, though in smaller adobe houses the addition of *portales*, or porticoes, and of chimneys reveals a Spanish influence. Everywhere, the continued use of the ceremonial *kiva* is evidence of the tenacity of the old religious practices. Nearby stands the mission church of the period (Fig. 11–13), sometimes of stone, more frequently of adobe, with thick, unbroken walls, massive buttressing, and roofs of wooden beams which project beyond the walls and are covered with twigs and a layer of adobe. Low, squat bell towers usually flank the façade, which has an open balcony above the entrance, quite possibly serving the same function as the open chapel in Mexico and Peru. This balcony, with its shadow-filled recesses, breaks the austere surface. The interiors with their whitewashed walls are as austere as the exteriors, except for the beams, or vigas, with their carved brackets, and the sanctuary, toward which the eye is inevitably guided through the dim light of the nave by the repetition of the vigas, by the focusing of light on the altar from a transverse clerestory, and by the painting and sculpture concentrated within the sanctuary.

In these paintings and sculptures we find Christian content given native form, producing what might well be called a folk art. While pictures and carvings were imported from Mexico and instruction was given the Indians in European arts, most of this work, together with the churches themselves, was destroyed in the rebellion of 1680. Thus for twelve years the Indians were free to express themselves without Spanish domination. Even after the return of the Spanish in 1692, the Indian artists, notably in the more isolated villages, were thrown upon their own resources. Within the limitations of local materials and of their own poverty they produced *santos* (sacred images) that are almost hypnotic in their emotional power. The *santos* took the form of *retablos* (paintings) and *bultos* (carvings in the round) which were used on the altar or carried in rites and festivals. The latter were the figures of saints, mostly Franciscan (as

11–13 SAN ESTEBAN REY. Acoma, New Mexico. *ca.* 1640. (Wayne Andrews)

the Franciscans were the chief missionaries in this region), of the Virgin as *Mater Dolorosa,* and of the Christ, with emphasis on the Man of Sorrows. Somber in color and passionate in mood, they partake strongly of the abstraction which permeates Indian art. The firm, clean-cut lines, the sharply contrasting light and dark areas, the large eyes, and the rhythmically repeated drops of blood create an effect of greater anguish than is conveyed by Spanish realism.

Except, perhaps, for the *retablos,* painting in Hispanic America, while prolific in quantity, did not show the same inventiveness nor reach the same high level of accomplishment as did architecture and carving.

Early fusion of Spanish and Indian art is more evident, however, in the postconquest illustrated books (codices).[7] Here appear experiments in the use of light and shade for modeling, in linear perspective, and in the intro-

duction of landscape and interiors in the backgrounds. These are found in combination with the traditional Indian flat linear style, in which depth was indicated by placing one figure above another with no diminution in size. There is a lively quality about many of these little drawings, as if the artist, though maintaining the integrity of his native style, was delighted to play with the new ideas. Given the opportunity, he might have been able to nurture an art rooted in native soil but branching out in new directions. This original growth, though submerged by the official art of the Church and the ruling class, was kept alive by the people, and in the twentieth century the Mexican mural painters have returned to its forms.

The official painters saw Spanish fashions only and followed first the current Flemish-Italian styles, or the tenebrist painting of Caravaggio and Ribera.

The clear bright color of Italianate painting and the melting light and color of Murillo made greater appeal to the Hispanic American than did the

[7] Codex: the book as we know it, consisting of leaves bound at one side or on alternating sides in the characteristic Mexican screenfold.

somber tenebrist style, and were in greater harmony with the sumptuously carved and gilded altarpieces. The Sevillian art of Murillo shaped the work of Gregorio Vasquez (1638–1711) of Bogotá, of Juan Rodríguez Juárez (1675–1728) of Mexico, and of the prolific Miguel Cabrera (1695–1768), often called the chief of Mexican painters, while José Ibarra (1688–1756) of Mexico reveals the influence of Rubens added to the sumptuousness of the local Baroque style.

There are two fields of painting, however, apart from that practiced in the viceregal centers of Mexico, Bogotá, Lima, and Quito, in which a more authentic expression of Hispanic-American life may be discovered. One is the so-called school of Cuzco; the other, the popular or folk art. Some painters followed the sequence of styles of the mother country; some, especially the mestizo artists, produced austere hieratic Madonnas, flat, strongly linear, and richly decorative, with many details of Inca derivation, especially in the garments and embroideries. And as we travel into Bolivia and northwestern Argentina we find, just as in the sculpture, further simplification, further intensity of feeling.

Another field of expression may be illustrated by the Mexican *ex voto* picture, which relates a miraculous escape from death or a recovery from illness through the intercession of some saint. The *ex votos* are small in size, painted on wood, tin, or canvas. Though some were made by well-known painters for the aristocracy, on the whole they were an art of the people. Some of the *ex votos* were flat and linear, dramatic arrangements of bright color areas, and highly conventional. Others were somewhat more naturalistic, indicating some acquaintance with European methods of expressing depth and mass. But in general they were infused with sincere, fervid feeling and a vitality expressed by a people with high aesthetic sensitivity.

Summary

Latin American colonial art was Spanish and Portuguese art transplanted to the Americas. It was often modified by climatic and geographical conditions and available materials, particularly in the viceregal capitals and coastal cities. Sometimes it was altered by contact with a people whose habit of mind and whose art were radically different from those of Europe. The modification was greater in areas where the aboriginal culture had reached a high level, as in Mexico and the Andean regions, and where the indigenous traditions were strong. Latin American art was largely at the service of the ruling aristocracy and of the Church, but was actually executed to a large extent by Indian craftsmen, who were endowed with considerable technical skill even before the coming of the Spaniard. A vast number of buildings were erected, at first chiefly ecclesiastical, later secular; and in style they passed through the contemporary European phases of Late Gothic, Plateresque, and Herreran, reaching a climax in the eighteenth-century Baroque, a style which permeated all the arts.

Sculpture, inextricably allied to architecture, consisted primarily of carvings for façades, *retablos*, and altars. It frequently showed Spanish realism modified by the Indian craftsman, who turned toward a simpler form. Painting was more definitely derivative than was sculpture, though in Cuzco, Bolivia, and the northern and southern fringes of the Hispanic domain the strong native element, blended with the Spanish influence, produced an original style. Among the Indians, especially away from the centers of Spanish culture, the native arts continued either in native form or with assimilated Hispanic elements. Thus a pure Indian or Indian-Hispanic art existed parallel to the European art, playing a decisive role in the twentieth-century revival of Latin American art.

New France

The first French explorers came to what is now Quebec and Montreal in search of a Northwest Passage to the Far East. Later, permanent colonies were established, and the settlers turned to commercial enterprise, particularly the fur trade. From Quebec and Montreal French traders pushed their explorations west and southwest until their forts and trading posts dotted a vast area from the mouth of the St. Lawrence to the mouth of the Mississippi. Other expeditions, exploratory or piratical, established French communities along the Gulf of Mexico, in Florida, in Haiti, and on the northern coast of Brazil. As with Spanish expeditions, missionaries accompanied the explorers or were themselves the exploring pioneers, seeking commercial relations with the Indians, if not their souls and their welfare.

Some of the French colonists were landed aristocracy. They constituted the ruling class in the government of the New World, which was patterned after the absolutism of France. The bulk of the population, however, were loyal peasant people of the Roman Catholic faith — farmers, fisherfolk, and craftsmen — who transplanted especially to the St. Lawrence valley the modes of life of their native Normandy and Brittany, with little attention to the culture of the native Indians. A woodland people with no cities, living in wigwams and skilled only in weaving, embroidery, and birchbark work, these Indians seem culturally to have been more strongly influenced by the white man than he was by them.

The vast extent of the French domain, with climatic conditions ranging from the rigorous cold of Quebec to the semitropical heat of New Orleans, required varied adaptation not only to climate but to local economies and materials as well. In the St. Lawrence valley stern economic conditions, as much as inherited aesthetic predilections, precluded nonessentials. The thrifty, industrious Norman and Breton peasants evolved simple, direct, and thoroughly adequate types of homes, churches, and convents from local material to meet their needs. Based on French prototypes a distinctive individual style arose. Out of local stone the builders constructed low, compact, rectangular houses, with walls several feet thick; small windows; steeply pitched roofs to shed the snow, sometimes broken by dormers and always by heavy chimneys. The *Château de Ramezay* (Montreal) is a somewhat elaborate version of the type.

The Church, a dominating element in the culture, gave importance to the building of churches, monasteries, and convents, which were of the same materials as the houses and as austerely simple. The early churches were devoid of ornament, but their roofs were distinguished by the "tin tiles" with which they were covered. These consisted of sheets of tin laid diagonally, producing a tilelike appearance. With time, the "tiles" acquired a silvery or

11–14 URSULINE CONVENT. Three Rivers, Quebec. 17th century. (S. J. Hayward)

bronze patina which made the roof pleasing as well as practical. The interiors of these churches were as unpretentious as the exteriors except for excellent wood carving around the altars. Because schools for artisans had been established in the colonies, craftsmanship was on a high level.[8] The designs were simplified versions of current French styles. The *Ursuline Convent* (Three Rivers, Fig. 11–14) well illustrates the neat, trim character of all this northern French colonial building and the peculiar harmony between the style and its cultural setting. The quiet dignity of its plain walls; its scorn, one is tempted to say, of ornament — these are peculiarly expressive of a simple, industrious people living in a harsh climate.

The large urban churches tended to flaunt twin towers, with classical porches reflecting the French neoclassic style. After the cession of Canada to England in 1763, the English Georgian versions of the classical styles came to replace the French, particularly in the mansions and churches of Montreal.

Buildings erected farther south in the vast French empire reflected gentler climates. Around St. Louis, for example, the combination trading post and home became an expansive structure. Double-pitched roofs sloped down on all four sides over the central rectangular core of the house and spread out beyond the walls to create porches or galleries often completely encircling the interior structure with a zone of breeze and shade. Walls were built of logs set vertically as a kind of palisade around the interior of the house. (This was in contrast to the horizontal placement of logs in the familiar frontier cabin which the westward-pushing English colonists had adopted from Swedish settlers in the Middle

[8] The first bishop of Quebec, Monseigneur de Laval, established the first such school at St. Joachim, near Cap Tourmente in Quebec in 1668.

11–15 CAST-IRON DOUBLE BALCONY. 805 Esplanade Avenue, New Orleans. *ca.* 1850. (Clarence John Laughlin)

Atlantic seaboard.) Clay plaster filled the interstices between these upright logs. Sometimes a regular half-timber frame replaced the palisade type of wall, the intervals between the timbers being filled with a soft clay brick which was in turn protected by a surface coat of lime plaster. Cabins situated on bottomlands tended to be raised on posts six to eight feet aboveground as a precaution against floods. The practice often appeared on more elevated sites, also, as a means of increasing the airiness of the living quarters.

Still farther south, at New Orleans, the semitropical climate combined with the French traditions and earlier Spanish influence to produce a style which reflects a mixture of French and Spanish elements.[9] Through-

[9] New Orleans was founded by the French in 1718 as a center for trade with the Indians, and was ceded to Spain by the treaty of 1763.

out most of the eighteenth century houses in New Orleans were generally built in a French folk tradition of simple cubic masses not too dissimilar from those in Quebec despite some differences in construction, roof silhouette, window area, and certain decorative details. From an early time, however, New Orleans also produced a distinctive type of urban residence, with the living floors raised to the top of the house and opening onto a porch overlooking the street. This so-called "raised cottage" style provided an urban parallel to the stilts of the country cabin, except that in New Orleans the first floor was given over to offices and stores which opened directly onto the street. It was the develop-

It suffered great fires in 1788 and 1794. In 1801 it was ceded by Spain to France. Thus as a result of the fires, most of the extant colonial building falls into the late Spanish and second French eras.

ment of this "raised cottage" style of house at the end of the eighteenth and throughout the first half of the nineteenth century which gives the *Vieux Carré* (Old Quarter) of New Orleans its distinctive architectural character today. The earlier mode of balconied living quarters upstairs with the shop front on the street was maintained; but increasingly the Spanish concept of the house, centered in a garden court, shaded by tropical foliage and cooled by fountains, exerted its influence on domestic planning. From Spain, too, derived the iron balconies which replaced the older wooden-posted porches. Whereas the old porches were usually recessed into the block of the house (so that the first floor projected to the sidewalk, while the living floor was set back under the roof behind its porch), the iron balcony almost always hung as a light cage directly above the street. With their lacelike quality and complex shadows, the balconies (Fig. 11–15) added grace and delicacy to the plain, rather stern walls. These iron balconies were of two kinds, wrought and cast. The older form, wrought iron, was simpler in design and of painstaking craftsmanship. Cast iron, largely mass-produced in standardized patterns and virtually all of it nineteenth-century, lent itself to more intricate designs, which often included monograms and motifs of local flora. Cast iron was also used for elaborately designed benches and street lamps, while wrought iron was used for gracefully ornamented grilled gates to protect the entrance to the court and at the same time to admit the breeze.

Within, the homes of the wealthy had high, stately rooms, with spiral staircases leading to the upper stories, and carved balusters, fine paneling and mantles, and crystal chandeliers. The furnishings were predominantly French. Much of the furniture — tables, chairs, chests, and great wardrobes — was imported, but much also was made locally of swamp cypress which thrived in the steaming bayou country of Louisiana.

The compactness of the New Orleans house, depending as it did on a small courtyard for contact with the outdoors, was ideally suited to the constricted space of what had originally been a fortified city. Outside the city, extending over great areas of rich farm land, plantations developed which produced great wealth for their owners and led to the building of houses as fine as those in the city but of a type adapted both in plan and arrangement to a different site. The plantation house was customarily only two stories high, the lower story a basement necessitated by the water-soaked soil, the upper the living quarters for the family. Built of brick on the lower story and wood above, the house was often a long, thin rectangle. Instead of facing an inner court, it opened outward onto wide, two-storied verandas shaded by the overhanging roof. Sturdy brick piers rising directly from the ground supported the upper porch, the slender wooden columns of this balcony in turn supporting the sheltering overhang of the roof above. Doors and windows opened wide on these verandas, thus linking the interior of the house to the airy shade of its porches. These plantation houses resembled those of Haiti and Santo Domingo, from whence refugees had fled to Louisiana at the time of the revolution on that island; they also recalled the plantation houses of northern Brazil. Likewise, the urban French style of New Orleans seems related to the colored stucco houses with delicate iron balconies seen in some of the older northern Brazilian cities. Although the precise degree of influence from South and Central America has yet to be determined, colonial building in Louisiana apparently represents the northern

11-16 THE COTTAGE (THE CONRAD PLACE). East Baton Rouge Parish, Louisiana. 1825. (A. E. Woolley from APA)

reaches of an architectural style part Spanish and part French in inspiration. With local variations, this hybrid style appeared wherever Europeans settled, from northern Brazil and the West Indies to the lower reaches of the Mississippi River valley. (See Fig. 11-16.)

The furnishings of French colonial houses tended to mirror the gamut of architectural styles. Furniture ranged from the simple, robust peasant types in Canada to the more elegant and aristocratic styles in New Orleans, often imported directly from Europe. Though secular art was predominant, ecclesiastical art was not neglected; but it did not dominate the community as in the Hispanic colonies — a reflection of the relative power of the Church in France and in Spain, as well as the differing degrees to which monastic orders had participated in the colonization of the two empires.

Summary

As the French colonies spread out loosely over a vast area whose climate varied from the harsh regions of Quebec to the semitropical conditions of New Orleans, French colonial art developed styles as diversified as the geography it encompassed. In Canada the style of Brittany and Normandy, adapted to a difficult climate, produced compact, thick-walled masonry structures. The direct and unpretentious quality of both houses and churches suggests the same qualities in the industrious, devout people who built them. In the middle Mississippi regions the closed quality of Quebec buildings gave way to more open structures under the influence of a milder climate. Finally, in semitropical and tropical regions the Mediterranean type of house appeared — in the cities as brightly colored stucco houses enclosing garden courts, with handsome iron balconies hung over the streets; in the rich agricultural sections as the plantation house opening onto shaded verandas.

The Seaboard Colonies

Unlike the colonial policies of Spain and France, which were largely determined by the need for filling the coffers of absolutist monarchies, English colonial policy unfolded under no centralized authority. English colonization followed instead a much more individualistic pattern of development. Whether pursued for the idealistic ends of religious or political freedom or, more often, for the materialistic ends of self-advancement, English colonization was characterized by a more dense community settlement and much more intensive development of economic resources than either the French or Spanish. Whereas the Spanish and French came to trade, the English came to live. Whereas royal companies or aristocratic landholders controlled vast areas of the Spanish and French sections of North America, all attempts to establish similar modes of control failed in the English colonies because of the relentless pressure of settlement. Only in the southern colonies did the concentration of property into a few hands suggest the enormous land holdings of Spanish aristocrats, and even in the South it was not impossible during the colonial period for the ambitious indentured servant to become a plantation owner.

Greater social and political equality existed in the English colonies, on the whole, than anywhere else in the New World, and greater homogeneity despite local diversity. The diversity between the northern and southern colonies was due to differences of climate and to differences in the cultural backgrounds of the first settlers. At one extreme, New England possessed a cold, nonagricultural, heavily timbered area; at the other, the tidewater areas of the southern colonies boasted fertile land and long growing seasons. While a town economy developed around the excellent New England harbors, the southern colonies developed the isolated agricultural unit with its manor house and cluster of outbuildings. Town life created opportunities for the specialized craftsman, and hence the best colonial furniture and crafts, as well as the most significant colonial painting, appeared in the northern colonies. The isolated planter simply could not keep such specialized craftsmen and artists as the cabinetmaker Goddard or the painter Copley employed, whereas the larger populations of such New England towns as Newport and Boston provided a considerable market for impressive furniture such as highboys or for family portraits. Moreover, the southern planter could export his tobacco, rice, or indigo (cotton was not a substantial southern crop until after 1800) directly to England quite as well as to the colonies further north. Hence furniture could be imported directly from the home country, and portraits obtained during an occasional business trip to London or ordered of itinerant

11–17 PARSON CAPEN HOUSE. Topsfield, Massachusetts. 1683. (Wayne Andrews)

European portraitists (or "limners," as they were usually called in colonial America — the term being a corruption of "delineator" or "illuminator"). The large plantation owners could thus furnish their houses in a manner appropriate to the style as it evolved. No group of houses built before the Revolution surpasses the greatest mansions of Virginia; perhaps only buildings in and around Charleston, South Carolina, and Annapolis, Maryland (both significantly planter-dominated towns) and some in what is now the Fairmount Park section of Philadelphia can equal them.

There was no indigenous influence on the arts of the colonists. Both North and South took the same attitude toward the Indians, who were woodland tribes with no cities and with an art expression limited to objects of daily life. There was no assimilation of cultures, no intermingling such as produced the mestizo class in the Spanish and Portuguese colonies, but rather a

consistent segregation, a pushing of the aborigines ever farther westward. Thus the arts of the colonists were European arts transplanted to primitive conditions and adapted to new climatic and cultural environments.

ARCHITECTURE

The English background is apparent in the types of buildings erected by the colonists. The earliest buildings were naturally in the style with which the colonists were familiar, the Late Medieval folk-building traditions of the Elizabethan and Jacobean eras translated, in the North, into a timber construction adaptable to a more severe climate than that of England. The developed type of these seventeenth-century houses in New England, such as the *Parson Capen House* (Fig. 11–17), appeared as a dark, high-roofed wooden mass. Small windows, the heavy barricade of the door, the huge central chimney core — all combined to

11–18 WESTOVER. Charles City County, Virginia. South front. *ca.* 1730–1734. (T. T. Waterman, from HABS, Library of Congress)

express a sense of shelter against an alien land newly redeemed from wilderness. The exterior clapboarded sheathing concealed a heavy frame in which the openings between the timbers were filled with an insulating material — either with lath and mud plaster (so-called "wattle and daub") or bricks ("nogging"). Inside, however, the timber frame was exposed in the low ceilings and the corner uprights. The impression of shelter conveyed by the exterior was fully realized inside by the heavy beams immediately overhead, the dim light from the small windows, and the cavernous fireplace. Furnishings shared the forthright vigor of the architecture in their sparse ornamentation and heavy, angular shapes.

During the seventeenth century not all colonies, of course, built in the New England manner. There were wide regional variations. In Virginia, for example, brick was much more widely used than in New England. The Virginian

tended to build his fireplaces, not in the center of the house but in the outer walls at either end of the building and, in the most elaborate plans, to create a breeze hallway in the middle of his space — precisely where the New Englander had placed his mammoth chimney mass. Regional variations depended upon climate, available building materials, and, above all, the traditions and personal preferences which each group of colonists brought from the Old World. Despite regional variations, however, seventeenth-century buildings possessed certain characteristics in common. They all represented old folk-building traditions emanating from the Medieval past. Moreover, all tended to be rather modest, relatively unadorned, boxlike masses enclosing limited, boxlike interior spaces with a directness which comprises their principal expressive quality.

As we have already seen, during the very years when the colonists were

11–19 ST. MICHAEL's. Charleston, South Carolina. 1752–1761. (Carolina Art Association)

transplanting Medieval building traditions to the New World, these traditions were undergoing change in England. With the gradual spread of Renaissance ideals throughout Europe, Renaissance concepts of symmetrical massing and classicized decorative details had progressively altered many essentially Medieval structures. By 1619 — almost sixty-five years before the *Parson Capen House* — Inigo Jones had

designed his *Banqueting Hall* in London as a fully classicized structure. With the advance of the seventeenth century, the Palladian neoclassicism of Jones tended to absorb certain Baroque architectural elements. This style first reached the colonies after 1690 by means of illustrated books. In this way learned or bookish styles replaced the old craft or folk traditions of building. Because the Georges ruled England throughout the eighteenth century, the style has come to be called "Georgian."

Early Georgian houses such as *Westover* (Fig. 11–18) (Charles City County, Virginia; *ca.* 1730–1734) reveal the same large, simple rectangular mass topped by tall roofs as do such seventeenth-century houses as the *Parson Capen House*. A new symmetry, however, appears in the forceful rhythm of the windows, which now open widely on the landscape. The horizontal molding above the first floor increases the geometrical organization of the façade by dividing the wall into long rectangular panels to echo the horizontal rhythm of windows above and below, while simultaneously indicating the two-story division inside. In the center of the façade, as its most conspicuous element, is the elaborate doorway, framed by pilasters and crowned by a scroll pediment. This frontispiece serves as the proper introduction to the ample space of the central hall, with its sweep of stairs rising to the second story. On either side of the hall, spacious rooms, paneled and plastered, tend to echo (although somewhat less precisely) the symmetry of the exterior. The Palladianized-baroque forms of Westover betokened the emerging wealth and cosmopolitanism of the colonies and created a setting appropriate to the social formality and ceremony which accompanied colonial prosperity.

In Charleston an unknown architect (perhaps Peter Harrison) used a plate in Gibbs' *Book of Architecture* as inspi-

11–20   PIERCE-NICHOLS HOUSE. Salem, Massachusetts. 1782. (Essex Institute)

11–21   STATE CAPITOL. Richmond, Virginia. Designed by Thomas Jefferson. 1785–1789. (Virginia Chamber of Commerce)

ration for the compelling tower of *St. Michael's* (Charleston, South Carolina; 1752–1761) (Fig. 11–19; cf. Fig. 10–48). Like its prototype *St. Michael's* displays a classical temple portico. This temple front indicated a tendency, beginning around 1750, toward the elimination of Baroque motifs in favor of a more rigorous Palladianism and hence toward classical forms more closely derived from the pre-Baroque buildings of the Italian High Renaissance and, beyond these, from the structures of the Classical past itself. Once again developments in the colonies reflected earlier developments in England where, from about 1720 to 1750, a coterie of architects and amateurs centered around Lord Burlington had dominated architectural taste in their attempt to exclude what they considered Baroque "impurities" from neoclassical architecture by a return to Palladio. Books published under the aegis of the wealthy lord began to appear in the colonies about the middle of the century. Late Georgian architecture in the colonies, exemplified by the *Pierce-Nichols House* (Salem, Massachusetts; 1782) (Fig. 11–20), therefore, tended to reject such Baroque elements as the scroll-pedimented doorway of *Westover* in favor of a porch which recalled a Doric temple complete with frieze and pediment, and preferred a flat balustraded roof to the tall, reminiscently Gothic gable of *Westover*. The emphasis on a flat, highly embellished roof line, the increased size of the windows with their prominent frames accentuating the vigor of the regular rhythm, and the three-storied pilasters decisively closing the corners — all these elements echoed Renaissance prototypes and can be traced, by way of England, to such distant ancestors as the *Farnese Palace* and Palladio's *Palazzo Valmarano*. In Salem, as in Italy, these buildings produce an impression of dignity, urbanity, and well-being.

11–22 THOMAS JEFFERSON. *University of Virginia*, Charlottesville, 1819–1826. As seen from Lewis Mountain in 1856,

Before the end of the eighteenth century, Thomas Jefferson revealed his deep feeling for the Classical past by suggesting the complete Roman temple form for the capitol at Richmond. He based the Virginia *Capitol* (Fig. 11–21) on the *Maison Carrée* (Fig. 6–24), which he had seen in Nîmes while serving in France as American ambassador. For his own house, Monticello, at Charlottesville, Virginia, Jefferson evoked the centralized-dome plan of Palladio's *Villa Rotonda* (Fig. 9–87) as his basic inspiration, but he transformed Palladio's formal Renaissance plan so that variously shaped rooms created a sense of ceremony combined with that of convenience, the rooms spreading parallel to the landscape axis. Finally, in the *University of Virginia* (Fig. 11–22), among his last major architectural works, Jefferson created what he termed an "academical

with later wing added to library at left. (From Lambeth, *Thomas Jefferson, Architect*, Houghton, Mifflin, 1913)

village." A group of two storied, temple-fronted buildings provided classrooms on the ground story and faculty apartments on the upper. These were linked by a one-storied colonnade fronting a row of student cubicles. The whole complex was closed at one end by a domed library and (originally) open at the other to the rolling countryside surrounding it. As each of the classroom buildings recalled a different temple structure, so the library dominating the "academical village" evoked, in wood and brick, the grandeur of the Roman *Pantheon* (Fig. 6–30). Here Jefferson transformed the Classical past into a modern program combining monumentality with human scale, geometrical order with the freer order of landscape.

Jefferson's enthusiasm for the Classical world and his adaptation of a wide variety of Classical structures to new programs reflected the increasing knowledge of Roman architecture, which excavations at the buried cities of Herculaneum and Pompeii (begun in 1738 and 1748, respectively) had revealed.[10] After 1787 the Adam style appeared in the colonies with the work of Charles Bulfinch in Boston (Fig. 11–23) and Samuel McIntire in Salem. This transplanted Adam style is often called "Federal" by Americans, partly because of its association with the early federal period and partly because patriotic devices such as eagles and stars were sometimes introduced into the light surface ornamentation. Originating in New England, the style rapidly spread throughout the country, thanks to such books as those by Owen Biddle and particularly by Asher Benjamin.

At the end of the colonial period, then, two influences were at work in American architecture, both largely transmitted from England, both ultimately deriving their inspiration from the Classical past. On the one hand, there were Palladianized versions of Roman monumental and Renaissance palace architecture; on the other, Adam-inspired interpretations of Roman domestic architecture. The two stylistic currents often intermingled. Meanwhile, as early as the 1750's, European archeologists were rediscovering Greek architecture and through their publications making the Greek past as readily available to modern architects as was the Roman. Only in the 1820's did the severe and ample ge-

[10] It is interesting to note that Jefferson, too, was interested in archeology, for he excavated Indian sites on his estates along the Potomac River. More important, though, to the development of archeological techniques is the fact that he discovered and applied stratigraphic methods in his excavations and explained them in his notebooks of 1809, which were studied by other scholars. This was about fifty years before other experts, notably the French, began to apply this important system for dating archeological finds.

11–23 DINING ROOM OF HARRISON GRAY OTIS HOUSE. Boston, Massachusetts. Designed by Charles Bulfinch. 1795. (Society for the Preservation of New England Antiquities)

ometry of the Greek temple become pervasive in the United States. Then, some three decades after political independence, the stylistic currents associated with the colonial period began to disappear in the emergent "Greek revival."

PAINTING

Although both frontier conditions and Puritan ideology militated against a rich painting tradition in the seventeenth century, the customary impression of a life of unembellished austerity has certainly been exaggerated. Painting appeared in the colonies with the growth of settled communities. The first painters seem to have been versatile. They not only painted portraits but also designed elaborate pictorial signboards for shops and inns, a neces-

sity when street addresses were unknown and businesses identified as being "at the sign of the whale" or the "rooster" or whatever device the entrepreneur fancied. The artisans painted banners and trappings for elaborate funeral processions, filling these with death's-heads or winged hourglasses to symbolize the passage of time, and often with portraits of the deceased. They doubtless contrived designs for tombstones and furniture. In short, the earliest colonial painter must have been something of a jack-of-all-trades, undertaking any task which required some artistic ability and permitted him to eke out a livelihood.

Unfortunately most of this early production has perished. Signboards and funeral trappings have almost completely disappeared. The major evidences of seventeenth-century artistry are tombstones, some furniture, and a few portraits preserved because of family pride. Among the earliest New England portraits known to us is that of the enchanting young *Alice Mason* (Fig. 11–1). As seventeenth-century buildings reflected Late Medieval traditions, so this portrait exemplified tendencies toward flat-patterned form as in Medieval English portraiture. Where Elizabethan portraiture often depicted extreme elegance of costume and suggested aristocratic demeanor through elongated figures and languid poses, *Alice Mason* confronts the spectator with a directness which resolutely proclaims a prosperous middle-class background beneath the "Sunday best" in which the child is clad. The simple background serves as a foil for the intricate curvilinear forms of lace and ribbons. The soft dull play of light as it moves slowly over the figure recalls the same kind of luminosity within the interior of the New England house as does the rather wooden directness of the figure.

Further south in New Amsterdam, a vigorous school of Dutch realists, largely anonymous, grew up. In contrast to the Medieval influences which dominated New England painting, Dutch limners seem to have been strongly affected from the beginning by the Baroque realism imported by the burghers of the New World. Perhaps nowhere in the painting of the colonies was a greater variety of subject matter to be seen in the seventeenth century. Still lifes, landscapes, figure pieces, Biblical and historical subjects — Dutch colonials reproduced all the manifestations of painting in the home country.

Still further south, in the plantation colonies, European imports were so extensive and the tradition of independent craftsman-artists so feeble that native painting failed to attain the vigorous expression of contemporary work further north.

About the beginning of the eighteenth century, in painting, as in architecture, Renaissance-Baroque ideals began to permeate the English colonies, partly through imported engravings and canvases, partly through the immigration of mediocre European painters to the colonies. Both influences accounted for the introduction to the colonies of the vocabulary of forms associated with the Van Dyck tradition of aristocratic portraiture, as later formularized by such fashionable seventeenth-century painters as Lely and Sir Godfrey Kneller. Diagonal arrangements of the figure into depth tended to replace the earlier frontality. A flickering light, moving abruptly from violent highlight to deep shadow, replaced the dull softness of earlier luminosity. A wider range of colors, the often awkward attempt to achieve a fluid brushstroke, and the multiplication of aristocratic accoutrements such as columns, balustrades, and drapery also characterized eighteenth-century painting.

The only interesting work done in the South during the later colonial period was the product of foreigners who migrated to the area, sometimes remaining briefly before returning home, sometimes settling for life. Painters such as the Englishman Charles Bridges (in Virginia for a few years after 1735), the German Engelhardt Kühn (active in Maryland from about 1708 to 1717), and the Swiss Jeremiah Theus (active around Charleston from 1740 until his death in 1774) depicted the planter aristocracy in provincial versions of the courtly style. Perhaps the most interesting of these expatriates in the southern colonies (although he painted in Delaware and Pennsylvania as well as in Maryland) was the Swede Gustavus Hesselius (1682–1755), who reached America in 1712. Hesselius' natural inclination toward realism, where he shows to best advantage, was usually thwarted by his

11–24   JOHN SMIBERT. *The Bermuda Group* (*Bishop Berkeley and his Entourage*). 1808. Yale University Art Gallery. (Yale Art Gallery)

clients' desire to see themselves decked out according to courtly formulas.

This conflict between a desire for realistic portrayal of man in a middle-class society and the arbitrary stylization implicit in the aristocratic tradition deriving from the home country is especially noticeable in New England, where colonial American painting was to produce its greatest masters. The dichotomy is apparent, for example, in the work of John Smibert (1688–1751), an English portrait painter who accompanied the famous philosopher Bishop Berkeley to America as part of an ill-fated expedition to establish a college for Indians in Bermuda. The venture collapsed for want of funds and Berkeley returned to England, but Smibert, who had meanwhile married a wealthy Massachusetts heiress, remained in Boston, where, from 1730 until his death, he was regarded as the city's foremost painter. His group portrait of *Bishop Berkeley and His Entourage* (Fig. 11–24) exhibits the mixture of middle-class realism and aristocratic formula characteristic of all Smibert's work. The two women sitting behind the table appear as doll-like generalizations. On the other hand, there are strong realistic elements in the painting: the scribe eagerly leaning forward to catch the bishop's words, the sensitive but rather discontented face of the artist in the left corner, and the confident, rather puffy face of the bishop himself as he clasps a volume in his pudgy hand. Smibert paid a price for daring the difficult task of placing a number of people around a table, for his composition is certainly somewhat disjointed. Awkwardness is apparent, too, in the linear strokes which he employed to catch the glitter of highlights on sumptuous fabrics and in the rather formless bulk of the bishop. Yet the painting does capture the liveliness of a social group and reveals considerable psychological insight.

Mediocre as Smibert may have been by European standards, his artistry appeared astonishing to the colonial Bostonian. It is not surprising therefore that two of the most significant of colonial painters were directly influenced by his work. Robert Feke (of whom little is known save the dates of his active career — from around 1741 to about 1750) used Smibert's portrait of *Bishop Berkeley* as a model in creating his group portrait of *Isaac Royall and His Family*. In this picture one perceives how Feke, by minimizing the strain of realism in Smibert, created rather stylized portraiture. This tendency in Feke's work, combined with a coolly harmonious range of color and a sensitive simplification of form, gives the best of his later works an abstract quality of design quite exceptional in colonial painting.

John Singleton Copley (1737–1815), together with Gilbert Stuart the greatest of colonial painters, was also influenced by Smibert. He worked in the realistic vein of Smibert but coupled this realism with a depth of psychological characterization and a capacity for compositional design which far surpass these qualities in the older master. It is true that his portrait of *Mrs. Thomas Boylston* (Fig. 11–25) reveals a certain stiffness in the figure due partly perhaps to propriety, but more to lack of ease on the part of a painter who was untrained professionally. There is a generally hard and linear effect, together with an overem-

11–25 JOHN SINCLETON COPLEY. *Mrs. Thomas Boylston.* 1766. Fogg Art Museum, Harvard University. (Fogg Art Museum)

phasis upon contrasting lights and darks. Hence the elements of the composition, skillfully as it is planned, do not completely fuse into a pictorial unity. These characteristics in Copley's painting doubtless are partly due to his necessary dependence for knowledge of European art on the hard linearity of engravings. Despite these handicaps in his training, however, he did achieve an intensity of realistic detail and of characterization which give his American portraits their forceful directness. After 1774 Copley established permanent residence in England, and in proportion as he gained professionally he lost in forthright candor of characterization. His talent, had it originally been grounded in the needed professional training, might conceivably have produced a truly indigenous art of high quality. Copley's decision to remain in England led to an increased facility in handling pigment but a general weakening of his genuine ability. His was the first of a long series of similar professional choices which have sapped a normal evolution of pictorial expression in this country.

The pull toward London proved irresistible to artists. To be sure, it was necessary for technical training. But few stopped at that. Benjamin West (1738–1820), for example, after an adventurous and now legendary youth, set out for Italy in 1760 with the financial assistance of a rich patron and arrived in London while Sir Joshua Reynolds was the revered president of the Royal Academy. Falling into the current styles, West became popular and wealthy, made a grandiloquent gesture by refusing knighthood, and upon the death of Sir Joshua in 1792 became president of the Academy. His studio was a mecca for American students during and for a generation after the War of Independence and thus brought American painting into close affiliation with English traditions. In addition, West introduced historical, mythological, and religious subjects in the "grand manner." Sometimes portraying subjects of moral stoicism in a neoclassical style, sometimes using visionary or apocalyptic themes in a romantic Baroque vocabulary of forms, West presaged both David (p. 651) and Delacroix (p. 654), though without their genius.

Although Copley as well as West was drawn to grandiose historical and visionary subjects while in England, there was little demand for such themes in the colonies, where the painter's standard commodity continued to be portraiture. Despite some influences from France toward the end of the century, English inspiration predominated. Of the portraitists [11] painting in

[11] Ralph Earle (1751–1801); Matthew Pratt (1734–1805); Charles Willson Peale (1741–1827); and Gilbert Stuart (1755–1828).

11–26 GILBERT STUART. *Mrs. Richard Yates.* 1793. Mellon Collection, National Gallery of Art, Washington, D. C. (National Gallery)

the colonies at the end of the eighteenth and the beginning of the nineteenth century, Gilbert Stuart was certainly the finest. Despite long residence in London he was freer than most English-trained provincials from imitation of the styles with which he came in contact. With genuine feeling for his medium, he built up a vibrant surface of loose, yet determined strokes which has its own esthetic value. *Mrs. Yates* (Fig. 11–26), for example, illustrates his sureness of technique and his use of it to set forth his subject with objective reality and interpretive probity. In contrast to the painfully intent vision which gives a somewhat static quality to Copley's portraits, the best of Stuart's work exhibits the lively vivacity of momentary gesture and glance. For this effect his nervous brushwork was particularly appropriate; but by the same token Stuart at his worst would dash off a merely facile likeness, structurally flabby, such as never marred Copley's American work.

Bibliography

LATIN AMERICA

Anderson, Lawrence L., *The Art of the Silversmith in Mexico, 1519–1936*, 2 vols., Oxford University Press, New York, 1941.

Benavides Rodríguez, Alfredo, *La Arquitectura en el Virreinato del Peru y en la Capitania General de Chile*, Santiago, Chile, 1941.

Cossio del Pomar, Felipe, *Pintura colonial, escuela Cuzqueña*, Cuzco, Peru, 1928.

Fernández, Justino, *El arte moderno en Mexico*, J. Porrúa, Mexico City, 1937.

Goodwin, Philip L., *Brazil Builds*, Museum of Modern Art, New York, 1943.

Kelemen, Pál, *Baroque and Rococo in Latin America*, Macmillan, New York, 1951.

Kubler, George, *The Religious Architecture of New Mexico*, Taylor Museum, Colorado Springs Fine Arts Center, Colo., 1940.

Navarro, José G., *Religious Architecture in Quito*, Metropolitan Museum of Art, New York, 1945.

Newcomb, Rexford, *The Old Mission Churches and Historic Houses of California*, Lippincott, 1925.

Smith, Robert C., "The Colonial Architecture of Minas Gerais in Brazil," *Art Bulletin*, June, 1939, p. 110.

——, "The Colonial Churches of Brazil," *Bulletin of the Pan American Union*, Washington, D. C., January, 1938.

——, "XIX Century Painting in Argentina," *Gazette des Beaux Arts*, Series 6, Vol. 22, No. 909, November, 1942, p. 99.

Solá, Miguel, *Historia del arte Hispano-Americano*, Editorial Labor, Barcelona, 1935.

Toussaint, Manuel, *Tres siglos de arquitectura colonial*, Mexico City, 1933.

Twenty Centuries of Mexican Art, Museum of Modern Art, New York, 1940.

Velázquez Chávez, Austín, *Tres siglos de pintura colonial Mexicana*, Editorial Polis, Mexico City, 1939.

Wethey, Harold E., *Colonial Architecture and Sculpture in Peru*, Harvard University Press, 1949.

Wilder, Mitchell A., and Breitenbach, Edgar, *Santos: The Religious Folk Art of New Mexico*, Taylor Museum, Colorado Springs Fine Arts Center, Colo., 1943.

NEW FRANCE

Carless, William, *The Architecture of French Canada*, McGill University Press, Montreal, 1925.

Carless, William, *The Arts and Crafts of Canada*, McGill University Press, Montreal, 1925.

Gowans, Alan, *Church Architecture in New France*, University of Toronto Press, 1956.

Laughlin, Clarence J., *Ghosts Along the Mississippi*, Scribner's, 1948.

Morrison, Hugh S., *Early American Architecture*, Oxford University Press, New York, 1952.

Ricciuti, Italo W., *New Orleans and Its Environs*, William Helburn, New York, 1938.

Spratling, William P., and Scott, Natalie, *Old Plantation Houses in Louisiana*, William Helburn, New York, 1927.

Traquair, Ramsay, *The Old Architecture of Quebec*, Macmillan, Toronto, 1947.

——, *The Old Silver of Quebec*, Macmillan, Toronto, 1940.

THE SEABOARD COLONIES

Bridenbaugh, Carl, *Cities in the Wilderness*, Ronald Press, New York, 1938.

——, *Peter Harrison, First American Architect*, University of North Carolina Press, Chapel Hill, 1949.

Briggs, Martin S., *The Homes of the Pilgrim Fathers in England and America, 1620–1685*, Oxford University Press, New York, 1932.

Burroughs, Alan, *Limners and Likenesses*, Harvard University Press, 1936.

Christensen, Erwin O., *The Index of American Design*, Macmillan, New York, 1950.

Davis, Deering, *Annapolis Houses, 1700–1775*, Architectural Book Publishing, New York, 1947.

Drepperd, Carl W., *American Pioneer Arts and Artists*, Pond-Ekberg, Springfield, Mass., 1942.

Flexner, James T., *America's Old Masters*, Viking, New York, 1939.

——, *First Flowers of Our Wilderness, American Painting*, Houghton, Mifflin, 1947.

Foote, Henry W., *Robert Feke, Colonial Portrait Painter*, Harvard University Press, 1930.

Forman, Henry C., *The Architecture of the Old South*, Harvard University Press, 1948.

Halsey, Richard T. H., and Cornelius, Charles O., *A Handbook of the American Wing*, Metropolitan Museum of Art, New York, 1932.

Hamlin, Talbot F., *The American Spirit in Architecture* (Pageant of America Series, Vol. 13), Yale University Press, 1926.

Hipkiss, Edwin J., *Eighteenth-Century American Arts*, Harvard University Press, 1941.

Kimball, Sidney Fiske, *American Architecture*, Bobbs-Merrill, Indianapolis, 1928.
——, *Domestic Architecture of the Colonies and of the Early Republic*, Scribner's, 1922.
——, *Mr. Samuel McIntire, Carver, the Architect of Salem*, Southworth-Anthoensen Press, Portland, Me., 1940.
LaFollette, Suzanne, *Art in America*, Harper, 1929.
Larkin, Oliver W., *Art and Life in America*, Rinehart, 1949.
Lipman, Jean, *American Primitive Painting*, Oxford University Press, New York, 1942.
Mather, Frank J., Jr., Morey, Charles R., and Henderson, William J., *The American Spirit in Art* (Pageant of America Series, Vol. 12), Yale University Press, 1927.
Morrison, Hugh, *Early American Architecture*, Oxford University Press, New York, 1952.

Murrell, William, *A History of American Graphic Humor*, Vol. 1, Whitney Museum of American Art, New York, 1934.
Park, Lawrence, compiler, *Gilbert Stuart*, with an appreciation by Royal Cortissoz, 4 vols., W. E. Rudge, New York, 1926.
Phillips, John Marshall, *American Silver*, Chanticleer Press, New York, 1949.
Pinckney, Pauline A., *American Figureheads and Their Carvers*, Norton, 1940.
Pratt, Richard, *A Treasury of Early American Houses*, McGraw-Hill (Whittlesey House), 1949.
Rogers, Meyric R., *American Interior Design*, Norton, 1947.
Waterman, Thomas T., *The Dwellings of Colonial America*, University of North Carolina Press, Chapel Hill, 1950.
——, *Mansions of Virginia*, University of North Carolina Press, Chapel Hill, 1946.
Wertenbaker, Thomas J., *The Founding of American Civilization: The Middle Colonies*, Scribner's, 1938.

CHAPTER 12

RUSSIAN

10TH–15TH CENTURIES

The people who first colonized the northern shore of the Black Sea and roamed the great Russian steppes were Hellenic or Iranian. Whatever their precise origin, these early pagans were settled in Kiev and other cities along the western rivers when Vladimir I (*ca.* 980–1015), through close relations with Constantinople, accepted Eastern Orthodox (or Greek) Catholicism and imposed this faith upon his subjects.

Russia at this time consisted of a group of loosely federated cities situated on the great water trade route between the Baltic and the Black seas. This route lay along the Dnieper and northern lakes and rivers, with Kiev the chief city of the south and Novgorod that of the north. In this land of vast southern steppes and unmeasured northern swamps and woodlands, the

natural trade routes of long navigable river systems connected by short portages determined the city sites. These great distances, as well as differences of climate and geography, which militated against political and cultural unity, enabled the northern cities to remain comparatively independent and out of reach of the Asiatic invaders who were surging west over the great steppes.

At first Byzantine influence was strong. But the Russians' inevitable expansion eastward, during the eleventh and twelfth centuries, into the valley of the Volga, another great trade route, and the transfer of the capital from Kiev to Vladimir (1109) brought contact with Caucasia and Transcaucasia. In the thirteenth century the great cultural development at Vladimir was halted by the invasion of the Mongols (1238),[1] who held sway over Russia

---

ILLUSTRATION ABOVE. **12–1** CHURCH OF THE ASCENSION. Kolomenskoe (near Moscow). 1532. (Grabar)

[1] The same westward movement of the Mongols under Jenghiz Khan which captured and destroyed Baghdad in 1258 and set up the Mongol dynasties in Persia.

12–2 CHURCH OF ST. DMITRI. Vladimir. View showing the three apses. 1194–1197. (Buxton)

12–3 CHURCH OF ST. NICHOLAS THE WONDER-WORKER. Panilovo, Archangel Oblast. 1600. (Grabar)

until the rising principality of Muscovy at first defied and then defeated the invaders (1480) and finally, under Ivan the Terrible, expelled the last of them (1552).

In the meanwhile northwestern Russia, centering at Novgorod and free from the Tatar domination, developed its native arts and brought the imported Byzantine traditions into comformity with them. Though Novgorod was a member of the Hanseatic League and was on the direct trade routes to the East, its arts evolved in comparative cultural isolation. In the fifteenth century, with the eviction of the Tatars, the Russians re-established close relations with the Byzantine empire. Byzantine painters came to Novgorod and Moscow, and Novgorod painters and Pskov builders helped build the new Moscow. As Moscow became a cultural as well as a political center, a truly Russian style, which translated borrowed forms into its own modes of expression, was consolidated here.

ARCHITECTURE

The chief architecture of medieval Russia was ecclesiastical, at first strongly under the influence of Constantinople, if not actually produced by Greeks. Examples are *Santa Sophia* at Kiev and a similar though less pretentious *Santa Sophia* at Novgorod. Both are built on the typical plan of the Second Golden Age Byzantine church (Fig. 7–21) — that at Kiev with five apses and some very fine Byzantine mosaics,[2] that at Novgorod with three apses, bulbous domes, and frescoes instead of mosaics, for Novgorod was not so affluent as Kiev, not being the seat of royalty. At Novgorod and at nearby Pskov the vividly colored bulbous dome was developed, as were external

[2] Only the central part of the present church at Kiev, with apses, belongs to the original church of 1037.

12–4 CHURCH OF THE TRANSFIGURATION. Kizhi, Lake Onega. Early 18th century. (Grabar)

galleries, covered stairways, and separate bell towers — all characteristic features of Russian churches.

Two churches at or near Vladimir, *St. Dmitri* (Fig. 12–2) and the *Church of the Intercession*, are built on the typical plan of a square enclosing a Greek cross and crowned with a dome — in these churches a single dome on a high drum. The churches are of stone, which is rare in Russia, where brick, stucco, and wood are the usual materials. Wall spaces, which have few openings, are decorated effectively with moldings. Some of these, rising unbroken from the ground to the roof, divide the wall into panels; others, much shorter, form blind arcadings. At *St. Dmitri* the surface within the arcadings is elaborately carved in low reliefs peculiarly adapted to stone, and in subject matter and form close to

Sassanian and other western Asiatic carvings.

A truly native style of church building originated in the north in the vast rural districts dotted with villages, where timber was abundant. Though these timber churches all date after 1600, they are the culmination of a long tradition, the earlier expressions of which have been lost through the perishable nature of the material, particularly its susceptibility to fire. Free from Byzantine and Eastern influences and undisturbed by the Mongols, the northern Russian evolved from his simple domestic buildings, constructed of tree trunks laid horizontally, the type of church seen in the octagonal "tent-roofed" church of *St. Nicholas* (Fig. 12–3), of which the *Church of the Transfiguration* at Kizhi (on an island in Lake Onega) is an elaboration (Fig.

12–5 CATHEDRAL OF THE ANNUNCIATION. Moscow. 1482–1490.

12–4). In the latter the octagon plan has been converted into a cross by extending four of its sides, and the mass of the church is as compact as its plan, notwithstanding the fantastic covering of roofs, which look like horizontally extended bulbous domes. Each roof carries a dome, and together they mount vivaciously to the crowning members — an extraordinary grouping of twenty-two domes into a compact conical mass.

So deeply traditional was the native wooden structure that, when the need for greater permanency demanded brick or stone, the type was translated quite literally into the new medium, as we see in the *Church of the Ascension* (Fig. 12–1) at Kolomenskoe, near Moscow. This practice reached its most elaborate expression in the *Cathedral of St. Basil* on the Red Square at Moscow (1555), in which all the elements noted above are used in exaggerated form and with intense color. Yet "a rare beauty of proportion emerges from apparent confusion — an impression of tranquility, not chaos," especially when the building is "seen

from the distance in some happy play of sun or moonshine."[3]

The fusion of Byzantine, Eastern, and native timber styles[4] took place in Muscovy, where at Moscow and Yaroslavl, from the fifteenth to the seventeenth century, the national style reached its climax. In Moscow the *Cathedral of the Annunciation* (Fig. 12–5) is an example. It is built on a square plan with eastern apses and is covered with bulbous domes. Around three sides run external galleries approached by covered stairways; on the roof are "encorbeled" arches[5] leading up to the

[3] D. R. Buxton, *Russian Mediaeval Architecture*, p. 44.

[4] The relation of the timber style to that of Moscow, like the origin of the bulbous dome, is controversial, as are, in fact, many points of origin and influence connected with this art, which has received but little attention up to the present time.

[5] This extraordinary external decorative feature originated in a structural device, on the part of builders in Pskov, of superposing corbeled arches above the four great arches of the crossing in order to make the transition from the square base to the dome — a problem solved by the Byzantine builders with pendentives.

domes. In this cathedral there is also evidence that as early as the late fifteenth century Italian architects were arriving in Moscow and were introducing Western elements, such as classical moldings, into the native style.

However, in Yaroslavl, a great trade center untouched by foreign influence, these Italian elements are lacking, and the church of *St. John the Baptist* (Fig. 12–6) is consistently Russian, following closely the standardized plan which, according to an edict issued in 1650 by the Patriarch Nikon, required all churches to use the square plan with five main domes – a central one over the crossing and one over each angle between the arms of the cross. Notable in this church are the external brickwork, the glazed tile decoration around the windows, the fine porches, and the general magnificence of the church as a whole.

As the window openings of these Russian churches are few and small, the interiors are dim. However, the great wall spaces lend themselves to mural decoration, as did those of their prototypes, the later Byzantine churches (Fig. 7–23). A few wealthy churches used mosaics, and lesser churches the fresco, but both followed a strict iconography.

An important feature was the iconostasis (Fig. 12–7), the many-tiered screen that separates the sanctuary from the main body of the church. It has three doors, the central one – the royal door – reserved for the priests only. The iconostasis contains the sacred images, arranged according to rigid regulation. It is decorated elaborately with carvings, gilding, and metalwork, and before it stand magnificent candelabra. Most resplendent is such an interior, its very dimness adding to the effect. The congregation stands, and the liturgy contains long chants and *a cappella* music, with frequent censing. In flickering candlelight

12–6   CHURCH OF ST. JOHN THE BAPTIST. Yaroslavl. 1687. (Buxton)

and through clouds of incense the rich vestments of the clergy combine with the brilliant color and ornament of the iconostasis to create a focal point, which is surrounded by dim walls covered with figures that rise in hieratic succession to the Pantocrator of the dome. Thus every element contributes to produce the effect of otherworldliness, the aim of Byzantine artists.

PAINTING

To decorate the walls of churches, to paint icons for private shrines and for iconostases and miniatures for the sacred books, were the functions of the Russian painter. Painting, like architecture, was an ecclesiastical art; and like the buildings, the early mosaics, frescoes, and icons are Byzantine in style.

12–7   ICONOSTASIS. Uspenski cathedral, Moscow. 17th century.

Some icons were probably imported from Constantinople or Greece. This was probably true of the *Vladimir Madonna* (Fig. 12–8), one of the icons held most sacred because it was believed to have protected the Russians against the Mongols, and for this reason held a place of honor in the lowest tier of the iconostasis of the church at Vladimir. It is a typical Byzantine painting,[6] in which two figures are compactly united into a majestic group that fills the panel with its flat pattern, a silhouette with unbroken sweep of virile contour within which the figures are united both in form and in sensitive feeling.

The development of the iconostasis into the elaborate screen with more than five tiers had an important effect on icon painting. The purpose of these paintings was to enable the worshiper to read pictorially. Clear pictorial legibility in wavering candlelight and through clouds of incense required strong pattern, firm lines, and intense color. Hence the relatively sober hues of the early Byzantine paintings gave way to the more characteristically Russian colors, intense and contrasting. We find this style in the work of the Novgorod and Pskov painters — in the *St. Basil* (Fig. 12–9), for example —

[6] There are at least six layers of repainting; only the faces show the original surface. As the icons were quickly blackened by incense, it was usual to repaint them, but the work was often done, unfortunately, by an inferior painter. For the cleaning of this and other icons by the Central National Restoration Workshops of the Soviet government, see M. S. Farbman, ed., *Masterpieces of Russian Painting*, 1930.

12–8 (Left, above) VLADIMIR MADONNA. 11th century. Historical Museum, Moscow. Formerly in the Cathedral of the Assumption at Vladimir but removed to Moscow in 1395 to protect the city from a Tatar invasion. (A. H. Barr, Jr.)

12–9 (Right, above) ST. BASIL THE GREAT. Right half of a pair of royal doors. 14th century. Museum of Kalinin. (A. H. Barr, Jr.)

which is dynamic in feeling and startling in its angularity and contrasts. The sharp angles and strong curves repeated in every detail, the precise outlining of parts of the head and of the features, the sharp color contrasts, the elongated proportions — each of these contributes to an abstract pattern of brusque forcefulness and vigorous movement that is little concerned with a representation of visual perception.

As in architecture, it was the assimilation of outside influences with this native dynamism which produced a Russian style. As in architecture, with the waning of the Mongol domination, during which Byzantine influence was cut off, Greek painters again appeared at Novgorod and Moscow, among them Theophanes of Mistra. Under this renewed Byzantine influence and through the requirements of the iconostasis, which was just at that time coming to its highest development, Russian painting reached a climax in the work of Andrei Rublëv (ca. 1370–1430), whose monumental *Old Testament Trinity* (Fig. 12–10) is a masterly design in line and color. About a table are seated the three angels who ap-

peared to Abraham near the oaks of
Mamre. The figures, each framed with
a halo and sweeping wings, almost fill
the panel, and are clearly related to
each other and to the space by a design of horizontals and peculiarly suave
curves, free from clashing oppositions,
which produces a tranquillity like that
of the *Vladimir Madonna*. Yet sufficient angularity in the table, the chairs,
and the folds of the garments provides
contrasting motifs. These forms are constructed of color, each detail an area of
color, which is frequently intensified by
the juxtaposition of a complementary
hue. The intense blue and green folds
of the cloak of the central figure stand
out starkly against the deep red robe
and gilded orange wings. In the figure
on the left, the highlights of the orange

cloak are an opalescent blue-green.

. . . one is amazed at a recurrent *gamme*
of color different from any that Western
art has produced or attempted to produce
until recent years, in the extraordinary
copy of Rublëv's *Trinity*, the unforgettable
Saint Demetrius robed in vermilion with a
vermilion shield, the black-winged arch-
angels, Michael and Gabriel. The dominant
scale of color is distinctly Oriental — parchment white, golden buff, turquoise, blue,
vermilion, malachite green, an occasional
note of plum heightened by the uncompromising accent of unrelieved black. It
could be matched by grouping Chinese,
Korean, and Persian ceramics. The enamel-
like purity and brilliance of the pigment
constitute an almost unparalleled triumph
in the technique of painting.[7]

[7] Lee Simonson, *Metropolitan Museum of
Art Bulletin*, January, 1931, p. 6.

We should not forget in considering this rich ecclesiastical art of Medieval Russia the indispensable part played by other arts in the entire ensemble of a church interior: the carvings and rich metalwork of the iconostasis; the finely wrought jeweled halos and other ornaments on the icons; the candlesticks and candelabra; the miters and ecclesiastical robes stiff with gold, embroidery, and jewels; the illuminated books bound in gold or ivory inlaid with jewels and enamels; the crosses, croziers, sacred vessels, and processional banners. Each contributed with its amazing richness of texture and color to the total effect.

16TH–18TH CENTURIES

Late in the fifteenth century, with the overthrow of the Tatars, Moscow became the capital of Russia. But it was not until the time of Peter the Great (1682–1725) that the Russian government, if not the nation, turned wholeheartedly toward the West and came within the periphery of the European nations. Symbolic of this reorientation was Peter's abandonment of Moscow, center of traditional Russian culture, in favor of a new capital to be built on the Neva, St. Petersburg (now Leningrad). He and his successors, Elizabeth (1741–1762), Catherine II, the Great (1762–1796), and Alexander I (1801–1825), opened the doors wide to the West and not only accepted but solicited Western influence by inviting artists from various countries to work in Russia and by sending their own students to Western capitals for training. The inexhaustible wealth of the extravagant, autocratic court made vast projects economically possible for the ruling class, who had no regard for the vast number of serfs. Even the French Revolution could not break through the hard crust of Russian reaction and absolutism, until 1861, when the serfs were emancipated and the social stirrings began which were to end in the revolution of 1917.

ARCHITECTURE

When Russia accepted Christianity in the tenth century, it accepted with it its outward expression, the Byzantine architectural style, to which it eventually contributed its own indigenous type of wooden construction. As we have seen, the assimilation of the two styles, translated into stone construction, is typified by the *Cathedral of St. Basil*. Before the building of *St. Basil*, however, Italian architects had been invited to Moscow to work on the design of walls of the *Kremlin* and on its churches and palaces. Although during the sixteenth and seventeenth centuries there was some attempt to integrate into the national style elements from the West — classical details and Baroque ornament from Poland and other northern European countries — the accession of Peter the Great flung the doors of Russia open to a whirlwind of lavish building based on Renaissance styles, though often in original Russian versions. In 1703 Peter began the erection of a capital that was to vie with, if not eclipse, every other capital of Europe. For more than a century work went on with the greatest intensity, as if to catch up with lost centuries, in laying out the city with wide avenues, open squares, and quays along the Neva, with monumental structures — churches, palaces with vast gardens, and civic buildings — placed so as to create fine ensembles, and all on a grandiose scale. Great manor houses rose in the country, not only around St. Petersburg (Leningrad) but in the Ukraine, in the Crimea, and in and about Moscow. In the early *Cathedral of Sts. Peter and Paul*, built by Peter the Great, a classical portico rises from a simple Baroque base to a lofty steeple (the tent roof of the Medieval style); other churches are crowned with the Russian "onion" dome, *St. Andrew* at Kiev, for example. With Elizabeth, the Rococo in an ostentatious version dominated. In her reign one of Russia's great architects, Count B. F. Rastrelli (1700–1771), built the *Winter Palace* under her direction, and rebuilt and decorated *Peterhof* (Fig. 12–11) and *Tsarskoe Selo*.

The climax of the eighteenth century was reached in the reign of Catherine II, whose personal taste for the simple classical style was largely responsible for the spread of the classical revival over much of Russia. Catherine maintained close relations in all cultural matters with France and staffed the Russian Academy of Arts, founded in 1758, with French instructors. She lured many artists from France and Italy with visions of vast building schemes supported by huge sums of money for carrying them out, and she sent Russian students abroad for training to fit them to share in the plans. Thus in her reign and in that of her successor, Alexander I, were erected: the *Academy of Arts,* which, with its rusticated ground story, central and end pavilions, and engaged

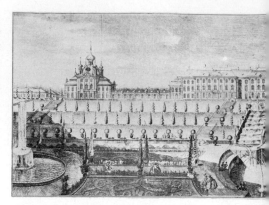

12–11 PETERHOF. Leblond's palace of 1716–1717 as remodeled by Rastrelli,

columns, is so strongly reminiscent of the Perrault façade of the *Louvre* (Fig. 10–32) that it does not surprise one to learn that a French architect collaborated in its design; the *Taurida Palace,* with its classical portico and colonnade; the *Cathedral of the Holy Trinity,* whose proportions contrast so markedly with the early lofty *Cathedral of Sts. Peter and Paul;* the *Kazan cathedral* (Fig. 12–12), a highly dignified domed edifice approached by curving colonnades, obviously inspired by Bernini's colonnades of *St. Peter's* in Rome; and *St. Isaac,* with its lavish use of rich materials, the *St. Paul's* of

12–12 A. N. VORONIKHIN. The cathedral of the Virgin of Kazan on the Nevski Prospekt, St. Petersburg (Leningrad). 1801–1811. (Courtesy G. H. Hamilton)

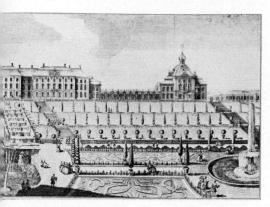

1747–1753. From an engraving by M. I. Makhaev, 1761.

Russia. Further foreign influence came from England through Charles Cameron (1740–1812), who, influenced by both Palladio and Robert Adam, produced a style consistent, in its sobriety and simplicity, with the classical revival of the time and, in its prodigality, with the autocracy which demanded it. Thus Russia followed, though tardily, the same sequence of styles from the Baroque to the classical revival as did the other countries of Europe, but on a scale and with a pompous magnificence possible only to an absolute monarch and with which only the palaces of the French absolutists at Versailles are comparable.

PAINTING

Medieval fresco and icon painting, with its exalted mood, symbolism, and mysticism, was zealously guarded by the authoritarian Eastern Orthodox church, which condemned Western innovations that were creeping into painting, as they were into the buildings in the *Kremlin*. As we have seen, Rublëv (Fig. 12–10) marked a high point in icon painting, but the state stifled any further growth through vitalizing influences. Copying of the traditional icon painters, with no opportunity for individual expression, was forced upon artists. Despite this, some naturalistic innovations crept in, such as changes in traditional poses and the introduction of architectural settings. Thus in the seventeenth century Russian painting seemed to be at the same stage as Italian in the fourteenth, when Cimabue and Giotto made a break from the Byzantine style. Natural development, however, came to a halt in the eighteenth century, when the Russian court introduced painters of the current academic schools of western Europe, exponents of the "grand style" of painting religious and historical subjects, nudes, and portraits. Though some Gainsborough-like portraits at the time of Catherine the Great were meritorious, this eclectic painting — created entirely at the bidding and in the style demanded by the court and the nobles — was, as a whole, an empty thing. An exception was a thread of genre painting, spontaneously naturalistic both in subject matter and in mode of treatment, known as "common art" and unrecognized by the academic proponents of the "grand style." This trend was important, as it sowed the seed of the realistic school of the nineteenth century.

Summary

The common objective of Russian art in the Middle Ages — to create visibly and emotionally an effect of transcendent otherworldliness — produced one of the loftiest expressions of Eastern Christianity. It was an art that took much from other cultures, but by adapting these borrowings to its own vernacular produced something strangely individual. In the quiet, almost monotonous, landscape a vivid, picturesque mass of domes and steeple-like tent roofs "gleams like a jeweled clasp on a sober robe." The dim, resplendent interior, to whose effectiveness builder, painter, and craftsman contributed, is perhaps the most comprehensive expression of the common objective.

Although Russia had accepted a few ideas from the West before the time of Peter the Great, this monarch made a direct break with Russian traditions and repudiated the native styles in favor of an imitation of Western modes, with slight modifications and with the retention, at least in the beginning, of a few traditional motifs. The entire eighteenth century and the first half of the nineteenth constituted a period of imitation, on a grandiose scale for the benefit of the absolute state and the ostentatious court, of Renaissance styles from its early phases through the Baroque and the classical revival. This imitative period was not, however, devoid of beneficial consequences, for it made a break in the hard shell of reactionary conservatism in all cultural life, and by revitalizing that life it played a part in the rise of a great independent age that reached a climax in the fields of literature, music, and the dance.

Bibliography

Bunt, Cyril G. E., *A History of Russian Art*, Studio Publications, New York, 1946.

Buxton, David R., *Russian Mediaeval Architecture*, Macmillan, New York, 1934.

A Catalogue of Russian Icons, with introduction by I. E. Grabar, Metropolitan Museum of Art, New York, 1931.

Eliasberg, Alexander, *Russische Baukunst*, Müller, Munich, 1922.

Farbman, Michael S., ed., *Masterpieces of Russian Painting*, Europa Publications, London, 1930.

Halle, Fannina W., *Alt-russische Kunst*, E. Wasmuth, Berlin, 1920.

Hamilton, George Heard, *The Art and Architecture of Russia*, Penguin Books, Baltimore, 1954.

Kondakov, Nikodim P., *The Russian Icon*, tr. by E. H. Minns, Oxford University Press, New York, 1927.

Lukomskii, Georgi P., *History of Modern Russian Painting*, Hutchinson, London, 1945.

Maskell, Alfred O., *Russian Art and Art Objects in Russia*, Chapman and Hall, London, 1884.

Miliukov, Paul N., *Outlines of Russian Culture*, 3 pts.; Part 3, *Architecture, Painting, and Music*, University of Pennsylvania Press, Philadelphia, 1942.

Muratov, Pavel Pavlovich, *Les icones russes*, J. Schiffrin, Paris, 1927.

——, *La peinture byzantine*, G. Crès et Cie., Paris, 1935.

Newmarch, Rosa J., *The Russian Arts*, Dutton, 1916.

Olsufiev, Yoori A., "The Development of Russian Icon Painting from the Twelfth to the Nineteenth Century," *Art Bulletin*, Vol. 12, No. 4, pp. 347–73. December, 1930.

Rice, David Talbot, ed., *Russian Art: An Introduction*, London, 1935.

Voyce, Arthur, *The Moscow Kremlin*, University of California Press, Berkeley, 1954.

——, *Russian Architecture*, Philosophical Library, New York, 1948.

NON-
EUROPEAN
ART

E VEN though the conquests and colonization of the sixteenth and seventeenth centuries carried Christianity well beyond the boundaries of western Europe, we may identify the non-European as the non-Christian world. Under such a large rubric it is not surprising to find a wide variety of ideas and forms, which we shall discuss in the following order: Islamic, Southeast Asian, Chinese, Japanese, Pre-Columbian and North American Indian, and Primitive (African Negro and Oceanic).

The art of Islam developed along the eastern shores of the Mediterranean at the same time as the Early Middle Ages in western Europe. Although Islamic armies threatened western Europe and the Byzantine empire in the eighth century and contacts between the Christian and Islamic cultures were frequent throughout the Middle Ages, Islam developed its own architecture and decorative vocabulary, which became even more distinctive as the centers of Islam moved farther toward the East.

There are Paleolithic and Neolithic art forms in the long history of the great Eastern civilizations in Pakistan, India, China, and Japan. Later, Buddhism provided the common denominator for the arts of these different countries in varying degrees at different periods, but each country developed a distinctive style, or rather a series of styles. Indian sculpture from its beginnings has been characterized by a pulsating vigor in reproducing the living body. In China, early bronzes display amazing technical virtuosity in presenting highly symbolic, though abstract, decorative motifs. In later dynasties, in sculpture and particularly in painting, carefully observed details are lyrically rendered, producing a haunting image of nature. The Japanese, in spite of recurring waves of foreign influences, especially from China, insistently returned to their native traditions. A sensitive understanding of relationships between decorative designs and natural forms distinguishes their painting and above all their architecture.

Prehistoric man presumably reached the Western Hemisphere by way of the Aleutians and Alaska. After several millennia of gradual development, highly cultured peoples emerged, grouped around centers in Mexico, Central America, and the Andean region of South America. With a Stone Age technology these peoples erected great temple complexes elaborately decorated with reliefs, and practiced the crafts of weaving and pottery with great skill. The North American Indian began to settle in agricultural communities about 500 A.D., with some tribes, such as the Pueblo, reaching a highly developed state in the eleventh, twelfth, and thirteenth centuries. Their stylized arts present an extraordinary understanding of the decorative qualities of abstract design.

The Negroes in Africa and the aborigines in the South Seas produced what we speak of as primitive art, until contact with Europeans either modified it or brought it to a halt. This art, far from being technically or aesthetically crude, is sophisticated in its presentation of conceptual rather than visual images. The rhythmical, abstract forms of the painted designs and carved figures have been of great interest to many modern artists.

◄   BUDDHA. Polychrome stone. Sui dynasty, 6th–7th centuries. H. 66 in. Winthrop Collection, Fogg Art Museum, Harvard University. (Fogg Art Museum)

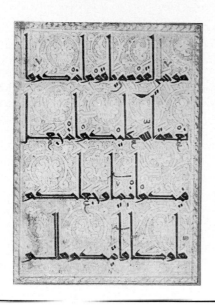

CHAPTER 13

ISLAMIC

Early Islamic

(7TH–12TH CENTURIES)

In 622 Mohammed fled to Me-dinet-en-Nabi ("City of the Prophet," now Medina). From this flight, known as the Hegira, Islam [1] dates its era.

When we think of the Mohammed-ans, we think not of a nation in the modern sense of the word, with sharp-ly defined boundaries, but of groups of people of varying cultures, widespread geographically but bound together by a burning and at times fanatical reli-gious faith. Their creed is embodied in the prayer chanted by the muezzin from the top of the minaret as he calls the faithful to worship:

Allah is great, Allah is great, Allah is great. I bear witness that there is no god but Allah. I bear witness that Mohammed is the Apostle of Allah. Come to prayer. Come to prayer. Come to security. Come to security. Allah is great. Allah is great. There is no god but Allah.

The religion thus epitomized, origi-nating in Arabia, spread both east and west with amazing rapidity, chiefly by means of the sword, for the creed also states that "the sword is the key to heaven."

Within thirty years this zeal had car-ried the faith of Islam to the eastern boundaries of Persia, north to Tiflis in the Caucasus and west to Tripoli in North Africa. Under the Ommiads

[1] Islam, "submission to the will of God," was Mohammed's name for his new religion. Mohammedan, Muhammadan, Moslem, Mus-lim, all refer to the same faith. Arab, or Arabic, refers specifically to the native tribes of Arabia, who first espoused Islam, and more generally to their style of writing and thus to Islamic literature. Saracen was the Greek and Roman name for Arab.

ILLUSTRATION ABOVE. 13–1 LEAF FROM KORAN, showing *Kufic* script. Iran. 12th century. Metropolitan Museum of Art, New York. (Gift of Horace Havemeyer, 1929; H. O. Havemeyer Collection)

(661–749), who had led a successful revolt against the successors of Mohammed, the capital was established at Damascus. Expansion continued to the east to include Samarkand and the Indus valley and to the west across North Africa and into Spain in 711, where victory in the battle of Jerez de la Frontera apparently opened all of western Europe to the Mohammedans. By 732 they had advanced north to Poitiers in France, where an army of Franks under Charles Martel, the grandfather of Charlemagne, opposed them so successfully that, although they continued to raid in France, their control was confined to the lands south of the Pyrenees. When the Abbasides, who claimed descent from Abbas, uncle of Mohammed, revolted in 749, they murdered more than ninety Ommiads. Only one, Abd-er-Rahman, escaped to flee west, where he founded the great Caliphate of Cordoba, which flourished in Spain until 1031. Indeed, it was not until 1492, when Granada fell to Ferdinand and Isabella, that Mohammedan influence and power in the West came to a close.

In the Near East under the Abbasides, the capital was moved to Baghdad, where Iranian influences dominated the Arabic and continued to do so after the Seljuk Turks entered Baghdad in 1055. In Egypt, meanwhile, another dynasty, the Fatimids (969–1171) of Berber origin, encouraged the development of Islamic art.

Because of its wide geographical extent and its lack of political unity, Islamic culture manifested itself in many different ways. Although the Koran [2]

[2] The Koran is the collection of Mohammed's revelations ordered to be gathered together by the caliph Othman (644–656) and practically unchanged down to the present day. The text contains all that a Mohammedan need know; and, although highly regarded as a piece of literature, it is hardly understandable without considerable exegesis.

strenuously forbade sumptuousness and license of all kinds, the caliphs and their courts managed in various ways to circumvent these decrees. Enormously wealthy, they adorned their homes, and even their travel tents of gold-shot silk, with rich hangings, fine rugs, and exquisite utensils; and they clothed themselves in the most splendid apparel. In spite of the many fastings, prayers, and pilgrimages demanded by the Koran, life was gay with festivals, feasts, and sports. In the midst of this leisure, learning was also encouraged, especially by the Abbasides. All available Greek, Persian, and Hindu scientific treatises were translated into Arabic. In mathematics Arab scholars adopted the Hindu numerals and system of arranging numbers — the basis of arithmetic as still taught in our elementary schools. The Arabs were also interested in astronomy and the natural sciences and were very active in medicine. In philosophy their translations of Aristotle and of other writers of Antiquity and their attempts to reconcile faith and reason were eagerly studied by Christian scholars in the twelfth and thirteenth centuries, while their love lyrics and poetic descriptions of nature inspired the early French troubadours.

Man and his environment were the Mohammedans' constant study, but, since the Koran forbade idols in any form, the image of man was excluded from their visual arts. Yet, in the decorative arts and in the development of a system of ornament allied with calligraphy (see p. 496), the Islamic artists created a vital style capable of endless variations on a simple theme (Fig. 13–9).

ARCHITECTURE

Since the Mohammedan was fanatical in religious belief and was also zealous in pursuit of pleasure, it is natural to find his architecture devoted chiefly to a place for worship, the mosque, and to the palace. For worship his needs were simple: a secluded place, away from the noise of the streets, where a fountain provided water for ablution (as he must bathe before going to worship), a place protected from the hot sun where, with face turned toward Mecca, he could pray. His religion was personal and direct, needing no liturgical ceremony. The direction toward Mecca was indicated by a small niche, the *mihrab*, in the wall of the mosque. To one side was a pulpit, the *mimbar*, from which the Friday (the Mohammedan Sabbath) sermon was preached; a little in front of these stood a raised platform from which the Koran was recited and prayers were chanted. These simple but universal features constitute the sanctuary of a mosque.

The early *mosque of Ibn Touloun* in Cairo presents all these features. There is a great open court with a fountain in the center, surrounded by covered ar

13–3 MOSQUE OF IBN TULOUN. Cairo. Arcades. 9th century. (Art G. Lekegian)

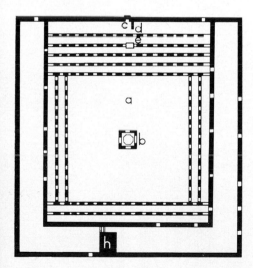

13–2 MOSQUE OF IBN TULOUN. Cairo. Plan. 9th century. *a.* Court. *b.* Fountain. *c.* Niche (mihrab), indicating direction of Mecca. *d.* Pulpit (mimbar). *e.* Tribune (dikkeh). *h.* Minaret.

cades two deep on three sides but five deep on the sanctuary side, the special place of prayer (Fig. 13–2). The arcades involved no difficult structural problem, since they were covered with simple wooden roofs. Thus the Islamic builders, searching for decorative forms, were able at an early date to experiment with different arch forms such as the pointed arch (Fig. 13–3) or the horseshoe arch (Fig. 13–4) to produce a more open, airy effect than could have been achieved with the ordinary round arch. A desire for more fireproof structures subsequently led to replacing of wooden roofs by vaults of light bricks or tiles. Stucco arches in complicated patterns were often placed, again for the decorative effect, under these vaults.

In Persia, stone or brick arches were included in the masonry of the vaults, evidently for structural reasons, but none of these vaults may be properly called ribbed vaults in the sense of the Gothic vault (see p. 247).

The exterior of a mosque was a plain massive wall with small windows and simple, originally unadorned doorways. At *Ibn Touloun* there is an exterior girdle wall, for added seclusion, and a single minaret, or tower, from which the muezzin called to prayer (Fig. 13–5). This early tower with its exterior ramps recalls the ziggurats of Mesopotamia (Fig. 3–2).

In later times the minarets became slender needles of masonry and were often several in number, providing the familiar mosque silhouette.

Only scattered remains of early palaces exist and these are more interesting for what they tell us of early decorative styles than for the architecture itself. A few wall paintings survive, from the desert palace at *Kuseir Amra* (712), and fragments of the carved stone façade from *Mschatta* (eighth century) (Fig. 13–6) show us how deeply indebted the early Islamic artists were to the traditions of Late Antiquity and of Sassanian Persia. In fact literary sources describe how the Ommiads requisitioned materials and craftsmen from many different provinces to build their new mosques, palaces, and cities. This is understandable, for the Arabs before the seventh century had no distinct artistic traditions except for poetry.

DECORATIVE SCULPTURE AND PAINTING

The strictures in the Koran against the worship of idols were so widely ac-

13–4 MOSQUE. Cordoba. 8th–9th centuries, with later additions. (Anderson)

13–5 MOSQUE OF IBN TULOUN. Cairo. 9th century. (Creswell)

cepted that the image of man seems to have been almost excluded from early Islamic art. In later times, especially in Persia, man's activities and pleasures were illustrated in superb miniatures accompanying secular texts; but in the early periods, if the figure of man appeared at all, it was only as an incidental part of a large ornamental design. For this reason also, sculpture, in the round or in high relief, and mural or panel painting as developed in Europe and in the Far East may be said to be nonexistent in the early art of Islam. But painting, as a decoration for manuscripts and architecture, and sculpture, in the form of low relief, stone or wood carving, and especially in modeled plaster designs, were important techniques. With them, Mohammedan artists developed one of the most distinctive decorative styles in the history of art.

Plaster, applied wet, was a particularly adaptable medium for the freely flowing line which distinguishes Mohammedan ornament, since the hand could move easily and spontaneously. It appears in the earlier buildings — for example, around the arches in the *mosque of Ibn Tuloun* — but later was largely replaced by stone or marble reliefs, beginning in the fourteenth century. Though plaster and stone were used largely in architectural ornament and even occasionally for a pulpit, wood was the material most favored for decorating the furnishings of both mosques and palaces. It was not only carved but frequently inlaid with ivory and ebony.

Islamic design is derived from floral motifs, which often became so stylized that the natural forms are lost in the purely decorative quality of the tendrils, leaves, or stalks. It is an all-over pattern, which covers the entire surface whether the object is a small utensil, a manuscript page, or the wall of a building. This *horror vacui* is similar to tendencies in Barbarian art (p. 218), and yet other principles in Islamic design distinguish it from the abstract Barbarian patterns. Islamic orna-

13-6 FRIEZE FROM MSCHATTA, a palace in the Syrian Desert. H. 15 ft. 8th century. (Berlin Museum)

scripts was always in direct harmony with Islamic ornament, with which they were frequently combined. The angularity of the Kufic (Fig. 13-1) is often an effective contrast to the over-all patterns, whereas the Naskhi blends perfectly with the basic curvilinear arabesques (Fig. 13-7). Indeed, the arabesque, which may be defined as a flowing, curving scroll derived from stylized, floral motifs often arranged in symmetrical palmette designs, best characterizes Islamic ornament; and it is easy to see how closely allied its flowing linear principles are to the art of calligraphy.

The precise origins of Mohammedan art may be hidden in the past, but it is not difficult to discern affinities both with the traditions of Late Antiquity in the Near East and with the heraldic devices of Sassanian art. The frieze from *Mschatta* (Fig. 13-6) has the same two-dimensional, crisp quality

ment is a repeat design which remains a surface ornament. The peculiar spatial qualities of the Irish interlace were never really investigated by the Moslem, for even when the fine patterns do intertwine in Islamic design, the stalks and leaves exist on distinct overlapping planes, without creating the enigmatic movement in a restricted space to be found in Irish manuscript decoration (cf. Fig. 8-1). Immediately noticeable in the page from the Koran (Fig. 13-7) is another fundamental characteristic of Islamic design — its intimate association with calligraphy.

Calligraphy is the art of fine handwriting, which we shall also discover as a major element in the art of China (see pp. 561-62). From the very beginning there were two principal styles of Arabic writing: *Kufic,* from the town of Kufa in Mesopotamia, a formal style with angular letters, and *Naskhi,* a cursive style with rounded letters. The linear and decorative quality of these

13-7 Leaf from Koran, showing *Naskhi* script. Egypt. 14th century. Metropolitan Museum of Art, New York. (Fletcher Fund, 1924)

which we noted in our discussion of some Early Christian reliefs (see p. 205), but the decoration has now spread over the entire surface.

Color and gilding played an important part in Mohammedan ornament. Both stucco and wood carvings were vividly painted, and marble or colored glass inlays were frequently used. Panels of variously colored marbles — red, yellow, black, green — perhaps combined with blue tile or bordered with a geometric pattern of colored glass and mother-of-pearl, faced the sanctuary of the mosque or formed a dado around the palace room. Another brilliant color effect came from the windows, which were made by filling a wooden frame with plaster about an inch thick, scooping out a pattern in the plaster while it was still soft, and then filling in the perforations with bits of colored glass. The process involved in making these colored windows is very simple and crude in comparison with the leaded windows of the Gothic period, but the masses of color when pierced by the southern sunshine are rich and jewel-like.

METALWORK, GLASS, TEXTILES

The furnishings of the palaces as well as of the mosques satisfied the Moslem's love of rich and sumptuous effects. The same motifs — the arabesque, floral, and geometric designs and calligraphy — which appear in all the crafts, reveal the inherent flexibility of this narrow range of ornament, for rarely does one find exact duplication. Islamic metalwork maintains the high quality which has characterized this art in the Near East throughout the ages. Basins, often huge in size, ewers, candlesticks, trays, perfume burners, jewel cases, writing boxes, and many other objects for use in the mosque and the home were made of

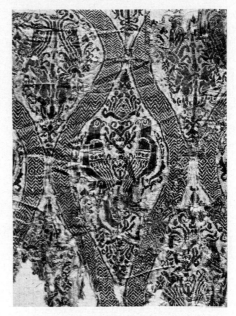

13–8 FATIMID SILK TEXTILE. 13th century. Metropolitan Museum of Art, New York.

wrought copper or brass, engraved and inlaid with silver, with the background sometimes covered with a black alloy to set forth the silver inlay more sharply and thus create a resplendent effect — a technique known as niello.

Enameled glass was also particularly effective in the mosque lamps. The glass of which these lamps is blown, with many bubbles and streakings, is usually slightly yellow or green. In a typical lamp the broad, tall neck tapers toward the rather squat body on which are set six loops or handles for the silver chains by which the lamp was suspended from the beam or ceiling of the mosque. The surface is covered with bands of arabesques with entwined inscriptions worked in enamel — in blue, white, yellow, green, and red, with a liberal use of gold. Inside the lamp a small glass vessel, with oil and wick, is hooked to the rim, so that the burning light brings out the decorations with a rich, soft glow. The effect of a considerable number of these lamps in a sanctuary must have been magnificent.

Woven fabrics and leather were also highly valued. When the Arabs overran Egypt, weaving had already reached a high level among the Copts, as it also had in Sassanian Persia. At first the Arabs employed the Copts to work for them, and from these experts learned the craft. By the time of the Fatimids,

Arab fabrics were famous and were widely exported (Fig. 13–8). The fabrics were usually made with a fine linen warp and silk weft, and the patterns were based upon the usual Islamic motifs — the arabesque and calligraphy — and upon Coptic and Sassanian designs of interlaced circles framing birds and animals or two bilaterally balanced figures.

Later Islamic

(13TH–18TH CENTURIES)

The distinction between Early and Later Islamic art may be an arbitrary one, and yet a number of important changes during the thirteenth century in most Islamic countries may best be interpreted as heralding the beginning of a new era. The basic vocabulary of Islamic art remained the same, but it was enriched by an elaboration of architectural forms and by an emphasis on secular themes, particularly in the paintings of Iran.

SPAIN

With the defeat of the Almohades in Spain in 1212 the political influence of the Moorish rulers was restricted to the small emirate of Granada in the south. Spanish art owes much of its particular distinction to influences from Islam which continued throughout the Middle Ages and into the Renaissance and whose traces may even be observed in the art of the Hispanic colonies of America.

Typical of this Moorish art, and of the Islamic pleasure palace in general, is the *Alhambra* (1309–1354) in Gra-

nada. Grouped around two rectangular courts, placed at right angles to each other, are various halls, chambers, and baths. The profuse ornamentation of the *Court of the Lions* (Fig. 13–9) creates an atmosphere of elegant fantasy, which is ordered, nevertheless, by the proportions of the court (interestingly enough, they are those of the Golden Mean), by the rhythmical spacing of the slender columns (alternately single and double), and by the placing of the different decorative motifs, which, in spite of great variety, recur regularly in their architectural setting. The wall decorations are executed in glazed tiles of subdued tones. The capitals, arches, and other surfaces above the columns are completely covered by molded stucco designs, whose effect is also heightened by color. Typically Islamic are the "stalactite" decorations of the arches and spandrels, so-called because of their resemblance to the natural hanging icicle-like formations in underground caverns. Rich as this architecture may seem even now, one must try to reconstruct its original furnishings of brightly colored rugs and textiles, lamps, and other adornments, which created, with the sound and movement

13–9 ALHAMBRA. Granada. *Court of the Lions.* 1309–1354. 115 ft. × 66 ft. (Linares, Yale Photo Collection)

of flowing fountains, a spectacle hardly equaled by the most impassioned lines of Omar Khayyám.

EGYPT

From 1250 to 1516 Egypt was ruled by Mamluk sultans, who strengthened the government against both Christian and Mongolian invaders. During this period Cairo was rebuilt, largely with limestone taken from the outer surfaces of the great Pyramids.

A typical building of the period is the *mosque of Sultan Hassan* (built 1356–1359), which shows changes in planning and structure of the mosque. The open court (Fig. 13–10), still pres-

ent, is now surrounded by four vaulted recesses (*liwan*), the largest of which is the sanctuary. Behind the sanctuary, in a square room covered by a dome, is the tomb of the sultan. The entire structure is known as a tomb or domed mosque. Crowded in the angles between the *liwans* are rooms for schools, offices, and apartments for the Moslem educational institutions usually connected with a mosque. The building is an austere mass of stone, with exterior decoration concentrated at the lofty portals and in a frieze beneath the crenelation. The interior, except the great arches, is made of brick stuccoed with decorative carvings, including a particularly fine border at the spring of

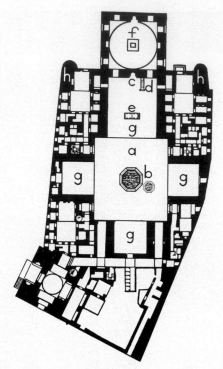

13–10 TOMB MOSQUE OF SULTAN HASSAN. Cairo. 1356–1359. *a.* Court. *b.* Fountain. *c.* Niche (mihrab), indicating the direction of Mecca. *d.* Pulpit (mimbar). *e.* Tribune. *f.* Tomb. *g.* Recess (liwan). *h.* Minaret.

the vault. Smaller mosques were decorated more lavishly, as we see in Figure 13–11.

The Cairene house was, and is today, a flat-topped structure of several stories built about an open court — the typical Mediterranean house plan — with one part reserved for the women, who live in seclusion. It stands flush with the narrow street and often has a carved, metal-studded wooden door and overhanging screened windows with infinitely varied wooden lattices. Although provided with these windows, the house faces the court, which in the more luxurious homes is a garden with fountains. The furnishings are extremely simple, but carpets and cushions, inlaid metal, and carvings produce the same

richness of effect that we have observed in the mosque.

TURKEY

By the end of the thirteenth century the Ottoman Turks controlled most of Asia Minor, threatening the Byzantine empire until Mohammed II, in 1453, succeeded in capturing Constantinople itself. By 1516 the Ottomans had conquered Syria and Egypt, thereby achieving both political and religious supremacy in the world of Islam.

In Constantinople, Hagia Sophia was converted into a mosque and its Christian mosaics were plastered over. This great structure so impressed the Turks that they adopted it as a model for other mosques. Two outstanding examples exist in Constantinople: the *Suleimaniyeh,* or mosque of Suleiman I, the Magnificent (built between 1550 and 1556) and the *Ahmediyeh,* or mosque of Ahmed I (1608–1614), also known as the *Blue Mosque* because of its blue tile decoration. Although no attempt was made to equal the majestic dimensions of Hagia Sophia, it is interesting to observe that in the *Blue Mosque* the structure was altered so that the central dome is flanked by four, rather than two, semidomes (Fig. 13–12). The windows, which perforate the dome and semidomes as well as the outside walls, create a startling effect of masonry pierced by light, quite unlike any other examples of Islamic architecture.

IRAN

In 1258, when Baghdad was captured by the armies of Jenghiz Khan, still another culture, the Chinese, was added to the Persian melting pot. The Mongol rulers of the thirteenth and fourteenth centuries, with their capital at Samarkand, accepted Islam. The dynasty of the Timurids (1396–1500), founded by Timur (Tamerlane), was a

13-11 TOMB-MOSQUE OF EL BARQUQ. 1472. Sanctuary showing the pulpit (mimbar), the niche (mihrab), and the richly colored glass windows. (Egyptian State Tourist Administration)

period of prosperity and wealth. Some of the finest books, carpets, and metalwork were produced under Timurid patronage and under the Safavids (1502–1736), especially at the time of Shah Abbas I (1586–1628). But a trend toward overelegance, easy grace, and naturalism foretold decline.

In the mosques and palaces built in the semidesert land of Islamic Persia, the garden assumed an extraordinary importance, reflected in poetry, in painting, and in the great flowered carpets. Persian art

is inseparable from the very land of Persia, where, against an ever-present background of mauve and golden desert, set in a frame of rosy mountains, a few dead mountains standing out against the horizon like some landscape in the moon, a slender stream of water, a few poplars, and an old crumbling wayside inn suddenly assume a totally unexpected artistic value.

And in addition to this incessant remind-

13-12 MOSQUE OF AHMED I (THE BLUE MOSQUE). Istanbul. 1608–1614. (Turkish Information Office)

13–13 ROYAL MOSQUE. Isfahan. 1612. (Arthur Upham Pope)

er of the desert there is the light air of the high plateaux with its incomparable purity, which adds an unvarying delicacy to every tone. Against this sky of a tender blue the favorite colors of the Persian architects acquire an extraordinary value — the mellow tone of the brick of the ancient mosques of Hamadan and Varamin or the fairylike blue of the great domes of Isfahan or the gold of the dome of Qum, brooding and solitary in the infinite space of the desert. A profound harmony exists between this country and its art, an intimate relation which transcends human factors and will survive them, for here ruin assumes the aspect of the very soil of the country, while the desert itself possesses the tones and appearance of its ruins.[3]

The *Royal Mosque* (*Masjid-i-shah*) of Isfahan (Fig. 13–13), mentioned in this description, faces a great open square on which are located the imperial palace, mosques, and markets. Rising from subsidiary cloisterlike buildings and courtyards with gardens and fountains, it presents a composition of pointed, bulbous dome, pointed arches framed by rectangles, and cylin-

[3] René Grousset, *The Civilizations of the East*, 4 vols., Knopf, 1931; Vol. 1, p. 393.

drical minarets — all sheathed in brilliantly colored glazed tile.

Our chief criterion for Persian painting and probably its greatest expression is found in the miniatures. The shahs, great lovers of fine books, maintained trained calligraphers at court; often these included the most famous artists of the day. Among the early books, in addition to splendid copies of the Koran, are copies of the *Manafi al-Hayawan* (or *Bestiary*).

The truly Persian style and some of the greatest triumphs of Persian painting are found in the secular books of the Timurids and the Safavids, such as the poems of Firdausi and Nizami illustrated by a whole galaxy of painters. Famous among them were Bihzad (*ca.* 1440–1536), Mirak and Sultan Muhammad, court painters of Shah Tahmasp (1524–1576), a great art patron. Although the shahs were Moslems, orthodox Islamic restrictions regarding the figure did not affect their secular arts, so that the gay scenes of their life of pleasure — the hunt, the feast, music, and romance — and battle scenes fill the pages of their books. In them we feel the luxury, the splendor, and the fleeting happiness of Omar.

Illustrating one of Nizami's romantic poems is the *Laila and Majnun* (Fig. 13–14). The scene represents a school, apparently in a mosque. Seated on a rug is the turbaned priest, the teacher, lash in hand, listening to a youth reading; around him are other youths studying, all seated on their knees and heels or with one knee raised, the customary sitting postures in the East. Here and there are cross-legged bookrests. In the foreground one boy is pulling his companion's ear, and at the left, near the large water jar, two are playing ball. In the middle distance are the lovers Laila and Majnun, each obviously aware of the other's presence. The figures are drawn expressively with delicate, flowing lines; but they are flat, with no chiaroscuro and with, but a hint of perspective; the tiles in the court and the rugs on the floor appear to be hanging vertically. The painting is conceived from the point of view not of natural appearance but of pattern and vivid color. To this end the tones are kept bright and clear. The decorative quality of the miniature is emphasized by the broad margins of the page, which is tinted pale blue and flecked all over with gold.

The twelfth and thirteenth centuries saw a revival of the art of metalwork. The craft was centered near great copper mines at Mosul, from which it spread to other localities. In the Mosul products, figure work is an important element, as we see in a ewer (Fig. 13–15) in which the figures of men, animals, and birds in hunting, fighting, and feasting scenes are inlaid in silver on an engraved brass ground. On the silver also were engraved details such as human features, drapery, plumage of birds, and manes of horses, so that the effect of the contrasting metals and the delicate chasing is one of rich splendor.

13–14 MIRAK. *Laila and Majnun*, illustration of a poem by Nizami. 16th century. Metropolitan Museum of Art, New York.

Ceramics of the highest quality were also produced in large numbers. Most of this pottery, because of its coarse base, required a slip or coat of opaque enamel to provide a surface for the painted decoration. An early example of a *Rhages* (Rayy) [4] bowl (Fig. 13–16) shows the sensitivity of the artist in adapting decorative designs to the shape of the utensil. Many of the jars and plates, such as this one, have a creamy glaze with decorations in a soft brown that has a peculiarly fleeting charm when covered, as it often is, by a transparent luster. For then, viewed at a certain angle, there appears an iridescence of violet, dull gold, and cop-

[4] So called from the city of Rhages (Rayy), near Teheran, a great center of pottery-making, and one of the most splendid cities of Persia before its destruction by Jenghiz Khan in the thirteenth century.

13–15 EWER. Brass inlaid with silver and ornamented with inscriptions and festal scenes. 1232. H. 11 in. British Museum, London. (Trustees of the British Museum)

per. Move slightly, and the sparkling color disappears. Thus is produced a subtle, evanescent form of decoration suggestive of the joy of the passing hour.

In some of these bowls we note that the faces are Chinese, and in other examples we find motifs (phoenixes, peonies, and scrolls) and color schemes of Chinese origin. The Persian shahs and nobles imported Chinese porcelain, which their ceramists succeeded in imitating. Yet the Persian potter, like other Persian artists, was able to assimilate these influences from the Far East and to produce his own designs.

Most of the fine pottery was made for the aristocrats, as were the richly decorated manuscripts. The art of weaving, of carpet-making, was, how-

13–16 LUSTERED RHAGES (RAYY). *ca.* 1200. Metropolitan Museum of Art, New York.

ever, peculiarly expressive of the people as a whole. Carpet weaving was an inherited craft. Many patterns and secrets for making particularly fine dyes were handed down from father to son. The wool came from the sheep which grazed on the mountainsides of this rugged country; and the dyes, few in number, came from plants.

The need of protection against the winter cold made carpets indispensable both in the nomad shepherd's tent and and in the shah's palace. And in each case the intimate relation of the carpet to its makers and to its function determined its design, as we realize in comparing a small shepherd rug of bold primitive pattern with the huge royal carpets of subtle richness. In the houses and palaces of Persia, built of brick, stone, plaster, and glazed tile, the carpets also contributed a contrasting texture as floor and divan coverings and wall hangings.

The success of a Persian carpet results from color massing and texture. The royal *Ardebil Carpet* (Fig. 13–17), a large example of the medallion type, depends for its effectiveness upon a simple massing of large elements of design enhanced by a wealth of subordi-

13–17 ARDEBIL CARPET. Detail. Wool. 34½ × 17½ ft. Made for Shah Tahmasp for the tomb-mosque of his family at Ardebil. Victoria and Albert Museum, London (Victoria and Albert Museum). The inscription at the top of the field reads:

"I have no refuge in the world other than thy threshold;
There is no place of protection for my head other than this door.
The work of the slave of the threshold, Maqsud of Kashan in the year 926 [A.D. 1540]."

nated detail. The field is a rich blue and is covered with leaves and flowers (chiefly peonies, a Chinese influence) attached to a framework of delicate stems which weave a spiral design over the whole field. The central medallion is of yellow, surrounded by small oval panels of yellow, red, and green, from one of which is suspended a mosque lamp; quarter-sections of the central medallion group fill the corners. The broad border has alternating medallions of red and yellow on a deep purple ground. In this carpet there are no human or animal figures, since it was made for a mosque; but other carpets from Ardebil illustrate how the Persian weavers used the animal form.

13–18 TOMB OF HUMAYUN. Delhi. Begun in 1564. Front view. (Department of Archeology, India)

These great royal carpets represent the joint work of a group of weavers, probably attached to the court. Pile weaving is a slow process at best, and, since a carpet like the *Ardebil* often has more than three hundred knots to the square inch, one skilled weaver by himself would have needed (according to an estimate) about twenty-four years to weave it.

INDIA

A descendant of Tamerlane, Babur, invaded India and founded the Mogul dynasty there in 1526. This Moslem conquest of India led to a virtual cessation of most major Hindu building in the north, but in its place the architecture of Islam was carried throughout India by the new rulers.

Nothing could be more antithetical than the Moslem and Hindu styles. The sculptural, three-dimensional mass of the Hindu temple with its mysterious cella was replaced by the two-dimensional screening and open columns of the Islamic mosque. As the mosque displaced the temple and the domed tomb and minaret supplanted the stupa (cf. p. 517), huge palaces burgeoned at the courts of sybaritic monarchs. Local styles and the passage of time varied the details, but the basic pattern was similar all over India. Flat geometric and arabesque decoration took the place of figural sculpture, and the dome displaced post and lintel construction.

The mosque was generally a long rectangular building, the interior forming a long arcade surmounted by one, three, or more domes set on squinches. The exterior is composed of an impressive screening wall and a massive dome, inviting an expectation of grandeur that is often disappointingly negated by the narrow interior volumes and the low

13-19 GATE TO AKBAR'S TOMB. Sikandra. 1593-1613. (Fritz Henle from Monkmeyer)

ceilings of the flattened dome. In the north and west the mosques, such as those at Ahmadabad and in Kashmir, have lofty columns, carved in the Hindu tradition, which enhance the interior volumes. But these are exceptions, for the aesthetic of the Indian mosque is usually established by the recessional movement of a series of pointed arches.

The tomb vied with the mosque in architectural importance, and changes in style can be traced most easily through a series of tombs in the Delhi area. The *tomb of Humayun,* second Mogul emperor, was begun in 1564. Though based on Persian prototypes, it used local red sandstone and white marble for structural and decorative purposes and introduced an important new feature: a prominent arcade which functioned as a high plinth for the tomb (Fig. 13-18). Another innovation

was the placing of kiosks in pairs above two lateral wings abutting the eight-sided hall or main chamber. The addition of a formal garden enclosed by a stone wall provided an imposing setting for the entire structure. The almost archaic simplicity of form in this monument contrasts sharply with the bold and more elaborate decorations of the emperor Akbar a generation later in the imperial city of Fatehpur Sikri and in Akbar's own tomb at Sikandra near Agra. The vitality of the period is mirrored here (Fig. 13-19), while the variegated coloring and greater delicacy at Fatehpur Sikri prepared the way for the exquisite, gemlike character of the *Taj Mahal* (Fig. 13-20).

The fabled *Taj,* built in 1634 by Akbar's grandson, Shah Jehan, as a tomb for his wife, Mumtaz, is symbolic of the classic moment in Mogul architec-

13-20 TAJ MAHAL. Agra. 1632–1653. (Kaufmann & Fabri)

ture. As at Akbar's tomb the mausoleum is approached through an impressive gate, but the power and restraint of the Sikandra entrance are no longer evident. The gateway of the Taj is profusely adorned with fanciful arabesques and an unbroken chain of graceful kiosks. The colorful interplay of red masonry and white marble inlaid with semiprecious stones is a perfect foil for the creamy white marble of the tomb itself which, as the spectator moves through the gateway, he sees outlined against the clear blue sky of north India. The shrine, rising at the end of a formal avenue of pools, trees, and flowers, seems not to be resting on the ground but to be motionlessly and magically floating in the clear atmosphere — an effect so startling that it has captivated the imagination of the world.

The jewel-like beauty of the Taj did not come from a sudden burst of creative genius but from the long and painstaking labors of many architects. The result was not an invention, but an incredible refinement of an old model, the *tomb of Humayun*. When compared, both monuments are found to have the same architectural elements, but, where these were combined for horizontal movement in the earlier structure, they were redistributed for vertical effect in the Taj. Later architects subordinated the arcaded plinth to the superstructure. At the same time they carefully related the kiosks on the roofs to the curve of the central onion-shaped dome which rested on a high drum. Voids, exaggerated by shadows in the deep arches, were made to enrich the surface with a quiet rhythmic beat, and as a final touch four minarets were placed at the corners of the plinth to repeat the upward movement and at the same time to stabilize the entire monument.

A generation later, Aurangzebe, last of the Mogul emperors, built a tomb for his mother, Rabi's Daurani. Although this imitated the Taj, it did so in a fashion which almost burlesqued the original. The forms which had been so perfectly balanced in the Taj were constricted and forced into manneristic tensions and thus were completely transformed. This tomb signaled the artistic decline of the culture in general. Aurangzebe's death in 1707 ended nearly 200 years of Islamic domination and was followed by a century of political chaos.

Summary

For more than a thousand years Islamic art was a vital force in countries ranging from Spain to India. Although its origins are obscure and the religious restrictions, which limited its early development, were severe, the Islamic style must be recognized as among the most original and distinctive in the history of art. The very restrictions of this art seem to have created its particular vitality. For with concentration upon decoration, closely associated with calligraphy, and with only a few fundamental geometric and floral motifs, the Moslem created an endless variety of designs. All the Islamic arts are inextricably interwoven, not only in creating an ensemble but in interchanging ideas and motifs: the pattern for geometric inlay on the helmet found its way to the carvings of the dome; the carved stone or stucco band on the mosque was transposed to the pages of a Koran; and the textile design, to the silver inlay of a bowl. The simple forms of the mosque were perfectly adapted both to their environment and to the needs of the religion. Their silhouettes, with minarets, remain unmistakable.

A careful study of the surface decorations in all the different media shows the degree to which simple abstract design may be elaborated and proves the inventiveness of these artists. One of the most interesting results of such a study is the recognition of an harmonious style, which was able constantly to renew its apparently restricted vocabulary over a long period of time.

Bibliography

Binyon, Laurence, Wilkinson, J. V. S., and Gray, Basil, *Persian Miniature Painting*, Oxford University Press, New York, 1933.

Blochet, Edgar, *Musulman Painting, XII–XVIIth Century*, tr. by C. M. Binyon, Methuen, London, 1929.

Brief Guide to the Persian Woven Fabrics, Victoria and Albert Museum, London, 1924.

Creswell, K. A. C., *Early Muslim Architecture*, Oxford University Press, New York, 1932–41.

Dimand, Maurice S., *A Handbook of Muhammadan Art*, Metropolitan Museum of Art, New York, 1944.

Firdausi, *The Shāh-nāmah*, described by J. V. S. Wilkinson, Oxford University Press, New York, 1931.

Gray, Basil, *Persian Painting*, Benn, London, 1930.

Guide to the Collection of Carpets, intro. by A. F. Kendrick, 3rd ed. rev., Victoria and Albert Museum, London, 1931.

Hannover, Emil, *Pottery and Porcelains*, 3 vols., Scribner's, 1925.

Hawley, Walter A., *Oriental Rugs, Antique and Modern*, new ed., Tudor, New York, 1937.

Koechlin, Raymond, and Migeon, Gaston, *Oriental Art: Ceramics, Fabrics, Carpets*, tr. by Florence Heywood, Macmillan, New York, 1928.

Marçais, Georges, *L'Art de l'Islam*, Larousse, Paris, 1946.

——, *L'Architecture Musulmane d'Occident*, Arts et Metiers Graphiques, Paris, 1955.

Mayer, Leo A., *Saracenic Heraldry*, Oxford University Press, New York, 1933.

Nizāmī, Ganjavi, *The Poems of Nizāmī*, described by Laurence Binyon, Studio Publications, New York, 1928.

Persian Fresco Paintings, American Institute for Persian Art and Archeology, New York, 1932.

Pope, Arthur Upham, *An Introduction to Persian Art Since the Seventh Century A.D.*, Scribner's, 1931.
——, *Masterpieces of Persian Art*, Dryden Press, New York, 1945.
——, and Ackerman, Phyllis, eds., *A Survey of Persian Art from Prehistoric Times to the Present*, 7 vols., American Institute for Iranian Art and Archeology, Oxford University Press, New York, 1939.
Rivoira, Giovanni T., *Moslem Architecture*, tr. by G. McN. Rushforth, Oxford University Press, London, 1918.

Ross, Sir Edward Dennison, ed., and others, *Persian Art*, Luzac, London, 1930.
Tattersall, Creassey E. C., *Notes on Carpet-Knotting and Weaving*, rev. ed., Victoria and Albert Museum, London, 1933.
Wilber, Donald N., *Architecture of Islamic Iran*, Princeton University Press, 1953
Wilson, Ralph P., *Islamic Art*, Benn, London, 1957.
Young, T. Cuyler, *Near Eastern Culture and Society*, Princeton University Press, 1951.

CHAPTER 14

SOUTHEAST ASIAN

(3RD MILLENNIUM B.C.–A.D. 19TH CENTURY)

India and Pakistan

India and Pakistan, which comprise a subcontinent, are surrounded by water except on the northern boundaries, the only gateway for invaders until recent times. There are three distinct geographical areas: in the northeast the massive Himalayas, the traditional home of the gods, rise as a barrier. In the northwest and to the south of the Himalayas, in the valleys of the Indus and the Ganges rivers, is the fertile, densely populated area generally known as Hindustan. And finally there is peninsular India, the Deccan and Tamil states, composed of tropical tablelands separated naturally from the northern rivers by mountains and forests (Fig. 14–2).

In these areas are great extremes

ILLUSTRATION ABOVE. **14–1** Finial of column erected by Emperor Aśoka (272–232 B.C.). Archeological Museum, Sarnath. (Department of Archeology, India)

of climate, from tropical heat to perpetual snow and glaciers; from desert conditions to the heaviest rainfall in the world. The northern river basins have a wonderfully productive soil, and the mountainous regions are rich in building stone, woods, ivory, gold, and precious stones. Economically, the greatest poverty stands opposed to the greatest wealth — wealth until recently kept in the form of the family treasure, gold and jewels.

The ethnic characteristics and religions of the peoples now living in this area vary as much as the geography. The northwestern languages have a strong admixture of Near Eastern elements; the most popular language of north central India is Hindustani, a Sanskrit derivative. Urdu, a related language infused with many Persian words, is spoken by most of the Moslem population. In the south, Dravidian languages, unrelated to Sanskrit, are

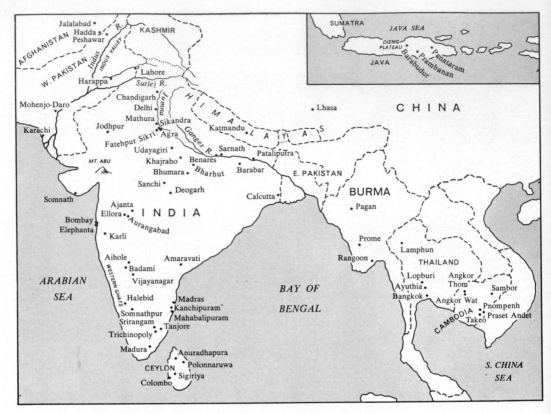

14–2 SOUTHEAST ASIA.

spoken, such as Tamil, Telegu, and Malayalam. Hinduism is the main religion of India, as Islam is of Pakistan, but Jainism, Christianity, and Judaism have many adherents, and Buddhism still has a few.

Unity is not lacking, however — a deeper and more fundamental unity than that manifested simply in political cooperation or in uniformity of dialect and custom. This unity is evident in the religious and cultural life of India. For perhaps no other people have felt so profoundly and pondered so deeply over the fundamental problems of life; and with no other people have spirituality and spiritual significance taken greater precedence.

The first major culture of India centered around the upper reaches of the Indus river valley during the third millennium B.C. Mohenjo-Daro and Harappa in Pakistan were the chief sites, though traces of the culture have been found as far south as Bombay state in India. The architectural remains of Mohenjo-Daro suggest a modern commercial center, with major avenues along a north-south orientation; with streets as wide as forty feet, multistoried houses of fired brick with wooden superstructures, and elaborate drainage systems. Strangely enough, no building has yet been identified as a temple, although a huge bath, much like the Indian "tank," may have been used for ritual bathing.

Some sculptures from this Indus civilization reflect foreign influences, while others indicate the presence of a thoroughly developed Indian tradition. A direct contact with Mesopotamia, for instance, is clearly shown by a limestone fragment of a male figure with striated beard and robe decorated with a trefoil design. The cylindrical treatment of this piece is unmistakably like that of the ancient Near East. Another, completely different, style is exemplified by a miniature torso from Harappa, which, at first glance, appears to be carved according to the precepts of Greek naturalism (Fig. 14–3). On closer study, though, the emphasis given to the surface of the stone and to the swelling curves of the abdomen reveals an interest, not in the logical anatomical structure of Greek sculpture, but in a fluid movement of a living body. This sense of pulsating vigor is Indian. It also permeates a fragmentary dancing figure from the same site and a copper statuette of a girl from Mohenjo-Daro. The emphasis on sensuous surfaces, expressed in these works, remained one of the chief characteristics of Indian sculpture for four thousand years.

Great numbers of steatite seals carved in intaglio have been found at Mohenjo-Daro which also exhibit a curious blend of Indian and Near Eastern elements (Fig. 14–4). Indeed, the finding of a Mohenjo-Daro seal at a datable Mesopotamian site enabled scholars to assign a date to the Indus valley cultures. A script which appears on the seals has not yet been deciphered, but we can learn much from the other varied devices worked into the stone, such as trees (sometimes associated with animals, and "human" figures), which are represented as objects of worship. The beasts most common on the seals are the humped Brahman bull, the water buffalo, the rhinoceros, and the elephant. Fantastic animals and anthropomorphic deities are also represented. On one seal a seated three-headed figure appears in what is later known as a yoga position. The heads are surmounted by a trident-

14–3 NUDE TORSO from Harappa. Third millennium B.C. H. 3⅞ in. Central Asian Antiquities Museum, New Delhi. (Department of Archeology, India)

shaped device which two thousand years later was to symbolize both the Buddhist trinity and the Hindu deity Śiva. Around the deity are various animals, including the bull and the lion, which were also to become symbols of Śiva. If the seal had been made three millennia later, the iconography would have been interpreted as symbolizing Śiva in the form of Mahādeva, the great Lord, Creator, Preserver, and Destroyer. Given its date, however, this seal probably represented a prototype of that god. Such continuity of iconography indicates the deep roots of religious tradition in India. Style, too, shows a continuous tradition. The animals on the Indus valley seals have the flowing contours and tactile surfaces characteristic of sculpture throughout most of Indian history.

14–4 SEALS FROM MOHENJO-DARO. Third millennium B.C. Central Asian Antiquities Museum, New Delhi. (Department of Archeology, India)

This artistic continuity is remarkable, not only because of its span of time but because, within the period between the disappearance of the Indus civilization (about 2000 B.C.) and the rise of the Maurya empire in the third century B.C., there are virtually no remains of the visual arts of India. The invasions of the Aryans, which began about 1800 B.C., might explain any break in the sequence of Indian art. Yet the amazing fact is that, despite the Aryan's profound effect on Indian culture, so many indigenous traits persisted. Wanton destruction and the decay of perishable materials undoubtedly account for the disappearance of many of the objects by which Indian traditions were kept alive during the two thousand years following the collapse of the Indus civilization. But evidence of these traditions may still be found by future archeologists.

When the Aryans arrived in India about 1800 B.C., they brought with them the religion known as Vedic. The term derives from the hymns (Vedas), which have survived to this day and which are addressed to gods who are personified aspects of nature. The warrior god Indra is thunder, Sūrya the sun, and Varuna the sky. There are many others. All were worshiped by means of hymns and sacrificial offerings in conformity to the strict laws of ritual. There were no temples, but fire altars, built according to prescribed

formulas, served as the focus of devotion. So important was the act of ritual that in time Agni, the sacrificial fire, and Soma, the sacrificial brew, became personified as gods in their own right. The rather simple form of religion and propitiation so beautifully expressed in the Vedic hymns was greatly elaborated in the Upanishads (800–600 B.C.), a series of treatises on the nature of man and the universe.

The Upanishads ostensibly developed from the Vedas, but they introduced a number of concepts alien to the simple nature worship of the northern invaders. Chief among the new ideas were those of saṁsāra and karma. Saṁsāra meant the transformation of the soul into some other form of life upon the death of the body. The type of existence into which the reborn soul entered depended upon karma, the effect of the past actions of the individual. A bad karma meant a dark future, rebirth in a hell or in this world as a lower animal, a reptile, or an insect. A good karma meant that the soul might go into the body of a king, a priest, or even a god, for gods also were subject to eventual death and to the endless cycle of rebirth. The goal of religion therefore became the extinction of individual life in the world soul, the undefinable state called nirvana, which was attainable only after an individual's karma had been perfected through countless rebirths. Penance, meditation, and asceticism were believed to speed the process.

The concepts developed in the Upanishads were grafted onto the imported Aryan doctrines of the Vedas. In this speculative atmosphere two major religions developed in India during the sixth century B.C. One of these was Buddhism, which exerted a profound influence on the culture and art of India from the third century B.C. to the sixth or seventh century A.D. The other was Jainism, which, although in many ways similar to Buddhism, never dominated the culture as its rival did. Jainism has continued, however, to the present day as a small but distinct religion in India, whereas Buddhism has been practically extinct in its mother country since the eleventh century, although it has survived in various forms in Tibet, China, Ceylon, southeast Asia, and Japan. Since the arts of so many Asian countries derive from Indian Buddhism, it is essential to have some understanding of its beliefs and practices.

The person called the Buddha Śākyamuni was born about 563 B.C. — the son of a king who ruled a small area on the border of Nepal and India. Legend tells how the child was miraculously conceived and how he was born springing from his mother's side as she supported herself against a tree in the Lumbini garden. The gods Indra and Brahma bathed the child while the whole universe rejoiced at the birth. Named Siddhārtha, and also known as Gautama, the child grew up displaying prodigious abilities. At birth a sage had predicted for him a future either as a universal king or as a Buddha — an "enlightened" holy man destined to achieve nirvana. The prince's father tried to lead the child toward the path of royalty, but after a series of confrontations with old age, sickness, and death, Siddhārtha renounced the life of courtly luxury and fled from the palace, determined to escape the natural sorrows of mankind. First he joined a group of ascetics who in traditional fashion were practicing austerities. After nearly dying of a self-imposed fast, the prince gave up severe penance and left his companions. Following a series of miracles and while meditating under a peepul tree in the city of Gaya, Gautama obtained illumination — the complete understanding of the universe that is Buddhahood. His teaching may be summed up in the formula that all existence implies sorrow; that the cause of existence is attachment to work and the self; that the cause can be removed through the elimination of desires which bind the self to existence and to an endless succession of rebirths. The cessation of rebirth can be accomplished by following the Eightfold Path, which prescribes simple practices of right thought, right speech, and right action.

The religion of Buddhism, so conceived, was not opposed to basic Hindu thought, but was rather a minor heresy deriving from the speculative thought of the Upanishads. What Buddhism actually did was to offer a specific method for solving the ancient Indian riddle of how to break the chain of existence so that the individual soul could find ultimate peace within the world soul.

ARCHITECTURE AND SCULPTURE

The first known examples of art in the service of Buddhism date from the middle of the third century B.C. They are both monumental and sophisticated. Emperor Aśoka (272–232 B.C.), grandson of Chandragupta, founder of the Maurya dynasty, was converted to Buddhism after witnessing the horrors of the brutal military campaigns by which he forcibly unified most of northern India. His palace at Pātaliputra (the modern Patna in Bihar) was designed after the Achaemenian palace at Persepolis (Fig. 3–21). Megasthenes, a Greek ambassador at Aśoka's court, has left a glowing report of Pātaliputra. Only the foundations of buildings and remnants of a wood palisade now remain, but we may draw some idea of the architectural details from a series of commemorative and sacred columns which Aśoka raised throughout much of northern India. These monolithic pillars were of polished sandstone, some as high as sixty or seventy feet. The finial of one now in the Sarnath Museum near Benares typifies the style of the period (Fig. 14–1). It consists of a lotiform capital, a derivative from the bases of the pillars at Persepolis. On the inverted lotus (not shown in the figure) rests a horizontal disk sculptured with a frieze of four animals alternating with carved wheels. Seated on the disk are four addorsed lions which originally were surmounted by another huge wheel. All the forms are symbolic. The lotus, traditional symbol of divinity, also con-

noted man's salvation in Buddhism. The wheel represented the cycle of life, death, and rebirth. This "wheel of life" often had other levels of meaning. In this instance it was the teaching of Buddha, the "turning of the wheel of the law." The wheel itself probably developed from ancient sun symbols, and the four animals (the four quarters of the compass), with which it is here associated, implied a cosmological meaning. In this sense the pillar, as a whole, symbolized the world axis which rose through holy Mount Meru to the heavens. The lions also had manifold meanings but were here specifically equated with Śākyamuni Buddha, who was known as the lion of the Śākya clan.

The pillars interest us not only for their symbolism but also because they exemplify continuity of style. The stiff heraldic lions are typical of Persepolis, but the low-relief animals around the disk are treated in the much earlier fluid style of Mohenjo-Daro. So too are the colossal figures of yakshas and yakshīs which were sculptured during Aśoka's time. These male and female divinities, originally worshiped as local nature spirits, gods of trees and rocks, were now incorporated into the Buddhist and Hindu pantheons. The huge yaksha from Parkham, with its smooth surfaces and swelling abdomen, is a direct descendant of the miniature torso from Harappa.

A lighter side of Mauryan art is found in a group of terra cotta dancing figures found at Pātaliputra. Elaborate coiffures, swirling robes, and smiling faces betoken a luxurious and pleasure-loving court.

The Mauryan period (*ca.* 321–184 B.C.) also witnessed the beginnings of unique architectural forms, such as sanctuaries cut into the living rock of stone cliffs. Unlike natural grottoes, parts of the exteriors (and later interiors) of these caves were carved to

14–5 ENTRANCE TO THE LOMAS RISHI CAVE. Barābar Hills. 272–232 B.C. (Department of Archeology, India)

14–6 SANCHI. The Great Stupa. *ca.* 10 B.C.–A.D. 15. (Department of Archeology, India)

imitate in accurate detail the wooden constructions of their period. In the Barābar Hills about seventy miles south of Patna, the *Lomas Rishi* cave was hollowed out during Aśoka's reign. This sanctuary differs from later examples in that the interior consists of two chambers (rather than one) and the entrance is on the long side rather than on the narrow end of the entrance hall. The entrance, however, is the basic type that was to be perpetuated for a thousand years (Fig. 14–5). A faithful replica of a wooden façade, it has a doorway with a curving eave which in stone reproduces a flexible wood roof bent over rectangular beams. Even the wooden screws which bind the roof to the column are translated into stone. A decorative frieze of elephants over the doorway carries on the indigenous sculptural traditions of the Indian culture.

The fall of the Mauryan dynasty around the beginning of the second century B.C. led to the political fragmentation of India and consequently to less contact with the West. In the succeeding period purely Indian features became more evident in the arts, which had previously combined foreign with native elements.

Under the Śungas and the Āndhras, who were the chief successors of the Mauryas, numerous *chaityas* (Buddhist assembly halls) and *vihāras* (monasteries) were cut into the hills of central India from Bombay in the west to the state of Orissa on the east coast. At the same time the *stupa*, which was originally a small burial or reliquary mound of earth, evolved as an important architectural program. (Aśoka is supposed to have built thousands of stupas throughout India.) By the end of the second century B.C. they had grown to huge proportions. Sculptured fragments from early stupas have been found at Mathura (modern Muttra) and at Bharhut (modern Satna) in north central India, but the grandeur of this type of structure can be seen only at Sanchi in the old state of Bhopal. There, on a hill overlooking a wide

14–7 SANCHI. Great Stupa. Detail of East Gate. 1st century B.C. (Department of Archeology, India)

the *yasti* or mast. The *yasti* is itself adorned with a series of *chatras* (umbrellas). Around the whole structure is a circular stone railing with ornamented *toranas* (gateways) at the north, east, south, and west.

The stupa, like most Indian structures, has more than one function. As a receptacle for relics it is an object of adoration, a symbol of the death of the Buddha, or a token of Buddhism in general. Devotion is given the stupa by the believer who circumambulates its dome. But in another sense, the stupa is a cosmic diagram, the world mountain with the cardinal points emphasized by the *toranas*. The *harmikā* symbolizes the heaven of the thirty-three gods, while the *yasti*, as the axis of the universe, rises from the mountain-dome and through the *harmikā*, thus uniting this world with the paradises above.

The railings and domes of some stupas were decorated with relief sculpture, but at Sanchi only the *toranas* were ornamented. These were covered with scenes from the *jātakas* (tales of the past lives of the Buddha) and from his most recent existence as Śākyamuni. The figure of the Buddha never appears in these scenes. Instead he is symbolized by such devices as an empty throne, as the tree under which he meditated, or as the wheel of the law. At Sanchi, as at other monuments prior to the second century, the great teacher was depicted only by a symbol, probably because his true form was considered too holy to be revealed.

The probity expressed in this iconographic restraint is echoed in the quiet mass of the dome itself, while simultaneously it is strikingly and paradoxically denied by the sculptural luxuriance which crowds the *toranas* (Fig. 14–7). Lush foliage mingles with the flowing forms of human bodies, and warm vitality pervades both animal and man. Sensuous *yakshīs* hang like

plain, several stupas containing sacred relics were built over a period of centuries. Of these, the *Great Stupa*, the tallest and finest, was originally dedicated by Aśoka. Enlarged and finally completed about the beginning of the first century B.C., it stands now as the culminating monument of an era (Fig. 14–6).

The base of this stupa consists of a circular drum about twenty feet high. Leading to this a double stairway at the south permits access to a narrow railed walk around the solid dome, which rises to a height of fifty feet from the ground. Surmounting the dome is the *harmikā*, a square enclosure, from the center of which arises

14–8 KARLE. Interior of carved chaitya cave. A.D. *ca.* 100. (Department of Archeology, India)

ripe fruit from tree brackets. This almost hedonistic expression is alien to the Buddhist philosophic renunciation of life. It is an expression, rather, of a basic Indian attitude which at all times unites and dominates almost all of Buddhist, Hindu, and Jain art throughout India.

As Sanchi is the greatest constructed monument of early Buddhism, so the *chaitya* at Karle is the finest of the sculptured cave temples. During the second and first centuries B.C. the cave sanctuaries had developed complexities far beyond the simple beginnings seen in the *Lomas Rishi* cave. Splendid façades reproducing wood architecture in exact detail were given permanence in stone. Around 100 A.D. at Karle, in the Western Ghats near Bombay, a peak was hollowed out and carved into an apsidal temple nearly 125 feet long and 45 feet high. The nave of the *chaitya* leads to a monolithic stupa in the apse, and on either side of the nave is an aisle formed by a series of massive columns crowned with male and female riders on elephants (Fig. 14–8). These great columns follow the curve of the apse, thus providing an ambulatory behind the stupa (Fig. 14–9). The inner wall of the narthex, despite some later additions, is almost intact, and today it functions as a magnificent façade. On each side of the entrance massive elephants, like atlantes, support a multistoried building, while flanking the central doorway are donors — male and female couples who enhance the already

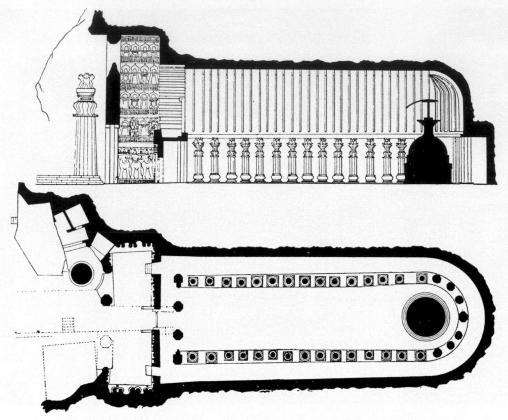

14–9 KARLE. Ground plan and elevation of cave temple. A.D. *ca.* 100. (From Benjamin Rowland, *The Art and Architecture of India*, Penguin Books, 1953)

rich surfaces with their heroic and voluptuous forms. These undulant figures contrast with the immobile severity of the stupa within and, like the *yakshīs* of Sanchi, they speak of life, not of death (Fig. 14–10).

The contradictions implicit in the conflict between style and philosophy, as seen at Karle, explain why Buddhism within a few centuries was to be absorbed by a resurgent Hinduism which was more congenial to basic attitudes of the Indian people. But before Hinduism triumphed, Buddhism still had one more important contribution to make which was to affect the arts of the entire Far East: the creation of the Buddha image.

For six hundred years before the

second century A.D., as we have seen, the Buddha was represented only by symbols. Then, simultaneously in Gandhāra and Mathura, he was suddenly depicted in anthropomorphic form. The explanation is partly to be found in the development of the Buddhist movement which, during the first century, was divided by two conflicting philosophies. The more traditional believers regarded the Buddha as a great teacher who had taught a method by means of which man might ultimately attain nirvana. The newer thought, called Mahāyāna (the Great Vehicle) as opposed to the older Hīnayāna (the Lesser Vehicle), deified the Buddha and provided him with a host of minor divinities (Bodhisattvas) to aid him in saving mankind. According to the older belief Śākyamuni was the last of seven Buddhas to have existed on earth. The Mahāyānists peopled the universe with thousands of Buddhas, of whom Amitābha, Lord of the Western Paradise, and Maitreya, a messiah who is to appear on this earth, soon rivaled Śākyamuni in popular favor. Symbols of the Buddha were too cold and distant to appeal to great masses of people and were not suitable for the pageantry of the new faith. In addition, Buddhism had borrowed from a reviving Hinduism the practice of *bhakti* (the adoration offered a personalized deity), which demanded the human figure as its focus. Thus Buddhism, out of emulation of its rival, produced its most distinct symbol, the Buddha image.

By the middle of the second century A.D. two different versions of the anthropomorphic Buddha had appeared, one in Gandhāra, the other in Mathura. Gandhara, which comprised much of Afghanistan and part of modern Pakistan, was the westernmost section of northern India, which in 327 B.C. had been conquered by the armies of Alexander the Great. Although the Greek occupation lasted only a short time, it led to continued contact with the Classic West. It is not surprising, then, to find that the Buddha image which developed at Gandhāra had Hellenistic and Roman sculpture as its model (Fig. 14–11). Indeed, the features of the Master often suggest those of a marble Apollo, while many details — such as drapery patterns and coiffures — recall successive styles in contemporaneous Roman carving. While the iconography was Indian, even the distinguishing marks of the Buddha (*lakshanas*) were sometimes translated into a Western idiom. Thus the *ushnisha*, a knoblike protuberance on the head, took on the appearance of a Classic chignon. At times even the robe of the

14–10 KARLE. Mithuna couple. Façade of *chaitya* cave. A.D. *ca.* 100. (Department of Archeology, India)

Indian monk was replaced by the Roman toga and minor divinities were transformed into Western water gods, nymphs, or atlantes.

While this intrusion of Western style was dominating the northwest, a purely Indian version of the Buddha figure was evolving in the holy city of Mathura, a hundred miles south of Delhi. This image derived directly from the *yaksha* of popular art and, like the *yaksha*, it was draped in a mantle so thin and clinging that at first glance it seems to be nude (Fig. 14–12). The *Mathura Buddha* also has broad shoulders, a narrow waist, and a supple grace. Only such iconographic details as the *ushnisha*, the *urna* (dot above the nose), and the long lobed ears distinguish the Buddha from the earlier *yaksha*.

By the third century A.D. the two Buddha types began to coalesce, and

14–11 SEATED BUDDHA. Late 3rd century A.D. Gandhāra. Yale University Art Gallery. (Yale Art Gallery)

14–12 SEATED BUDDHA. 2nd–3rd centuries A.D. Curzon Museum of Archeology, Muttra (Mathura). (Department of Archeology, India)

by the fifth century A.D. a perfect blend was produced which was to typify the Indian Buddha and to become the prototype of most Chinese and Japanese images of the deity (Fig. 14–13). This Buddha conveys both the abstract idealism of the religion and the sensuousness of Indian art, the first in the simplified planes of the face, the second in the clinging drapery which reveals the human form.

While Buddhism was at its height, Hinduism was slowly gathering the momentum which was eventually to crush its heretical offspring. Buddhism owed its original victory to the clear definition of a method by which salvation could be attained. About the first or second century B.C., Hinduism's answer appeared in the *Bhagavad-Gita*,

a poetic gospel which ever since has been fundamental to Hindu doctrine. According to the *Gita*, meditation and reason can lead to ultimate absorption in the Godhead; so too can the selfless fulfillment of everyday duties. Since the *Gita* also stressed *bhakti*, which focused on a personalized deity as a means of achieving unity with this deity, and since this answered a fundamental emotional need, the *Gita* swept Hinduism to final supremacy in the sixth and seventh centuries.

Sporadic examples of Hindu art dating from the last centuries B.C. have been found, but we know of no great monuments before the fifth century A.D., which evidently was an age of extensive Hindu building. The basic forms elaborated in all later Hindu

14–13 SEATED BUDDHA. 5th–6th centuries A.D. Archeological Museum, Sarnath. (Department of Archeology, India)

temples had already been established by the end of the fifth century A.D., when a Vishnu temple was built at Deogarh in north central India (Fig. 14–14). All later developments of the Hindu temple were no more than elaborations upon the principles embodied in Deogarh.

The Hindu temple is not a hall for congregational worship; it is the residence of the god. The basic requirement is a cubicle for the cult image or symbol. This most holy of places is called the *garbha griha*, or womb chamber (Fig. 14–15). It has thick walls and a heavy ceiling to protect the deity and at the same time to hold him within the shrine. A doorway through which the devotee may enter is the only other architectural neces-

sity. As in the stupa, the temple has other meanings, for it is also the symbol of the *purusa*, or primordial man. In addition it is a *mandala*, or magic diagram of the cosmos. The magic properties of the temple are also expressed in its proportions, which are based on specific modules. Thus the temple itself is a symbol to be observed from the exterior. It shelters god, not man. Contemporary Western theories of architecture as a space-enclosing form within which man carries on his activities do not apply to the Hindu temple, which is to be appreciated as sculpture rather than as architecture.

In early temples such as Deogarh, the decoration is limited and restrained and the architectural form is a simple cube which originally was surmounted by a tower (*sikara*). All the walls, save that of the entrance, are solid, but include sculptured panels like false doorways framed in the walls. On these panels are scenes from Hindu mythology with figures, relaxed and supple, which carry on the Indian tradition of ease and poise.

In the territory of the Chalukyas in central India, the Hindus seem to have emulated the Buddhists by building cave sanctuaries. During the sixth century, in the rocky hillsides at Badami and nearby Aihole, they hacked out rectangular temples and carved the pillars, walls, and ceilings with figures of their favorite deities. In a temple dedicated to Śiva — one of the two chief divinities of the Hindu pantheon — the god is shown in his cosmic dance with numerous arms spread fanlike around his body (Fig. 14–16). Some of the god's hands hold objects while others are represented in prescribed gestures (*mudrā*), each object and each *mudrā* signifying a specific power of the deity. The arrangement of the limbs is so skillful and logical that it is hard to realize that the sculptor conceived of

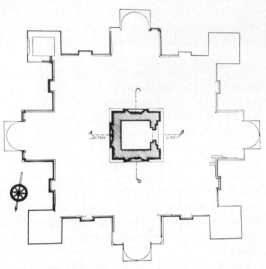

14–14 DEOGARH. Vishnu temple. 5th century A.D. Plan. (Department of Archeology, India)

14–15 DEOGARH. Vishnu temple. Gupta period, 5th century A.D. Side view. (Department of Archeology, India)

the figure as a symbol, not as an image of a many-armed being.

Also at Badami, in a cave dedicated to Vishnu, the other chief god of the Hindus, we see a different aspect of Hindu mythology. According to Indian belief, Vishnu has appeared in this world at many times but in different forms (*avatars*). One of the various *avatars* carved at Badami is that of the god as a huge boar rescuing the earth goddess from a devastating flood. The iconography of this scene derives from a somewhat earlier Gupta version made to the north at Udayagiri in Gwalior, but the style derives from the south.

The beginning of this southern style may be seen in Buddhist art early in the first century A.D. at Amarāvatī, one of the great cultural centers of India, situated near the mouth of the Kistna river on the Bay of Bengal. Here from the first to the third century workmen erected one of the finest of all stupas. This Buddhist monument was elaborately ornamented in a style of great elegance (Fig. 14-17), whose attenuated figures and rhythmic grace con-trasted sharply with the robust forms of the north. The fusion of these two manners, which finally took place in the Chalukyan monuments at Badami, Aihole, and Pattadakal in southern India, produced an art at once delicate and powerful.

The Hindu architects of the Chalukya dynasty, unlike their sculptors, however, did not combine in any one monument the southern and northern styles. Instead, temples of both types were built side by side, each distinguishable by its individual form of *śikara* rising above the *garbha griha* at the rear of the structure. From a distance the northern tower resembles an ear of corn for, although the *śikara* is basically four-sided, it is often so laden with vertical strips of masonry that it seems octagonal or even round. Furthermore, because of the masonry strips which repeat the strong vertical forms of the *śikara*, the mass creates an emphatic upward movement despite the horizontal organization of the carved decoration. The culmination of the *śikara* is the *amalaka,* a mushroom-shaped block which, pierced by a rod representing the axis of the universe, symbolically links the world mountain and the heavens.

The southern or Dravidian temple differs from the northern mainly in the form of the tower, which lacks the soaring quality of its northern equivalent, partly because the tower is generally less lofty, partly because its horizontality is emphasized by a succession of heavy rolled cornices clearly defining each receding story. The whole is crowned by a solid dome (*stupika*), usually octagonal, which substitutes for the northern *amalaka* (Fig. 14–18).

By 600 A.D. both types had evolved beyond the simple combination of cella and tower which the Vishnu temple at

14–17 AMARĀVATĪ. Relief from stupa. 1st–3rd centuries A.D. Musée Guimet, Paris. (J. LeRoy Davidson)

Deogarh exemplified. In some instances the Buddhist *chaitya* cave (in itself a modification of a free-standing wood structure) became the model for masonry temples. The symbolic stupa which had filled the apse of the *chaitya* was replaced by the Hindu *garbha griha,* but the apse itself and the ambulatory around the stairs were retained. At Bhumara in central India a more specifically Hindu form of the temple was evolved. There the *garbha griha* was placed within a large square ambulatory before which a rectangular assembly hall was added to shelter a small group of worshipers. During the seventh century in both north and south the hall and porch preceding the shrine became a general feature of most temples.

A cross-section of architecture existing in south India at the beginning of the seventh century may still be seen at Māmallapuram (modern Mahabalipuram), once the seat of the Pallava kings and now a magnificent archaeological site at the rocky edge of the ocean not far from the city of Madras. Here, near a miscellany of monuments — including cave shrines, carved cliff-

14–16 BADAMI. *Dancing Śiva.* Relief from cave temple. 6th century A.D. (Department of Archeology, India)

14–18 MAHAKUTESVARA. Northern and southern temples. A.D. *ca.* 600. (J. LeRoy Davidson)

sides, and a masonry temple — is a unique group of five small free-standing temples sculptured, perhaps as models, from some of the huge boulders which litter the landscape (Fig. 14–19). The largest of these models is thirty feet high and is in typical southern style. One of the temples is apsidal, another is a long vaulted shape with a barrel roof, the ends of which reproduce the bent wood curves of the ancient *chaitya* halls. The smallest is a square shrine crowned with a pyramidal roof which copies in stone the thatch of primitive shrines as they appear in reliefs on the rails of early stupas.

Further development of the south Indian temple is best seen in the Virūpāksha temple at Pattadakal, which was built under the Chalukyas around 740. The interior of this shrine consists of a dimly lighted ambulatory surrounding the cella, which is entered through a large columned assembly hall (*mandapa*) and two subsidiary shrines. Light entering the *mandapa* through narrow windows and two projecting porches plays over elaborate relief carvings on the columns and walls. The devotee who entered through an open porch walked from the blazing light through a cool, softly lighted, and spacious area until he reached in darkness the enigma of the *garbha griha* itself. There in the austere chamber, having passed through a *mandapa* carved with the visible manifestations of his faith, he came face to face with the dimly revealed symbol of his deity. The sense of mystery offered the worshiper in such a setting was as satisfactory for Hinduism as was the soaring exultation of the Gothic cathedral for Christianity.

The exterior of the Virūpāksha and

14–19 MĀMALLAPURAM. Rock-cut temples. 7th century A.D. (J. LeRoy Davidson)

other eighth-century temples was not so successfully organized as the interior, mainly because the *śikara*, when seen in direct profile, appears to be perched too awkwardly on the end of the long hall. It was a century or two before the architects in the north — at Gyraspur, Bhuvanesvar (Bhubaweswar), and Khajuraho (Khajraho) — combined the exterior and interior into a visual unity.

Hindu art in the north during the seventh and eighth centuries was at its best in the cave temples of Ellora in the northwestern part of Hyderabad state and in the Elephanta caves on an island in the harbor of Bombay. At Ellora the Hindus usurped a cliff in which Buddhist artists, active from the first to the sixth century, had carved a series of their own cave temples. There, in the following two hundred years, the Rāshtrakūta rulers elicited some of the most powerful expressions of Indian art. The most astonishing technical achievement was the Kailāsanātha tem-

ple, or the *Kailāsha*, for which workmen were impressed from conquered territories as far south as Madras. These craftsmen chiseled out of the cliff a huge three-story temple on the model of the Virūpāksha. Both interior and exterior were lavishly carved and painted with the legends and deities of India. The main effort took four decades, and additions were made for at least a century.

The triumph of the *Kailāsha* is that of craftsmanship rather than of art. The full vigor of Hindu art had already reached its peak in the earlier caves at Ellora and in the Śiva cave at Elephanta. Indeed, perhaps the supreme achievement of Hindu art is at Elephanta. There, in the seventh or early eighth century, craftsmen excavated a hilltop and carved out a huge pillared hall almost a hundred feet square. On entering this sanctuary, the visitor peers through rows of heavy columns, until, adjusting to the dark, he sees, emerging from the end wall, the gigantic

14–20 ELEPHANTA. Śiva with guardians in rock-cut temple. 8th century A.D. (Department of Archeology, India)

forms of three heads (Fig. 14–20). These represent Śiva as Mahādeva, Lord of Lords and incarnation of the forces of Creation, Preservation, and Destruction. The concept of power is immediately transmitted by the sheer size of the heads, which, rising nearly fourteen feet from the floor, dwarf the onlooker. Each of the three faces expresses a different aspect of the eternal. The central, neither harsh nor compassionate, looks beyond humanity in the supreme indifference of eternal meditation. The other two faces, one soft and gentle, one angry and fearsome, speak of the sequence of birth and destruction which can be ended only in union with the godhead. The assurance of the period is manifest in the guardians of the shrine, who stand tall and relaxed in the certainty of their power. Around the walls deeply cut panels, illustrations of the legends of Śiva, carry on the robust and sensuous

traditions of both Harappa and Karle.

During these centuries Buddhism borrowed heavily from Hindu doctrines. Elaborate rituals and incantations, inspired by similar Hindu practices, replaced the simple activities which the Buddha had prescribed. Esoteric sects sprouted, and the popular Hindu worship of Śakti, the female power of the deity, was adapted for Buddhist usage. A seventh-century relief in a Buddhist cave temple at Aurangabad depicts worship of the Buddha through music and dance (Fig. 14–21). The scene might have been taken from a Hindu temple, for the volatile and rapturous figures of the musicians and dancer represent an Indian, not a truly Buddhist, way of life. With little to distinguish it from Hindu art, Buddhist art in India gradually withered and within a few centuries virtually disappeared.

The victory of Hinduism carried with

14–21 AURANGABAD. Relief with dancers and musicians. 7th century A.D. (J. LeRoy Davidson)

14–22 KHAJURAHO. Temple. 10th–11th centuries. (India Office)

it the germs of decay. The rigid caste system and religious taboos imposed by its powerful Brahman priests congealed the social structure and stifled creative thought. It is interesting to note that the Hindu art of the tenth and eleventh centuries sometimes reminds us of the works of sixteenth-century Mannerist painters in Europe.

The great temples of Khajuraho in central India are typical of the finest work of the period (Fig. 14–22). They were larger and more elaborate than earlier temples and were given even greater prominence by being placed on a high plinth. Two and sometimes three *mandapa* were put before the cella. The greatest aesthetic advance was made in the roofs of these *mandapa* and their pyramidal eaves, which unite with the *śikara* to create a rapid and torrential sequence of cascading forms. The lower sections of the build-ing, bound by a series of horizontal registers, were filled with sculptured deities, legends, and erotic scenes. It is in the figures that the weakening of a tradition can be detected. Their beauty lies in their attenuated forms and in the way in which they are contorted and often locked together in a sinuous mass. But the warm humanity of earlier sculptures, so well expressed in the Aurangabad musicians, is no longer present. It has been lost in the very mannerisms which characterize the Khajuraho figures.

In the year 1000 the first of a series of Moslem invasions sounded the knell of Hindu architecture in northern India. But in the south — first under the Chola kingdom (846–1173) and later under the Hoyśala (1022–1342), the Vijayanagar (1336–1565), and Nayak (1420–1736) dynasties — sculpture and architecture continued to flourish.

14–23 ŚIVA AS NATARĀJA, LORD OF THE DANCE. Bronze. 14th–16th centuries. H. 46 in. Museum of Art, Cleveland. (Museum of Art)

Enormous temple compounds grew around the nucleus of earlier temples. The Mīnākshi temple at Madura and the Śrīrangām temple at Trichinopoly (Tiruchirapalli) eventually covered acres of ground. "Thousand-pillared" halls were built almost one beside the other, acquiring the aspect of a continuous structure interrupted only by open courtyards and sacred water tanks for ritual bathing. Elaborate monolithic columns, carved with high- and low-relief figures, evoke a solemn mood, the stone sculpture giving the effect of iron castings.

Typical of the Chola and Vijayanagar periods are the many superb bronzes designed to be carried out of their shrines during important ceremonies. The figures of Śiva as *Natarāja*, *Lord of the Dance*, reached their highest point of perfection by the twelfth century, although almost identical figures were made as late as the sixteenth and seventeenth centuries (Fig. 14–23). The exquisite balance achieved in the relationship of the four arms and the complete equilibrium of the revolving movement are triumphs of three-dimensional sculpture.

The spread of Moslem domination throughout India gradually sapped the Indian tradition even in the south. By the seventeenth century the harmonious proportions of earlier figures were lost, and even the metal suffered from inferior casting.

PAINTING

The art of painting was probably as great in India as the art of sculpture but, unfortunately, less of it survives. The earliest traces are a few fragments in cave X at Ajanta, which date from approximately the first century B.C. Like the *toranas* at Sanchi, to which they are related in style, they illustrate scenes from the past lives of the Buddha.

14–24 AJANTA. *Great Bodhisattva*. Wall painting from cave I. 5th–6th centuries. (Department of Archeology, India)

At Ajanta, again, in caves I and XVII, we find the next and most magnificent examples of Indian painting. These murals, which belong to the fifth and sixth centuries A.D., embody all the clarity, dignity, and serenity of Gupta art; and they must rank among the great paintings of the world. The *Great Bodhisattva* in cave I moves with the subtle grace of the Deogarh sculptures, while the glow of color imparts an even more spiritual presence (Fig. 14–24). The Ajanta paintings, however, are more than the manifestations of Buddhist devotion. Their genre-like scenes and worldly figures, although illustrating Buddhist texts, reflect a sophisticated and courtly art. The elegant *apsara* on the veranda of cave XVII would be as much at home in a Paris setting as she is in the Indian jungle. The urbane character of the Ajanta paintings is expressed not only in the

14–25 Scene from *Gītā-Govinda* poem. Ink and gouache on paper. 19th century. Museum of Fine Arts, Boston. (Courtesy, Museum of Fine Arts, Boston)

imagery but also in the compositional devices. Architectural and landscape settings were abstracted into cubist forms which relate the paintings to the wall surfaces and enliven the spatial movement through a prismatic shifting of planes. Decorations on the ceilings demonstrate the same sensitivity for controlled animation. The regularity of their basically rectangular pattern gives cohesion to the broad surfaces, while an ingenious interweaving of the coffer-like motifs adds variety. Representations of flowers, animals, and deities within the individual rectangles pick up the movement of the wall paintings and play a whimsical counterpoint against the melodic repeat of the framing squares.

The Ajanta painting tradition in all its colorful vitality was continued under Chola rule (846–1173) in the south. We know this from a recent discovery of wall paintings in the Great Temple at Tanjore (built about 1000 A.D.). The dancing figures in these murals — though drawn in vivacious postures made familiar by bronzes of the same time — are modeled in the soft tonalities of the Gupta style. No contemporary paintings of corresponding importance have been found in the north and, in order to follow the development of the art there, we must turn to illuminated manuscripts. These fall into two stylistic groups, one distinguished by a rigid formality and an almost Byzantine severity, the other by the freshness and freedom of folk art.

Although the Moslems prevented the evolution of sculpture and architecture in northern India after the thirteenth century, they revitalized the art of painting. In the sixteenth century, especially under the reign of Akbar, who tried to unite Hinduism with Islam, traditional Indian painters were exposed to the delicate and conventionalized miniatures of the great Persian artists. During the seventeenth and eighteenth centuries the Indian painters synthesized the so-called Rajput style, rooted in Ajanta, with the almost purely Persian painting of the Mogul overlords. Local schools of painting arose on islands of Hindu rule in the Himalayas and in the fortified courts of rocky Rajasthan. Native artists in these isolated areas added sparkling color and spacious background to the subtle Persian style. The richness of this new style was particularly well suited to newer Hindu cults which were dedicated to the worship of Krishna, an avatar of Vishnu whose praises were sung in the erotic poetry of the *Gītā-Govinda*. The love of the rich and the sensuous, which the earliest sculptures had expressed, thus found an entirely new medium in exquisitely colored and tender illustrations which were still a vital art in the early nineteenth century (Fig. 14-25). Faint traces of this delicate style sometimes occur today.

The Expansion of Indian Art

The vigorous culture which generated the great achievements of art in India overflowed its borders. The great tide of Buddhism in the early centuries of the Christian era carried Mahāyāna beliefs and the art of Gandhara-Mathura through Afghanistan, across the desert trade routes of Turkestan into China, and eventually into Japan. The path of Hīnayāna Buddhism during the second and third centuries led in another direction — southward from Amarāvatī to Ceylon across the narrow straits. From that time on, sculpture in Ceylon followed the Indian pattern, dominated at first by the style of Amarāvatī and then by the successive styles of the Guptas, the Pallavas, and the Cholas. The great sites are Anurādhapura (second and third centuries) and Polonnāruwa (eighth to thirteenth centuries). The influence of Amarāvatī was still active at Polonnāruwa, where it is particularly evident in the colossal figures of the dying Buddha (nearly 50 feet long) and of the disciple Ānanda. The stupas in Ceylon, unlike any extant stupa in India, consist of an elaborate base, a bell- or bubble-shaped dome, and a unified *harmikā* and mast. It is this stupa, so typical of Ceylon, that was carried to Siam and to Burma, where the magnificently gilded *Shwe Dagon* pagoda helps us to imagine what the Ceylonese stupa looked like in its prime.

The earliest and most important paintings in Ceylon belong to the late fifth century and are basically like the murals at Ajanta. These are at Sīgiriya, a fortress city uniquely situated on a cliff. The heavenly beauties which were painted on the escarpment of the fortress were intended not only to decorate the stronghold but also to suggest a parallel between the dwellings of the gods and the royal palace on the crest.

14–26 STUPA OF BARABUDUR. Java. 8th century.

By the fifth century a series of emigrations from India had totally transformed the countries of southeast Asia. The island of Java, as well as Burma, Siam, and Cambodia, felt the impact of the imported culture. Buddhism and Hinduism abroad continued their struggle for supremacy, but each brought with it the art of India. While Buddhism was dying in south India, one of its greatest monuments was ris-

ing at Barabudur in Java (Fig. 14–26). There, in the eighth century, a huge stupa approximately a quarter-mile long at the base was built in a series of nine terraced levels. The basement and the first four tiers above it have a rectangular plan. The stupa, as we have seen, was a cosmic diagram — a magic *mandala* — which must be complete to be effective. Thus, for iconographic reasons scenes from man's lowest activ-

14–27 STUPA OF BARABUDUR. Buddha expounding the law to his mother, Maya (detail). 8th century A.D.

ities were carved on the basement walls, even though they were hidden from sight. These represent beings caught in the cycle of life, death, and rebirth through "desire" and the workings of karma.

The next four tiers depict scenes from the *jātakas* and from different *sūtras* which tell of the many ways in which man may arrive at enlightenment (Fig. 14–27). Above the rectangular terraces, which represent the world of sensation, are four circular levels which represent the spiritual plane of esoteric Buddhism. No scenes of man and his activities intrude upon this area. The only forms are those of the Buddhas (some enclosed in reticulated stupas) lost in eternal meditation. Standing alone on the topmost terrace is a stupa, symbol of the ultimate, which once enclosed a single figure. According to an inscription on the stupa, that figure was a portrait of the reigning king in the form of the Buddha. Esoteric Buddhism believed that all beings carry within them the seeds of Buddhahood, and in southeast Asia the king was regarded as a Buddha incarnate.

The forms of the Barabudur sculptures parallel their symbolism to a great extent. The basement designs and those of the *jātakas* are crowded with figures and exuberant foliage, whereas the scenes from the higher paths of salvation are more quiet and restrained. This progression of purity in style and purity in mind culminates in the Buddhas on the topmost levels. These, though deriving ultimately from Pallava art, are without the sensuous emphasis which in India invariably contradicted the spirit of Buddhism.

On the mainland other groups of immigrants from India introduced their arts into Siam and neighboring Cambodia. From north central India they brought the Gupta sculptural style, with the flowing planes and sensitive surfaces of Mathura, Sarnath, and Ajanta. In the eighth century we find the pre-Khmer peoples of Cambodia, who had earlier worked with ease in the south Indian manner of the Pallavas, producing such sculpture as Figure 14–28, the Harihara (combined form of Śiva and Vishnu) from Prasat Andet. In this figure the elegance and rigidity of Pallava forms have been only slightly modified, but in such a way as to increase the sense of tautness and springlike tension.

The earliest architecture (sixth to eighth centuries) of the pre-Khmers was modeled, like their sculpture, on south Indian examples. The basic forms

14–28 HARIHARA FROM PRASAT ANDET. 8th century. Musée Albert Sarraut, Pnompenh. (*Life* photo by Eliot Elisofon)

14–29 ANGKOR THOM. Dance relief. 12th–13th centuries. Musée Guimet, Paris. (J. LeRoy Davidson)

of their temples are like those of the Pallava monuments at Māmallapuram even to such details as the sculptured lintels over the entrances. In the twelfth and thirteenth centuries the Khmers (i.e., the Cambodians), who had conquered the country in the eighth or early ninth century, built two tremendous temple "cities": *Angkor Wāt* and *Angkor Thom*. Some idea of the size of the earlier, Angkor Wāt, may be obtained from simple statistics. This monument is surrounded by a moat two and a half miles long. One of its many courtyards contains half a mile of sculptured reliefs, and the foundations of the central shrine alone measure more than three thousand feet on each side. The temples comprising this great complex are set at the corners of two

14–30 ANGKOR THOM. *Bayon.* 13th century. (Marie Mattson, Black Star)

14–31 ANGKOR THOM. Tower of *Bayon*. 13th century. (Elizabeth Lyons)

concentric walls which gird the central shrine. Each of the eight temple towers repeats the form of the main spire, which rises in the center from a raised platform like the apex of a pyramid. The towers themselves resemble in outline the śikara of north India, but their star-shaped plan and some of their ornament probably have as their source the eleventh-century art of Mysore in south India.

Relief carvings, set in panels in the walls at Angkor Wāt, illustrate Hindu legends and at the same time express the Khmer predilection for melodic design. The juxtaposition, wherever possible, of one, two, three or more almost identical figures, and the repetition of their flowing contours, create a linear pattern. The graceful forms, thus locked together, move in the harmonious rhythm which so distinguishes these reliefs and Cambodian art in general (Fig. 14–29) — even their dance forms today.

The *Bayon* in Angkor Thom (Fig. 14–30), built in the thirteenth century, is in many ways the culmination of the Indian building tradition, particularly in the complete integration of sculpture and architecture. This temple was placed in the center of a new capital in an area four times that of Angkor Wāt and was composed according to the same general pyramidal grouping of structures. The uniqueness of the Bayon lies in the size and disposition of four colossal human heads, each of which covers a side of the square central tower. These faces — their features composed of large almond eyes, full squared mouth, and high cheekbones — smile enigmatically from their lofty height. They represent the omnipresent Bodhisattva Lokeśvara, Lord of the Universe, and together with numerous smaller versions on subsidiary towers, symbolize the infinity of the Bodhisattva's powers, which extend to all points of the compass (Fig. 14–31).

As at Barabudur, the Bayon's central shrine originally held a statue of a Buddha who, like a king, a Bodhisattva, or a God, was believed to be only a manifestation of the supreme power. The Bayon itself was the world mountain. On it and around it a tropical luxuriance of decorative and narrative carvings intensified its magic symbolism. The creative force which had been waning in India since the tenth century left its last great record in these compassionate faces of Lokeśvara surveying from eternity the riot of mortal history carved on the temple walls below.

Bibliography

Archaeological Survey of India, Annual Reports, Office of the Superintendent of Government Printing, Calcutta, 1904 – .

Archaeological Survey of India, Memoirs, Office of the Superintendent of Government Printing, Calcutta, irreg.

Archer, W. G., *Indian Painting in the Punjab Hills,* Her Majesty's Stationery Office, London, 1952.

Bachhofer, L., *Early Indian Sculpture,* 2 vols., Harcourt, Brace, 1929.

Barrett, Douglas, *Sculptures from Amaravati in the British Museum,* London, 1954.

Bhandarkar, R. G., *Vaisnavism, Saivism, and Minor Religious Systems,* K. J. Trubner, Strasbourg, 1913.

Brown, P., *History of Indian Architecture,* Bombay, no date.

Brown, W. Norman, *A Descriptive and Illustrated Catalogue of Miniature Paintings of the Jaina Kalspasutra,* Lord Baltimore Press, Washington, D. C., 1934.

Coomaraswamy, Ananda K., *Buddha and the Gospel of Buddhism,* Putnam, 1916.

——, *Catalogue of the Indian Collections in the Museum of Fine Arts, Boston* (Part 5), Harvard University Press, 1926.

——, *Dance of Śiva,* Sunwise Turn, New York, 1918.

——, *History of Indian and Indonesian Art,* E. Weyhe, New York, 1927.

——, *The Mirror of Gesture,* Harvard University Press, 1917.

——, *Rajput Painting,* 2 vols., Oxford University Press, New York, 1916.

——, *Yaksas,* 2 vols., Smithsonian Institution, Washington, D. C., 1928–31.

Cunningham, Gen. Sir Alexander, *The Stupa*

of the Bharhut, W. H. Allen, London,
1879.
Eliot, Sir Charles, *Hinduism and Buddhism,*
3 vols., Longmans, Green, New York,
1921.
Getty, Alice, *The Gods of Northern Bud-
dhism,* Oxford University Press, New
York, 1928.
Gray, Basil, *Rajput Painting,* Pitman, New
York, 1949.
Groslier, B. P., *Angkor,* Arthaud, Grenoble,
1956.
Grousset, René, *Civilizations of the East,* tr.
by C. A. Phillips, Knopf, 1931.
Hackin, J., "The Colossal Buddhas of Bami-
yan: Their Influence on Buddhist Sculp-
ture," *Eastern Art,* Vol. 1, 1928, pp.
109–16.
Hall, D. G. E., *A History of South-East Asia,*
Macmillan (St. Martin's Press), New
York, 1955.
Ingholt, Harald, *Gandhāran Art in Pakistan,*
Pantheon Books, New York, 1957.
*Journal of the Royal Asiatic Society of Great
Britain and Ireland* (quarterly), London.
Jouveau-Dubreuil, G., *Iconography of South-
ern India,* P. Geuthner, Paris, 1937.
Kar, Chintamoni, *Classical Indian Sculpture,*
Tiranti, London, 1950.
Kramrisch, Stella, *The Art of India,* Phaidon
Publications, New York, 1954.
——, *The Hindu Temple,* University of Cal-
cutta, 1946.

Marshall, Sir John H., *Mohenjo-daro and the
Indus Civilization,* A. Probsthain, Lon-
don, 1931.
——, *Taxila,* 3 vols., Cambridge University
Press, 1951.
Mus, Paul, *Barabudur,* Imprimerie d'Ex-
trême-Orient, Hanoi, 1935 –.
Rawlinson, H. G., *A Concise History of the
Indian People,* Oxford University Press,
London, 1940.
Rowland, B., *The Art and Architecture of
India: Buddhist, Hindu, Jain,* Penguin
Books, Baltimore, 1953.
——, "A Revised Chronology of Gandhāra
Sculpture," *Art Bulletin,* Vol. 18, 1936
(and other articles in the *Art Bulletin*
and the *American Journal of Archaeol-
ogy,* 1940 and later).
——, and Coomaraswamy, A. K., *The Wall
Paintings of India, Central Asia, and
Ceylon,* Boston, 1938.
Singh, Madanjeey, *India: Paintings from the
Ajanta Caves,* New York Graphic So-
ciety and UNESCO, New York, 1954.
Thomas, E., *History of Buddhist Thought,*
London, 1933.
Vogel, Jean P., *Indian Serpent-Lore,* A.
Probsthain, London, 1926.
Wheeler, Sir M., *The Indus Civilization,*
Cambridge University Press, 1953 (sup-
plementary vol. of the *Cambridge His-
tory of India*).

CHAPTER 15

CHINESE

Although most Westerners realize that China has the longest continuous history in the civilized world, few are aware of the complexity of this history or are capable of interpreting it. It is commonplace in the West to speak of Chinese art as though it were a specific style which persisted with only slight modifications for some 5000 years. This is a fallacy, for the changes in Chinese art from 1000 B.C. to 1000 A.D. were even greater than those in the art of Europe during the same period. In spite of these complexities, our task here is to identify the spirit of Chinese art and to trace at least in outline its major developments and styles.

China is geographically vast and topographically varied. Although China proper is about the size of the United States, its political and cultural boundaries have spread at times to double that area, encompassing Tibet, Chinese

Turkestan (Sinkiang), Mongolia, Manchuria, and parts of Korea. The country includes great stretches of sandy plains, mighty rivers, towering mountains, and fertile farmlands. North China, centering around Peking, has a dry and moderate to cold climate, whereas south China is moist and tropical. (See Fig. 15–2.)

The unifying factor in Chinese history has been the written language. While the spoken language varies so much as to be unrecognizable in different areas, its written characters have remained uniform and intelligible in all parts of the country. Thus literary, philosophic, and religious traditions were shared by people thousands of miles apart.

A similar uniformity is observable in artistic expression, for only slight modifications are apparent in the art forms from different parts of China at any given epoch except during the prehistoric period. This uniformity arose from fundamental relationships between the art of writing, or calligraphy (see p. 562), and the brushwork of the painter, and from a common attitude

ILLUSTRATION ABOVE. **15–1** YU. Bronze. Early Chou dynasty, 10th–7th century B.C. Freer Gallery of Art, Washington, D. C. (Courtesy, Smithsonian Institution, Freer Gallery of Art)

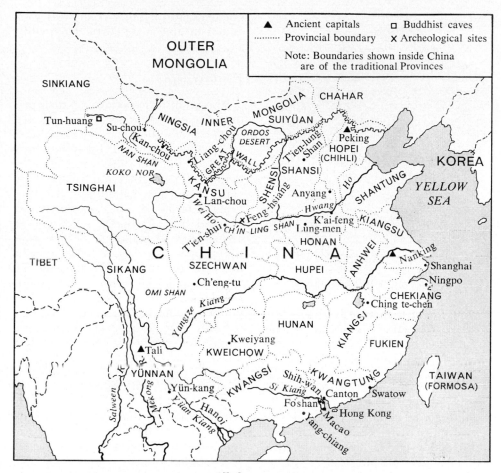

15–2   CHINA.

which regarded painting specifically, but all art in general, as a superior form of self-expression.

Other common denominators inherent in this art are only now being analyzed by Chinese and Western scholars in terms comprehensible to the Western mind. In addition to the technical and stylistic characteristics discussed in the chronological survey which follows, we should also be aware of the Chinese attitude toward time and of the artist's direct participation in his design. Careful observation proves that no traditional design motif is ever absolutely symmetrical

or suggestive of a complete entity with a finite beginning or end. There are seemingly geometrical designs, but the straight lines and curves are never true to any measurement. Their origin was in a concept of squares, spirals, meanders, or such, but they were never constructed by rulers or compasses. Even in the apparently symmetrical animal motifs on early bronzes, the left is never identical with the right. This is a matter of organic growth, recalling the imperfect symmetry of the human body. As visual forms, these motifs were more perfectly depicted in what might be called dynamic equi-

15–3 YANG SHAO POTTERY JAR. Neolithic period. Museum of Fine Arts, Boston. (Courtesy, Museum of Fine Arts, Boston)

librium rather than axial symmetry. Instead of subjecting his design to tools of measurement, the artist merges himself with it to avoid being merely its creator. He becomes part of the total expression of his art; this explains his lack of interest in creating a frame for a painting, a beginning or an end for his decorative motifs, or the interior and exterior of his architecture. The lack of finite measurements, of symmetry, or of a beginning and an end is not a negative value. It is evidence of a positive desire to include time through growth, to create a dynamic equilibrium and rhythm of movement.

Characteristic as well of the Chinese attitude toward art was the preparation of the artist's materials, which often became almost ritualistic. The best ink, for instance, was derived from soot or lampblack mixed with animal glue and pulverized clay, oyster shells, or powdered jade which was evidently added primarily as a gesture of respect for the ink. From these ingredients, each of which had symbolic as well as physical properties, an ink stick was formed; and musk, camphor,

pomegranate or other fragrances were added to give it its particular quality.

Prehistoric

The prehistoric period in China produced many artifacts of a style similar to those of other Stone Age cultures throughout the world. Little has been found of the Paleolithic period other than the rough stone implements typical of man's first handicrafts. The earliest material of any artistic significance dates from the Neolithic period, about 3000 to 1500 B.C. At this time the people were agriculturalists who domesticated the pig and the dog and who hunted and fished. They made polished stone implements and painted pottery, twin hallmarks of Neolithic cultures (see p. 43). The earliest examples of Neolithic Chinese pottery are decorated with bold spirals, gourd-shaped designs, and representations of human arms and legs stylized into chevrons (Fig. 15–3). The spirals, which resemble those on painted pottery of the Near East and central Europe, and the gourd patterns, which recall those from the Indus valley culture of India, were apparently brought to China from the outside, while the chevron ornament was probably indigenous to China.

Many other styles of Chinese prehistoric pottery have been found. Some, such as the *li*, a hollow-legged tripod which was originally an invention of the Chinese potter, later reflect the decorative motifs developed in metal techniques. Most Neolithic pottery was made between 3000 and 2000 B.C., but in some provincial areas production probably continued for another thousand years. An unpainted ware of thin, finely polished black pottery was made, for instance, in the east and north just before the Shang dynasty, when Chinese recorded history begins.

Shang

(ABOUT 1500–1050 B.C.)

The very early history of China is clothed in legends, repeated again and again by Chinese writers and represented by symbolic forms in art. The first presumably ordered society is identified as the Hsia, before which there was a long, nebulous age during which civilization was gradually introduced. Although the Hsia state is still a matter of historical conjecture, the remains of a considerable kingdom, specifically identified as being ruled by the Shang dynasty, have only recently been discovered. As late as 1929 many scholars doubted the historical existence of the Shang dynasty, but in that year excavations at Anyang in northern China brought to light not only one of the last capitals of the Shangs but also evidence of their earlier development. Among the astounding discoveries were large numbers of inscribed bones, once used for divination, which tell us much about the Shang people. Their script was basically pictographic but developed sufficiently to express abstract ideas. These fragmentary records, together with other finds from the excavations, reveal an advanced if barbaric civilization. They indicate that the king was a feudal ruler and that some of his wives were also his vassals, living in different cities. Warfare with neighboring states was frequent, and cities were protected by surrounding walls of pounded earth. Royal tombs were extensive, and the beheaded bodies of servants or captives accompanied the deceased rulers to the grave. Chariots, trappings of horses buried alive, weapons, and ritual objects found in these

15–4 LIBATION BEAKER (KU). Bronze. Shang dynasty, 12th century B.C. H. 11¾₆ in. Freer Gallery of Art, Washington, D. C. (Courtesy, Smithsonian Institution, Freer Gallery of Art)

15–5 COVERED LIBATION VESSEL (KUANG). Bronze. Shang dynasty, 12th century B.C. H. 6⁹⁄₁₆ in. Freer Gallery of Art, Washington, D. C. (Courtesy, Smithsonian Institution, Freer Gallery of Art)

graves have enabled us to describe the art of this period.

Although sculpture in marble and small carvings in bone and jade exist, the great art of the Shang was that of ritual bronze vessels, many of which have come down to us in imperial collections and through other recent discoveries. These bronzes were made by the *cire perdue* method, or in piece molds. Even the earliest of them are as advanced in technique as any casting ever produced in the East or West, so that this art must have been practiced for many centuries before the Shangs. The bronze vessels were intended to hold wine, water, grain, and meat used in sacrificial rites. As containers they were generally made in three standard shapes: the *ku*, a tall narrow beaker (Fig. 15–4); the *ting*, a hemisphere on three solid legs; the *li*, a hollow-legged tripod derived from earlier pottery. There are other vessels, some in the shape of birds or animals. The major elements of decoration are zoomorphic, but usually the background and sometimes the animals themselves are covered with round or squared spirals, believed to symbolize clouds, rain, or water — all fertilizing aspects of nature. Such conventions, which obviously evolved during a long period of time, rigidly governed the stylistic representation of animals, so that images or symbols are often involved and difficult to decipher. A major zoomorphic motif is that of an animal divided in half and arranged symmetrically on the body of a vessel. On the central zone of a covered libation vessel (Fig. 15–5) such an animal is shown; its complexity may be understood by realizing that the nose is represented by two spiral motifs and the eyes by stylized horns. A specific animal may be identified by one major attribute, such as the curved horns of a ram or the bent horns of a bull. More complex ideas were symbolized by combining certain of these motifs, so that an animal or a bird in the mouth of another animal signifies birth. At times, also, the entire animal or bird was represented by an isolated detail such as a beak or a horn. The multiple designs and their enigmatic fields of spirals are so closely integrated with the total form of the vessel that they are not merely an external embellishment but an integral part of the sculptural whole. The tense outline of the bronze compactly encloses the forces symbolized on its surface. These vessels not only were ritual containers but also, in their very form and decoration, served as a kind of sculptural icon or visualization of the early Chinese attitude toward the powers of nature.

We know little about Shang architecture since the remains at Anyang are meager, consisting chiefly of an imperfect rectangular plinth of pounded earth on which rested a series of bronze disks for the support of columns. This structure, which may have been a royal palace, seems to have had screening walls and a roof resting on columns, much like later Chinese buildings.

Chou

(ABOUT 1050–249 B.C.)

About 1050 B.C. the Shangs were overthrown by the Chous. Although the Chous were a more barbaric people from the west, their culture apparently resembled that of the Shangs. Fragments of Chou literature, preserved in the *Shu Ching* (*Book of History*) and the *Shih Ching* (*Book of Odes*), show, however, that the Chous tried to revise history in order to justify their conquest of the Shangs.

The very earliest Chou period bronzes are indistinguishable from those of the Shang. Indeed they were probably made by the same craftsmen. But within a generation the new and bolder spirit of the conquerors was unmistakably imprinted on the ritual vessels. Whereas the Shang silhouette had been suave and compact, the Chou was explosive and dynamic (Fig. 15-1). Gradually this vitality diminished, and in a hundred years the shapes became more utilitarian and the zoomorphic shapes more ornamental. The animal forms were distorted and twisted into interlaces until, by the beginning of the Late Chou period (600–249 B.C.), almost all evidence of the original awesome motifs was lost in an exuberance of playful rhythms over the surface of the bronzes. What had once expressed the power of magic and religion was transformed into a secular display of technical skill and fantasy.

During the sixth century B.C. the Chou empire began to dissolve into a number of warring feudal states. As old values were forgotten, Confucius and other philosophers strove to analyze the troubles of their day. While Confucius urged intelligent and moral action upon his followers, his famous contemporary, Lao-tzu, favored meditation, inaction, and withdrawal from society. Neither philosophy, however, was to affect the arts for several centuries.

The art of Late Chou, whether in bronze, jade, or lacquer, was produced to satisfy elaborate demands of ostentatious feudal courts, which vied with each other in lavish display. At this time the technique of niello inlay in gold and silver became common, and jade carving reached a peak of technical perfection (Fig. 15-6). Metal mirrors of polished bronze decorated on the reverse with designs similar to those on contemporaneous bronze vessels made their appearance.

About the fourth century B.C. an entirely new system of narrative decora-

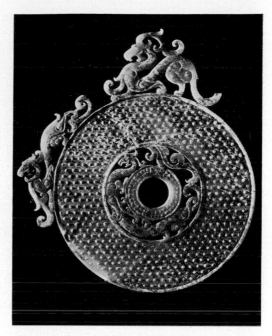

15–6 JADE PI (symbol of Heaven). Late Chou dynasty, 5th-3rd centuries B.C. William Rockhill Nelson Gallery of Art, Kansas City, Missouri. (Nelson Gallery of Art, Atkins Museum of Fine Arts)

tion was introduced on ritual bronzes. Hunting scenes, religious rites, and magic practices now decorated the surfaces. The scenes on the bronzes are necessarily small, but they nevertheless reveal new subject matter and compositions, which may have been taken from lost paintings mentioned in the literature of the period. An unusual bronze illustrates another aspect of the change which was taking place — a t'ou, in the Freer Gallery, in Washington, D. C. This vessel is decorated with the traditional dragon motifs but the style has greatly altered. The dragons are drawn in an undulating line, sometimes thick, sometimes thin — a line that is no longer the line of the bronze craftsman but is the calligraphic line of the Chinese painter. The culture which produced the great bronzes and jades of Shang and Chou

15–7 PAINTED TILE (detail). Han dynasty, 206 B.C.–A.D. 221. Ross Collection, Museum of Fine Arts, Boston. (Courtesy, Museum of Fine Arts, Boston)

was dying, and during the next four hundred years a radically different art developed.

Ch'in and Han

(249 B.C.–A.D. 221)

The political chaos of the last few hundred years of the Chou dynasty was temporarily halted by Shih Huang Ti, ruler of the state of Ch'in, who established dictatorial control over most of China in the third century B.C. In an attempt to eradicate old traditions, this emperor ordered the burning of all historical books and established totalitarian controls which seem only too familiar today. At his death the people revolted, and in 206 B.C. a new dynasty, the Han, was founded. A powerful centralized government now extended the southern and western boundaries of China. Chinese armies penetrated far into Turkestan, and indirect trade was maintained with distant Rome. Confucianists struggled with Taoists (followers of the mystic philosophy of Lao-tzu) for control of governmental powers. The Confucianists eventually won, though the formalized Confucianism which triumphed was far removed from the teachings of the master. The Confucian legends of filial piety and the folklore of Taoism together provided most of the subject matter of Han art.

Fragments of Han painting which have survived, supplemented by reliefs carved in stone or stamped in pottery tiles, enable us to reconstruct the pictorial style of the period. In the set of painted tiles in the Museum of Fine Arts in Boston (Fig. 15–7), the outlines of the figures are rendered in typically Chinese calligraphic line whose elasticity also conveys depth and mass. The overlapping of arms and drapery further emphasizes the third dimen-

15–8 RUBBING OF A STONE RELIEF FROM WU TOMB, Shantung province. Mythological scenes. Later Han dynasty, A.D. 147–168. L. *ca.* 5 ft. (Chavannes)

sion, while the rhythmic relationship of the different figures is accented by flat colors applied within contours. There is no background or any other indication of environment.

Numerous stone reliefs in the Wu tombs in Shantung (*ca.* A.D. 150) also reflect modes of painting. A whole history of the world, from the time of creation to the burial of the deceased, is depicted on these slabs. The story unfolds in images of polished stone against an equally flat though roughly striated ground. As in the Boston paintings, the massive figures are related to each other by the linear rhythms of their contours. In addition, buildings and trees now indicate a milieu. Space, though, is conceptual as in Egyptian painting; and distance is suggested by the superimposition of one figure above another, although, curiously enough, chariot wheels overlap. Individuals of importance are shown hieratically in larger size than their subordinates. Most interesting are the trees, which are highly stylized as a mass of intertwined branches bearing isolated, overlarge leaves (Fig. 15–8). Yet within this schematic form some accidental variation in a twisted branch or broken bough shows how the designer's generalization derived from observation of specific trees and how a detail of the particular could individualize the general. It is this subtle relationship between the specific and the abstract which became one of the most important aesthetic attributes of later Chinese painting.

Another group of Han stone carvings was only recently discovered in the southwestern province of Szechwan. These reliefs, although similar in technique to the Shantung examples and probably of the same date, are rather more advanced in style (Fig. 15–9). Rhythms are more rapid, spatial organization more three-dimensional, and the environment is more fully stated. Some of the subjects, such as pictures of salt-making, show an interest and observation of daily existence in contrast to the earlier preoccupation with mythological or historical subjects. Others may even be Buddhist and therefore the first reference to the new religion which was to dominate Chinese thought for the next thousand years.

15–9 RUBBING OF TOMB TILE from Chengtu, Szechwan province. *Rice Paddy and Hunting Scene.* Later Han dynasty, A.D. 25–221. (From R. C. Rudolph, *Han Tomb Art of West China,* University of California Press, 1951)

Three Kingdoms, Six Dynasties, and Sui

(A.D. 221–618)

Buddhism (see p. 515), whose spirit was a profoundly different one from the ancient and native philosophies of China, was introduced by the first century of the Christian era. During the last hundred years of Han rule and the succeeding period of the Three Kingdoms, China was splintered by strife and her people grasped eagerly at a new ideal by which to live. The Confucian system of ethics had proved unable to adapt itself to the anarchy of the times, and Taoism, having degenerated into magic and superstition, no longer appealed to the philosophic mind. Buddhism offered the Chinese masses the promise of hope beyond the troubles of this world. In addition, it attracted the intellectuals by its fully developed logical system, whose refinements surpassed those of any pre-

vious Chinese system of thought. Buddhist missionaries from India, working at first with the ruling families, spread their gospel so successfully that their teachings ran like wildfire throughout China.

The arts flourished in the service of the imported religion. A new aesthetic was developed in imitation of Indian or central Asian models, in harmony with the prescribed formalism of Buddhist doctrine. The earliest important Buddhist image, a gilt bronze statuette of *Śākyamuni Buddha,* dated by inscription in the year 338 (Fig. 15–10), is clearly related, in both style and iconography, to the prototype which had been conceived and developed at Gandhāra in northwest India (see p. 521).[1] The heavy concentric folds of the robe, the *ushnisha* on the head, and

[1] Yet so new was the icon and its meaning that the Chinese craftsman, although endeavoring to make an image faithful to prescription, nevertheless erred in representing the canonical *mudrā* of meditation: the Buddha's hands are clasped across his stomach, whereas they should be turned palms upward, with thumbs barely touching.

the cross-legged position all derived ultimately from the Indian prototype, examples of which had been brought to China by pilgrims and priests who had made the hazardous journey along the desert trade routes of central Asia.

The Chinese artist transformed the basic Indian pattern during the following century or so. These changes may be observed in a series of great cave temples which were carved into the hillsides after the fashion of the early Buddhists in India. At Tun-huang, westernmost gateway to China, over three hundred sanctuaries were cut into the loess cliffs, the walls decorated with paintings, and the chambers adorned with images of clay. This site was dedicated in 366, but the earliest caves we know belong to the late fifth century. About the same time, in 460, sculptors at Yün-kang, near Ta-t'ung in northern China, were carving temples in cliffs of sandstone. Although the materials are different, both sites have an archaic style similar to the sculpture of the sixth century B.C. in Greece and of the early twelfth century in France. Like their Western counterparts, the cave figures have faces carved in sharp planes and drapery conventionalized into angular patterns, and as a whole they, too, express the intense and noble dignity of a deeply felt religion (Fig. 15–11). The Buddhist concept of divinity in its most perfect form may be seen in the caves of Yün-kang, where the image of the Buddha, a blend of conventional restraint and religious fervor, became human enough for popular recognition, while remaining sufficiently idealized to carry the worshiper beyond the image to the abstraction it symbolized.

In 494 the Wei Tatars, staunch Buddhists who had supported the colossal program at Yün-kang, moved their court southward to Lo-yang in Honan. Near there, in the limestone cliffs of Lung-men, another series of caves was started where work continued until the first part of the sixth century. The new carvings, despite their undeniable charm, were mannered reworkings of the Yün-kang formula. The religious ardor reflected in the earlier caves was softened by sophistication. The elegance of the Lung-men figures, as compared with the austerity of those at Yün-kang, may be seen in the attenuation of the bodies and in the tightened drapery folds which resemble the facile line of the painter's brush.

While the Lung-men caves were being worked on, the people's imagination was captured by a new form of Buddhism, which gave promise of rebirth in a Buddhist Paradise rich in the

15–10 ŚĀKYAMUNI BUDDHA. Six Dynasties, A.D. 338. Gilt bronze. Collection Avery Brundage, Santa Barbara Museum, Santa Barbara, California.

15–11 MAITREYA. Yün-Kang caves. *ca.* 460. (J. LeRoy Davidson)

desired material pleasures which are denied to most in this world. As an idyllic existence in this paradise could be gained merely by faith in the word of the Buddha, many who might have failed to appreciate the goal of nirvana and the ultimate extinction of personality were won over to Buddhism by the more tangible and attractive goal of the Paradise sects. Glories beyond those even of the imperial court were thus offered to every man who put his trust in the Buddha. The pleasant aspirations of these Buddhists were reflected in the greater naturalism of their arts, particularly in the humanization of the deity. It is no wonder that, when the Paradise sects reached their peak during the Sui dynasty (581–618), the Buddha was transformed from an archaic image of divine perfection into a gentle and human saviour such as the marble figure

in the Grenville Winthrop Collection (p. 489).

A comparable development of Buddhist images can be observed in the wall paintings of Tun-huang. The richly painted walls of the Tun-huang sanctuaries were calculated to inspire the worshiper with the splendor of Buddhism and also, like Medieval paintings, to instruct the illiterate. Impressive Buddhas, hieratic figures serving as a focus of devotion, were surrounded by scenes illustrating colorful stories about the past lives of the Buddhas (*jātaka*). The formalized patterns of the individual Buddhas are equivalent to those of the sculptured images at Yün-kang and Lung-men. But the narrative scenes, freed from the prescriptions which firmly dictated the forms of the icons, carried on the traditions of Han painting. We see this in the cell-like composition, in the leaping rhythms, and in the disproportionate relationship of figures to diminutive, conventionalized settings. While the Tun-huang artists thus translated Indian legends into a Chinese idiom, they continued to paint the principal figures in heavy contour lines according to central Asian models which were in turn provincial modifications of Indian painting.

By the year 539 most traces of central Asian influence had disappeared. Like sculpture of the time, Buddhist painting responded to the happy credo of the Paradise sects with increasing naturalism and grace. Although the Buddha groups retained the strict frontality and rigid balance of ritualistic art, the *jātaka* tales expanded haphazardly over the temple walls, and their figures, now slim, elegant, and emancipated from their compartmental designs, move freely over the plane surface. By the end of the century the same forces which were humanizing the sculptured deity began to transform the abstract environment of the painted figures into a three-dimensional world. The simple device of overlapping was used to create depth, and the sense of reality was further heightened by surrounding the celestial groups with such earthly phenomena as trees, pavilions, lotus ponds,[2] and bridges.

T'ang

(618–906)

The short-lived Sui dynasty was overthrown in 618, and under the T'ang empire, which followed, China entered a period of unequaled magnificence. Chinese armies marched to the

[2] According to the *sutras* the believer was reborn as a lotus in the waters of the Sukhāvatī lake in Amitābha's Paradise. In course of time the lotus opened, and the Buddha received the newborn soul.

ends of central Asia, opening a path for the flow of wealth, ideas, and differing peoples. Arab traders, Nestorian Christians, and other travelers journeyed to the cosmopolitan capital of the T'ang, and the Chinese in turn adventured westward. During the middle of the seventh century Hsüan-tsang, a Chinese monk, visited India, as had some earlier devotees, and returned from the mother country of Buddhism with revolutionizing doctrines of more recently developed esoteric sects. It was a critical moment for Buddhism, which was being brought into disrepute by a lax court and a corrupt clergy. Under the notorious Empress Wu, who had usurped the throne, the religion was used as an instrument for political power and as a cloak for personal excesses. The material rewards promised in heaven by the Paradise cults offered no effective antidote to the troubles of the time. But the elaborate and mysterious rituals which the new esoteric sects practiced provided an attraction by giving the worshiper in his daily life many of the sensory pleasures which the Paradise sects had promised him in heaven. As the new cult spread, the Chinese craftsman again looked to India, where he found appropriate models in the sculpture of the time.

Some influence from Gupta India had already affected Chinese sculpture during the late sixth century, and by the end of the next century Buddhist sculpture in China had lost much of its own character in its borrowing from the sensuous carvings of India. Fleshiness increased even more, and drapery was made to cling as if wet against the bodies. The new wave of influence from India brought not only stylistic changes but also the iconography of the esoteric sects which we see in figures with multiple arms and heads, symbolizing various aspects of the deities as described in the new gospels.

The early T'ang style under Indian influence is admirably exemplified by a *Bodhisattva* (Fig. 15–12). The sinuous beauty of this figure has been accented by the hipshot pose and revealing drapery, as in Gupta sculpture. At almost the same time, around 700, carvings in the caves of T'ien-lung Shan anticipated the style of later T'ang. These cave figures might seem gross were it not for the graceful postures and the soft drapery which falls in rhythmic patterns over the plump bodies.

Esoteric Buddhism, with its emphasis on detailed and complicated ritual, placed the deity in a formal relationship to the worshiper. The followers of Amitābha Buddhism, in stressing salvation by faith, had visualized a warm and human Buddha, but by the ninth century the arduous discipline of the esoteric sects had inspired an austere, heavy-set, almost repellent icon. At times fleshiness was exaggerated almost to the point of obesity, and yet sufficient restraint lent the figures a somber dignity.[3]

The westward expansion of the T'ang empire increased the importance of Tun-huang. Here the desert routes converged and the cave temples profited from the growing prosperity of the people. By the eighth century wealthy donors were demanding larger and more elaborately decorated caves. The comparatively simple Buddha group in paintings of the previous century was enlarged to include crowds of attendant figures, lavish architectural settings, and minor deities who worshiped the resplendent Buddha with

[3] Few sculptures survived the terrible persecutions of Buddhism which occurred during a revival of Confucianism in 845. Many wooden temples were destroyed by fire and their bronze images melted down. Fortunately, we are able to reconstruct the style of the period from Buddhist art in Japan, which was then under direct Chinese influence (cf. pp. 573–74).

15–12 BODHISATTVA. Marble. Early T'ang dynasty, 7th–8th centuries. Private collection, New York. (Charles Uht)

music and dance. The opulence of the T'ang was reflected in the detailed richness of these brilliantly colored *Paradise paintings* (Fig. 15–13). Vignettes flanking the Buddha group illustrate incidents from specific *sūtras*. These little scenes, like the *jātaka* tales in earlier caves, are usually set in landscapes painted in an altogether different style from that of the hieratic groups. Mountains stacked one behind the other and painted in graded washes give the impression of distance. Although each mountain is related to the adjacent peak through the device of atmospheric perspective, there is still no spatial continuum.

The persecutions of 845 did not affect Tun-huang, which was then under Tibetan rule. But elsewhere, from the middle of the ninth to the beginning of the eleventh century, the T'ang style of painting remained fairly static. Meanwhile a vital and sophisticated tradition of secular painting had produced the landscape scroll, which is one of China's unique contributions to the world. The early development of these scrolls remains an unsolved mystery, because the silk and paper on which they were painted have not survived. It is difficult to correlate the glowing early accounts of such an art with the fact that similar forms do not appear in other media, such as relief sculpture. Wang Wei, for instance, wrote in the fifth century:

I unroll a picture and examine the inscription, and meditate upon mountains and water which are foreign to me. Verdant forests raise the wind; foaming waters stir the torrent of the streams. Wonderful indeed! [4]

Statements such as this lead to the conclusion that fully developed landscape painting existed as early as the fifth

[4] For this and other excerpts from essays on painting which are quoted below, see Shio Sakanishi, *The Spirit of the Brush*, Murray, London, 1948.

century. Yet as late as 600 in the murals at Tun-huang nature was expressed only in the most rudimentary terms.

Landscape painting, we have learned from history, appears when man begins to question his place within the natural order of the world. Conversely, it is either absent or of little importance when man's thoughts are directed primarily toward the relationship of man to man or of man to God. In China the pantheistic love of nature which the Taoists professed permeated Chinese thought during the fourth century so that conditions favorable to a landscape art existed at this early date.

From the writings of Ku K'ai-chih (*ca.* 344–*ca.* 406), who was an essayist and a painter, and from later paintings believed to be imitations or even copies of Ku's original designs, we learn something about such late fourth-century art. Ku wrote of "tawny rocks, wrinkled with fissures as if torn by the lightning" and of crags which were "fang like and tapering." Painting for him transcended reality, and landscapes, while existing in material substance, soared "into the realm of the spirit." [5] "Human eyes," Wang Wei declared a few decades later, "are limited in their scope. Hence they are not able to perceive all that is to be seen; yet with one small brush I can draw the vast universe."

Two horizontal scrolls, although they are later copies, probably give some clue to Ku K'ai-chih's style. The first, *Admonitions of the Instructress to the Young Ladies of the Palace*, a watercolor on silk, is composed of a sequence of unconnected scenes, each illustrating a different maxim. One of

[5] Chinese critics have always insisted that a painting be more than an image of nature. About 500 A.D. Hsieh Ho formulated his famous "Six Principles" of painting, which have guided Chinese artists ever since. The first principle required that a picture be imbued with its own life.

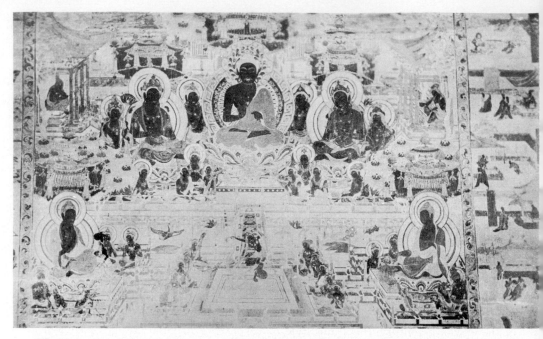

15–13 PARADISE OF AMITĀBHA. T'ang dynasty, 9th century. Cave 139A, Tun-huang. (Courtesy Langdon Warner and J. LeRoy Davidson)

these depicts a well-known act of heroism in which the Lady Feng saved the life of her emperor by placing herself between him and a runaway bear (Fig. 15–14). The figures move in an undefined space and are delicately drawn in slender lines enclosing washes of color. The second painting is a long scroll, *The Nymph of the Lo River* (Freer Gallery), which was done in the eleventh century and is also associated with Ku's style.

Scrolls such as these have a continuous composition and were intended to be viewed slowly in sections of about eighteen inches at a time. As in many early Tun-huang narrative scenes, there is a series of cell-like units bounded by trees or mountains. The different parts — trees, mountains, and figures — have no relationship in scale. Yet, as in all Chinese art, there is a harmony between abstract design and the image of nature which is achieved by the lyric rendering of carefully observed details.

It is questionable, though, whether Ku or any other pre-T'ang artist ever painted the magnificent panoramas which are so eloquently described in writing. More than a century after Ku's lifetime, around 525, even the most advanced landscape we know of still falls short of his descriptions. This landscape, which is engraved on a stone sarcophagus (Nelson Gallery), probably reproduces the design of a painter who was certainly more sophisticated than his contemporaries at Tun-huang. The cell-like structure we have seen in the cave paintings of the same time is still in use, but in addition a sense of distance has been created by diminishing mountain ranges in the background. Nevertheless, the space given to man is so limited by artistic conventions that it is like a stage, and the universe, instead of expanding in the manner lauded by Wang Wei, is constricted as if it were a backdrop.

During the following two centuries

15–14 KU K'AI-CHIH. *Lady Feng and the Bear*. Detail of the "Admonitions of the In-structress." Copy of an original design done in the Six Dynasties, late 4th or early 5th centuries A.D. British Museum, London. (Trustees of the British Museum)

landscape paintings, called by the Chinese "mountain-water pictures" and regarded by them as their supreme artistic achievement, reached full stature. Indeed, Chinese historians regard the T'ang dynasty of the eighth and ninth centuries as their golden age of painting. Glowing accounts by poets and critics and a few remaining examples of the paintings themselves permit us to understand this enthusiasm.

Such an example may be seen in the *Portraits of the Emperors*, which has been attributed to Yen Li-pen, a celebrated painter and statesman of the seventh century. The first six of the portraits are restorations, but the remaining seven are masterfully drawn and in perfect accord with descriptions of the robust T'ang style. Each emperor stands in a space as limitless as in the *Admonitions* scroll, but these figures bulk larger than the slender forms of Ku K'ai-chih's supposed style, and in their greater strength they express the expanding power of Early T'ang. The eminence of the emperors is clearly indicated by their size, which is larger than that of their attendants, and

their personalities are defined by carefully distinguished, individual features. Yen Li-pen's style is also known from many copies of his works and from a series of monumental and spirited stone horses which he designed for the approach to the tomb of the T'ang emperor T'ai-tsung.

The statuary of the *tomb of T'ai-tsung* (reigned 627–649) was a reflection not only of the emperor's interest in fine horses but also of a long tradition. In Han times emperors had sent missions westward to Bactria to procure blooded stock for their stables. The practice of importing horses continued, and Ming Huang, who reigned from 713 to 756, had paintings made of the finest among his 40,000 steeds. The picture of a tethered horse in the collection of Sir Percival and Lady David (Fig. 15–15) fits descriptions of paintings by Han Kan, who was Ming Huang's favorite painter of horses. The fiery stallion evokes the sense of power and authority which was also expressed in Yen Li-pen's *Emperors* scroll, and both pictures have the dynamic "inner vitality" so stressed by Chinese critics.

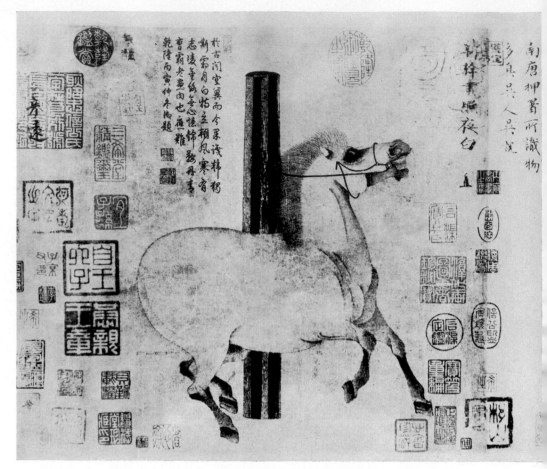

15–15 HAN KAN. *Horse*. T'ang dynasty, 8th century. Collection Sir Percival and Lady David, London. (By courtesy of Sir Percival and Lady David)

Two of the most famous artists of the T'ang period were Wang Wei (699–759), who is not to be confused with Wang Wei of the fifth century, and Wu Tao-tzu (active *ca*. 725–*ca*. 750), both of whom are now almost legendary figures although none of their paintings has survived. Wang was not only a painter; like so many Chinese artists he was also a poet and a critic. His poems are mellow and lyrical, as his paintings are said to have been. Although none of his painting survives, numerous imitations have the peaceful lyricism of his poems. Many of these copies are of snow scenes, a favorite subject of Chinese artists, probably because of its adaptability to monochrome painting, an art of infinite variation and contrast in black and white. Wu's work, according to reports of his time, was very different. He painted with such lightning speed and "ferocious energy" and over such large surfaces that people watched with awe the rapid appearance of vast landscapes and images which seemed frighteningly real. His bold brushwork and expansive forms were frequently copied, and rubbings made from engraved replicas. Later artists looked to Wu's virtuoso brushwork and to Wang's subtle harmonies for their models.

15–16 T'ANG TOMB FIGURINES. 7th–9th centuries. (Left) *Horse*. Fogg Art Museum, Harvard University. (Center) *Peddler*. Portland Art Museum, Portland, Oregon. (Right) *Dancer*. William Rockhill Nelson Gallery of Art, Kansas City, Missouri. (Fogg Art Museum; Portland Art Museum; Nelson Gallery of Art, Atkins Museum of Fine Arts)

Another distinctive style was developed by Li Ssu-hsün and was carried on by his son Li Chao-tao, both of whom flourished in the first half of the eighth century. They were famous for their pictures in the "green (or blue) and gold" style, for which they used delicate lines of gold and flowing pigments made from malachite and lapis lazuli. Their landscapes are described as being filled with mountain formations so fantastic as to suggest a dream world, yet they were actually decorative distillations of the rugged and variegated terrain of the Yangtze valley.

The T'ang rulers also embellished their empire with extravagant wooden structures, all of which have disappeared. Judging from records, however, they were of colossal size and as colorfully painted as Li Ssu-hsün's landscapes. Bronze mirrors with decorations in strong relief added to T'ang luxury and to the furnishings of a court already enriched by elaborate gold and silver ornaments.

The potter met the demand for display by covering his wares with color-ful lead glazes and by inventing robust shapes with clearly articulated parts — base, body, and neck. Earlier potters had imitated bronze models, but the T'ang craftsman derived his directly from the character of clay. Ceramic figures of people, domesticated animals, and fantastic creatures were also made by the thousands for burial in tombs. The extraordinarily delicate grace and flowing rhythms of these figures have a charm and vivacity seldom equaled in ceramic design. Their subject matter, which included such diverse figures as Greek acrobats and Semitic traders, is proof of the cosmopolitanism of T'ang China (Fig. 15–16).

Five Dynasties and Northern Sung

(906–1127)

The last century of T'ang rule witnessed the gradual disintegration of the empire. When in 906 the dynasty

15–17   FAN K'UAN. *Travelers Among Mountains and Stream*. Five Dynasties, 10th century. Palace Museum, Taichung, Taiwan.

Ching Hao, who flourished during the first half of the tenth century, left an essay in which he listed his criteria for judging paintings. Under the classification of "divine" he grouped the greatest paintings. In these, he wrote, "there appears no trace of human effort; hands spontaneously reproduce natural forms." In the lowest category he placed the "skillful" artist who "cuts out and pieces together fragments of beauty and welds them into the pretense of a masterpiece. . . ." "This," he added, "is owing to the poverty of inner reality and to the excess of outward form." Although these ideas were not original with Ching Hao, his restatement of them shows the continuity of thought underlying Chinese painting regardless of changing styles. The artist who painted the truth beneath surface appearances had to be imbued with *ch'i*, the "divine spirit" of the universe. The man who achieved this had done so through years of self-cultivation. Originality in the Western sense was not a necessary virtue; truth, it was believed, could be revealed in old forms. Ching Hao and his equally famous contemporary, Li Ch'êng, did little to alter T'ang formulas, but through the inherent power of their personalities they breathed life into every twig and rock they painted. Succeeding generations went to their works for inspiration — great artists to catch the spirit, lesser painters to copy tricks for drawing trees and hills.

We know enough about the art of the Five Dynasties to be able to distinguish the styles of individual masters, such as Tung Yüan, Chü-jan, and Fan K'uan of the late tenth century. Paintings by these artists and by Kuo Hsi, who lived at the beginning of the following century, express very different personalities and yet exhibit a common feeling for monumentality. A characteristic painting in this style presents vertical landscape of massive moun-

finally fell, China was once more left to the ravages of civil war. Conflicting claims between rival states were not resolved until the country was consolidated under the early Sungs, whose court was at Pien-liang (modern K'ai-fêng in Honan). Strangely enough, during the interim of internal strife known as the Five Dynasties, painting seems to have been unaffected by the turbulence of the times.

tains rising from the middle distance (Fig. 15–17). Human figures, reduced to minute proportions, are dwarfed by overwhelming forms in nature. Numerous roads and bridges penetrate the distant heights, and vanish only to reappear in such a way as to lead the spectator on a continuous journey through the landscape — a journey facilitated by shifting perspective points. No single vanishing point organizes the entire perspective, as in many Western paintings, and as a result the observer's eye moves with freedom, focusing on intricate details and on the character of each line. An ability and a willingness to expend considerable effort to see are necessary if such paintings are to be appreciated fully.

In this period in China the gifted amateur began to displace the professional artist. The amateur's support came either from a government sinecure or from his family, and the full development of the horizontal handscroll may be ascribed to the leisurely atmosphere which consequently surrounded such an artist and his associates. The scroll, which might measure as long as fifty feet, had to be unrolled from right to left; only a small section could be seen at a time and then, properly, by only two or three persons. The organization of these paintings has been compared to the composition of a symphony because of the way in which motifs are repeated and moods are varied in the different sections. The temporal sequence of the scroll involved memory as well as vision. It was an art of contemplation and leisure. Yet to appreciate how it also expressed the vitality of the period we have only to look at Kuo Hsi's views of towering ranges with "peaks like cumulus clouds," and at Mi Fei's mountains looming starkly out of the mist.

Mi Fei (d. 1107) was one of a galaxy of artists who lived about the be-

15–18 MI FEI. *Landscape.* Northern Sung, ca. 1102. Collection, Palace Museum, Tokyo. (Elizabeth Lyons)

ginning of the twelfth century. He was not only a painter but also a brilliant calligrapher and an enthusiastic antiquarian. As a painter he worked in heavy blobs of ink, masses of which defined powerful forms. His landscapes, which curiously combine both impressionistic and architectonic elements, became the link between the strong style of early, or northern, Sung and the more delicate manner of the twelfth and early thirteenth centuries (Fig. 15–18).

Among the versatile figures clustered around the court at this time were Su T'ung-p'o (Su Shih), one of China's greatest poets, a celebrated painter and statesman. Another was Li Lung-mien, who was famous for his original Buddhist compositions and for his outline drawings of horses. The emperor Hui-tsung, an avid collector and patron of artists, was himself an important painter. He is known particularly for his meticulous pictures of birds in which almost every feather was carefully drawn in sharp lines. Lesser artists attached

to the imperial court functioned as a sort of academy and in general followed the detailed and colorful style of the emperor. Lines of poetry to be illustrated in painting often served as examinations for court offices. Fans painted by master artists were treasured in albums. But while the court spent its energy on aesthetic refinements, less cultured neighbors were assaulting the frontiers of China.

Southern Sung

(1127–1279)

In 1127, because of increasing pressure from the Tatars and Mongols in the west and north, the capital of China was moved to the south. From then until 1279 the Southern Sung court lived out its days amid the tranquil beauties of Hangchow. Neo-Confucianism, a blend of traditional Chinese thought and some Buddhist concepts, became the leading philosophy. Accordingly, orthodox Buddhism declined. Buddhist art continued to develop in the north, where a Tatar tribe had established itself as the Liao dynasty, but it stagnated in the south. Buddhist sculpture in the Southern Sung period merely added grace and elegance to the T'ang style. Paintings, however, reflected a new and more intimate relationship between man and nature.

A typical Southern Sung landscape is basically asymmetrical. It is composed on a diagonal and consists of three distinct parts — foreground, middle distance, and far distance — separated from each other by a field of mist. The first is marked by a rock which, by its position in the foreground, gives emphasis to the more distant ones; the middle distance is marked by a flat cliff, and the far distance, by mountain peaks which are usually tinted in pale blue, suggesting the infinity of space. To this basic composition, of which there were many variations, the artist frequently added the figure of a philosopher meditating under a gnarled pine tree and accompanied by an attendant. Such paintings expressed the artists' ideal of peace and pantheistic unity. The manner in which great voids were used to hold solid masses in equilibrium was one of China's unique contributions to the art of painting.

The chief painters in the Southern Sung style were Ma Yüan (*ca.* 1190–1224) and Hsia Kuei (*ca.* 1180–1230). Ma was a master of suggestion, as is demonstrated by a small fan-shaped album leaf — a picture of tranquillity stated in a few sensitively balanced and half-seen shapes (Fig. 15–19). Hsia Kuei's misty landscapes were often so like those of Ma Yüan — though sometimes more delicate and sometimes bolder — that the Chinese refer to them and their followers as the Ma-Hsia school. But the Ma-Hsia tradition, despite its gentle beauty, could not be maintained. It perpetuated an ephemeral, classic moment, but the serenity of its beliefs was soon threatened by political realities.

As orthodox Buddhism lost ground under the Sung, a new school of Buddhism, called Ch'an in China but better known by its Japanese term, Zen, gradually gained importance, until it was second only to Neo-Confucianism. The Zen sect traced its semilegendary origins to Bodhidharma, an Indian missionary of the sixth century. By the time of the Sixth Patriarch, who lived in early T'ang, the pattern of the school was already established, and Zen remains an important religion in Japan today.

The followers of Zen repudiated texts, ritual, and charms as instruments of enlightenment. They believed, instead, that the means of salvation lay within the individual, that meditation was useful, but that direct personal experience with ultimate reality was the

15–20 LIANG K'AI. *The Sixth Patriarch Tearing up a Sutra.* Southern Sung dynasty, 13th century. Ink on paper. National Museum, Tokyo. (National Commission for Protection of Cultural Properties of Japan)

necessary step to enlightenment. Zen enlightenment was conceived as a sudden, almost spontaneous act. These beliefs shaped a new art.

Liang K'ai, a Zen painter of the thirteenth century, has left us two portraits of Hui Neng, the Sixth Patriarch. In one, the patriarch is a crouching figure chopping bamboo; in the other, he is tearing up a Buddhist *sūtra* (Fig. 15–20). Both are informal sketches which look as though they were caricatures of the revered figure. The brush strokes are staccato and splintery. Such paintings correspond to the spontaneous process of Zen enlightenment. They probably were painted in a few minutes, but, like enlightenment, they required years of preliminary training. The full impact reaches the spectator with a shock, much as the shock of Zen understanding.

The spontaneity of Zen painting, with its rapid and economical brushwork, emphasizes the calligraphic quality of Chinese painting. One reason for the importance of calligraphy in China was the vast number of characters (word symbols) which had to be used in writing and the subsequent necessity of being able to distinguish between them. The Chinese had always regarded calligraphy as a major art, and most painters were also fine calligraphers. The quality of Chinese calligraphy depends on the dynamic relationship of each stroke in a character (word symbol), on the relationship of character to character, and on the spacing of all the characters within a given format. In addition, each stroke of the brush must have its own vitality. Up to the time of Zen, skillful brushwork had been regarded as only one of the components of a good painting. The Zen artist, however, found that bold brushwork was paramount for his succinct pictorial statements. His experiments with brush stroke so emphasized its importance that it became, in later periods, the dominating interest of the Chinese painter.

Southern Sung artists also produced superb ceramics with monochrome glazes. The most famous of the single-glaze wares are known as celadon, *Yin-ching*, and *Ting*. The first is a mat gray-green, the second a subtle pale blue, and the last a fine white proto-porcelain. Designs were usually incised or pressed into the clay before glazing (Fig. 15–21). Other experiments produced the heavier *Chün* ware, in which a blue transmutation glaze, splashed with red and purple, flowed over a stoneware body. A quite different kind of pottery is loosely classed as *Tzu-chou*. Some of these ceramics were boldly painted in brown or black against a cream ground. Others were covered with a white slip which was incised or scraped off in such a way as to create a design. The shapes of Sung ceramics were more suave than those of T'ang; some, however, were affected

15–21 SOUTHERN SUNG VASE. Ting technique. 12th–13th centuries. Metropolitan Museum of Art, New York. (Gift of Mrs. Samuel T. Peters, 1926)

15–22 HUANG KUNG-WANG. *Landscape* (detail). Yüan dynasty. 1347. Collection, Palace Museum, Tokyo. (J. LeRoy Davidson)

by a prevailing interest in archeology and imitated the powerful forms of Shang and Chou bronzes. Other crafts, particularly jade carving, were also subjected to the influence of archeological or antiquarian interests.

Yüan

(1279–1368)

The artistic vitality of Southern Sung was not a true reflection of its political weakness, for in 1279 the dynasty crumbled beneath the continued onslaughts of Kublai Khan. Yüan, the dynasty of the invaders, dominated China only until 1368, and yet it profoundly affected the culture of the country and particularly the art of painting. Many of the scholar-painters chose exile in the provinces rather than service to the barbarian usurpers in Peking. Forced by their exile to reappraise their place in the world, the artists no longer looked at a landscape as an idyllic retreat, but as part of a formidable environment. The new austerity is evident in a paint-

ing (Fig. 15–22) by one of the great masters of Yüan, Huang Kung-wang (1269–1354). Here the misty atmosphere of the Sung landscapes has been replaced by clearly articulated forms. The pine which had previously shaded the philosopher has become a symbol of a harsh terrain.

The Yüan painter, unlike his predecessors, and perhaps again because of his need to grapple with reality, was interested in texture. This is clearly evident in a painting of a sheep and a goat (Fig. 15–23) by Chao Meng-fu (1254–1322). The artist's intention obviously was to contrast the woolly texture of one animal with the long coarse hair of the other, and he succeeded admirably. The quality of texture was also developed in the landscapes of such artists as Wang Meng (d. 1385). Most of these painters rejected the mellow harmonies of Southern Sung as being no longer valid in their new situation; for their sources they went back to the more monumental works of the tenth century. But a few, notably Ni Tsan (1301–1374), continued in the tranquil pattern of the previous period. The bare landscapes of Ni Tsan, however, are permeated

15–23 CHAO MENG-FU. A *Sheep and a Goat*. Yüan dynasty, 13th–14th centuries. Ink on paper. Freer Gallery of Art, Washington, D. C. (Courtesy Smithsonian Institution, Freer Gallery of Art)

with a new note of sadness. They contrast with paintings by Wu Chen (1280–1354), who adapted the bold brushwork of the Zen artists to conventional subjects.

Ming and Ch'ing

(1368–1912)

In 1368 a popular uprising drove out the hated Mongol overlords, and from that time until 1644 China was ruled by the native Ming dynasty. Many of the fifteenth-century Ming masters, such as Wu Wei (1459–1508) and Tai Chin (active mid-fifteenth century), reverted to Sung models. Tai Chin, although he followed the style of Hsia Kuei, was also a virtuoso in calligraphic brushwork and an astute observer of river life, which he painted with spirit. But the greatest master of early Ming was Shen Chou (1427–1509), who painted brilliantly in many styles and moods (Fig. 15–24). Some of his paintings are strikingly economical and serene, while others, composed of vibrant darks and lights, are bold and quixotic. Shen Chou's life, as well as his free style, greatly influenced succeeding generations of painters, for he broke with the custom of working at

15–24 SHEN CHOU. *Landscape with Farm Buildings*. Ming dynasty, 15th century. Ink and color on paper. H. *ca*. 12 in. Museum of Fine Arts, Boston. (Courtesy, Museum of Fine Arts, Boston)

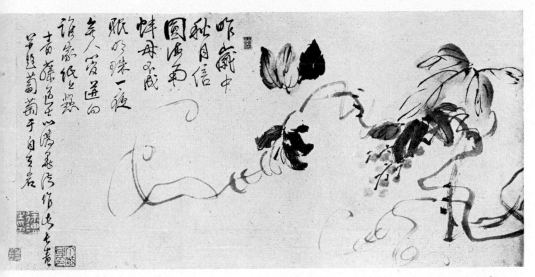

15–25 HSÜ WEI. *Grapevine.* Detail of the "Four Seasons" Scroll. Ming dynasty, 15th–early 16th centuries. National Museum, Stockholm. (National Museum)

the court. As we have noted, the distinction betwen amateur and professional artists became more and more artificial. Too often "amateurs" were appointed to government posts because of their painting abilities rather than for their administrative talents, and they might, therefore, more properly have been identified as artists-in-residence. Shen Chou, who came from a distinguished family of painters and scholars, set a new pattern by completely spurning government support in order to devote himself entirely to painting and literature.

During the sixteenth century increasing corruption in the Ming court drove some of the best minds from court circles. Tung Ch'i-ch'ang (1555–1636) and Mo Shih-lung (active *ca.* 1567–1582), who were among the dissidents, subsequently became the leaders of a group of artists whose standards were those of the "antique style." Actually this group, designated as the "gentleman's" or "ink-flinging" school, experimented in both brushwork and composition; in order to show their disdain for the finicky paintings of the profes-

sionals, they consciously created pictures which, though they appear crude, required great skill. Calligraphic drawing was also developed to such a degree that the subject merged almost imperceptibly with the writing. This blending may be seen in Hsü Wei's bravura painting of a grapevine in which the tendrils seem to be characters and the characters themselves appear to be tendrils (Fig. 15–25). Other Ming artists painted long horizontal scrolls which carry the viewer on a circuitous journey through constantly changing landscapes. This effect — which contrasts with that of the clear spatial organization of Southern Sung and Yüan paintings — was produced by a rapid sequence of different perspectives and an abrupt shifting of distances. The uneasy sensation created by these paintings recalls a totally different art — that of the Mannerists who were then painting in Italy and who were also disregarding established conventions. It is interesting to note that both countries were undergoing social and intellectual readjustments. Many of the extreme experiments of Chinese sixteenth-century art appear to have been perverse, but they helped to establish artistic freedom. The artists who lived into the next dynasty were the beneficiaries.

The internal decay of Ming bureaucracy permitted another group of invaders, the Manchus, to overrun the country. Established as the Ch'ing dynasty (1644–1912), the northerners quickly adapted themselves to Chinese life. The early emperors cultivated a knowledge of China's arts, but their influence seems merely to have encouraged academic work. While the Yüan style of painting continued to be fashionable among the conservatives, other artists carried the calligraphic experiments of Ming to excess, and some, contemptuous of professional skills, painted with their fingers, while eccentrics went so far as to use their noses, or even their beards.

Two artists with intensely personal styles stand out against a mass of lesser painters. Chu Ta (1626–after 1705), a descendant of Ming royalty, assumed the name of Pa-ta Shan-jen and, living as a cultivated recluse, adopted the pattern of life which so many Yüan artists had followed. His sketchy brush and wet ink technique was derived from sixteenth-century forerunners, but his subjects — whimsical animals or petulant birds tensely balanced on an album page — demonstrated his discontent with conventional themes. Chu Ta's great contemporary, Shih-t'ao (1630–1707), was another whose individuality led him in search of the unusual. Although Shih-t'ao (also known as Tao-chi) adapted the standard landscape to his splashy ink style, his more interesting album leaves were devoted to small segments of nature often viewed from an unusual angle. As in some modern photography, the familiar, and thus fragmented, appears unfamiliar.

Some twentieth-century artists, such as Ch'i Pai-shih and Chang Ta-chen, have found the free brush expressive, and the calligraphic tradition still manifests its vitality. Ju Peon, known for his heavily outlined pictures of horses and mules, has imbued his work with social content, in keeping with China's current political developments. The coming decades will reveal whether a popular art is able to assimilate the traditions of aristocratic painting which have dominated Chinese art for over a thousand years.

CERAMICS, TEXTILES, SCULPTURE

In ceramics the technical ingenuity of the Ming and Ch'ing potters exceeded the skill of even the Sungs. In general, porcelain was favored over pottery, with the exception of Ming stonewares, which were broadly decorated in "three-color" enamels. More delicate designs were painted in a "five-color" underglaze on fine clay. The celebrated blue-and-white porcelains owed their quality as much to the distinction of their painted decoration as to the purity of the imported cobalt pigments. Experiments with glazes led to the invention of the superb imperial yellow and oxblood monochromes. Craftsmen also ingeniously devised a "secret," or barely visible decoration which they carved into porcelain as thin as paper.

When the Manchus came into power in 1644, they continued to support the great kilns at Ching Te-chen, where enormous quantities of excellent porcelains were made until the destruction of the kilns during warfare in the middle of the nineteenth century. In the K'ang-hsi period (1662–1722) delicate glazes known as clair de lune (a silvery blue) and peachbloom (pink dappled with green) vied with the polychrome wares. A brief revival of Sung simplicity occurred during the reign of Yung-cheng (1723–1735), but under Ch'ien-lung (1736–1795) a reaction led to a style which was sometimes more elaborate than artistic.

Fine embroidered and woven textiles, created for lavish court ceremonies, followed the general style of the age, becoming more intricate and at the same time more delicate.

During this long period sculpture consisted primarily of charming but inconsequential porcelain bibelots and jade and ivory carvings of an almost unbelievable technical perfection. Huge workshops, much like our own production-line factories, provided masses of materials for imperial use. Specialists, instead of designer-craftsmen, worked on each stage of manufacture. By the middle of the nineteenth century this system had drained all vitality from the crafts.

ARCHITECTURE

Little has been said about Chinese architecture, partly because few early buildings still exist and partly because Chinese architecture over the centuries did not display distinctive changes in style. The modern Chinese building closely resembles its prototype of a thousand years ago. Indeed, the dominating silhouette of the roof which gives Chinese architecture much of its specific character may go back to Chou or Shang times. Even the simple buildings depicted on Han stone carvings reveal a style and a method of construction still basic to China. The essentials consist of a rectangular hall, dominated by a pitched roof with projecting eaves supported by a bracketing system resting on wooden columns. Walls served no bearing function but acted only as screening elements.

Within this limited formula the Chinese architect focused his attention on the superstructure. As early as the Han dynasty combinations of projecting brackets and impost blocks on columns were devised to support the weight of massive tiled roofs. Animation was added to the exterior by varying the shapes of the brackets: some were straight, while others curved in different directions. From these simple beginnings later architects developed very intricate systems of support. Some brackets were placed parallel to the walls, while others reached outward to support a beam or other brackets, until the multiplication of units created a rich pattern of light and shade. The effect was intensified by decorations in red and gold lacquer. Functionalism was often subordinated to ornamental effects; complicated bracket systems were sometimes introduced for interior decoration where only minimal support was required.

On the exterior the coloristic interplay of the supports formed a pleasing contrast to the uninterrupted sweep of the pitched roof. Overhanging eaves became so wide during the T'ang period that builders found it advisable, for aesthetic reasons, to turn up the corners. These slightly curving eaves were exaggerated in later buildings, especially in south China, where they produced a riotous fantasy of upswept lines. But in most areas the gentle curves of the roofs give an air of grace to the otherwise severe rectangular form and rigid symmetry which were imposed by the ground plan and by the order of the architectural complex. For centuries the orientation of buildings, even of whole cities, had been ordered on a strict north-south axis, providing a uniformity related to nature. Houses, palaces, temples, and official buildings all fell within one formal pattern. In addition, structures such as the infinitely varied bridges and pavilions were scattered throughout carefully devised informal gardens.

Buddhist architecture contributed a specific form, the pagoda, which to many has become a symbol of China. These towers, which dot the countryside and seem so native to the land, were derived from the Indian stupa (see p. 517). Most of the wooden pagodas, with their multiplicity of winged eaves, bear little resemblance to the solid domes of Sanchi or Amarāvatī; but their origin, like that of the Chinese Buddha, is to be found in Gandhāra, where terraced and towering variants of the stupa had once impressed Chinese pilgrims with their grandeur. So quickly was the stupa structure assimilated by the Chinese that, even in the earliest pagodas (sixth to eighth century), only a few traces of its Indian source appear. In the Chinese wooden idiom all that remained of the Indian stupa was the *yasti* and parasols which crowned that structure. The circular pattern of the stupa was made angular by the Chinese architects, who designed four-, six-, or eight-sided towers and added story upon story until the pinnacle reached a height of as much as three hundred feet. Each story was marked by its own projecting eaves, the curved lines of which soared into the sky.

Modern Chinese architecture has attempted, as has painting, to combine the components of its own tradition with those of the West, but with little success. Chinese culture, disrupted by the introduction of Western thought and technology during the last century, must once more form a coherent unity before a renaissance of her arts can be expected.

Bibliography

Andersson, Johan G., *Children of the Yellow Earth*, Kegan Paul, Trench, Trubner, London, 1934.

Archives of the Chinese Art Society of America, New York, 1955 ff.

Artibus Asiae (quarterly), Institute of Fine Arts, New York University.

Bulletin of the Museum of Far Eastern Antiquities (Astasiatika Samlingarnen), Stockholm, 1929 ff.

Chavannes, Eduard, *Mission Archéologique dans la Chine septentrionale*, 3 vols., Ernest Leroux, Paris, 1909–15.

Creel, H. G., *The Birth of China*, Jonathan Cape, London, 1936; rev. ed., Ungar, New York, 1954.

Davidson, J. LeRoy, *The Lotus Sutra in Chinese Art*, Yale University Press, 1954.

Fêng, Yu-lan, *A Short History of Chinese Philosophy*, Macmillan, New York, 1948.

Harada, Jiro, *The Pageant of Chinese Painting*, Obukakegeisha, Tokyo, 1936.

Kelley, D. F., and Ch'en Mêng-Chia, *Chinese Bronzes from the Buckingham Collection*, Art Institute of Chicago, 1946.

Kue, Hsi, *An Essay on Landscape Painting*, tr. by S. Sakanishi (Wisdom of the East Series), Murray, London, 1935.

Lee, Sherman, *Chinese Landscape Painting*, Cleveland Museum of Art, 1954.

Lodge, J. E. A., and Pope, J., *A Descriptive and Illustrative Catalogue of Chinese Bronzes* (Oriental Series, No. 3), Freer Gallery of Art, Smithsonian Institution, Washington, D. C., 1946.

Mizune, Seiichi, *Yün-Kang, The Buddhist Cave Temples of the Fifth Century A.D. in North China*, text in Japanese with English summary, Kyoto, 1952; Vols. 1, 3, 4, 7, 8, 9, and 10 published; other vols. in preparation.

Pelliot, Paul, *Les Grottes de Touen-Houang*, 6 vols., portfolio plates, Mission Pelliot en Asie Centrale, Paris, 1914–24.

Priest, Alan, *Chinese Sculpture in the Metropolitan Museum of Art*, New York, 1944.

Rowley, George, *Principles of Chinese Painting*, Princeton University Press, 1947.

Rudolph, Richard, *Han Tomb Art of West China*, University of California Press, Berkeley, 1951.

Sickman, Laurence, and Soper, Alexander, *The Art and Architecture of China*, Penguin Books, Baltimore, 1956.

Sirén, Osvald, *Chinese Sculpture from the Fifth to the Fourteenth Centuries*, 4 vols., Scribner's, 1925.

——, *A History of Early Chinese Painting*, 2 vols., Medici Society, London, 1933.

——, *A History of Later Chinese Painting*, 2 vols., Medici Society, London, 1938.

Soper, Alexander C., *Kuo Jo-Hsü's Experiences in Painting*, American Council of Learned Societies, Washington, D. C., 1951.

Stein, Sir Mark Aurel, *The Thousand Buddhas*, B. Quaritch, London, 1921.

Suzuki, D. T., *An Introduction to Zen Buddhism*, Philosophical Library, New York, 1949.

Tokiwa, Daijo, and Sekino, Tadashi, *Shina Bukkyo Shiseki* (*Buddhist Monuments in China*), text in English; 6 vols., Kenkyu-Kwai, Tokyo, 1926–38; 6 portfolios of plates.

Vincent, Irene V., *The Sacred Oasis*, Chicago University Press, 1953.

Waley, Arthur, *The Way and Its Power*, Allen & Unwin, London, 1934.

Waley, Arthur, *A Catalogue of Paintings Recovered from Tun-huang by Sir Aurel Stein*, Dept. of Prints and Drawings, British Museum, London, 1931.

Warner, Langdon, *Buddhist Wall Paintings . . . at Wan Fo Hsia*, Harvard University Press, 1938.

Willets, William, *Chinese Art*, 2 vols., Penguin Books, Baltimore, 1958.

Yetts, W. Perceval, *The Cull Chinese Bronzes*, Courtauld Institute of Art, University of London, 1939.

CHAPTER 16

JAPANESE

(1ST MILLENNIUM B.C.–19TH CENTURY A.D.)

The arts of Japan have neither the stylistic continuity of the Indian nor the wide variety of the Chinese. A series of foreign influences sporadically affected the course of Japan's artistic evolution. Yet, no matter how overwhelming the impact of new forms and styles, the indigenous tradition invariably reasserted itself. Hence the artistic pattern evolved in a rhythmic sequence of marked periods of borrowing, of absorption, and of return to native patterns.

Japan and its nearby islands are of volcanic origin (Fig. 16–2), so that there is little stone suitable for carving or building. In architecture this lack led to the development of wooden construction, carefully devised to withstand the frequent earthquakes and tempests. In sculpture, figures were either modeled in clay, which was often left unfired, or cast in bronze by the *cire perdue* process, familiar to many other cultures, or constructed of lac-

quer. Although the technique of lacquer probably originated in China, Japanese artists excelled in creating large, hollow lacquer figures by placing hemp cloth soaked in the juice of the lacquer tree over wooden armatures. The surfaces were gradually added to and finished, but the technique remained one of modeling rather than of carving. Such figures were not only light but very durable, being hard and resistant to destructive forces. Hollow lacquer was gradually superseded by carved sculpture done in wood, with unusual sensitivity for grain and texture.

The earliest arts of Japan were produced by a people of an ethnic group different from that of the later Japanese. The first artifacts known in Japan are pottery vessels and figurines from a culture designated as Jomon, which apparently flourished in the first millennium B.C. These objects are associated with Neolithic tools, although they persisted in northern Japan as late as the fourth or fifth century A.D. while a metal culture was being fully developed in the south. The

Jomon arts may have been produced by the Ainus, a people who still survive on Hokkaido, Japan's northernmost island. The Ainus did not paint their pottery, as most Neolithic peoples did. Instead, they carved the clay with geometric and curvilinear patterns, some of which were apparently taken from designs on Chinese bronzes of the Late Chou period. Grotesque figurines with stubby arms, accentuated hips, and goggle-shape eyes are another strikingly original aspect of Jomon pottery which contrasts strangely with later Japanese art.

The development of more typically Japanese forms began about the same time as the advent of the Christian era. Objects from this period fall into three categories: (1) those imported from the Asian mainland, (2) those copying imported articles, and (3) those of Japanese invention. There are, for instance, bronze mirrors from Han China as well as replicas made in Japan. Some of the replicas are adorned with a Japanese innovation — spherical rattles attached to the perimeter of the disk. From Korea, on another wave of continental influence, came a gray pottery known as *yayoi*, which was soon copied, and small comma-shaped stones (*magatama*) used as necklaces. A third area — Indo-China — was the source of motifs used on bell-shaped bronzes known as *dōtaku*. Houses and boats depicted on these bronzes are the same as those on contemporaneous drums of Annam in Indo-China.

Within this heterogeneous culture the Japanese spirit began to assert itself in the production of *haniwa*. These are sculptured tubes made of pottery and placed fencelike around burial mounds, possibly to control erosion and also to act as protectors of the dead. The upper parts of these curious objects are usually modeled in human form, but sometimes they are in the shape of a horse, a bird, or even a

16–2 JAPAN.

house (Fig. 16–3). Simple pottery cylinders were used similarly in Indo-China, but the sculptural modeling of *haniwa* is uniquely Japanese. The form of the tube so conditioned the representation that arms and legs as well as the mass of the torso in most instances recapitulated the cylindrical base of the *haniwa*. The tubelike character of some later monumental sculpture and even of the common wooden dolls may have been derived from these remote ancestors.

16-3 HANIWA FIGURINE. A.D. *ca.* 200. H. 17 in. National Museum, Tokyo. (National Commission for Protection of Cultural Properties of Japan)

Architecture was first limited to pit dwellings and simple constructions of thatched roofs on bamboo stilts, but we learn from *haniwa* models that wooden architecture was fully developed by the fifth century, some buildings containing such features as two stories, saddle roofs, and decorative gables. There may have been monumental constructions of wood, but nothing remains from this early period except for colossal mounds which were the tombs of rulers. The *tumulus of Nintoku,* who, according to legends, reigned from *ca.* 395–427, has an over-

all length of 1600 feet and rises 130 feet from the ground. Three concentric moats protect the mound, which once must also have been surrounded by *haniwa* guardians.

The native traditions which were being established at this time were interrupted in 552 by an event of paramount importance to Japan. In that year the ruler of Kudara (Paikche), a kingdom in Korea, sent a gilt bronze figure of the Buddha to Kimmei, emperor of Japan. With the image came the gospels. For half a century the new religion met with opposition, but at the end of that time Buddhism and its attendant arts were firmly established in Japan. Among the earliest examples of Japanese art serving the cause of Buddhism are a bronze sculpture of Yakushi, the Buddha of medicine, and a triad of Shaka (Śākyamuni); the first was cast in 607, the second in 623 (Fig. 16–4). Both were made by Tori Busshi, a third-generation Korean living in Japan. Tori's style is that of the mid-sixth century in China. His work proves how tenaciously the formula for a "correct" representation of the icon had been maintained since the introduction of Buddhism almost a century earlier. Yet at the same time a new influence was coming from Sui China. This may be seen in the cylindrical form and flowing draperies of the wood sculpture known as the Kudara Kwannon (Chinese: Kuan-yin). The two styles were blended, and in the middle of the seventh century they coalesced in one of Japan's finest sculptures, the *Miroku* (Sanskrit: Maitreya) of the Chūgūji nunnery at Hōryūji (Fig. 16–5). In this figure the Japanese artist combined a gentle sweetness with formal restraint in a manner unknown in Chinese sculpture.

Within a little more than half a century, however, all the archaisms of the fused style (loosely called Suikō after the empress who reigned from 593 to

16–4 TORI BUSSHI. *Shaka Triad* from Hōryūji. Bronze. Asuka period, A.D. 623. H. 5 ft. 9¼ in. (National Commission for Protection of Cultural Properties of Japan)

628, or Asuka after the site of the capital from 552 to 710) were swept aside by a new impact from T'ang China. The T'ang style, which found its way to Japan at the end of the Hakuhō period (673–685), dominated Japanese art during the following periods of Nara (710–784) and Early Heian (784–797). Chinese models were followed not only in sculpture and painting but also in architecture, literature, and even in etiquette.

The mature style of T'ang, as seen in the Lung-men caves, appeared suddenly in Japan in the bronze *shrine of Lady Tachibana* (Fig. 16–6). This consists of three full round figures, the Buddha Amida seated on a lotus between the smaller figures of Kwannon and Dai Sesshi, each standing on a lotus and all three rising from a plat-

16–5 MIROKU. Wood. Asuka period, mid-7th century. H. 5 ft. 2 in. Chūgūji Nunnery, Hōryūji. (National Commission for Protection of Cultural Properties of Japan)

form representing the stylized waters of the Sukhāvatī lake in the Paradise of the Buddha. Behind them is a three-fold screen on which are modeled in low relief the graceful forms of apsaras seated on lotuses and the tiny figures of souls newly born into heaven. The upswept scarves of the apsaras and the petals, tendrils, and pads of the lotuses create an exquisite background for the three divinities, while a detached openwork halo of delicate design frames the head of the Buddha. The ensemble gives some idea of the

16–6 AMIDA TRINITY of the shrine of Lady Tachibana. Bronze. Early 8th century A.D. Hōryūji.

glorious T'ang bronzes which were melted down in China during the Buddhist persecutions of 845. It also demonstrates the remarkable adaptability of the Japanese artist, which permitted him to seize upon a new art form and make it his own.

The development of painting paralelled that of Buddhist sculpture. The earliest surviving example of Japanese painting dates from the first half of the seventh century and is found on the Tamamushi (beetle-wing) shrine.[1] The sides and doors of the wooden

cabinet are decorated with scenes from the *jātakas* in the style of the Tun-huang caves a century earlier, as may be seen in the cell-like composition, the crystalline rock formations, the attenuated figures, and free linear movement. There is also the same delight in surface pattern to the disregard of naturalism in scale and spatial relationships. Quite a different influence from China — the Indian style of the paintings in the cave temples decorated at the end of the seventh century (see p. 552) — affected the artists who, in 710, painted the famed cycle of murals in the Kondō of Hōr-

[1] So called because it once was decorated with the iridescent wings of beetles.

yūji. These, tragically destroyed by fire in 1949, consisted of four major tempera panels, each representing a Buddha group. The style of the Hōryūji murals was so completely Chinese that many experts believe them to have been the work of a Chinese rather than of a Japanese painter. In either case they showed how completely the culture of Japan was influenced by China at this time. The same is true of a portrait of Shōtoku Taishi, the prince-regent who consolidated Buddhism's position in Japan early in the seventh century. Painted about a hundred years after his death, it was closely modeled on the style of Yen Li-pen's *Portraits of the Emperors* (see p. 555), the figures having the same hieratic relationship and the drapery the same treatment of colored washes over line.

Throughout the eighth century, paintings in Japan reflected the rapidity with which Chinese styles were transmitted to Japan. The Japanese even adopted the ideal of plump beauty which had been made fashionable by Yang Kuei-fei, concubine of Ming Huang, a T'ang emperor. We see the new type glorified in several paintings on screens in the Shōsōin and in a picture of *Kichijōten,* goddess of beauty (Fig. 16-7).

The Shōsōin is a storehouse in Nara where the belongings of Emperor Shōmu were placed after his death in 756 and carefully preserved thereafter as a national treasure. Lacquer objects, bronze mirrors, textiles, enameled wares, and musical instruments are only a few of the treasured articles which illustrate the almost total dependence of eighth-century Japan on the arts of China. The wooden building itself, however, is purely Japanese. The form is that of a box 108 feet long which is raised nine feet from the ground by wooden piles. Constructed of triangular logs, it was designed to

16–7 KICHIJŌTEN (GODDESS OF BEAUTY). Painting on hemp cloth. 8th century. H. *ca.* 22 in. Shōsōin, Nara. (National Commission for Protection of Cultural Properties of Japan)

meet changing weather conditions. During the rainy season the wood swells, locking out the damp, while in the dry hot season, it obligingly shrinks to permit circulation of air. Contrasting with the strong horizontal pattern of the logs and the accent of the projecting floor beams is the vertical countermovement of the pilings, the whole a series of repeated motifs which even in this austerely functional building expresses the Japanese love of pattern.

For a more unusual type of Japanese structure we must refer to the shrines of the Shintō religion, the indigenous

16–8 THE SHŌDEN. Ise shrine. Rebuilt in 1953, reproducing 3rd-century type. (The Ise Grand Shrine Bureau, Ise City, Mie-Ken)

faith of the Japanese people.[2] These shrines were customarily destroyed every twenty years and then replaced by exact duplicates, a process which has been repeated since the third century. Thus, we may assume that such a construction as the *Ise shrine*, which was last rebuilt in 1953, reproduces with a great measure of accuracy the original method of building (Fig. 16–8). This, the greatest of all Shintō shrines, covers an area of 55 by 127 yards, enclosed by four concentric fences. The Shōden, the main building, like the Shōsōin, rests on piles and has a thatched roof. Massive columns, once the great trunks of cypress trees, and

[2] The Shintō religion, or "the Way of the Gods," was based on love of nature, of the family, and, above all, of the ruling family, as direct descendents of the gods. Extremely nationalistic in character, Shintō was embodied in symbolic forms and shunned pictorial representation.

planks of the same golden-hued wood were burnished to mellow surfaces, their color and texture contrasting with the white gravel which covers the ground of the sacred precinct. In the characteristic manner of the Japanese artist, the thatched roof was transformed from a simple functional element into one which established the aesthetic of the entire structure. The thatch itself, browned by a smoking process, was sewn into bundles and carefully laid in a decreasing number of layers, the thickness gradually diminishing toward the ridgepole. The entire surface was then sheared smooth, creating a gently changing contour. The roof line was further enhanced by decorative elements which once had been structural, i.e., the *chigi* or crosspiece at the gables and cylindrical wooden weights placed at right angles across the ridgepole. The repeats and echoes of the various parts

16–9 HŌRYŪJI. Near Nara. A.D. 586–607. In the center is the kondo, containing the shrine, and behind it the pagoda. At the right is the entrance, and at the left the preaching hall. (Consulate General of Japan, J.P.M.S.)

of the main building and of the related structures are a quiet study in rhythmic form. The shrine in its setting is an expression of purity and dignity, effectively emphasized by the extreme simplicity of its carefully planned proportions, textures, and architectural forms.

Buddhist architecture, unlike that of Shintō, adhered strictly to Chinese models, so much so that we are able to reconstruct the lost style of T'ang from such temple complexes as those of Hōryūji (Fig. 16–9) and Tōdaiji, which still stand in Japan.

A new style in representation made its way into Japan at the beginning of the ninth century. Under the influence of esoteric Buddhism (p. 551), a heavier image with multiple arms and heads was introduced, which in China was then replacing the earlier classic grace of T'ang figures. The bloated forms of the new style, while repellent, nevertheless have the merit of somber dignity. In paintings these bulky figures, often cut off at the sides, give the effect of a mighty force expanding beyond the pictorial format.

From the middle of the ninth century relations between Japan and China deteriorated so rapidly that by the end of the century almost all intercourse had ceased. No longer able to reflect the fashions of China, the artists of Japan began to create their own forms during the Later Heian or Fujiwara period (898–1185). At this time the court at Heian (Kyoto) was refined to the point of preciosity. A vivid

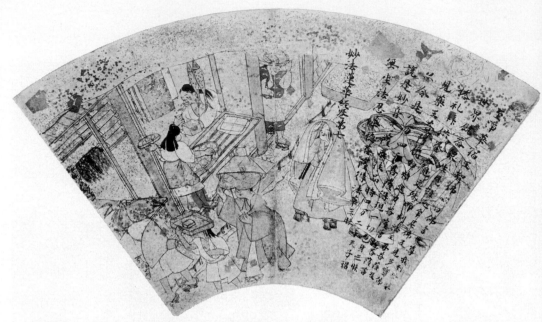

16-10 HOKKE-KYŌ (LOTUS SŪTRA) FAN. On paper, in color. Later Heian period, 10th–12th centuries. W. *ca.* 19 in. Osaka Municipal Art Gallery. (National Commission for Protection of Cultural Properties of Japan)

and detailed picture of the period appears in the eleventh-century novel, *The Tale of Genji,* by Lady Murasaki (which has been beautifully translated by Arthur Waley), a work of superb subtlety. The picture is of a court society in which etiquette overwhelmed morality, a society which considered as a cardinal sin any expression of poor taste in such matters as the selection of color combinations of robes, the choice of paper for the endless writing of love letters, or the quality of the script itself. The very essence of this court is reflected in a series of fan paintings illustrating, with text, the *Hokke-kyō* (the *Lotus Sūtra*) — exquisite pictures which at first glance fail to give the slightest indication of representing one of the world's great religious documents, so luxurious is the decorative display of brilliant hues and ornamental calligraphy (Fig. 16–10). The same may be said of the scrolls of the *Hokke-kyō* in the Itsukushima

shrine, which are flecked with gold and silver and designed in a pattern of rich colors.

Paintings of this type are small in size, rarely more than ten by eighteen inches, and are often mounted in a series, alternating with the text which they illustrate, on a horizontal scroll (*makimono*). At this time the artist seemed to be content with such a series of scenes. Continuous composition in paintings, as in contemporary China, was apparently adopted later, toward the very end of the Fujiwara period.

Takayoshi, a twelfth-century court artist, illustrated *The Tale of Genji* in a set of scrolls consisting of separate scenes painted in the decorative style of the *Hokke-kyō*. In each of these we find the artist employing a distinctly Japanese technique for representing space within the picture plane. The scenes have been viewed as from a high point, the ceilings removed from the interiors, and the ground plane

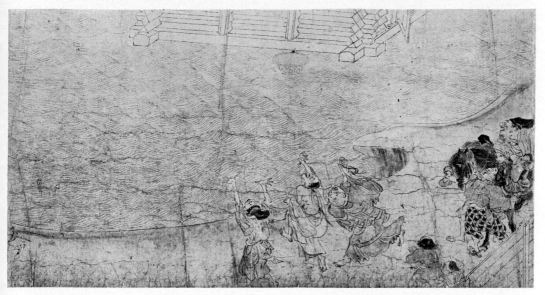

16–11 SHIGISEN ENGI. *Flying Warehouse* (detail). On paper and in color. Three scrolls. Later Heian period, 10th–12th centuries. Chogosonshi-ji, Nara Prefecture. (National Commission for Protection of Cultural Properties of Japan)

sharply tilted to a horizon so high that it often lies above the pictorial boundary. Thus the area of representation was both expanded and abruptly compressed. Flat fields of unshaded color emphasize the two-dimensional character of the paintings, as do accented diagonal lines which direct the eye more along the surface plane than into the picture space. Human figures appear as if they were constructed of stiff layers of contrasting fabrics, and, although they represent specific characters in the novel, their features are scarcely differentiated. The formula for such aristocratic faces consisted of a brush stroke for each eye and eyebrow, one for the nose, another for the mouth. The last was sometimes even omitted. Individuals were thus depersonalized. Paintings in this purely Japanese style, known as Yamato-e,[3] re-

flect the sophisticated mannerisms of the Fujiwara nobility for whom they were created.

A different facet of Yamato-e painting is represented by the *Shigisen Engi*, painted at the end of the period (Fig. 16–11). This is one of the first Japanese scrolls designed as a continuous composition. It illustrates the story of the Flying Warehouse, in which a rich merchant, having forgotten to provide a Buddhist monk with his daily meal, was made to watch his warehouse and goods sail away into the sky. The gaping merchant, his attendants, and several onlookers are shown in various poses, some grimacing, others wildly gesticulating and scurrying about in frantic astonishment. Such display of feelings was considered by the Fujiwara aristocracy to be crude and ill-bred, and was therefore an appropriate subject for humorous caricature. The faces — so unlike the generalized masks in the Genji scrolls — are drawn with each feature exaggerated, thus conforming to a convention of the

[3] The name means "paintings of Yamato," the area around Kyoto and Nara which is regarded as the cradle of Japanese culture. The term is used in painting to signify a native as distinguished from an imported style.

16–12 ANIMAL CARICA-
TURES (detail) from a scroll
attributed to Toba Sōjō. Later Heian period, 10th–12th
centuries. H. *ca.* 12 in.
Kozanji.

period to distinguish the lower classes from the nobility. Cartooning of this kind was to remain an important element in Japanese painting.

From the same period or slightly later are three horizontal scrolls of animal caricatures, painted in monochrome with a free calligraphic brush more typical of Chinese Zen painting than of the refined style of Yamato-e. One of these scrolls, often attributed to the Buddhist Abbot Toba (Toba Sōjō), depicts a medley of frogs, monkeys, and hares in a hilarious burlesque of Buddhist practices. In one section a monkey dressed as a priest is paying homage to a Buddha in the shape of a frog sanctimoniously seated on a lotus throne with a nimbus of luxuriant banana leaves (Fig. 16–12). In another more animated passage, the animals tumble and frolic while washing each other in a river. Throughout this whimsical satire the Japanese predilection for decoration asserts itself in charming clumps of foliage which play a delicate counterpoint to the vigorous movement of the animals.

The more conservative style of Buddhist art continued through the Later Fujiwara period, but paintings of a new subject, known as Raigō, also made their appearance. These represented the Buddha Amida descending through clouds amid a host of Boddhisattvas to assist beings on this earth. Such paintings were products of the Paradise cults (see p. 550) which

eased the rigors of religion for the luxurious courtiers in Kyoto.

Even more than Buddhist painting, Buddhist sculpture maintained its conservative character. The refinement of the period was expressed nevertheless in the application of delicate ornament, frequently of cut gold leaf, and in the creation of forms that were more graceful and slender, if somewhat less vigorous, than those of the preceding period.

A series of civil wars led to the downfall of the decadent Fujiwara rulers, and their successful rivals established a new capital at Kamakura, the city which gave its name to the period from 1185 to about 1392. The new rulers, reacting against what they considered to be the effeminacy of the Fujiwaras, supported an art emphasizing strength and realism. The style of the Nara period was revived by Unkei (died 1223), perhaps the greatest sculptor of Japan, and his school. Unkei and his followers went even further than the earlier realists by carefully reproducing their observations of every accidental variation in the folds of drapery and by using crystal for the eyes of their sculptures. That they were able, nonetheless, to keep a sensitive balance between the spiritual and the realistic is shown by the superb figure of *Basu* (preserved in the Sanjūsangendō). Another example is a portrait of *Kūya*, a sage who is represented as he walked about invoking the name of Amida

Buddha (Fig. 16-13). Not only is every detail meticulously rendered, but the epitome of sculptural realism appears in the six small Buddha images which are issuing from the saint's mouth. These, as in a cartoonist's balloon, represent the words "Amida, Amida, Amida. . . ." Realism was thus carried to the point at which the sculptor attempted to animate his figures by personifying the spoken word.

Painting during the Kamakura period is most interesting for the advances which were made in the Yamato-e style, although all the different types of Fujiwara art were also continued. Perhaps the greatest Yamato-e painting of this time is a *makimono, The Burning of the Sanjō Palace* (Museum of Fine Arts, Boston), one of a series of horizontal scrolls illustrating tales of the Heiji insurrection (*Heiji Monogatari*). In this the artist, using and even perfecting the symphonic composition of the Chinese landscape scroll, has added the element of drama swiftly and violently described in staccato brushwork and vivid flashes of color. At the beginning of the scroll the eye of the observer is caught by a mass of figures rushing toward a blazing building — the crescendo of the painting — then led at a decelerated pace through swarms of soldiers, horses, and bullock carts, and finally, it seems, arrested by a warrior on a rearing horse (Fig. 16-14). But the horse and rider, used as a deceptive cadence, are a prelude to the single figure of an archer which picks up and completes the mass movement of the soldiers and so draws the turbulent narrative to a quiet close.

The power of the Kamakura rulers ceased in 1333, after which internal warfare persisted until 1392, when the Ashikaga shoguns (military dictators) imposed a brief peace. Civil war soon broke out again, though the shoguns managed to maintain control, amid almost continuous insurrections,

16-13 THE SAGE, KŪYA, invoking the name of Amida Buddha. Painted wood. Kamakura period, 13th century. Rokuharamitsuji Temple, Kyoto. (National Commission for Protection of Cultural Properties of Japan)

until 1573. The arts, nevertheless, flourished. New painting styles imported from China coexisted with conventional Buddhist pictures and with paintings in the Yamato-e style carried on by artists of the Tosa family. The monochrome landscape style of the Sung masters Ma Yüan and Hsia Kuei was belatedly adopted by Shūbun at the beginning of the fifteenth century. Chō

16–14 HEIJI MONOGATARI. *The Burning of the Sanjō Palace* (detail). Kamakura period, 12th–14th centuries. Museum of Fine Arts, Boston. (Courtesy, Museum of Fine Arts, Boston)

Densu (1352–1431) and other painters went directly to Yüan models. But the most powerful current to come from China was that which accompanied Zen Buddhism.

It is only through a knowledge of Zen that we are able to understand the efflorescence of art during the troubled Ashikaga period. The new philosophy appealed to the samurai, a caste of professional warriors composed of men who held a relatively high position in society and who were followers of the feudal nobility. They lived by rigid standards which placed high values on such virtues as loyalty, courage, and self-control. The self-reliance required of adherents (see p. 561) made Zen the ideal religion for the samurai.

Because the samurai found Zen attractive, the arts which had been associated in China with this Buddhist sect swept into the country. Sculpture, as in China under Zen, lost importance, and painting widely imitated the bold brush of the Sung masters of Zen. Early in the Ashikaga period the artist Kao worked in the style of Liang K'ai, while his contemporary Mokuan painted almost indistinguishably from his Chinese predecessor, Mu Ch'i. Of all the Zen artists in Japan at this time Sesshū (1420–1506) is the most celebrated. He had several different styles, but is best known for paintings in the Ma-Hsia manner (p. 561). He greatly admired Sung painting and, although he studied in China, he decried the work of contemporary Ming painters. Nevertheless he was affected by the Ming style, for two of his masterpieces, *The Four Seasons* and an ink-splash *landscape* in the National Museum, Tokyo (Fig. 16–15), contain elements basic to the Ming style as well as to the Sung. Although the ink-splash landscape recalls the wet style of Hsia Kuei, the brushwork is more abstract and the tonal contrasts more startling, after the Ming manner.

The Four Seasons, a *makimono* fifty-five feet long, is in a drier, less dramatic style, and yet it is an outstanding example of symphonic composition. A panoramic landscape, it begins with spring, imperceptibly merges into summer, then into autumn, and finally ends with a view of winter. In the three seasons of mildness we see many different figures busy with their everyday lives and moving through a changing background of jagged pines and rocks, soft distant hills, or quiet seascapes. But in the snow-clad winter there are only houses giving a sense of comfortable shelter to the now unseen figures. This scroll may not have the Zen spontaneity so evident in the ink-splash painting, but it reveals the deep understanding and love of natural beauty which the Japanese added to the Zen tradition.

The influence of Zen went considerably beyond painting. It gave rise during the Ashikaga period to the tea ceremony, a unique custom which, among other things, provided a new outlet for the products of the Japanese artist-craftsman. This ceremony soon became a major social institution of the aristocracy. Special teahouses were built in the marvelously mannered gardens of the period. The teahouse itself was small and was designed to give the appearance of refined simplicity. Even its exterior was carefully planned to blend with the calculated casualness of the garden. A flagstone path led past moss-covered stone lanterns to an entrance where the guests, after washing at a "natural" spring, crawled through a low doorway into the room itself. There the host and a group of four guests sat in an atmosphere of almost unadorned simplicity. Scaled to create a feeling of intimacy, the room formed a rectangle broken only by an alcove (*tokonoma*) which held one painting — most appropriately one in the free monochrome style of Zen — and perhaps a stylized flower arrangement. The ritual of tea drinking in this setting imposed on all the participants a set of mannered gestures and even certain topics of conver-

16–15 SESSHŪ. *Landscape*. On paper. ▶ Ashikaga period, 15th century. H. *ca.* 54½ in. National Museum, Tokyo. (National Commission for Protection of Cultural Properties of Japan)

16–16 UJI BRIDGE. Artist unknown. On paper in color. Momoyama period, 16th–17th centuries. National Museum, Kyoto. (National Commission for Protection of Cultural Properties of Japan)

sation. Every effort was made to prevent any jarring note which might shatter a perfectly planned occasion.

Each object employed in the ceremony was selected with utmost discrimination. The connoisseur preferred a tea bowl, a flower container, a lacquer tray, or any other ritual utensil which appeared to have been made without artifice. The same effect was sought in the room itself, which was constructed of unpainted wood. Although the supporting columns were made to keep their natural appearance, and thus remained rounded and knotty as tree trunks, all the surfaces were painstakingly rubbed and burnished to bring out the beauty of grains and textures. Potteries used in the ceremony were covered with heavy glazes seemingly applied in a casual manner, belying the skill which had controlled the colors and textures. Lacquers followed the same aesthetic code, avoiding the mechanical perfection of later examples. To the simplest utensil the artist brought a sense of individuality and impeccable artistry.

The artistic understatement of the tea ceremony was counterbalanced by the continuing Yamato-e style of decorative painting. Tosa Mitsunobu (1434–1525), the foremost exponent of this tradition during the Ashikaga period, retained the coloristic patterns of his native style, but also emphasized ink outline after the fashion of Chinese painting. The new manner of painting resulting from this combination is most apparent in pictures of the Kanō school. Motonobu (1476–1559), who was probably the grandson of the founder of the Kanō school, worked so closely in the Sung tradition that some of his paintings have been mistaken for those of Hsia Kuei (p. 561). He had a more personal style in which we find the new emphasis on brushed outlines and strong tonal contrasts — features which became distinctive of the Kanō school. In addition he often used Tosa coloring and at times even painted in a purely Tosa manner. As a result the Tosa and Kanō schools became less distinguishable after the end of the sixteenth century.

16–17 HASEGAWA TŌHAKU. *Cryptomeria Trees.* Momoyama period, 16th–17th centuries. T. Fukuoka Collection. (National Commission for Protection of Cultural Properties of Japan)

In the Momoyama period (1575–1614), which followed the stormy Ashikaga, a succession of three dictators finally imposed peace on the Japanese people. Huge palaces were erected, partly as symbols of power, partly as fortresses. The grand scale of the period is typified by *Nagoya Castle*, built about 1610. This castle also exemplifies how well the new style of painting suited the tastes of the Momoyama nobility. The sliding doors and large screens within the mammoth structure were covered with gold leaf on which were painted a wide range of romantic and historic subjects, even exotic portrayals of Dutch and Portuguese traders. Traditional Chinese themes were frequent, as were the more commonplace subjects of everyday experience. But all were transformed by an emphasis on two-dimensional design and striking color patterns (Fig. 16–16). The anecdotal or philosophical content of the subject matter was almost completely lost in a grandiose decorative display.

Not every Momoyama artist worked exclusively in the colorful style exemplified by the Nagoya paintings. Hasegawa Tōhaku (1539–1610), for instance, carried on the Zen manner of Mu Ch'i with brilliant success. His versatility, which was shared by most artists of the time, is evident in a screen painting, *Cryptomeria Trees,* whose strong verticals and diagonals are distinctively Japanese (Fig. 16–17).[4]

In 1615 Ieyasu Tokugawa, last of the Momoyama rulers, consolidated his power as shogun of Edo (Tokyo) and established the Tokugawa or Edo rule, which lasted until 1857. Screen painting was continued in all its Momoyama magnificence by such artists as Kanō Sanraku (1561–1635), Kōetsu (1556–1637), and Sōtatsu (d. 1643), whose lives spanned both periods. Kōetsu and Sōtatsu also composed numerous scrolls in which pictorial forms — those of flowers or of animals — were interlaced with strokes of a free-flowing calligraphy.

[4] It should be noted that, although screens were used in many other countries, it was in Japan that their decoration was especially developed and often exhibits the highest quality of painting.

16–18 SHŌHAKU. *The Four Sages of Mount Shang* (detail). Post-Ashikaga idealistic school, 18th century. Museum of Fine Arts, Boston. (Courtesy, Museum of Fine Arts, Boston)

Kōrin (1658–1716) and his brother Kenzan (1663–1743) carried the decorative tradition on into the eighteenth century. The first was primarily a lacquer designer, the second a master potter, but each was also a painter of note, Kōrin famous largely for his dramatic renderings of rocks and waves, Kenzan for the sophisticated economy of his austere compositions. Both artists harmonized the decorative styles of Momoyama and early Edo with the studied simplicity required of art in the service of the tea ceremony.

Meanwhile the older Tosa and Chinese traditions persisted with only a slight diminution in quality. The painter Shōhaku (1730–1783), for example, was able to draw upon both streams of influence, the one providing virtuoso brushwork, the other, wit and decorative pattern (Fig. 16–18). At the same time the varied demands of the feudal lords who still dominated the country gave impetus to the formation of several new movements in painting. One of these was devoted to naturalism and was led by Maruyama Ōkyo (1732–1785), Mori Sosen (1747–1821), and Mori Tessan (1775–1841). Another and more eclectic movement strove to combine the decorative elements of Kōrin's work with the new realism of the naturalists. Prominent among the followers of the latter movement were Itō Jakuchū (1713–1800) and Hōitsu (1761–1828).

The policy of the Tokugawa shoguns was to maintain as static and stratified a society as possible. They attempted, in edict after edict, to prevent any intermingling of classes, and as a result the different classes developed their own distinctive cultures. The center of the new plebeian culture was the Yoshiwara entertainment area of Edo, where the popular idols were the talented courtesans of the tea houses and the actors of the Kabuki theater. Kabuki itself was a popular and lusty form of drama which developed in response to a demand for a more intelligible and more easily enjoyed theater than that of the highly stylized Nō plays. The latter were patronized exclusively by the nobility and a small number of the *nouveau riche*.

During the sixteenth and seventeenth centuries a new form of Japanese art developed, which was to influence

Western art in the nineteenth century. This new art was known as *ukiyo-e,* or "pictures of the floating world." Largely centered in Kyoto, it was first exemplified in paintings of man and his daily activities (genre painting). Later in the seventeenth century the center of production shifted to Edo, and the medium became predominantly that of printmaking, which reflected the tastes and pleasures of the lowest social groups in a feudal society.

That there should have been a print tradition at all, that this tradition should be far grander, more varied, and more sophisticated than any folk art, and that these prints should be acclaimed as one of the most remarkable of art achievements poses a difficult problem. It argues for the homogeneity of Japanese culture, one of the most positive and permanent blessings of the shogunate, and it proves the penetration of the civilization through all the classes. That the sons of firemen, superintendents of tenement houses, and embroiderers should be counted among the great artists of the world is not surprising today, but that these men of little education should have arisen in the feudal age in Japan is only explicable if one admits that artistic sensibility can be quite independent of other aspects of education.[5]

The woodblock as a device for printing had been invented in China during the T'ang dynasty. The technique was introduced into Japan during the eighth century, when it was employed chiefly to reproduce inexpensive religious souvenirs or charms. In the seventeenth century, Chinese woodblock book illustrations inspired the production of low-priced illustrated guidebooks of the Yoshiwara district.

The art of block printing as it ultimately developed in the eighteenth century was a triumph of collaboration. The artist, having been selected and commissioned by a publisher, pre-

[5] Paine, R. T., and Soper, A., *The Art and Architecture of Japan,* p. 139.

pared his design in ink, merely adding color notations. Next a specialist in woodcutting transferred the lines to the blocks. A third man applied the appropriate color to each block and did the printing. The quality of the finished picture depended as much on the often anonymous cutter and printer as on the painter of the original design.

Moronobu (*ca.* 1625–*ca.* 1695) was probably the first to employ everyday subjects for illustrating books in woodblock and also for individual prints. The latter had their origin about 1673. The woodblock quickly evolved as a cheap reproductive medium for wide distribution. Moronobu's woodblocks were simply in black outline against a plain white paper, as were the prints produced for the next fifty years, but often they were hand-colored by their purchasers. Moronobu's designs of large and simple forms had the exuberance of a young art. The same vitality was expressed in prints of the Torii school by such artists as Kiyonobu I (1664–1729), Kiyomasu I (1694–1716), and Kiyotada (active in the early eighteenth century) (Fig. 16–1). These artists specialized in portraying Kabuki actors (Kiyonobu I was the son of an actor). They worked with a broad rhythmic outline and for emphatic pattern used the bold textile designs of the actors' robes.

At about the same time, members of the Kaigetsudō family were painting and making designs for woodblocks of elegant courtesans. Their figures had more grace but somewhat less power than those of the Torii painters. In general the print style gradually acquired more delicacy during the eighteenth century. The invention of a process of printing in color directly from blocks brought the "primitive" period of *ukiyo-e* printmaking to an end about 1741–42.

Masanobu (1691?–1768) had earlier experimented with what is called "lac-

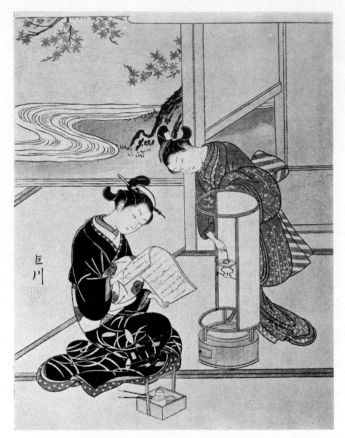

16–19 SUZUKI HARUNOBU. *The Evening Glow of the Ando.* Print. 1765. Art Institute of Chicago. (Art Institute of Chicago)

quer technique" in order to increase the luster of the ink in his black-and-white prints. He later used the new two-color method for printing in pink and green, a style called *benizuri-e*, in which the dominant pink contrasts with patches of pale green and still smaller areas of black to produce a color vibration so strong as to belie entirely the very limited palette. Coincident with the use of color printing the artists began to work in smaller, more delicate scale. In 1765 an improved device for obtaining an accurate register permitted the successful use of even smaller color areas. This led to the development of the *nishiki-e* or "brocade picture" which was a true polychrome print. The new technique encouraged greater refinement and delicacy, characteristics evident in prints by the two leading print masters of the time, the incomparable Harunobu (1725–1770) and Koryūsai (active 1764–1788). In their work we find a new loveliness replacing the monumentality of earlier compositions. The figures are of slighter proportions, the colors more muted, the line lyric rather than dramatic (Fig. 16–19).

After the death of Harunobu, prints changed rapidly in style, shape, subject, and color. Kiyonaga (1752–1815) and Utamaro (1753–1806) revived the taste for tall, willowy figures. Utamaro, who later concentrated on half-length figures, was fortunate in having the services of craftsmen skilled enough in woodcutting to allow him to create extraordinary nuances in color, texture, and line. Bunchō (active 1766–1790), working in another vein, made many

16–20 HOKUSAI. *Fuji Above Storm. ca.* 1823. (From *Japanese Prints in the Collection of Louis V. Ledoux,* Princeton University Press)

striking portraits of well-known figures. Even more dramatic are the prints of Sharaku, who was active for a brief ten months during 1794–1795. Sharaku was a unique and enigmatic figure among print artists. About one hundred and thirty of his prints survive, all of them piercing, rather acid, psychological studies of actors, wrestlers, or managers. Toyokuni I (1769–1825) followed in a similar, less biting manner, but the strength of this style was dissipated in the hands of later artists.

Dozens of other artists contributed to the popular art of printmaking, but during the nineteenth century Hokusai (1760–1849) and Hiroshige (1797–1858) were outstanding. Increasing political and moral censorship, which was to contribute to the decline of this art, led Hokusai to landscape for his *ukiyo-e* subjects. His brilliant and ingenious compositions, such as his *Thirty-Six Views of Mt. Fuji,* always succeeded in avoiding mannerisms which might have congealed his individual style (Fig. 16–20). Nature was his primary subject, but in its setting he also included genre and anecdote as minor themes. Hiroshige, too, specialized in landscape and like Hokusai painted birds, flowers, and legendary scenes. In general, however, his prints did not evoke the sense of grandeur implicit in Hokusai's work.

These prints show the instinctive Japanese attitude toward nature, which regarded natural forms in their utmost simplicity as a point of departure for an interpretation of reality and which resulted in abstract pictorial design.

Another important aspect of Japanese art, deeply rooted in native traditions, is domestic architecture. Modest homes and pretentious mansions employ basically the same structural and aesthetic principles which we have found in the Shintō shrines and in the tea ceremony houses. The Japanese dwelling almost invariably is intimately related to the land around it, and wherever possible it is set in a garden closed off by a handsomely designed bamboo fence, a thing of beauty in itself, securing a sense of privacy and intimacy even in the most crowded environment. Uniformity and harmony of proportions is achieved by using the dimensions of the sleeping mat as a module for the areas of different rooms as well as for their heights.

The construction of the Japanese

16–21 INTERIOR OF A JAPANESE HOUSE. 20th century. (Japan Tourist Association)

house is essentially a series of posts supporting a roof. The walls, which are thus screens rather than supports, either slide open onto the outside or open one room into another. Space is designed with the idea of being continuous and harmoniously divisible: it could be made small or large, enclosed and private or expanded and shared (Fig. 16–21) — concepts which have revolutionized architectural theory in the West. But it is difficult to borrow the tradition of taste and patient craftsmanship which the Japanese express in their choice of woods, proportions of volumes, and scale of garden to building.

Summary

Japanese art has demonstrated, since its early beginnings in prehistoric times, an originality and vitality which has constantly reasserted itself even at times when foreign influences have seemed predominant. Indeed, it is this ability to assimilate ideas and forms, particularly those of China, to reinterpret them in keeping with the traditional tenets arising from Shintoism, which has given Japanese art its insular and national character. An instinct for decorative design and a sensitive understanding of harmonious relations between these designs and nature in both painting and architecture have produced an art of profound significance for the development of European art within the last century. It is even more significant in its own environment, for the people of Japan of all walks of life accept and enjoy artistic expression as an integral part of their daily existence.

Bibliography

Bijutsu Kenkyu (*Journal of Art Studies*) (bimonthly), Institute of Art Research, Tokyo.

Drexler, Arthur, *The Architecture of Japan,* Museum of Modern Art, New York, 1955.

Eliot, Sir Charles, *Japanese Buddhism,* Longmans, Green, New York, 1935.

Ernst, Earle, *The Kabuki Theatre, Japan's Spectacular Drama,* Oxford University Press, New York, 1956.

Henderson, Harold G., and Ledoux, Louis V., *The Surviving Works of Sharaku,* Weyhe, New York, 1939.

Hirano, Chièko, *Kiyonaga,* Harvard University Press, 1939.

Ledoux, Louis V., *Japanese Prints of the Collection of Louis V. Ledoux,* 5 vols., 1942–51; Vols. 1–3, Weyhe, New York; Vols. 4–5, Princeton University Press.

Michener, James A., *The Floating World,* Random House, 1954.

Minamoto, Hoshu, *An Illustrated History of Japanese Art,* tr. by H. G. Henderson, K. Hoshino, Kyoto, 1935.

Murasaki, Shikibu, *Tale of Genji,* tr. by Arthur Waley, 2 vols., Houghton Mifflin, 1935.

Okakura, Kakuzo, *The Book of Tea,* Duffield, New York, 1906.

Pageant of Japanese Art, ed. by staff members of Tokyo National Museum, 6 vols.; Vol. 2, *Painting;* Tōto Bunka and Co., Tokyo, 1952.

Paine, Robert T., and Soper, Alexander, *The Art and Architecture of Japan,* Penguin Books, Baltimore, 1955.

Reischauer, Robert K., *Early Japanese History,* 2 vols., Princeton University Press, 1937.

Sansom, George B., *Japan, A Short Cultural History,* Century, New York, 1931.

Soper, Alexander C., *The Evolution of Buddhist Architecture in Japan,* Princeton University Press, 1942.

Toda, Kenji, *Japanese Scroll Painting,* University of Chicago Press, 1935.

Warner, Langdon, *The Craft of the Japanese Sculptor,* McFarlane, Warde, McFarlane, New York, 1936.

——, *The Enduring Art of Japan,* Harvard University Press, 1952.

——, *Japanese Sculpture of the Suiko Period,* Yale University Press, 1923.

CHAPTER 17

PRE-COLUMBIAN

MAYA, MEXICAN,

AND ANDEAN

(ABOUT 1500 B.C.–A.D. 1492)

While the early cultures of India and China were emerging from the Neo-lithic stage, a parallel process was under way in America. About the close of the last glacial age (*ca.* 25,000 to 10,000 B.C.) there began a series of migrations from Asia by way of the Aleutians (then probably a land passage) and Alaska. The migrants were Mongoloid nomads of the Stone Age, with no knowledge of agriculture but possibly some of basketry. They were big-game hunters, and their only tools were of bone, pressure-flaked stone, and wood. They dressed in hides and skins, had control of fire and probably built rude shelters. Much of the energy of these early men was focused upon prepara-tory hunting rituals and upon those forms of magic which keyed their fac-ulties to the pitch needed for a success-ful kill. Over the centuries the nomads spread out until they occupied the two

ILLUSTRATION ABOVE. **17–1** MAIZE GOD. Limestone figure. *ca.* 6th century A.D. Co-pan, Honduras. (American Museum of Natural History, New York)

American continents. They were few in numbers — the total population of the hemisphere in 1492 probably did not exceed 15 million. By 3000 B.C. some of these nomads had learned to cultivate wild grasses, thus starting the maize culture which was basic to aboriginal America. As agriculturists they became a settled people, and learned to make pottery utensils and lively, realistic fig-urines of clay. They probably also wove textiles. With these skills as a base there arose, over long periods of time, many cultures, of which several reached a high level by the early cen-turies of the Christian era. Throughout some 20,000 years of pre-Columbian civilization, however, the only beast of burden domesticated in South America was the llama; the wheel appeared on-ly on ancient toys in Mexico; and met-als were used for ornament rather than for tools. Ancient American technology remained a Stone Age one.

The main outlines of pre-Columbian chronology in Middle and South Amer-ica, where the major cultures flourished, are fairly clear. Carbon 14 testing (see

	Andes of Peru	Central America	Mexican	North American
EARLY to 1 A.D.	Chavin		Olmec	
MIDDLE 1–800 A.D.	Nasca Mochica	Classic Maya (Central and North)	Teotihuacan Monte Alban (Zapotec)	Adena-Hopewell culture
LATE 800–1300	Tiahuanaco	Toltec Maya	Mixtec Toltec	Mimbres pottery Pueblo III (Mesa Verde, Pueblo Bonito)
TERMINAL 1300–1530	Chimu Inca		Aztec	Pueblo IV
COLONIAL 1530–1800				Sikyatki pottery Awatovi murals
MODERN				Northwest Coast Modern Pueblo pottery Navaho art Eastern woodland of North America

17–2   CHRONOLOGY FOR PRE-COLUMBIAN CIVILIZATIONS.

p. 37, note 1) confirms evidence regarding the following four principal stages, although authorities still debate the exact dating (Fig. 17–2).

Early — from the fourth millennium B.C. to about the beginning of the Christian era. At this time the first great temple groups and pyramidal forms were being built by farmers under the rule of a priestly caste.

Middle — first century A.D. to A.D. 800. This has been called the classic period of American antiquity. The central Maya cities flourished, and the ritual centers of Teotihuacan, near Mexico City, and Monte Alban, to the south in Oaxaca, were built. In South America the potters and weavers of the Peruvian coast were active, as we know from the well-preserved Nasca and Mochica burial finds on the arid coastal deserts of Peru.

Late — about 800 to about 1300. Profound disturbances marked the history of all areas. These troubles arose from protracted soil exhaustion; from the incursions of nomadic tribes, and from civil wars and class struggles. New dynastic states of warrior groups were formed, which sometimes settled on the ruins of the older theocratic cities of the classic age. A growing population gave rise to the first densely inhabited urban centers, such as Mayapan in Yucatan, and Chanchan on the north coast of Peru.

Terminal — 1300 to about 1530. Both in Mexico and Peru, certain nomadic groups emerged as the military and economic masters of vast territories — the Aztecs in Middle America, and the Incas in Peru. These imperial states expanded steadily until their destruction by the Spanish conquest of 1520–1530.

Middle American

Middle America (a geographical term frequently used by archeologists) includes what is now Mexico and Central America (Fig. 17–3). In highland Mexico great reaches of arid plateau land, fertile for maize and wheat wherever water can be secured, lie between heavily forested mountain slopes which, at some places, rise to perpetual snow. The moist tropical jungles of the coastal plains yield rich crops when man can clear the land. The Mexican highland is a volcanic region; in Yucatan a subsoil of limestone furnishes abundant material both for building and for carving. Indians speaking the Maya language still inhabit Yucatan and Guatemala. The Mexican peoples belong to a different linguistic family, and their arts display different traditions. The following discussion will treat first the arts of Maya cultures of Central America and then those of Mexico.

Central Maya

In the early centuries of the Christian era the Maya Indians who occupied the moist lowlands of Guatemala, British Honduras, and Yucatan had already reached a stage of civilization which presupposes a development for many centuries. Although, during the classic period between A.D. 450 and 700, they possessed only tools of stone, bone, and wood, they erected huge structures with richly carved decora-

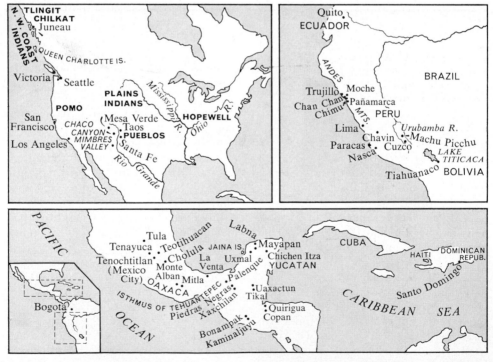

17–3 THE WESTERN HEMISPHERE, showing principal artistic centers of Pre-Columbian, colonial, and modern Indian peoples.

tions at such centers as Copan, Tikal, Uaxactun, Yaxchilan, and Palenque. Then followed a period of resettlement, perhaps because of soil deterioration in the peninsula of Yucatan, during which the cities of the central Maya began to revert to the jungle.

An upper class of priests, astronomer-priests, and nobles constituted a theocratic government which dominated the mass of the people, who were farmers and artisans. Agricultural activities were regulated by religious practices; and the people, scattered over the countryside, visited the ceremonial centers for festivals and markets. Such gods as the sun god, the wind god, the maize god, and the death god personified processes of nature. The intricate Maya calendar expresses the interaction of these numerous gods in astrological combinations for purposes of prophecy and divination. This calendar necessitated a system of writing, only the numerical parts of which have yet been deciphered. Its characters are the central elements in Maya ornament.

Although good quarries of limestone, an abundance of weathered stone for making cement and concrete, and huge forests to furnish timber and firewood for the preparation of lime were everywhere available, all classes of Mayas dwelt by preference in wattled and thatched houses, which were drier and cleaner than stone buildings in the high humidity and tropical vegetation of the region. The so-called Maya palaces were many-chambered buildings of stone, used for state occasions and for civil functions rather than for human habitation.

In a theocratic culture temple building is important. Maya temples, on their pyramidal platforms, were decorated with sky symbols. Between the platforms were east-west sight-lines which marked the solstices and equinoxes of the solar year. At sunrise on

17-4 Section of a North Maya structure with concrete hearting, twin corbeled vaults, flying façade, and roof comb. Chichen Itza. *ca.* 9th century A.D. (After Holmes)

such days, the priestly observer saw the sun emerge at the point fixed by these sight-lines. Such observations, with their calendrical references, helped the priests to govern the agricultural cycle of the farmers; and their symbolic expression forms the main substance of Maya art. Maya pyramid temples may be seen in Figures 17–5 and 17–9. Here the temples stand upon a terraced pyramidal base and are approached by a broad flight of steps. Some, but not all, pyramidal platforms covered burial chambers. For example, at Palenque, the pyramidal platform of the *Temple of Inscriptions* conceals a vaulted stairway descending by three ramps to a richly furnished burial chamber below ground.

In the temples, or elsewhere, when an enclosed space was required in durable stone construction, a type of corbeled vault structure was used. Above the vertical walls the masonry courses projected inward (Fig. 17–4) until they met, framing an interior space whose upper part was triangular in

17–5 UAXACTUN. Guatemala. Reconstruction drawing by T. Proskouriakoff as of A.D. *ca.* 700. (Carnegie Institution of Washington)

section. Rooms so constructed were never more than about fifteen feet wide, but might be of any length. Hence the temples consisted of one or more long, narrow compartments. In some buildings a pierced roof crest or decorative comb rose above the roof.

Uaxactun has a temple group (Fig. 17–5) which was part of a larger assembly of temples and buildings on hilltops, all connected by roadways and covering many square miles. The base of the group consisted of a series of receding terraces, with stairways leading up to the temple court. The massive temple roofs were surmounted by ornate and towering roof combs. Both roofs and combs were polished and painted so that the surface shone brilliantly. The walls inside were probably also painted. In 1947 a three-chambered temple with paintings intact was discovered at *Bonampak* not far from Yaxchilan in the western part of this central Maya area. The paintings are discussed below (p. 601).

Wealth of ornament is characteristic of Maya architecture. At *Copan* or *Tikal* the stone was carved with exuberance and vitality but with a tendency to fill the space to overflowing. This is seen in the stelae, commemorative or calendrical stone shafts, from five to twenty-five feet high, erected in the plazas. Many bear dates, often recording the day of the erection of the stone. Such stelae were carved over a span of time from about the first century A.D. to the seventh or eighth centuries A.D., so that a stylistic sequence can be accurately charted. Most of them are crowded with relief carvings, usually a figure in ceremonial dress surrounded by hieroglyphs and other motifs in lower relief. At Copan the reliefs cover the four sides of the shaft. Sometimes each side is treated as a unit in itself; sometimes the carving is continued from one side of the stele to another. Flowing rather than angular lines characterize Maya art of the central region.

The sculptures in the western river valleys, where large stones were less easily available, are thin, tall slabs, like the *Corn Stele* from Piedras Negras (Fig. 17–6). On this shaft the profile figure of the corn priest kneels with a bag in one hand, to sow the kernels. In the surrounding border a rope motif, decorated with corn leaves, leads the eye from the priest's head down to the enthroned bust of the god below.

The huge boulder at *Quirigua* (Fig. 17–7), which may have been an altar, is entirely covered with intricate carvings in both high and low relief. The most conspicuous part of the design on the north face is a human figure, dressed in rich garments with an enormous elaborate headdress. He is seated in the mouth of a great dragon. Serpent forms often symbolize the sky; such placing of a human figure in the jaws of a reptile is quite common in Maya art and perhaps indicates the supernatural or godlike character of the human represented.

Maya sculpture in the round, or in high relief, is rare. When it occurs it is usually closely associated with architecture, as in the head and torso of the *Maize God* (Fig. 17–1) from Copan in the east central area. This figure, which rested with others upon a cornice, was meant to be seen from below. Note how the inward concentration of an incantation or prayer is conveyed by the parted lips, the closed eyes, the rapt expression. The gesture of the hands, palms out and pointing up and down, evokes the stylized emotion of a dance. The head is a sensitively proportioned oval volume whose contour is clearly defined by the framing hair which sweeps back in repeated curves. The light and shadow afforded by the broad plane of the forehead and the softly modulated features are accentuated by the deeply cut curves of the hair and the countercurves of the lofty headdress.

17–6 CORN STELE from Piedras Negras, with priest above and corn god below. Limestone. A.D. *ca.* 470. H. 13 ft. University Museum, Philadelphia. (University Museum)

17–7 GREAT DRAGON OR TURTLE OF QUIRIGUA. Carved stone monolith. Front view. 6th century A.D. H. 7¼ ft. (Courtesy of the Archaeological Institute of America)

This treatment of the face, the pose of the body, and the vital intensity of the figure are strangely reminiscent of early Buddhist sculpture in China and Japan.

North Maya

The flat, low limestone peninsula of Yucatan lies north of the rolling and densely forested habitat of the central region. During the classic period this northern region had been sparsely inhabited, around such centers as Uxmal and Labna, by Maya-speaking peoples. But after the eighth century, when for unexplained reasons the central region was abandoned, many new temples still were built here. They show strong influence from the highlands of Mexico, 800 miles to the west. This new style, which can be seen at Chichen Itza, is contemporaneous with the political ascendancy of the Toltecs from Tula, northwest of Mexico City, who ruled at Chichen Itza during the twelfth and thirteenth centuries A.D.

Uxmal in Yucatan was a classic city which flourished before 1000 A.D. and was abandoned to the forest at the same time as the central Maya cities. But, unlike the central Maya builders, the architects of the northwestern area experimented with piers and columns in the doorways, and with encrusted decorations of stone mosaic on the outer façades. They also invented a new type of concrete construction: a solid core of coarse material, faced inside and out with a veneer of thin square limestone plates. Inside, the overhanging vaults were faced with specialized stones tenoned far back into the core for great stability. *The Nunnery* (as it has been called by travelers since the nineteenth century, because of its cloistered space) consists of four separate buildings (Fig. 17–8) set about a court, all on a broad platform. Each building is a long rectangular mass. The walls are broken

17–8 UXMAL. *The Nunnery*, East Building. 9th century. (Middle American Research Institute, Tulane University, New Orleans)

mainly by doorways, since windows are very rarely found. Each façade is divided into a lower band broken by several doorways and faced with stone, finely cut and laid, and an upper band of uninterrupted stonework. The design of the upper consists of an inverted triangular shape made up of bars set over against a uniform diaper pattern. A series of masks appears over the main doorway, and at the corners hieroglyphs and masks with projecting hooked noses round off the corners,

breaking their angularity. This same type of decoration is even more intricate in the *Governor's Palace*. Here the rich band of ornament above, whose chief motif is a bold fret pattern, is effectively set off by the fine unbroken stonework below.

At Chichen Itza, the majestic pyramid temple of *El Castillo* (Fig. 17–9) rose above the nearby jungle to dominate the site. Four stairways, oriented to the four cardinal points, lead up from the nine terraces to the tem-

17–9 CHICHEN ITZA. *El Castillo.* Pyramid temple of Kukulcan. 12th or 13th century. H. 105 ft.; the base covers one acre. (Carnegie Institution of Washington)

17–10 CHICHEN ITZA. *Temple of the Warriors.* 12th or 13th century. (Carnegie Institution of Washington)

ple — stairways alarmingly steep to the modern visitor. Their radial symmetry recalls the analogous arrangement of the oldest known Maya pyramidal platform at Uaxactun (built about 1000 years earlier) in the central Maya area.

Near *El Castillo* stands the *Temple of the Warriors* (Fig. 17–10), so named because of the figures of the warriors carved on its piers. The approach to this temple is across a plaza and through a great open hall, whose roof was supported by rectangular piers decorated with life-sized figures of priests and warriors in ceremonial costume, carved in low relief and painted in vivid color. The temple itself rests on a base of four superimposed diminishing platforms, each faced with a carved frieze. A broad stairway with carved stone balustrades rises to the temple. At the entrance are feathered-serpent columns, and immediately before the doorway is a reclining human figure of stone. On the façade are serpent masks with feathers spreading out in relief from heads in the round. All this carving was painted and, with the frescoes on the interior depicting do-

mestic, military, and religious scenes, constituted an elaborate and brilliant decorative entity. The entire arrangement of colonnade, terraced platform, and temple closely recalls similar buildings 800 miles away at Tula, northwest of Mexico City. The structures at Tula were built by the Toltec highlanders, during the same period — the twelfth and thirteenth centuries A.D. — when Toltec warriors were the ruling class of north Maya society.

MAYA PAINTING

The work of the Maya painter, like that of the sculptor, was closely coordinated with building and can hardly be considered separately, for most of the reliefs were colored. The inside of the temple walls was smoothed and given a coat of fine plaster for frescoes. Here the painter first outlined his figure in red, then filled in the areas with flat colors, and finally outlined the figure again in black — a process (reminiscent of the Ajanta frescoes, p. 531) which makes line emphatic and tends to make the design two-dimensional. This method appears both in the cen-

17–11 BONAMPAK. Mural. Maya warriors surrounding captives on a terraced platform. *ca.* 6th century. Carnegie Institution of Washington. Water color copy by Antonio Tejeda. (Photo by Giles G. Healey, courtesy Carnegie Institution of Washington)

tral Maya area, at Bonampak, and again at Chichen Itza in Yucatan, perhaps 500 years later.

In both the Bonampak and Chichen Itza areas Maya painting, in murals and on pottery, gave a factual record of daily life much like that of Egyptian narrative art. The restrictions to flat local color, to linear outlines, and to horizontal registers in the composition also recall the formal properties of Egyptian art, though no historical link of any kind connects the two cultures.

In the temple discovered at *Bonampak* in 1947, narrative murals cover the walls of the three chambers. In each chamber, lower, middle, and upper registers correspond respectively to the people, to priests and nobles, and to

celestial symbols in scenes of rich color and moving narrative. The color was applied in a watery medium on dry plaster. The principal scenes in the three chambers are (1) preparations for a dance, (2) a raid on a town and capture of prisoners, (3) the sacrifice of prisoners (Fig. 17–11), and (4) a dance.

Besides murals, the Maya painters made codices, which like the stelae, recorded both religious and historical events. A codex was a long sheet of fig-bark paper, about six inches wide, which folded in accordion pleats and was protected by wooden covers. Unfortunately only three Maya codices are in existence, because the Spanish friars, in an effort to destroy "pagan-

range of high-key colors. A vase of the classic period, now in Philadelphia (Fig. 17–12), is banded top and bottom by a black and white chevron recalling basketry techniques. Around the cylinder appear attendants, bearers, a dog, and a corpulent personage in a litter, whose fan marks his high social rank. Written forms, still unciphered, occupy the background.

17–12 MAYA CYLINDRICAL VASE of the classic period, showing a litter-borne dignitary. *ca.* 6th century. Painted in brown and red on cream slip. *ca.* 8 in. high. University Museum, Philadelphia. (Rendering by M. L. Baker)

Olmec

The Olmecs, who were quite distinct from the Mayas, were tropical lowlanders who inhabited the east coast of Mexico at its southernmost point. The name Olmec signified "the rubber people"; the area where they lived was an ancient source of rubber for balls, ritual offerings, and garments. The Olmecs convened from their scattered farms at regular intervals for religious observances at such temple centers as *La Venta,* where earthen platforms and stone enclosures mark out two great courtyards. Here, facing out from the plaza, are four colossal heads of basalt, weighing about ten tons each, and standing between 6 feet and 8 feet 5 inches high. The supple modeling, achieved with only stone tools, suggests flesh as well as waterworn boulders.

The worship of a jaguar monster, with the features of a human infant, is suggested by the Olmec's frequent portrayal of this figure in stone, jadeite, and pottery. The figure reappears throughout Mexico in preclassic periods. The Olmec sculptor's predilection for independent full-round sculpture distinguished his work from the Maya, whose architecture governed the emplacement and form of sculpture.

Teotihuacan

Contemporaneous with the period of early classic Maya art, but later than Olmec, was the civilization called Teo-

ism," burned many, as the Ch'in of China burned the Chinese classics. All of the three remaining record the astrological divisions of Maya time, each with its patron deities. The most elaborate codex, now in Dresden, includes calculation tables for the revolutions of certain planets.

The central Maya potter, like all ancient American potters, had no knowledge of the wheel but constructed his pottery by hand shaping, by coiling, or by the use of a mold. Nor did he know of glazing, but obtained a polish and a certain degree of imperviousness by rubbing. The cylindrical vases of the Maya are painted with outlines in black against a yellow or orange ground, with details of red, brown, and white. Low firing temperatures prevented the achievement of a wide

tihuacan, from the name of the great ritual center near Mexico City. The builders of its temples were an agricultural people who attained a distinctive art style during the first centuries of the Christian era. They worshiped many nature gods and made innumerable clay figurines of humans to place in their fields, perhaps to ensure fertility. They also established colonies or daughter-cities, such as *Cholula*, on the Mexican plateau. Other colonies were adjacent to the southern borders of Maya civilization, in the highlands of Guatemala, near Guatemala City, some 800 miles from Teotihuacan. At *Kaminaljuyu* pyramidal edifices identical with those of Teotihuacan have been excavated, but no figurines have been found. The pottery from this site resembles and probably influenced the ceramics of the central Maya early in the classic era.

Teotihuacan ("Place of the Gods") was a great sacred city, carefully laid out in such a way that all its pyramid temples in symmetrical groupings flanked a broad avenue. The largest and most imposing was the *Temple of the Sun*. Though the temple itself is entirely gone, its pyramidal base remains with five tiers and one broad stairway, alternately single and double, leading up from the base to the temple. A smaller temple, the *Citadel*, lay at the center of a great quadrangle marked by terraced mounds. Its sculptured panels are in an excellent state of preservation because they have been covered over by subsequent building. The temple pyramid here consists of six terraces, each decorated with boldly projecting heads of the feathered serpent. These heads alternate with a masklike motif, and the two are connected by the feathered bodies of rattlesnakes and by seashells carved in low relief (Fig. 17–13). Traces of color differentiating the parts of the design still glow under the brilliant sunshine

17–13 TEOTIHUACAN. *Temple of Quetzalcoatl* (The Citadel) (detail). 3rd century A.D.(?).

of this dry valley, more than 8000 feet above sea level.

Zapotec and Mixtec

The Zapotecs and Mixtecs lived west of the Yucatan peninsula, in the province of Oaxaca in Mexico.

The Zapotecs, earlier in date, inhabited the fertile valleys of eastern Oaxaca and the isthmus of Tehuantepec, whereas the Mixtecs originated in the mountainous western part of Oaxaca. The Zapotecs resembled the Etruscans in their concern with great tombs; the Mixtecs may be compared to the early Roman successors of the Etruscans because of their expansive political and military behavior. The peak of Zapotec civilization occurred at the same time as classic Maya culture; then the Mixtec hill people descended into the valleys and conquered the Zapotecs some time before 1000 A.D. The archeology of both groups may be studied at *Monte Alban* ("The White Mountain") and at *Mitla* nearby. Ultimately the en-

17–14 MITLA, Mexico. *Palace of the Columns.* Wall of inner chamber. Fine cut stone laid in clay mortar. Zapotec or Mixtec, *ca.* 8th century (?). (Sheila Hicks)

tire region was conquered by Aztec armies about 1480 A.D.

The Zapotecs were great builders. As among the Mayas, the Zapotec cities were ceremonial centers rather than places of habitation. At Monte Alban the structures stand on terraced platforms grouped around rectangular courts, and broad stairways rise from the plaza floor to the colonnaded temples. At Mitla, the palace is a simple closed quadrangle. Its walls are paneled with a stone mosaic of geometric motifs resembling textile design (Fig. 17–14). These mosaics are composed of triangular stone tesserae at most a few inches in size. The apex of the

triangular stone was left rough so that it would adhere more firmly to the clay in which it was embedded, while the base of the triangle was cut and set so that it projected about one and one-half inches from the background. Each panel of mosaic is framed by finely cut stone moldings.

The Zapotec attitude toward a future life is manifested in innumerable tomb buildings and records of elaborate burial rites. At Monte Alban the tombs were small stone chambers of cruciform plan, with painted walls. Over the doorway was a niche in which rested a funerary urn, and other urns stood in the tomb chambers. A common design for such urns of red-dish clay is in the form of an ornately garbed seated figure with crossed legs. The body itself is the cylindrical jar (Fig. 17–15). Sometimes the face is naturalistic enough to suggest a por-trait; sometimes it is covered by a mask with a long hooked nose. These urns with their plumed headdresses form unusually powerful clay figurines.

The Mixtec successors of the Zapo-tecs, although not great builders, were probably the earliest metallurgists in Middle America. The gold-work-er's craft in the Americas is be-lieved to have originated in the Ande-an region of South America, though how it was transmitted to Middle America is still unknown. The skillful use of gold by Mixtec artists may be seen in a pectoral (Fig. 17–16) which suggests filigree work, but is actually entirely made by the cire-perdue proc-ess. The total design is contained with-in a rectangular shape with rounded corners, and consists of an interplay of rectangular and circular motifs, of straight and curving lines. The head, representing a death god, emerges from the low relief of the base and headdress. The strong, almost natural-istic modeling of the face contrasts with the intricate details of the rest of the pectoral and gives it a fierce, cere-monial power, especially striking in such a small object.

Like the Mayas, the Mixtecs pre-pared genealogical and ritual manu-scripts in pictorial shorthand, drawn in colors on sized deerhide with screen-fold pages. Manuscripts such as the *Codex Zouche-Nuttall* in the British Museum record some twenty genera-tions — perhaps the longest genealogi-cal records in existence. Figure 17–17, a page of the *Codex Zouche-Nuttall,* shows a princely couple on a platform. The place names are indicated in the temple-base mosaic and by the crenel-ations. Men are seated and the women

17–15 FUNERAL VASE OF EFFIGY FORM. From the Zapotec ritual center, Monte Al-ban. Middle period, 5th century A.D.(?). *ca.* 12 in. high. Museo Nacional, Mexico City. (Museum of Modern Art, New York)

kneel. At the sides are aligned the named children of the marriage, and each figure is identified by the birthday calendar sign nearby.

Tomb VII at Monte Alban, discov-ered in 1932, plays the same role in the knowledge of Mixtec art that the tomb of Tut-ankh-amen plays in Egyptian art. It was built by Zapotec masons for a Zapotec burial and reused centuries later by the Mixtecs. There the Mixtecs deposited a wealth of gold and silver armlets and necklaces enriched with pearls and turquoise; gold pectorals; onyx and rock crystal vessels cut by stone tools to unbelievable thinness; carvings in obsidian, jade, jet, and am-ber; and bone intricately carved with historical and mythological scenes.

17–16 GOLD PECTORAL. From Tomb VII, Monte Alban. Mixtec, 14th century A.D. (?). H. 4½ in. Museo Nacional, Mexico City. (Museo Nacional)

Toltec

The name Toltec, which signifies "builder," pertains to a powerful tribe of barbarian invaders from the north, whose arrival in south central Mexico toward the end of the first millennium A.D. followed great disturbances among the older civilizations. The Toltec capital, *Tula,* about 40 miles northwest of Mexico City, flourished from about 900 to after 1200 A.D. The buildings excavated in 1940 at Tula are like the colonnaded *Temple of the Warriors* at Chichen Itza. The detailed resemblances between the sculptures of the two sites reinforces the belief that the builders of Tula were the same as the Toltec masters of the Mayas at Chichen Itza in Yucatan. Unique at Tula, however, and expressive of the harsh character of the Toltecs, are colossal caryatid sculptures of armed warriors, built up of several stone drums to support a temple roof. These figures wear a feather headdress; on their breasts hang geometric butterfly pectorals, and in their hands are throwing sticks which are called *atlatl* in Mexico.

Aztec

The Aztecs were a small and fiercely warlike tribe from the north who set set up their capital in the Valley of Mexico about 1325, at Tenochtitlan (now Mexico City), and became dominant in the region. They were as fierce in their religious as in their military life, practicing human sacrifices. Their

17–17 CODEX ZOUCHE-NUTTALL. *Wedding Scene.* Mixtec genealogical manuscript. 14th century (?). Painted on deerhide. British Museum, London. (Peabody Museum, Harvard University)

religion demanded that, since the gods had sacrificed themselves to create man, man was obliged to repay the gods by supplying them with nourishment — human blood. The ritual required not only a splendid temple setting but magnificent costumes and accessories, which, like much of Aztec culture, continued customs already established by the Toltecs and the Mixtecs.

Pyramid temples continued to be built. The one at *Tenayuca*, frequently rebuilt from Toltec to Aztec times, is a double temple dedicated to the war god and the rain god. A double stairway leads up the pyramid to the two temples, and fringing the base on a narrow platform is a row of massive stone serpents.

It was in the massiveness of their sculpture that the Aztecs excelled. In contrast to the Mayas, who subordinated a sculpture of rich surface to the architectural setting, the Aztecs treated sculpture as independent, full-round form, endowing it with expressive intentions which still move us. A tragic and sensitive head of a dead warrior, carved in coarse volcanic stone, suggests the flaccid muscles and final relaxation of death. The Aztec's intensely religious nature, combined with his theocratic organization, also impelled him toward powerful monumental form. We see an example in statues of *Coatlicue* (Lady of the Skirt of Serpents), mother of the gods and earth goddess, in her double role of creator and destroyer. Possibly the most forceful is Figure 17–18, a ponderous block of stone shaped into rectangular masses, upon which have been carved in both low and high relief the entwined serpents of the skirt, the necklace of hands and hearts with a skull pendant, the claw feet and hands, and the tusked mask — all symbolic of sacrificial death. This Mother of the Gods combines both savagery

17–18   COATLICUE (Lady of the Skirt of Serpents), goddess of earth and death. Aztec, 15th century. Andesite. H. *ca.* 8½ ft. Museo Nacional, Mexico City. (Museo Nacional)

and tenderness, for the Aztecs believed that out of destruction arose a new life — an ideology analogous to that found in the Hindu dancing Śiva (see p. 523).

Another important example of Aztec sculpture is the calendar stone, a broad disk placed before the *Temple of the Sun* in the central plaza of Tenochtitlan. It lay in a horizontal position, probably for sacrificial use connected with the cult of the sun god. In the center is the face of the sun; from it radiate four squares which illustrate four former suns, or epochs, which were destroyed by tigers, wind, a rain of fire, and flood. On either side of the sun god are claws clutching human hearts, symbolic of the belief that the sun god lived on human blood. Around this central group are concentric bands, containing days of the calendar, solar rays, ornaments, and the serpents who carry the sun across the sky and whose heads, at the base, hold human faces in their jaws. Every detail has meaning, all expressed with clarity and in a conventional form of great decorative quality.

Andean

The Andean region in South America lies between Ecuador and northern Chile. It consists of three well-defined geographic zones, running north and south, roughly parallel to one another: (1) a narrow western coastal plain, where a hot desert is crossed by rivers, creating habitable, fertile valleys; (2) the great Cordillera of the Andes, whose high peaks hem in plateaus of a temperate climate; and (3) the eastern slopes of the Andes, a hot, humid jungle. Both on the coast and in the highlands highly developed cultures flourished, the origins of which, as in Middle America, are still obscure.

These cultures, with their arts, succeeded one another in a manner similar to those of Mexico (see Fig. 17–2). They are identified as Chavin in the early period; Mochica and Nasca styles in the middle period; the style of Tiahuanaco in the late period; and the Chimu and Inca civilizations in the terminal period before the Spanish conquest.

Chavin

As in Mexico an early theocratic social organization developed in the first millennium B.C. Its art centered upon a feline monster with human attributes, best known in the carvings of Chavin. At Chavin in the highlands of central Peru, pyramidal platforms surround a sunken plaza. The principal platform is honeycombed with stone-lined passages and rooms. The facing is coursed masonry with sculptured human and feline heads set at intervals. In one gallery was found a ceiling slab (Fig. 17–19) of green diorite carved in shallow relief. Its design is a central standing figure, from which upward radiating lines terminate alternately in spirals and serpent heads. The human figure is in frontal view, short, and angular. Each hand holds a sheaf of staves. The panel above this figure is occupied by masks with decorated protruding tongue and fangs. In each mask or face the eye can be read as belonging both to a profile view and to a frontal view simultaneously, as in the animal forms of Chinese ritual bronzes (cf. Fig. 15–5).

Mochica and Nasca
Early Coastal

The art of Chavin was replaced, during the centuries near the beginning of the Christian era, by two different coastal styles belonging to the Mochica and the Nasca peoples. The Mochica, who lived on the north coast of Peru, were makers of a lively, realistic pottery with strong sculptural feeling. The Nasca, who occupied the south coast valleys, produced ceramics of a more colorful and conventional style and also textiles of a high aesthetic and technical quality.

Coastal architecture consisted of pyramidal platforms of sun-dried brick, of immense size as at *Moche*, on the north coast, and of diminishing magnitude in the south, toward the Nasca valley. Here ancient people laid out long sighting lines on the desert plateaus, presumably to mark the rising and setting points of certain stars on the horizon, as in the Maya temple groupings.

The Mochica people (also called Early Chimu) lived in one of the fertile valleys of the coastal plain. They were agriculturists, but their proximity to the sea made them fishermen also, as the sea motifs on their pottery reveal. They were also hunters and warriors. Their proud chieftains, whose portraits have survived in the pottery, lived in fine houses in large fortified towns. These houses were of adobe, as stone was not available, so that only mounds of ruin remain; many are still to be excavated. The Mochica seem to have been a vigorous, dramatic people, who translated a lively interest in the daily activities of life and in the world of nature into clay vessel forms. As the wheel was unknown, their pottery was either coiled or hand-shaped. Mochica vessels are flat-bottomed, unlike the rounded Nasca forms to the south. A progression from stiff and unarticulated representations of the human form to more and more exact anatomical reporting can be traced during the six centuries of Mochica ceramic production. Exact representations are common. Parrots, owls, ducks, frogs, fish, and crabs, a fruiting branch of a plant, the head of a llama, people singly or in groups pursuing various activities — all this material is adjusted to the walls of a jar. One constant element, almost a mark of Mochica style, is the stirrup handle, the branching tubes of which allow easy pouring. Evaporation of the water, so precious on the arid coast, was reduced by con-

17–19 Ceiling slab of greenish diorite, from principal pyramid at Chavin in the Central Andes. Drawing of incised relief. 1st millennium B.C. H. 6 ft. National Museum of Archaeology, Lima.

17–20 PORTRAIT JAR. Mochica, 5th–6th centuries A.D. Henna and brick reds on cream. H. 11½ in. American Museum of Natural History, New York. (AMNH)

densation inside these tubes and by the small vent.

The highest attainments of the Mochica sculptor-potters were the portrait jars (Fig. 17–20), which depicted chieftains or nobles. Like the central Maya potters, the Mochica craftsmen were unable to achieve a wide range of colors because of low firing temperatures. But recently discovered Mochica murals at Panamarca show monumental designs in many colors, from which the pottery paintings, like those of Maya vases, are derivatives.

The Nasca of the south coast reveal in their pottery a very different habit of mind from the Mochica. In Nasca pottery a globular shape is common, vented by a double spout and bridge handle. Flat, linear designs are achieved with highly conventionalized motifs of plant, animal, and sea life, gods, and demons, which follow the curving surfaces. A wide range of color was used: white, yellow, black, violet, blue-gray, and intermediate tones on a ground of white, red, or black.

Many textiles, found in graves and preserved by the dry climate, show that the south coast weavers were among the world's greatest. Cotton was used for the warp, and the wool of the llama and vicuña for the weft and for embroidery. The textiles were not *objets d'art,* but articles of everyday use — pouches, girdles, mantles, tunics. Since the backstrap looms were of the simplest construction, the weavers depended largely upon skilled fingers to produce a great variety of weaves — tapestry, pile, gauze — and minute embroidery. About 180 hues of red, brown, blue, and green were used with the greatest subtlety of relationship and variation.

Embroidery in wool on a cotton base characterizes the textile found at *Paracas,* an arid burial ground near the Nasca area. In chromatic range these textiles are outstanding. A characteristic one has a light border surrounded by a dark ground; the figure on the ground is equally spaced in even rows and carries the border colors into the dark ground. This motif, which is often based on a human figure, never exactly repeats, but each time shows unique variations in color and tone.

Tiahuanaco

The bleak highland country around Lake Titicaca in southeastern Peru contrasts with the warm valleys of the coast. Isolated in these mountains another culture named for *Tiahuanaco,* the principal archeological site, developed independently of the coastal cultures until about 1000 A.D., when the style spread to the coastal as well as to

17–21 TIAHUANACO. Monolithic gateway. 9th century (?). (Chicago Natural History Museum and Archive of Hispanic Culture, Library of Congress)

the highland areas from northern Peru to Chile. At Tiahuanaco on Lake Titicaca an imposing architectural center was built of the fine stones of the region: sandstone, andesite, and diorite.

The gateway at Tiahuanaco (Fig. 17–21) is monolithic, with a doorway cut through and a sculptured frieze across the top. Above the doorway, in the center of the frieze, is the image called Viracocha, the sky god, a short, squat figure standing on a terraced step

facing directly forward and holding staffs in both hands. From his angular face project rays terminating in circles and puma heads. The form recalls the ceiling slab (Fig. 17–19) in the frontal aspect and symmetrical staffs as well as in the geometrical conventions used for human and animal representations. This figure is in high relief and stands out prominently against the low-relief border of rows of condors and winged men with weapons, running toward the

Chimu

The north coast of Peru is dotted with many large ruined cities which were built during the Chimu period from about 1000 to 1400. *Chanchan* is the largest: not less than 60,000 people lived there in walled districts, each containing several hundred dwellings with public gardens and artisans' workshops. The Chimu cities had a feudal and dynastic social organization and each was under the lordship of one family, some of whose descendants still farm the fields surrounding the nearby modern city of Trujillo.

At Chanchan the sun-dried brick walls of the courtyards were decorated in carved clay, with patterns of geometric shapes of fishes, birds, and men, which recall textile designs. Pottery, textiles, and metalwork of Chimu manufacture all show derivation from Mochica prototypes, but are inferior technically. The building of vast cities with their immense irrigation works may account for the poor quality of the Chimu arts, for urban life and its technological problems probably absorbed most of the people's energies. Yet metalwork in gold and silver was abundant, and there is good reason to believe that much of the great metallic treasure of the Inca conquerors in the fifteenth century A.D. came from these north-coast centers.

17–22 TEXTILE, probably section of a large shirt. Coast of Peru. Tiahuanaco style, 11th century. Museum of Primitive Art, New York. (Courtesy, Museum of Primitive Art)

center. A border of frets interspersed with masklike heads gives the design unity. Each of the running figures with his weapons forms a square panel, as in a textile, and the movement within the square contributes action to what would otherwise be a static design.

Characteristic of the middle period of Andean textile history are tapestries, of extraordinarily fine weave, in which the chief motif is a figure repeated at equal intervals but infinitely varied in its details, as in the arrangement of the light and dark strips forming the body. The fine slits not only help to define the color areas clearly but also give the fabric a vibrant texture (Fig. 17–22).

Inca

The Incas were a small highland tribe who set up their rule in the valley of Cuzco, with the city of *Cuzco* as their capital, and who gradually extended their power until, in the fifteenth century, it stretched from Quito in Ecuador to Chile. Their religion centered upon the powers of nature, primarily the sun, whose temple in Cuzco, the *Coricancha* (Court of Gold), was

17–23 PONCHO, from an island in Lake Titicaca. Cotton and vicuña wool. Inca, 15th–16th centuries. H. 39 in. Red, green, black, buff, and violet with silver tinsel yarn in the border figures. American Museum of Natural History, New York. (AMNH)

the most splendid building of the Inca empire.

From its beginnings about the fourteenth century, the authoritarian Inca state sought to adjust the subsistence needs of a vast population to an environment of limited resources by holding the people's wants to a minimum. Thus the crafts tended towards the utilitarian in stereotyped productions of monotonous likeness. Only occasional works for the nobles display inventiveness and individuality. Figure 17–23 reproduces a poncho worked in squares, each filled with a geometric motif probably heraldic in meaning, which, by variations in color value and a stress upon diagonal line, vivifies an otherwise monotonous checkerboard design. The same simplicity, bordering on geometry, permeates the goldwork

and silverwork which, according to the chroniclers, was produced in unbelievable quantities — ornaments and utensils of all kinds and sizes, as well as images such as the *Alpaca* (Fig. 17–24). In this figure smooth *repoussé* surfaces of the head and feet contrast with the vertical ridges of the metal, which suggest heavy wool and accent the long neck.

The Incas were supreme masters of shaping and fitting stone. As a militant, conquering people, they selected sites fortified by nature, and strengthened them further by various defensive structures; as a religious people, they built temples, especially to the sun god, whose cult constituted the state religion; for their kings they erected palaces befitting their status.

Machu Picchu (Fig. 17–25) is an In-

17–24 ALPACA. Of sheet silver modeled in *repoussé*. Inca, 15th century. H. 9 in. American Museum of Natural History, New York. (AMNH)

ca city built to protect the highlanders from the attacks of lowland tribes from the Amazonian jungles. The city perches on a ridge between two jagged peaks high above the canyon of the Urubamba River in the heart of the Andes, some fifty miles north of Cuzco. The city is so ingeniously adapted to

the site that it seems a part of the mountains themselves.

Cuzco still preserves the somber walls of Inca temples and palaces. Some walls curve, like the sickle-shaped construction (Fig. 17–26) built as part of the Inca *Temple of the Sun* and used by the Spaniards as the base for the apse of the Dominican church. The close joints of Inca masonry were achieved by abrasion alone. Each stone was swung in slings against its neighbors until the surfaces were ground to a precise fit. This method was also used in the Khmer monuments (Angkor Wat) of Cambodia.

The decoration of this impressive architecture was of gold and silver, applied rather than sculptured. Gold was symbolic of the sun god. His temple in Cuzco was, according to the chronicles, covered on the interior with sheets of gold beaten thin and encrusted with emeralds.

Summary

Until 1492 the American continents remained isolated and unknown to Europe, but their peoples arrived inde-

17–25 MACHU PICCHU. Inca, early 16th century. (National Geographic Society-Yale University Peruvian Expedition. Copyright National Geographic Society)

pendently at many of the inventions of Neolithic and early urban civilizations of Europe and the Near East. The Olmec people of southeastern Mexico and the builders of Chavin in the central Andes are the earliest of these American innovators.

The Maya Indians, like early agricultural peoples the world over, lived under theocratic rule. In the service of ritual and agriculture, they evolved one of the most accurate of calendars and a system of writing. Their cities were chiefly ecclesiastical centers and, though the Mayas built some secular buildings, their principal concern was the erection of temples raised on lofty pyramidal bases and decorated in reliefs and color to serve as stages for an elaborate ritual. Wealth of ornament appears in the commemorative stelae and boulders, highly conventional in style, dominated by curving lines and intricate movement. In northern Yucatan, under Mexican domination, the Maya peoples continued to build groups of pyramidal temple-platforms, with concrete hearting and mosaic veneer or mural decorations. In southern Mexico the Zapotecs built stone "palaces" and tombs with stone mosaic decoration; they were masters of clay sculpture. Their Mixtec successors produced jewelry of great elegance and technical skill.

Another Middle American center of civilization was Teotihuacan, in the Valley of Mexico. Here also was an agricultural people whose life was dominated by pyramid temples, but these were less luxuriantly adorned than the Maya. When Teotihuacan fell in ruins, for reasons still unknown, the Toltec people rose to dominance at Tula, northwest of Mexico City. This warrior state, much like the Mixtec dynasties in southern Mexico, was finally replaced by the militant Aztec tribe, who like the Romans, appropriated aspects of the many civilizations they

17–26 TEMPLE OF THE SUN (now church of Santo Domingo). Cuzco. 15th century. (A. Guillen)

conquered. Like the Toltecs, the Aztecs were master stonecutters and built massive pyramid temples. They also produced magnificent free-standing stone sculpture.

In South America, during the first ten centuries of the Christian era, three civilizations were dominant in the Andean region.

The Mochica of the northern coastal valleys modeled stirrup-handled pottery jars of great vitality in the form of highly realistic representations of the life around them: animals, birds, human figures, and groups, perhaps the finest being the expressive, individualized portrait heads of warriors.

The Nasca in the coastal valleys to the south produced less realistic, more geometric and decorative designs on pottery, which was often globular, with twin spouts joined by a handle. The colorful painted motifs are stylized, fanciful representations of plant, animal, and human forms. Nasca textiles, though produced by primitive means, were supreme in the finesse of the weaving and in the rich, imaginative coloring of the embroidered designs.

The highland people of Tiahuanaco are notable for the austere monumental grandeur of their stone sculpture and architecture. After A.D. 1000 their forms fell into disuse, and about 1300, when the Tiahuanaco style vanished, the coastal peoples re-established their own political and artistic forms.

A long period of confused local history (when the Chimu dynasty of the north coast was ascendant) ended in the Andean area with the rise to imperial power of the Inca tribe in the southern highlands. The Incas were masters in stonework, in erecting fortifications, temples, and palaces with magnificently cut masonry, ablaze on the interior with gold and jewels. They were also expert gold- and silversmiths and weavers. Both the Inca and Aztec empires succumbed in the sixteenth century to the invading Spaniards.

Bibliography

GENERAL READINGS

Keleman, Pál, Medieval American Art, 2 vols., Macmillan, New York, 1943.

Lothrop, S. K., Foshag, W. E., Mahler, J., Pre-Columbian Art (Robert Woods Bliss Collection), Phaidon Publishers, New York, 1957.

MIDDLE AMERICAN

Covarrubias, Miguel, The Eagle, the Jaguar, and the Serpent: Indian Art of the Americas, Knopf, 1954.

——, Mexico South, Knopf, 1946.

Holmes, William H., Archaeological Studies Among the Ancient Cities of Mexico, Field Columbian Museum, Chicago, 1895–97; issued in parts.

Kidder, Alfred V., Jennings, Jesse A., and Shook, Edwin M., Excavations at Kaminaljuyu, Guatemala, Carnegie Institution, Washington, D. C., 1946.

Kubler, George, The Arensberg Collection, Philadelphia Museum of Art, Philadelphia, 1954.

Landa, Diego de, "Relación de las cosas de Yucatan," tr. by A. M. Tozzer, Peabody Museum Papers, Vol. 18, 1941.

Linné, Sigvald, Archaeological Researches at Teotihuacan, Mexico, Oxford University Press, New York, 1934.

——, Mexican Highland Cultures, Statens Etnografiska Museum, Stockholm, 1942.

——, The Technique of South American Ceramics, Elanders Boktryckeri Aktiebolag, Göteborg, 1925.

Marquina, Ignacio, Arquitectura prehispánica, Instituto Nacional de Antropología e Historia, Mexico City, 1951.

The Maya and Their Neighbors, Appleton-Century, 1940.

Morley, Sylvanus G., The Ancient Maya, Stanford University Press, 1946.

Médioni, Gilbert, and Pinto, Marie-Thérèse, Art in Ancient Mexico, Oxford University Press, New York, 1941.

Morris, Earl H., The Temple of the Warriors, Carnegie Institution, Washington, D. C., 1931.

Porter, Muriel N., Tlatilco and the Pre-Classic Cultures of the New World, Viking Fund Publication 19, New York, 1953.

Proskouriakoff, Tatiana A., An Album of Maya Architecture, Carnegie Institution, Washington, D. C., 1947.

——, A Study of Classic Maya Sculpture, Carnegie Institution, Washington, D. C., 1950.

Roys, Lawrence, "The Engineering Knowledge of the Maya," Contributions to American Archaeology, Vol. 2, No. 6, 1934.

Sahagún, Bernardino de, General History of Things of New Spain, Florentine Codex, tr. by A. J. O. Anderson and C. E. Dibble, New Mexico School of American Research, Santa Fe, 1950.

Spinden, Herbert J., A Study of Maya Art, Peabody Museum, Cambridge, Mass., 1913.

Thompson, John E., Maya Hieroglyphic Writing: Introduction, Carnegie Institution, Washington, D. C., 1950.

——, The Rise and Fall of Maya Civilization, University of Oklahoma Press, Norman, 1954.

Toscano, Salvador, Arte precolombino de México y de la América Central, Instituto de Investigaciónes Estéticas, Universidad Nacional Autónoma de Mexico, Mexico City, 1944.

Twenty Centuries of Mexican Art, Museum of Modern Art, New York, 1940.

Vaillant, George C., *Aztecs of Mexico,* Doubleday, Doran, 1941.

ANDEAN

Bennett, Wendell E., *Ancient Arts of the Andes,* Museum of Modern Art, New York, 1954.

——, and Bird, Junius B., *Andean Culture History,* American Museum of Natural History, New York, 1949.

Lehmann, Walter, and Doering, Heinrich, *The Art of Old Peru,* Benn, London, 1924.

Posnansky, Arthur, *Tihuanacu, the Cradle of American Man,* tr. by James F. Shearer, 3 vols., J. J. Augustin, New York, 1945.

Stafford, Cora E., *Paracas Embroideries,* J. J. Augustin, New York, 1941.

Wassermann, B. J., *Cerámicas del antiguo Perú de la Colección Wassermann-San Blas,* J. Peuser, Lda., Buenos Aires, 1938.

CHAPTER 18

NORTH AMERICAN INDIAN

(A.D. ABOUT 100–1900)

The art of the North American Indians may be studied in two distinct groupings: that of the tribes (Pueblo, Adena-Hopewell) which developed before the coming of the white man, and that of the tribes whose art benefited or was transformed by European contributions (Northwest Coast, Plains Indians, and Navaho).

Pueblo

Of the many tribes inhabiting the great area north of the Rio Grande, the Pueblo[1] people were the most highly developed in a cultural sense. The region in which they lived — around the Four Corners, where Colorado, Utah, New Mexico, and Arizona meet — is a semiarid plateau, cut by canyons and buttes, an austere land of brilliant color

[1] Their Spanish name, meaning "village."

ILLUSTRATION ABOVE. **18–1** HOPEWELL HAWK EFFIGY PIPE. Tremper Mound, Ohio. L. 3½ in. A.D. *ca.* 500. Ohio State Museum, Columbus. (Courtesy, Ohio Historical Society, Columbus, Ohio)

and tremendous spaces. The ancestors of the people were nomadic hunters and seed-gatherers, who are known as the "Basket-Makers" because of their skill in this craft. The introduction of maize, probably from Middle America, and later of beans and squash (possibly about A.D. 500) led them to a more settled, agricultural life, to the building of permanent houses, and to the making of pottery and textiles. The classic age of the Pueblo peoples occurred about A.D. 1050–1300. Each village lived a self-contained communal life — profoundly religious but not theocratic. Like their contemporaries in Mexico and Central and South America (at Teotihuacan, Monte Alban, among the central Mayas, and in the Andean area), the Pueblos worshiped the powers of nature, especially those related to rain and fertility — winds, clouds, and rainbow — with elaborate ceremonial. All the daily activities of life — religious, social, and creative — combined in a happy unity. The planting of corn, for example, was a religious ceremony; and prayers for rain were expressed

18–2 CLIFF PALACE. Mesa Verde National Park, Colorado. A.D. *ca.* 1100. (National Park Service)

not only in chants but also in dances as well as in the decorative themes of textiles and ceramics.

ARCHITECTURE AND PAINTING

Unlike the Middle and South American peoples, the Pueblos built no great religious centers and no temples. The men and boys gathered in an underground room, the kiva, for ceremonies which did not involve dancing. All other ritual took place in the open, with elaborate costumes, chants, and dances. Pueblo architecture in New Mexico and Arizona consists of terraced houses of many stories, of which a modern example is the pueblo of *Taos* in New Mexico. The ancient entrances to such dwellings were holes in the roofs, with ladders descending into the interiors.

Adobe, timber, and local sandstone were the building materials. The stonework is remarkable, considering that it was dressed by stone axes and moved without the aid of draft animals.

In the canyons of New Mexico and Utah, rimmed by mesas, many groups lived in the caverns in the cliffs. These shelflike spaces provided areas large enough for entire villages, accessible only by a system of ladders which could be withdrawn in times of war. Such villages are preserved in Colorado at Mesa Verde National Park (which takes its name, "Green Tableland," from its unusually thick covering of piñon). The largest of these villages, the *Cliff Palace* (Fig. 18–2), built *ca.* 1100, occupies a sheltered ledge high above the valley floor. It has about two hundred rooms, superimposed in several stories, built of skillfully laid

18–3 WALL PAINTING FROM A KIVA. Awatovi, Arizona. 1300–1700. Detail from a continuous decorative band. 7 × 11 ft. Replica. Peabody Museum, Harvard University. (Museum of Modern Art, New York)

stone or of adobe and timber. These chambers constitute a communal tribal dwelling. Along the outer edge of the cavern floor are twenty circular kivas, the ritual chambers.

Not all Pueblo houses were built in cliff caverns. Many villages rose in the river valleys, as in the Chaco Canyon (New Mexico) with its eighteen or more major, and innumerable minor, villages. Along these river bottoms the villagers farmed with the help of irrigation. *Pueblo Bonito,* in Chaco Canyon (*ca.* 1100 A.D.), one of the largest and wealthiest of these villages, consisted of nearly a thousand rooms built on a semicircular plan about a court, terraced back from one story in front to five at the back, where it abutted the canyon wall. In the court were twenty large kivas. These kivas, together with those of *Chetro Ketl* ("Rain Village"), are among the most notable achievements of the Pueblo masons. This masonry was made either of smooth blocks of local sandstone, irregular in size and widely spaced with chips filling the interstices, or of square-cut blocks nearly uniform in size and more closely set. At the corners, where large stones and smaller ones often alternate, the deco-

rative and textural effects are particularly rich.

In later Pueblo history (Period IV – 1300–1530) the interior walls of the kivas were sometimes painted, as excavations have shown, in a highly conventional, if at times naturalistic, style. Figure 18–3 is a part of a continuous band circling the walls of a kiva at *Awatovi.* In representing deities and offerings it shows the color and the flat, yet lively, pattern sense which have distinguished Pueblo pottery designs from the sixteenth century to the present. This angular art of line and of light and dark color on a flat surface suggests the influence of textile design. Some of the costume details are almost identical with those worn by these people in ceremonies today. The costumes with their ornaments are in marked contrast to the plain and barren architecture – a contrast persisting even today in Pueblo villages.

BASKETRY AND POTTERY

Early in their history the Pueblos became expert in making finely coiled baskets for household and burial use, decorated with designs of zigzag, terrace, and other geometric motifs in red and black. The design of this red and black basketry (*ca.* 800), whose angular decoration is not always suited to its curving surfaces, suggests a textile prototype, as do the murals at *Awatovi*.

By the classic (Pueblo III) period these geometric motifs were adapted to the pottery forms, and the highest technical excellence was reached. The practice of ceramic art was confined to women, who made all pottery by the coiling method, for the potter's wheel was unknown in the Southwest. A variant of this Pueblo pottery occurred in the Mimbres valley of southwestern New Mexico (A.D. 900–1200). Although most *Mimbres bowls* are decorated with purely geometric abstractions, others have zoomorphic designs which are exceptional in the art of prehistoric North America. Such designs are treated so individually by the potter that each differs entirely from all others excavated (Fig. 18–4). Each design is created by fundamental linear rhythms, and every aspect of the pattern has significance. The balance and control thus achieved promote tensions inside the figured area, creating extraordinary relationships within a clearly defined frame.

A later development, in the sixteenth and seventeenth centuries, was

18–4 MIMBRES BOWL. Black on white. D. *ca.* 9 in. 13th century. Peabody Museum, Harvard University. (Peabody Museum)

Sikyatki ware (Fig. 18–5), which became a prototype for styles perfected in different pueblos and surviving even today in the pottery of Ácoma Pueblo and of the Zuñi Indians. These more recent wares consist chiefly of large bowls with a broad flattened shoulder, and shallow bowls of a yellow or orange clay decorated with geometric designs or highly conventionalized red and black birds and animals. Such decorations reveal once more the predilection for angularity in design native to the Southwestern area.

18–5 HOPI JAR. Sikyatki ware. Red and black on yellow. D. 13 in. H. 7 in. 16th century. National Museum, Washington. (Bureau of Ethnology, Smithsonian Institution)

Adena-Hopewell

Of other Indians north of the Rio Grande, we should mention at least two closely connected Eastern Woodland groups, the Hopewell and the Adena.[2] Both centered in southern Ohio, though the Hopewell art forms spread to West Virginia and Wisconsin. Archeology has established general dates for these arts, about A.D. 100 for the Adena and about A.D. 500 for the Hopewell. There is little doubt, how-

[2] These groups derive their names from the sites near Chillicothe, Ohio, where their remains were first discovered and properly identified.

18–6 THE ADENA PIPE. A.D. *ca.* 100–500. H. 8 in. Ohio State Museum, Columbus. (Courtesy, Ohio Historical Society, Columbus, Ohio)

ever, that the classic periods of both overlapped and that the *Adena pipe* (Fig. 18–6) may be contemporary with most Hopewell material.

The most imposing architectural expressions of the Hopewell group were great mounds and earthworks. Some of these mounds served for burial. The core was a filled-in charnel house, which was repeatedly enlarged until the mound achieved the dimensions we see today, as in the Seip Mound, Ross County, Ohio. These mounds, sometimes in complex groupings, varied in height from a few feet to upwards of seventy feet. The "effigy" mounds represent animal forms, of which the huge *Great Serpent Mound* (Adams County, Ohio) is the best known, its serpentine bends measuring approximately 1400 feet from end to end. Some mounds of the Hopewell group, in addition to social or religious functions, probably served as defenses for the neighboring villages, as at Fort Ancient, which is, however, of contemporary Adena style.

The copper ornaments and stone effigy pipes found in these mounds are especially noteworthy. Copper, secured from the Lake Superior region, was hammered, cut, engraved, or embossed by the *repoussé* method into two-dimensional ornaments with geometric and conventional human, bird, and animal motifs. Mica sheets were cut into human hand patterns whose purpose is at present unknown. The Hopewell people were, above all, sculptors of effigy pipes, representing birds and animals, which they carved from Ohio pipestone with flint tools (Fig. 18–1).

The Adena people, on the other hand, produced no animal pipes, and their works are usually less pleasing than Hopewell art. Yet the most subtly modeled specimen of sculpture from southern Ohio is actually of Adena workmanship. This is the Adena human effigy pipe (Fig. 18–6), eight inches high, probably representing a deified member of the tribe. The ear spools and facial features of this pipe betray an influence from Middle America (see Fig. 17–15). Hopewell carved shell gorgets and stone disks also reveal in their designs a similarity to perforated shell ornaments from the Vera Cruz region of Mexico.

Several American Indian groups profited culturally by the coming of the Europeans. As the white man penetrated into Indian territories at the end of the eighteenth century, he brought with him many techniques and materials which enriched the native arts. The groups chiefly affected were the Indians of the Northwest Coast, the Plains, and the Navaho tribes.

Northwest Coast

The Indians of the coasts of British Columbia and southeastern Alaska were a fishing and hunting people who lived on an irregular rocky coast from which heavily timbered mountains rose abruptly. Shell, bone, horn, and skins were abundant. They were skillful hunters who traded furs for the steel axes of the Europeans. With these they felled the enormous native cedars to make their houses, furniture, and canoes, thus becoming the best woodworkers in America. The wealth of the tribes allowed a leisurely cultivation of ceremonial and heraldic art. The finest examples of Northwest Coast Indian art were generally executed between 1840 and 1890, though carvings of good quality were produced up to 1910. Since then these crafts have deteriorated beyond recall.

The forms of Northwest Coast art were determined by religious and social patterns of behavior. The designs were taken directly from nature — beaver and seal, hawk and eagle, killer whale and shark, bear, wolf, frog, snail, raven, and dragonfly. It was a highly stylized art, of which an American anthropologist, Franz Boas, has written the most illuminating interpretation:

The fundamental idea underlying the thoughts, feelings, and activities of these tribes is the value of rank which gives title to the use of privileges, most of which find expression in artistic activities or in the use of art forms. Rank and social position bestow the privilege of using certain animal figures as paintings or carvings on the house front, on totem poles, on masks and on the utensils of everyday life. Rank and social position give the right to tell certain tales referring to ancestral exploits; they determine the songs which may be sung. There are other obligations and privileges related to rank and social position, but the most outstanding feature is the intimate association between social standing and art forms. A similar relation, although not so intimate, prevails in the relation of religious activities and manifestations of art. It is as though the heraldic idea had taken hold of the whole life and had permeated it with the feeling that social standing must be expressed at every step by heraldry which, however, is not confined to space forms alone but extends over literary, musical, and dramatic expression.[3]

The Haida Indians of the Queen Charlotte Islands were famous for their canoes, carved or painted with the heraldic devices of the owner. From the abundant timber they also built sturdy wooden houses of planks as much as sixty feet long. In front of them they set up single poles, eighty feet high, carved with totems, heraldic designs (derived usually from animals or birds) which were the mark and prerogative of the family or clan, often illustrating a story from the rich mythology of the Northwest Coast (Fig. 18–7). The totem pole, as we know it today, was a nineteenth-century form, based upon earlier and cruder proto-

[3] Franz Boas, *Primitive Art*, H. Aschehoug, Oslo, 1927 (Capitol Publishing Co., N. Y., 1951), p. 280, by permission of the publishers.

18–7 HAIDA TOTEM POLES at Masset, Queen Charlotte Islands, British Columbia. (American Museum of Natural History, New York)

types which have now rotted away. The cylindrical mass and the rounding surface of the pole were never lost in the carving. Only enough was cut away to define the totems, conventionally colored, large in scale, and imposing in their simplified forms. Other totems, adapted to flat design, were painted on the front wall of the house, or on interior partitions, as in Fig. 18–9.

The woodcarver also made masks, worn by actors in ceremonial dances, which often were dramatic presentations of legends. An integral part of the ceremony, the masks had a magical function. The masks were sometimes of humans, more often of birds or of animals or legendary monsters. They were frequently very large and were made of several parts. Thus among the Kwakiutl tribe the masks could be manipulated with strings to achieve strange effects, such as opening the mouth of one monster to disclose another monster hidden within.

In making objects for household use, the Indians considered not only the purpose of the object and the available material but also the rank of the owner. As pottery was unknown, wood was the chief material. From single pieces they carved their killing clubs, grease and food trays, bowls, spoons, and ladles. Large utensils were for ceremonial use, small ones for everyday. Since fat was important in the diet, the grease dish for fish and seal oil was more elaborate than other dishes, often heavily carved, painted, and inlaid with pieces of abalone shell. Spoons and ladles had horn handles or were made entirely of the horn of the mountain goat. The horn was softened by boiling and was then shaped in a mold before being carved with totemic designs. Among the sparse household furnishings boxes and chests played an important part. Even in large chests the four sides were made of one plank, steamed until pliant and then bent to form the corners. These boxes and

18–8 TLINGIT INDIAN. Carved and painted wooden chest. L. 33 in. American Museum of Natural History, New York. (AMNH)

chests were carved and painted in red, black, and, less often, blue (Fig. 18–8).

The carvings, whether on wooden dishes, spoon handles, boxes, or totem poles, show a unity of style, a common attitude toward the forms of nature. For it was not the animal's appearance from which the artist drew his material, but his knowledge of its essential parts, each of which he reduced to a conventional unit and combined according to the space to be filled. Each unit recorded a characteristic aspect, disregarding a consistent point of view in the combination of front view, profile, and bird's-eye views. So stylized were these parts that cedar stencils were made for each unit, allowing a great variety of groupings, depending on the shape and size of the space to be filled. Often an animal was bilaterally split, and his limbs, sometimes stylized beyond recognition, were flattened to fit the picture plane (see Figs. 18–8 and 18–9). This treatment of the figure also appears in Chinese bronzes (Fig. 15–5).

So conventional a style could be used interchangeably in various mediums. Thus the woven blankets are similar in style to the carvings and to the paintings on skins. The *Chilkat blankets* (Tlingit tribe) of mountain goat's wool and cedar bark were woven in designs with totemic significance. Figure 18–10 has the bear design, woven in yellow, white, blue, and black. The central panel contains the front view of the face and various parts of the body; the side panels contain the stylized profile view. These blankets, together with those woven by the Navahos, are the finest aboriginal North American textiles. They were used only on ceremonial occasions and were worn about the shoulders over a tunic woven with a similar pattern. The accompanying leggings were painted and decorated with bits of bone or ivory which clinked with the movements of

18–9 TLINGIT INDIAN. Carved and painted wooden screen representing a bear. H. *ca.* 15 ft. Denver Art Museum. (Taylor Museum)

the dance; and there was an elaborate headdress (called the *amalaid*) of abalone shell and ermine — a costume of elegance and taste, worthy of the dignity of the family or the clan. These blankets were woven by the women on primitive looms according to designs drawn on boards by the men.

The Tlingit baskets, exclusively the work of women, were woven from grasses and fern stems for various household purposes, for berrying in particular. The weave was fine and tight enough for use in drinking cups. The baskets were decorated by varying the weave or by the introduction of colored weft, or by wrapping colored grasses around the weft strand on the outside. Many baskets, especially those used for berrying, are cylindrical, with the decoration concentrated in zones.

The Plains

The Plains Indians, numbering more than thirty tribes, occupied the Great Plains and Rocky Mountain regions. Before the arrival of the Europeans they were seminomadic peoples, small farmers and short-range hunters, dependent chiefly upon the buffalo for food, clothing, and coverings, and using only the dog for a draft animal. Their life moved in narrow bounds. However, the introduction of the horse by Coronado in the sixteenth century changed the whole pattern of their life. They became wide-ranging hunters and, with the rise of competition among the tribes, fierce warriors, raiding afar to hunt the great buffalo herds. They proclaimed their wealth and economic status by the numbers of their horses and by the splendor of their costumes and trappings. In the new, wholly nomadic life, they could use only durable and portable articles. Even the houses, tipis of skins, were easily portable. With the exception of weapons and peace pipes, or calumets, decorated with hair, beads, and feathers, Plains Indian art was therefore restricted to the embellishment of everyday objects. On their clothing they lavished their decorative skill and craftsmanship so that they evolved a costume which was not only adapted to the climate but also so expressive of their daring spirit that it has become associated throughout the world with the American Indian. Buffalo, deer, elk, and various smaller animal skins, such as beaver, were ornamented with fringes, porcupine quills, beads, and painting, and the costume was crowned by an elaborate headdress of feathers which fell from the head to the feet.

18–10 CHILKAT BLANKET with bear design. Of wild goat's wool and cedar bark. Light yellow, turquoise blue, white, and black. Such blankets were used as ceremonial cloaks. Chicago Natural History Museum. (American Museum of Natural History, New York)

Quillwork was a peculiarly North American craft, found among other tribes as well as among the Plains Indians. It was an embroidery on buckskin with dyed and flattened porcupine quills, whose designs are angular and geometric because of the nature of the medium. For the same reason the rare motifs which are based on natural forms were equally angular and abstract.

In the second half of the nineteenth century beadwork, using glass and porcelain beads introduced from Europe, replaced quillwork. Before the white man, shells, stones, and seeds had been used in embroidered decoration. The new material, however, provided both color and flexibility of design, and, while the patterns continued to be chiefly angular and geometric, some floral motifs appeared with curved flowing lines, probably under the influence of the French, with whom the Plains Indians traded in the Mississippi valley.

Painting was used to decorate not only clothing but also tipis, shield covers, and buffalo skins, commemorating some fight or hunt by pictorial representations of warlike acts and running horses. A design on a *Kiowa shield cover* (Fig. 18–11), depicting a bear about to be shot, juxtaposes light with dark areas and geometric with naturalistic shapes to produce a striking effect. This art of line and flat color, full of life and vitality in the fighting and hunting scenes, contrasts with the abstract quality of the nonrepresentational designs. These two distinct kinds of painting reflect a sex differentiation in the practice of the craft. The men produced the representational scenes on the shields and hides. The women made the nonrepresentational or geometric designs on clothing, bags, and containers.

18–11 KIOWA painted shield cover. Oklahoma. D. 20 in. National Museum, Washington, D. C. (National Museum)

Navaho

Another Indian tribe whose art owed its flowering to the presence of the white man was the Navaho. The Navaho entered the Pueblo area from the northwest about seven hundred years ago, and as raiding nomads they harassed the Pueblos. The art of the Navaho was negligible until the Spaniards introduced them to domestic animals, tools, plants, and somewhat later, silver. The sheep and the horse became essential to their economy: the sheep both for food and wool, the horse for mobility, enabling them to range more widely for pasturage in their semiarid plateau land. The Spanish introduction of many plants led some Navahos to become farmers, but the majority remained pastoral, roaming widely with their sheep in summer, and staying close to their hogans in the cold months. They had no villages. In this environment they developed three arts: weaving, silverwork, and ceremonial sand painting.

Rudiments of the weaving craft were learned by the Navaho from the Pueblo Indians with whom they came into close contact during the Indian Rebellion of 1680. Weaving was done by women only and could be carried on under the conditions of semi-nomadic life. A loom of logs could be set up in the open, often attached to a supporting pole of the summer tent. The blankets and rugs woven upon this loom were of tapestry weave, thick and strong, with boldly geometric patterns (Fig. 18–12). Until approximately 1860 the blankets were designed in stripes, and the colors were usually the natural black, white, and gray of the wool. Later the introduction of bayeta, an English flannel cloth, which the Navahos unraveled to secure its threads, enriched their color schemes. The art reached its best moments about 1880.

Silver, introduced from Mexico about 1850, was used in bracelets, buttons, necklaces, and bridles, enriched with contrasting turquoise and coral. The finest pieces were hand-hammered or cast; the turquoises were hand-cut and

18–12 NAVAHO BLANKET (detail). Museum of the American Indian, Heye Foundation, New York. (Museum of the American Indian, Heye Foundation)

polished to a dull finish; and the designs were as boldly simple as those of the blankets.

In Navaho ceremonial rites, notably in sand painting, we find a unique aboriginal art. The rudiments of sand painting may have been learned from the Pueblos, but in the hands of the Navaho the art reached a lofty expression in which ancient religious significance and high aesthetic value mingled. Sand painting was one phase of a curative ceremony which included chanting, dancing, and costuming. Some of the more elaborate rites, such as the Mountain Chant or the Night Chant, lasted as long as nine days. The sand paintings, also called dry paintings, were made by the medicine man and his assistants on the floor of a hogan especially constructed for the purpose. Colored sands — white, red, yellow, black, and blue — were secured by grinding stones from nearby cliffs. With exquisite dexterity the "painter" made the designs freehand from memory, squatting on the ground and dropping the colored sand with his thumb and forefinger upon a smoothed surface of ordinary sand. He followed

strict rules in the composition as well as in the single figures, with individual variations permissible only in small details. The designs were abstract and highly symbolic, signifying gods and spirits, the rainbow, mountains, plants, and animals. After the painting had served its function in the ceremonial, it was destroyed with the same traditional precision. By these ceremonials the Navahos (who lacked a written language) kept alive their legends and beliefs, preserved the rich mythology and poetry of the tribe, and provided a focus for the social life of a semi-nomadic people.

Eastern North America

During the nineteenth century the old Indian preserves in the eastern United States were engulfed by the white settlers, and those tribes who had not moved west were confined to small reservations. In their New York State reservations the Iroquois gave an increased emphasis to the curative ritual. Carved masks with facial distortions were used in this ritual for emo-

18-13 SENECA INDIAN. False face society mask. American Museum of Natural History, New York. (AMNH)

tional effect. The finest masks, dating from only 1890 or 1900, were made by the Seneca tribe of the Iroquois Confederation (Fig. 18-13). To the north and across Canada other tribes, such as the Cree, the Penobscot, and the Micmac, turned to embroidering clothing with elaborate designs which often show the influence of French floral motifs. The Cree became particularly adept at making small birchbark boxes painted with these designs. In the comparative isolation of Nova Scotia the Micmac Indians developed a highly original and decorative design system using a repeated double-C curve. They applied this design to jackets, trousers, and even to canoe paddles. The resili-ency of these tribes is shown in the high craft standards they were able to preserve against white encroachment until after 1900.

Summary

A distinction must be made among the Indian groups north of the Rio Grande. The early Pueblo and Adena-Hopewell tribes developed their arts independently of the white man, whereas the other groups show influences of European cultures in varying degrees. The Pueblos built great communal domestic structures. They reached a high level of skill in pottery and weaving. The Hopewell peoples built imposing mounds for religious and defensive purposes. They were skilled designers of copper ornaments and carved stone pipes based on birds and human and animal forms. This sculpture approached naturalism within the conventional limit of the function of the object.

The white man brought new plants, animals, and tools which enabled several of the Indian tribes of North America to expand their crafts. The Northwest Coast fishermen, living with an abundance of fine timber, already possessed tools of stone and some fashioned from free metallic copper. With the acquisition of steel tools they produced an extraordinary art of wood-carving: canoes, totem poles, and objects for everyday and ceremonial life. This conventional art was abstract and decorative. The Plains Indians, with the advent of the horse, became wide-ranging hunters and warriors who developed an art of costume, elaborated with feathers, porcupine quills, and bead embroidery. On shields, tipis, and buffalo skins they portrayed their vigorous way of life in paintings of hunts and fights. The nomadic Navaho, with the introduction of sheep, horses, and crop plants, became pastoral sheep-raisers who brought woolen weaving to a high level. The importation of silver from Mexico enabled them to make jewelry, either using the silver alone or combining it with turquoise or coral. The Navaho welcomed innovations, such as sand painting as part of a curing ceremony, at the same time retaining intact their traditional ways of thinking and living. In the latter part of the nineteenth century various Indian tribes in eastern United States and Canada maintained their artistic integrity against the pressures of the white man's civilization. The masks carved by the Seneca tribe of the Iroquois Nation were the most original manifestation of this flowering of American Indian art in the East.

Bibliography

Adair, John, *The Navaho and Pueblo Silversmiths*, University of Oklahoma Press, Norman, 1944.

Amsden, Charles A., *Navaho Weaving*, Fine Arts Press, Santa Ana, Calif., 1934.

Armer, Laura A., *Sandpainting of the Navaho Indians*, Exposition of Indian Tribal Arts, New York, 1931.

Barbeau, Marius, *Haida Myths Illustrated in Argillite Carvings*, National Museum of Canada Bulletin 127, Anthropological Series 32, 1953.

——, *Totem Poles*, National Museum of Canada Bulletin 119, No. 1, 1950.

Boas, Franz, *Primitive Art*, H. Aschehoug, Oslo, 1927. (New editions, Capitol Books, Irvington-on-Hudson, New York, 1951; Dover Publications, New York, 1955.)

Bunzel, R. L., *The Pueblo Potter*, Columbia University Press, 1929.

Bushnell, Geoffrey H. S., and Digby, Adrian, *Ancient American Pottery*, Pitman, New York, 1955.

Chapman, Kenneth M., *Decorative Art of the Indians of the Southwest*, Laboratory of Anthropology, Santa Fe, N. M., Bulletin 1, 1934.

Cosgrove, H. S. and C. B., *The Swarts Ruin*, Papers, Peabody Museum of American Archeology and Ethnology, Vol. 25, No. 1, 1932 [Mimbres pottery].

Covarrubias, Miguel, *The Eagle, the Jaguar, and the Serpent: Indian Art of the Americas*; Vol. 1, *North America, Alaska,* *Canada, the United States,* Knopf, 1954.

Davis, Robert T., *Native Arts of the Pacific Northwest, from the Rasmussen Collection of the Portland Art Museum*, Stanford University Press, 1949.

Douglas, Frederic H., *Plains Beads and Beadwork Designs*, Denver Art Museum Leaflets 73 and 74, December, 1936.

——, *Totem Poles*, Denver Art Museum Leaflets 79 and 80, December, 1936.

——, and d'Harnoncourt, René, *Indian Art of the United States*, Museum of Modern Art, New York, 1941.

Earle, Edwin, *Hopi Kachinas* (with text by Edward A. Kennard), J. J. Augustin, New York, 1938.

Emmons, George T., *The Chilkat Blanket*, American Museum of Natural History, New York, 1907.

Ewers, John C., *Plains Indian Painting*, Stanford University Press, 1939.

Gilpin, Laura, *The Pueblos*, Hastings House, New York, 1941.

Griffin, James B., ed., *Archeology of Eastern United States*, University of Chicago Press, 1952.

Inverarity, Robert B., *Art of the Northwest Coast Indians*, University of California Press, Berkeley, 1950.

Klah, Hasteen, *Navajo Creation Myth*, recorded by Mary C. Wheelwright, Museum of Navajo Ceremonial Art, Santa Fe, N. M., 1942.

Krieger, H. W., *Aspects of Aboriginal Decorative Art in America*, Annual Report, 1930, Smithsonian Institution, Washington, D. C.

Mason, Otis T., *Aboriginal American Basketry*, Annual Report, 1902, Smithsonian Institution, Washington, D. C.; Part 2, *Report of the U. S. National Museum*, 1904.

The Maya and Their Neighbors, Appleton-Century, 1940.

Mera, Harry P., *Navajo Blankets*, Laboratory of Anthropology, Santa Fe, N. M., General Series, Bulletins, 2–16, 1938–45.

——, *Style Trends of Pueblo Pottery in the Rio Grande and Little Colorado Cultural Areas from the Sixteenth to the Nineteenth Century*, Memoirs of the Laboratory of Anthropology, Santa Fe, N. M., Vol. 3, 1939.

Newcomb, Mrs. Franc J., *Sandpaintings of the Navajo Shooting Chant*, with text by Gladys A. Reichard, J. J. Augustin, New York, 1937.

Reichard, Gladys A., *Navajo Shepherd and Weaver*, J. J. Augustin, New York, 1936.

Shetrone, Henry C., *The Mound-Builders*, Appleton-Century, 1930.

CHAPTER 19

PRIMITIVE

(13TH–20TH CENTURIES)

Primitive art is that produced by peoples who have no written literature, whose social organization is tribal in nature, and who are often still in a Neolithic cultural state. The arts of Negro Africa, of the South Seas, and of the American Indian (see Chapter 18) fall into this category, that is, until contact with Europeans modified the art, or in some cases brought it to a halt altogether.

Use of the word "primitive" need not imply crudity or a lack of artistic quality. Works of art such as Benin bronzes from Africa (Fig. 19–5) or wood carvings from New Ireland (Fig. 19–16) are actually of complex design and high technical refinement.

It has been said that primitive man generally has a feeling for rhythm in art superior to that of other peoples.[1] Primitive man's attitude toward technique is less intellectual than ours. His interests are narrower, his social patterns more fixed. His art is based directly upon the materials of use in his society: hence the emphases upon basket-making, pottery, weaving, and carving. He sees and creates in conceptual rather than in purely visual terms, and thus his idea of reality is often far removed from ours. His sense of form, with some notable exceptions, is non-naturalistic, emphasizing abstract conventions rather than illusionistic reality. To understand the primitive artist also requires recognition of his rhythmical way of seeing.

Consider two portraits of the same Maori chief, one a self-portrait and the other painted by a Western artist (Fig. 19–2). While the English artist drew a conventional likeness, the Maori self-portrait is a flat, bilaterally symmetrical, abstract design in which the chief identifies himself with the ornamental pattern of the facial tattoo. But it is also a true portrait, since the tattoo marks are individual with the owner, setting him apart from all other tribe members.

[1] See Franz Boas, *Primitive Art*, for an excellent discussion of the aesthetics of primitive art.

ILLUSTRATION ABOVE. **19–1** ANTELOPE HEADDRESS. Bambara tribe, French Sudan. Wood. L. 21 in. Private collection, Cleveland, Ohio. (Cleveland Museum of Art)

19–2 (Left) The Maori chief, Tupai Kupa, after a drawing by John Sylvester, *ca.* 1800. (Right) The Maori chief, Tupai Kupa, after his own self-portrait drawing. (Both from Leo Frobenius, *The Childhood of Man*, Lippincott, 1909)

African Negro

African Negro sculpture was first known to Europeans in the fifteenth century, but little serious attention was given it until its rediscovery about the turn of the twentieth century.

European colonial administrators in Africa during the late nineteenth century first drew attention to the art which they found there. For example, *Benin* bronzes (Fig. 19–5) were unknown until a British army expedition discovered them in Benin City, Nigeria, in 1897. Shortly after 1900 painters such as Picasso and Vlaminck began to collect African sculpture. Other painters in France, seeking to enlarge the traditional forms in European art, also looked outside their own environment, and found in the abstract rhythms of African sculpture a fresh and totally new inspiration. But before 1920 African art was studied chiefly by anthropologists, seeking to understand primitive magic and technology. Today,

finally, African art is studied on its own merits, as design of high formal excellence.

African Negro art comes primarily from the central part of the continent extending from its western coast far into the interior (see map, Fig. 19–3). The inhabitants of the east coast of Africa (of Arabic extraction) and the Bushmen and Pygmies of South Africa were not notably artistic peoples. The north coast of Africa (Hamitic peoples) was always under Mediterranean influences and does not concern us here.

South of the barrier of the Sahara Desert, along the Niger and Congo river systems of central Africa, live a great number of Negro tribes whose early history is largely unknown. Local traditions tell us of the early movements of these tribes; and it is known that as late as the eighteenth century, and even the early nineteenth, many

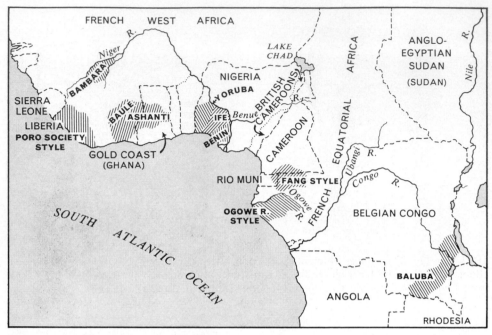

19–3 AREAS OF AFRICAN NEGRO SCULPTURE. Major styles or traditions are indicated by shading.

were still migrating northward and southward in an effort to extend their territorial claims.

Some of these tribes, in the Sudan and Cameroons areas, use the grasslands fringing the forests for sheepherding, and their existence is sometimes seminomadic. But most of the tribes living along the Gold Coast (now Ghana) and Ivory Coast, in Nigeria, and through the Belgian Congo inhabit tropical rain forests, supplementing village agriculture by hunting.

In central Africa social organization is clearly defined: a number of small, family units form a village, each village with its subchief. Each village is in turn a part of a larger tribal complex with a head chief. The tribes vary from a few hundred members to more than thirty-five thousand. The Yoruba tribe of Nigeria, an aggregate of many subtribes, actually contains over five million members.

Often such tribes formed a nation under a king. Of these kingdoms, that of Ife in Nigeria probably flourished in the fourteenth century; that of Benin reached its artistic zenith in the sixteenth and seventeenth centuries; and the kingdom of Dahomey in the late eighteenth century. These kingdoms maintained law courts, standing armies, and urban centers of considerable size. In social organization, kingdoms such as Benin and Dahomey resembled the early city-states of Europe.

Religion in tribal Negro Africa was a combination of nature and ancestor worship. Dwelling in close contact with the forces of nature, the Negro found a magical explanation for natural phenomena. Nature deities were propitiated to ensure crops and good hunting, as well as to watch over the birth of fellow humans and animals. Special deities inhabited the streams and fields, and even the trees: before a tree was cut, prayers were often said to placate the spirit and invite it into its new home — the sculptured image made from its wood.

Even more widespread than belief in nature deities was ancestor worship. Since the ancestor was aware of all the acts of his descendants and also in contact with the spirits of still more powerful ancient ancestors and gods, he was in a position to aid or to bring misfortune on his descendants. Two classes of ancestors were propitiated: those of the tribe and those of the family. Tribal ancestors were deceased kings or chiefs and therefore the most powerful; the less powerful family ancestors were informally worshiped within the privacy of dwellings.

Ancestor worship was a powerful discipline for the Negro mind; it encouraged a respect for traditions, which accounts for the continuance of fixed and traditional styles in sculpture. The ritual involved fostered a magical relationship between the worshiper and the image of his ancestor. This relationship, intensely emotional in nature, provided the aesthetic motivation for much African sculpture, which must always be considered in relation to its religious purpose.

As the tribes vary in language, customs, and social organization, so the particular styles of their carvings vary, although similar habits of visualization, and hence a similar basic style, is observable. Practically none of the carving in wood has the copying of nature as its objective. On the contrary, parts of the human or animal figures were distorted and reassembled, not according to nature but according to an aesthetic pattern related to the material used, the spaces to be filled, and the function of the object for ritual use. These aesthetic patterns were established by tradition and were thoroughly intelligible to both the artist and his public.

The oldest datable African cultures

19–4 IFE BRONZE HEAD. Nigeria. *ca.* 14th century. (Photo from cast in American Museum of Natural History, New York; courtesy Nigerian Government)

have thus far been found in Nigeria, where specific styles of court art were encouraged. Small terra-cotta heads have been found near the town of *Nok* in a geological level estimated to be more than two thousand years old. These small pieces are the point of departure for the study of subsequent African sculpture. While the portrait-like quality of the Nok heads foreshadows the later court art of Ife and Benin, their angular modeling anticipates the abstract character fundamental to African tribal sculpture as we know it today.

About twenty royal portrait bronzes were unearthed at *Ife*, Nigeria, between 1910 and 1948 (Fig. 19–4), together with a number of terra cottas which may have served as models for other cast portraits. These heads, cast by the *cire-perdue* method, are of a

cased by bronze plaques depicting royalty, hunting, and battle scenes. Over 2400 of these plaques have been recorded. Figure 19–5 illustrates one of the *oba* and his entourage, of probable seventeenth-century date. The strict frontality and the emphasis upon armor and standards of rank indicate the pomp and splendor by which the *oba* maintained his rule. Here we can see how the portrait tradition of Ife still distinguished between individual people but how, nevertheless, conventional distortions and an interest in surface ornament led to the characteristically abstract quality of primitive art. The rich art of Benin also included bronze heads for the royal altar, ivory gongs, and small masks as well as musical instruments and staff heads.

19–5 BRONZE PLAQUE from Benin, Nigeria, representing the *oba* (king) of Benin and attendants. *ca.* 17th century. University Museum, Philadelphia. (University Museum)

surprising realism, the scarification marks of the individuals portrayed being utilized as part of the surface design. Most scholars agree in attributing them to the fourteenth century A.D. Ife portraiture has often been compared with that of the Mediterranean Classical world, though there can be no doubt that the tradition of sensitive realism which Ife sculpture represents was an indigenous one, perhaps owing something to Egyptian precedent, as well as to the tradition of Nok.

The other important early kingdom was that of *Benin*. A local Benin tradition maintains that about 1280 A.D. the *oba* (king) of Benin applied to the ruler of nearby Ife for artisans skilled in bronze casting. Benin art flourished until the end of the seventeenth century, and inferior casting continued in Benin City until the middle of the nineteenth century.

The buildings of the palace complex at Benin were surrounded by colonnades of wooden pillars completely en-

The tradition of metal casting did not die at Benin but continued until very recent times among the *Ashanti* in British West Africa, who were famed for their gold weights, pendants, and miniature masks of gold. The Ashanti (or Ashanti-influenced) gold crocodile pendant illustrated as Figure 19–6 demonstrates how the bold style of Benin ended in a later tradition of small-scale, delicate work carried on by neighboring tribes.

In contrast to the African kingdoms, the sculpture of the tribes was generally more abstract in nature. Most tribal sculptures produced in Africa are of wood, and will not usually resist jungle rot or the ravages of white ants for more than half a century. For this reason most of the tribal carvings in museums date from 1825 to the end of the nineteenth century. The few examples collected before 1825, however, differ very little from the African sculptures of more recent decades. Works of similar style have been collected consistently among the same tribes for many years, evidence of a tradition as conservative as ancestor worship itself.

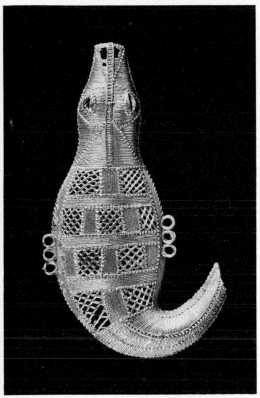

19–6 GOLD PENDANT in the shape of a crocodile. Ashanti or tribe under Ashanti influence. Ivory Coast. Gold. L. 4¼ in. John L. Severance Collection, Cleveland Museum of Art. (Cleveland Museum of Art, John L. Severance Fund)

Tribal sculpture in the form of figures or masks was made to propitiate ancestors, to procure material benefits from nature deities, or to transfer magical powers to individuals or things (fetishes). The fetish figures were usually cruder in execution than the ancestor figures or dance masks, and were studded with nails or rubbed with "medicine" in order to effect the desired transfer of power.

The different tribal styles in Africa are too numerous for specific analysis here; [2] rather let us indicate the range

19–7 MALE ANCESTOR GUARDIAN FIGURE. Gabun. Wood. Probably Mavai of the Fang tribes. In the Brooklyn Museum Collection. (Courtesy, Brooklyn Museum)

and richness of these styles by citing several typical works of art, both from western Africa and from the Congo region.

In the *Bambara* tribe (French Sudan) the antelope was worshiped as a symbol of fertility and good hunting. At festivals headpieces representing

[2] Paul Wingert, in *The Sculpture of Negro Africa*, gives the stylistic differentiations between tribes. His book is in effect an objective handbook to the art styles of the major tribes.

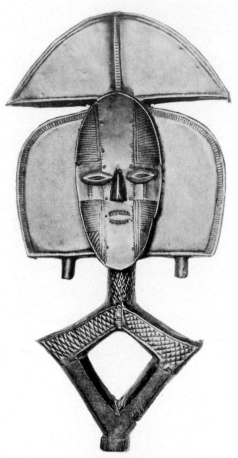

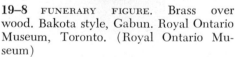

19–8 FUNERARY FIGURE. Brass over wood. Bakota style, Gabun. Royal Ontario Museum, Toronto. (Royal Ontario Museum)

19–9 FIGURE SUPPORTING A CHIEF'S STOOL. Baluba tribe. Belgian Congo. Wood. Barnes Foundation, Merion, Pa. (Morgan Photo)

the antelope were worn by Bambara dancers (Fig. 19–1), whose steps also imitated the leaping antelope. The rhythm of this dance is echoed in the headpiece; the animal is in springing posture, with the curve of his head repeated in the flowing line of back and haunches. The head is balanced by the scroll-like tail, while horns, projecting boldly into space, are deliberately exaggerated for emotional effect.

The *Fang* tribes of Gabun developed a specific type of ancestor figure called a skull-barrel guardian. A barrel of

bark containing the skulls of ancestors was attached below the torso of the figures, and the distinctly different forms of these figures adopted by two neighboring tribes accents the instinctive sense for appropriate, harmonious forms so insistently present in primitive art. In one tribe the container was cylindrical, and the guardian figure was therefore round (Fig. 19–7). Unity in the elongated torso is achieved by the subtle, rhythmical repetition of pear-shaped and bulbous forms. Another tribe of the Upper Ogowe river

19–10 PORO SECRET SOCIETY MASK. Dan tribe, Liberia. H. 8 in. Yale University Art Gallery. (Yale Art Gallery)

19–11 PORO SECRET SOCIETY MASK. Dan tribe, Liberia. H. *ca.* 9 in. James M. Osborn Collection, New Haven. (Yale Art Gallery)

used rectangular containers, and their guardian figures, instead of being in the round, are flat abstractions (Fig. 19–8). The Fang guardian figures are among the oldest that have survived in African wooden sculpture, some of them dating back as far as two hundred years.

A chief's stool from the *Baluba* tribe (Belgian Congo) shows how the Negro artist resolves zigzag rhythms and conic forms into a structural and aesthetic unit (Fig. 19–9). Such command of structure is implicit in the power of this sculpture. The most remarkable gifts of the Negro artist are his unerring sense of rhythm and form and his ability to integrate separate parts into a balanced composition. In his best work, no matter how distorted any part of it may be, this sense of form and underlying order prevails.

No African art is more varied than the making of masks for dancing and for secret society initiation rites. Consider the differences between the delicate surfaces shown in Figure 19–10 and the rough carving shown in Figure 19–11, both of which are Poro Secret Society masks. Yet in each one there is an architectonic feeling for the integration of parts.

The machine age has made it increasingly difficult for the Negro to retain the tribal religious beliefs which have been the spiritual impetus for his art. In certain areas (the Cameroons and parts of Nigeria) traditional work of good quality is still being executed, but over the larger part of Negro Africa the old art has become debased, particularly in the coastal areas, where nearly all trace of the traditional artistic cultures has been lost.

Oceanic

Another major area producing primitive art is Oceania, a vast island-studded section of the Pacific Ocean including Australia and New Zealand and extending from Java and Sumatra eastward to Hawaii and Easter Island (see map, Fig. 19–12).

For the last three centuries Oceania has been open to European trade. Only in remote areas, as in the mountainous interior of New Guinea or Arnhem Land in northern Australia, are natives still living in their original cultural state. Many examples of Oceanic art were originally collected by sailors and traders during the first half of the nineteenth century and deposited in European ethnological museums. Although eighteenth- and nineteenth-century datings may be assigned to most of the Oceanic art which has come down to us, its origins lie deep in the past. A leading authority has traced Oceanic art to probable, if remote, beginnings on the southwestern Asiatic mainland, suggesting that the early forms were altered as successive migrations moved eastward from Asia across the Oceanic islands. It is generally held by anthropologists that Oceania was the latest area to be populated by modern man. While remains in Java, Sumatra, and the Celebes indicate human habitation as far back as Paleolithic times, there is no evidence of prehistoric types of man east of Java. The people of Oceania are a mixed race compounded of the aboriginal settlers who presumably migrated in Paleolithic times, and other Asiatics who later followed their path.

The ancestors of the present aborigines of Australia appear to have been among the very first settlers. Anthropologists have found other pockets of these oldest racial elements, such as

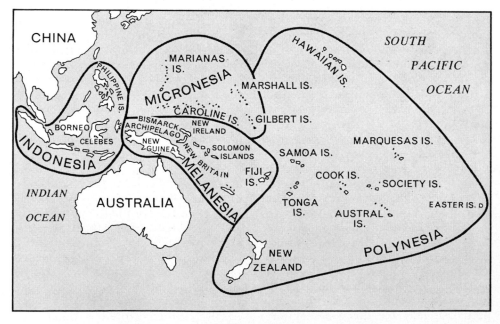

19–12   OCEANIA.

the fuzzy-headed, dark-skinned Papuans; and the path of migration is generally so distinct that the Oceanic peoples have been assigned to three distinct groups: Melanesians, Polynesians, and Micronesians.

Evidently the first people to move to the islands north and east of Australia were the Melanesians (black people), who settled New Guinea and the islands from the Bismarck Archipelago southeast to the Fiji Islands. They were followed by the Polynesians, who arrived from the extreme southeastern section of the Asiatic mainland by the same route. This, apparently, was about three thousand years ago. The Polynesians, finding the islands near Australia already occupied by the Melanesians, pushed further out into the Pacific. By canoe they went from island to island, slowly settling the vast area from New Zealand north to the Hawaiian Islands and east to Easter Island, Samoa, the Society Islands, and the Marquesas. According to local tradition Hawaii was not settled until sometime after 1200 A.D., and Easter Island probably even later.

The equatorial island groups north and northeast of New Guinea, including the Caroline, Mariana, Marshall, and Gilbert Islands, were settled by the Micronesians. These people, also of Asiatic origin, included a strong Polynesian strain. As Micronesian culture approached a settled state, the outlying fringes of Polynesia were probably still being explored by the Polynesians during the same period when Medieval civilization flourished in western Europe.

All these Oceanic peoples were generally organized into clans and families, ruled by chiefs to whom divine birth was attributed. Systems of social rank were more strictly established in Oceania than in Africa. In the economy fishing ranked first, and agriculture was carried on where the land

could be tilled. Warfare (sometimes with head-hunting as its objective) was frequent.

Oceanic religion consisted of spirit and ancestor worship. Nature deities were also sometimes worshiped. Religious beliefs were strongly conditioned by two concepts: "mana" and "taboo." Mana was a universal spirit power, whereas taboo expressed the related idea of prohibition. As Paul Wingert has said,

In differing degrees it (mana) was contained in all animate and inanimate things. The degree of potency of mana in an object, such as a weapon, was determined or revealed by its performance or efficacy, and in a person by his high birth or skill in his vocation. Gods also had mana depending upon their rank. Since objects and persons with great mana were dangerous to those with less, taboos were established to protect against it. To break a taboo was fatal.[3]

Taboo also kept matters of social rank clearly defined, preventing a person from assuming a rank which did not belong to him.

It is even more difficult to make valid generalizations about Oceanic than about African art because the cultures diverged widely in an area so immense and because the varying physical environments produced different materials for artistic expression. The forests supplied wood for houses, canoes, utensils, and sculpture, as well as bark and pulp for cloth and mats. The fauna provided colorful feathers for ceremonial robes and bone for small objects of personal adornment. From the sea came shells, such as abalone, for inlays. The Oceanic peoples developed very little pottery. Their tools were primitive, and metal was unknown until it was introduced through trading with Europeans. Adzes with blades of jade or shell, knives of flaked obsidian or

[3] Paul Wingert, *Art of the South Pacific Islands*, p. 22.

Melanesia

Melanesian art centered in New Guinea, one of the largest islands in the world (1200 miles in length). Here an elaborate ceremonial life developed with an art of corresponding intensity accompanying its rituals. There are a number of distinctly different styles in New Guinea. Examples from three of them are presented here.

Along the *Sepik River* art always played an important role; the anthropologist Margaret Mead has observed, for instance, that the Tchambuli tribe found a principal focus for their life in art. The Sepik River style is richer and more varied than any other in Oceania, including as it does ancestor figures, sacred flutes, carved stools, neck rests, shields, drums, and suspension hooks among its numerous forms. The basic attributes of its sculpture, which include a sharply pointed head, a prominent nose, and an elongated trunk, may be seen in Figure 19–13, where an ancestor figure has been carved as part of a stool. The painted designs upon the face of this carving do not follow the sculptural contours, so that a tension arises between the carved forms and the applied surface decoration. The Melanesian believed that by touching such an image as they talked, chiefs could gain eloquence.

Two more objects illustrate the variety of styles to be found on New Guinea: a memorial tablet from the *Papuan Gulf* (Fig. 19–14) and a mask from the *Torres Straits* area (Fig. 19–15). The memorial tablet is essentially a facial image, presenting on its surface actually a double image, since it can also be read as two profiles divided at the nose. Though carved of wood, the Torres Straits mask derives in style from others in the same area made of thin plates of tortoise shell. The brittle nature of shell is expressed even in the wood translation.

19–13 CARVED STOOL from the Sepik River area, New Guinea. Wood, partially painted. H. 36¼ in. University Museum, Philadelphia. (University Museum)

with blades set with sharks' teeth, and drills with points of stone or shell originally composed the artist's repertory of tools.

Whereas the African Negro was concerned with the formal properties of sculpture, the Oceanic artist was preoccupied with its decorative effect. The dramatic imagery, as much as the formal invention, strikes the Westerner who looks at Oceanic art. Throughout this art a highly developed feeling for surface design heightened the visual effect, even though these designs were often applied to three-dimensional sculpture. These qualities can best be understood by a consideration of the art produced in the three major areas of Oceania: Melanesia, Polynesia, and Micronesia.

While the Sepik River style is the most varied in Melanesia, the most spectacular manifestation of Melanesian art is to be found on the island of New Ireland, immediately northeast of New Guinea, in carving executed for the Malagan festival, staged to commemorate dead ancestors. Preparations for the Malagan festival cycle were the most elaborate in Oceania. An enclosure was built together with one or more sheds. For six months or longer, sculptors worked within the enclosure on the memorial boards, crested masks, and tall upright memorial poles used in the ceremony. On pain of death women were forbidden within the enclosure until the moment its walls were knocked down. Then all the carvings were displayed amid general acclaim, and for two to four days dances and processions took place in which the

19–15 WOODEN MASK from the Torres Straits area, New Guinea. H. 20 in. Collection Nelson A. Rockefeller, New York. (Charles Uht)

masks and smaller carvings were used. The symbols on the Malagan carvings, such as pig, bird, and crocodile, often had a totemic significance. These symbols were intertwined with geometric motifs in a continuous fashion, with the hollow spaces producing an openwork effect. The carvings and masks were painted bright red, yellow, white, blue, and black. Shell decorations and the opercula of sea snails were used to indicate eyes. Figure 19–16 illustrates the openwork Malagan style; the bird at the top of this pole symbolizes the spirit power.

The neighboring island of New Britain produced distinctive masks made of pith and bark cloth, while New Caledonia was noted for its doorposts, sea spirit masks, and carved housetop

19–14 MEMORIAL TABLET from the Papuan Gulf area, New Guinea. Painted wood. Chauvet Collection, Paris.

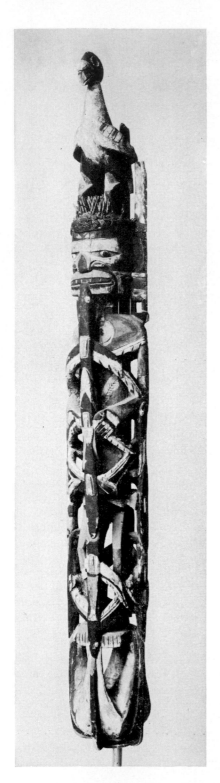

spires. The Solomon Islanders were known for skillful shell inlays, inserted in bowls and especially in small figureheads affixed to the prows of canoes to bring good luck to head-hunting parties (Fig. 19–17). These canoe prow figureheads were an elaboration in wood of the actual skulls of ancestors which the Melanesians preserved and revered.

Polynesia

The group of islands including Tonga, Samoa, and the Cook, Society, and Austral islands may be identified as central Polynesia. In this region a tradition of small-scale geometric surface design prevailed. These schemes were carved on paddles and adzes. Geometric devices (sometimes in combination with floral motifs) were also used to decorate tapa cloths made from beaten bark. Tapa cloth was decorated by spreading it over a surface bearing raised designs; it was then rubbed with red earth or soot so that the underlying design was transferred to the cloth.

In the Cook and Austral Islands adzes, paddles, and spears, too large and elaborate for use, were designed as works of art rather than as objects of utility. The finest of these (see Fig. 19–18) were carefully balanced in form, beautifully made, and decorated with a sensitively scaled over-all pattern. Central Polynesia also had a tradition of figural sculpture, but it was a restricted one in comparison to that of Melanesia, being limited to the carving of fishermen's gods on the Cook Islands. These figures were decorated with conventional geometric devices similar to those of the cult objects.

The art of the natives of the nearby Marquesas Islands was close to that of central Polynesia. It was, however, more highly developed, and it made constant use of a single decorative motif, a stylized head, which appeared on headbands, bone earrings, strangling cords, and clubs. Although the Marquesans also carved images, both large and small, in stone as well as in wood, Marquesan design tended, in its use of repetitively similar ornamental schemes, toward uniformity and lack of invention.

The other major islands of Polynesia — New Zealand, Easter Island, and Hawaii — form a huge triangle enclosing the central Polynesian area (see map, Fig. 19–12). On New Zealand a temperate climate and an abundance of timber provided a rich variety of materials. The most elaborate carvings

19–18 CEREMONIAL ADZE from the Cook Islands. Wood. L. 34 in. National Museum, Washington, D. C. (Smithsonian Institution)

in Polynesian art were those made by the Maori of this island to decorate their canoes, communal houses, orator staffs, feather boxes, and war clubs. Most of these were carved of wood but jade was also used for the war clubs and for small amulets called *heitikis*. Since the Maori had no sacred precincts and since the ancestor images

19–19 ANCESTRAL MALE FIGURE from Easter Island. Wood. H. 17 in. University Museum, Philadelphia. (University Museum)

19–20 WOODEN STATUE of the war god Ku, Hawaii. H. 79 in. Peabody Museum, Salem, Massachusetts. (Courtesy Peabody Museum)

carved upon the house posts and coffins of chiefs were not worshiped, their art was secular in nature and marked by virtuosity, in the most exacting sense of the term. The gable ends, sides, and house posts provided the Maori artists with ample space to exercise this virtuosity in curvilinear design. Their large canoes, up to eighty feet in length, were also decorated at the prow and stern with heavily carved boards whose scrollwork was often pierced. Here a florid inventiveness prevailed, curtailed only by the forms to be deco-rated, which never varied in type. The sweeping quality of Maori spiral designs depends upon their organization in terms of the whole field. They are without parallel in Oceanic art, although a distant kinship with Marquesan art can be discerned.

Although New Zealand offered an abundance of wood, Easter Island, the eastern outpost of Oceania, lacked native wood altogether. Its inhabitants were forced to quarry stone from the crater of the volcano Rano-raraku for their great ancestor images. These co-lossal stone heads, some as high as fifteen feet, were set along the outer slopes of the volcano. On Easter Island also, driftwood, which was regarded as an extremely valuable material, was carved with a jewel-like precision into statuettes, other small carvings, and breast ornaments. The emaciated and

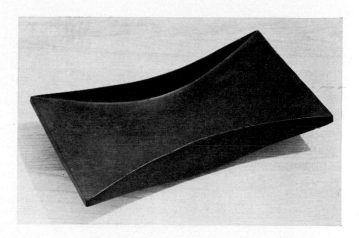

19–21 WOODEN DISH from Matty Island. L. *ca.* 10 in. Collection Nelson A. Rockefeller, New York. (Charles Uht)

grotesque ancestor statuettes (Fig. 19–19) were based upon the appearance of mummified bodies.

In Hawaii, religion centered in the worship of the war god Ku, whose ritual was financed by the Hawaiian kings. The temple enclosures dedicated to Ku were surrounded by six-foot walls with a single entrance. Only priests and chiefs entered the sacred part of the enclosure to view the aggressive and powerful images of the god displayed there. Just three of these wooden statues have survived; one is illustrated as Fig. 19–20. Up to 1819, when the native religion was replaced by Christianity, feather cloaks (for the chiefs), images of wickerwork clothed in feathers, and figure-bowls were also made.

Micronesia

The modest and utilitarian Micronesian art forms contrast with the dramatic and inventive art of Melanesia and with the complex decorative and sculptural traditions of Polynesia. The poor resources on the Micronesian islands retarded cultural development. Micronesian art is simple, consisting of ornaments, dishes, gable masks, and occasional figurines. Decorative patterns and painted surfaces are virtually unknown. All objects display utilitarian form. The inhabitants of the Marshall Islands, for example, were noted for navigational maps constructed of wooden strips arranged in a grid. The Caroline Islanders, the most warlike of Micronesian peoples, made excellent swords with cutting edges of shark's teeth. On Matty Island were the best woodworkers in Micronesia; dishes from this island, with their thin edges and concave sides, are of elegant craftsmanship (Fig. 19–21).

Summary

While primitive art has often appeared to the outsider as merely crude or barbaric, it is actually the product of complex and refined artistic traditions. Primitive sensibility, which was expressed in conceptual rather than natural images, created distorted and abstract forms which differ radically from the Western tradition of pictorial illusion. Form and decoration were determined, within broad limits, by tradition and available material, which in both Africa and Oceania was chiefly wood. In Africa wood-carving attained a remarkable three-dimensional quality; in Oceania it was exploited for flat pictorial effect.

Bibliography

GENERAL READINGS

Adam, Leonhard, *Primitive Art*, Penguin Books, Baltimore, 1949.

Benedict, Ruth, *Patterns of Culture*, Houghton, Mifflin, 1934.

Boas, Franz, *Primitive Art*, H. Aschehoug, Oslo, 1927 (new editions, Capitol Books, Irvington-on-Hudson, N. Y., 1951; Dover Publications, New York, 1955).

Burland, C. A., and Hooper, J. T., *The Art of Primitive Peoples*, Fountain Press, London, 1953.

Christensen, Erwin O., *Primitive Art*, Crowell, 1955.

Herskowitz, Melville J., *Man and His Works: The Science of Cultural Anthropology*, Knopf, 1948.

Kroeber, Alfred L., *Anthropology*, Harcourt, Brace, 1948.

——, "Primitive Art," *Encyclopedia of Social Sciences*, Macmillan, New York, Vol. 2, 1930–44, pp. 226–29.

Linne, Sigvald, ed., *Primitiv Konst*, Statens Ethnografiska Museum, Stockholm, 1947.

Linton, Ralph, "Primitive Art," *Kenyon Review*, Vol. 3, No. 1, 1941.

——, *The Tree of Culture*, Knopf, 1955.

AFRICAN NEGRO

"Exhibition of African Art," *Allen Memorial Art Museum Bulletin*, Oberlin College, Ohio, Vol. 13, No. 2, Winter, 1955–56.

Fagg, William, *The Webster Plass Collection of African Art*, British Museum, London, 1953.

Griaule, Marcel, *Folk Art in Black Africa*, Tudor, New York, 1950.

Lem, F. H., *Sudanese Sculpture*, Arts et Métiers Graphiques, Paris, 1949.

"Masterpieces of African Art," *Exhibition Catalog*, Brooklyn Museum, 1954.

Olbrechts, Frans M., "Contributions to the Study of the Chronology of African Plastic Art," *Africa*, London, October, 1945.

Plass, Margaret, *African Tribal Sculpture*, University Museum, Philadelphia, 1956.

Radin, Paul, and Marvel, Elinore, *African Folktales and Sculpture*, Pantheon Books, New York, 1952.

Read, Charles H., and Dalton, Ormonde M., *Antiquities from the City of Benin and from Other Parts of West Africa in the British Museum*, Longmans, London, 1899.

Schmalenbach, Werner, *African Art*, Macmillan, New York, 1954.

Segy, Ladislaw, *African Sculpture Speaks*, A. A. Wyn, New York, 1952.

Sweeney, James Johnson, *African Negro Art*, Museum of Modern Art, New York, 1935.

Sydow, Eckart von, *Afrikanische Plastik*, G. Wittenborn, New York, 1954.

Trowell, Margaret, *Classical African Sculpture*, Frederick A. Praeger, New York, 1954.

Underwood, Leon, *Bronzes of West Africa*, Tiranti, London, 1948.

——, *Figures in Wood of West Africa*, Tiranti, London, 1949.

——, *Masks of West Africa*, Tiranti, London, 1948.

Wieschoff, H. A., "Africa" (The African Collections of the University Museum), *University Museum Bulletin*, Philadelphia, Vol. 2, Nos. 1–2, March, 1945.

Wingert, Paul S., *The Sculpture of Negro Africa*, Columbia University Press, 1950.

——, *The Wurtzburger Collection of African Sculpture*, Baltimore Museum of Art, 1954.

OCEANIC

Covarrubias, Miguel, *Pageant of the Pacific*, Pacific House, San Francisco, 1940.

Davidson, Daniel Sutherland, "Oceania" (The Oceanic Collections of the University Museum), *University Museum Bulletin*, Philadelphia, Vol. 12, Nos. 3–4, June, 1947.

Emory, Kenneth P., *Hawaii: Notes on Wooden Images*, Ethnologia Cranmorensis, Cranmore Ethnological Museum, Chislehurst, England, 1938.

Firth, Raymond W., *Art and Life in New Guinea*, Studio Publications, New York, 1936.

Krieger, H. W., "Design Areas in Oceania Based on Specimens in the U. S. National Museum," *Proceedings of the U. S. National Museum*, Washington, D. C., Vol. 79, 1931–32, pp. 1–47.

Linton, Ralph, and Wingert, Paul S., *Arts of the South Seas*, in collaboration with René d'Harnoncourt, Museum of Modern Art, New York, 1946.

Reichard, Gladys A., *Melanesian Design*, 2 vols., Columbia University Press, 1933.

Read, Sir Herbert E., *Australia: Aboriginal Paintings from Arnhem Land*, New York Graphic Society and UNESCO, 1954.

Tischner, Herbert, *Oceanic Art*, Pantheon Books, New York, 1954.

Wingert, Paul S., *Art of the South Pacific Islands*, Beechhurst Press, New York, 1953.

——, *An Outline Guide to the Art of the South Pacific*, Columbia University Press, 1946.

The Wurtzburger Collection of Oceanic Art, Baltimore Museum of Art, 1956.

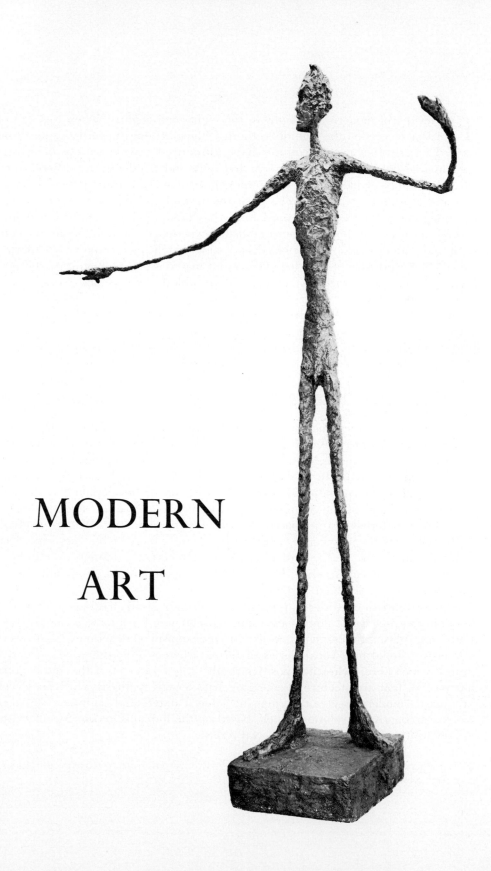

MODERN

ART

THE history of modern art begins in the eighteenth century, when the Age of Reason succeeded the Age of Authority. New attitudes toward the past and toward other, often exotic, cultures have introduced a wide variety of artistic vocabularies, which have been interpreted quite independently by different artists. The history of modern art is complex, but there are certain general tendencies and attitudes which provide a basis for its study. In painting and sculpture the image of nature and of natural forms has gradually been transformed into abstract or intuitive interpretations of man's experience. In architecture, eclecticism and variety have been replaced by a new search for a common or international style expressive of new techniques and materials. In photography the perfection of technical processes has made it possible to explore and record man's decisive moments.

Since the late eighteenth century the two opposing views of reality, originally clarified by Plato and Aristotle, also provide a key for the recognition and identification of different stylistic interpretations. In Neoclassicism, as in Constructivism, reality is an abstract order imposed by the mind of man on the world of nature. In the Romanticism of the early nineteenth century, as in the Expressionism of the twentieth, the emotional factor of man's experience is emphasized and given an organic order.

During most of the nineteenth century artists were concerned with varying images of man and nature with the different stylistic results which we identify as Neoclassicism, Romanticism, Realism or Naturalism, and Impressionism. It was also the time when the Revival styles in architecture were greatly favored, although original interpretations and syntheses led to the development of the Picturesque style and of the Shingle style. Experiments with iron, steel, and glass as building materials also prepared the way for the new forms of the twentieth century. Late in the nineteenth century a desire for a more stable, less superficial order produced the highly individual and provocative paintings of the Post-Impressionists and in America the architecture of Richardson, Sullivan, and the early work of Frank Lloyd Wright.

As the twentieth century has progressed a series of "isms" has appeared, which may be interpreted as different experiments searching for a new, coherent style. Fauvism, Cubism, Futurism, Surrealism, Expressionism were serious, constructive attempts to build new vocabularies of forms, whereas Dadaism was a negative protest which nevertheless had positive results. It would seem, as the mid-century has passed, that architecture is emerging with a new synthesis which may well produce a "modern" style of permanent value. Painters and sculptors still seem to be searching for a solution which, based on the humanistic concerns of Western civilization, states them in universal terms.

◀ ALBERTO GIACOMETTI. *Man Pointing*. 1947. Bronze. H. 70½ in. Museum of Modern Art, New York. (Museum of Modern Art)

CHAPTER 20

PAINTING

19th-Century European

France

After 1750 many thoughtful persons were aware that the political and economic structure of French society was no longer equal to the serious internal strains which it had developed. The national treasury was approaching bankruptcy. The energetic middle class was no longer willing to accept its traditional subordination to the privileged nobility. Throughout the country, peasant and shopkeeper looked for more equitable taxation and some voice in government. As a result the gay fantasies of Rococo art were no longer an adequate expression of experience. During the reign of Louis XVI (1774–1790) this more serious mood led to the intensive study and interpretation

ILLUSTRATION ABOVE. **20–1** HENRI DE TOULOUSE-LAUTREC. *At the Moulin Rouge*. 1892. *ca.* 3 ft. 11 in. × 4 ft. 7 in. Art Institute of Chicago. (Courtesy of the Art Institute of Chicago, Helen Birch Bartlett Memorial Collection)

of Classic art. It was also felt that in the history of ancient Rome there might be ethical lessons for the present. Enthusiasm for such studies was fostered by the systematic excavations at Pompeii and Herculaneum (after 1748) and by the publication of objects found there, as well as by the extensive circulation of Piranesi's engravings of Roman ruins. J. J. Winckelmann's *History of Art Among the Ancients* — the first history of art in the modern sense — appeared in 1764 and provided a new methodical account of classic art.

Among the first of the artists to use Classic themes for the interpretation of modern life was Jacques Louis David (1748–1825), also considered the most creative of the Neoclassicists. In his *Oath of the Horatii* (Fig. 20–2), painted several years before the outbreak of the French Revolution, he constructed a spare architectural framework for the tense figures, directly inspired by the Classic sculptures he had admired in Rome. Instead of sinuous Rococo

20–2 JACQUES LOUIS DAVID. *Oath of the Horatii.* 1784. *ca.* 14 ft. ½ in. × 11 ft. ½ in. Louvre, Paris. (Archives Photographiques)

rhythms, David developed a movement parallel to the picture plane in a space so shallow and with such controlled modeling that the effect resembles bas-relief sculpture. The public which flocked to see the painting in 1785 found in it more than pictorial significance; they interpreted this dramatic account of three Roman brothers, swearing to save the fatherland or perish, as an attack on the profligate behavior of the upper classes, who seemed unaware of the disasters threatening France. After the outbreak of the Revolution in 1789 David became the artistic dictator as well as the official painter of the Republic. His *Death of Marat* (Brussels), with its sharply defined shapes and cold light, remains the

most forceful statement of the Neo-classic artistic faith in the relevance of the clarity and order of ancient forms for the expression of modern political meanings (Fig. 20–3).

The ultimate definition of the Neo-classic manner was achieved by J. A. D. Ingres (1780–1867), the most notable of David's followers and the leader of conservative painting in France for half a century. To David's clarity of form Ingres added a profound feeling for nature, whose most beautiful aspects he selected after a comparison of living forms with the finest examples of Greek sculpture and High Renaissance painting. Although he chose classic poses as often as possible even for his modern figures, nothing he touched is devoid of an immediate feeling for life. Since he believed that line was the principal medium of expression, and color only a secondary means of clarifying and distinguishing forms, his portrait drawings, executed with the hardest of pencils, are among his most successful works. In the painting *Mme. Rivière* (Fig. 20–4) we see his mastery of harmonious rhythms in the sweeping lines of the shawl as it winds over the shoulders and falls across the figure in a large curve composed of several minor harmonies — a typical Neoclassic pose.

David's and Ingres's strict sense of form, based upon their studies of Antique sculpture, their vital and descriptive line, their selective use of nature, and their choice of noble subjects soon became an exclusive pattern for conservative painters throughout the nineteenth century. Coherent as such a program was for instructing students, it stifled more independent artists while helping many a mediocre one to conceal his own lack of talent and imagination. A typical example of such later academic painting, so-called because it was officially taught and practiced by the faculties of government art schools, is Alexandre Cabanel's *Birth of Venus* (1863) (Fig. 20–5). It shows us how tawdry the classic tradition became in the hands of those who practiced it without conviction — "cream-puff and pastry" painting, Emile Zola called it. The fact that this was one of the most popular pictures of its day and was acquired by Napoleon III for the imperial collections sharpens the contrast between official public, academic art and the work of those painters who were seeking a more meaningful expression for their times.

A distinction as to true artistic qualities must be made between such imitative, academic art and nineteenth-century conservative painting. Thus the idyllic scenes by Pierre Puvis de Chavannes (1824–1898) may seem at first

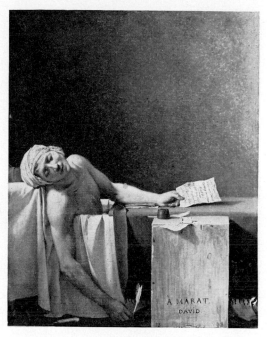

20–3 JACQUES LOUIS DAVID. *Death of Marat.* 1793. Musées Royaux d'Art et d'Histoire, Brussels. (Copyright, A.C.L., Brussels)

20–4 JEAN AUGUST DOMINIQUE INGRES. *Mme. Rivière.* 1805. *ca.* 3 ft. 10 in. × 3 ft. Louvre, Paris. (Archives Photographiques)

20–5 ALEXANDRE CABANEL. *The Birth of Venus.* 1863. *ca.* 4 ft. 3½ in. × 7 ft. 5 in. Metropolitan Museum of Art, New York.

glance only pale reflections of the tradition of David and Ingres, but closer inspection reveals a very personal treatment of the classic subject. The linear design and dreamlike effect of his small canvases also distinguish his larger murals, as in the scenes in the Panthéon illustrating the life of St. Geneviève, patron saint of Paris, or the allegorical subjects adorning the main staircase of the Boston Public Library. Chavannes' arrangement of flat, simplified, figures with cool silvery colors reinforcing the plane of the wall contributed much to the aesthetic of modern mural painting.

Meanwhile the lofty classicism of David and Ingres was not unchallenged in their own lifetime. In 1819 Théodore Géricault (1791–1824) exhibited his *Raft of the Medusa* (Fig. 20–6), a vivid account of a disastrous shipwreck in which hundreds of French emigrants traveling to North Africa perished as a result of official negli-

gence. The controversial subject matter, with its overtones of political criticism, was as unexpected in the midst of the reign of the placid Louis XVIII as was the young artist's intensely dramatic use of classically nude figures arranged in a monumental pyramidal design. In the few major works Géricault executed before his premature death, this uneasy combination of classic forms, romantic expression, and realistic technique epitomizes the major trends of French painting until almost 1875.

Géricault's position of leadership in the romantic movement was assumed by Eugène Delacroix (1798–1863), who encouraged the small group of artists to challenge the ideals of Ingres and his followers. Had Delacroix's talent been less than the majestic instrument it was, this struggle would have been most unequal. For Ingres, representing, as we have seen, the conservative painters, could muster to his support the

20–6 THÉODORE GÉRICAULT. *Raft of the Medusa.* 1818–1819. 16 ft. 2 in. × 23 ft. 3 in. Louvre, Paris. (Archives Photographiques)

majority of the faculties and students of the official schools; indeed, he himself was director of the French Academy in Rome. The romantics, on the other hand, could neither claim so many adherents nor present so united a front. The reason is clear; the classic program was intended for wide public acceptance; romantic art was necessarily personal and individual. Its merit depended more on each artist's intensity of personal expression than on an appeal to the general public.

The difference between the two schools must be sought in execution and expression rather than in subject matter. Both Delacroix and Ingres painted classic scenes and Turkish subjects. But the romantic artist usually preferred exotic subjects. In turbulent episodes from Medieval history he found opportunities for sumptuous displays of costume and color. In this respect much romantic painting suffers from an excess at an opposite extreme from classicism: the subject is suffocated in an accumulation of historical details such as we find in the contemporaneous novels of Victor Hugo and the elder Alexandre Dumas. Delacroix clarified his themes through his power of expression, the grandeur of his design, and his poignant treatment of tragic subjects. He rejected the rigid order of High Renaissance principles of design which guided the Neoclassicists for the spatial effects of Baroque art. Only in this way could he achieve the deep space enlivened by the passage of tumultuous forces which we see in his *Entrance of the Crusaders into Constantinople* (Fig. 20–7). The contrast between the foreground crowded with pathetic crouching fig-

20–7 EUGÈNE DELACROIX. *Entrance of the Crusaders into Constantinople.* 1840. *ca.* 13 ft. 5½ in. × 16 ft. 4 in. Louvre, Paris. (Archives Photographiques)

ures and the deep background stretching beyond the city to the waters of the Golden Horn communicates the anguish of the Byzantine patricians humbled before the arrogant intruders. A strong movement sweeping inward from the foreground and repeated again and again defines a space in which the figures are organized by light and dark, warm and cool spots of color.

In his small canvases for private collectors Delacroix often treated dramatic episodes from literature. His illustrations for *Hamlet, Faust,* and Byron's poetry are penetrating revelations of the texts, expressed in inimitable line and color. Delacroix thought no one a

draftsman who could not sketch a body falling from a fourth-story window, and he declared that "gray is the enemy of all painting." His sinuous, agitated line, which permits the most expressive distortions, and his acrid color contrasts, frequently between blue-greens and a variety of reds, demonstrate his mastery as a colorist.

To a certain degree both the romantic and classicist nineteenth-century painters increasingly neglected contemporary subject matter. In 1846 the poet Charles Baudelaire denounced this attitude in a review of the Salon [1]

[1] The annual art exhibition sponsored by the French government was commonly called

20–8   JEAN FRANÇOIS MILLET. *The Gleaners.* 1851. Louvre, Paris. (Giraudon)

exhibition in which he called for painting that, as he somewhat sardonically demanded, should express "the heroism of modern life." It was easier to ask for than to find such subjects, and the techniques with which to express them. Somewhat earlier, a group of landscape and figure painters who had settled near the village of Barbizon in the forest of Fontainebleau had begun to paint scenes of peasant life which in their own quiet way might be considered "heroic." Chief amongst the

the Salon after the great hall (*salon*) in the palace of the Louvre where it had been held in the eighteenth century. Throughout the first half of the nineteenth century this was the most important European exhibition; an artist's reputation could be made if his work was accepted, favorably hung, and awarded a prize. Rejection by the jury could adversely affect a painter's career.

"men of 1830" (known as such because they had left Paris after the July Revolution that year, discouraged by the confusion and the cost of city life) were Théodore Rousseau (1812–1867) and Jean François Millet (1814–1875). Rousseau's contemplative landscapes were based on studies made out of doors and later arranged in compositions reminiscent of the seventeenth-century Dutch landscape tradition he so much admired. Himself of peasant stock, Millet's sympathies for such life seem close to those of the seventeenth-century French realist master, Louis Le Nain (Fig. 10–40). The quiet design of Millet's paintings accents his scrupulous truth of detail and contributes to the dignity with which he invests even the simplest rural tasks (Fig. 20–8). Although this presentation of the sol-

20–9 CAMILLE COROT. *The Port of La Rochelle*. 1851. 19⅞ in. × 28 in. Stephen C. Clark Collection, New York. (Courtesy of Stephen C. Clark Collection)

emn grandeur of the working classes caused Millet to be charged with socialism in his lifetime, it is actually a late echo of the romantic intuition which, like Wordsworth's, found a touch of nobility in the humblest lives.

In close association with the painters of Barbizon, Camille Corot (1796-1875) developed his own vision of landscape. A man of simple, generous impulses, his canvases are often as unassuming as their author. His early work, including many Italian scenes, is notable for the precise definition of landscape and architectural forms. In his later, more imaginative paintings his green-gray palette, sensitively adjusted for the slightest changes of value, created effects often reminiscent of the early photographs in which he was so much interested. Midway in his career he

painted the spacious *Port of La Rochelle* (Fig. 20–9). Here the interplay of dark and light areas in the foreground, through which the figures move unhurriedly, is prophetic of the later Impressionist interest in climate and atmosphere. The calm geometric shapes in the background suggest the concern which such painters as Cézanne would later feel for solid structural design.

Corot and his friends in Barbizon were little concerned with the course of events in Paris, where the rapid development of an urban industrial civilization created acute political and social unrest. But in a Parisian studio only a few steps from Notre Dame, the lithographer Honoré Daumier (1808–1879) was in close touch with this social ferment. For forty years, from the July Monarchy through the Second Empire,

20–10 HONORÉ DAUMIER. *The Third-Class Carriage.* 1860's. *ca.* 2 ft. 2 in. × 3 ft. Metropolitan Museum of Art, New York.

he contributed satirical lithographs each week to the leading humorous journals. In this prodigious output of some four thousand prints his keen insight, coupled with his sympathy for human beings, was constantly expressed in brilliant draftsmanship. Even when we are no longer amused by the point of his story, our sympathies are engaged by the warmth of his characterization and our admiration is equally excited by his mastery of line. In his lifetime Daumier was known principally for his lithographs; only his intimate friends were aware that he was also a very powerful painter. His *Third-Class Carriage* (Fig. 20–10) exemplifies his insight into human behavior, patient under adversity. In this large easel painting he achieved an ef-

fect of solemn monumentality through the contrast between the broad triangular design of the persons seated in the foreground with the generalized figures behind them. Never before had the peculiar pressures of modern life, especially as they affect the classes so largely cut off from the benefits of a materialistic culture, been so penetratingly and persuasively depicted.

Daumier's technique is also of interest, since he carried into oil his searching draftsmanship, defining his forms in crisp outlines before covering the linear pattern with oil glazes as freely brushed as water color. In a sense Daumier may be said to have painted for himself at a time when the Salon jury required too tight and finished a surface to suit him. By his un-

20–11 GUSTAVE COURBET. *The Stone Breakers.* 1849. *ca.* 5 ft. 5 in. × 7 ft. 10 in. Formerly in Museum, Dresden.

derstanding of the effects to be secured from a surface which his academic contemporaries thought "unfinished," Daumier prepared the way for our own concern with varied techniques and surface treatment.

A more aggressive attitude toward subjects chosen from the life of the lower classes is conspicuous in the work of Gustave Courbet (1819–1877). In 1848 Europe was wracked by revolution. Twice within six months the barricades were thrown up in Paris. Courbet was suspected, perhaps not without reason, of socialist tendencies, and some of the opposition to his paintings may well have sprung from such suspicions. Yet today his methods and intentions are considered irreproachable. In his *Burial at Ornans* (1849, Louvre) he painted the funeral of his grandfather on a scale hitherto reserved for the depiction of great public occasions. The *Stone Breakers* (Fig.

20–11) stirred violent protests because of the allegedly commonplace character of the subject. But his bold, somber palette was essentially traditional and certainly in harmony with his subject matter. Lights and darks converge abruptly along the edges of simplified planes, and a surface richness results from the various ways he used his pigments, often modeling his forms with the palette knife or his fingers. To his contemporaries such methods seemed unbearably crude. Since he intentionally sought the simplest and most direct methods of expression, in composition as well as in technique, he was accused of being a primitive. Courbet insisted that he wished only to paint the life of his own times in the costumes of the day, and that toward such an end he studied "without prejudice the art of the old and modern masters." We know from his own statement that the *Stone Breakers* was inspired by the sight of an old man and a boy working on the roads. Although their poverty touched him and he thought he was presenting his own vision as directly as possible, we can see how much he instinctively relied on tradition by comparing the figures with those of the shepherds in Poussin's *Et in Arcadia Ego*, painted two centuries before. But to the public, which believed that only the ideal or imaginary subject was suitable for such important paintings, Courbet's insistence that he could not paint an angel because he had never seen one sounded blasphemous.

To define such paintings of everyday life and of landscapes interpreted without sentimentality, a leading modern critic has introduced the term "naturalism." Courbet preferred the word "realism," which he used as a slogan for a large one-man exhibition of his work in 1855. There is something to be said, however, for the newer word, since remarkably realistic techniques had been used much earlier, notably in Roman art and in Flemish and Dutch painting (see p. 414). By "naturalism" we understand a kind of art in which subject and expression are strictly contemporary. In naturalistic art the artist portrays only objects and situations which he has seen and experienced himself.

The climax of this naturalistic movement was reached with the work of Edouard Manet (1832–1883) and the Impressionists. Although the term "Impressionism" was first used in 1874 by a journalist ridiculing a landscape by Claude Monet (1840–1926) called *Impression — Sunrise*, the beginning of the bitter controversy which raged for twenty years over the merits of Impressionism appeared ten years earlier, in 1863 at the *Salon des Refusés*. This exhibition received its name because the works rejected by the jury for the Salon that year were so numerous and the artists' protests so vigorous that the

20-12 EDOUARD MANET. *The Dead Christ with Angels*. 1864. 69⅞ in. × 61 in. Metropolitan Museum of Art, New York.

government was obliged to hold a separate exhibition of the rejected paintings. Here Manet shocked the public with his *Déjeuner sur l'herbe*, the portrayal of a nude woman and two clothed men seated in a wood. Like Courbet, Manet had tried to combine the modern subject with an earlier design, for the composition, and even the theme, were derived from sixteenth-century Italian art. But Manet's refusal to idealize the figures or to minimize the contemporary character of the event was offensive to many. Two years later his *Olympia*, another frank treatment of the nude, again aroused protest. In viewing his *Dead Christ with Angels* (Fig. 20-12) we can still sense something of the public's bewilderment, for here the nude is treated with all the power of Manet's searching vision, but without a shred of religious mysticism or idealization. Had he wished, Manet might have urged that there were precedents for his vision, and even for his technique, in such earlier realists as Hals, Velasquez, and Goya, on whom he certainly relied more than once for inspiration. But, although he would have welcomed official recognition, he would not attempt to justify his principles in public, nor would he compromise them. It was not until the twentieth century that the intrinsic quality of his work and its importance for the development of modern art were fully appreciated.

From the middle 1860's such painters as Claude Monet (1840–1926), Edgar Degas (1834–1917), Camille Pissarro (1830–1903), and Auguste Renoir (1841–1919) followed Manet's lead in depicting scenes of contemporary life and landscape. Their desire for a more modern expression led them to prize the immediacy of visual impression and persuaded the landscapists, especially Monet and Pissarro, to work out of doors. From this custom of painting directly from nature came the spontaneous revelation of atmosphere and climate characteristic of Impressionist painting. Their rejection of idealistic interpretation and of literary anecdote was paralleled by their scrutiny of color and light. Recent scientific studies of light and the invention of chemical pigments had increased their sensitivity to the multiplicity of colors in nature and gave them new colors with which to work. Their eight cooperative exhibitions, held between 1874 and 1886, usually irritated the public. But their technique was actually less radical than it seemed at the time; in certain respects they were merely developing the color theories of Leonardo and the actual practice of Rubens, Constable, Turner (see pp. 678–80), and Delacroix. The Impressionists sought to create the illusion of forms bathed in light and atmosphere. This required an intensive study of light as the source of our experience of color. The Impressionists

revealed the important visual truth that local color — the actual color of the object — is usually modified by the quality of the light in which it is seen, and by reflections from other objects and modifications produced by juxtaposed colors. Complementary colors, for example, if used side by side in large enough areas, intensify each other. In small quantities, though, or mixed, they fuse into a neutral tone. Shadows are not gray or black, as earlier painters had thought, but are composed of colors complementary to the hue of the object casting the shadow, if not modified by reflections or other conditions. Furthermore, the juxtaposition of colors on the canvas for the eye to fuse at a distance produces a more intense hue than the mixing of the same colors on the palette. Although it is not strictly true that the Impressionists separated the primary hues, such as blue and yellow, and juxtaposed them to create green, they achieved remarkably brilliant effects with their characteristically short, choppy brush strokes which so accurately caught the vibrating quality of light. The fact that at close range the surfaces of their canvases look unintelligible, and that forms and objects appear only when the eye fuses the strokes at a certain distance accounts for much of the adverse criticism which they received at first.

Of the Impressionists Claude Monet carried this method furthest, especially in a series of paintings of the same scene, such as his twenty-six views of *Rouen Cathedral*, or the sixteen views of *Waterloo Bridge* (Fig. 20–13). In each case the cathedral or the river scene was observed from the same point of view at differing times of day and under various climatic and atmospheric conditions. If Monet is charged with an attitude which is too impersonal and almost scientific, we may reply that he has given us a record of the passing of time, as seen in

20–13 CLAUDE MONET. *Waterloo Bridge, London.* 1903. 25½ in. × 36 in. Worcester Art Museum, Worcester, Massachusetts. (Worcester Art Museum)

the movement of light over identical forms, unparalleled and unexcelled in the history of art. Later critics accused Monet and his companions of destroying form and order for the sake of evanescent atmospheric effects, but we may feel that the study of light is properly the "form" of Monet's finest paintings, rather than the narrower definition which recognizes "formal" properties only in geometrical shapes.

Although such landscapes are the most strictly "impressionist" works of the group, the figure paintings of Renoir and Degas, and those executed by Manet in the last decade of his life, are revelations of the beauty and interest in everyday surroundings. After 1870 Manet put aside his dark, Spanish palette and half-traditional subjects for the brighter Impressionist color and

scenes from daily life. His last work, the *Bar at the Folies-Bergères* (Fig. 20–14), is in some respects his most successful interpretation of a modern scene restricted now through his own tastes to the world of fashion and pleasure, a world far removed from the pressures of poverty and toil depicted by Millet, Daumier, and Courbet. Indeed, never before or since have the pastimes of the middle classes been portrayed with so much sympathy and charm as by the Impressionist masters in the 1870's and '80's. The surface of Manet's canvas vibrates with the reflections of light spilling from the gas lamps over the figures and the brilliant still life of fruit and bottles on the counter. In this study of artificial light, both actual and reflected in the mirror background, the subject matter has lost

20–14 EDOUARD MANET. *The Bar at the Folies-Bergères.* 1882. 37¾ in.× 51⅛ in. Home House Society, Courtauld Institute of Art, University of London. (Copyright *Country Life*)

all its earlier importance. Manet tells us little about the barmaid, and less about her customer, but much about his own visual experience. Because of this transference of the center of interest from the subject to the artist's own feelings and because of the way in which he has painted them, Manet has sometimes been considered the pioneer of modern painting, and even of abstraction.

Among Manet's contemporaries Renoir and Degas present two differing, even opposed, attitudes toward figure painting. Renoir had an absorbing interest in people; he delighted in unaffected feminine charm and expressed his joy in it in a hundred beguiling studies. But by 1880 he had grown dis-

satisfied with the dissolution of form in light and sought a stricter discipline. The change in his art is marked in his *Luncheon of the Boating Party* (1881) (Fig. 20–15). Over the figures and still life in the foreground plays the inimitably iridescent sheen of Renoir's rainbow palette, but his instinctive knowledge of color is now controlled by a strong sense of design. The line of the table swung at an angle to the picture plane is reinforced in depth by the railing and the awning above. Within this space, which is plastically as well as atmospherically convincing, the figures move as casually as in actual life. Indeed, the way they turn across each other creates an almost photographic sense of movement much like the mod-

20–15 AUGUSTE RENOIR. *Luncheon of the Boating Party.* 1881. 51 in. × 68 in. Phillips Gallery, Washington, D. C. (Phillips Gallery)

ern candid camera shot, reminding us that Renoir and his colleagues studied photography with care in search of the new compositional devices it suggested.

After a trip to Italy, where he studied Raphael and the Pompeiian frescoes, Renoir devoted more attention to drawing and three-dimensional design. His color, too, grew in depth and meaning from his admiration for Rubens and Delacroix. From their reds he derived the dominant coloration which became almost an obsession in his last years. His interest in abstract rhythms in deep space is often expressed in bathing scenes, so monumental in scale and generalized in treatment that it is no surprise to find him restoring to the twentieth century a specific link with the classic tradition when he gave to

his nude subjects such titles as the *Judgment of Paris.*

We find in the sudden angles and abrupt spatial recession of Renoir's *Canoers* a suggestion of the influence of Japanese art[2] which became a more prominent factor in the work of Edgar Degas. Degas' selective vision, trained in the tradition of Ingres's linearism and refined by a careful study of photography and of the asymmetrical designs and diagonal or angular perspective of Japanese prints, was analytical, impersonal, and often mordantly

[2] Japanese prints had become known in Europe in the early 1860's and were collected and studied by many artists who admired the clear, flat patterns, the unexpected points of view, and the informal glimpses of contemporary life.

20–16   EDGAR DEGAS. *Place de la Concorde (Portrait of M. le Vicomte Lepic and His Daughters). ca.* 1873. 31¾ in. × 47⅝ in. Location unknown. (Durand-Ruel)

critical of human beings. Whatever his subject, Degas saw it as clear line and pattern, observed from a new and unexpected visual angle, so that the first impression, which is what the picture seems to record, appears as casual as the theme itself. Yet such effortlessness was not achieved without enormous research. In such a scene as *Vicomte Lepic and His Daughters* (Fig. 20–16) Degas has created a skillful artistic equivalent for the camera eye. In the divergent movements of the father and his small daughters, of the man entering the picture from the left, and of the horse and carriage passing across the background, we have a vivid pictorial account of a moment in time at a particular position in space, much as Monet in his own way defined such space and time in landscape painting. In another instant there would be no picture, for each of the figures would have moved in a different direction,

and the harmony of the particular moment would have dissolved into nothing. Certainly much of Degas' effect resides in his magical sense of the significance of empty space. Although his earlier works are in oil, his most characteristic medium came to be pastel, which he was obliged to use when his eyesight began to fail. The chalks enabled him to record his reactions to form and movement more quickly than did oil, and with the bright dry colors he created a new variation of Impressionist sensitivity to light in spaces which are carefully ordered and constructed.

In the work of Henri de Toulouse-Lautrec (1864–1901), who deeply admired Degas, the older master's cool scrutiny of contemporary life was transformed into mordant satire and deft character analysis. Unlike the earlier satirists Goya and Daumier, who saw beyond the personal to the impersonal, the generic, and the universal, Lautrec dealt with definite individuals, especially those whose lives were spent either as entertainers or spectators, in the unnatural gaiety of the music halls and cafés of Paris. In his *At the Moulin Rouge* (Fig. 20–1) the influence of Japanese prints can be seen in the oblique and asymmetrical composition, the diagonals in space, and the strong patterns of line and color. But each element, although closely studied in actual life and already familiar to us in the work of the older Impressionists, has been so emphasized or exaggerated that the tone is new. Compare, for instance, the mood of this painting with the relaxed and casual atmosphere of Renoir's *Luncheon of the Boating Party* (Fig. 20–15). In addition to his paintings and drawings in many media, Lautrec was a prolific printmaker. He was the first major painter to design for commercial art. His posters (Fig. 0–24), in which his feeling for linear design was expressed on a large scale, and his book illustrations had considerable influence on other contemporary art.

By 1886 the Impressionist painters were accepted as serious artists by most of the critics and by a large portion of the public. But just at the time when their gay and colorful studies of contemporary life no longer seemed crude and unfinished, the painters themselves and a group of younger followers came to feel that too many of the traditional elements of picture-making were being neglected in the search for momentary sensations of light and color. Renoir restudied the formal principles of Rubens, as we have seen, and also of the Venetian masters. A more systematic examination of the properties of three-dimensional space, of the expressive qualities of line, pattern, and color, and of the symbolic character of subject matter was undertaken by four men in particular: Seurat, Cézanne, Van Gogh, and Gauguin. Since their art diverges

so markedly from earlier Impressionism, although each painter had at first accepted the Impressionist methods and never rejected the new and brighter palette, they have come to be known as the Post-Impressionists, a term which signifies simply their chronological position in nineteenth-century French painting. Without a sound understanding of their individual styles and achievements it would be impossible to comprehend fully the art of the twentieth century.

At the eighth and last Impressionist exhibition in 1886 Georges Seurat's (1859–1891) large canvas, *Sunday Afternoon on Grande Jatte Island* (Fig. 20–17), set forth the Impressionist interest in holiday themes and in the analysis of light in a new and monumental synthesis which at the time seemed strangely rigid and remote. Seurat had studied the color theories of Delacroix and of the color scientists Helmholtz and Chevreul, and had worked out a system of painting in small roundish dots, of about equal size, with scientific exactness in the relation of primary and complementary colors (a method which he called divisionism, but which is often incorrectly described as pointillism). It was a difficult procedure, disciplined and painstaking as the Impressionist method had been spontaneous and exuberant. Thus Seurat transformed the Impressionist illusion of natural appearance into a precise organization composed of people and objects that are solid and arranged with mathematical regularity in a deep space filled with sunlight and air, yet which paradoxically is also seen as an effective surface pattern. In the *Grande Jatte* the pattern is based on the verticals of the figures and trees, the horizontals in the shadows and the distant embankment, the diagonals in the shadow and shore line, each of which contributes to the psychological effect. At the same time, by

20–17   GEORGES SEURAT. *Sunday Afternoon on Grande Jatte Island.* 1884–1886. 81¼ in. × 120¼ in. Art Institute of Chicago. (Courtesy of the Art Institute of Chicago, Helen Birch Bartlett Memorial Collection)

the use of meticulously calculated values the painter carves out a deep rectangular space, and in creating both pattern and suggested space he plays upon repeated motifs: the profile of the lady, the parasol, and the cylindrical forms of the figures, each so placed in space as to set up a rhythmic movement in depth as well as from side to side. The picture is filled with sunshine but not broken into transient patches of color. Light, air, people, and landscape are fixed in an abstract design in which line, color, value, and shape cohere in an organization as precise as a machine. This is a calculating, intellectual art — in no sense a mechanical procedure — but an art which, in the lineage of Paolo Uccello and Piero della Francesca, moves us by its serene monumentality.

The early works of Paul Cézanne (1839–1906) were romantic in content, baroque in design and painted with the tempered palette and thick pigment of Courbet. But after he met the Impressionists, especially Pissarro, who instructed him in the intricacies of their technique, he accepted their theories of color and their faith in subjects chosen from everyday life. Yet his own studies of the old masters in the Louvre persuaded him that Impressionist painting lacked form and structure. As he said: "I want to make of Impressionism something solid and lasting like the art in the museums." Impelled by his knowledge of Tintoretto and Poussin, who had so magnificently conquered the problems of spatial organization, he sought not to copy but to create equally compelling space relationships by new uses of the old means. The basis of his art was his study of nature, observed at length with his own peculiarly intense powers of visual concentration. In his ability to sustain this process of examining the motif, whether landscape, still life or figure, through days and months and even years, Cézanne resembled the contemporary scientist who could not rest until repeated tests had proved his hypothesis. Cézanne explored with especial care the properties of line, plane, and color, and their interrelationships: the effect of every kind of linear direction, the capacity of planes to create the sensation of depth, the intrinsic qualities of color, and the power of colors to modify the direction and depth of lines and planes. Through the recession of cool colors and the advance of warm, he controlled volume and depth. Having observed that the point of saturation or of highest intensity of color produces the greatest fullness of form, he painted apples, for example, chiefly in one hue — such as green — and by his meticulously exact intensities of green he achieved convincing solidity and structure by the control of color alone, in place of the more usual method of modeling in values of light and shade.

Although nature was Cézanne's point of departure, and the presentation of nature his goal, his object was not verisimilitude but the creation of a pictorial reality parallel to nature and more essential, in a philosophical sense, than any mere appearance could be. His search for essential reality led him to consider closely the fundamental forms of natural objects. Although Cézanne never reduced natural objects to geometrical abstractions, the monumental effect of his forms suggests that they have been stripped of the accidental variations of individual appearance. In this sense we can read his famous remark to a young follower, that the painter should "treat nature in terms of the cylinder, and the sphere and the cone," as an injunction to generalize natural forms in terms of their simplest and broadest dimensions, rather than to replace them by geometrical constructions. Yet simultaneously this tendency toward simplifying individual forms was counteracted by his discovery of a new and more complex space.

Since the spatial construction in Cézanne's paintings was not laid out in line and value before the colors were applied, but was developed only gradually as the painting progressed through the most sensitive adjustment of innumerable small planes of color, it follows that usually there is not a single over-all perspective point of view, as had prevailed from Renaissance painting down to and including Impressionism. Instead, there are several or even many different perspectives combined, juxtaposed, and overlaid within a single composition. The adjustment of these different perspectives, which may be thought of as the bringing together of several views of an object upon a single surface, was not accomplished without difficulty. The frequent distortions, which resulted when these different views were combined, led the public at first to believe that Cézanne could not draw. The truth would seem to be that he was creating a new kind of drawing, just as he had created a new kind of space (Plate 7).

Cézanne's method, at once simple and complex, may be seen at its best in his mature work after 1885. In his still-life arrangements, such as Figure 20–18, the individual forms have lost something of their private character as bottles and fruit and approach the condition of cylinders and spheres, for it is only in this way that they can most effectively contribute to that intricate interplay of volumes moving in space which is the real subject of the painting. The spectator cannot fail to marvel

20–18 PAUL CÉZANNE. *Still Life. ca.* 1890. 25½ in. × 31½ in. Chester Dale Collection, National Gallery of Art, Washington, D. C. (National Gallery)

at the skill with which Cézanne has constructed a design as monumental as any in Western painting out of the most commonplace facts of daily life.

Just as landscape had been the principal source of Impressionist theory and experiment, so it became the subject for Cézanne's most complete transformation of Impressionism. In his many views of *Mont-Sainte-Victoire* (Fig. 20–19), the mountain near his home in Aix-en-Provence, we can see how the transitory effects of changing atmospheric conditions have been replaced by a more concentrated and lengthier analysis of a large lighted space. This space stretches out behind and beyond the plane of the canvas,

which is emphasized by the pattern of the pine tree in the foreground, and it is made up of numerous small elements such as roads, fields, houses, and the aqueduct in the far right, each seen from a slightly different point of view. Above this shifting, receding perspective rises the largest mass of all, the mountain, with an effect of being simultaneously near and far away. Is it erroneous to suggest that this effect is much closer to the actual experience each of us might have of such a view, when the forms of the landscape grow gradually within our vision rather than being fixed once and for all by a strict one- or two-point perspective such as a photograph would show us?

20·10 PAUL CÉZANNE. *Mont-Sainte-Victoire*. 1885–1887. 26¾ in. × 36¼ in. Home House Society, Courtauld Institute of Art, University of London. (Home House Copyright)

The ability to endow everyday experience with grandeur and dignity also distinguishes Cézanne's figure compositions, such as the *Card Players* (Fig. 20–20). Cézanne painted many portraits, but scarcely any do we now remember for the individual personality of the sitter. Yet to claim that his method depersonalizes his sitters is to overlook the significance of his accomplishments. The four men absorbed in their game may not be very interesting persons, taken one by one, but in the very process of generalizing their appearances Cézanne seems to have discovered something meaningful about their relation to humanity. He has painted not men, but Man, and in so doing justifies his own hope of recovering the great tradition. Studying the *Card Play-*

ers we think, not of specific individuals living in the later nineteenth century, but of the greatest masterpieces of figural representation of the past, of Poussin and Le Nain, of Gothic and even of Greek sculpture.

Vincent van Gogh (1853–1890) was a Hollander by birth, the son of a Protestant pastor. He believed that he too had a religious vocation and worked as a missionary in the slums of London and the mining districts of Belgium, but repeated failures exhausted his body and brought him close to despair. Only after he turned to painting and mastered the Impressionist technique did he find a means to communicate his experience of a world illuminated by God's love, which he represented pictorially in terms of his favorite col-

20–20 PAUL CÉZANNE. *The Card Players.* 1892. 25⅝ in. × 31⅞ in. Stephen C. Clark Collection, New York. (Museum of Modern Art)

or, yellow. His insistence on the expressive values of color led him to develop his characteristic surface textures. The thickness, shape, and direction of his brush strokes create a tactile counterpart to his intensely vibrant color schemes. Now a thickly loaded brush moves vehemently back and forth or at right angles, giving a textile-like effect; now the palette knife or a finger rubs on or smoothes the pigment; now the tube squeezes dots or streaks upon the canvas. Everywhere we feel the impetuosity with which Van Gogh approached each work, and which might have led to disaster if it had not been controlled by an innate sensibility. Col-

or is used in its highest intensity, color area meeting color area abruptly, thus creating an effect of emphatic line and silhouette — an influence from Japanese prints.

But for Van Gogh the act of painting always meant more than the skillful manipulation of the artistic elements. He thought of each work as a symbolic equivalent of his own experience, which would in turn lead the spectator to a more profoundly spiritual understanding of life. His own description of his *Woman Rocking a Cradle* (*Mme. Roulin*) (Fig. 20–21) shows how he thought of color both as an abstract relationship of hues and at the same time as expressive of the symbolic as well as representational values of the subject:

I have in hand the portrait of Roulin's wife, which I was working on before I was ill. In it I have ranged the reds from rose to orange, which rise through the yellows to lemon, with light and sombre greens. . . . I have just been saying to Gauguin about this picture that when he and I were talking about the Icelandic fishermen and of their mournful isolation, exposed to all dangers, alone on the sad sea . . . the idea came to me to paint such a picture that sailors, who are at once children and martyrs, seeing it in the cabin of their boat should feel the old sense of cradling come over them and remember their own lullabies. Now, if you please, it's like a chromolithograph from a cheap shop. A woman in green with orange hair stands out against a background of green with pink flowers. Now these discordant sharps of crude pink, crude orange, and crude green are softened by flats of red and green.[3]

And on another occasion he wrote that the color in one of his paintings was "not locally true from the point of view of the stereoscopic realist, but color to suggest any emotion of an ardent temperament."

Van Gogh's body and mind, physically weakened by years of poverty, isolation, and neglect, could not long sustain his burning desire to achieve through his art an evangelical expression of psychic experience. But before his early death he created a series of canvases in which color and texture approach abstraction and yet communicate, as immediately as material substances can, the intensity of his awareness of nature. In his *Wheatfield with Blackbirds* (Fig. 20–22), painted just before his death, the intense color, the long horizontal shape which is Oriental in feeling, and the short, sharp brush strokes combine to create, as he himself wrote, "vast stretches of corn

[3] *Further Letters of Vincent van Gogh to His Brother, 1886–1889*, Houghton Mifflin, Boston, 1929, Letters 573,574.

20–21   VINCENT VAN GOGH. *Woman Rocking a Cradle* (Mme. Roulin). 1889. 36⅜ in. × 28¾ in. Rijksmuseum Kröller-Müller, Otterlo, Holland (Rijksmuseum)

under troubled skies, and I did not need to go out of my way to express sadness, and the extreme of loneliness."[4]

A similar rejection of objective representation in favor of subjective expression is found in the work of Paul Gauguin (1843–1903). He, also, used color in new and unexpected combinations, but his art is very different from Van Gogh's. It is no less tormented, perhaps, but more learned in its combination of rare and exotic elements, and more broadly decorative. Gauguin had painted as an amateur, but after taking lessons with Pissarro he resigned from his prosperous brokerage business in 1883 to devote his time entirely to painting. When his work did not sell his savings were soon exhausted, and he and his family were reduced to pov-

[4] *Op. cit.*, Letter 649.

20–22 VINCENT VAN GOGH. *Wheatfield with Blackbirds.* 1890. 19⅞ in. × 39½ in. Ir. V. W. van Gogh Collection, Stedelijk Museum, Amsterdam.

erty. Not even suffering could make him abandon his painting, however, for he felt that in spite of ridicule and neglect he was called to be a great art-

20–23 PAUL GAUGUIN. *The Yellow Christ.* 1899. 36⅛ in. × 25⅝ in. Albright Art Gallery, Buffalo, New York. (Albright Art Gallery)

ist. In his search for provocative subjects as well as for an economical place to live he visited Martinique, and lived also for some time in small villages in Brittany. Thus even before he settled in Tahiti in 1891, tropical color and subjects drawn from primitive life had entered his art. In the *Yellow Christ* (Fig. 20–23) he combined an image of folk sculpture with his recollections of the Breton peasants' piety. Gauguin's companions briefly called such painting "Synthetist-Symbolist," an awkward term which we may take to mean that the various elements of color, line, and form were symbols of experience and recollection arranged in an artistic synthesis, distinct from the Impressionists' direct analysis of visual appearance.

In his attitude toward color Gauguin broke with the Impressionists' studies of minutely contrasted hues. As he said, "A meter of green is greener than a centimeter if you wish to express greenness. . . . How does that tree look to you? Green? All right, then use green, the greenest on your palette. And that shadow, a little bluish? Don't be afraid. Paint it as blue as you can." [5] His influence was felt especially by members of the younger generation, such as Maurice Denis, who declared:

Gauguin freed us from all the restraints which the idea of copying nature had placed upon us. For instance, if it was permissible to use vermilion in painting a tree which seemed reddish . . . why not stress even to the point of deformation the curve of a beautiful shoulder or conventionalize the symmetry of a bough unmoved by a breath of air? Now we understood everything in the Louvre, the Primitives, Rubens, Veronese.[6]

Gauguin's art, too, can be understood as a complex mixture of Eastern and Western elements, of themes common to the great masters of the European Renaissance treated in a manner based on his study of earlier arts and of non-European cultures. In Tahiti and the Marquesas, where he spent the last ten years of his life, he expressed his love of primitive life and brilliant color in a series of magnificent, decorative canvases. The design is often based, although indirectly, on native motifs, and the color owes its peculiar harmonics of lilac, pink, and lemon to the tropical flora of the islands. But the mood of such works is that of a sophisticated modern man interpreting an ancient and innocent way of life already threatened by European colonialism. Although the figures and costumes in his *Maternity* (Fig. 20-24) are Tahitian, the theme of the nursing mother and child is familiar in Western art. The simplified linear pattern and broad areas of flat color recall the Byzantine enamels and Medieval stained glass which Gauguin admired, and the slight distortion of the flattened forms is not unlike similar effects in Egyptian and

20-24   PAUL GAUGUIN. *Maternity.* 1896. 36¾ in. × 23½ in. Private American collection, New York.

Cambodian sculpture. Through the decorative character of the vertical design and the subject matter, in the presentation of fruit and flowers to the mother, Gauguin presents a content whose meaning is wider and deeper than mere appearance.

Gauguin's interest in the so-called "primitive" arts, whether of Europe or of Polynesia, and Van Gogh's insistence that his *Woman Rocking a Cradle* was "like a chromolithograph from a cheap shop" are indicative of a fundamental shift in artistic values which was occurring toward the end of the nineteenth century. The Renaissance tradition of the artist as a highly trained professional had been compromised by the huge numbers of well-educated but

[5] Maurice Denis, "L'Influence de Paul Gauguin," *L'Occident*, October, 1903, reprinted in *Theories, 1890–1910*, Rouart et Watelin, Paris, 1920, p. 167.
[6] *Op. cit.*, p. 169.

20–25 HENRI ROUSSEAU. *The Waterfall*. 1910. Art Institute of Chicago. (Courtesy of the Art Institute of Chicago, Helen Birch Bartlett Memorial Collection)

merely competent graduates of innumerable schools and academies whose uninspired works were technically irreproachable but dull. The work of Van Gogh and of Gauguin suggested that since authentic artistic experience could be found in the art of peoples who had not been influenced by European culture, it might also be looked for in the art of the amateur, of the person who has true artistic instincts but who has never had the opportunity to acquire a professional education. The first such inspired amateur was Henri Rousseau (1844–1910), called "le Douanier" because he earned a living as a minor official in the Paris customs. Rousseau possessed an instinctive and extraordinary gift for arranging colors and shapes in patterns of great aesthetic power, in which a bold design was never overwhelmed by his fondness for minute detail. In his spare time he painted astonishing visions of tropical scenery (he is said to have served in the French army in Mexico in his youth), where wild animals are often seen in jungles composed of mammoth house plants (Fig. 20–25). Rousseau himself venerated professional craftsmanship and always hoped that his paintings would be accepted at the official exhibitions. But his work encountered only ridicule and scorn from his contemporaries. His lasting importance was understood only toward the end of his life, by younger artists who incorporated his contributions into the fabric of modern art.

Painting, from Cimabue to Rubens, had evolved toward complexity of design, especially design in space, and richness of palette where color melts into color until, with the Impressionists, everything was dissolved into scintillating light broken up into an infinite number of color spots. Whereas Seurat and Cézanne sought structure, solidity, and organization in depth, Van Gogh and Gauguin revived flat pattern design, the use of harmonious and contrasting areas of color, and emphatic line such as one finds in Byzantine and Mohammedan, Oriental and primitive, art. The emotional intensity of Van Gogh and Gauguin also served as a corrective to the intellectual, scientific approach of Seurat and Cézanne, which could be used successfully only if held under a perfect and sensitive control. Van Gogh's and Gauguin's non-naturalistic tendencies were also particularly opposed to the influence of the camera, which was inciting many painters to vie with science in producing verisimilar recordings of nature. Thus the green horses in Gauguin recall the arbitrary color schemes of the green pigs of the Prodigal Son or the blue hair on the head of the Christ in the thirteenth-century stained glass at Chartres cathedral.

The great diversity found in Seurat, Cézanne, Van Gogh, and Gauguin is symbolic of the "many-mindedness" of modern painting and of its challenge to a new kind of seeing. Impressionism failed to be accepted as a legitimate, not to say orthodox, method of painting until people had finally caught up with the painters' vision, as they had in the case of Courbet and the Barbizon group. Always late,

a tradition, like an old family, must constantly renew itself with the body and soul of each new age. Otherwise the end is in sight. A tradition in art simply means the heritage of qualities which deserve not only to endure but to develop. If a tradition is not also an evolution it is unworthy of the reverence which we accord to it.[7]

These ideas we inherit — they form the tradition of our civilization. Such traditional ideas are never static. They are either fading into meaningless formulae, or are gaining power by the new lights thrown by a more delicate apprehension. They are transformed by the urge of critical reason, by the vivid evidence of emotional experience, and by the cold certainties of scientific perception. One fact is certain, you cannot keep them still. No generation can merely reproduce its ancestors. You may preserve the life in a flux of form, or preserve the form amid an ebb of life. But you cannot permanently enclose the same life in the same mold.[8]

England

By 1800 the two major currents which were to prevail through earlier nineteenth-century English painting became apparent in the work of two great painters, Constable and Turner. Both were predominantly landscape painters, but each approached the problems of form and expression in a remarkably different way. John Constable (1776–1837), like Wilson and Crome before him, found delight in a direct contact with his native landscape — in the light and warmth of the sunshine, the cool of the shadow, and the movement of wind and rain. The freedom of his brushwork, his spontaneous evocation of transient sunlight and rain, of storms and passing clouds, shows so searching an analysis of these effects that he is sometimes considered a forerunner of the Impressionists. In

[7] Duncan Phillips in *Leaders of French Art Today*, Phillips Memorial Gallery, Washington, D. C., December, 1927–January, 1928.

[8] A. N. Whitehead, *Science and the Modern World*, Macmillan, New York, 1925, p. 269.

20–26 JOHN CONSTABLE. *The Hay Wain.* 1821. National Gallery, London. (Courtesy of the Trustees of the National Gallery, London)

1824, indeed, when his painting of the *Hay Wain* was exhibited at the Paris Salon, French artists were astonished at the new vision of landscape, and it is said that Eugène Delacroix actually repainted the landscape background of his *Massacre at Scio* in emulation of the English painter. The *Hay Wain* (Fig. 20–26) reveals the quiet charm of the countryside in an informal and unconventional composition. In the foreground a hay wagon is fording a stream near a house behind which are luxuriant trees that cast cool shadows; at the right stretch meadows glowing in sunshine; masses of clouds move rapidly through the spacious sky. A new vibrant quality of light and air appears in this picture, and a rich varied texture. These Constable secured by a method known as broken color, whereby he substituted short thick strokes laid over the ground color for the traditional smooth surface of greens, grays, and browns. These effects he sometimes enhanced by manipulating the pigment with the palette knife as well as with the brush.

Constable's studies of nature are so objectively analytical that they may be compared to scientific notes. Indeed, at the end of his life he expressed an opinion which reads prophetically like the later pronouncements of the mid-century realist artists who insisted that their art was not so much interpretative as descriptive. "Painting," Constable declared, "is a science, and should be pursued as an inquiry into the laws of nature. Why, then, may not landscape painting be considered as a branch of natural philosophy?" [9] In his love of the

[9] C. R. Leslie, *Memoirs of the Life of John Constable, R.A.,* p. 403.

20-27 JOSEPH M. W. TURNER. *The Fighting Téméraire.* 1839. National Gallery, London. (Courtesy of the Trustees of the National Gallery, London)

beauties of nature and of country life Constable also reminds us of his friend and contemporary, the poet William Wordsworth. For Wordsworth's poetical program is not unlike Constable's painting. What the one achieved with words the other sought in the pictorial image. The poet's intention, as he stated it early in his career, had been "to choose incidents and situations from common life, and to relate or describe them, throughout, as far as was possible in a selection of language really used by men." But Wordsworth then added that he wished "at the same time, to throw over them a certain coloring of imagination, whereby ordinary things should be presented to the mind in an unusual aspect." [10]

[10] Preface to *Lyrical Ballads,* 1798.

The investment of the commonplace with imaginative coloring is an apt description as well of the work of the other great English landscape painter. Joseph Mallord William Turner (1775–1851) was also interested in light and air. In his early atmospheric studies he too anticipated the Impressionists by specifying even the time of day and the direction of the compass from which the view had been taken. But in contrast to Constable's intimate and rather detailed transcription of nature, to the solidity of Constable's composition and the reticence of his expression, Turner, after a preliminary direct study of nature, swept off into the world of imagination, into limitless space filled with light in which forms lost structure and definition in the golden misty light and

20–28 WILLIAM BLAKE. *When the Morning Stars Sang Together and All the Sons of God Shouted for Joy.* From *The Book of Job.* Published 1826. (Courtesy Yale University Library)

air which enveloped them. His subjects were often as dramatic as his color, yet whatever literary title he bestowed on his work, the majesty of sun, sky, sea, and mountains and the vastness, power, and grandeur of light-filled space were his actual themes. Since he was extraordinarily prolific — there exist thousands of his oils, water colors, drawings — a selection is particularly difficult, but in the *Fighting Téméraire* (Fig. 20–27) we can see many of his greatest qualities. The imagination which invests the ordinary with the unusual appears in this poignant account of the evening on which one of England's grand old ships of the line was towed off to demolition by a dark little steam tug. In the conjunction of the types of ships Turner's imagination created a romantic reverie on the passing of the old order, which he saw as

one of beauty and grace, and the coming of the new day with its bustle and dirt. He developed the contrast even in the atmospheric space of the painting, for while the tug is illuminated by the last rays of the setting sun the warship is bathed in silver moonlight. In this painting a romantic subject has found a consistent expression, with the structure in harmony with the emotional content. Although human interest is here associated with the landscape in a highly imaginative way, later Turner paintings are almost abstract visualizations of space and light. In *Rain, Steam and Speed* (National Gallery, London), the structure and solidity of all objects are lost in the effect of the swift movement of the train through a driving rainstorm — an effect secured by using a rather thick pigment in broken color. In such a work and in his *Fighting Téméraire*, Turner showed himself a true romantic by his ability to endow even the most up-to-date forms of transportation and industry with imaginative coloring.

A solitary in English painting was William Blake (1757–1827), the mystic who lived the largest part of his life in the world of his visions (Fig. 20–28).

There assuredly never was a more singular, more inexplicable phenomenon than the intrusion, as though by direct intervention of Providence, of this Assyrian spirit into the vapidly polite circles of eighteenth-century London. The fact that, as far as the middle classes of England were concerned, Puritanism had for a century and a half blocked every inlet and outlet of poetical feeling and imaginative conviction save one, may give us a clue to the causes of such a phenomenon. It was the devotion of Puritan England to the Bible, to the Old Testament especially, that fed such a spirit as Blake's directly from the sources of the most primeval, the vastest and most abstract imagery which we possess. Brooding on the vague and tremendous images of Hebrew and Chaldean poetry, he arrived at such indifference to the actual material world, at such an intimate perception of the elemental forces which sway the spirit with immortal hopes and infinite terrors when it is most withdrawn from its bodily conditions, that what was given to his internal vision became incomparably more definite, more precisely and more clearly articulated, than anything presented to his senses. His forms are the visible counterparts to those words, like *the deep, many waters, firmament, the foundations of the earth, pit* and *host,* whose resonant overtones blur and enrich the sense of the Old Testament.[11]

With intuitive sensitivity for linear rhythms he projected his internal visions in woodcuts, engravings with a wash of color added, and wash drawings, composed of symbols by which he wished to convey concretely the elemental forces with which he lived. His drawings and paintings are not illustrations of an incident but the final forms reached by a man who has struggled to see through the incident to its fundamental implications. In his claim that the Byzantine style was revealed to him one discerns a realization that his own objective and that of the Byzantines were similar: "to render visible the mysteries of the supra-natural world."

A later movement in English painting which is perhaps of greater value historically than for its intrinsic artistic quality was that of the Pre-Raphaelite Brotherhood. The Industrial Revolution had plunged the country into a turbulent state, socially, economically and artistically, from which it was only gradually emerging after the passage of the various reform laws of the 1830's. Most significant for many artists had been the loss of the older traditions of craftsmanship and patronage. Without secure training and without steady support the artist had little hope of

[11] Roger E. Fry, *Vision and Design,* Meridian Books, New York, 1956, pp. 214–15.

20–29 DANTE GABRIEL ROSSETTI. *The Annunciation.* (*Ecce Ancilla Domini*). 1850. 28½ in. × 16½ in. Oil on canvas, mounted on panel. Tate Gallery, London. (Courtesy of the Trustees of the Tate Gallery)

regaining the position he had held in the past. The ambition of a group of young men who banded together in 1848 under the name of the Pre-Raphaelite Brotherhood [12] was to revive the best traditions of workmanship in painting and to renew an understanding of its possibilities through attention to serious subject matter. Their title

[12] The best known of the group were Dante Gabriel Rossetti (1828–1882) and William Holman Hunt (1827–1910); in close sympathy were Ford Madox Brown (1821–1893), Sir Edward Burne-Jones (1833–1898), and William Morris (1834–1896).

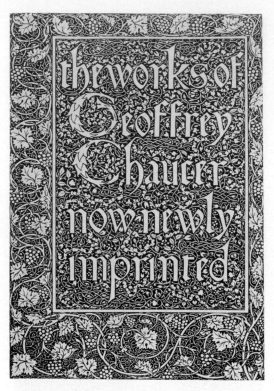

20–30 WILLIAM MORRIS. Title page of *The Kelmscott Chaucer*. 1896. (Courtesy Yale University Library)

signified their intention of reaching back beyond the Renaissance to the glories of Medieval painting for technical and symbolic inspiration. Their leader, Dante Gabriel Rossetti, was a far better poet than painter; in his best-known work, the *Annunciation* (Tate Gallery, London), the consciously archaic qualities of his work are evident (Fig. 20–29). The abrupt perspective, the simplified planes, and the dominant linear pattern are ultimately derived from Rossetti's studies of Sienese painting. The Virgin's expression, however, suggests that the Pre-Raph-

aelites, for all their admiration of the past, were men of the nineteenth century, for in the drawn and haunted features there are qualities of psychic introspection which Rossetti could not have found in Medieval art.

Pre-Raphaelite painting soon attracted the enthusiastic support of John Ruskin (1819–1900), the greatest English critic of the day, who also hoped to bring some order into the confused aesthetic conditions of industrial manufacture. Under the influence of Ruskin's earnest pleadings for the revival of the conditions of Medieval craftsmanship William Morris developed a program of social reform designed to permit the revival of the guild system and the establishment of handicraft industries. Although it was too late, for the individual worker could no longer compete on economic terms with the processes of mass manufacturing, Morris's ideas were significant in that he called attention to the possibilities of improving design in industrial articles. Through his tapestry works at Mortlake, his printing shop known as the Kelmscott Press (Fig. 20–30), and his decorating shop in London, Morris made the public familiar with his fresh designs for all kinds of interior decoration and household articles. The Arts and Crafts movement, as it came to be called, engaged the support of many followers of the Pre-Raphaelites who made stained-glass windows, designed cartoons for tapestry and wallpaper, and printed and illustrated books. The value of the movement lay chiefly in its protest against the segregation of art from life, and in its efforts to make art a vital, spontaneous expression, manifest in a chair or a book as well as in a building or a painting.

19th-Century American

United States

Painting in the United States in the nineteenth century (about 1815 to 1913) was noticeably influenced by its patronage. The commercial aristocracy of the North and the landed aristocracy of the South, which had supported the colonial painter, declined during the era of great expansion toward the West and gave way to an industrial plutocracy devoid of a cultural tradition. On the whole these new patrons considered the goal of painting as merely the reproduction of the object seen in nature treated in meticulous detail or sentimentalized; they also tended, especially after the Civil War, to equate aesthetic excellence with the physical size of grandiose compositions produced by such painters as Albert Bierstadt and Frederick Edwin Church.

Portrait painting, the chief expression in painting in the colonial age, lingered on in the East in the work of Thomas Sully (1783–1872), who painted technically accomplished but structurally rather weak portraits imbued with all the mannerisms of the late English portrait painters. His contemporary, Samuel F. B. Morse (1791–1872), trained in France, attained a vigorous and romantic style occasionally capable of such forceful characterization as his *Lafayette* (Fig. 20–31). But disillusioned by his lack of commissions, Morse abandoned painting for scientific study. It is ironic that the rising vogue for the daguerreotype, which he was among the first to introduce to America, absorbed much of the demand for the painted portrait.[13] More-over, those portraits which were painted usually revealed the daguerreotype as the new standard for likenesses. Painterly qualities disappeared in the effort to mimic photographic effects in color.

Meanwhile, the new spirit of nationalism briefly stimulated historical painting. John Trumbull (1756–1843) had painted from life a series of miniatures of most of the leaders of the Revolutionary War period and composed, as small sketches, his well-known *Battles of Yorktown* and *Bunker Hill* and his even better-known *Signing of the Declaration of Independence*. When he enlarged these as mural decorations for the rotunda of the national capitol some years later, however, they lost their vitality, becoming loose and flabby in both composition and construction.

20–31 SAMUEL F. B. MORSE. *The Marquis de Lafayette*. 1825. 30⅜ × 25⅛ in. New York Public Library. (New York Public Library)

[13] Other important portrait painters were Chester Harding (1792–1866) and Eastman Johnson (1824–1906), especially toward the end of the latter's career.

Closely related to historical painting was the moralistic Neoclassicism which Benjamin West had explored in the late 1760's and David had so powerfully developed during the 1780's and 1790's in France. In America this approach produced only some feeble works by John Vanderlyn (1776–1852) and some beautifully elegiac landscapes with figures by Washington Allston (1779–1843). The intimate and poetic romanticism of Allston, however, was unhappily thwarted by his desire to realize grandiose themes. Thus by mid-nineteenth century two of the most significant trends emerging from colonial American painting had withered away: portraiture floundering both for lack of artists with the competence of a Copley or a Stuart and because of competition from the daguerreotype; historical painting dying before it was fairly born, again in part for lack of competence, but also for want of patronage and encouragement.

A general feeling of patriotism, inspired by the recent independence from British control, accounted for the nationalistic strain in the writings of Bryant, Irving, and Cooper, and simultaneously gave rise to schools of native landscape and genre painting. The landscape tradition found its beginning in the so-called Hudson River school.[14] A true love of nature and a fine feeling for man's place in nature permeate the work of this group. Many of their

paintings, though realistic in detail, are composed with large masses of trees and hills at the sides through which the eye is guided into space in the manner of Claude Lorrain (Fig. 10–43). Their green and brown tonality recalls the Dutch and early English landscape painters. Doughty and Durand favored intimate scenes; Cole was more grandiose and romantic as a result of European travel and the influence of Turner. Still others, notably Lane and Heade, were primarily tonalists who sought, as did the French Impressionists, to catch the quality and nuance of weather, but sought it in terms of the tight meticulousness which characterized the whole Hudson River school. Finally, panoramists such as Church, Bierstadt, and Moran found their subject matter in the newly discovered scenery of the Rockies and the Sierras, in Mexico, and in South America. They attempted to express the grandeur of these landscapes, and often their dramatic composition compensated for the accumulation of tiny details.

From the Hudson River school emerged Homer D. Martin (1836–1897), Alexander Wyant (1836–1892), and George Inness (1825–1894), men who joined native ability with a technical proficiency gained chiefly through study of the Barbizon painters. The comparison of an early Inness such as *Peace and Plenty* (Metropolitan Museum) with his late *Home of the Heron* (Fig. 20–32) shows how he eventually rejected the panoramic vision and painstaking detail characteristic of his early work. In *Home of the Heron* Inness conveyed his special feeling for landscape by means of pigment freely brushed and delicately modulated within a narrow range of dull browns and subdued greens which establish a painterly equivalent to nature—evoking, not imitating, what he saw and felt.

[14] This name was loosely applied to a large group of painters many of whom lived in the vicinity of the Hudson and the Catskills, though (especially later in the century) they painted in various parts of the country and even in Mexico, South America, and the Mediterranean countries. Customarily associated with this group are Thomas Doughty (1793–1856), Asher Brown Durand (1796–1886), Thomas Cole (1801–1848), Fitz Hugh Lane (1804–1865), Martin Johnson Heade (1814–1904), John Frederick Kensett (1818–1872), and the panoramists Frederick Edwin Church (1826–1900), Albert Bierstadt (1830–1902), and Thomas Moran (1837–1926).

20–32 GEORGE INNESS. *Home of the Heron.* 1893. 30 in. × 45 in. Art Institute of Chicago. (Courtesy of the Art Institute of Chicago, Edward B. Butler Collection)

A similar attitude toward the local scene is observable in the work of the genre painters,[15] who found their inspiration in everyday life within the home, the yard, the city street, the country, the Western frontier. Their honest, if sentimental, pleasure in such scenes manifested itself in truth to objective appearance. With the advent of the camera they tended, as did the portraitists, to compete in seeking verisimilitude. Other paintings of the period became merely storytelling illustration. Not so some of the work of Johnson, and especially that of Homer

[15] John L. Krimmel (1787–1821), Henry Inman (1801–1846), William S. Mount (1807–1868), George Caleb Bingham (1811–1879), Thomas Hovenden (1840–1895), Frederic Remington (1861–1909), Eastman Johnson, and the early work of Winslow Homer (1836–1910) and Thomas Eakins (1844–1916). These last two will be more thoroughly discussed in association with the "solitaries," where their style rightly places them.

and Eakins, in which the genre content was expressed in larger, weightier forms dependent on formal organization rather than on a reproduction of actuality.

Another type of painting closely related in feeling to the affectionate interest which the genre painter exhibits toward everyday existence is still-life painting. Raphael Peale (1774–1825) carefully arranged household objects on a table, creating compositions with considerable abstract quality due to the intensity of his vision and his discriminating simplification of forms. Later, still-life painters such as William Harnett (1848–1892) tended to view their subjects more externally than Peale, sacrificing his emotional absorption with the object for clever *trompe-l'oeil* ("fool the eye") effects, in which the painted object in its exactitude uncannily mimicked its counterpart in nature.

During the last quarter of the nineteenth century patronage, however, tended to move away from this interest in local and national subject matter. The rise of the "Gilded Age," with its wealth, its insistence upon European products, and its scorn of American wares had made "European" synonymous with "artistic." To Europe, therefore, American artists flocked partly to improve their painting, partly perhaps to enhance their prestige in the hope of better sales. Some went to Düsseldorf and Munich,[16] where they developed a technique of bold vigorous brushwork reminiscent of Hals, the use of black or dark colors, and strong contrasts in value. More went to Paris [17] into the ateliers of the popular academic painters and learned the formulas governing "proper" subject matter and a suave technique expended chiefly upon figure painting.

Although these young men acquired a sound routine training in both Germany and France and became able technicians, they were faced with an unfortunate predicament if they returned home. In spite of their ideals, inspired by the European salons, which should have met with the approval of the taste for European art in the United States, they discovered that their potential American patrons were quite blind to any role that the artist might play in the development of American culture. These patrons, indeed, were unconscious of, if not snobbish toward, the value of vigorous artistic activity. In view of this unfavorable situation at

home some of the painters chose to remain in Europe.

In their work some of these painters assimilated their European training better than others—a repetition of the contrasting effect of European experience on Stuart and Copley in the previous century. Elihu Vedder, for example, made his strongly linear style personal even though it was firmly based upon Ingres and the latter's Italian prototypes. John LaFarge (1835–1910) was another independent who from his wide travel in the Far East as well as in Europe brought home a breadth of outlook and a feeling for sound craftsmanship seen particularly in his work in stained glass. Opposing the practice of painting pictures on glass, he revived the Medieval conception of a mosaic of small units of glass colored in the pot and leaded into a flat decorative design.

Of the painters who remained permanently abroad, Whistler and Sargent were the most prominent examples. James Abbott McNeill Whistler (1834–1903) worked with the progressive French painters active in the late fifties and early sixties, with the result that Courbet, Manet, Degas, the early Impressionists, and through them Velázquez and Japanese prints, are all easily discernible influences in his work. Reacting against the popular anecdotal painting, whose objective was storytelling and naturalistic imitation, Whistler became a champion of "art for art's sake." [18] He subordinated content for "Harmonies," "Arrangements," "Nocturnes." In *Miss Alexander* (*Harmony in Grey and Green*) (Fig. 20–33), the young girl stands before a paneled background of gray and black, wearing a white dress with a green sash and carrying a hat with a green plume. Gray and green, black and white — these color combinations dominate the

[16] Notably William Merritt Chase (1849–1916), Frank Duveneck (1848–1919), John W. Alexander (1856–1915), and Walter Shirlaw (1838–1909).

[17] Outstanding among this large group were Kenyon Cox (1856–1919), Elihu Vedder (1836–1923), Abbott H. Thayer (1849–1921), Thomas W. Dewing (1851–1938), Edwin H. Blashfield (1848–1936), Edwin A. Abbey (1852–1911), Edmund C. Tarbell (1862–1938), and George de Forest Brush (1855–1941).

[18] For his theories see his *Ten O'Clock*, Marion Press, Jamaica, New York, 1908.

composition. In some parts the pigment appears in large, flat, opaque areas; in others as light, transparent brush strokes. Compositionally, rectangles, triangles, and circles repeat and contrast. Whistler's use of the high horizon line, the informal asymmetrical composition, the flowers breaking into the frame, the color relationships, and the sense of flat pattern are evidences of the same influence of the Japanese print which may be found in Degas. On the other hand the full-length figure, so characteristic of Whistler's portraits, the use of black and neutrals, the emphasis upon color values, and the brushwork also reveal the strong influence of Velázquez. Despite his somewhat effete insistence on "art for art's sake," Whistler was important in nineteenth-century painting because he struggled for the reinstatement of formal criteria in an art which was in

20–34   JOHN SINGER SARGENT. *The Wyndham Sisters*. 1900. 115 in. × 84⅛ in. Metropolitan Museum of Art, New York.

20–33   JAMES A. MC N. WHISTLER. *Portrait of Miss Alexander*. 1872. W. C. Alexander Collection, London.

danger of losing them as it tried to vie with the new realism of the camera.

John Singer Sargent (1856–1925), born in Florence and trained in the academic Parisian atmosphere, became the popular portrait painter of socially prominent wealthy patrons. A virtuoso in handling pigment, he created brilliant surface effects with his dashing brushwork. If his paintings are largely devoid of formal significance and penetrating interpretation, they often astonish by their compositional daring and unerring sense of the elegant. In his *Wyndham Sisters* (Fig. 20–34), Sargent has suggested with amazing economy the suave image of the Gilded Age — that image of personal assurance and urbane cultivation exuded by the old wealth to which the new wealth aspired.

In contrast to the Europeanized painters there were the "solitaries," who assimilated whatever, if any, European training and travel they had obtained

20–35 THOMAS EAKINS. *The Pathetic Song.* 1881. 45 in. × 32½ in. Corcoran Gallery of Art, Washington, D. C. (Corcoran Gallery)

and often pursued their profession in obscurity or isolation, without regard to the popular tastes and fashions of the day. Characteristic of this group were George Fuller (1822–1884), Ralph Albert Blakelock (1847–1919), Thomas Eakins (1844–1916), Albert P. Ryder (1847–1917), and Winslow Homer (1836–1910). Eakins, though thoroughly trained in Europe, kept his feet firmly planted on local ground and his attention fixed unwaveringly upon whatever he was painting — chiefly the people and scenes of his own Philadelphia environment. Although a "realist," he was so not in the sense of literal verisimilitude. Eakins' objective vision was based upon a thorough understanding of structure which enabled him to translate the human figure into large, weighty forms reminiscent of Courbet, whom he came to admire. In short, he was a realist in the sense in which his other mentors, Rembrandt

and Velázquez, had been. His sober color and uncompromising fidelity to objective reality make his art austere. At times, when Eakins became so interested in realizing his subject that content dominated form, there are weak passages or a lack of complete compositional unity. But at his best Eakins was probably the most profound painter in America during the nineteenth century. His portraits, with their agonized perception of human character and personality — so displeasing to the fashionable public who delighted in Sargent's superficial elegance — are certainly among the great paintings of the century (Fig. 20–35).

Another major American painter of the latter part of the nineteenth century, though, like Eakins, too little appreciated in the midst of the Gilded Age, was Winslow Homer. His work as an illustrator for *Harper's Weekly* until 1875 perhaps determined the strongly illustrative character of much of his painting. After European travel, during which he purposely avoided art centers, and a sojourn in the tropics, during which he produced some of his best water colors, he settled on the Maine coast and in isolation largely devoted himself to the interpretation of the dramatic energy of the sea in its more violent moods. Like Eakins, he was firmly rooted in his own environment and did not scorn to use it as his raw material. While visual perception was his starting point and his objective, he painted with economy and with as much concern for the organization through which he expressed this raw material as for the material itself. In the *Northeaster* (Fig. 20–36), for example, the relationship of lines and light and dark areas, the contrasts of movement and immobility, are largely responsible for the expressive power of this storm-resistant shore. The reduction of naturalistic experience to a bold color pattern even recalls the styliza-

20–36 WINSLOW HOMER. *Northeaster.* 1895. 34⅜ in. × 50¼ in. Metropolitan Museum of Art, New York.

tion of Japanese prints by which Homer seems to have been influenced.

If Eakins and Homer were realists in basing their art upon experiences directly perceived in nature, Ryder was a visionary, a mystic. [Clumsy in the use of his medium, for he was untrained even in the fundamentals of his craft, he reduced the elements of his composition to the simplest pattern and color and labored over the surface, building it up thickly into boldly abstract patterns. [The sea, especially by moonlight, was a favorite subject, drawn from his own experience as a youth on the shore of Long Island Sound. Such a painting as *Moonlight Marine* (Fig. 20–37) reduces boat, sailors, and swollen sea to silhouettes, but silhouettes creating a subtle sense of three-dimensional space and gliding movement beneath the bold, and almost animate, pattern of the lunar sky.

As isolated as the "solitaries," and as untrained as the mystic Ryder, were

the so called primitives of the late nineteenth century. Their work constituted a folk art, in which the subject matter was set forth with spontaneous directness. The untrained worker had to reach his objective in his own way, usually by means of conventions rather than naturalistically. Some of these paintings, in which intuitive aesthetic feeling was joined with sound craftsmanship, were of high quality. In landscape the work of Joseph Pickett (1848–1918) illustrates the type. Still life was also popular. Such paintings reveal the tendency of the amateur to translate commonplace experience into abstract patterns and rhythms. It is this characteristic of abstract design and color which explains the appeal of the naïve painter to the twentieth-century eye, conditioned as it is to a non-naturalistic vision. The work of these folk artists is found in many mediums besides painting. It is largely anonymous, local, and much of it utilitarian: weath-

ervanes, hitching posts, ships, figureheads, decoys, textiles and embroideries, and furniture.

Though Impressionism had won recognition in Paris before 1886 and an exhibition of Impressionistic pictures was held in New York in 1885, it had almost no effect upon the United States until the last decade of the century, when a few pioneers [19] began using the technique and thus introduced novel uses of pigment and a more intense and varied color. Basically, however, American painters contributed little that was new to Impressionism. To be sure, Prendergast's tapestry-like decorative style of gay city scenes certainly represented an individual approach to Impressionism; so, too, did Twachtman's canvases capturing the intimate

quality of shadowy corners of nature through subtly modulated color harmonies, or Hassam's depictions of the strident quality of American sunlight. But on the whole American Impressionism tended toward naturalistic illustration, and hence toward academic formulas, rather than toward further plastic exploration as it had done in France.

Professionally, many American painters were well equipped by the end of the century, but their position in American culture was still anomalous. Many were too readily beguiled by European accomplishment. Thus they lost vital contact with American experiences or, more damaging, lost the power of self-expression in creating pastiches of European work. They were encouraged to ape European styles because affluent patrons continued to purchase European pictures, Dutch or French salon or Barbizon styles being particularly popular among those who prided themselves (often naïvely) on their sense of discrimination. Meanwhile, the general public was captivated by

[19] John H. Twachtman (1853–1902); J. Alden Weir (1852–1919); Willard L. Metcalf (1858–1925); Childe Hassam (1859–1935); Maurice B. Prendergast (1859–1924); Ernest Lawson (1873–1939); Gifford Reynolds Beal (1879–1956); Jonas Lie (1880–1940); and Mary Cassatt (1845–1926), who, however, clung more to the style of Degas and Manet than to Monet's style of Impressionism.

the anecdotal, photographic picture, usually sentimental in theme, such as Jozef Israel's (1824–1911) *Alone in the World,* or Thomas Hovenden's *Breaking Home Ties* (the prize painting by popular vote of the 1893 World's Columbian Exposition). Hence, apart from a few commissions for murals and portraits, there was no function for the painter and little demand for his product.

In protest against this excessive patronage of European painters, in 1898 "The Ten"[20] organized and held an exhibition of their work. The seemingly radical program of this rather conservative group soon evaporated, however, as their styles were accepted in academic circles. Another, and more significant, line of attack was developing among the young painters of the last decade of the century, with Robert Henri as their somewhat older leader. Henri, although a rather mediocre painter in the tradition of Hals and Manet, was among the most gifted teachers in America at the end of the century. Intensely humanitarian, he inspired students with the importance of the relation of art to life. On his return from study abroad, Henri taught in Philadelphia in the nineties and had among his students four young newspaper artists, John Sloan, William Glackens, George Luks, and Everett Shinn. At a time when photography was only beginning to appear in the press, these four illustrators provided their editors with dramatic sketches depicting news events. Inevitably, the fervent love of life which infused Henri's teaching struck a responsive chord in pupils whose own work was saturated with the same kind of vitality. The teacher's idealism gradually won the students away from journalism.

[20] Merritt Chase, Thomas W. Dewing, Childe Hassam, Edmund C. Tarbell, John H. Twachtman, and Alden Weir are the best known.

Henri and his protégés had meanwhile drifted to New York, where they worked in close proximity to one another and talked evenings of an art which would depict the realities of everyday American life. These five were eventually joined by three other painters, equally independent in spirit although not realists, and in 1908 they organized a group exhibition as "The Eight."[21] Although some critics were immediately hospitable to the scenes of everyday city life featured in the exhibition, others opposed the use of subject matter which had been customarily regarded as "anti-aesthetic." Hostile criticism dubbed The Eight the "Ash Can school." To the young painters the "ash can" epithet became a badge of freedom to flaunt before conservatives who demanded that the artist restrict himself to genteel subject matter.

Although The Eight painted in various personal styles, the early work of John Sloan has come to epitomize the spirit motivating the group. His *Sunday, Women Drying Their Hair* (Fig. 20–38) exhibits Sloan's dependence on Manet (and perhaps Goya) by way of Henri. Although Sloan depicted a rather sordid urban environment, there was no sense of social protest in his paintings. He captured instead the picturesque aspect of the city, the warm

[21] Robert Henri (1865–1929); Maurice B. Prendergast; Arthur B. Davies (1862–1928); George B. Luks (1867–1933); William J. Glackens (1870–1938); Ernest Lawson; John Sloan (1871–1955); and Everett Shinn (1873–1953). In addition to Henri and the four ex-Philadelphia newspaper illustrators, Prendergast might be considered something of a realist since he depicted city scenes, but with such a decoratively patterned effect as to minimize the importance of subject matter. Lawson's impressionistic landscapes occasionally dealt with city subjects in a rather idyllic mood. Davies was not a realist at all, being interested in allegory and symbolism. Without exception, every one of The Eight moved away from the realist position in his later works.

20–38 JOHN SLOAN. *Sunday, Women Drying Their Hair*. 1912. Phillips Collection, Addison Gallery of American Art, Andover, Massachusetts. (Addison Gallery)

sense of community which develops among the inhabitants of urban slums. Hence his work appears humanitarian in spirit rather than revolutionary, in this respect suggesting the mild humanitarianism characteristic of liberal reform during the Progressive Era. George Bellows (1882–1925), who was influenced by Henri and The Eight although he did not participate in their famous group exhibition, was equally enthusiastic about depicting the American life around him. His scenes of the robust side of life—boxing, vaudeville, the swimming hole, the farm—were often a bit too grandiose in composition for their subject matter. But it was pre-

cisely this compositional ability and his technical fluency which made Bellows readily acceptable to the conservatives, and he was admitted to the National Academy [22] at an early age. Thus his

[22] A meeting on November 8, 1825, founded the New York Drawing Association, from whose membership emerged the National Academy of Design on January 19, 1826; it was founded "for the purpose of mutual improvement and the instruction of their pupils, and all others who wish to become students of the Arts of Design." It was in opposition to the well-established American Academy of the Fine Arts, which thereafter rapidly declined. (*National Academy of Design Exhibition Record, 1826–1860*, printed for the New York Historical Society, New York City, 1943.)

work reinforced the position taken by The Eight, and this within the very citadel of gentility.

While The Eight were revolutionizing the conception of subject matter appropriate to art, other artists were simultaneously bringing the new European concepts of form and color to America. Actually some of the members of The Eight were among the most active organizers of a huge exhibition of modern European art held in a New York armory in 1913. Generally known as the "Armory Show," it presented for the first time to most of the American public, and to many American artists as well, a comprehensive showing of the work of the Post-Impressionists, Fauves (p. 695), and Cubists (p. 702).

Canada

In Canada the nineteenth century was a period of expansion, confederation of the provinces (1867), and a growing national consciousness. This may be seen in art beginning with such topographical draftsmen as Fanny Wright Bayfield (active 1838) and William Henry Bartlett (1809–1854), whose illustrations for *Canadian Scenery* are much sought after. Then came the pioneer painters: Paul Kane (1810–1871), who traveled widely over the Western plains, where he recorded Indian life, and whose work reflected some acquaintance with the French romantics. Cornelius Krieghoff (1815–1872), who arrived in 1840 from Amsterdam, became an indefatigable and humorous recorder of habitant life. Georges Theodore Berthon (1806–1892), who had studied with Jacques Louis David, brought to Canada a polished classical style.

The period following confederation heralded an even wider development. Native-born artists were more numer-

ous. James Wilson Morrice (1865–1924) studied in France with Henri Harpignies, was befriended by Matisse, and knew the Fauves, particularly Marquet, to whom his painting owes some debt. Maurice Cullen (1866–1934) also traveled and studied in France. He too absorbed the message of Impressionism, using it with understanding and moderation in his landscapes. Marc-Aurèle Suzor-Coté (1869–1937), Paris-trained, introduced aspects of pointillism into his work.

Latin America

Early in the nineteenth century, Miranda, Bolivar, and San Martín led the Spanish colonies in America to independence. The ecclesiastical art of the colonial age was superseded by an art which was secular both in content and in control, as power passed to lay institutions, frequently to the government itself. Government-sponsored academies were established, manned by Europeans, and pupils were sent to Paris or Rome for further training. Thus art, no longer dominated by the Church, was under the direction of the state, with official exhibitions, salons, and collections.

Pupils of David came to the important Latin American cities both as painters and as instructors in the academies. But, as in Europe, the liberalizing effect of romanticism was more in accord with the spirit of the independence movement than were the tenets of classicism.

One cannot generalize about the complex art movements in this large number of countries, all of which were living through revolutions and periods of chaos. But, although no major art expression emerged from these upheavals in the nineteenth century, we can still discern three distinct currents or trends.

First, there was academic salon art, frequently but not always dull, derived in style and largely in content from Europe to satisfy the tastes of European-guided academies. Apart from some church murals, the subjects were portraits and battle or historical scenes or genre. The style, even with such local subjects, was European.

A second movement was that of the regionalist and *costumbrista* painters. This trend was a result of the revolutions and the romantic movement, which inspired both individuals and scientific expeditions to seek out exotic peoples and places for observation. Though in general the level was not that of great art, a few of the landscapes, street and country scenes, and studies of costumes and customs show freshness and a quality far above mere recording.

A third current was that of the arts of the people combining both indigenous and derivative elements. These arts, though affected by European influences, carried on long-lived native traditions.

In painting this is well illustrated by the Mexican *retablos* and by the decoration of shop façades. Some of the folk painters showed a knowledge of European principles of perspective and sculptural use of light and shade. They were more likely, however, to reflect the native tradition of flat linear design and at times to display a startling juxtaposition of brilliant colors. This folk art helped to perpetuate indigenous forms which served as one of the bases for the Mexican painting of the twentieth century.

The folk arts were as varied as the needs of daily life which they satisfied. All were rooted in ancient traditions of technique and design but were capable of absorbing new methods and motifs brought by the Spaniards. In Mexico, ceramics, textiles, and lacquer were perhaps the most important of the folk arts, though leatherwork, silver, straw inlay, and basketry were also notable.

Almost as widespread as the ceramic art was the art of the weaver. In the more isolated regions primitive looms continued to produce traditional weaves and patterns, though at times Spanish motifs crept in. The articles woven were for everyday use, chief of which perhaps were the serape, a man's cloak and blanket, usually of wool; the *rebozo*, the woman's shawl and headdress, sometimes made of silk, a fiber introduced after the conquest; and smaller articles such as belts, sashes, and carrying bags. Every region had its special design and its own distinctive color, which ranged from the neutral colors of the wool itself to the most brilliant hues daringly juxtaposed and interwoven. Both design and color identify the origin of the fabric. The designs tended to be geometric, as in many of the serapes; or to use highly conventional bird, animal, and flower motifs, as in the cotton and wool embroideries of the Huichol and Otomi tribes.

The art of lacquering continued in two centers, Olinalá in Guerrero and Uruapan in Michoacán, both of which were situated where the needed materials were available. Gourds and wooden objects afforded a base, which was entirely covered with a black lacquer coating in which the design was cut and in which the different colors were inlaid and then polished. Alternatively a sgraffito process was used, producing a raised design in two colors.

The textiles of Guatemala; the clay figurines of Ecuador, representing people or fruit and flowers; and the silver artifacts of Peru and Chile are other outstanding examples of the native arts found throughout Middle, Central, and South America. This folk art is in sharp contrast to the crafts of Europe and the United States, where during the nineteenth century the impact of the machine and of mass production brought an end to making articles by hand. It remains true, nevertheless, that the formal properties of Latin American folk art are similar to those of the folk arts of central Europe and Scandinavia, where an analogous reduction of metropolitan styles took place after 1500 A.D.

20th-Century European

The first signs of a new and specifically twentieth-century movement in painting appeared in Paris as early as 1905. In that year, at the third Salon d'Automne, a group of younger painters under the leadership of Henri Matisse (1869–1954) exhibited a group of canvases so simplified in design and so brilliant in color that a startled critic described the artists as *fauves* (wild beasts). The Fauves were encouraged by the newly discovered exotic arts to seek more personal forms of expression. In African fetishes, Polynesian decorative wood-carvings, and in the sculptures and textiles from the ancient cultures of Central and South America, they saw unexpected shapes and colors which suggested new ways of communicating emotion. This led them individually into various paths of free invention. Deft, spirited painters, they produced canvases of great spontaneity and verve, with a rich surface texture, with lively linear patterns and boldly clashing effects of primary colors. Their subject matter was as varied as their methods of painting, although many subjects familiar in Impressionist and Post-Impressionist painting, such as landscapes, still lifes, and nude figures, still appeared. Thus the Fauves carried on and expanded the trends instigated by Van Gogh and Gauguin, whose works had become better known through extensive retrospective exhibitions held in Paris in 1901 and 1903.

The Fauves brought color to a new intensity with startling discords of vermilion and emerald green, cerulean blue and vivid orange held together by sweeping brushstrokes and bold patterns. Relationships to the past and contributions to the present can be seen in a painting such as the one exhibited in the 1905 Salon d'Automne as *London Bridge* (Fig. 20–39) by André Derain (1880–1954), whose Fauve work remains among his finest achievements. We can judge how thoroughly the Fauve painters had broken with the art of the late nineteenth century when we recall that Monet had completed his series of views of Waterloo Bridge in London only three years before. Derain rejected entirely the subtle harmonies so expressive of atmospheric and climatic conditions in favor of a distorted perspective emphasized by clashing yellows, blues, greens, and reds against the black accents of the arches. Implicit in such work is the concept that the artist's emotional reaction to the subject and his presentation of such feeling in the boldest color and strongest linear pattern is more important than any objective representational values. In this way the Fauves freed color from its traditional role as the description of the local tone of an object and helped prepare both artists and public for the use of color as an expressive end in itself.

The Fauve movement was never an official organization of painters and

20–39 ANDRÉ DERAIN. *London Bridge.* 1906. 26 in. × 39 in. Museum of Modern Art, New York. (Museum of Modern Art)

was short-lived; within five years most of the artists modified their violent colors and found their own more personal treatment of subject matter.[23] Thus Raoul Dufy (1878–1953), by transforming his rather heavy Fauve color and patterns into a delicate system of light washes of color over a skeletal outline, was enabled to comment wittily upon the gayer aspects of modern social and sporting life. In landscape Maurice de Vlaminck (1877–1958), and in scenes of Paris and French provincial towns Maurice Utrillo (1883–1955), continued the Fauve tradition, but they too by 1920 had developed their own particular manners of painting. In quite another vein Georges Rouault (1871–1958), who had always

[23] Other prominent members of the group were Kees van Dongen (1877–); Othon Friesz (1879–1949); Albert Marquet (1875–1947).

preferred more somber tonalities of glowing reds, greens, and purples, treated social and religious themes. His studies of clowns and prostitutes and his long series of religious paintings are Fauve in their simplified designs, constructed with black outlines like the leads in Medieval stained glass which Rouault, who had worked as a glass-maker's apprentice in his youth, had always admired. To this he added his own special feeling for sorrowing humanity, his hatred of injustice and authority, and his deep piety. In expressing such feelings Rouault developed a personal iconography based on a set of interchangeable symbols. His figures of the Christ, the clown, and the workman are often seen in almost identical poses, suggesting that each human being, no matter how humble, has about him something of the divine, even as the Christ was made manifest in hu-

20–40 GEORGES ROUAULT. *Three Clowns*. 1917. 36¼ × 28½ in. Collection Mr. and Mrs. Joseph Pulitzer, Jr., St. Louis.

20–41 HENRI MATISSE. *Le Luxe, II*. 1907 or 1908. 82½ in. × 54¾ in. Statens Museum for Kunst, Copenhagen. (Statens Museum for Kunst)

man form. In his *Three Clowns*, for instance (Fig. 20–40), the larger figure in the foreground sits in the position of the artist's frequent representations of Christ as the Man of Sorrows.

The artist who remained most faithful to Fauve principles, and yet who, through his extraordinary sensitivity for color, transformed them into one of the strongest and most influential personal expressions in modern art, was Henri Matisse. Throughout his long life his gift for combining colors in unsuspected ways and for inventing new combinations never flagged, and still never fails to astonish the spectator. But Matisse was also an accomplished pictorial designer. He preferred working in two dimensions, but by the subtlest of color accents his surfaces, no matter how apparently flat, convey effects of three-dimensional space. In his

early painting, *Le Luxe* (Fig. 20–41), the background of sea, hills, and sky seems to stretch out behind the figures although it is executed in the simplest method by overlapping planes of undifferentiated color. In the schematic drawing of the figures Matisse showed his mastery of human anatomy. To his contemporaries in 1906 such apparent distortion and elimination of detail seemed horrifyingly unnatural. We can now understand that only through such extreme simplifications could Matisse convey his expression of a serene, detached world of forms wherein line, shape, and color exist almost independently of the subject; where the subject, so to speak, is only a comment upon the artistic elements.

20–42 HENRI MATISSE. *Still Life: Apples on a Pink Tablecloth.* 1924–1925. 23¾ in. ×
28¾ in. Chester Dale Collection, National Gallery of Art, Washington, D. C. (National
Gallery)

Although much in *Le Luxe* recalls
Gauguin, and especially his *Maternity*
(Fig. 20–24), Matisse also admired
Cézanne, in whom he saw a master of
poetic expression. This same poetic
spirit can be seen in Matisse's still-
lifes, such as the *Apples on a Pink Tablecloth* (Fig. 20–42), so typical of his
later, more lyrical work. The warm-
hued, rather solid foreground group,
with its combination of broad quiet
curves and angles, acts as a foil to the
cool blues and exciting movement of
the jagged motifs above. The two parts
are united by the pitcher and by the
lines, the motif, and the colors of the
vertical bands and circular disks.

Much modern art, as we shall see, is
based upon severely intellectual prem-
ises frequently publicized in written
doctrines and manifestos. And it may
require for its enjoyment some understanding of the artist's relation to contemporary currents of thought. Matisse's art, however, is founded upon his
instinctive love of nature, of color, and
of joyous subjects. For this reason it is
sometimes disparaged as too decorative and lacking in profound meaning.
But this is to overlook its very special
and very French qualities, those which
an early critic of Matisse expressed as
"simplicity, serenity and clarity." These
qualities found magnificent expression,
at the very end and climax of his life,
in his designs and decorations for the
chapel of the Holy Rosary in the Dominican convent at Vence in southern
France (Fig. 20–43). In a severe
white-walled room Matisse installed

20–43 CHAPEL OF THE HOLY ROSARY. Vence. Architecture, stained glass windows, tile figure of St. Dominic, and altar decorations by Henri Matisse. 1950–1951. (Photo Helene Adant)

stained glass windows in floral patterns of green, yellow, and blue which flooded the space with a soft, springtime light. Upon three walls he placed glazed tiles inscribed in black outlines with figures of St. Dominic, the Virgin and Child, and abbreviated, almost stenographic, notations of the stations of the cross. The altar, its furnishings, and all the vestments were also designed by Matisse. Simple, severe, and clear, each element contributes to the harmonious whole. Matisse's profound artistic convictions and his sense of the continuity of art are expressed both in the chapel and in the beautiful letter he wrote at the age of eighty-two in which he said: "Whatever weakness this expression of

human feeling may contain will fall away, but there will remain a living part which will unite the past with the future of plastic tradition." [24]

The element of immediate personal expression in Fauve painting appealed to artists elsewhere in Europe, especially in Germany where two groups of painters, the members of "The Bridge" in Dresden,[25] and of "The Blue Rider" in Munich [26] carried even further the

[24] A. H. Barr, Jr., *Matisse, His Art and His Public*, p. 288.
[25] E. L. Kirchner (1880–1938); Erich Heckel (1883–); Karl Schmidt-Rottluff (1884–); Emile Nolde (1867–1956).
[26] Heinrich Campendonk (1889–); Alexei von Jawlensky (1864–1941); Paul Klee (1879–1940); August Macke (1887–1914).

tendencies in the work of Derain and Matisse. In Germany there was less concentration than in France on purely formal problems. German Expressionism was a manifestation of subjective feeling toward objective reality and the world of the imagination. With bold, vigorous brushwork, emphatic lines, and bright color the German painters produced splendid, almost savagely powerful canvases, concisely organized and particularly expressive of intense human feeling. German Expressionism is in the direct line of descent from earlier German painting and engraving, especially in its strong color, linear pattern, emphasis on subject matter of a highly emotional character, and its frequent transcendental overtones. These elements appear most effectively in the work of Emile Nolde, whose religious paintings continue the mood of intense exaltation so familiar in German Late Gothic art. Although Nolde's colors, and even his abrupt linear rhythms, can eventually be traced back to the influence of Matisse, the profoundly religious conviction in such works as the *Pentecost* is closer to the spirit of Grünewald's *Isenheim Altarpiece* (Fig. 9–88) than to contemporary French painting.

Perhaps the most sensitive of the German Expressionists was Franz Marc (1880–1916). In many respects his color is reminiscent of the Fauves, but he carried further the separation of local color from the original object, in such paintings as his *Red Horses*. His transcendental interests can also be seen in his studies of animal life, his favorite subject matter, wherein he sought to penetrate the dynamics of the animal kingdom.

An associate of Marc's in the Blue Rider group, the Russian painter Vassily Kandinsky (1866–1944), carried his research into the emotional and psychological properties of color, line, and shape to the point where subject

matter and even representational elements were entirely eliminated. In 1910 he painted a composition in brilliant color, apparently based on landscape studies of the previous year, but in which no recognizable natural objects appear. By 1911 he succeeded in creating a composition based upon the artistic elements of color, shape, and line without any reference to the visible world. Now that abstract art has become so much a part of our experience, we tend to forget the courage such a step required, and the creative imagination needed to undertake so completely new a direction in the art of painting. By 1914 Kandinsky had perfected his methods and established his two principal kinds of painting. He called one kind *Compositions,* the title implying that such arrangements of geometrical shapes were consciously planned and intellectually ordered. In his *Improvisations,* on the other hand (Fig. 20–44), he approached the canvas with no preconceived theme but allowed the colors to come as they would, prompted by subconscious feelings. In these works the brilliant colors flow effortlessly across the canvas with as little conscious order or control as possible on the artist's part. In thus exploiting subconscious sensations Kandinsky uncovered an area of feeling which was soon to be exploited by other artists, notably by the Surrealists.[27]

Just as European Expressionism, with its emphasis on subjective experience, can be traced back through all its branches to the examples of Van Gogh and Gauguin, so two other important currents in modern art, the investigations leading to Cubism and

[27] Kandinsky described his methods and the philosophical connotations of his art in his important treatise, *Concerning the Spiritual in Art* (latest English translation published by Wittlenborn, Schultz, New York, 1947). Also see pp. 709–14 for further discussion of the philosophical backgrounds of abstract art.

20–44 VASSILY KANDINSKY. *Improvisation.* 1912. 44 in. × 64¼ in. Solomon R. Guggenheim Museum, New York. (The Solomon R. Guggenheim Museum)

Constructivism, descend from another Post-Impressionist, Paul Cézanne. Although Matisse and other members of the Fauve group had been familiar with Cézanne's work, they admired it chiefly for the color and expressive linear distortions. Cézanne's death in 1906, the retrospective exhibition of his work held the following year at the Salon d'Automne, and especially the publication by Emile Bernard that year of the famous letter in which Cézanne wrote of treating nature "in terms of the cylinder, sphere, and cone," enabled the younger painters for the first time to see that Cézanne's principal preoccupation had been to establish substantial forms within a space in which the actual properties of the two-dimensional picture surface and the illusionary effects of three dimensions were consciously and subtly adjusted.

This aspect of Cézanne's practice and theory became the chief concern of a group of younger French painters soon to be known as the Cubists. They were encouraged by the remarkable personality and achievements of the Spanish painter Pablo Picasso (1881–), whose adult life has been spent in France and whose works are inseparably connected with the history of modern French art.[28] From his earliest studies in the Barcelona Academy of Art, where his father was a professor, Picasso had demonstrated precocious ability. At an age when other artists

[28] Other members of the group were Georges Braque (1882–); Albert Gleizes (1881–1953); Jean Metzinger (1883–); Fernand Léger (1881–1955); Juan Gris (1887–1927); Robert Delaunay (1885–1941); Jacques Villon (1875–); and Roger de la Fresnaye (1885–1925).

20–45 PABLO PICASSO. *Portrait of Gertrude Stein*. 1906. Metropolitan Museum of Art, New York.

have only learned the rudiments of their craft, Picasso had mastered all aspects of late nineteenth-century realist techniques. For one so greatly gifted, not only in terms of manual dexterity but also in powers of pictorial visualization, there could be no question of quietly following conventional methods of painting. Consequently it is not surprising that Picasso should have investigated more than one aspect of picture-making, but, even so, the public was ill prepared for the astonishing variety of his "styles" and "periods." In some respects Picasso is characteristic of the modern age in his constant experimentation, in his startling shifts from one kind of painting to another, and in his invention of the most surprising innovations in painting and even in sculpture.

When Picasso settled permanently in Paris in 1904, his work had evolved from the sober realism of Spanish painting, through a brightening of col-

or in an Impressionistic manner, into the so-called Blue Period (1901–1905), in which he painted pathetic figures of his native Spain in a predominantly blue tonality. There followed a series of acrobats, harlequins, and other figures with more varied color, and then in the Rose Period (1905–1906) he constructed in pinkish hues more impersonal forms which at times showed influences from Classic sculpture. The predominantly terra-cotta coloring suggests a study of Tanagra figurines. In 1906 his *Portrait of Gertrude Stein* (Fig. 20–45), with its masklike face and solid forms, reveals an acquaintance with African sculpture, in which Picasso saw new possibilities for the construction of forms. In the abrupt dislocations of this sculpture Picasso found one of the clues for the dissection of natural forms into their essential volumes and planes, a task which occupied him for the next few years. By 1910 Picasso, with Georges Braque, had laid the basis for a new kind of painting which was soon nicknamed Cubist by a critic who was amused by the approximately geometrical forms in many of their paintings. The name stuck and was soon accepted by the painters and their critics, but it suggests very little of the seriousness and originality of the Cubists' achievements. This consists in their discovery of a new kind of pictorial space. Like Cézanne's, it is based on the principle of multiple points of view, but the Cubists carried Cézanne's researches to the point where they were able to present an object as seen from several different angles simultaneously.

It is often said that Cubist space thus surpasses the three dimensions as they had been known heretofore in painting, and adds a fourth, a temporal dimension, since objects appear not as they are seen at any given moment but as their varying aspects are known at different moments in time. Philosophically such a procedure may be said to be an attempt to present the essential reality of forms in space, rather than their merely ephemeral appearance. Since the concept of reality thus became separated from that of appearance, the resemblance of essential form to ordinary vision was no longer important.[29] Cubist paintings at first seemed confused and bewildering to those who expected them to resemble their titles, which still referred to familiar objects or figures. Nevertheless the title is important as a clue to the source in the everyday world of the new pictorial reality.

To create this new kind of painting was also not easy, and the early stages of Cubism, often described as analytical because of the experimental character of the research, are marked by a severe discipline, almost complete abolition of color in favor of black, white, and ochre, and an impersonality so pervasive that the works of Braque and Picasso between 1910 and 1914 are often almost indistinguishable.

Picasso's *Accordionist* (Fig. 20–46) is a construction of large intersecting planes in which the longer edges and large angles suggest the original subject, a man playing such an instrument. Within these planes a host of small shapes hover and interpenetrate. Although we assume that each of these smaller forms is a simplified equivalent of some aspect of the original subject, the total effect is that of a new kind of pictorial reality. We are no longer obliged to contemplate merely a man playing an accordion; we can let our eyes set out on another kind of adventure as they probe the manifold aspects of an object which has been decomposed, so to speak, and then recomposed in a space which has multiple dimensions.

[29] For the philosophical implications of Cubist painting see Christopher Gray, *Cubist Aesthetic Theories.*

20 46 PABLO PICASSO. *Accordionist.* 1911. 51¼ in. × 35¼ in. Solomon R. Guggenheim Museum, New York. (The Solomon R. Guggenheim Museum)

This first stage of Cubism was so ascetic and disciplinary, however, that the painter soon demanded more freedom for personal expression and invention. This Picasso found by taking the parts into which he had separated the figure or object and combining them very freely into compositions which may only remotely resemble the original subject. In this method, which is sometimes known as synthetic Cubism, analysis has yielded to a more spontaneous mingling of views of the object — views selected for their decorative rather than their exclusively spatial significance. An early and superbly decorative example of this aspect of Picasso's work is the *Three Musicians* (Fig. 20–47; another version is in the Museum of Modern Art in New York).

20–47 PABLO PICASSO. *Three Musicians.* 1921. 80 in. × 74 in. A. E. Gallatin Collection, Philadelphia Museum of Art. (Philadelphia Museum of Art)

Here the space is much flatter, scarcely deeper than a series of planes laid like playing cards one upon another. There is also a strong tendency to reduce each form to a simple rectangular shape, but for all that the figures of the clown, the harlequin, and the monk, their instruments and music, and the table at which they are sitting can be detected without effort.

Another aspect of the Cubists' search for a new kind of picture appears in their attention to surface texture. They not only built up the paint structure in various ways, but even added sand and other materials to the medium in an attempt to convey as vividly as possible certain tactile values. Surface texture is a most important element in the sober harmonies and elegant shapes of Braque's *Musical Forms* (Fig. 20–48). In another version of this same theme he used various cloths and papers, including corrugated paper and wallpaper simulating wood graining. In such *papiers collés* (pasted papers) or collages, the use of actual materials

not only created unexpected varieties of surface texture, but reinforced the artist's contention that his work had an independent artistic reality divorced from the objects in actual life which had provided the original inspiration.

Although the invention of Cubism must be considered one of Picasso's greatest achievements, he has never been content to work for long in any one mode. While still painting synthetic Cubist pictures he also made Ingres-like drawings, and painted figure subjects, in a broadly realistic manner often influenced by Antique sculpture. In the late 1920's with heavy swirling lines and rich color, he created visual distortions which seemed related to contemporary Surrealist painting. The climax of this personal style came in 1937 in his large mural *Guernica* (Fig. 20–49), painted for the Spanish pavilion of the Paris International Exposition of that year to commemorate the bombing of the open town, Guernica, during the Spanish Civil War. In this allegorical presentation of the plight of his native country, where brute force seems momentarily triumphant over innocence and truth, Picasso used all the resources of his Cubist experience. The severe colors, blacks, whites, and grays, emphasize the marvelously complex design of interpenetrating planes; the unexpected and violent linear distortions communicate the full horror of the tormented women and children. And in the figures of the dead warrior, the dying horse, and the unyielding bull, Picasso created impressive and public symbols for the plight of his native country.[30] The contention that modern forms of expression in art were unequal to the task of interpreting the humanistic values of modern society was contradicted by

[30] For an analysis of the symbolism in *Guernica* see Juan Larrea, *Guernica*, tr. by Alexander H. Krappe and ed. by Walter Pach, Curt Valentin, New York, 1947.

this painting, for in it Picasso set forth in masterly terms an indictment of the evils of modern totalitarianism and his conviction that art is the best means for affirming the pre-eminent worth of individual human beings.

In contrast to Picasso's violence, of form as well as of expression, Georges Braque worked in a more lyrical and even, one might say, more French manner. The rhythmic effect of his Cubist painting (Fig. 20–48) indicates his admiration for the great masters of French decorative painting; such a work, although entirely contemporary, would not be out of place in an eighteenth-century drawing room. Much of the effect of his work depends upon his mastery of two-dimensional design, for he maintains that painting is a flat surface and should remain a flat surface, animated by line, color, and texture. He worked within a narrow range of restrained but subtly related colors, often using grays and whites to advantage, with frequent unexpected passages of modulated textures.

"The aim of painting," said Braque, ". . . is not to reconstruct an anecdotic fact, but to constitute a pictorial fact. . . . We must not imitate what we want to create. The aspect of things is not to be imitated, for the aspect of things is the result of them."[31]

Fernand Léger is the third leading painter among the original Cubists. His works have the sharp precision of the machine, whose beauty and quality Léger was one of the first to discover. He has been pre-eminently the painter of modern urban life, incorporating into his work the massive effects of modern posters and billboard advertisements, the harsh quality of electric lights, the noise of traffic. An early work in which these effects appear — modulated, however, by the aesthetic

[31] Maurice Raynal, *Modern French Painters*, tr. by Ralph Roeder, Brentano's, New York, 1928, pp. 51–52.

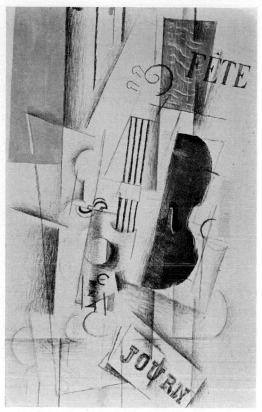

20–48 GEORGES BRAQUE. *Musical Forms.* 1913. 36¼ in. × 23½ in. Oil, pencil, and charcoal on canvas. Louise and Walter C. Arensberg Collection, Philadelphia Museum of Art. (Philadelphia Museum of Art)

of synthetic Cubism — is *The City* (Fig. 20–50). Its large size and even more monumental scale prove that Léger, had he been given the opportunities, would have been one of the great mural painters of our age.

Outside France the most significant instance of Cubist influence appeared in the Italian Futurist movement, inaugurated in 1909 by the manifesto of the poet Filippo Marinetti, who proclaimed a new art of "violence, energy, and boldness." In principle the Futurist painters attempted to present aspects of modern society seen in moments of energetic movement; in practice they adapted the Cubist analysis of space,

20–49　PABLO PICASSO. *Guernica*. 1937. 11 ft. 6 in. × 25 ft. 8 in. Owned by the artist.
Museum of Modern Art, New York. (Museum of Modern Art)

but by repetition of forms across the
plane of the canvas they gave emphasis
to the element of time, and thereby
added another dimension to the vocabulary of modern art. This method had
first been worked out by the French
painter, Marcel Duchamp (1887–),
in his *Nude Descending a Staircase* of
1912 (Philadelphia Museum of Art).
Futurism is best known today through
The Dog on Leash, also called *Leash
in Motion* by Giacomo Balla (1871–
) (Collection of A. Conger Goodyear, New York). The sculpture of

Umberto Boccioni (1882–1916) remains the best work of the group (see
p. 758).[32]

The special effect of Cubist painting
is found in the balance maintained between the appearance of the original
object or figure, as the spectator may
remember it, and the relative degree of
abstraction with which it has been
transformed into a work of art. The extent to which Cubist technique almost

[32] Other members of the group were Carlo
Carrà (1881–); Luigi Russolo (1885–
1941); Gino Severini (1883–).

inevitably led to a greater and finally absolute degree of abstraction is implicit in Juan Gris's remark:

Cézanne turns a bottle into a cylinder, but I begin with a cylinder and create an individual of a special type: I make a bottle — a particular bottle — out of a cylinder. Cézanne tends towards architecture, I tend away from it. That is why I compose with abstractions (colors) and make my adjustments when these colors have assumed the form of objects.[33]

But what, one may wonder, would happen if one started with the geometrical shape and did not develop the resemblance, no matter how remote, to any actual object? Such was the proposal of the Dutch painter, Piet Mondrian (1872–1944), who felt, as he later wrote, that "Cubism did not accept the logical consequences of its own discoveries; it was not developing abstraction toward its ultimate goal, the expression of pure reality."[34] Mondrian himself had begun painting as an Expressionist, influenced by his famous countryman, Vincent van Gogh. But after studying in Paris just before World War I, he turned to a stricter

[33] D. H. Kahnweiler, *Juan Gris, His Life and Work*, p. 138.

[34] Pieter C. Mondriaan, *Plastic Art and Pure Plastic Art*, p. 10.

20–50   FERNAND LÉGER. *The City.* 1919. 91 in. × 117½ in. A. E. Gallatin Collection, Philadelphia Museum of Art. (Philadelphia Museum of Art)

conception of pictorial design. When hostilities commenced he was obliged to return to Holland, where he remained during the war, meditating upon the theories of Cubist painting and continuing his own researches into the absolute properties of artistic order. This led him to renounce all representational elements and to concentrate upon a severely limited vocabulary of forms; he discarded all colors but the primaries, red, yellow, and blue, to which he added black and white; he abandoned all lines but straight lines and reduced all shapes to the square and rectangle. With these elements he constructed two-dimensional designs arranged in such subtle asymmetrical

balances of line, color, and area that no change, however slight, is possible without disturbing the equilibrium of the whole. The entire composition is also so carefully adjusted that no single portion of the surface is more important than any other; the tension between the rectangles is maintained to the very edges. Such a work is *Fox Trot A* (Fig. 20–51), where even primary colors are omitted, the whole consisting of three black lines of varying widths against a white background. But for all its extreme simplicity the painting is complex; the attentive observer finds continual interest in contemplating the balance established between the white areas, in this instance irregular in shape, and the black lines, which may be thought of as meeting invisibly somewhere beyond the boundaries of the canvas. The apparently irrelevant title refers to Mondrian's interest in the syncopated rhythms of modern jazz. We may also think of such a composition as an exceptionally concentrated effort to impose upon the disordered world of actual life, by means of the fewest possible elements, in a syncopated rhythm so to speak, the clarity and definition of the artist's own vision of reality. Contrary to the popular belief that Mondrian was exclusively concerned with artistic problems, his writings indicate that he was constantly seeking to express his conception of ultimate reality. As he himself said:

. . . true reality is attained through dynamic movement in equilibrium. Plastic art affirms that equilibrium can only be established through the balance of unequal but equivalent oppositions. The clarification of equilibrium through plastic art is of great importance for humanity. . . . It is the task of art to express a clear vision of reality.[35]

Mondrian's art was the most conspicuous but not the sole example of this search for a new basis for the arts of design. During the war years in Holland he worked in association with a group of painters, architects, and designers who were seeking to establish a new style for modern times based, as were Mondrian's paintings, on the fewest elements of design.[36] Under the leadership of Théo van Doesburg (1883–1931), who wrote and edited the journal *de Stijl* (*Style*), the mem-

[35] *Ibid.*, p. 15.
[36] Other members were the painters Bart A. van der Leck (1876–   ) and Vilmos Huszar (1884–   ); the sculptors Georges Vantongerloo (1886–   ) and C. Domela-Nieuwenhuis (1900–   ); and the architects Cornelis van Eesteren (1897–   ), J. J. P. Oud (1890–   ), and G. T. Rietveld (1888–   ).

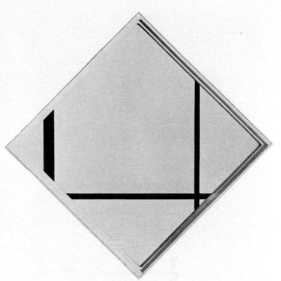

20–51   PIET MONDRIAN. *Fox Trot A.* 1930. 43¾ in. on the diagonal. Société Anonyme Collection, Yale University Art Gallery. (Yale Art Gallery)

bers of the group designed furniture, household articles, typography, and industrial objects in the same spirit of strict simplicity and geometrical order. Certain aspects of *de Stijl* design affected modern art elsewhere, most noticeably through the influence of Mondrian and Van Doesburg at the *Bauhaus* in Dessau, Germany (see p. 780).

In Russia the influence of Cubist painting led to a somewhat similar concern with basic elements of design. Before 1914 Cubist and even Futurist paintings had been exhibited in Moscow and St. Petersburg, and the younger generation of Russian artists were anxious to contribute to the modern movement. Kazimir Malevich (1878–1935), after working in the Cubist and Futurist manners, created what he called Suprematist paintings in which his intention was the expression of nonobjectivity, a form of expression removed as far as possible from the world of natural forms, in this way arriving at "the supremacy of pure feel-

20–52 EL LISSITZKY. *Proun 99*. 1924–1925. 50½ in. × 38¾ in. Société Anonyme Collection, Yale University Art Gallery. (Yale Art Gallery)

ing or perception," for "the essential thing [in pictorial art] is feeling — in itself and completely independent of the context in which it has been evoked." [37] The most nonobjective of all Malevich's work is his famous *White on White*. Here color, shape, and line are reduced to the elements of a white square superimposed upon a larger white square, the two shapes being differentiated only by slight modulations in texture.

With the outbreak of the Russian Revolution in 1917 Malevich and other artists hastened to support the short-lived Kerensky government with the promise of a new and "constructive" art for the "new" social order. But after the emergence of the Com-

munists the Russian peasants and workers found such art incomprehensible and the Constructivist movement was soon suppressed, many of the members emigrating to other countries. In this way Constructivist art and philosophy became known throughout Europe and America. The character of later Constructivist painting can be seen in El Lissitzky's (1890–1947) *Proun 99* (Fig. 20–52). The clear colors, predominantly red, black, and white, suggest the influence of *de Stijl*, but there is a livelier concern for the three-dimensional tensions set up between the cube and the triangular grid. The geometry is apparently correct, but closer study reveals inexplicable dislocations in perspective which contribute to the artistic effect of the painting.

The artists of the Constructivist and *de Stijl* movements were each in their own way reacting to the chaos and disillusionment of the first great war. They tried to create a new art of clarity and order as an expression of a more stable social order. But elsewhere quite another attitude toward the war led to an essentially destructive artistic expression. In several places and at approximately the same time, in Zurich, Barcelona, and New York in the years 1916 and 1917, a number of artists independently stated their disgust with the course of the war by making works of non-art.[38] This movement was early christened Dada, a meaningless infantile word indicating the artists' conviction that European culture had lost all meaning. Those who professed to respect the art of the past had been unable to prevent the outbreak of the holocaust and were now eagerly destroying each other. Since the artists'

[37] Translated from Malevich's *Die gegenstandslose Welt* (1927) in Robert J. Goldwater and Marco Treves, *Artists on Art*, Pantheon Books, New York, 1945, pp. 452–53.

[38] In addition to Duchamp and Schwitters, discussed here, other Dadaists were Francis Picabia (1878–1953), Man Ray (1890–   ), Max Ernst (1891–   ), and Hans Arp (1887–   ).

intentions were fundamentally nihilistic, Dada works are difficult to interpret and are best approached with their creators' avowed spirit of non-art or even anti-art in mind. In this sense they may be considered as criticism of previous and present artistic expression. Such a critical attitude appears in Marcel Duchamp's famous photograph of the *Mona Lisa,* upon which he drew a moustache, just as billboards are defaced in our subways. The public was shocked and interpreted the defacement as an outrage upon the *Mona Lisa* itself, but we can now see that Duchamp's intention was rather an indirect and witty attack upon those who he felt had betrayed the humanistic ideals of the Renaissance, of which the *Mona Lisa* remains one of the noblest expressions. After 1918 the Dada movement spread quickly through Europe, especially in France and Germany, where it appealed to the respective national moods of victory and despair.

Since the Dadaists claimed that they were not creating art, it is perhaps unfair to examine their works in a critical spirit, but nevertheless certain positive contributions emerged from their intentionally negative attitude. Among these are the collage compositions by the German artist Kurt Schwitters (1887–1948), which he called by the meaningless name of "Merz Pictures." ("Merz" is one of the syllables of the German word for "commercial," which Schwitters "accidentally" discovered when cutting the word in pieces.) Although the "Merz" pictures were put together from the contents of the gutter and trash basket, they always show Schwitters' innate sensitivity for texture and design (Fig. 20–53). The typical Dada disdain for conventional techniques accounts for the materials used, but truly artistic feeling for color and form endows these works with an appeal which has survived their historical significance.

20–53   KURT SCHWITTERS. *Merz Picture 19.* 1920. 7¼ in. × 5⅞ in. Collage. Société Anonyme Collection, Yale University Art Gallery. (Yale Art Gallery)

In Marcel Duchamp (1887–) the Dada movement found its most provocative and witty champion, as well as its most eloquent philosopher. Dada, according to Duchamp, was "a metaphysical attitude . . . a sort of nihilism . . . a way to get out of a state of mind — to avoid being influenced by one's immediate environment, or by the past: to get away from *clichés* — to get free." [39] This escape from conventional forms and modes of expression can be seen in Duchamp's glass constructions. Unlike the painting and sculpture of the Russian Constructivists, who had a profound sense of public responsibility, Duchamp's painted glass is his own private jest about the world and art. And if its meaning is inextricable from its non-meaning, as in the title of *To be looked at with one eye, close to, for almost an hour* (Fig. 20–54), at

[39] *Museum of Modern Art Bulletin,* Vol. 13, Nos. 4–5, 1946, p. 20.

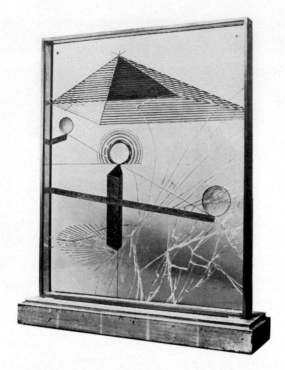

20–54 MARCEL DUCHAMP. *To be looked at with one eye, close to, for almost an hour.* 1918. 20⅛ in. high × 16⅛ in. wide × 1⅜ in. deep. Oil, collage, etc., on glass. Museum of Modern Art, New York. (Museum of Modern Art)

least we can admire the perfection with which he has designed and painted the geometrical shapes in such irrational perspective upon the sheet of plate glass. Not the least perplexing aspect of Duchamp's work is his scrupulous regard for craftsmanship combined with apparently utterly irrelevant subject matter. When at a later date this and other glass objects by Duchamp were accidentally cracked, Duchamp insisted that the unexpected pattern of the fractures completed his original designs.

Although much Dada work was intentionally ephemeral and the movement came to a sudden end in 1922, it had important consequences for later art. It reinforced the trend away from the reasoned, formal aim, and cool disciplinary requirements of Cubism and abstract art toward a spontaneous intuitive expression of the whimsical, fantastic, humorous, sardonic, and absurd. These are aspects of experience which had been neglected by Cubism

and Constructivism, but which had played an important part in earlier art. Thus it is not surprising that when they reappear in the twentieth century they are frequently supported by reference to the art of the past. In the early work of the Greco-Italian painter, Giorgio de Chirico (1888–   ), the squares and palaces of Roman and Renaissance Italy are visualized in a mood of intense and mysterious melancholy. In his *Soothsayer's Recompense* (Fig. 20–55) he suggests a new kind of spatial reality by the enigmatic relationship of the foreground to the background, by the inexplicable discrepancy in scale between the statue and the train, and by the foreboding sense of departure in the clock and the darkened arches. The impact of this is not only visually disturbing but also philosophically so puzzling that De Chirico's works between 1911 and 1919 are considered to belong to the short-lived "scuola metafisica" in modern Italian art. De Chirico himself has supplied

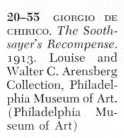

20–55 GIORGIO DE CHIRICO. *The Soothsayer's Recompense.* 1913. Louise and Walter C. Arensberg Collection, Philadelphia Museum of Art. (Philadelphia Museum of Art)

some evidence for a philosophical interpretation by remarking that he was inspired to paint such architectural scenes by Nietzsche's poetic interpretation of autumn afternoons in north Italian cities. Although such "metaphysical painting" does not, strictly speaking, introduce supernatural elements, it does communicate a feeling of reality very different from our ordinary experience. And for that reason De Chirico has been considered a source of inspiration for those artists who created the Surrealist movement in the early 1920's.[40]

The Surrealists' intention was to discover and explore the "more real than real world behind the real" — in other words, the world of psychic experience as it had been revealed by psychoanalytical research. In 1924 the French poet André Breton formulated their intentions in his *Surrealist Manifesto.* The aim was to resolve the two contra-

dictory states of dream and reality into a new and absolute reality, a super-reality (*surréalité*), and so "to re-establish man as psychology instead of anatomy." The dominant motivation of their paintings and constructions is to bring together into a single composition aspects of outer and inner "reality" in much the same way that seemingly unrelated fragments of life combine in the vivid but startling world of dreams. The projection in visible form of this new conception required new techniques and new ways of pictorial construction. At first the Surrealists adopted some of the devices discovered by the Dadaists, but they gave them a new meaning. Thus they used automatic writing and various types of planned accidents not so much to reveal a world without meaning as to provoke in the spectator reactions closely related to his subconscious experience. And since the appearance of Surrealism followed so soon upon the formulations of abstract and nonobjective art,[41]

[40] The leading Surrealist painters have been Salvador Dali (1904–   ), Max Ernst, René Magritte (1898–   ), André Masson (1896–   ), Joan Miró (1893–   ), and Yves Tanguy (1900–1955).

[41] The terms "abstract" and "nonobjective" are often confused, but they refer to different kinds of art. An abstract work has been "ab-

20–56   JOAN MIRÓ.
Composition. 1933.
68½ in. × 77¼ in.
Museum of Modern
Art, New York. (Museum of Modern
Art)

the techniques of the latter and even some of the artists themselves were enlisted in the cause. The abstract paintings of Joan Miró incorporate aspects of biological imagery which lend them a weird and disturbing humor. Intensive work in collage in various mediums as a study in forms and textures led Miró to a greater simplification of shapes, with stress on the curved lines and amoeba-like organisms which seem to float in an immaterial space. In *Composition* (Fig. 20–56), against a dark background of closely related reds, blues, and greens, appear his black shapes, some solid and others only in outline, with dramatic accents of white and vermilion. These elements give the canvas, which is large, a handsome decorative qual-

ity. Several figures are recognizable, such as a dog and an ox. But as Miró often attempts to work automatically, and as his brush moves over the surface with as little direction as possible from his conscious mind — as in automatic writing — he cannot himself always explain the meaning of his pictures. They are in the truest sense spontaneous and intuitive expressions of the little-understood submerged unconscious life.

A new interest in subject matter was perhaps the most important contribution of the Surrealists to modern painting. As Miró said:

I am attaching more and more importance to the subject matter of my work. To me it seems vital that a rich and robust theme should be present to give the spectator an immediate blow between the eyes before a second thought can intervene. In this way poetry pictorially expressed speaks its own language.[42]

stracted" from nature, and vestiges of figures or objects may sometimes still be detected in it (as in Cubist paintings). A nonobjective work has no reference, in conception or execution, to natural appearances (as in the later paintings of Kandinsky and Mondrian).

[42] J. J. Sweeney, *Joan Miró*, p. 13.

20–57 SALVADOR DALI. *Apparition of Face and Fruit Dish on a Beach*. 1938. 45 in. × 57½ in. Wadsworth Atheneum, Hartford. (Courtesy Wadsworth Atheneum, Hartford)

Dream imagery is, of all forms of psychic experience, the most common and the most vivid, but its presentation requires more than a mastery of abstract design. In order to project the world of dreams as convincingly as possible the Catalan painter, Salvador Dali (1904–   ) restudied the masters of seventeenth-century realism, especially the Dutch masters of genre. Since in dreams objects and even situations collide and interpenetrate in a ceaseless process of metamorphosis, Dali uses multiple images of multiple symbolic meaning to suggest evocations from his subconscious. He has also developed a fundamental Surrealist method, the juxtaposition of seemingly irrelevant and certainly unrelated

objects in unexpected situations. This method was suggested to the Surrealists by a metaphor in the work of the little-known nineteenth-century French poet Isadore Ducasse, known as the Comte de Lautréamont. In his *Chants de Maldoror* Ducasse had stated that a situation was "as beautiful as the encounter of an umbrella and a sewing-machine on a dissecting table." The surprising effect of Dali's work depends upon his presentation of such situations in a meticulous, miniature-like technique. These several aspects of his style can be seen in his *Apparition of Face and Fruit Dish on a Beach* (Fig. 20–57), in which the foreground is simultaneously a beach and a table, while the bowl of the fruit dish is part of the

20–58 MARC CHAGALL. *Crucifixion.* 1943. Collection of the artist. (Pierre Matisse Gallery, New York)

body of a large dog. Throughout the background smaller figures move restlessly through a landscape which is now a village street and again a distant shore. In his famous *Persistence of Memory* (Museum of Modern Art) Dali created his most haunting allegory of empty space in which occurs the end of time, if we may so interpret the limp watches which are being incongruously devoured by ants.

Although it is a challenge for the artist to paint his dream images, he is handicapped by the fact that each dream is the experience of a single individual and depends for its meaning on the events in the private life of that one person; the clearer and more detailed its description, the less likely that it will be comprehensible to others. Thus Surrealist art inevitably presented feelings so private that communication

became difficult if indeed not impossible except when the artist, through his choice of familiar symbols, described experiences common to groups of people. Such a broader use of symbol and fantasy occurs in the work of Marc Chagall (1887–   ), who was born in Russia but has studied and worked in Paris, Berlin, and New York. Although he accepted many aspects of the most sophisticated theory and practice of the times, Chagall has never forgotten his early life in an obscure Russian village. Themes from his childhood return as if in dreams and memories; some, gay and fanciful, suggest the simpler pleasures of folk life; others, somber and even tragic, recall the trials and persecutions of his Jewish ancestors. In his *Crucifixion* (Fig. 20–58) the terror of wars and pogroms is suggested by the pitiful little figures and the village in the background, while resignation and hope are expressed in the flying angel, the Torah scroll, and the rabbi-Christ figure on the cross. The very free composition with unexpected juxtapositions of the actual and the unearthly is Surrealist in the sense that it perpetuates the fantastic movement of a dream, but the individual symbols refer to much more than Chagall's personal psychic life. Each of us may be moved by so sensitive a portrayal of the artist's feeling that faith is important in a world of war and brutality.

The most subtle and certainly the most influential of all the masters of fantasy was the German-Swiss artist, Paul Klee (1879–1940). In his contempt for illusionistic art he turned to the art of children and primitive people, and sought to put upon canvas or paper, in terms of the most delicate line and color, and infinite varieties of texture, a graph, as it were, of his emotional reactions to his environment and his materials. His paintings and drawings reveal a world of strangely real unreality, wherein the lives of human beings, birds, animals, and even of inanimate objects are discovered with wit and charm. Klee was also a most ironic commentator on all contemporary artistic styles. In turn he used aspects of Cubism, nonobjective art, Dada, and Surrealism to make his points, so that often a painting by Klee is simultaneously a shrewd comment on human and animal folly, and also a penetrating analysis of some phase of modern art. Although his paintings and drawings are usually very small in size, and although they would seem at first to be the most private of all visual communications, they are charged with meaning which gradually becomes clearer to the imaginative spectator. In a water color such as *At the Mountain of the Bull* (Fig. 20–59), the interpenetrating planes of Cubism, the geometrical character of nonobjective art, and the instinctive linear structure of children's drawings satirize those current modes, but the oddly sacrificial feeling of the subject matter probes deep into the sources of religious experience as old as human history.

By now most of us accept the fact that much recent art, and even a good deal of older art, is not comprehensible at first sight. Like great works of literature, serious painting and sculpture may incorporate ideas which require considerable thought and even learning to be properly understood. For this reason modern art surprised and disturbed many people when it was first exhibited, and there were those who reproached the artist for creating objects which he himself did not take the trouble to understand. But in spite of many difficulties, modern artists in most democratic countries have seen the gradual growth of public interest and understanding until today in the United States, England, and Europe there are important and active museums and galleries devoted to show-

20–59 PAUL KLEE. *At the Mountain of the Bull.* 1923. 18⅛ in. × 13⅜ in. Water color and oil. Private collection, Berlin. (From W. Grohmann, *Paul Klee*, Abrams, New York)

ing works of modern art to a large and appreciative audience. This remarkable increase in understanding, however, has not been universal. In undemocratic countries a feeling has prevailed that the public has the right to enjoy all works of art without previous preparation, and that the artist has an obligation to create works which the public can easily understand. In countries where art is supported by large state subsidies, rather than by private patronage, the artist who fails to conform soon finds himself forbidden to exhibit, and occasionally even his personal liberty is endangered. This was especially true in Germany during the 1930's, when every artistic expression which did not conform to official standards was rigorously suppressed, as it was in Russia after the progressive artists were expelled in the 1920's. Even works of modern art purchased from public funds by previous German governments, and which had been enjoyed by the public, were removed from museums and sold. The results of such a program were twofold: artistic poverty at home and unexpected artistic enrichment abroad. After Hitler's rise to power in 1933 many German artists emigrated, and with the outbreak of war in 1939 even more artists from other countries were displaced. Many came to the United States, where the temporary residence of such men as Léger, Mondrian, and Chagall, among others, proved most stimulating to American artists. Others chose to remain permanently, such as the German Expressionist master, Max Beckmann (1884–1950) and the German nonobjective painter, Josef Albers (1888–   ). Their presence and their work, as artists and as teachers in American schools and universities, has immeasurably increased the nation's understanding of the modern movement. In Soviet Russia all aspects of modern art have been officially suppressed in favor of "social realism,"

whereby contemporary Russian painters and sculptors have been required to treat banal subjects of supposedly general public interest in a realistic technique.

In conclusion it is appropriate to recognize the debt which so many modern artists, both painters and sculptors, have owed to the titanic genius of Pablo Picasso. Although he himself has said that all his work is based on the experience of nature, he has at times adventured so far from the visual appearance of actual objects that his work seems thoroughly abstract, and yet the next day he may produce an image almost literally representational. In each of his phases he has created work so powerful in feeling and so imaginative in design that it contains inexhaustible suggestions for further development. This factor, a characteristic of the work of only the very greatest artists, is alone sufficient to guarantee his position as the dominant artist of the first half of the twentieth century.

2oth-Century American

United States

Two exhibitions — one of "The Eight" in 1908 and the other, the "Armory Show" in 1913 — dramatized for the twentieth century a debate which has persisted in American cultural life since the mid-eighteenth century. Should American art be rooted in the American environment? Or should the American artist take a more cosmopolitan point of view and look to Europe for inspiration? Because of the predominant interest of The Eight in urban reportage, this group has come to repre-

sent the ideal of an American art inspired by American subject matter. On the other hand, the Armory Show provided the American public with its first comprehensive view of the nature of the formal revolution wrought by modern painters in Europe. In effect, then, the moral of the earlier exhibition seemed to center in subject matter; of the second, in formal values — *what* was painted in the first, and *how* it was painted in the second.

Those who championed the cause of subject matter argued that the painter could create a vital modern art only if he immersed himself in modern life, and, that, for the American, this search for life implied a scrutiny of America. Such at least was the reasoning of those who believed that "American" art demanded American subject matter. All too frequently, however, the pleas for American subject matter reflected naïveté, provinciality, or, at worst, chauvinism. If the attack on an overly precious attitude toward the forms of art was quite legitimate, the extreme position that subject matter should predominate over form was nonsense — and doubly absurd to specify that the subject *must* be American. For the artist can create only in terms of his own meaningful experience and the forms appropriate to it, regardless of whether this experience happens to require the depiction of native themes.

The first direct contact in America with European modernism came from exhibitions in New York galleries. Alfred Stieglitz (1864–1946), the notable photographer (see p. 748), presided over the most famous of these galleries, established in 1905 to exhibit progressive photography. Beginning in 1908 Stieglitz interspersed his photographic shows with the initial American exhibitions of French moderns such as Matisse, Cézanne, Picasso, Toulouse-Lautrec, and Henri Rousseau. In his small upstairs gallery (which came to be called "291" because of its Fifth Avenue address) Stieglitz also introduced the work of some of the young American painters studying in Paris, such as Alfred Maurer (1868–1932), Max Weber, and John Marin.

Although "291" gradually attracted a devoted coterie, it was the International Exhibition of Modern Art, held in New York in the Sixty-Ninth Regimental Armory from February 17 to March 15, 1913, which provoked the attention of a large public, making the problem of "modern art" a *cause célèbre*. Immediately dubbed the "Armory Show" by press and public, no other single exhibition in America has ever matched its impact. The idea of a comprehensive exhibition of modern art had originated in 1910 with a small group of forward-looking painters. Working against tremendous odds, they gathered an estimated 1600 works of painting and sculpture particularly representative of the major modern movements in France, although including some non-French works as well. Contemporary American artists, for instance, were shown, but it was the Europeans who attracted the greatest attention. To most Americans the Armory Show was a revelation. The sprawling exhibition defied indifference. Most came to rage, to chortle, to ridicule — the *succès de scandale* being Marcel Duchamp's *Nude Descending a Staircase* (see p. 706). Some, however, came and discovered fresh insights, new possibilities.

Travel abroad and exhibitions at home began to influence even painters of a conservative temperament, who flirted tentatively with the new forms, just as the conservatives of a previous generation had embraced Impressionist forms. Thus Cézanne's innovations made a superficial appearance in academic still life and portraiture, while Renoir's late figure style spawned numerous derivative idylls. For the more independent American painters of the period, however, certainly the most important influences were Cubism and Fauvism, the one inevitably evoking Cézanne, the other sometimes reinforced by German Expressionism. Whereas Cubism as it originally developed in France had tended to emphasize stable compositions, American Cubism often revealed dynamic qualities in both movement and color. This dynamic characteristic doubtless owed much to the fact that Americans simultaneously absorbed the architectonic emphasis of Cubism with the violent color and movement of Fauvism and Expres-

20–60 JOSEPH STELLA. *Brooklyn Bridge*. 1917–1918. 48¼ in. × 29¼ in. Yale University Art Gallery. (Yale Art Gallery)

sionism. Moreover, many Americans reached France after the initial Cubist explorations, when Duchamp was dissecting human movement in cubistic and mechanistic terms.[43] But the American environment itself also accounted for the energetic styles of many of the Cubist-inspired Americans – the vigorous activity of the American city, the blatant color of its advertising, and the hard forms of its buildings in the intense sunlight so different from the softer atmosphere conditioning Paris.

The American painter was little interested in the purely formal problems which the French painter often set himself. Americans used these formal dis-

coveries for personal expression. Stella, Marin, Hartley, Davis, and Weber represent diverse approaches to dynamic Cubism. In his *Brooklyn Bridge* (Fig. 20–60), Joseph Stella (1880–1946) broke up the piers and cables of the bridge into faceted forms, creating deep corridors of space against the outward radiation of long diagonals. The engineering forms merge with the night environment to create a prismatic sparkle epitomized by the jewel-like radiance of the conical shape in the foreground. John Marin (1870–1953) also felt the pulsating energy of New York after his return from Europe. In his earliest American water colors, he shattered skyscrapers into twisting pyramids of planes in Fauvist color. In his later work he abandoned the city to express the vitality of nature. Like Winslow Homer before him, Marin was particularly attracted to the Maine coast. Whereas Homer had chosen large motifs rather

[43] Duchamp's influence on the development of modern American art was increased by his living in New York from 1916 to 1920 (and again in later years). Although the Italian Futurists also particularly concentrated on the creation of dynamic forms of Cubism, only one American painter of importance, Joseph Stella, appears to have come directly into contact with them.

20–61   JOHN MARIN. *Maine Islands.* 1922. 16¾ in. × 20 in. Phillips Gallery, Washington, D. C. (Phillips Gallery)

close to the spectator, such as a single breaker dashing on rocks (Fig. 20–36), Marin preferred panoramic views such as his *Maine Islands* (Fig. 20–61). Here the slashing diagonals in the foreground create transparent planes through which the spectator peers, as through a foreground window, at the sun-drenched sweep of ocean beyond, dotted with crisp island shapes. Marin's calligraphic style was borrowed from Chinese landscape painting, just as Homer's large sea patterns owed something of their simplicity to Japanese prints. The contrast, however, between the naturalism of Homer and the abstract qualities of Marin marks the extent of the revolution in vision which the French moderns had wrought.

We may also compare Winslow Homer and Marsden Hartley (1877–1943). Attracted, like his predecessor, to the Maine motif of waves against rocks and the hard life of the fisherman, Hartley simplified the forms and greatly intensified the color characteristic of Homer's realism, thereby attaining an expressive clash of form and color similar to that of the German Expressionists. Stuart Davis (1894–   ), too, delights in a violent clash of forms, but he usually concentrates on the strident juxtaposition of city buildings and billboards as his expression of American life. In *Report from Rockport* (Fig. 20–62) he saw a small New England seaport town in terms of a tumbled pat-

20–62 STUART DAVIS. *Report from Rockport.* 1940. Collection Mr. and Mrs. Milton Lowenthal. (The Downtown Gallery, New York)

tern in strong color. The flat pattern of form and color creates tensions in space reminiscent of Léger (cf. Fig. 20–50). Characteristically American, however, is Davis' greater emphasis on subject matter as compared to the more abstract and formal quality of Léger's work.

None of the dynamic Cubists has been more eclectic in his sources, nor has better fused his eclecticism into a personal style than Max Weber (1881–). Among the first Americans to paint with both Fauvists and Cubists in Paris, he also became interested while abroad in various non-Western and primitive arts which enriched the sumptuousness of his color and in-

creased the depth of his pictorial symbolism. In his developed style, Weber establishes the basic structure of his canvases in a calligraphic mesh of black paint, reminiscent of Rouault though looser and freer and, therefore, suggestive of the influence of Chinese brushwork. Somberly exotic color bejewels the paint surface, intensifying the religious quality of his Old Testament and rabbinical scenes.

If certain American painters developed the dynamic aspects of Cubism, others — such as Sheeler, Demuth, O'Keeffe, Blume, and Hopper — continued in the tradition of the stable, architectonic compositions which characterized the beginnings of that move-

ment. Charles Sheeler (1883–   ),
Charles Demuth (1883–1935), and
Georgia O'Keeffe (1887–   ) all express their vision in terms of sharply
bounded, meticulously shaded, immac-
ulately precise forms, rather cool in col-
or. Despite some formal characteristics
in common, however, each has viewed
different aspects of America in differing ways. Sheeler delights in the elegant precision of modern industry and
engineering, and the large simplicities
of Pennsylvania barns or early American interiors. He organizes his pristine
worlds into an elegant equipoise of
stripped forms. Demuth, too, often
used architectural themes, but he generally preferred older buildings and
country factories to the vast industrial
panoramas which attract Sheeler. In
My Egypt (Fig. 20–63) long diagonals
and transparent planes unite the geometry of a pair of grain elevators with
the surrounding sky. Demuth's penciled
lines and thinly applied color — especially in his landscapes and flower
pieces — recall Cézanne water colors,
but his paintings are stylized into larger, simpler, more frozen patterns.

Employing the same kind of forms,
O'Keeffe prefers bold curvilinear
shapes to the angularities predominat-
ing in the work of Sheeler and Demuth. Her colors are more intense; her
themes usually organic: the sweep of
the New Mexican desert or enormously
enlarged flowers pushed up so close to
the picture plane that one sees only the
pattern created by a few petals.
O'Keeffe's "close-ups," her textureless
surfaces, and their subtle gradation in
light and shade reflect, as do Sheeler's
forms, the influence of the photograph.
Whereas Sheeler is himself a distinguished photographer as well as a
painter, O'Keeffe as the wife of Alfred
Stieglitz has been profoundly influenced by her husband's photography
(see p. 748).

Peter Blume's (1906–   ) meticu-

20-63   CHARLES DEMUTH. *My Egypt.* 1927.
Whitney Museum of American Art, New York.
(Whitney Museum of American Art)

lously elaborate compositions show the
influence of Surrealism as well as Cubism. The trancelike clarity of his forms
and his unlikely juxtaposition of subject matter create an unreal world
where man seems engulfed in an un-
controllable mechanization. If in the
machine Stella found an exultant dynamic and Sheeler the basis for a new
order, Blume sensed in it the threat of
dehumanization. Edward Hopper
(1882–   ), too, sees the darker side
of modern life with its capacity to create physical obsolescence and human
loneliness. The bold simplification of
his *Early Sunday Morning* (Fig. 20–
64) reflects the influence of Cubism,
while this influence on such a realist
indicates how profoundly the French
modernists have conditioned twentieth-
century vision. It is the strength and
austerity of Hopper's forms which give
his tawdry subject matter its haunting
power.

Hopper was not alone in his critical
realism during the twenties. Charles

20–64 EDWARD HOPPER. *Early Sunday Morning.* 1930. 35 in. × 60 in. Whitney Museum of American Art, New York. (Whitney Museum of American Art)

Burchfield (1893–   ) also portrayed the crassness of American small-town life at a time when Sinclair Lewis created Babbitt and the critic H. L. Mencken attacked the American "booboisie" in the pages of the *American Mercury*. Less detached than Hopper, Burchfield expresses his more emotional point of view by smaller forms in more abrupt relationships. His paintings suggest Burchfield's ambivalent attitude toward subject matter, at once romantic and realistic. The same ambivalence appears in his career. He forsook his early fantasies on landscape themes for social realism during the twenties and especially during the thirties, only to return to his earliest themes in the forties.

The economic depression of the thirties inevitably encouraged social satire. Whereas The Eight, at the turn of the century, had been essentially optimistic in their picturesque approach to the urban slum, the thirties saw many painters strike out against social injustice.

Poverty, political corruption, strikebreaking, totalitarianism: these provided themes for an expression of indignation. The social painting of the revolutionary Mexican muralists — especially José Orozco and Diego Rivera (p. 730), both of whom received important commissions in the United States during the thirties — strongly attracted American painters. Influenced by the Mexican example and encouraged by funds from the Works Progress Administration, the revival of mural painting epitomized the social awareness engendered by the depression.

Varied artistic sources inspired these social paintings of the thirties. The quickly brushed, flat planes of Goya and Daumier, for example, influenced the left-wing pictorial criticism of William Gropper (1897–   ). For Jack Levine (1915–   ) and Hyman Bloom (1913–   ) it was the violent distortions and color of Van Gogh, Chaim Soutine, and German Expressionism which fed the bloated countenances of their

20–65 BEN SHAHN. *Handball*. 1939. 22¾ in. × 31¼ in. Museum of Modern Art, New York. (Museum of Modern Art)

bankers and stockbrokers. For Philip Evergood (1901–   ) the conscious awkwardness of folk art offered a prototype for his poignant views of slum and factory life. For others, such as Ivan Albright (1897–   ), a pitiless realism recorded the sordid side of life. Perhaps the most profound social painter of the period is Ben Shahn (1898–   ). Eclectic in his sources, he has fused his varied borrowings into a personal style which is at once socially and formally expressive. His *Handball* (Fig. 20–65), for example, recalls the geometry of Cubism, the haunted space of Surrealism, the hypnotic perspectives of Quattrocento painting, the striking juxtapositions and changes of scale of the candid photograph.

If the thirties saw much criticism of America, this was but one aspect of the tendency for the American artist to scrutinize what came to be called the "American scene." Protest in some was matched by praise in others. In either case, prevailing opinion held that, whereas excessive concern with European modernism encouraged effeteness in the arts, immersion in the American scene promised vitality. The old (and somewhat puerile) dilemma as to whether the American artist should look to Paris or to Paducah for inspiration was momentarily resolved in favor of a nationalistic bias.

The artists most widely publicized among the "American scene" painters — Grant Wood (1892–1942) and Thomas Hart Benton (1889–   ) — began as social satirists at the opening of the decade, but only later in the thirties did they tend to celebrate what

20–66　GRANT WOOD. *American Gothic*. 1930. 29⅞ in. × 24⅞ in. Art Institute of Chicago. (Courtesy of the Art Institute of Chicago, Friends of American Art Gift)

they had earlier ridiculed. Wood's *American Gothic* (Fig. 20–66) illustrates this curious duality between love and hate which the American artist has often felt toward his country. When Wood first conceived of this painting he thought of the Iowa farmer and his wife standing before their stark Gothicized farmhouse as the embodiment of narrow prejudice and self-righteous morality. He endeavored to suggest these qualities by means of gaunt forms and meticulously simplified detail, based in part on recollections of fifteenth-century Flemish painting, in part on the woodenness of American folk productions. The public, however, completely missed the satirical intent of the painting, praising the couple instead as the embodiment of American virtue and self-reliance. Wood himself seems later to have adopted the public interpretation of his painting. He gradually abandoned the social satire of his

earlier painting to glorify, in archaic stylization, the rolling fields of Iowa, the celebration of Arbor Day at the one-room schoolhouse, and patriotic mythology such as Washington's chopping the cherry tree. Much the same transformation occurred in Thomas Hart Benton's attitude toward America. His painting of the late twenties and early thirties depicted the crassness of American urban life in tortured, elongated figures reminiscent of El Greco. By the mid-thirties his subject matter had shifted to Ozark farmers dancing to the fiddle or plowing beside log shacks. As Wood and Benton turned to the Middle West for inspiration, so did John Steuart Curry (1897–1946), who depicted the sweep of the countryside, the terror of the tornado, and the vigor of prairie life in large forms and surging movement reminiscent of Rubens. Reginald Marsh (1898–1954) is also frequently included with "American scene" painters. He concentrated on New York street and slum scenes in a Rubensian technique. His subject matter links him to Sloan, but his point of view is less picturesque and more critical of urban conditions. While these "American scene" painters were at work, other artists, under WPA sponsorship, ferreted out the American folk arts — glass, needlework, furniture, iron casting, whatever it was and wherever it existed — and created the invaluable *Index of American Design.*

Although the "American scene" painters garnered most of the publicity during the thirties, other painters continued to explore and develop the tradition of modern form which they had inherited from Europe. Perhaps the increasing importance of international problems at the end of the decade tended to make American artists once again more conscious of Europe and less patient with the extreme chauvinism of much "American scene" propaganda. Certainly the influx of foreign

20–67 JACKSON POLLOCK. *Number 29.* 1950. Oil paint, wire mesh, string, shells, pebbles on glass. Collection Lee Krasner Pollock, Springs, New York. (Museum of Modern Art)

artists to America as a result of Fascist persecution encouraged a cosmopolitan approach to the arts. These refugees, as we have noted, not only enriched with their own creations the cultural life of their adopted country, but many of them, through their teaching, infused a new generation of Americans with their creative idealism. Finally, foreign contacts (many of them non-European) during World War II and the proliferation of grants for travel since the war have enabled many American artists to study abroad, whereas they had necessarily remained at home during the depression.

Recently a new development in abstract art indicates the continuing vitality of the modern movement here and abroad. The terms "abstract Expressionist" (in New York) and "action painting" (in London) suggest the artists' intention of projecting immedi-

ate emotional experience within the technique of abstract art. The premeditated structure of earlier abstract art, as it developed from Cubism, has been replaced by a handling of the medium which exploits, through dripping, spatters, and other accidental effects, the possibilities of emotional expression within the actual physical texture of the painted surface. Foremost among such painters was Jackson Pollock (1912–1956), whose impassioned treatment of the paint seemed at first to lack all conscious control, but is now seen to be an instrument for the accurate projection of his particular experience (Fig. 20–67). In breaking the boundaries of traditional attitudes toward the easel picture, Pollock and other leaders of the movement, such as Willem de Kooning, Clyfford Still, and Robert Motherwell, have also enlarged the actual size of their works. Many modern paintings approach in size, and

20–68 WILLIAM RONALD. *In Dawn the Heart.* 1954. Collection, the Art Gallery of Toronto. (McLean Fund)

search in pictorial art are proof of a vigorous and original school of painting, the first in American history which has been independent of European influence and which has had, in turn, a significant effect on painting abroad.

Distinguished work has also been recently done in representational painting, although here too the intensity of Expressionist art and certain technical procedures derived from abstract painting are in evidence. In England, Graham Sutherland and Robert Bacon have made important contributions to modern religious painting and to portraiture. Sutherland frequently develops intense designs from such natural forms as tree roots and thorns, whereas Bacon has introduced a profound psychological mood into his portraits.

Canada

In the twentieth century Canadian art may be said to have come of age. European dependency has been rejected, and a national school of painting has asserted itself, followed by a preoccupation with forms of abstract Expressionism. Tom Thomson (1877–1917), a self-trained north country fire ranger, has become a legend, and he has left an impressive legacy of colorful landscape paintings.

Led by Lawren Harris (1885–), the "Group of Seven" held their first exhibition in 1920. Their crusade, against a redundant tradition and in support of an essentially national school of painting, was dedicated to an interpretation of the Canadian environment. Their contribution too was largely in the realm of landscape painting. Having achieved their objective, this vigorous and talented group dissolved in 1933. Their heirs are the "Canadian Group of Painters." Two noted independents, David Milne (1882–1953) and Emily Carr (1871–1945), developed concurrently with, but apart

in monumental scale, the dimensions of earlier mural painting.

A further development and a possible new direction to modern painting may be seen in the work of such painters as Corrado Marca-Relli and Grace Hartigan. In these paintings, although each object may have been begun as a problem in the abstract arrangement of color and shape, the emergence of images suggesting natural forms or evoking personal experience is encouraged. The diversity of theory and practice and the number of younger talents committed to unremitting re-

20–69 JOSÉ GUADALUPE POSADA. *Calavera: Don Quixote*. Early 20th century. 5¹³⁄₁₆ in. × 10¾ in. Relief engraving on metal. Art Institute of Chicago. (Courtesy of the Art Institute of Chicago)

from, The Seven. Milne was a protégé of Maurice Prendergast, but his accomplishments are unique. Emily Carr was a West Coast mystic who dreamed in the forests and employed the imagery of the aboriginal totems in her painting.

Today Canadian art is diverse and cosmopolitan. Its national character has yielded to the new international disciplines of the twentieth century. In painting, sculpture, architecture, and the minor arts there is a preoccupation with the new forms of contemporary expression and complexity of style and influence. Among others, Jean-Paul Riopelle (1923–   ) and William Ronald (1926–   ) (Fig. 20–68) have achieved international repute as nonobjective abstract Expressionists.

Mexico

Modern painting in Mexico made its appearance with the Mexican Revolution of 1910. Although a complete break with Spain in 1810 had established Mexico's independence, it was not until a century later that exploitation by the Díaz regime caused the revolution to burst forth which created a modern government.

Mexico remains a complex land, one of marked contrasts and contradictions. Indian and Hispanic traditions are everywhere in evidence, and the influence of foreign artistic training vies with this native heritage in the formation of a vigorous idiom, which has established a recognizable Mexican style of monumental mural painting and lithography. The traditional arts of the craftsman, producing articles of daily use, have at the same time been maintained to a marked degree in spite of the inroads of industrial techniques.

The work of José Guadalupe Posada (1851–1913), an engraver who supplied illustrations for a publishing house during the Díaz regime, was a prelude to this modern Mexican style. He was prolific, illustrating songs, ballads, stories, and romances as well as

20–70 DAVID ALFARO SIQUEIROS. *Proletarian Victim.* 1933. Museum of Modern Art, New York. (Museum of Modern Art)

murders and current news items — usually with caustic satire — and his work appealed directly to an illiterate audience (Fig. 20–69). Contemporary society — often presented in the guise of skulls and skeletons — came under his lash. This style was quite comprehensible to the Mexican, for the macabre has been firmly fixed in his life, as, for example, in the celebrations of All Saints' Day, with food and drink in family feasts at the cemetery.

With the fall of Díaz in 1910, students of painting revolted against the established authority of the National Academy. They followed varied paths. Some artists, notably David Alfaro Siqueiros, joined the revolutionaries. José Clemente Orozco, in isolation, painted caricatures and scenes of suffering. Other painters, especially Diego Ri-

vera, were in Europe, acquiring technical proficiency and assimilating ideas from French painting. Carlos Mérida came from Guatemala with paintings based on Guatemalan Indian themes, not to illustrate the picturesque peoples and costumes of that country, but to provide a starting point for the creation of abstract forms. Dr. Atl (pseudonym of Gerardo Murillo, 1884–), Roberto Montenegro (1885–), and Adolfo Best-Maugard (1891–) were concerned with the folk arts and with educational methods.

The formation of the Syndicate of Painters and Sculptors in 1922 gave these forces an opportunity for expression. The new government encouraged their activity by commissioning them to cover the walls of public buildings with murals whose content should be of their own choosing. In the decade of feverish activity which followed, Rivera, Montenegro, Siqueiros, Orozco, Jean Charlot (1898–), and others painted murals depicting scenes of revolutionary struggle. A very important result was the revival of the fresco technique.

Though these painters were linked in motivation, they were highly individual in their mode of expression. Siqueiros (1898–), who participated actively in the revolutionary movements, recalls preconquest sculpture in his *Proletarian Victim* (Fig. 20–70). The figure is painted on burlap in Duco. Some of his more expressive murals are at Chillan, Chile, and in the Electricians' Union building and school buildings in Mexico City. Another startling example of his work, bordering on Surrealism, can be seen in the Museum of Modern Art in New York City (Fig. 20–71).

Diego Rivera (1886–1957) went to Europe in 1907 and, except for a brief return to Mexico, remained there until 1921, studying not only the work of the Cubists but also the long tradition of mosaics and frescoes of Italy. On his

DAVID ALFARO SIQUEIROS. *Echo of a Scream.* 1937. 48 in. × 36 in. Museum of Modern Art, New York. (Museum of Modern Art)

to-hand battle between Indian foot soldiers and a Spanish horseman. Rivera's influence upon mural painting in the United States, in particular upon the revival of fresco, was due to his frescoes in San Francisco (1930–1931), Detroit (1932), and New York City (1933–1934). Although those in New York were destroyed because of political prejudice, they exist in replica in the Palace of Fine Arts in Mexico City.

José Clemente Orozco (1883–1956), though imbued with the same ideology as other members of the Syndicate, presented an entirely different personality and manner of expression. He was a retiring, passionate humanitarian and a caustic satirist. Orozco had intense energy, a violence of feeling, expressed in a frequent use of diagonals and violent clashes of color. His frescoes at Guadalajara cover two domes and the walls beneath. In the Chapel of the Orphanage the figures represent Earth, Air, Sea, and Fire in one great rhythm with many minor contrasting movements. In the Assembly Hall of the

return to Mexico he, too, immediately became involved in the revolutionary movement.

While some of Rivera's earlier paintings were in encaustic, most of them were true frescoes. This technique limited his palette to the earth colors, to which he added green, blue, and black. At Chapingo a pervading warm tonality results from the earth reds obtained from *tezontle*, a native red volcanic stone widely used in Mexican building. This tonality is an important element of unity in a decorative scheme which covers walls and ceiling with massive figures.

In a fresco in Cuernavaca showing a scene from the conquest (Fig. 20–72) Rivera revealed his command of mural design in the deft unification of two walls at the corner to portray a hand-

20–72 DIEGO RIVERA. *Siege of Tenochtitlan.* 1930. Palace of Cortes, Cuernavaca. (Elliott H. Kone)

20–73 JOSÉ CLEMENTE OROZCO. *Man in Four Aspects.* 1935. Fresco in the dome of the Assembly Hall, University of Guadalajara. (Frances Toor)

University of Guadalajara, in a lunette beneath the dome, hordes of emaciated, starving people, against a background of fire, rush with angry gestures toward a cowering group of their oppressors. Chaotic movement and vivid color and value contrasts diminish as the gestures and flames carry the eye to the brilliantly colored dome, which is filled with four figures, gigantic in size relative to those below, representing *Man in Four Aspects: Scientist, Worker, Philosopher, and Skeptic* (Fig. 20–73). Orozco has here implied a universal protest against injustice and exploitation in the tradition, indeed, of Michelangelo.[44]

The traditions so expressive of the Mexican heritage are being continued, with the individual interpretation characteristic of modern art, by such artists as Rufino Tamayo (b. 1900), in Mexico and the rest of Latin America.

[44] Orozco also painted murals in the United States: in Pomona College, Claremont, California (1930); in the New School for Social Research, New York City (1931); in the library of Dartmouth College (1932–1934).

Bibliography

19TH-CENTURY EUROPEAN

France

Baudelaire, Charles, *The Mirror of Art,* Phaidon Press, London, 1955.

Berger, Klaus, *Géricault and His Work,* University of Kansas Press, Lawrence, 1955.

Boas, George, ed., *Courbet and the Naturalistic Movement,* Johns Hopkins Press, Baltimore, 1938.

Cartwright, Julia Mary, *Jean François Millet,* Macmillan, New York, 1910.

Cooper, Douglas, ed., *The Courtauld Collection,* Athlone Press, London, 1954.

——, *Toulouse-Lautrec,* Abrams, New York, 1956.

Duret, Théodore, *Manet and the French Impressionists,* Lippincott, Philadelphia, 1910.

Friedlaender, Walter, *From David to Delacroix,* Harvard University Press, 1952.

Gauss, Charles K., *Aesthetic Theories of French Artists,* Johns Hopkins Press, Baltimore, 1949.

Hamilton, George Heard, *Manet and His Critics,* Yale University Press, 1954.

Hunter, Sam, *Modern French Painting, 1855–1956,* Dell, New York, 1956.

The Intimate Journals of Paul Gauguin, tr. by Van Wyck Brooks, Heinemann, London, 1931.

The Journal of Eugène Delacroix, ed. and tr. by W. Pach, Crown Publishers, New York, 1948.

Lassaigne, Jacques, *Daumier,* Hyperion Press, New York, 1938.

Laver, James, *French Painting and the Nineteenth Century,* Scribner's, 1937.

Leymarie, Jean, *Impressionism,* tr. by J. Emmons, 2 vols., Skira, New York, 1955.

Mack, Gerstle, *Paul Cézanne,* Knopf, 1935.

——, *Gustave Courbet,* Knopf, 1951.

——, *Toulouse-Lautrec,* Knopf, 1938.

Pach, Walter, *Ingres,* Harper, 1939.

——, *Renoir,* Abrams, New York, 1950.

Pissarro, Camille, *Letters to His Son Lucien,* Pantheon Books, New York, 1943.

Rewald, John, *Degas: Works in Sculpture,* Kegan Paul, Trench, Trubner, London, 1944.

——, *History of Impressionism,* Museum of Modern Art, New York, 1946.

——, *Post-Impressionism from Van Gogh to Gauguin,* Museum of Modern Art, New York, 1956.

——, *Seurat,* G. Wittenborn, New York, 1943.

Rich, Daniel Catton, *Degas,* Abrams, New York, 1951.

Richardson, Edgar P., *The Way of Western Art,* Harvard University Press, 1939.

Schapiro, Meyer, *Paul Cézanne,* Abrams, New York, 1952.

——, *Vincent van Gogh,* Abrams, New York, 1950.

Sloane, Joseph C., *French Painting Between the Past and the Present,* Princeton University Press, 1951.

Van Gogh, Vincent, *Letters to Emile Bernard,* Museum of Modern Art, New York, 1938.

Wildenstein, Georges, *Ingres,* Phaidon Press, London, 1954.

England

Binyon, Laurence, *The Drawings and Engravings of William Blake,* The Studio, London, 1922.

Figgis, Darrell, *The Paintings of William Blake,* Benn, London, 1925.

Finberg, Alexander J., *The Life of J. M. W. Turner, R.A.,* Oxford University Press, New York, 1939.

Fry, Roger, *Reflections on British Painting,* Macmillan, New York, 1934.

Ironside, Robin, *Pre-Raphaelite Painters,* Phaidon Press, London, 1948.

Klingender, Francis D., *Art and the Industrial Revolution,* Noel Carrington, London, 1947.

Leslie, Charles R., *Memoirs of the Life of John Constable,* ed. and enl. by Andrew Shirley, Medici Society, London, 1937.

Pevsner, Nikolaus, *The Englishness of English Art,* Architectural Press, London, 1956.

Redgrave, Richard and Samuel, *A Century of British Painters,* Phaidon Press, London, 1947.

Ritchie, Andrew C., *Masters of British Painting, 1800–1950,* Museum of Modern Art, New York, 1956.

Rothenstein, John K. M., *An Introduction to English Painting,* Cassell, London, 1933.

19TH-CENTURY AMERICAN

American Folk Art, Museum of Modern Art, New York, 1932.

Barker, Virgil, *American Painting, History and Interpretation,* Macmillan, New York, 1932.

Baur, John I. H., *American Painting in the Nineteenth Century,* Praeger, New York, 1953.

Born, Wolfgang, *American Landscape Painting,* Yale University Press, 1948.

——, *Still-Life Painting in America,* Oxford University Press, New York, 1947.

Cowdrey, Mary B., and Williams, Hermann W., Jr., *William Sidney Mount, 1807–*

1868, An American Painter, Columbia University Press, 1944.

Drepperd, Carl W., American Pioneer Arts and Artists, Pond-Ekberg, Springfield, Mass., 1942.

Flexner, James T., The Light of Distant Skies, Harcourt, Brace, 1954.

Frankenstein, Alfred V., After the Hunt: William Harnett and Other American Still Life Painters, University of California Press, Berkeley, 1953.

Goodrich, Lloyd, John Sloan, Macmillan, New York, 1952.

——, Thomas Eakins, His Life and Work, Studio Publications, New York, 1933.

——, Winslow Homer, Macmillan, New York, 1944.

Inness, George, Jr., Life, Art, and Letters of George Inness, Century Co., New York, 1917.

Janis, Sidney, They Taught Themselves, Dial Press, New York, 1942.

M. and M. Karolik Collection of American Paintings, 1815–1865, published for Boston Museum of Fine Arts by Harvard University Press, 1947.

Larkin, Oliver W., Art and Life in America, Rinehart, 1949.

Lipman, Jean, American Primitive Painting, Oxford University Press, New York, 1942.

Mather, Frank J., Jr., Morey, Charles R., and Henderson, William J., The American Spirit in Art (Pageant of America Series, Vol. 12), Yale University Press, 1927.

Mumford, Lewis, The Brown Decades, . . . , Harcourt, Brace, 1931.

Pennell, E. R., and Pennell, Joseph, The Life of James McNeill Whistler, 6th ed. rev., Lippincott, 1920.

Peters, Harry T., Currier & Ives, Printmakers to the American People, Doubleday, Doran, 1942.

Richardson, Edgar P., American Romantic Painting, Weyhe, New York, 1944.

——, Washington Allston, A Study of the Romantic Artist in America, University of Chicago Press, 1948.

——, The Way of Western Art, 1776–1914, Harvard University Press, 1939.

Sweet, Frederick A., The Hudson River School and the Early American Landscape Tradition, Whitney Museum of American Art, New York, 1945.

Trumbull, John, The Autobiography of Colonel John Trumbull, Patriot-Artist, 1756–1843, ed. by Theodore Sizer, Yale University Press, 1953 (orig. ed. 1841).

Whitney Museum of American Art, monographs by various authors on Bellows, Davies, Glackens, Luks, Prendergast, Twachtman, and others.

Canada   See books listed under
Latin America   these headings on p. 736.

20TH-CENTURY EUROPEAN

Apollinaire, Guillaume, The Cubist Painters, Wittenborn, Schultz, New York, 1949.

Barr, Alfred H., Jr., ed., Cubism and Abstract Art, Museum of Modern Art, New York, 1936.

——, Fantastic Art, Dada, Surrealism, new ed., Museum of Modern Art, New York, 1936.

——, Masters of Modern Art, Museum of Modern Art, New York, 1954.

——, Matisse: His Art and His Public, Museum of Modern Art, New York, 1951.

——, Picasso, Forty Years of His Art, Museum of Modern Art, New York, 1939.

Bell, Clive, Art, Chatto & Windus, London, 1949.

Blanshard, Frances M. B., Retreat from Likeness in the Theory of Painting, Columbia University Press, 1949.

Deknatel, Frederick B., Edvard Munch, Institute of Contemporary Art, Boston, 1950.

Duthuit, Georges, The Fauvist Painters, Wittenborn, Schultz, 1950.

Fry, Roger, Vision and Design, Meridian Books, New York, 1956.

Goldwater, Robert, Primitivism in Modern Painting, Harper, 1938.

Gray, Christopher, Cubist Aesthetic Theories, Johns Hopkins Press, Baltimore, 1953.

Grohmann, Will, Paul Klee, Abrams, New York, 1954.

Hope, Henry R., Georges Braque, Museum of Modern Art, New York; dist. by Simon & Schuster, 1949.

Jaffé, H. L. C., de Stijl, 1917–1931, London, n.d.

Kahnweiler, Daniel Henry, Juan Gris, His Life and Work, tr. by Douglas Cooper, Valentin, New York, 1947.

——, The Rise of Cubism, tr. by Henry Aronson, new ed., Wittenborn, Schultz, New York, 1949.

Kandinsky, Vassily, Concerning the Spiritual in Art, Wittenborn, Schultz, New York, 1947.

Kuh, Katharine, Léger, Art Institute of Chicago, 1953.

Martin, J. L., Nicholson, B., and Gabo, N., eds., Circle, Faber & Faber, London, 1937.

Moholy-Nagy, László, The New Vision, 4th rev. ed., Wittenborn, Schultz, New York, 1949.

Mondriaan, Pieter C., *Plastic Art and Pure Plastic Art*, G. Wittenborn, New York, 1945.

Motherwell, Robert, *The Dada Painters and Poets*, Wittenborn, Schultz, New York, 1951.

Pevsner, Nikolaus, *Pioneers of Modern Design*, 2nd ed., Museum of Modern Art, New York, 1949.

Read, Sir Herbert, *Art and Society*, Faber & Faber, London, 1950.

——, *Art Now*, Faber & Faber, London, 1948.

——, *The Philosophy of Modern Art*, Horizon Press, New York, 1952.

——, *Surrealism*, Faber & Faber, London, 1936.

Ritchie, Andrew C., ed., *The New Decade: 22 European Painters and Sculptors*, Museum of Modern Art, New York, 1955.

Rothschild, Edward F., *The Meaning of Unintelligibility in Modern Art*, University of Chicago Press, 1934.

Seuphor, Michel, *Piet Mondrian, Life and Work*, Abrams, New York, 1956.

Soby, James Thrall, *After Picasso*, Dodd, Mead, 1935.

——, *Contemporary Painters*, Museum of Modern Art, New York, 1945.

——, *Georges Rouault*, Museum of Modern Art, New York, 1945.

——, *Modern Art and the New Past*, University of Oklahoma, Norman, 1957.

——, *Salvador Dali*, Museum of Modern Art, New York, 1946.

——, and Barr, Alfred H., Jr., *Twentieth-Century Italian Art*, Museum of Modern Art, New York, 1949.

Sweeney, James Johnson, *Joan Miró*, Museum of Modern Art, New York, 1941.

——, *Plastic Redirections in Twentieth-Century Painting*, University of Chicago Press, 1934.

Tannenbaum, Libby, *James Ensor*, Museum of Modern Art, New York, 1951.

20TH-CENTURY AMERICAN

United States

American Artists Series, Whitney Museum of American Art, New York, 1931–32.

Baur, John I. H., *Charles Burchfield* (Whitney Museum of American Art), Macmillan, New York, 1956.

——, *Revolution and Tradition in Modern American Art*, Harvard University Press, 1951.

Boswell, Peyton, Jr., *Modern American Painting*, Dodd, Mead, 1939.

Brown, Milton, *American Painting from the Armory Show to the Depression*, Princeton University Press, 1955.

Charles Sheeler: Paintings, Drawings, Photographs, Museum of Modern Art, New York, 1939.

Cheney, Martha C., *Modern Art in America*, McGraw-Hill, 1939.

Garwood, Darrell, *Artist in Iowa: A Life of Grant Wood*, Norton, 1944.

Hall, William S., *Eyes on America*, Studio Publications, New York, 1939.

Helm, MacKinley, *John Marin*, Pellegrini & Cudahy, New York, 1948. (Biography is included in *John Marin*, tributes by William Carlos Williams and others, University of California Press, Berkeley, 1956.)

Janis, Sidney, *Abstract and Surrealist Art in America*, Reynal & Hitchcock, New York, 1944.

——, *They Taught Themselves*, Dial Press, New York, 1942.

John Marin, Museum of Modern Art, New York, 1936.

Kootz, Samuel M., *Modern American Painters*, Brewer & Warren, New York, 1930.

——, *New Frontiers in American Painting*, Hastings House, New York, 1943.

Max Weber: Retrospective Exhibition, Whitney Museum of American Art, New York, 1949.

McCausland, Elizabeth, *Marsden Hartley*, University of Minnesota Press, Minneapolis, 1952.

Mellquist, Jerome, *The Emergence of an American Art*, Scribner's, 1942.

Pagano, Grace, *Contemporary American Painting* (Encyclopaedia Britannica Collection), Duell, Sloan & Pearce, 1945.

Painters and Sculptors of Modern America, introduction by Monroe Wheeler, Crowell, 1942.

Pearson, Ralph M., *Experiencing American Pictures*, Harper, 1943.

Ritchie, Andrew C., *Charles Demuth*, Museum of Modern Art, New York, 1950.

Rodman, Selden, *Portrait of the Artist as an American: Ben Shahn*, Harper, 1951.

Sweeney, James Johnson, *Stuart Davis*, Museum of Modern Art, New York, 1945.

Watson, Forbes, *American Painting Today*, American Federation of Arts, Washington, D. C., 1939.

Wight, Frederick S., *Milestones of American Painting in Our Century* (Institute of Contemporary Art, Boston), Chanticleer Press, New York, 1949.

Zigrosser, Carl, *The Artists in America*, Knopf, 1942.

Canada

The Arts in French Canada (exhibition catalogue), Musée de la Province, Quebec, 1952.

The Arts of French Canada (exhibition catalogue), Institute of Arts, Detroit, 1946.

Biennial Exhibition of Canadian Painting (exhibition catalogue), National Gallery of Canada, Ottawa, 1955.

Buchanan, D. W., *Canadian Painters,* Phaidon Press, London, 1945.

——, *The Growth of Canadian Painting,* Collins, London, 1950.

Canadian Abstract Paintings (exhibition catalogue, circulated in the U. S. by the Smithsonian Institution, 1956–57), National Gallery of Canada, Ottawa.

Canadian Art (quarterly), Ottawa, 1943–present.

Canadian Painting (exhibition catalogue), National Gallery of Art, Washington, D.C., 1950.

Comfort, C. F., "Canadian Painting," *Royal Commission Studies,* King's Printer, Ottawa, 1951.

The Development of Painting in Canada (exhibition catalogue), National Gallery of Art, Washington, D. C., 1950.

Emily Carr, 1945; *Lawren Harris,* 1948; *Arthur Lismer,* 1950; *A. Y. Jackson,* 1953; *F. H. Varley,* 1954; *David Milne,* 1955; *Maurice Cullen,* 1956; and other catalogues of one-man exhibitions, Art Gallery of Toronto, Toronto, 1945–present.

Duval, Paul, *Canadian Drawings and Prints,* Burns & MacEachern, Toronto, 1952.

——, *Canadian Water Colours,* Burns & MacEachern, Toronto, 1954.

Forty Years of Canadian Painting (exhibition catalogue), Museum of Fine Arts, Boston, 1949.

The French in America (exhibition catalogue), Institute of Arts, Detroit, 1951.

Housser, F. B., *A Canadian Art Movement: The Story of the Group of Seven,* Macmillan, Toronto, 1926.

McInnes, G. C., *A Short History of Canadian Art,* Macmillan, Toronto, 1950.

MacTavish, N., *The Fine Arts in Canada,* Macmillan, Toronto, 1925.

Latin America

American Artists Group Monograph Series, American Artists Group, 1945 –.

Brenner, Anita, *Idols Behind Altars,* Payson & Clarke, New York, 1929.

Chilean Contemporary Art, Toledo Museum of Art, Toledo, Ohio, 1942.

A Comprehensive Exhibition of the Contemporary Art of Argentina, Virginia Museum of Fine Arts, Richmond, 1940.

Fernández, Justino, *El arte moderno en México,* J. Porrúa, Mexico City, 1937.

——, *José Clemente Orozco,* J. Porrúa, Mexico City, 1944.

Fine Arts in Argentina, National Committee New York World's Fair and Golden Gate Exposition, Buenos Aires, 1939.

Frescoes of Diego Rivera, Museum of Modern Art, New York, 1933.

Gamboa, Fernando, Schniewind, Carl O., and Edwards, Hugh L., *Posada, Printmaker to the Mexican People,* Art Institute of Chicago, 1944.

Gómez Sicre, José, *Cuban Painting of Today,* English version by Harold T. Riddle, María Luisa G. Mena, Havana, 1944.

Kirstein, Lincoln, *The Latin-American Collection of the Museum of Modern Art,* Museum of Modern Art, New York, 1943.

"Modern Cuban Painters," *Bulletin of the Museum of Modern Art,* New York, Vol. 11, No. 5, April, 1944.

Portinari of Brazil, Museum of Modern Art, New York, 1940.

Schmeckebier, Laurence E., *Modern Mexican Art,* University of Minnesota Press, Minneapolis, 1939.

Smith, Robert C., "Brazilian Art," in *Concerning Latin American Culture,* ed. by Charles G. Griffin, Columbia University Press, 1940.

Velásquez Chávez, Agustín, *Contemporary Mexican Artists,* Covici Friede, New York, 1937.

Zalamea, Jorge, *Nueve artistas colombianos,* Litographía Colombia, Bogotá, 1941.

CHAPTER 21

PHOTOGRAPHY

In photography, science and art merge to create new kinds of pictorial experience. This relatively new method of picture-making requires its own criteria of analysis and criticism. It is not enough that a photograph should, in its general composition and distribution of values or of color remind us of similar qualities in a painting; it must present a different kind of design, and a different realization of values and of color peculiar to the technical nature of the medium itself. The development of such new qualities constitutes the artistic history of photography.

The first camera was actually a room, "camera obscura" (literally, "dark room"), large enough to enter. Danielo Barbaro, an Italian living in 1568, tells us of such a room with a lens in one wall so that if a piece of white paper was held about a foot away "you will see the whole view [outside reproduced] as it really is, with its distances,

its colors and shadow and motion, the clouds, the water twinkling, the birds flying. By holding the paper steady you can trace the whole perspective with a pen, shade it and delicately color it from nature." [1] Thus from the very beginning a relationship between the "camera" and "art" existed, although the former was originally only a step in achieving the latter. The degree to which the *camera obscura* was used by artists of the seventeenth and eighteenth centuries and its influence on their vision, or even, as with Vermeer, on the finished painting, is still a matter of some debate. Our problem, though, is the history of photography rather than of the camera; and, since a photograph is a camera image recorded by chemical means, our study begins in the early nineteenth century. [2]

[1] In this chapter the sources for all quotations not otherwise identified will be found in Beaumont Newhall, *History of Photography*.

[2] Since the art of the cinema is essentially a theatrical art and since the drama is not studied in this volume, the development or history of the moving picture is not treated in this chapter.

The first attempt to capture the camera image by chemistry was made by Thomas Wedgwood (1771–1805), son of the famous English potter, who experimented with a solution of silver nitrate. Meanwhile in France an amateur inventor, Nicéphore Niepce (1765–1833), was, without knowing it, repeating the work of Wedgwood. In 1816 he wrote his brother, "This is but an imperfect trial. . . . The background of the picture is black, and the objects white, that is, lighter than the background." Today we know that Niepce had made the first negative. While he was perfecting this technique, he heard about experiments which Louis Jacques Mandé Daguerre (1787–1851), a showman of Paris, was making along the same lines. Daguerre and Niepce became partners in 1828, but before they worked out a process together, Niepce died. Daguerre went on alone, and by the winter of 1838–1839 he announced a new technique.

THE DAGUERREOTYPE

Daguerre named his new technique the daguerreotype, whose process he kept secret. He was hoping to form a company to sell stock, but the French government bought the process outright and published the information to the world.

Daguerreotypes were literally mirror pictures. A silvered copper plate buffed to a brilliant polish was put over the top of a box containing a few particles of iodine. The fumes from the iodine reacted with the silver of the plate to form silver iodide, a light-sensitive chemical. The plate was exposed in a camera for about twenty minutes. After this exposure the plate was put over mercury and heated to a temperature of 167° F., when an image gradually appeared as a whitish amalgam formed on the surface of the plate in proportion to the amount of light received.

The plate then was bathed in sodium thiosulfate of soda to remove the unaltered silver salts, so that further exposure to light would not cause them to turn dark and spoil the picture. All that remained was to wash the picture in water, dry it, and put it behind glass, as the surface was so fragile that the slightest friction would spoil it.

It was a unique picture and hard to look at, for it had to be held in such a way that the mirror surface did not reflect anything light in tone. The exposure was so long that at first people could not be photographed, for no one could remain still for half an hour.

But in spite of these disadvantages, the new technique was immensely popular. The detail which could be recorded seemed incredible (Fig. 21–2).

There was a view of Paris . . . the minutest details, the interstices of pavements and brickwork, the effects of humidity from falling rain – all were reproduced as in nature. On viewing the same scene through an eye glass, the inscription over a distant shop, altogether invisible on the model, was brought forward in its proper degree of perfection.[3]

This was a new kind of picture-making; it was not a substitute for the artist's brush, but a new art.

Joseph Petzval (1807–1891) then designed a lens which admitted sixteen times more light than the one used by Daguerre. When this lens was used with a hypersensitized plate, invented by J. F. Goddard (1795–1866), portraits could be regularly taken at exposures of less than a minute. The best daguerreotype portraits are straightforward and penetrating. This is partly due to the fact that they could not be retouched, except for delicate tinting. Such a daguerreotype as that of *Chief Justice Lemuel Shaw* (Fig. 21–3) is as revealing as any portrait painted

[3] *The United States Magazine and Democratic Review*, Langtree and O'Sullivan, Washington, D. C., Vol. 5, p. 517, 1839.

21–2 *Paris Boulevard.* Daguerreotype by L. J. M. Daguerre. 1839. Perpignan Museum, Perpignan, France. Presented to the Perpignan Museum by François Arago, to whom it was given by Daguerre. The dark sky and the scratches across the plate were caused by physical damage. (George Eastman House, Rochester, New York)

by a contemporary artist. Indeed, most of the greater painters of the nineteenth century were aware of the potentialities of the camera and were enthusiastic students and collectors of photographs. Ingres and Delacroix, Corot and Degas are only four among many who adapted in their works aspects of nature and its representation as revealed by photography. Of the thousands of daguerreotypes still existing, those by A. S. Southworth (1811–1894) and J. T. Hawes (1809–1901) of Boston are the finest and show the highest point reached by the technique. By the time of the Civil War the daguerreotype process was obsolete. It had been replaced by the less expensive negative-positive technique.

THE CALOTYPE

William Henry Fox Talbot (1800–1877), English scientist and scholar, first recognized the value of a negative; for that reason his invention is the cornerstone of photography as we know it today. His first successful results date from 1835 and were published in 1839.

His innovation was to make paper light-sensitive by treating it with common salt and silver nitrate: these chemicals reacted to form silver chloride in the fibers of the paper. He also found

21-3 *Lemuel Shaw*, Chief Justice of the Massachusetts Supreme Court. Daguerreotype by Josiah Johnson Hawes. 1851. Metropolitan Museum of Art, New York. (George Eastman House, Rochester, New York)

a way to keep the images from darkening. His first "preserving process" was simply to soak the paper in a strong solution of common salt. This rendered the unused, and consequently undarkened, silver chloride so much less sensitive to light that the image was relatively stable. Later his friend, Sir John Herschel, suggested that the undarkened silver salts could be dissolved and washed away with a solution of sodium thiosulfate. Such a solution has been used as a fixing bath for photographic processing ever since.

Talbot also found that he could reverse the order of light and dark in a negative by simply making another "photographic drawing" from it, by exposing to sunlight a fresh sheet of silver chloride paper beneath the negative. From one negative any number of positive prints could now be made. In 1840

21-4 *The Ladder*. Calotype by William Henry Fox Talbot. Plate XIV of his series of original prints published as *The Pencil of Nature,* 1844. Collection Miss M. T. Talbot, Lacock Abbey, England. (George Eastman House, Rochester, New York)

Talbot improved his process radically. Instead of leaving the paper in the camera until it darkened, he brought out the latent image by development. This brought exposures down to a matter of seconds instead of minutes. He named his new process "calotype" or "talbotype" (Fig. 21-4). Photography now lacked only a transparent support for negative material to correspond to present-day techniques.

In 1844 Talbot published *The Pencil of Nature,* the first book illustrated with photographs; in each copy twenty-four calotype prints were pasted as illustrations. The pictures were chosen to show various ways that photography could be used: to record architecture, botanical specimens, the pages of rare books, and the aspect of foreign places.

The calotype process was used by David Octavius Hill (1802–1870) and Robert Adamson (1821–1848) in Edinburgh to make some of the finest photographic portraits ever taken. Though their work was limited to the five years between 1843 and 1848, their results have seldom been excelled. Again and again, throughout the history of photography, we find that the work of the pioneers is unexcelled; improvements in technique have increased the scope of photography but not necessarily its quality. In the best of the hundreds of portraits which the partners took, the interpretation of character and the play of light and shade may be considered models of photographic excellence (Fig 21–5). They were forced to compose their pictures in broad masses, however, as the calotype process would not give the fine detail so easily recorded by the daguerreotype.

Portraiture, however, was the exception, since most calotypists took architectural scenes and travel pictures. Maxime Du Camp (1822–1894) made a trip to Egypt and the Middle East with Gustave Flaubert, the writer; he took along a calotype camera and made in 1849–1850 a series of pictures of the famous monuments of Egypt which appeared in book form. Most of the famous French cathedrals also were photographed for the government with Talbot's process: the pictures taken by Henry Le Secq (1818–1882) were greatly admired, and it was said that one could actually see more in these photographs than if one visited the cathedral, so well had Le Secq succeeded in capturing the wealth of fine detail which escapes the eye of the spectator.

WET PLATES

Photographers were not satisfied with calotype, however, because the paper base was not transparent. In 1851, an English sculptor, Frederick Scott Archer (1813–1857), discovered that collodion, a viscous solution of guncotton in alcohol and ether, when spread upon a glass plate, dried to form a thin, tough skin. Archer mixed potassium iodide with the collodion and poured it over a glass plate. While

21–5 *John Henning and Alexander Handyside Ritchie.* Calotype by David Octavius Hill and Robert Adamson, *ca.* 1845. Collection Heinrich Schwarz, Middletown, Connecticut. (George Eastman House, Rochester, New York)

the coated plate was still tacky, he plunged it into a solution of silver nitrate. The plate was put into the camera before it had dried, was exposed, and developed immediately. The new technique almost at once replaced both the daguerreotype and the calotype and became the universal way of making negatives up to 1880.

The new technique had drawbacks. The plates had to be prepared and processed on the spot. To work outdoors meant taking along a portable darkroom of some sort: a wagon, a tent, or a box with light tight sleeves through which the operator could thrust his arms. Yet with the wet plate remarkable photographs were secured of battlefields, the Alps, and even of the flow of traffic in crowded streets.

21–6 *Eugène Delacroix.* Photograph by Nadar. *ca.* 1855. Modern print from original negative in Bibliothèque Nationale, Paris. (George Eastman House, Rochester, New York)

The first popular use of the new wet plate was for portraiture. In Paris magnificent portraits were made of celebrities, particularly by Gaspard Félix Tournachon (1820–1910), who called himself Nadar (Fig. 21–6). A colorful figure in the Bohemian world of Paris, Nadar began to take photographs as models for his caricatures, but soon became more famous as a photographer. He was a pioneer in the use of electric light in photography, and also took the first photograph from a balloon.

In order to keep up with the demand for portraits, a new kind of camera was invented in 1854 by another Frenchman, Adolphe Eugène Disdéri (1819–1890?). It had four separate lenses, and by exposing first one half and then the other of a glass plate, he made eight small portraits on one negative. Prints from these negatives were cut apart

and mounted on small cards which, because of their size (4 x 2½ inches) were called *cartes de visite* or visiting cards. These little pictures were made by the thousands. They were cheap, so that friends could exchange pictures. The familiar plush-covered photograph albums which graced every Victorian parlor table were made to hold them.

It was also soon realized that photography was of unrivaled importance for the historical record. For the first time great events could be recorded on the spot and the views preserved. The photographs taken of the Crimean War by Roger Fenton (1819–1869), and of the American Civil War by Mathew B. Brady (1823–1896) and Alexander Gardner (1821–1882) are still unsurpassed as incisive accounts of military life, unsparing in their truth to detail, poignant as expressions of experience.

Of the Civil War photographs the most moving are the inhumanly objective records of ruins (Fig. 21–7) — architecture and men, the bleak and ravaged fields, shattered houses, stiff and gruesome corpses, the pathetically homely pictures of camp life. Neither words nor even the most detailed painting can evoke a moment of vanished time so powerfully or so completely.

The camera also witnessed the development of the Far West. Major John Powell's cumbersome equipment was "a special sorrow" for an exploration of the Grand Canyon in 1871. T. H. O'Sullivan recorded the exploration of the 40th parallel in 1867, and then studied the interior of the Comstock Lode mines, as well as the shifting sand dunes of Carson Sink. In 1870 O'Sullivan went to Panama and ventured with his camera into previously almost inaccessible regions.

Perhaps the most heroic efforts were made by William Henry Jackson (1843–1942). In 1875 he packed a 20 x 24 inch camera on a trip into the

21–7 *Ruins of the Railroad Depot, Charleston, S. C.* Photograph by George N. Barnard. 1865. (George Eastman House, Rochester, New York)

Rocky Mountains; the almost two-foot square glass plate had to be coated wherever he set up his camera. His first successful negative, of Lake Cristobal, Colorado, cost him three days' work. Perhaps the very despairs of the collodion photographer worked, in the long run, for him. Casual, promiscuous snap shooting was impossible. Every exposure was an effort, every piece of glass carried by pack mule, boat, or human was precious. If a negative was a failure, the silver image was washed off and the glass used again. Only successes survived to be brought back to the studio for printing.

One of the most popular forms of photography in the 1850's was the "stereograph," twin pictures which, viewed through a "stereoscope," give a startling illusion of three dimensions. Stereographs are taken with a camera fitted with two lenses, separated by 2½ inches, the average distance between our eyes. The stereoscope enables us to look at the picture taken with the right-hand lens with the right eye and the one taken with the left-hand lens with the left eye. Stereograph pictures of New York and Paris, taken in the later 1850's, show the streets and boulevards crowded with traffic and pedestrians.

The technical developments of the 1850's encouraged photographers to rival the achievements of painting. Multiple negatives were printed on a single paper, for instance, by O. G. Rejlander in 1857, to illustrate the *Two Paths of Life* (Fig. 21–8); and his example was followed by Henry Peach Robinson (1830–1901), who produced similar "composition pictures" annually for years. In 1869 he wrote *Pictorial Effect*

21–8 *The Two Paths of Life.* Combination print by O. G. Rejlander. 1857. Collection Royal Photographic Society, London. (George Eastman House, Rochester, New York)

in Photography, which was to run into edition after edition. It was the parent of countless books which attempt to

21–9 *Sir John Herschel.* Photograph by Julia Margaret Cameron. 1867. (George Eastman House, Rochester, New York)

tell how art may be produced by the camera.

Julia Margaret Cameron (1815–1879) made many photographs inspired by Pre-Raphaelite paintings of such subjects as "Venus Chiding Cupid and Removing his Wings" or "The Foolish Virgins." But this English lady also made some fine portraits. She photographed Tennyson, Sir John Herschel (Fig. 21–9), Carlyle, Darwin, Browning, and Longfellow. "When I have had such men before my camera," she wrote in her autobiographical *Annals of My Glass House,* "my whole soul has endeavored to do its duty towards them in recording faithfully the greatness of the inner as well as the features of the outer men. The photograph thus taken has been almost the embodiment of a prayer."

Photography was also called upon to record scientific facts. In 1878 Eadweard Muybridge (1830–1904) made, in California, a series of photographs of a galloping horse (Fig. 21–10). Along one side of the racetrack he ranged a battery of cameras. Opposite

21–10　*Galloping Horse*. Photographs by Eadweard Muybridge. 1878. (George East-man House, Rochester, New York)

them he built a reflector. Threads, attached to electromagnetic shutters on the cameras, were stretched across the track. The horse, as he rushed by, broke the threads in succession, thus tripping the shutters. The pictures were hardly more than silhouettes, but they created a sensation when they were published in scientific journals in America and abroad. Nobody had ever seen the legs of a rapidly galloping horse "frozen." The conventional attitude favored by painters, front legs thrust forward and rear legs backward, as on a rocking horse, was shown to be incorrect. Muybridge invited friends and the press to see a unique demonstration in 1880. With an ingenious device he projected his pictures on a screen, one after the other in quick succession. The horse moved again: moving pictures were born.

DRY PLATES AND FILMS

The chief drawback to the collodion process was that it chained the photographer to a darkroom. He had to make his sensitive material on the spot, and

develop it, fix it, and wash it immediately after exposure. Many dry-plate processes were tried, but none was successful until Richard Leach Maddox (1816–1902), a British physician, found in 1871 that gelatin could be substituted for collodion.

The discovery was revolutionary. Now it became possible to coat plates well in advance of exposure, and process them long afterwards. More importantly, the new gelatinobromide plates were so much more sensitive than the old wet plates that exposures could be made in a fraction of a second. For the first time the photographer was freed from his tripod; he could hold the camera in his hands. Action, which previously could be arrested only under the most favorable circumstances, could now be recorded with ease: the era of the snapshot was born.

George Eastman (1854–1932), a bank clerk in Rochester, N. Y., was enthusiastic about photography as a hobby, and he experimented with the new dry-plate technique. About 1880 he began to develop a system by which the sensitive material would be applied to

21–11 *Setting the Bow Net.* Photograph by Peter H. Emerson. 1886. (George Eastman House, Rochester, New York)

a flexible support, which in turn could be rolled up to save space. He devised a way of stripping the gelatin emulsion from the paper support after development and drying it between sheets of clear gelatin. He called this material "American Film" and put it on the market with a simple roll holder which could be fitted to any camera. In 1888 Eastman began to market a simple box camera to which he gave the name "Kodak." The Kodak, when loaded with his "American Film," could take one hundred pictures, each 2½ inches in diameter. The instructions were simple: Pull the String (to set the shutter), Press the Button (to make the exposure), Turn the Key (to wind on fresh film).

Eastman's invention made every man

a photographer. The significance of popular photography lies less in the fact that innumerable snapshots have been taken by millions of people than in the efforts of amateurs to search out the artistic potentialities of the medium. For many to whom the art of painting was too difficult a craft, the camera offered the possibility of expressing their interest in composition through careful study of the scene or object to be photographed and subtle manipulation of the printing process. Beginning in the 1890's societies for the exhibition and criticism of photography appeared in all countries, and the general standard of photography was immeasurably raised.

By the end of the nineteenth century a bitter discussion had arisen between

21–12 *Shop Window, Paris.* Photograph by Eugène Atget. *ca.* 1914. (George East-man House, Rochester, New York)

those who advocated a "pictorial" art (to be distinguished from earlier "imitative" ideals) and those who favored "pure" photography. In 1891 an American living in England, Peter H. Emerson (1856–1936), who had been a staunch advocate of "pictorial" photography as "second to painting only because it lacked color and the ability to reproduce exact tonal relationships" recanted his belief (Fig. 21–11). Due to the influence of an artist (presumably Whistler) he admitted that photography was not an art. But his followers belied him and in 1893 they formed a new society, the "Linked Ring," for the "establishment of a distinct pictorial movement."

It was while such photographers in Europe and America were exploring the possibilities of establishing photog-

raphy as a fine art by ingenious new printing techniques that other photographers were using the camera in a much simpler way.

Jean-Eugène-Auguste Atget (1846–1927) spent a lifetime photographing the face of Paris in all its aspects. His technique was utterly simple: a tripod camera for glass plates, contact prints on paper toned deep brown. In an Atget photograph every detail stands forth with a clarity which is remarkable. For Atget's vision found a human quality although no human being was present (Fig. 21–12).

When Atget's work was first shown in America, younger photographers found it an inspiration, for it revealed the power of the straightforward, direct use of the camera. The photographs came to their attention at a time

21–13 *Gare Saint-Lazare, Paris.* Photograph by Henri Cartier-Bresson. 1932. (Reproduced by courtesy of the photographer)

when the word "functional" was being applied to architecture and to the arts of design. Atget's attitude was not a discovery as much as a recognition of a tradition as old as photography itself.

It was Alfred Stieglitz, however, who proved the validity of the photograph, and of art in general, at a moment when the American public was peculiarly confused about this problem. Although he championed many "pictorial" photographs (because he had studied with the "Linked Ring" in Europe), he created his own style of photography. By means of publications and through his gallery at 291 Fifth Avenue, New York, Stieglitz presented the best work of contemporary photographers, and he campaigned tirelessly for serious consideration of their artistic merits. His own photographs are still among the most sensitive and revealing ever taken.

Borrowing from a friend a 4 x 5 inch box camera, Stieglitz waited three hours on Fifth Avenue, New York, in a blinding snowstorm in 1893 to photograph a horse-drawn coach; the next day he photographed the steaming horses of the Harlem streetcar as they started uptown. In this early work,

Stieglitz relied upon purely photographic controls. He did not retouch or alter in any way the camera image.

Stieglitz always considered *The Steerage* his masterpiece (Fig. 21–1). On a trip to Europe in 1907 he was promenading on deck when he saw a striking scene of immigrants on the deck below. He rushed to his cabin for his Graflex camera and then recorded

a round straw hat, the funnel leaning left, the stairway leaning right, the white suspenders crossing on the back of a man in the steerage below, round shapes of iron machinery, a mast cutting into the sky — I saw a picture of shapes, and underlying that the feeling I had about life.

In these words, Stieglitz has told us how the photographer works. He recognizes, almost instantaneously, a particular moment of time.

The technical developments — miniature cameras, increasingly sensitive films and papers, and improvements in artificial lighting — allow an almost infinite number of opportunities to seize the *moment décisif*, as Henri Cartier-Bresson (1908–) has so vigorously defined the opportunity of photography. The photographer has been able to seize the split second when the subject stands revealed in its most significant aspect and most evocative form (Fig. 21–13). He has brought the camera into action almost instinctively as "an extension of the eye," so that every picture has a framework, an organization of shapes, to carry the image.[4]

[4] The editors regret that the demands of limited space have forced them to eliminate discussion of such talented photographers as Edward Weston (1886–1957); Paul Strand (1890–); Ansel Adams (1902–); Walker Evans (1903–); Dorothea Lange (1895–); Margaret Bourke-White (1904–); Barbara Morgan (1900–); and others, who were included in Mr. Newhall's original manuscript (see Preface). Reference to their works may be found in the bibliography.

Conclusion

During its relatively brief development, photography's scope has been enormously expanded. Pictures which only a few decades ago seemed beyond the camera's capacity are now within the reach of all. But if the scope has expanded, the traditions remain the same. Yesterday's photographer would be amazed that pictures can be taken in the hundred-thousandth part of a second, but put a camera in his hands and he would know exactly how to use it. Behind our present techniques, and behind our ways of seeing the world, lie the experiments of thousands upon thousands of photographers who believed that with the camera they could best say what was in their minds and, in a few instances, in their hearts.

Bibliography

Adams, Ansel, *Artificial-Light Photography*, Morgan & Morgan, New York, 1956.

——, *Camera and Lens*, Morgan & Lester, New York, 1948.

——, *Natural-Light Photography*, Morgan & Lester, New York, 1952.

——, *The Negative: Exposure and Development*, Morgan & Lester, New York, 1948.

——, *The Print: Contact Printing and Enlarging*, Morgan & Lester, New York, 1950.

Atget, *Photographe de Paris*, preface by Pierre MacOrlan, Weyhe, New York, *ca.* 1930.

Doty, Robert, "The Interpretive Photography of Lewis W. Hine," *Image*, 6:112–19, May, 1957.

Evans, Walker, *American Photographs*, with an essay by Lincoln Kirstein, Museum of Modern Art, New York, 1938.

The Focal Encyclopedia of Photography, Focal Press, London, 1956.

Fouque, Victor, *The Truth Concerning the Invention of Photography: Nicéphore Niépce, His Life, Letters and Works*, tr. by Edward Epstean, Tennant & Ward, New York, 1935.

Frank, Waldo, and others, eds., *America and Alfred Stieglitz: A Collective Portrait*, Doubleday, Doran, 1934.

Freund, Gisèle, *La Photographie en France au dix-neuvième siècle,* La Maison des Amis des Livres, A. Monnier, Paris, 1936.

Gernsheim, Helmut, *Julia Margaret Cameron: Her Life and Photographic Work,* Fountain Press, London, 1948.

——, and Gernsheim, Alison, *L. J. M. Daguerre (1787–1851), The World's First Photographer,* World Publishing, Cleveland, 1956.

——, *Roger Fenton, Photographer of the Crimean War: His Photographs and His Letters from the Crimea, with an Essay on His Life and Work,* Secker & Warburg, London, 1954.

——, *The History of Photography from the Earliest Use of the Camera Obscura in the Eleventh Century up to 1914,* Oxford University Press, London, 1955.

Horan, James D., *Mathew Brady, Historian with a Camera,* Crown Publishers, New York, 1955.

Jackson, Clarence S., *Picture Maker of the Old West: William H. Jackson,* Scribner's, 1947.

Kirstein, Lincoln, and Newhall, Beaumont, *The Photographs of Henri Cartier-Bresson,* Museum of Modern Art, New York, 1947.

Lécuyer, Raymond, *Histoire de la photographie,* Baschet et Cie, Paris, 1945.

Newhall, Beaumont, *The History of Photography from 1839 to the Present Day,* Museum of Modern Art, New York, 1949.

Newhall, Nancy, *Paul Strand Photographs, 1915–1945,* Museum of Modern Art, New York, 1945.

——, *The Photographs of Edward Weston,* Museum of Modern Art, New York, 1946.

Potonniée, Georges, *The History of the Discovery of Photography,* tr. by Edward Epstean, Tennant & Ward, New York, 1936.

Robinson, Henry Peach, *Pictorial Effect in Photography,* E. L. Wilson, Philadelphia, 1881.

Sandburg, Carl, *Steichen the Photographer,* Harcourt, Brace, 1929.

Schwarz, Heinrich, *David Octavius Hill,* tr. by Helene E. Fraenkel, Harrap, London, 1932.

Taft, Robert, *Photography and the American Scene,* Macmillan, New York, 1942.

SCULPTURE

CHAPTER 22

During the nineteenth century painting was the dominant form of expression. Sculpture was relatively unimportant for at least two reasons: the invention of photography, with the resulting concern among public and artists for images faithful to visual experience, and the difficulty of achieving a realistic image of contemporary life in sculptural materials. The majority of those with a talent for sculpture avoided such a challenge and took refuge in imitations of Antique and Renaissance works of art, executed in marble or bronze according to the idealistic canons taught in the official art schools. It was not sculptors but rather painters, such as Daumier, Degas, and Renoir, who produced some of the most convincing sculpture of the nineteenth century. Only occasionally did a professional sculptor create a work which was equal or superior to contemporary

ILLUSTRATION ABOVE. **22-1** WILHELM LEHMBRUCK. *Standing Youth*. 1913. 7 ft. 8 in. high. Cast stone. Museum of Modern Art, New York. (Museum of Modern Art)

painting. One such man was the French sculptor, François Rude (1784–1855). In his relief for the Arc de Triomphe in Paris, the *Departure of the Volunteers* (Fig. 22-2), he infused the Neoclassical forms of contemporary painting with a romantic energy which recalls Delacroix. The figure of his screaming Victory, soaring on a diagonal, is so convincing an image of patriotism that it has become indelibly associated with the French concept of political liberty. In a less heroic vein the sculptor Antoine Louis Barye (1796–1875) joined the scientific studies of the age with a personal and romantic interest in animals. His animal groups are masterpieces in which great technical knowledge of anatomy is subordinated to a generous handling of form. Each minor detail contributes to the larger synthesis. Barye's concern with surface modulation and realistic detail were first worked out in clay and then cast in bronze, a method typical of the modeling technique used by the best nineteenth-century sculptors. Even their stone sculptures were mechanically copied from a clay original.

22–3 AUGUSTUS SAINT-GAUDENS. *Adams Memorial*. 1891. Bronze. Rock Creek Cemetery, Washington, D. C. (Ewing Galloway)

22–2 FRANÇOIS RUDE. *Departure of the Volunteers*. 1836. 41 ft. 8 in. × 26 ft. Marble. Arc de Triomphe, Paris. (Archives Photographiques)

The technique of direct carving in stone nearly disappeared.

A sensitive treatment of bronze surfaces distinguishes the work of the leading American sculptor of the period, Augustus Saint-Gaudens (1848–1907). In a long series of portraits and monuments he held in delicate balance the public's demand for naturalistic likenesses and his own feeling for the movement of large three-dimensional masses. Saint-Gaudens' achievement is most remarkable in such a figure as his standing *Lincoln* (Grant Park, Chicago), where the wrinkles and creases of the clothing are not allowed to distract one's attention from the grave, brooding figure. In the *Adams Memorial* (Fig. 22–3) Saint-Gaudens' ability to generalize detail into a sequence of broad, simplified planes is in perfect accord with the philosophical overtones of the nameless, grieving figure.

Toward 1880 the French artist Auguste Rodin (1840–1917) emerged as the greatest sculptor of the century, an artist whose international reputation in his own lifetime rivaled that of Michelangelo and Bernini. Rodin shared his public's taste for literary, even sentimental, subjects, and statuary such as *The Kiss* and the *Hand of God* became all too familiar through numerous replicas mechanically executed in marble. But Rodin was also a contemporary of the Impressionists, and his aesthetic was based upon a similar acceptance of the world of appearances revealed through light. If he was an Impressionist in his study of light and its effects on marble and bronze, he was also a powerful Expressionist in his discovery of new forms in which to cast his themes. Even today when we are not

22–4 AUGUSTE RO-
DIN. *The Burghers
of Calais.* 1884–
1886. 82 in. × 94
in. × 75 in. Bronze.
Calais, France. (Ar-
chives Photographi-
ques)

so interested in the subjects of his work
we can admire his masterly handling
of three-dimensional forms in space.
His great personal gifts, as well as the
limitations imposed upon his talents by
the age in which he lived, can be seen
in the group of life-sized figures, the
Burghers of Calais (Fig. 22–4), commemorating a tragic episode in the
Hundred Years' War. Each of the individual figures is a convincing study of
despair, achieved through the movement of a few simplified planes whose
rugged surfaces catch and disperse the
light, much as does the surface of a
painting by Renoir or Monet. But moving though the work is, it is difficult to
believe that Rodin ever visualized the
group as a unit; indeed, the separate
figures were conceived as individual
pieces and then placed in various relations to one another until the scheme
was considered satisfactory.

Rodin was also a great teacher. His
reputation brought to his studio in Paris, as pupils or admirers, many of the
younger generation who were to develop new kinds of sculpture, either influenced by Rodin or rejecting his
ideas. The Expressionist element
proved most sympathetic to the younger German sculptors. Wilhelm Lehmbruck (1881–1919), inspired by elements of distortion in Rodin's later
work, developed strangely attenuated
figures (Fig. 0–4). His *Standing Youth*
(Fig. 22–1) is his most impressive work,
reminding us, in the elegant elongations
of the limbs, of the similar distortions
in Matisse's *Le Luxe* (Fig. 20–41),
painted only a few years before. A
Gothic strain in Lehmbruck's sculpture, not unlike that in the work of the
German Expressionist painters, is also
found in an even more marked degree
in the work of Ernst Barlach (1870–
1938) and Gerhard Marcks (1889–).
Barlach's floating figure (Fig. 22–5),
designed as a memorial for the cathedral in Güstrow, Prussia, is one of the

22–5 ERNST BARLACH. *War Memorial for the Güstrow Cathedral.* 1927. Bronze. Replica now in the Antoniterkirche, Cologne. (Bildarchiv, Rheinisches Museum, Cologne)

22–6 SIR JACOB EPSTEIN. *Madonna and Child.* 1927. 64½ in. high. Bronze. Museum of Modern Art (on extended loan from Miss Sally Ryan), New York. (Museum of Modern Art)

most poignant monuments of World War I. The transcendental strain in German Expressionist art, which we have already observed in painting, is found in the sculptor's intention of representing a dying soul at the moment when it is about to awaken to everlasting life. Under the Nazis the figure was removed from Güstrow and destroyed, but a replica has recently been placed in the Antoniterkirche in Cologne.

The Expressionist tradition has been carried on in England by the American-born sculptor, Sir Jacob Epstein (1880–   ), who has lived in London since the age of twenty-six. His portrait busts reveal a nervous energy, an

intensity of life, because of his highly individual, excitable manner of handling clay and bronze. These portraits, although solidly constructed, receive special surface emphasis, partly in an attempt to indicate all the minute surface planes of the head, partly for the interpretation of personality, and partly for the aesthetic pleasure in the handling of clay, just as the painter depends for certain effects upon his method of handling pigment. In his *Madonna and Child* (Fig. 22–6), Epstein's technique is apparent in his poignant treatment of the theme of the Virgin and Child, a contemporary yet ageless rendering of the two figures. Ep-

22–7 CARL MILLES. *The Meeting of the Waters Fountain.* 1940. Bronze. Aloe Plaza,
St. Louis. (Photo Jean Jackson, in M. R. Rogers, *Milles,* Yale University Press, 1940)

stein has also worked in stone, often on a monumental scale with startlingly simplified planes, and he has created important architectural sculpture for modern buildings in London.

Toward the close of the nineteenth century interest in primitive and archaic art introduced new currents into the predominantly naturalistic sculpture of the period, as similar influences did in painting. Many sculptors sought to dispel the lingering remnants of romanticism and eclecticism by greatly simplifying their forms in the manner of early Greek sculpture. Breadth and sensitivity based on profound learning characterize the work of Carl Milles

(1875–1955), the Swedish sculptor who lived for many years in the United States. In his figures are many reminiscences of early Greek and Medieval art, but he always found an original and very personal solution for each problem. His reputation may well rest on his many fountains, composed of numerous figures, which he created in America and in Sweden. The *Meeting of the Waters* (Fig. 22–7), in the center of a large square in St. Louis, is a particularly happy combination of bronze forms which seem to gain the dimension of movement when the waters play about them. In addition to the inherent qualities of his sculptures,

22-8 ARISTIDE MAILLOL. *Mediterranean. ca.* 1901. Oskar Reinhart Collection, Winterthur, Switzerland. (Max P. Linck, courtesy Dr. Oskar Reinhart)

Milles' insistence on the public use of sculptural groups has been an important contribution to the art of civic planning. A somewhat similar interest in simplified classical forms, often incorporated in figures of heroic stature and emotional force, is found in the work of the French sculptor Emile Antoine Bourdelle (1861–1929) and the Yugoslav Ivan Mestrovic (1883–   ).

The French sculptor Aristide Maillol (1861–1944) began his career as a painter, executing broadly decorative designs in the manner of Gauguin, and was also known as a graphic artist through his book illustrations. About 1900 he turned to sculpture and until the end of his life scarcely deviated from his chosen subject, the female figure, which he interpreted in massive planes and volumes devoid of historical stylization. One of his first and certainly his most important work was the seated figure, *Mediterranean* (Fig. 22–8). It is conceived as an organization of almost abstract volumes provided by the human figure. It has the weight and solidity inherent in the marble, and the largely unbroken surfaces of the simply modeled masses take the light evenly and quietly. But it is not just an abstract treatment of the subject, for the title indicates Maillol's intention of creating a symbolic form to express his conception of the inherited cultures of the Mediterranean countries. In this use of the figure for purposes of symbolic communication Maillol proves his relationship to the Symbolist painters and poets (such

as Gauguin, Odilon Redon, and Mal-
larmé) of the 1890's rather than to the
younger sculptors of the twentieth century who were soon to cast off such
literary overtones.

Gaston Lachaise (1882–1935), of
French descent but active most of his
life in the United States, treated the female figure with a similar breadth and
abundant vital energy. His life-size
Standing Woman (Fig. 22–9) is as
broadly modeled as Maillol's figures,
but with a more sensuous treatment of
the anatomy. The strongly felt movement swells from the lightly posed feet
to the large rounding hips; thence, after a sharp accent in the angle of the
waist, it again swells into the broad
shoulders and bent arms. This abstract
rhythm, suggestive of some profound
power rising to a climax, is the content
of the statue, and persuades us that it
ranks among the most powerful nude
figures in modern American sculpture.
Bronze is peculiarly suitable for expressing this upward movement. On the
other hand weight and solidity, the
feeling of the play of gravity, are seen
in the stone carving of William Zorach
(1887–   ), an American who com-
poses complex arrangements of spherical and cylindrical volumes into clearly
and firmly integrated structures filled
with movement and enlivened by contrasts of texture.

Interest in Archaic Greek art had
turned sculptors' attention toward formal problems involving the geometry
of the human figure; on the other
hand, the discovery of the arts of primitive people, especially of African Negro sculpture, suggested many new
ways of treating human and other natural forms in a more abstract manner.
Some of Epstein's early work resembles in this respect the paintings of Picasso's so-called "Negro Period" in the
imitation of fetishlike forms, and especially of the concave surfaces found in
African sculpture. Something of this

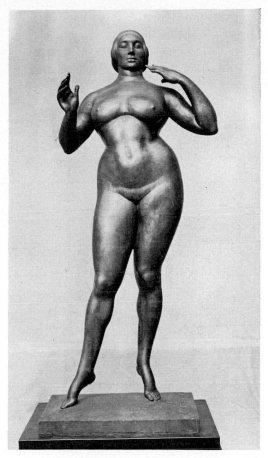

22–9 GASTON LACHAISE. *Standing Woman.*
1912–1927. 70 in. high. Bronze. Albright Art
Gallery, Buffalo. (Albright Art Gallery)

research into the structure of concave
and transparent forms was taken over,
as we have seen, into Cubist painting,
and Cubism in turn suggested various
sculptural possibilities. Picasso himself
modeled a head in 1909 which is a significant demonstration in three dimensions of the properties of Cubist painting at that time. But since Cubism,
properly speaking, was concerned with
the creation of effects of three-dimensional space on a flat surface, its aesthetic was not easily adapted to sculptural problems. The earlier works of
Jacques Lipchitz (1891–   ) — born in
Poland but long resident in France and

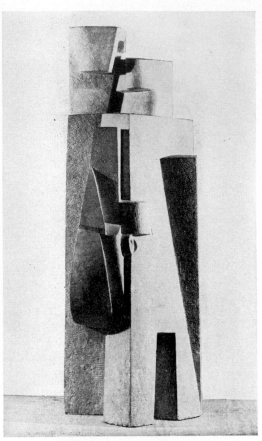

22–11   UMBERTO BOCCIONI. *Unique Forms of Continuity in Space.* 1919. 43½ in. high. Bronze. Museum of Modern Art, New York. (Museum of Modern Art)

22–10   JAQUES LIPCHITZ. *Man with Mandolin.* 1917. 29¾ in. high. Stone. Société Anonyme Collection, Yale University Art Gallery. (Yale Art Gallery)

the United States — such as his *Man with Mandolin* (Fig. 22–10), are among the most successful solutions to the problem of developing in three dimensions the spatial feeling of Cubist painting.

Just as Cubist painting contained implicit abstract tendencies, so sculpture executed within the Cubist orbit tended to cast off the last vestiges of representation. By 1913 the Italian Futurist painter and sculptor, Umberto Boccioni (1882–1916), had pushed his forms so far toward abstraction that in his *Unique Forms of Continuity in Space* (Fig. 22–11) the title calls our

attention to the formal and spatial effects rather than to the fact that the source for these is the striding human figure. Boccioni's search for plastic means with which to express dynamic movement here reached a monumental expression. In its power and sense of vital activity this sculpture surpasses similar experiments in painting by Boccioni and his Futurist companions to create images symbolic of the dynamic quality of modern life. The broad treatment of these restless planes has suggested to many a resemblance to similar shapes and energetic movement in the *Victory of Samothrace* (Fig. 5–47).

The Rumanian sculptor Constantin Brancusi (1876–1957) carried abstraction as far as possible without entirely losing the representational element. At the same time he extracted from the

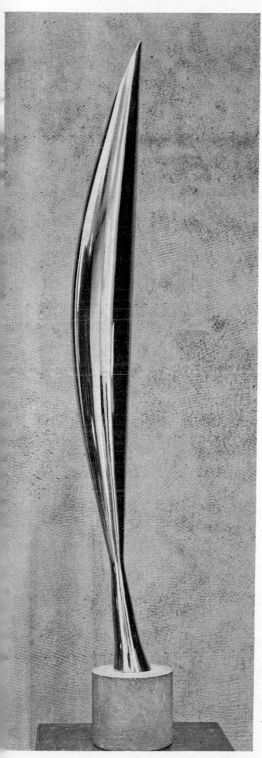

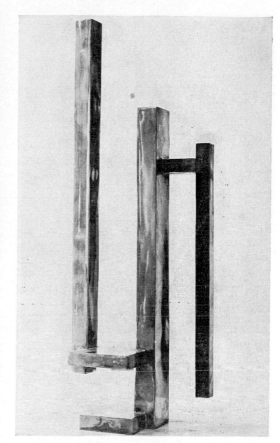

22–13 GEORGES VANTONGERLOO. *Construction* $y = 2x^3 - 13.5x^2 - 21x$. 1935. Nickel silver. Kunstmuseum, Basel. Emanuel Hoffmann Fund. (Kunstmuseum)

material, whether marble, metal, or wood, its maximum effect. Brancusi visualized an extended ovoid shape as the most basic natural form. He then simplified the most complex natural forms, and even natural movements, so that they were reduced to variations on this fundamental theme. In his famous *Bird in Space* (Fig. 22–12) everything accidental has been eliminated or compressed into the most direct and economical expression, and yet the form as a whole suggests the essence of a

◀ 22–12 CONSTANTIN BRANCUSI. *Bird in Space*. 1919. 54 in. high. Bronze. Museum of Modern Art, New York. (Museum of Modern Art)

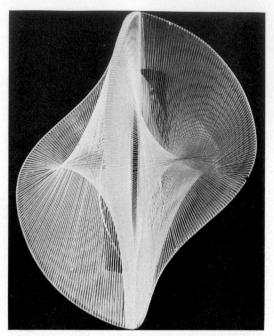

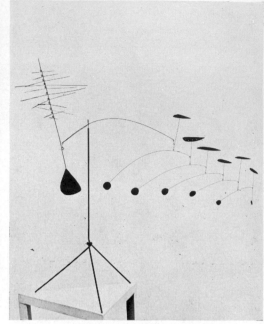

22–14 NAHUM GABO. *Linear Construction.*
1950. Collection Mrs. George Heard Hamilton, New Haven, Connecticut. (Yale Art Gallery)

22–15 ALEXANDER CALDER. *Horizontal Spines.* 1942. 54 in. high. Addison Gallery of American Art, Phillips Academy, Andover, Massachusetts. (Andover Art Studio)

bird's sudden upward movement through space. The means which Brancusi used to stress the concept of flight are not unrelated to those which the modern engineer uses in designing "streamlined" industrial forms. There is the same study of the nature of the material, the same meticulous attention to proportions, contour, and surface finish.

More completely nonrepresentational sculptural forms were created by the artists of the *de Stijl* and Constructivist movements. The constructions of Georges Vantongerloo (1886–) resemble the paintings of Mondrian. There is the same careful manipulation of rectangular elements, in this case in three dimensions and often related to mathematical equations, as in his *Construction* $y = 2x^3 - 13.5x^2 - 21x$ (Fig. 22–13). The Russian sculptors Antoine Pevsner (1886–) and Naum Gabo

(1890–) reached similar conclusions by 1920. In their *Realist Manifesto*, published that year, they declared that

Mass and space are two concrete and measurable things. We consider and use space as a new and absolutely sculptural element, a material substance which really enters into construction.[1]

In their concern with the properties of space they created objects in which voids acted as forcefully as the elements of solid mass. Gabo turned to the new synthetic plastic materials, at first celluloid and later nylon and lucite, for constructions in which space seems even to flow through as well as around the transparent materials. In his *Linear Construction* (Fig. 22–14) space is caught and held, as it were, in

[1] Quoted by Andrew C. Ritchie, *Sculpture of the Twentieth Century*, New York, 1952, p. 44.

22–16 THEODORE ROSZAK. *Whaler of Nantucket.* 1952. 35 in. × 48 in. Steel. Art Institute of Chicago. (Courtesy of the Art Institute of Chicago, Edward E. Ayer Fund)

suspension by the most delicate combination of hovering planes. Like Mondrian, Gabo believes that through art the artist may express his conception of ultimate reality, that indeed such "artfully constructed images are the very essence of the reality of the world which we are searching for." [2]

This transparence of mass, with the consequent creation of visible interior volumes, seems but a step toward the attempt to create actual movement in space. One of Gabo's earliest works, his *Kinetic Construction* of 1920, consisted of a vertical metal rod agitated by an electric motor. Its vibrations created an apparent volume more extensive than the actual dimensions of the slen-

[2] K. D. Dreier, J. J. Sweeney, and N. Gabo, *Three Lectures on Modern Art,* Philosophical Library, New York, 1949, p. 70.

der rod. The American sculptor, Alexander Calder (1898–   ), was the first to set his works in continuous and unmechanical motion. His *mobiles,* as they are appropriately called, are made of rods, wires, and metal disks so balanced that in the slightest current of air the parts move within a carefully planned pattern, creating constantly shifting definitions of space. Calder's work, although usually entirely nonrepresentational, is so gay and witty, and it contains such unexpected felicities of line and shape, that it is anything but remote from human concerns. In this respect it often reminds us of the paintings of Joan Miró. In *Horizontal Spines* (Fig. 22–15), the delicate grace and precision of pure line in the fine steel wires contrasts and combines in constantly changing relation-

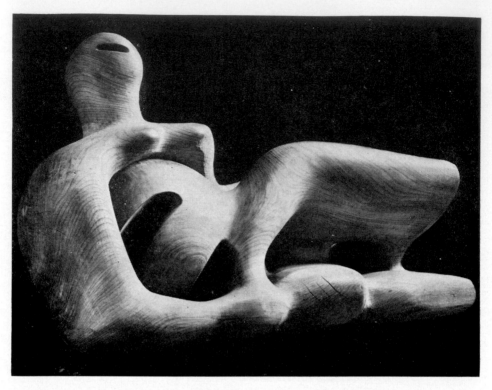

22–17 HENRY MOORE. *Reclining Figure.* 1945–1946. L. 6 ft. Elm wood. Galleries, Cranbrook Academy of Art, Bloomfield Hills, Michigan. (Buchholz Gallery)

ships with the bold dash and vigor of the flat shapes.

In recent years many abstract sculptors have placed considerable emphasis on the subject matter of their work through forms which seem related to human experience. This is not a return to realistic representation as such, but rather a tendency to present forms and spatial constructions which derive meaning and value from the spectator's memory of natural objects and situations, or of human or literary associations. Calder, for instance, has created mobiles in which variegated colors and a slightly naturalistic treatment of the metal shapes suggest natural forms, such as snowstorms or trees in an autumn wind. In direct succession to the Constructivists the American sculptor Richard Lippold (1915–) uses an austere vocabulary of rods and wires, but through colorful materials, such as copper and brass, he introduces a new sense of poetic symbolism.

Many sculptors have also turned to the new metallic alloys which fuse at a low temperature so that they may be easily wrought directly by the sculptor without recourse to the tedious and costly process of casting a plaster or wax model in bronze. Notable work in this medium has been done by Herbert Ferber (1906–), an American sculptor whose abstract shapes convey a profound emotional content. In his *". . . and the bush was not consumed"* he created a sculpture of profound religious symbolism for a synagogue in New Jersey. Many Hebrew congregations in this country are now acquiring abstract sculptures by the younger generation of American artists with promise of a revival in completely modern terms of the great traditions of religious art.

A similar interest in incorporating meaningful content in abstract forms is seen in the work of Theodore Roszak (1907–). Until 1945 he worked in the Constructivist idiom, but since then his style has undergone a marked change. Out of welded and brazed metals, often steel, he constructs monstrous forms, menacing and yet infected with vitality. His *Whaler of Nantucket* (Fig. 22–16) is a remarkable example of his ability to infuse nonrepresentational shapes with the poetic meaning of universal symbolism which Roszak himself felt in reading Melville's *Moby Dick*. Such sculpture fulfills the artist's intention as he has stated it:

The forms that I find necessary to assert, are meant to be blunt reminders of primordial strife and struggle, reminiscent of those brute forces that not only produced life, but in turn threatened to destroy it. I feel that, if necessary, one must be ready to summon one's total being with an all-consuming rage against those forces that are blind to the primacy of life-giving values. . . . Perhaps, by this sheer dedication, one may yet merge force with grace.[3]

Such a "dedication to life-giving values" marks the work of sculptors who are interested in more directly representational forms. The English sculptor Henry Moore (1898–) has created a long series of variations upon the reclining human figure, some more abstract than others but all with an instinctive warm feeling for the dignity of the human form. Like many Englishmen Moore has a profound love for and knowledge of natural forms and materials. In such a work as the *Reclining Figure* (Fig. 22–17) the mas-

[3] Quoted by Ritchie, *Sculpture of the Twentieth Century*, p. 46.

22–18   JACQUES LIPCHITZ. *Sacrifice II*. 1948–1952. 48¼ in. high. Bronze. Whitney Museum of American Art, New York. (Collection of Whitney Museum of Art)

sive interlocking shapes reflect the discipline of abstract art, but their total visual reality relates the human being to the enduring world of natural experience, even as the smooth, polished wooden surfaces suggest the action of wind and water upon natural materials. More specific symbolism has appeared in the later work of Jacques Lipchitz, whose Cubist sculpture has been discussed above. His *Sacrifice II* (Fig. 22–18) reaches back through historic time to an ancient Hebrew religious rite, and in the combination of ritual solemnity and intense devotion the mysterious masses project an almost overpowering sense of destiny. Quite another treatment of the human figure is found in the work of Alberto Giacometti (1901–). This Swiss sculptor, long a resident of Paris, participated in the Abstract and Surrealist movements and contributed significant works in each mode. But in 1947 he turned to representational sculpture and produced unexpectedly poignant figures which seem immediate projections of modern experience of bewilderment and loss. His *Man Pointing* (p. 649), with the extreme elongations of the limbs and the sensitively treated surface, is typical of this new manner. At times the forms are so attenuated that they almost disappear, and yet the communication of the human condition is always present.

It is interesting to observe that in this way the search of contemporary sculptors for a reality in the absolute relationships of forces in space returns, again and again, to the image of man as a point of departure.

Bibliography

Barr, Alfred H., Jr., ed., *Cubism and Abstract Art,* Museum of Modern Art, New York, 1936.
——, *Masters of Modern Art,* Museum of Modern Art, New York, 1954.
Gabo, Naum, *Constructions, Sculpture, Paintings, Drawings, Engravings,* Harvard University Press, 1957.
Giedion-Welcker, Carola, *Modern Plastic Art,* Zurich, 1937; new edition as *Contemporary Sculpture,* Wittenborn, Schultz, New York, 1954.
Hope, Henry R., *Jacques Lipchitz,* Museum of Modern Art, New York, 1954.
Kahnweiler, Daniel-Henry, *Les Sculptures de Picasso,* Editions du Chêne, Paris, 1948.
Olson, Ruth, and Chanin, Abraham, *Naum Gabo [and] Antoine Pevsner,* Museum of Modern Art, New York, 1948.
Read, Herbert, *Art Now,* Faber & Faber, London, 1948.
——, *Henry Moore, Sculpture and Drawings,* C. Valentin, New York, 1944.
Rewald, John, *Maillol,* tr. by P. Montagu-Pollock, Art Book Publications, New York, 1939.
Rich, Jack C., *The Materials and Methods of Sculpture,* Oxford University Press, New York, 1947.
Ritchie, Andrew C., *Abstract Painting and Sculpture in America,* Museum of Modern Art, New York, 1951.
——, *Sculpture of the Twentieth Century,* Museum of Modern Art, New York, 1952.
Seymour, Charles, Jr., *Tradition and Experiment in Modern Sculpture,* American University Press, Washington, D.C., 1949.
Sweeney, James J., *Alexander Calder,* Museum of Modern Art, New York, 1951.
Valentiner, Wilhelm R., *Origins of Modern Sculpture,* Wittenborn, Schultz, New York, 1948.

CHAPTER 23

ARCHITECTURE

During the two centuries from the mid-eighteenth to today a new Western architecture has gradually emerged, created in an environment increasingly dominated by the revolutions which established industrialism and democracy as major economic, social, and spiritual factors.

Two hundred years ago the momentum which had sustained the principles of the Renaissance through three centuries expired. The Age of Authority was succeeded by the Age of Reason, and, as the laws of the Church and the king were questioned, so the academic laws of architecture began to be challenged. This challenge, however, did not give rise then or later to a single body of architectural law. Numerous disparate theories were, instead, proposed successively and concurrently. From the mid-eighteenth century forward a self-conscious desire both to be original and to find new roots led at

ILLUSTRATION ABOVE. 23–1 FRANK LLOYD WRIGHT. *Johnson Wax Company.* Racine, Wisconsin. Begun 1936. (S. C. Johnson & Son, Inc.)

once to variety and to revivalism. Eventually certain architects tried to develop original styles from the new materials that were coming into use, such as iron, steel, and concrete. But at the same time ancient styles continued to be revived seriatim or simultaneously, and some more than once. Thus nineteenth-century architecture appears chaotic, and, at first glance, attempts to describe the growth of modern architecture by strictly chronological analysis lead to confusion. Another approach is obviously necessary, and the following discussion recognizes the complexity of the history of the last two hundred years.

Certain trends may be identified in the development of modern architecture. The first may be called that of Picturesque Eclecticism; the second, Romantic Naturalism; and the third, Romantic Classicism. These trends occurred simultaneously, and it must not be forgotten that they did not exist independently and that the totality of architecture of the last two hundred years represents the sum of their effects. Before approaching the architecture of today, we must attempt to understand the nature of these trends.

PICTURESQUE ECLECTICISM

Many periods of architecture have been more or less eclectic. But in the mid-eighteenth century eclecticism became exceptionally varied in its interpretation and overt in its expression.

A first principle of eclecticism is reliance on the past. Although such reliance seems to imply lack of initiative, the revival of an earlier style, or use of an individual building or idea as a more or less specific example to be followed, does not necessarily constitute slavish imitation. The concept of revival is certainly implicit in an eclectic attitude, but even more important is the fact that a new synthesis is produced by the selection of certain features for emphasis. Often the earlier elements are reinterpreted or reconsidered to such a degree that they bear only superficial resemblance to the prototype. This was true in the eighteenth and nineteenth centuries, as it was in other eclectic moments during Late Antiquity or during the Renaissance.

In England, particularly, it is often difficult to distinguish between the survival or revival of traditional forms. The use of Medieval details, for instance, never completely stopped. Indeed, Sir John Vanbrugh, highly regarded as one of England's outstanding Baroque architects, used crenellations, round towers, and other familiar Medieval forms when he built his own country house in Blackheath as late as 1717–1718.

Horace Walpole's country seat near London — *Strawberry Hill*, begun in 1747 — is one of the first examples of deliberate revival of Medieval art. It is interesting to note that Walpole, surrounded as he was by the fanciful forms of Rococo art, instinctively preferred the similar highly decorative forms of Late Medieval art for the ornamentation of his library and other rooms. Such predilections for one type of form or another usually provide the impetus for a revival; and it is the degree of sensitive intuition, of affinity, for the earlier forms which determines whether the results will be successful or not.

Similar re-use of earlier styles occurred during the second half of the eighteenth century. Robert Adam (1728–1792) is usually regarded as the initiator of the Classic Revival, but an examination of his work reveals how much more Rococo it is than either Greek or Roman. Yet the spirit of the times encouraged greater and greater interest in the past. A new attitude toward history may be seen, for example, in the Society of the Dilettanti in London, who introduced archeological methods by actually measuring monuments and publishing them in the *Antiquities of Athens* in 1762. Similarly, Winckelmann's famous *History of Ancient Art* (1764) for the first time attempted to reappraise Greek art in its own terms. Winckelmann, for this reason, is usually regarded as the father of all historians of art.

Interest in the past, in its history and monuments, increased as time went on, and the startling excavations at Herculaneum and Pompeii (after 1748) gave it popular appeal. It is not surprising, therefore, that revival of many different styles should have occurred and recurred as the nineteenth century advanced. In many instances the motives for such revivals reveal interesting characteristics of eclecticism. Symbolic eclecticism, for instance, is the practice of selecting a style for its associations. The followers of this theory today would insist that college buildings and churches be Gothic, and banks and capitols Greek or Roman, while shopping centers might be "modernistic." But less superficial associations often

23–2 SIR CHARLES BARRY, assisted by A. N. PUGIN. *Houses of Parliament*. London. Designed 1835. (British Information Services)

existed, as in Thomas Jefferson's selection of the Roman *Maison Carrée* at Nîmes as the model for the *Virginia State Capitol* at Richmond (Fig. 11–21). Jefferson's choice was based on the admiration he felt for the original, both as an embodiment of the pure beauty of Antiquity and as representing idealized Roman Republican government. Its selection reflects as well the attempt, also found in the thought of Jefferson's contemporary French revolutionaries, to rediscover in Antiquity certain principles of life which had presumably been distorted during the intervening centuries.

Eclecticism also fostered the typical nineteenth-century growth, nationalism. This was not a malady confined to the architectural profession, since poets, novelists, and politicians were likewise infected. In seeking forms to be revived, each country turned toward its own past and, by reviving forms nostalgically linked with its earlier days of glory, encouraged patriotism and thus separatism. In London, when the old

houses of Parliament burned in 1834, the Parliamentary Commission decreed that designs for the new building should be "either Gothic or Elizabethan." Sir Charles Barry with the assistance of A. N. W. Pugin submitted the winning design in 1835, and the work was carried on through the 1840's and '60's. (Fig. 23–2). Their concept was thoroughly eclectic, since it combined a formal axial plan with detailing which was English Perpendicular.

Medieval styles were also considered ideally Christian and therefore morally pure. Some "Gothic" churches of the mid-nineteenth century recapture to a surprising degree the Rayonnant spirit, as in Ste. Clotilde in Paris (1846–53). But some Anglican cathedrals, begun within the last fifty years or so, such as those in Liverpool, or St. John the Divine in New York, or in Washington, and which are all still under construction, show how stereotyped forms may become when executed on a drafting board and produced by the aid of machinery.

The moral values of Medieval art were strongly emphasized by William Morris (1834–1896) (see p. 682) and his architect and friend, Philip Webb, in the famous Red House at Bexley Heath (1859–60). Repelled by the meretricious nature of most of the early machine-age products, they turned instead to traditional methods and materials, honestly used and hand-crafted, thus reintroducing simplicity and what they called "truth" into later nineteenth-century architecture. Earlier, "Gothic" designs were also engraved in a number of handbooks, which crossed the Atlantic to produce the delightful fantasies often called "carpenter's" or "gingerbread" Gothic of such resorts as Kennebunkport, Maine, or Oak Bluffs on Martha's Vineyard.

Although Revived Gothic in different forms continued to be popular during most of the nineteenth century, the styles of Antiquity had, to begin with, an even greater vogue. It seemed appropriate in an era of increasing democracy to install governmental bodies, customs offices, banks, educational institutions, and even Christian churches in structures derived from Greek temples. On the other hand, since the Romans had enjoyed republican government, their architecture, notably the Corinthian order, could also be used with propriety, as in the additions to the *Capitol* at Washington or on subsequent government buildings in the national capital.

A shorter-lived fashion with a different vocabulary, derived from the French Renaissance, was known as the "Second Empire," as reinterpreted by French, English, and American architects. Enormous prestige was attached for a time to the physical environment created by architects and city planners for Napoleon III and his empress, Eugénie — an environment that made Paris the symbol of magnificence and luxury. This style swept briefly through the world and has left us such monuments as railroad hotels all over England, the *Philadelphia City Hall*, and the *State, War, and Navy Building* in Washington, D. C.

Some of the more talented architects turned easily from one style to another and could synthesize expertly. Sir Charles Barry, who used Gothic forms in designing the *Houses of Parliament* in London, as we have mentioned, actually preferred the formal Italian Renaissance models such as the Farnese Palace, on which he based his Reform Club building (1837) in London. As a result the Italian Palace style enjoyed a considerable vogue in the mid-century and was again revived in the '80's.

France, Germany, and America shared in this passing Italianate phase. In Paris various government buildings, such as those that line the rue de Rivoli and even Henri Labrouste's Bibliothèque Sainte-Geneviève are more Italian than *néo-grec*. The Bavarian Capitol, at Munich, received harmonious additions with a Quattrocento flavor, and in the United States many seaboard towns built libraries and post offices in this formal Italianate manner.

The work of Karl Friedrich Schinkel (1781–1841), the greatest German architect of the early nineteenth century, is typical of these varied eclectic modes: Revived Greek, Romanesque, or Gothic. His *Altes Museum* in Berlin demonstrates the original quality an able architect could give to a building even when he was synthesizing (Fig. 23-3). Here the long façade, derived from the Greek stoa — originally a modest commercial building — is elevated to the grandeur of a temple by its colossal scale. Behind the colonnade, but visible through it, rises a Renaissance double staircase. Within, the galleries are dominated by a domed rotunda resembling the Roman Pantheon. These

23–3 KARL FRIEDRICH SCHINKEL. *Altes Museum.* Berlin. 1824–1828. (Deutscher Kunstverlag, Munich)

recombined elements, freshly handled, create an edifice neither Greek nor Roman but Nineteenth-Century.

Although Schinkel and a few others were capable of creating original forms with the vocabulary of earlier styles, such talent was not widespread, so that prosaic imitations of earlier buildings, or of contemporary ones, became only too frequent. In reaction against such pedantry and as a natural outgrowth of other characteristics of revivalism, a new style arose, based on a daring aesthetic. This style was the Picturesque, which valued qualities considered barbarous by an earlier generation. "Intricacy, variety, irregularity, roughness, and movement" were admired, wherever they might be found: in natural landscapes, whether mountain scenery or gardens, in ruins, accidental or contrived, or in historic styles that emphasized them. "Sensibility," rather than the academic skills of formal training, was admired; and, since this offered an avenue of escape, it was, and has been, espoused by many whose spontaneous talents seemed fettered by arduous study.

Picturesque qualities were present in many of the Revived Medieval buildings, but they were even more apparent in other more exotic styles, such as the Moorish, Indian, or Oriental. Even the Italian villa provided inspiration for a combination of slender classical columns, loggias, cupolas, and picturesque towers. John Nash (1752–1835) was successful in his use of Classical themes in old Regent Street in London, and equally so in Gothic terms for country houses; but his *Cronkhill villa* near Shrewsbury (*ca.* 1802) established the Italian Villa mode, which was popular especially in Germany and continued to be so in America until the Civil War. This concept afforded freedom, variety, and picturesqueness for comparatively small cost, and it was so particularly useful in the design of small railroad stations that it is sometimes referred to as the "Railroad style."

The values attributed to Romanesque and Gothic art have already been mentioned, especially in connection with William Morris and Philip Webb. These qualities were enhanced both by the archeological approach of Pugin, who extolled the qualities of thirteenth- and fourteenth-century buildings, and by a "scientific" interpretation whose greatest exponent was Eugène Viollet-le-Duc in France. This mixture of sci-

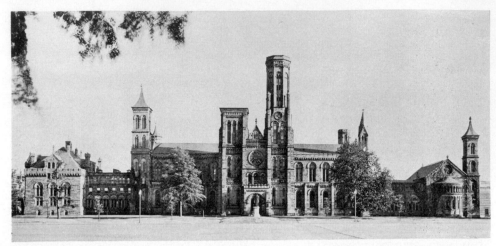

23–4 JAMES RENWICK. *Smithsonian Institution.* Washington, D. C. 1852. (Smithsonian Institution)

entism and sentiment produced a series of buildings and monuments which seemed to meet the demands for "truthful" as well as "picturesque" building — the basis of John Ruskin's widely admired analysis of art.

The universality of this picturesque style, with its opportunities for elaboration and variety of silhouette, is shown in surviving examples from Berlin to Bombay, Copenhagen to Melbourne, Rome to Ottawa. A list of its familiar buildings would include such seemingly disparate examples as the Museum at Oxford, over which Ruskin himself exercised a direct influence; Alfred Waterhouse's *City Hall* and *University* buildings in Manchester; G. E. Street's *London Law Courts;* Sir Gilbert Scott's innumerable churches and his *Albert Memorial* in London; churches in Paris and Nancy; the *Votivkirche* and *town hall* in Vienna; and city halls and churches throughout the United States. One of the few surviving railroad stations in this style, *St. Pancras Station* in London, is one of its high points; and the epitome of nineteenth-century taste is to be found in James Renwick's *Smithsonian Institution* in Washington, D. C. (Fig. 23–4).

Built with funds from an English gift and designed to be surrounded by a parklike landscape, its vigorous picturesqueness has quality and an undeniable charm.

In domestic architecture the goals of variety and novelty could be achieved more easily. Nineteenth-century houses reflect this freedom in their planning, construction, and wide-ranging eclecticism. The newly enfranchised and enriched classes welcomed increasing comfort and installed such innovations as running water, water closets, central heating, illuminating gas, and service areas placed in more functional proximity to living areas. Flexible planning evolved, which made possible the combination of several rooms for occasional large functions (with a continuity of space) and their subsequent separation by means of folding or sliding doors into smaller, more easily heated private areas for daily living. The rapidly expanding frontier of the United States also welcomed structural inventions such as the balloon frame, invented in the 1830's. This system of nailed two-by-fours coincided with the industrial development of the drawn nail. It facilitated cheaper construction by relatively unskilled labor by eliminating heavy timbers and thus the highly trained craftsmen required for the traditional pegging or mortise-and-tenon structure. Architects even had the courage to find an aesthetic expression for these new building methods in the "Stick style." Men such as A. J. Downing and A. J. Davis in America, or J. C. Loudon in England, were advocates of this common-sense "real" approach. They promoted informal, simple designs which emphasized the wooden structure, soon to be covered with continuous shingles, expressive of interior spaces as well as the exterior wooden sheath. Similar effects are to be found in much of H. H. Richardson's building and in Frank Lloyd Wright's earliest structures.

Picturesque Eclecticism thus prepared a way and developed forms which were to emerge as part of the vocabulary of modern architecture. Without some attention, however, to another important attitude, which was concerned with continuity, our preparation for its study is incomplete.

ROMANTIC NATURALISM

Romantic Naturalism, by its interest in asymmetry and natural surroundings, emphasized the Baroque principle of freedom and sought to develop an organic unity in planning, structure, materials, and site. One of its greatest exponents, Frank Lloyd Wright (1869–   ), has identified the principle of continuity as fundamental to its understanding. He has written:

Classic architecture was all fixation. . . . Now why not let walls, ceilings, floors become seen as component parts of each other, their surfaces flowing into each other. . . . You may see the appearance . . . in the surface of your hand contrasted with the articulation of the bony structure itself. This ideal, profound in its

architectural implications . . . I called . . . continuity."[1]

The concept of flux, of constant change, of evolution and progress, is inherent in this principle, as it was in the "Open Road" of Walt Whitman, who has also been hailed as a prophet of continuity. We shall understand Wright's architecture better if we first briefly trace the development of Romantic Naturalism.

In Piranesi's powerful *Carceri*, or prison, etchings of the late 1740's (Fig. 10–59), the Baroque balance between freedom and order was disrupted by violent explorations of vistas deep into space, which were given continuity by the organic relation of the multiple foci. The massive masonry of these fantastic structures lacks any detail with which man might associate himself and thereby achieve a sense of scale. Man seems overwhelmed by the immensity of these limitless galleries, crowded with weird, foreboding machines; and it is man's insignificance in these never-ending spaces which emphasizes the infinite continuity of the universe. At almost the same time Lancelot ("Capability") Brown (1715–1783) was redesigning the great parks around *Blenheim Palace* and *Stowe House;* and, although his "perspectives" have none of Piranesi's violence, their axes are constantly changing and his deliberately placed masses of trees, shrubs, lawns, and lakes create a similar organic continuity. Here is the carefully studied English "informality," which has influenced landscape gardening all over Europe and America.

Another important factor in this whole development was the new materials which the Industrial Age was producing. Among the early important engineering advances were those in the structural use of iron for fireproof roof-

[1] Quotations from F. L. Wright, *An American Architecture,* ed. by E. Kaufman, Horizon Press, New York, 1955, pp. 205, 208.

23–5 SIR JOSEPH PAXTON. *Crystal Palace.* London. 1850–1851. From a lithograph made in 1851. (Victoria and Albert Museum, London)

ing and in bridge construction. The perfection of these techniques may be traced from the early cast-iron bridge at *Coalbrookdale* (1775) through suspension and girder types to the Roeblings' great triumph, the *Brooklyn Bridge* (1868–1883), and the giant cantilever over the Firth of Forth. The tensile qualities of iron and particularly of steel allowed new concepts of vast enclosed, or spanned, spaces. Important advances were also made in the great train sheds of railroad stations and in exposition halls. A startling technological development, due to the versatile genius of Sir Joseph Paxton, led to the standardization of parts which could be prefabricated. This permitted the erection in 1850–1851 of the enormous *Crystal Palace,* in London, almost entirely of iron and glass, in the unheard-of time of six months (Fig. 23–5). Such industrialized practices led to a new business, the export of entire prefabricated buildings from England to Australia and the two Americas. But the climax of nineteenth-century enterprise in wide-span construction occurred at the Paris Exhibition of 1889, in the 360-foot single span for the *Galerie des Machines* (Fig. 23–6). Alexandre Eiffel's daring tower was also built at this time; and these two feats by engineers

jolted some of the architectural profession into a realization that the new materials and new processes might contain the germ of a completely new style, a goal which Picturesque Eclecticism had failed to attain.

The desire for greater speed in building, increased economy, and reduction of fire hazards, all characteristic of the new age, encouraged the use of cast and wrought iron for many other building programs, especially commercial ones. Both England and America enthusiastically developed cast-iron architecture until a series of disastrous fires in the early 1870's in New York, Boston, and Chicago demonstrated that cast iron by itself was far from fireproof. This led to the practice of encasing the metal in masonry, thus combining the strength of the first with the safety of the second.

Meanwhile, urban congestion required buildings to be closely grouped, and increasing demands for office space forced architects literally "to raise the roof." Attics, even, could command high rentals if the newly invented elevator was also provided, as was done first in the *Equitable Building* in New York (1868–1871). Metal could support such structures, and the tall building was finally developed by William

23–6 *Galerie des Machines* in Palais des Machines. International Exhibition, Paris. 1889. C. L. F. Dutert, architect; Contamin, constructor. (Photo Chevojon)

Le Baron Jenney in the *Home Insurance Company* office building in Chicago (1883–1885). Here, for the first time, conscious use was made of novel structural possibilities. Isolated footings supported a skeleton of wrought and cast iron encased in masonry, with fireproof floors, numerous fast elevators, and gas light. The traditional masonry-bearing walls now became weather curtains or skins, largely of glass, supported by the metal skeleton. The American skyscraper was born, although it was only with rare exceptions, as in the work of Louis Sullivan, that this original type of building was treated successfully. In fact, it is to Sullivan and to his predecessor, Henry Hobson Richardson, that we must now turn in our discussion of Romantic Naturalism.

The use of free, asymmetrical plans closely related to the natural environment was characteristic of buildings in the style of the Gothic Revival, which we have already discussed. Similar principles are also fundamental in the precepts of Romantic Naturalism. This interest in carefully organized interior spaces distinguished the "Shingle style," which also aimed at expressing the intimate relations between interior volumes and exterior sheathing. It was in this environment that Henry Hobson Richardson (1838–1886) grew up, although his formal training had been received in the traditional manner at the Ecole des Beaux-Arts in Paris.

Because Richardson frequently used heavy round arches and massive masonry walls, and because he himself was particularly fond of the Romanesque architecture of the Auvergne in France, his work has usually been described as "Romanesque Revival." Those who have studied Romanesque architecture will realize that this does not emphasize properly the true originality and intrinsic quality of almost every one of Richardson's buildings during the brief sixteen years of his practice. While Trinity Church in Boston and his smaller public libraries and residences in New England best demonstrate his vivid imagination and the solidity, the sense of enclosure and permanence so characteristic of his style, his most important and influential building was the *Marshall Field Warehouse* in Chicago, begun in 1885 (Fig. 23–7). Here the rich texture of the masonry, the rhythmical treatment of the opening voids and of their relation to the multistoried structure of the interior are typically Richardsonian.

Early in his own career Louis Sulli-

23–7　HENRY HOBSON RICHARDSON. *Marshall Field Warehouse*. Chicago. Begun 1885. (Museum of Modern Art, New York)

van (1856–1924), recognizing the quality of Richardson's work, applied some of the same principles to the new "tall buildings." This was brilliantly exemplified in the *Wainwright Building* in St. Louis (1890–1891) and especially in the *Guaranty Building*, Buffalo (1894–1895; Fig. 23–8). The fact that the interior of the skeleton was filled with identical spatial units was here, for the first time, expressed on the exterior. Sullivan provided his building with a firm visual base, treated the intermediate office floors as a unit, and crowned the whole with a bold cornice. Although the twentieth century departed from this formula for a while, the Wainwright Building remains a glorious and revolutionary expression of

Sullivan's dictum, "form follows function."

After the turn of the century and the apparent entrenchment of Eclecticism as a result of the Chicago World's Fair of 1893, skyscrapers were clothed in styles of the past, as were most other buildings. The verticality of the office towers, for instance, was thought to be suitably expressed by the vertical forms of Gothic, as in the *Woolworth Building* (1912) or the *Chicago Tribune Tower* (1924–1926). The architect of the latter, Raymond Hood, went on to seek a more logical solution to the problem of height in his *Daily News* and *McGraw-Hill* buildings in New York. Even more successful was the *Philadelphia Savings Fund Society* building by George Howe and William Lescaze. Its form, materials, and structural system were completely interrelated.

Some sensational achievements, such as the world's tallest building, the *Empire State* building, completed in 1932, or the largest planned complex of office buildings, *Rockefeller Center*, begun in 1931, contribute to the magnificence of New York City's famous skyline, which is as changing as the "open road" (Fig. 0–13). The more recent "curtain walls," such as the *United Nations' Secretariat* (1953) or *Lever House* on Park Avenue (1949–1952), glitter in the maze of new buildings, themselves sheathed in a wide variety of metal or stone veneers.

To return to problems more directly concerned with principles of Romantic Naturalism, we must mention the decorative ornamentation devised by Louis Sullivan and used on some of his office buildings. Based on floral motifs but organized in a manner closely resembling the Irish interlace of the early Middle Ages, these metal and stucco designs were among the more original creations of the late nineteenth century. Equally decorative and original, although more carefully integrated in terms of a coherent style, was the *Art Nouveau* which flourished in Europe during the 1890's. The *People's Palace* in Brussels (1897–1899) by Victor Horta shows how this architecture, which was hailed enthusiastically as a modern style, emphasized the late nineteenth-century interest in decorative forms. A number of influences can be identified, ranging from the rich foliated two-dimensional ornament and craftsman's respect for materials of William Morris' Arts and Crafts movement (see p. 682) to the free sinuous whiplash curve of Japanese designs. The bold use of metal may also be seen in the light supports, the ductile curving ornament, and the candor with

23–8 LOUIS SULLIVAN. *Guaranty Building.* Buffalo. 1894–1895. (J. Szarkowski, *The Idea of Louis Sullivan,* University of Minnesota Press, 1956)

which design and structure were integrated.

From 1896 to 1914 *Art Nouveau* in one or another of its national manifestations (the Italians had a *stile floreale*) was the fashionable expression of good taste from Constantinople to Lima. Although many buildings were designed in this style, still more individual rooms were redecorated in it, and all the arts of design were under its sway. The Catalan architect, Antonio Gaudi (1852–1926), was able to use similar continuities in his concrete buildings in profoundly moving ways (Fig. 23–9).

The work of Horta and Gaudi provides the components for a new and deeply searching art. These elements lead us into the modern world, and it is the architecture of that world which we should now attempt to identify.

The most striking and original personality in the development of a "modern" architecture unquestionably is Frank Lloyd Wright, who was born in 1867 and whose projects still startle the world. He has always been a fervid exponent of Romantic Naturalism, although his own term "organic" is more descriptive of his vigorous originality. His first houses in Oak Park, Illinois, show his indebtedness to the earlier "Shingle style" and to the work of Richardson and Sullivan; but by the beginning of this century his cross-axial plan and the interwoven building fabric of continuous roof planes and screens defined a new domestic architecture. He attacked the concept of the skeleton frame in his studies of other systems, including the cantilever, and he said, "Have no posts, no columns. . . . In my work the idea of plasticity may now be seen as the element of continuity." And he acclaimed "the new reality that is *space* instead of matter." All

these elements were fully expressed in his *Robie House* in Chicago (1909; Fig. 23–10), which was called, as were his other houses of the time, a Prairie House. Although a few discerning clients commissioned his work, his reputation was greater in Europe, especially in Holland and Germany, than in America. The United States did not appear to be ready for the innovations proposed by Wright, but in 1915 he was summoned to Tokyo to build the Imperial Hotel (1916–1922). To erect a structure capable of withstanding frequent earthquakes, he mastered the principles of cantilever construction and explored further the "nature" of building materials. During the 1920's he had few commissions, but some of his designs reveal an appreciation of the massive temples of Maya architecture (p. 599). It was not until the 1930's that Wright achieved the recognition that ranks him among the great architects of the Western world.

23-10   FRANK LLOYD WRIGHT. *Robie House*. Chicago. 1909. (Ryerson Library)

A comparison of Wright's *Robie House* (Fig. 23-10) with his *Falling Water* (Fig. 23-11) shows how his style developed. The *Robie House* is "modern," with its long, low horizontal masses and its projecting roofs, creating accents of deep shadows, and, above all, in the integration of interior volumes as well as of interior and exterior spaces. At *Falling Water* concrete and

23-11   FRANK LLOYD WRIGHT. *Falling Water*, built for E. S. Kaufman. Bear Run, Pennsylvania. 1936. (Hedrich-Blessing Studio)

23–12 FRANK LLOYD WRIGHT. *Taliesin West*. Phoenix, Arizona. 1938–1940. (Peter E. Guerrero)

steel made it possible to build over-hanging slabs which harmonize perfectly with the rocky ledges of the stream but create their own sharply defined planes in a space which is treated in as fluid a manner as the continuously falling water itself. The strong textural contrasts of the concrete slabs with the vertical masses of native stone emphasize an organic relation with the natural site, which is given a new significance by the presence of the building. Although there is a machine-like clarity in the definition of the planes, which we shall see as well in the "International style" of Gropius and Le Corbusier, Wright's architecture is so organically related to its site and to the materials of which it is built that land and building become inseparable.

Wright's inventiveness and sensitivity to different programs may also be seen in the administration building for

the *Johnson Wax Company* in Racine, Wisconsin, begun in 1936, and in his own residence and school, known as *Taliesin West*, near Phoenix, Arizona (1938). In the Johnson Wax building, curvilinear masses of brick with stone trim are accented by bands of glass tubing. The rhythm of these masses has a compelling flow, which seems resolved in the interior by an extraordinary diffusion of light (Fig. 23–1). The unique, hollow shafts of reinforced concrete support circular concrete "pads," which seem to float above a space so free and uniform that it is more real than the defining matter itself.

At *Taliesin West* Wright has created a spectacularly original house of canvas, redwood, and massive masonry of desert rocks and coarse, granulated cement (Fig. 23–12). On a base as solid and earthbound as the Central American temple platforms, the fabric of the structure is arranged with ceremonial corridors and terraces constantly opening on the surrounding desert — "the man-made building heightening the beauty of the desert and the desert more beautiful because of the building." A monumental stability created from the most violent oppositions gives these buildings of Wright's the grandeur of Picasso's *Guernica*, which was painted at the same time.

Not all "modern" architecture, however, has the organic continuity of Wright's buildings. We must retrace our steps to define Romantic Classicism as distinct from Romantic Naturalism, in order to analyze the work of Gropius, Mies van der Rohe, and Le Corbusier.

ROMANTIC CLASSICISM

In contrast to the accent on freedom implicit in Romantic Naturalism, the principle of order identifies Romantic Classicism. The "classicists" found satisfaction in the abstract terms of geometry, in "pure" relationships which create their own environment and whose meaning can be sought only in the forms themselves. Such preoccupations, ultimately found to be expressive of the non-natural world created by the machine, were embodied in the "International style" of the 1920's. Yet the principles of "classicizing" may be observed as early as the eighteenth century, although they continued with less emphasis during the nineteenth.

Sir John Soane (1753–1837) in England, Claude Nicholas Ledoux (1736–1806) in France, and Friedrich Gilly (1772–1800) in Germany are usually identified with the Neoclassic movement. Although it is true that the Doric column and other Classical motifs constantly appear in their work, their projects or buildings broke with tradition in most original ways. The severity of their abstract forms is much more easily understood in terms of a classical

purity than in those of revivalism. Some of Ledoux's unrealized projects present early solutions for industrial complexes and urban centers, which because of their simple geometrical forms, such as the sphere, the cube, and the pyramid, present most unexpected eighteenth-century vistas. In Soane's *Bank of England* (1788) ornamentation such as molding was reduced to a minimum, so that walls or piers seem to combine with vaults and domes in continuous, flowing surfaces. To this degree the early "classicists" participated in the search for continuity, but it was in abstract rather than organic forms, and infinite, stable relationships rather than in those concerned with change and movement.

Although the enthusiasm for Picturesque Eclecticism in the nineteenth century seemed to overshadow the interest in such "classically pure" forms, the order and simple integrity of many Greek Revival buildings, particularly in the United States, are deservedly regarded as classic. They create their own environment, quite independently of their natural surroundings, and establish an abstract order in their own terms.

We must return to Europe, though, in order to discover an interest in technological determinism. A synthesis of these functional principles ultimately combined with classicizing tendencies to produce a new style. It was Viollet-le-Duc, in France, for instance, who, in spite of his seemingly romantic interest in the restoration and rebuilding of Medieval monuments, insisted in his original works and in his stimulating *Discourses* on the use of new materials and on their direct expression in structure. This rational approach, in which form *and* function receive equal emphasis, provided European architects in the early twentieth century with a new philosophy. The results may first be seen in the work of Auguste Perret

23–13 WALTER GROPIUS. *Bauhaus.* Dessau. 1926.

(1873–1954) in France, and of Peter Behrens (1868–1940) and Walter Gropius (1883–) in Germany. In a sense Romantic Classicism and a new romanticism of the machine seem to coalesce here. The reinforced-concrete structures of Perret have the clarity of French classicizing, while emphasizing a rectangular skeleton which is self-contained and yet is designed as a series of unrelated or discontinuous elements. In the factories and industrial buildings of Behrens and Gropius a similar regard for individual units reveals a profound sensitivity for the machine, whose multiple parts are minutely tooled but which are visually unrelated and have their function only as part of the whole. This may be seen in the *Bauhaus* in Dessau, Germany, a school founded by Gropius in 1919.

The *Bauhaus* was formed by Walter Gropius as a design school aimed at finding solutions for the problems of housing, urban planning, and high-quality, utilitarian mass production, all vitally needed in impoverished Germany. The *Bauhaus* nevertheless constantly nurtured imagination and inspiration by emphasizing music and drama and in particular painting, under the guidance of Lyonel Feininger, Kandinsky, and Klee. In design, handicraft was considered the natural training device for mass production and the natural technique for experimental models leading to industrial products. In these respects, and in the noticeable playing down of philosophy and other verbal techniques, the *Bauhaus* was the earliest working example of much that is still sought in design education. Its training was rooted in the Arts and Crafts movement of earlier generations and in Friedrich Froebel's and others' work with children's art, but its vision was firmly fixed on the requirements and potentialities of its day.

Gropius' design for the *Bauhaus* buildings, which included a workshop, a studio, a school, and an administrative office, established the principles of the International style, which is expressive of the Machine Age as the Europeans of the 1920's wished to see it. Planned as a series of cells, each with its own specific function, it is the direct expression, in glass, steel, and thin concrete veneer, of the technical program. It bespeaks the methodical precision not only of the machine but of the German temperament as well. The forms are clear, cubic units — the epitome of classicizing purity (Fig. 23–13).

23–14 MIES VAN DER ROHE. *German Pavilion.* International Exposition, Barcelona. 1929. (Mies van der Rohe) (See also Fig. 0–15.)

It is in the work of Mies van der Rohe (1886–) that the International style found its most imaginative solutions and perhaps a new order as well. His *German Pavilion,* built for the International Exposition at Barcelona in 1929, has a program — an information center and rest house — which was, paradoxically, so simple that the architect was able to concentrate almost exclusively, as in many "Fair" buildings, on the dramatic principles of the new style. Fine stone and marble, chromium and glass, water and sculpture molded the space and led the visitor subtly through a succession of areas which varied in their degree of enclosure, now open on several sides, now closed by two, three, or four walls (Fig. 23–14). Grace and elegance, refined and subtle harmonies were realized to a degree comparable to those eighteenth-century masterpieces, the *Amalienburg* near Munich, or the *Petit Trianon* at Versailles, but in this instance in a language and spirit wholly of the twentieth century (Fig. 0–15).

Since 1937, however, when Mies van der Rohe came to the United States, he has been aware of a desire to create a more fixed and symmetrical type of design. Mies' early classicism has served him well, as may be seen at the *Illinois Institute of Technology* (Fig. 23–15) where he established a sense of continuity by natural expansion from a sym-

23–15 MIES VAN DER ROHE. *Illinois Institute of Technology.* Chicago. 1956. (Bill Engdahl, Hedrich-Blessing Studio)

23–16 LE CORBUSIER. *Unité d'Habitation.* Marseilles. 1946. (Lucien Hervé, by permission Spadem, Paris)

metrically conceived central space. In this way his cubic buildings are in modular harmony with the rectangular spaces created by them, and he rejected the International style's compromise between structure and design to insist upon the skeleton cage of the steel frame. He clarified Sullivan's emphasis on the vertical and horizontal elements of girder construction and achieved the absolute order and simplicity of the lines and planes of Mondrian's paintings. Mies' designs of the 1940's and 1950's, in their modularity and urbanity, have often been compared with Renaissance townscapes and the permanent order of the urban piazza. But Mies' forms in steel frames are thinner, less sculptural, than those of Renaissance buildings, and they have also the sharp linearity which seems typical in all ages of classicizing or neoclassic work. In a sense the detachment and anonymity of much of modern life seems to be expressed in them.

The French architect Charles Edouard Jeanneret-Gris (born in 1887), who calls himself Le Corbusier, also contributed to the development of the International style during the 1920's. His later buildings, however, seem to search more deeply into the complicated and challenging nature of man's existence in the modern world. His *Vers une Architecture (Towards a New Architecture)*, published in 1923, remains one of the outstanding statements on modern architecture, reassessing, as well, the past, especially the monuments of Antiquity, in terms of a new "modern" architecture, which he is still defining in his own work.

In his *Citrohan* houses of 1922, a "machine for living" is proposed, which recalls the very early megarons of Antiquity, with their open ends and closed sides. The design of the interior spaces, though, is the tense, constructed space of Cubist painting rather than the organic, continuous space of Frank Lloyd Wright or of *de Stijl.* In 1929 his *Villa Savoie*, at Poissy-sur-Seine, is a lightly enclosed space, supported, at least visually, on thin columns so that there is a deliberate analogy to the isolated but "machined" space of an ocean liner. His use of color — dark green base, cream-colored walls, and rose and blue superstructure (a wind screen) — are also deliberate analogies to contemporary painting, in which he was also actively engaged. Early in the 1930's Le Corbusier gave these membranes enclosing living spaces new solidity by using massive, supporting "pilotis," which may be seen under his *Swiss Pavilion* at the *Cité Universitaire* in Paris, although the box of rooms above remains thin and taut.

Immediately following World War II, in 1946, Le Corbusier designed the *Unité d'Habitation* in Marseilles (Fig. 23–16) as an answer to one of modern man's insistent problems: communal living. Here a new modular, the standing man, gives a powerful scale and an immediate reference to the program. The mighty pilotis support a framework in which each apartment is an integral unit. The individual porches, each with a *brise-soleil*, create a new sculptural mass, so that the building does not exist as a skeletal framework enclosed in a membrane, nor as a solid mass. The solids and voids are in direct relation, as in Greek temples, which to Le Corbusier sound "clear and tragic like brazen trumpets." Geoffrey Scott's definition of the humanist architecture of Antiquity and the Renaissance, in his *Architecture of Humanism* (Scribner's, 1914), is pertinent here. He wrote:

The center of that architecture was the human body; its method to transcribe in stone the body's favorable states; and the moods of the spirit took visible shape along its borders, power and laughter, strength and terror and calm.

As the confident nineteenth century sought security in organic, continuous forms, the beleaguered twentieth seeks

23–17 LE CORBUSIER. *High Court Building*. Chandigarh, India. 1956. (Ernst Scheidegger, Magnum)

23–18 LE CORBUSIER. *Notre Dame du Haut*. Ronchamp. 1955. (François Bucher)

it in a new image of man (p. 1).

More recently Le Corbusier has built the new capitol of the Punjab at *Chandigarh*, in India, which he designed in 1952 (Fig. 23–17). Here he has given architecture and man a new, or should we say, an old, pre-industrial relationship with nature, with the landscape. Man no longer dissolves into this landscape as he may in the lonely dreams of Wright, nor is he an intruder separated from nature, as in classicizing, self-sufficient forms of Mies van der Rohe. In a manner similar to the Greek temple this architecture, because of its sculptural masses and volumes, its human scale, brings the natural landscape into human focus.

The startling forms of Le Corbusier's *Notre Dame du Haut*, at Ronchamp, in France (1955; Fig. 23–18), present us with a challenge. Here, in his own terms, is a "vessel" on a "high place," intended to respond to a *psycho-physiologie de la sensation* ("a psycho-physiology of the senses") to *une acoustique paysagiste, prenant les quatres horizons à temoin* ("a reverberating landscape, holding the four hori-

zons as witness"). In these powerful, surging masses, these sculptural solids and voids, there is a new environment in which man, as a human being, may find new values, new interpretations of his sacred beliefs and of his natural environment.

The reconstruction of devastated areas in Europe and the Far East, as in the pressing necessities following the Great Fire of London in 1666, have not always followed the projects of urban planners, but they do show a respect for the past as well as an intent to create a contemporary environment, although too often the result is still a dreary compromise. In Latin America, where progress and the future are still shining avenues, modern architecture shares this optimism. The work of Oscar Niemeyer, of Lúcio Costa, and a host of others reflects and interprets this contemporary environment, which found its beginnings in the disappearance of the Renaissance world and is still searching for an equilibrium between man, man-made forces and techniques, and nature.

This summary of trends in modern architecture has, of necessity, stressed the contributions of those men who, in our foreshortened historical perspective, appear to have been pioneers. It seems certain that Frank Lloyd Wright, Mies van der Rohe, and Le Corbusier will be recognized as such by future generations. But our review, again of necessity, has not mentioned the many architects who, by their own interpretation of an organic or of an absolute architecture, have proved that these new vocabularies of form have had meaning for the generations of this century. In the free countries of the world the past decade has witnessed an energy expended in building, which recalls the words of Raoul Glaber who, after the end of the first millennium, saw the earth covered by a "white robe of churches" (see p. 231). Perhaps not all of our new buildings have been churches, but as one surveys the landscape, urban or rural, of the Western world, there is no denying that a new environment has been created and is, in fact, still in the very process of creation. Future historians will evaluate more accurately than we the true significance of these contributions to the history of man's willed environment. If we identify such men as Philip Johnson, Erro Saarinen, Marcel Breuer, Paul Rudolph, or Joseph Esherick, Jr., in the United States, it is only to emphasize the wide variety of creative interpretations available in the vocabulary of "modern" architecture. A survey of the Western hemisphere also proves that the "modern" idiom is no longer an idiom but a common language.

Bibliography

Behrendt, Walter C., *Modern Building*, Harcourt, Brace, 1937.
Clarke, Kenneth, *The Gothic Revival*, Constable, London, 1928 and 1950.
Condit, Carl W., *The Rise of the Skyscraper*, University of Chicago Press, 1952.
Fitch, James Marsden, *American Building*, Houghton Mifflin, 1948.
Giedion, Sigfried, *A Decade of New Architecture*, Girsberger, Zurich, 1951.
——, *Space, Time and Architecture*, Harvard University Press, 1943.
Goodhart-Rendel, H. S., *English Architecture Since the Regency*, Constable, London, 1953.
Goodwin, Philip L., *Brazil Builds*, Museum of Modern Art, New York, 1943.
Gropius, Walter, *The New Architecture and the Bauhaus*, tr. by P. Morton Shand, Museum of Modern Art, New York, 1937.
——, *Scope of Total Architecture*, Harper, 1954.
Hamlin, Talbot F., *Architecture Through the Ages*, Putnam, New York, 1953.
——, *Greek Revival Architecture*, Oxford University Press, 1944.
Hitchcock, Henry-Russell, *The Architecture of H. H. Richardson and His Times*, Museum of Modern Art, New York, 1936.
——, *Early Victorian Architecture in Britain*, 2 vols., Yale University Press, 1954.
——, *In the Nature of Materials: The Buildings of Frank Lloyd Wright, 1887–1941*, Duell, Sloan & Pearce, New York, 1942.
, and Drexler, Arthur, *Built in U. S. A.: Post War Architecture*, Museum of Modern Art, New York, 1952.
——, and Johnson, Philip, *The International Style: Architecture Since 1922*, Norton, 1932.
Howarth, Thomas, *Charles Rennie Mackintosh and the Modern Movement*, Wittenborn, Schultz, New York, 1953.
Hussey, Christopher, *The Picturesque*, Putnam, London and New York, 1927.
Kaufmann, Emil, *Architecture in the Age of Reason*, Harvard University Press, 1955.
Le Corbusier (pseud. for Jeanneret-Gris, Charles E.), *Towards a New Architecture*, tr. by Frederick Etchells, Payson & Clarke, New York, 1927.
——, and Jeanneret, Pierre, *Oeuvre Complète:*
    Vol. 1, *1929–34*, Boesiger, Zurich, 1935.
    Vol. 2, *1934–38*, Girsberger, Zurich, 1939.
    Vol. 3, *1938–46*, Boesiger, Zurich, 1946.
    Vol. 4, *1946–52*, Girsberger, Zurich, 1953.
    Vol. 5, *1910–29*, Les Editions d'Archi-

tecture Erlenbach, Zurich, 1937 (5th. ed., 1948).

Lees-Milne, James, *The Age of Adam*, Batsford, London, 1947.

Meeks, Carroll L. V., *The Railroad Station*, Yale University Press, 1956.

Morrison, Hugh, *Early American Architecture*, Oxford University Press, New York, 1952.

——, *Louis Sullivan*, Peter Smith, New York, 1935.

Mumford, Lewis, *The Roots of Contemporary American Architecture*, Reinhold, New York, 1952.

Neutra, Richard, *Survival Through Design*, Oxford University Press, 1954.

Pevsner, Nikolaus, *Pioneers of Modern Design*, Museum of Modern Art, New York, 1949.

Pilcher, Donald, *The Regency Style, 1800–1830*, Batsford, London, 1947.

Richards, J. M., and Mock, Elizabeth, *An Introduction to Modern Architecture*, Penguin Books, New York, 1947.

Roth, Alfred, *The New Architecture*, Girsberger, Zurich, 1940.

Sartoris, Alberto, *Encyclopédie de l'Architecture Nouvelle*, Hoepli, Milan, 1948.

Scully, Vincent, *The Shingle Style*, Yale University Press, 1955.

Smith, G. E. K., *Italy Builds*, Reinhold, New York, 1955.

——, *Sweden Builds*, Bonnier, New York, 1950.

——, *Switzerland Builds*, Bonnier, New York, 1950.

Sullivan, Louis, *Kindergarten Chats and Other Writings*, Wittenborn, Schultz, New York, 1947.

Taut, Bruno, *Modern Architecture*, The Studio, London, 1930.

Tunnard, Christopher, *American Skyline*, Houghton Mifflin, 1955.

——, *The City of Man*, Scribner's, 1953.

Turner, Reginald, *Nineteenth Century Architecture in Britain*, Batsford, London and New York, 1950.

Whittick, Arnold, *European Architecture in the Twentieth Century*, Crosby Lockwood, London, Vol. 1, 1950; Vol. 2, 1953.

Wright, Frank Lloyd, *An Autobiography*, rev. ed., Duell, Sloan & Pearce, 1943.

——, *Modern Architecture*, Princeton University Press, 1931.

Zevi, Bruno, *Storia dell' architettura Moderna*, Einaudi, Turin, 3rd ed., 1955.

——, *Towards an Organic Architecture*, Faber & Faber, London, 1949.

GLOSSARY

GLOSSARY

Abacus. A flat block forming the upper member of the capital of a column. Fig. 5-5.

Aesthetic. Literally, sensitive to art and beauty. Used generally as a philosophy of beauty, or as the distinctive vocabulary of a given style.

Agora. An open square, for public meetings or business, in Greek cities. Fig. 5-42.

Amalaid. An elaborate ceremonial headdress of abalone shell and ermine used by the Tlingit Indians.

Ambulatory. A passageway. It may be outside, as in a cloister (*see* Cloister) or inside; used especially of the passageway around the chevet. Fig. 8-34.

Amphora. A jar with two handles for general storage purposes. Figs. 5-33, 5-36.

Apsara. Indian: nymph of the sky or atmosphere, courtesan of Indra's heaven. Chinese: Buddhist heavenly maiden, dwelling in the paradises.

Apse. The recess, usually semicircular, at the end of a Roman basilica or a Christian church. Fig. 7-6.

Aqueduct. A channel for conducting water; frequently supported by arches. Fig. 6-23.

Arabesque. Literally, like the Arabian. Strictly, a Mohammedan decorative motif; a flowing, curving scroll derived from stylized floral motifs often arranged in symmetrical palmette designs.

Arcade. A series of arches supported on piers or columns. Figs. 8-15, 9-32.

Arch. A constructional device to span an opening. A true arch is curved and is made of wedge-shaped blocks (voussoirs). Fig. 6-23.

Archeology. The scientific investigation and reconstruction of past cultures.

Architrave. The lintel or lowest division of the entablature. Fig. 5-5.

Archivolt. One of a series of arches framing a Romanesque or Gothic portal. Fig. 8-37.

Area. An enclosed, or limited, flat space. P. 6.

Artesonado. Coffered wooden ceilings employing Moorish geometric schemes.

Atlantes. Sculptured male supporting figures.

Atrium. The court of a Roman house, near the entrance and partly open to the sky. Fig. 6-14. The open court in front of a Christian basilica. Fig. 7-6.

Axial plan. See Plan.

Axis. The organization of the component parts of a building, or of any work of art, or of an interrelated group of them, along a given line, or lines, of direction in space. P. 8.

Baldachino (baldachin). In Italy, a canopy on four columns, frequently built over an altar. Fig. 10-3.

Barrel vault. See Vault.

Basilica. In Roman architecture, a public building for assemblies, especially tribunals, rectangular in plan, entered on a long side. Fig. 6-22. In Christian architecture, an early church somewhat resembling the Roman basilica; usually entered from one end with an apse at the other, creating an axial plan. Figs. 7–6, 7–9.

Bas relief. See Relief.

Batik. A process in which cloth, usually white, is temporarily covered with wax, so that the covered areas remain white after dyeing.

Batter. The inward slope of a wall, often almost imperceptible.

Bay. A compartment that serves as a unit of division in a building. In a Gothic cathedral the transverse arches and adjacent piers of the arcade divide the building into bays, the design of which is an architectural unit repeated in each bay. Fig. 8–42.

Bayeta. An English flannel cloth of bright colors, exported to the colonies and used by the Plains Indians. P. 628.

Blind arcade (wall arcade). An arcade, applied to a wall surface, with no actual openings, to serve as a decoration. Fig. 8–21.

Bottega. A shop. The studio-shop of an Italian artist. P. 291.

Bulto. In New Mexico, the statue of a saint.

Bracket. A projecting wooden construction supporting eaves.

Broken color. A painting technique of short, thick strokes laid over a ground color to create vibrant effects of light and rich textures. P. 678.

Broken pediment. A pediment in which the cornice is broken at the apex. Fig. 10–8.

Buttress. A masonry support to counterbalance the lateral thrust of an arch or vault. A pier buttress is a solid mass of masonry. Fig. 8–18. A *flying buttress* is an arch or series of arches that carry the thrust over the aisles to the solid buttresses. Fig. 8–29.

Calumet. A tobacco pipe with a bowl carved out of stone or modeled in clay. In use among North American Indians.

Campanile. Italian word for a bell tower. Sometimes it is free-standing; sometimes it is a part of the building. Fig. 8–21.

Capital. The upper member of a column, usually decorated, that serves as a transition from the shaft to the lintel. Fig. 5–5.

Cardo. The north-south road in Etruscan and Roman towns, intersecting the *decumanus* at right angles. Fig. 6–3.

Cartoon. A preliminary drawing for a painting.

Caryatid. A draped female figure which, as a column, serves as a support. Fig. 5–10.

Cella. An enclosed chamber, the essential feature of a Classical temple, in which the cult statue usually stood. Fig. 5–4.

Centering. A wooden framework to hold an arch or vault during its construction.

Central plan. See Plan.

Ceramics. A general term for the art of making pottery.

Chaitya. Buddhist assembly hall. Fig. 14–8.

Chalice. A cup or goblet, especially that used in the sacraments of the Christian church. Fig. 7–1.

Chamfer. The surface formed by cutting off a square angle; a bevel.

Champlevé enamel. A process of enameling in which the design is cut out of a metal plate, leaving thin raised lines that create compartments to hold the enamel. Plate 3. P. 241.

Chevet. The term applied to the eastern end of a Romanesque or Gothic church, including choir, ambulatory, and radiating chapels. Figs. 8–29, 8–40.

Chevron. A zigzag or V-shaped motif of decoration.

Chiaroscuro. Literally, clear-obscure. The treatment of light and dark in a work of art. P. 13; Fig. 0–12.

Chiton. A Greek tunic, the essential (and often only) garment of both men and women, the other being the mantle (*see* Himation). There were two kinds of tunics, the Doric and Ionic. The Doric was a rectangular piece of woolen stuff, usually folded over at the top, wrapped about the body so that it was open at the left side, sleeveless, fastened on the shoulders with buckles, and girdled. The Ionic was longer, more voluminous, of soft goods such as cotton or linen, and often caught at intervals by fastenings to form sleeves. Fig. 5–29.

Choir. The space reserved for the clergy in a church. Usually it lies east of the transept, but in some instances extends into the nave. Fig. 8–40.

Choir stalls. Seats for the clergy, usually ranged along the sides of the choir.

Chroma. The relative purity of a color, identified by the degree of its adulteration. P. 13.

Ciborium. A canopy, usually standing free and supported on four columns, erected over an altar (*see* Baldachino). Fig. 7–7. Also a covered cup used in the sacraments of the Christian church.

Cire-perdue process. Literally the "wax-lost" process. In bronze casting, a method of melting away the wax in which the figure is modeled and filling the space thus left with molten bronze. P. 605.

Clerestory. That part of a building which rises above the roofs of the other parts and whose walls contain openings for light. Fig. 8–42.

Cloison. Literally, a partition. A metal wire or narrow strip, usually gold, soldered to a metal base to form cells for holding enamel or other decorative materials. Fig. 8–2.

Cloisonné enamel. A process of enameling in which strips of metal (cloisons) are soldered to a base, forming cells into which the enamel is poured and fused. Fig. 7–29.

Cloister. A court, usually with covered walks or ambulatories on the sides. Fig. 8–23.

Closed form. A mass limited by space. P. 7.

Clustered pier. See Compound pier.

Codex. A manuscript in the form of a volume with pages bound together.

Coffer. A sunken ornamental panel in a soffit, vault, or ceiling. Fig. 6–31.

Coin type. The pattern or design used to decorate a coin.

Collage. A composition made by pasting together various materials, such as newspaper, wallpaper, printed text and illustrations, photographs, and cloth. Sometimes used interchangeably with "montage," which refers specifically to combinations of photographs. Fig. 20–53.

Colonnade. A series or range of columns, usually spanned by lintels. Fig. 5–9.

Colonnette. A small column. Fig. 8–35.

Colophon. An inscription at the end of a book or manuscript which gives the title, possibly the name of the writer or illustrator, the place of writing or printing, and the date – information now usually placed on title and copyright pages.

Column. A vertical, circular weight-carrying architectural member, consisting of a base (sometimes omitted), a shaft, and a capital. Fig. 5–5.

Complementary colors. Those colors which lie opposite each other on a color diagram. Colors which complement or complete each other. Pp. 13–14.

Compound or *clustered pier.* A pier composed of a group or cluster of members. Especially characteristic of Gothic architecture. Fig. 8–41.

Connoisseur. An expert who seeks criteria for attributing works of art to given artists. By extension, one whose disciplined sensibilities have been highly developed. Pp. 27–28.

Contour. The visible border of a mass in space. A line which by its subtlety creates the illusion of mass and volume in space. P. 8; Fig. 0–6.

Cool color. Blue and the hues that approach blue, blue-green, and blue-violet. P. 14.

Corbel. A projecting stone used as a support.

Corbeled arch. A constructional device for spanning an opening by projecting successive courses of masonry inward until the opening is closed. Figs. 0–16, 4–8. Not a true arch (*see* Arch).

Corbel table. A projecting course of masonry supported by corbels, frequently connected by arches. Fig. 8–18.

Cornice. The projecting crowning member of the entablature. Fig. 5–5. Also used for any crowning projection. Fig. 9–33.

Cosmati. Cut stone inlay decorations.

Costumbrista. A painter of customs and daily life in Latin America.

Cramp. A device, usually metal, to hold blocks of stone together.

Crocket. A projecting foliate ornament that decorates a capital, pinnacle, gable, buttress, or spire. Fig. 8–62.

Cromlech. A circle of monoliths. Fig. 1–13.

Crossing. The space in a cruciform church where the nave and transept intersect. Fig. 8–40.

Crown of an arch or vault. The topmost part of an arch or vault.

Crypt. A vaulted space under part of a building. In medieval churches, normally the portion under an apse or chevet. It may be wholly or partly underground.

Cuneiform. Literally, wedge-shaped. A system of writing, used in Babylonia-Assyria, in which the characters were wedge-shaped. Fig. 3–6.

Dado. A horizontal band, often decorated, at the base of a wall or pedestal.

Damascene. To inlay metal with another kind of metal or other material for decorative purposes. Fig. 13–15.

Decumanus. The east-west road in an Etruscan or Roman town, intersecting the *cardo* at right angles. Fig. 6–3.

Diptych. Consisting of two leaves. A Roman two-hinged writing tablet; used also for commemorative purposes by the Christian church.

Dolmen. Several large stones capped with a covering slab, erected in prehistoric times. Fig. 1–13.

Donjon. A massive tower forming the stronghold of a medieval castle. Fig. 8–13.

Dowel. A wooden or metallic pin to hold together two pieces of stone or other material.

Drum. The circular wall which supports a dome. Fig. 7–22. An individual circular stone of which a built shaft is made. Fig. 5–9.

Dry point. Engraving in a soft metal, such as copper, with the raised burr retained to produce a soft, richly black effect.

Echinus. Literally, a sea urchin. The convex member of a capital directly underneath the abacus. Fig. 5–5.

Emboss. To ornament a surface with raised work.

Embrasure. The flared opening of a doorway or window. Fig. 8–37.

Enamel. A vitreous, colored paste which solidifies when fired. *See* Champlevé, Cloisonné.

Encaustic. Painting with colored wax, which is afterwards fused with hot irons, thus fixing the colors.

Engaged column. A column-like member forming part of a wall and projecting more or less from it. Fig. 8–43.

Engraving. The process of incising a design upon a substance with a sharp in-strument (*see* Incising). Also the impression made from such a plate. P. 24.

Entablature. The part of a building between the capitals of the columns and the roof or upper story. Fig. 5–5.

Entasis. A slight, almost imperceptible, curvature in the shaft of a column. Fig. 5–5.

Etching. The process of engraving a design upon a copper plate with an acid or mordant. Also the impression from a plate so made. Fig. 10–22.

Façade. Usually, the front of a building. The term also refers to the other sides when they are emphasized architecturally. Fig. 8–36.

Faïence. From Faenza, Italy, a center for the manufacture of majolica. By some authors used exclusively for tin-glazed pottery (except porcelain); used by others as a general term for all kinds of glazed earthenware.

Fan vaulting. A development of lierne vaulting, found in English Perpendicular Gothic, in which the ribs radiate in such a way that they form an inverted cone. Fig. 8–53.

Fenestration. Strictly, the arrangement of the windows in a building; by extension, the arrangement of all the openings (windows, doors, arcades) in architectural design.

Ferro-concrete. See Reinforced concrete.

Figure-ground. The relative clarity with which a form is distinguished from the background against which it is shown; the relationship of figure to background.

Filigree. Delicate and intricate metallic ornament made of fine wire.

Finial. A knoblike ornament, usually with a foliate design, in which a pinnacle terminates. Fig. 8–62.

Flamboyant. Meaning flamelike, applied to the late Gothic style. Fig. 8–57.

Flush. On the same level or plane as the adjoining surfaces.

Flute (fluting). Vertical channeling, usually semicircular. Used principally on columns and pilasters. Figs. 5–5, 5–9.

Flying buttress. See Buttress.

Fresco. A method of painting on freshly applied, moist plaster. The pigments are mixed with water and become chemically incorporated with the plaster. Also a painting so executed. Fig. 8–61.

Fret or *meander*. An ornament consisting of interlocking angular motifs. Frequently in bands but also covering surfaces. Fig. 5–1.

Gargoyle. A waterspout, usually carved, often in the form of a grotesque and used, as part of the general decoration, to throw the water from roof gutters away from the walls.

Genre. Style or subject matter dealing realistically with scenes from everyday life. Fig. 10–24.

Gesso. Prepared plaster mixed with a binding material, used as a ground for painting or for relief.

Glaze. A vitreous coating applied to pottery; used to seal the surface for decorative purposes. For Chinese variants, *see* p. 19.

Golden Mean or *Golden Section*. A system of proportional relationships obtained by dividing a line in such a way that the shorter part is to the longer part as the longer part is to the whole. P. 10.

Gouache. Opaque watercolor; a picture painted in this medium. P. 20; Fig. 13–14.

Granulation. In jewelry a method of ornamenting, in which small grains of metal, usually gold, are soldered to a flat surface.

Greek cross. A cross consisting of two equal bars meeting at right angles.

Groin. The edge formed by the intersection of two vaults. Fig. 8–17.

Groin vault. *See* Vault.

Guilloche. An ornament consisting of interlacing curving bands.

Hammer-beam ceiling. An English Gothic open-timber ceiling.

Haunch. The part of an arch, from a third to two-thirds the distance from the spring to the crown, where the lateral thrust is most strongly exerted.

Heraldic. (a) Relating to the science of heraldry, or to devices, such as coats of arms, which signify genealogical relationships. (b) Symmetrical designs with human figures or animals confronting each other. Figs. 3–8, 3–28.

Herreran style. Architectural style named

for Juan de Herrera (*ca.* 1530–1597), the designer of the Escorial in Spain, whose severe manner displaced the Plateresque style after 1560.

Hieroglyphs or *hieroglyphics*. A system of writing derived from picture writing; used by the ancient Egyptians. By extension, other writings such as the Maya. Fig. 2–25.

High relief. *See* Relief.

Himation. A Greek mantle worn by men and women over the tunic and draped in various ways. Fig. 5–12.

Historiated. Ornamented with figures that have a representational or narrative function, such as plants, animals, or human figures, as distinct from purely decorative elements. Historiated initial letters were a popular form of manuscript decoration in the Middle Ages. Fig. 8–50.

Hogan. An earth-covered lodge of the Navaho Indians.

Hue. The name of a color. The primary hues are blue, red, and yellow, which, together with green, orange, and violet, form the chief colors of the spectrum. Between these lie the intermediates, which partake of the qualifications of both adjacent hues: red-orange, yellow-orange, yellow-green, blue-green, blue-violet, and red-violet. P. 13; Plate 8.

Hydria. A Greek water jar with three handles, two for lifting and one for carrying. Fig. 5–33a.

Hypostyle hall. A hall whose roof is supported by columns. Applied to the colonnaded hall of the Egyptian pylon temple. Figs. 2–18, 2–19.

Icon. Literally, a portrait or image. Used especially in the Greek church for the panels containing representations of sacred personages, which are regarded as objects of veneration. P. 27, note 6; Fig. 12–8.

Iconography. The study of pictorial images and of their symbolic interpretation. P. 27.

Iconology. The study and interpretation of the intrinsic meaning or content of a work of art. P. 27.

Iconostasis. In East Christian churches, a screen or partition, with doors and many tiers of icons, which separates the sanctuary from the main body of the church. Fig. 12–7.

Illumination. To decorate with gold, silver, and bright color, especially the initial letters of a manuscript. An illuminated manuscript may or may not contain miniatures. Fig. 8–1.

Image. The visual impression of what something looks like. In art, an imitation or representation of a person or thing. Pp. 26–27.

Impost block. A truncated, inverted pyramidal-shaped stone placed between a capital and the arch above. Fig. 7–19.

Incising. To cut into a surface with a sharp instrument. A method of decoration, especially on metal and pottery.

Intaglio. A design sunk below the surface so that an impression made from it is in relief. Used especially on gems, seals, and dies for coins. Also applied to an object so decorated. Fig. 5–40.

Intensity. In color, the relative density or opaqueness of a pigment. Pp. 12–13.

Intercolumniation. The space between the columns in a colonnade.

Isocephaly. Literally, heads equal or on a level. A principle by which natural proportion is distorted so as to bring all the objects in a composition to an equal height for the purpose of design. Fig. 5–28.

Jākata. Tales of the past lives of the Buddha. P. 518.

Jube. A choir screen treated as an architectural ornament.

Kakemono. A Chinese or Japanese painting in the form of a hanging, not framed but mounted on brocade.

Keystone. The uppermost voussoir in an arch (*see* Voussoir).

Kiva. The underground ceremonial chamber in Pueblo villages. P. 620.

Krater (*crater*). A large bowl for mixing wine and water. Fig. 4–14.

Ku. A tall, narrow beaker; a ritual Chinese bronze. Fig. 15–4.

Kylix (*cylix*). A Greek drinking cup. Fig. 5–33(*e*).

Lacquer. A resinous varnish. The Chinese and Japanese lacquer is obtained by making incisions in the bark of the *Rhus vernicifera* tree. P. 570.

Lantern. A small structure that crowns a dome, turret, or roof. It has openings for lighting, though frequently the primary purpose is decorative. Fig. 9–13.

Latin cross. A cross consisting of two bars meeting at right angles, the lower part of the vertical bar longer than the upper.

Li. A hollow-legged tripod. Originally in prehistoric China a pottery form; later used in ritual bronzes.

Lierne. In architecture, a short crossrib inserted between the main ribs of a vaulting.

Light. The illumination that defines the forms of matter in space. P. 11.

Line. The identifiable path of a point moving in space. P. 8.

Lintel. A horizontal beam of any material used to span an opening. Figs. 0–16, 5–9.

Lithograph. The impression of a design made on stone with a greasy pencil or crayon. Fig. 0–24.

Local color. The actual color of an object. P. 662.

Loggia. A gallery that has an open arcade or colonnade on one side. Fig. 9–84.

Lunette. Literally, little or half-moon; especially a wall space over an arched door, niche, or window. Fig. 9–14.

Luster. A thin glaze, usually metallic, sometimes used on pottery to produce a rich, often iridescent, color when it catches the light. Found especially in Persian wares and in Spanish and Italian majolica.

Majolica. Specifically, a kind of Italian pottery coated with a whitish tin enamel, brilliantly painted and often lustered.

Makimono. A Chinese or Japanese painting in the form of a long scroll.

Mandala. A magic diagram of the cosmos in Hindu symbolism. P. 523.

Mandorla. An almond-shaped nimbus, or glory, surrounding the figure of Christ. Fig. 8–6.

Mandapa. In Hindu architecture, an assembly hall attached to a temple.

Mass. The effect and degree of bulk, density, and weight of matter in space. Pp. 6–7.

Mastaba. Literally, a bench. A bench-shaped Egyptian tomb.

Medallion. A decorative, medal-shaped panel, usually enclosing a figure, portrait, or ornament. Figs. 7–17, 9–14.

Medium. The vehicle or liquid with which pigment is mixed, such as water, egg, oil, wax. In a more general sense, the substance, material, or agency through which an artist expresses his idea, such as stone, pigment, metal, wood, enamel, words, tones, movements.

Megaron. A large, rectangular living hall, traditional in the Aegean area. Fig. 4–9.

Menhir. Prehistoric monoliths, uncut or roughly cut, standing singly or in rows or circles. Fig. 1–14.

Mestizo. Half-breed. Used of the provincial architecture of the Spanish colonies in America (the term confuses ethnic and artistic conceptions).

Metope. The space between two triglyphs in a Doric frieze. Fig. 5–5.

Mihrab. The niche in a mosque which indicates the direction of Mecca. Figs. 13–2, 13–10.

Minaret. A tall slender tower belonging to a mosque, with one or more balconies from which the summons to prayer is chanted. Fig. 13–13.

Miniature. A small picture illustrating a manuscript. Derived from the Latin verb *miniare,* to decorate with vermilion. By extension, any small portrait, often on ivory or porcelain. Fig. 8–4.

Mithuna. Term for an amorous couple in Hindu art. Fig. 14–10.

Modeling. Gradations of light and shade reflected from the surfaces of matter in space, or the illusion of such gradations on a two-dimensional surface as in a drawing or painting. P. 13.

Module or *modular.* The use of a common denomination in the measurements of different parts of a site, building, piece of sculpture, or other work of art. P. 10.

Molding. An architectural term for a continuous narrow surface, either projecting or recessed, plain or ornamented, whose purpose is to break up a surface, to accent, or to decorate by means of the light and shade it produces.

Monolith. A single stone block, large in size. Fig. 1–13.

Montage. A composition made by fitting together parts of various photographs. Also motion picture effects produced by superimposing images (*see* Collage).

Monumental. In this text, used as an adjective to describe the effect of unpretentious grandeur in a work of art, irrespective of its size.

Morphology. The study and interpretation of the forms of matter in space. P. 28.

Mosaic. A surface of decoration made of small pieces of stone or glass (tesserae) set in cement. Plate 2.

Mosque (masjid). A Moslem place of worship. Fig. 13–13.

Mudejar. A Moslem who, though subject to a Christian ruler, still retains his religion, laws, and customs. By extension, the Moorish-influenced art of Christian Spain and the Spanish colonies.

Mudra. Mystic ritual gestures of Hindu deities, signifying various actions and powers. Fig. 14–12.

Mullion. A vertical bar that separates a window into sections with more than one light. Fig. 8–39.

Narthex. A porch, generally colonnaded or arcaded, forming the vestibule of a church. Figs. 7–6, 7–9.

Nave. From *navis,* ship, an early symbol of the Church. The part of a church located between the chief entrance and the chancel, and separated from the aisles (if they are present) by piers or columns. Figs. 8–40, 8–41.

Necking. A gorge at the bottom of the Greek Doric capital between the echinus and the grooves, which masks the junction of capital and shaft. Fig. 5–5.

Niello. Inlay of gold or silver in other metals, such as bronze or steel.

Obverse of a coin or medal. The side of a coin or medal that bears the principal type or inscription. The opposite side is the *reverse.*

Ogee. A molding having a double or S-shaped curve. An arch of this form.

Oenochoë. A Greek wine pitcher. Fig. 5–33 f.

Open form. Matter which has been perforated or treated in such a way that space acts as its environment rather than as its limit (*see* Closed form). Pp. 7–8.

Order. In classical architecture, the design of the column and entablature. Fig. 5–5. *See also* Superimposed order.

Pagoda. In China and Japan, a tower of several stories, usually associated with a temple or monastery. Fig. 16–9.

Pastel. Pigments, in the form of powders, compressed into sticks. Also the work of art which results from their use. P. 20.

Patina. An incrustation that forms on bronze through chemical action. The term is also applied to incrustation on other materials.

Patio. In Spanish architecture, a court open to the sky.

Pediment. The triangular space (gable) at the end of a building, formed by the sloping roof. Fig. 5–23. Also an ornamental feature of this character.

Pendentive. A concave, triangular piece of masonry (a triangular section of a hemisphere). By means of pendentives a dome can be erected over a square area, and the pendentives carry its load to the isolated supports at the four corners. Fig. 7–10.

Peripteral. Surrounded by a colonnade. Fig. 5–4.

Peristyle. A continuous range of columns surrounding a building or a court. Fig. 2–17.

Perspective. A scheme, or formula, for representing, on one plane, distance and distant objects. P. 9.

Photomontage. A combination of several photographs or parts of photographs into one composition. *See* Montage.

Pi. Chinese jade disk, the symbol of Heaven. Fig. 15–6.

Piano nobile. The principal story, usually the second, in Renaissance buildings. P. 361.

Pier. A vertical masonry support to carry the load of a superstructure.

Pilaster. A flat rectangular member projecting from the wall, of which it forms a part. It usually has a base and a capital and is often fluted. Figs. 8–17, 9–14.

Pile fabric. A textile in which extra warps or wefts, looped above the surface and then cut, form a pile or nap, as in velvets and carpets.

Pillar. A general inclusive term used for a weight-carrying member of any kind. It may be a pier or a column. Also an isolated structure used for a commemorative purpose.

Pinnacle. An upright architectural member generally ending in a small spire, often ornamental, but used functionally in Gothic architecture to give additional weight to a buttress or an angle pier.

Plan. A drawing or diagram showing a horizontal section of a building or site. *Axial plan*: one in which the parts of a building are organized longitudinally, or on a given direction in space. *Central plan*: one which radiates around a given point. P. 15.

Plane. A flat, continuous surface which does not change direction. P. 6.

Plastic. Literally, the molding or shaping of matter. Often used to describe the quality of matter which lends itself to molding, or to the effect of this molding (*see* Modeling).

Plateresque. A style of architectural decoration in Spain (*ca.* 1470–1560), including both Medieval and Renaissance ornamental systems. The term alludes to jewel-like enrichment (*platero* – silver-smith).

Plinth. The lowest member of a base; also a block serving as a base for a statue.

Porcelain. Strictly speaking, pottery, made on a base of kaolin, that is translucent, impervious, and resonant. By extension the term is sometimes applied to pottery which is translucent, whether made of kaolin or not.

Pottery. Objects of any kind which are made of clay and hardened by firing.

Predella. Literally, a footstool. In Italian art the narrow panel, at the back of the altar, on which the altarpiece rests.

Primary colors. Red, yellow, and blue hues. P. 13.

Program. The architect's solution for problems arising from the site of a building and its surroundings, from the purpose of the building, the special requirements of the client, or the materials available for construction. It is the totality of a building, and by extension may also refer to the same totality in any work of art. P. 16.

Pronaos. The enclosed space in front of the cella of a Greek temple.

Proportion. The mathematical relation or ratio of the parts of a building or of an object to each other and to the whole. P. 10.

Putto (pl., putti). A young boy. A favorite subject in Italian painting and sculpture. Fig. 9–37.

Pylon. The monumental entrance of an Egyptian temple. Fig. 2–17.

Quoin. A large, slightly projecting stone at the angle of a building, sometimes rusticated. Fig. 9–72.

Raking cornice. The cornice on the sloping sides of a pediment. Fig. 5–5.

Ramp. An inclined plane that takes the place of steps in the ascent of a structure.

Reinforced concrete (ferro-concrete). Concrete strengthened by iron or steel networks or bars embedded before the concrete hardens.

Reja. Wrought iron grille in Hispanic lands.

Relief. In sculpture, figures projecting from a background to which they are attached. They may be cut deeply (high relief) or shallowly (low or *bas relief*), or sunk into the surface (hollow relief or *intaglio*). P. 16.

Reliquary. A small receptacle for holding a sacred relic. Usually of precious material richly decorated.

Repoussé. The process of decorating metal by beating it into relief from the back, leaving the impression on the face. The metal plate is hammered into a hollow mold of wood or some pliable material with hammer and punch and finished with the graver. Fig. 0–19.

Respond. An engaged column, pilaster, or similar projection in a pier or other supporting architectural device. Fig. 8–42.

Retable or *Retablo.* Shortened form of *retrotabulum,* behind the altar. An architectural screen or wall facing set up behind an altar, usually containing painting, sculpture, carving, or other decorations. The Spanish retable is especially elaborate. Figs. 9–46, 11–19.

Reverse of a coin or medal. The side opposite the obverse (*see* Obverse).

Rib. A molded masonry arch, projecting from the surface. In Gothic architecture the ribs form the framework of the vaulting. Fig. 8–31.

Rinceau. An ornamental design composed of undulating, foliate vine motifs. Fig. 6–34.

Roof comb. A pierced wall rising above the roof. Found in Maya architecture. Fig. 17–4.

Rose or wheel window. The round window with tracery frequently found on the façades of Gothic churches. Fig. 8–36.

Rusticated stone. Stone masonry with beveled joints and roughened surface. Fig. 9–79.

Santo. In New Mexico, the painted image of a saint.

Sarcophagus. A stone coffin. Fig. 7–17.

Scale. The mathematical relation or ratio of the parts or totality of a building or of an object to its use or function or to the size of the original form. P. 10.

Sculpture in the round. Free-standing figures, carved or modeled in three dimensions.

Secondary colors. The colors (green, orange, purple) which result from mixture of the primary colors. P. 13.

Serdab. A tiny secret chamber in a Pyramid to hold the statue of the deceased. Fig. 2–7.

Sgraffito. Decoration produced by scratching through a surface layer of plaster, glazing, etc., to reveal a differently colored ground. Also pottery or other ware so decorated.

Shaft. The part of a column between the capital and base. Fig. 5–5.

Sign. A form which, by convention, has an independent, specific meaning (*see* Symbol). Pp. 26–27.

Sikara. In Hindu architecture the high tower that rises over the shrine of the temples of Vishnu. Fig. 14–15.

Silhouette. A two-dimensional outline of an object in space. P. 8.

Soffit. The underside of an architectural member, such as an arch, lintel, cornice, or stairway.

Spandrel. The triangular space between

the curve of two arches. It is frequently decorated. Fig. 8–23.

Splayed opening. A splay (a shortened form of display) is a large chamfer. In splayed openings the wall is cut away diagonally so that the outer opening is wider than the inner. Fig. 8–36.

Squinch. An architectural device to make a transition from a square to a polygonal base for a dome. It may be composed of lintels, corbels, or arches. Fig. 7–10.

Stalactite. A pendant architectural ornament common in Mohammedan architecture. Fig. 13–9.

Stele. A stone slab or pillar used as a gravestone, or to mark a site. Fig. 17–6.

Stilted arch or dome. An arch or dome having its springing higher than the level of the impost. Fig. 7–22.

Stoa. In Greek architecture, a building whose roof is supported by a row of columns parallel to the back wall.

Stone mosaic. A kind of decoration made with small pieces of cut stone embedded in cement. Used most effectively by the Maya. Fig. 17–14.

Stoneware. A kind of pottery of the nature of porcelain but with a coarser base.

Strapwork. A carved or molded decoration which looks like cut and rolled leather. Fig. 9–98.

Stringcourse. A horizontal molding to indicate a division in the architectural design. Fig. 9–33.

Stucco. Fine plaster or cement used as a coating for walls or for decorations.

Stupa. In the Buddhist architecture of India, a domelike structure which marks a sacred site. Fig. 14–6.

Style. (a) A special and superior quality in a work of art. (b) A coherent grouping of forms united by reciprocal fitness, which is expressive of a civilization, of a people, or of an individual. P. 27.

Stylobate. The upper step of the base of a Greek temple which forms a platform for the columns. Figs. 5–5, 5–6.

Superimposed order. The placing of one order of architecture above another in an arcaded or colonnaded building: usually Doric on the first story, Ionic on the second, and Corinthian on the third. Found in Greek *stoas,* used widely by the Romans, and thence by Renaissance builders. Fig. 6–26.

Sutra. Sacred Buddhist text, usually one attributed to Buddha himself.

Symbol. An object or its image or a sign which has meanings other than its own. Pp. 26–27.

Tactile. Referring to the sense of touch. P. 17.

Technique. Method or procedure involved in transforming matter or artistic media into a work of art. P. 20.

Tempera. A technical method of painting upon an especially prepared panel with pigment mixed with egg, glue, or milk. P. 21.

Tenebrist. Among seventeenth-century European painters, those who used violent contrasts of light and dark. Fig. 10–39.

Terra cotta. Hard baked clay used for sculpture and as a building material. It may or may not be glazed or painted. Fig. 15–16.

Tesserae. Small pieces of glass or stone used in making mosaics.

Texture. The sensuous or tangible quality of a surface. The simulation of such qualities in drawing or painting. P. 14.

Tholos. A circular Greek building.

Thrust. The outward force exerted by an arch or vault which must be counterbalanced by abutments.

Tierceron. In a Gothic vault, a supplementary arch or rib which joins two other ribs. Its function is decorative.

Ting. A Chinese ritual bronze, a hemisphere on three solid legs.

Tonality. The relative purity of a color. *See* Chroma. P. 13.

Tondo. A painting or piece of relief sculpture in circular format. Fig. 9–59.

Toranas. Gateways at cardinal points of the compass in the circular railings surrounding Buddhist stupas. Fig. 14–6.

Torus. A convex molding, or part of a molding, which is semicircular in profile.

Totem. An animal or object, its representation or image, considered as a symbol of a given family or clan. Fig. 18–7.

Trabeated. Built with horizontal beams, or lintels.

Tracery. Stone ornament that decorates a window and holds the glass; particularly characteristic of Gothic.

Transept. In a cruciform church, the arm

at right angles to the nave. Fig. 8–40.

Triforium. In a Gothic cathedral, the passageway in the thickness of the wall, opening on the nave through an arcade, situated between the principal nave arcade and the clerestory. Fig. 8–42.

Triglyph. The projecting grooved member of the Doric frieze separating the metopes. Fig. 5–5.

Trumeau. A median jamb or support in the center of a Romanesque or Gothic portal. Fig. 8–22.

Tympanum. The space over a doorway enclosed by the lintel and the arch. Fig. 8–22.

Ushnisha. Protruberance on the head of Buddha emblematic of his more than mortal knowledge and consciousness. Fig. 14–11.

Value. The amount of light and dark in a color. The greater the amount of light, the higher its value; the greater the amount of dark, the lower its value. P. 13.

Vault. A stone, brick, or concrete roof constructed on the arch principle. A barrel vault is semicylindrical in shape. Figs. 6–21, 8–15. A groin vault consists of two barrel vaults intersecting at right angles. Figs. 6–21, 8–17. A ribbed vault is one in which there is a framework of ribs or arches under the intersections of the vaulting sections. Figs. 8–33, 8–34. A dome is a hemispherical vault. Fig. 7–10.

Volume. The manner in which space is organized by mass. Pp. 6–7.

Volute. A spiral scroll, especially charac-

teristic of the Greek Ionic capital. Fig. 5–5.

Voussoir. A wedge-shaped block used in the construction of a true arch. The central voussoir, which sets the arch, is called the keystone (*see* Arch). Fig. 0–16.

Wainscot. A wooden facing for an interior wall, usually paneled.

Wall arcade. *See* Blind arcade.

Warm color. Red and the hues that approach red, orange, yellow, and possibly yellow-green. P. 14.

Warp. The lengthwise threads with which a loom is strung.

Water color. Pigments mixed with water and applied to an absorbent surface, or the painting produced by this means. P. 20.

Weft (woof). The thread which is inserted in the warp at right angles in the process of weaving.

Westwork. A multistoried mass, usually surmounted by towers, at the western end of a Medieval church. Fig. 8–20.

Woodcut. A design engraved upon a block of wood in such a way that all the wood is cut away to a slight depth except the lines forming the design. Also the printed impression made from the wood block. Fig. 0–23.

Yaksha (m.), *yakshi* (f.) Male and female divinities originally worshiped as local nature spirits, and later incorporated into the Buddhist and Hindu pantheons.

Ziggurat. In Babylonia-Assyria, a staged tower with ramps for ascents. Fig. 3–2.

INDEX

INDEX

(Page numbers in italic indicate illustrations.)

arcade: Islamic, 493, 507, 509; Renaissance, 319; Romanesque, 231, 232, 233, 235
arch: Babylonian, 74; corbeled, *16*, 480; diagrams of, *16*; Etruscan, 156; Gothic, 246–47; horseshoe, 493; Islamic, 493, 507; pointed, 231, 247, *247*; Roman, 168–73, *169*, *171*, *172*; Romanesque, 231; Sumerian, 74 (*see also* vaults and vaulting)
Arch of Constantine, Rome, 183, *183*
Arch of Septimius Severus, Africa, 177: relief from, 182, *182*
Arch of Titus, Rome, 172, *172*: relief from, 180, *181*
Archaic style, of Greek art, 108, 117, 119, 121, 123, 135, 145, 149
archeology, 33: art and, 27; 18th-century developments in, 469
Archer, Frederick Scott, 741
Archers of St. Adrian (Hals), *409*, 410
architect, 15–16
architectural ornament: Greek, 111, 115–17; Inca, 614; Islamic, 495, 498; Maya, 596, 598–601; Mexican, 603; Roman, 176–77; Romanesque, 234; of Romantic Naturalism, 775; Spanish, 390–91 (*see also* frieze; relief sculpture)
"Architectural" style, of Roman wall painting, *162–65*, 165–66
architecture, 14–16: Achaemenian, 86–87; Aegean, 96–99; Andean, 608–09, 611, 612, 613; Assyrian, 81–82; Babylonian, 74–75; Barbarian, 220; Baroque, 398–401, 416, 421–23; Byzantine, 208; Carolingian, 224–27; Chaldean, 84–86; Chinese, 544, 549, 552, 557, 567–68; Early Christian, 194–201; Egyptian, 49–53, 58, 59–64, 69; 18th-century, 438–40; English, 234, 265–67, 280, 432–35, 438–40, 766–72, 779; English colonial, 464–70; Etruscan, 154–56; French, 224–25, 229–34, 245–49, 256–59, 262–63, 280–81, 385–87, 420–25; French colonial, 458–62; German, 234, 268–69, 780–81; Gothic, 246–49, 256–59, 261–63, 266–74, 280–81; Greek, 110–17, 140–41; Hispanic American, 454–55; of India, 515–20, 523–31; Islamic, 492–94, 498–502, 506–09; Italian, 234–35, 273–74, 300–01, 314–19, 356–62, 366–69, 373–77, 398–402; Japanese, 570, 572, 575–77, 585; Maya, 594–600; Mexican, 444–47; 19th-century, 765–74, 779; North American Indian, 619–20; prehistoric, 44–45; Renaissance, 300–02, 314–19, 343, 356–62, 365–69, 373, 374–76, 377, 385–87, 390–91; Rococo, 423–25; Roman, 168–77, 185; Romanesque, 228–29, 231–35, 241–42; Russian, 478–81, 485–87; Sassanian, 91; sculpture

and, 16; South American, 447–54; Southeast Asian, 533–38; Spanish, 235, 270–71, 377, 390–91, 492, 498–99, 775–76; 20th-century, 709, 774–84; United States, 767–79, 781–82 (*see also* domestic architecture)
architrave: Doric, *110*, 115; Ionic, *110*, 116
archivolt, 237 *n.*
Ardebil carpet, 504–05, *505*
area, 6
Arena chapel, Padua, 273–74; fresco, *276*, 277
Argentina, 451
Aristotle, 140
Armory Show, 693, 718, 719
Arp, Hans, 710 *n.*
Arrentine bowls, 184
ars et scientia, 245, 248
art: as abstraction, 4; definition of, 3; form in, 5–11; forms of, 14–26; light in, 11–14
art academies (*see* academies of art)
Art Nouveau, of 19th-century architecture, 775
Artemis, temple of: Corfu, pediment, 123, *123*; Eleusis, plan, *109*; Ephesus, 140
artist: attitude of, in China, 541–42; attitude of primitive, 632; creative process of, 327; role of 19th-century, 675–76, 686; role of, in Renaissance Italy, 290–91
Arts and Crafts movement, 682
Arundel Psalter, 268
Ascension church, Kolomenskoe, 477, 480
Ascension of Christ (Tintoretto), *374, 374*
"Ash Can school," 691
Ashanti goldwork, 636, *637*
Ashikaga period of Japanese art, 581–85
Asia, Southeast, art of, 533–38 (*see also* India)
Asia Minor, 107, 140, 150: map, *106, 190*
Aśoka, Emperor of India, 515–18: columns of, *511*, 516; stupas of, 517–18
Assisi church, 277 *n.*
Assumption of the Virgin (El Greco), 392–93; (Titian), 355, *356*
Assurbanipal, palace of, 82, *82–84*
Assurnasirpal II, palace of, *81*, 82, 83
Assyrian art, 72, 79–84, 93
Asuka style in Japan, 572–73
At the Moulin Rouge (Toulouse-Lautrec), *651, 667*
At the Mountain of the Bull (Klee), 717, *717*
Atget, Jean-Eugène-Auguste, 747–48: *Shop Window, Paris, 747*
Athena, 150
Athena Nike (Nike Apteros), temple of: parapet, 130–31, *130*
Athena Promachos (Phidias), 113
Athens, 107, 131, 150 (*see also* Acropolis; Parthenon)

Atl, Dr., 730
atrium: of Early Christian basilica, *194*, *195*; Etruscan, 156; Roman, *161*, 163
Augustan Age, 178–79
Augustus, statue of, 178, *178*
Aurangabad cave temple, relief from, 528, *529*
Aurangzebe, 509
Aurignacian period: sculpture in, 42, *42*; toolmaking in, 36
Autun cathedral: aisle, 233, *233;* tympanum, 238, *240*
avatars of Vishnu, 524
Avebury Circle, 44–45, *45*
Averlino, Antonio (*see* Filarete)
Ávila cathedral, 270
axis, 8–9
Aztec culture, 593, 604, 606–08, 615

Babylon, 73, 84–86
Babylonian art, 72–79, 93: architecture, 74–75; bibliography, 93; metalwork, 77–79; sculpture, 75–77 (*see also* Chaldean art)
Baciccio (*see* Gaulli, Giovanni Battista)
Bacon, Robert, 728
Badami cave temple, India: Śiva relief, 523, *525;* Vishnu relief, 524
Baghdad, 492, 500
Bakota ancestor figure, 638, *638*
Baldovinetti, Alleso, 305
Balla, Giocomo, 706: *The Dog on Leash*, *706*
Baluba stool, *638*, 639
Bambara antelope headdress, *632*, 637–38
Bamberg cathedral, 268
Banco, Nanni di, 292–93, 304: *Isaiah*, 293; *Quattro Santi Coronati*, *293*
Bank of England, London, 779
Baptism of Christ (della Francesca), 305, 306
Bar at the Folies-Bergères (Manet), 663, *664*
Barabudur, Java: stupa, 534–35, *534:* detail, *534*
Barbarian nations and Barbarian art, 217–20: metal work, 218–19; painting, 219–20; sculpture, 220
Barbaro, Danielo, 737
Barbizon school, 657–58: influence of, in United States, 684
Bare Willows and Distant Mountains (Ma Yüan), *560*, 561
Barlach, Ernst, 753–54: *War Memorial for the Güstrow Cathedral*, *754*
Barnard, George N., 743: *Ruins of the Railroad Depot*, *743*
Baroque art, 360–61, 376, 377, 397–438: architecture, 398–401, 416, 421–23; bibliography, 443; in England, 432–38; in

France, 420–23, 425–30; in Hispanic America, 456–57; in Low Countries, 406–15; 19th-century romanticism and, 655; painting, 402–15, 416–19, 426–30; sculpture, 401–02, 415–16, 425; in Spain, 415–19
Barquq, El, tomb mosque of, *501*
Barr, Alfred H., Jr., 699 *n.*
barrel vault: Babylonian, 74; Etruscan, 154; Renaissance, 319; Roman, 168–69, *168*, *169*, *173*, 175; Romanesque, 231, *232* (*see also* vaults and vaulting)
Barry, Sir Charles, 767, 768: Houses of Parliament, *767;* Reform Club building, 768
Bartlett, William Henry, 693
Bartolommeo, Fra (Baccio della Porta), 346
Barye, Antoine Louis, 751
bas relief, sculpture in, 16 (*see also* relief sculpture)
basilica, 112: Early Christian, *194–96*, 195–98, *198–200*, 200, 207; Greek, 140–41; Roman, 171–72 (*see also* churches)
Basilica of Maxentius (or Constantine), Rome, 169, *169*, 175
Basilica Ulpia, 172
basketry, North American Indian, 618, 620–21, 626
Basu, Sanjūsangendō, 580
Bathers (Picasso), 8, *8*
baths, Roman, 172–73, *173:* plan, *172*
Baths of Caracalla, Rome, 172, *172:* plan, *172*
batik, 26
battening, 26
Battle of Anghiari (da Vinci), 344
Battle of Bunker Hill (Trumbull), 683
Battle of the Cascina (Michelangelo), 344
Battle of the Nudes (Pollaiuolo), 321
Battle of Yorktown (Trumbull), 683
Baudelaire, Charles, 656–57
Bauhaus, Germany, 709, 780
Bayeux Tapestry, 229
Bayfield, Fanny Wright, 693
beadwork, Plains Indian, 627
Beal, Gifford Reynolds, 690 *n.*
Beatus, illumination of *The Apocalypse of St. Sever*, 240, *242*
Beauvais cathedral, 253, 262–63: choir, *263*
Beckmann, Max, 718
beehive tomb, Mycenaean, 99, *100*
Belgium, 382, 408 (*see also* Low Countries)
Belle Jardinière (Raphael), 345 *n.*
Belleville Breviary (Pucelle), *264*, 265
Bellini, Giovanni, 352–53, 355: San Giobbe altarpiece, *353;* San Zaccaria altarpiece, 353
Bellows, George, 692

Bend in the Road (Cézanne), Plate 7
Benin bronzes, 633, 636, *636*
Benjamin, Asher, 469
Benton, Thomas Hart, 725–26
Berenson, Bernard, 28
Bermejo, Bartolomé, 342
Bernard, Emile, 701
Bernini, Giovanni Lorenzo, 6, 359 *n.*, 398, 399, 401–02, 409, 415, 425: baldachino over altar of St. Peter's, *399; Cardinal Scipione Borghese, 403; Ecstasy of St. Teresa, 402;* piazza of St. Peter's, 399
Berruguete, Alonso, 391: *St. Peter,* 391
Berthon, Georges Theodore, 693
Bertoldo, Giovanni, 348
Bertrand du Guesclin, tomb of, 281, *282*
Bhagavad-Gita, 522
Biblical history: in Byzantine art, 209; in Early Christian art, 193, 203, 204
Bibliothèque Sainte-Geneviève, 768
Biddle, Owen, 469
Biema, Carry van, 13 *n.*
Bierstadt, Albert, 683, 684
bifacial toolmaking, 35–37
Bihzad, 502
Bingham, George Caleb, 685 *n.*
Bird in Space (Brancusi), 759–60, *759*
Birth of Venus (Botticelli), 323
Birth of Venus (Cabanel), 653, *654*
Bishop Berkeley and His Entourage (Smibert), 472–73, *472*
Bison with Turned Head, Magdalenian, *33,* 38
Black Death, 272, 279
Blade tradition, of toolmaking, 36
Bladelin altarpiece (van der Weyden), 335, *336*
Blake, William, 680–81: *When the Morning Stars Sang Together, 680*
Blakelock, Ralph A., 688
blankets: Chilkat, 625, *627;* Navaho, 628, *629*
Blashfield, Edwin H., 686 *n.*
Blenheim Palace, 434–35, *435:* parks of, 771
Blois chateau, 386: Orleans wing, *420,* 421
Blondeel, Lancelot, 383
Bloom, Hyman, 724
Blue Mosque (Ahmediyeh), Constantinople, 500, *501*
Blue Rider group, 699–700
Blume, Peter, 722, *723*
Boas, Franz, 623
Boccioni, Umberto, 706, 758: *Unique Forms of Continuity in Space, 758*
Bodhisattva, 520: Angkor Thom, *538;* T'ang dynasty, 552, *552 (see also* Buddha images)
Boffrand, Germain: Hotel de Soubise, decorations, *423*
Bogotá, 457

Bologna, Giovanni da, 371 72: Fountain of Neptune, sea nymphs, 371; *Mercury, 371*
Bonampak, Central America, 596, 601: mural at, *601*
bone, Paleolithic artifacts of, *37, 38*
book covers, Carolingian, *20, 223, 223*
book illustration: in Hispanic America, 456; in 16th century, 380 (*see also* engraving; manuscript illumination; woodcuts)
Book of Job, Blake's illustration for, *680*
Book of Kells, 219
Borromini, Francesco, 398, 399, 425: San Carlo alle Quattro Fontane, 399: plan, *400*
Bosch, Hieronymus, 384: *Temptation of St. Anthony, 383*
Boscoreale Treasure, 183
Botticelli, Sandro, 310, 321–24, 336: *Adoration of the Magi, 323; Birth of Venus,* 323; *"Calumny" of Apelles, 323, 324;* drawings for *Divine Comedy, 322–23, 322; Garden of Venus,* called *Primavera,* 323; Sistine Chapel frescoes, 324
Boucher, François, 430: *Toilet of Venus, 397*
Bound Slave (Unfinished) (Michelangelo), *5, 6*
Bourdelle, Emile Antoine, 756
Bourges cathedral, 16, 256–58: nave and aisles, *256;* plan, *255, 256;* royal portals, 250 *n.;* stained glass, 261
Bourke-White, Margaret, 749 *n.*
Bouts, Dirck, 337
brackets in Chinese architecture, 567
Brady, Mathew B., 742
Bramante, Donato, 318–19, 325, 346, 358–60
Brancacci Chapel, Florence: Masaccio's frescoes, 297–99
Brancusi, Constantin, 758–60: *Bird in Space, 759*
Braque, Georges, 701 *n.*, 702–05: *Musical Forms, 705*
Brazil, 452–54
Breakfast Scene (Hogarth), 437, *437*
Breaking Home Ties (Hovenden), 691
Breasted, James H., 49 *n.*
Breton, André, 713
Breuer, Marcel, 785
Breughel the Elder, Pieter, 384–85: *Wedding Dance, 384*
brick, use of: Assyrian, 81–82; Early Christian, 200; English colonial, 465; Etruscan, 155; French colonial, 461; Islamic, 499; Roman, 168, 172, 173; Russian, 479, 480; Sassanian, 91; Sumerian, 74
Bridge group, the, 699
Bridges, Charles, 471
bridges, 19th-century, 772

Carrà, Carlo, 706 n.
Carracci, Annibale, 402–03, 407, 426: *Polyphemus Hurling Rocks at Acis*, 403
Carter, Howard, 59 n.
Cartier-Bresson, Henri, 749: *Gare Saint-Lazare, Paris*, 748
cartoon, in fresco, 21
Carucci, Jacopo (*see* Pontormo, Il)
carving: as sculptural technique, 17; Paleolithic, 38–39 (*see also* gem carving; sculpture; woodcarving)
Caryatids (Goujon), 388
Casa Milá, Barcelona, 771
Cassatt, Mary, 690 n.
Castagno, Andrea del, 303–04: *Last Supper*, 304
Castelfranco Madonna (Giorgione), 354, 354
Castiglione, Baldassare, 329
Castillo, El, Chichen Itza, 599–600, 599
castle, feudal, 229, 229
Catalonia, churches of, 235
cathedrals, Gothic, 243–54; Le Secq's photographs of, 741; plans, 254–55 (*see also specific cathedral* and Gothic art)
Catherine II, Russia, 486
Catholicism (*see* Early Christianity and Early Christian art; Eastern Orthodox Church; Roman Catholic Church)
Catholicon, Hosios Lucas, mosaic bust of Christ, 211, 211
Cavallini, Pietro, 275–76
cave paintings, Paleolithic, 39–42
cave temples: Chinese Buddhist, 549; Hindu, 523, 527–28, 528; Indian Buddhist, 516–17, 519, 528, 529
ceilings: decoration of, in Moorish style, 452; painting of, in Baroque period, 405; in Perpendicular style, 280 (*see also* dome; Sistine Chapel)
celadon ware, 562
cella, 109
Cellini, Benvenuto, 18, 371, 372, 377, 388, 389: *Diana of Fontainebleau*, 388; *Perseus*, 372
Celtic design, 219–20
Cenninni, Cennino, 291 n.
Cenno di Pepi (*see* Cimabue)
Central American arts and culture, 594–608, 615: 19th-century, 693–95
central-plan church, 399–400: Byzantine, 208; Early Christian, 198–200; Renaissance, 318, 358
ceramics, 18–19: Chaldean, 85–86, 85; Chinese, 557, 557, 562–63, 562, 566–67; Islamic, 503–04; Latin American, 694; Mexican, 446–47 (*see also* pottery and pottery-making)
Ceylon, India, stupas, 533
Cézanne, Paul, 23, 167, 658, 667–71, 677, 701, 702, 707, 719, 723: *Bend in the Road*, Plate 7; *The Card Player* (drawing), 3; *The Card Players*, 672; *Mont-Sainte-Victoire*, 20, 671; *Still Life* (ca. 1890), 670

Chaco Canyon, New Mexico, 620
Chagall, Marc, 716, 718: *Crucifixion*, 716
chaitya cave, 525: at Karle, India, 519–20, 519–21
Chaldean art, 84–86, 93: architecture, 84–86; bibliography, 93
Chalice of Antioch, 189, 206
Chalukyan temples, 524
Chambord, chateau de, 385, 386
Chanchan, Peru, 612
Chandigarh capitol building, India, 783, 783
Chang Ta-chen, 566
Chao Meng-fu, 563: *A Sheep and a Goat*, 564
chapels, in Romanesque church, 230, 231 (*see also specific chapel*)
charcoal, 23
Chardin, Jean-Baptiste Siméon, 431: *Still Life*, 431
Charging Mammoth (Paleolithic) 38, 38
Charioteer of Delphi, 5, 31, 119–20
Charlemagne, 221
Charlot, Jean, 730
Charonton, Enguerrand, 340: *Coronation of the Virgin*, 340
Chartres cathedral, 243, 256–58: air views of chevet, 243; nave, 257; plan, 254, 256; royal portals, 249–51, 250–51; stained glass, 261, Plate 4; statue columns, 251, 252; statues, 187
Chase, William Merritt, 686 n., 691 n.
chasing in metalwork, 19
Chateau de Ramezay, Montreal, 458
Chateau Gaillard, 229, 229
chateaux: Baroque, 420, 421; Renaissance, 385–87, 385; Romanesque, 229, 229
Chavannes, Pierre Puvis de, 653–54
Chavin: culture, 608, 615; sculpture, 608, 609
Cheops (*see* Khufuw)
Chetro Ketl, 620
chevet, 243: plan, 254–55; Romanesque, 233, 234
Ch'i Pai-shih, 566
chiaroscuro, 12
Chicago Tribune Tower, 744
Chichen Itza, Yucatan, 598–600: *El Castillo*, 599; *Temple of the Warriors*, 600
Ch'ien-lung, 567
Chile, pre-Columbian culture in, 608, 611, 612
Chilkat blankets, 625, 627
Chimu culture, 593, 612
Ch'in dynasty, 546–47
China and Chinese art: architecture, 544, 549, 552, 557, 567–68; bibliography,

manesque, 234, 239–40; sculpture, 267, 754–55; 20th-century, 728–29, 754–55

English colonial art, 463–74: bibliography, 475–76

engraving: of Blake, 681; of Dürer, 380, *380, 381;* in metalwork, 19; Paleolithic, 38–39; of Posada, 729–30; printmaking by, 24–25

Entrance of the Crusaders into Constantinople (Delacroix), 655, *656*

eoliths, 35

Epstein, Jacob, 754–55: *Madonna and Child, 754*

equilibrium, Mondrian's views on, 709

Equitable building, New York, 772

Erasmo da Narni, called *Gattamelata* (Donatello), *313,* 314, 321

Erectheum, 113, 114, *115,* 116: carving from, *115;* plan, *113*

Ernst, Max, 710 *n.,* 713 *n.*

Escorial, near Madrid (De Herrera), 391, *391, 446*

Esherick, Joseph, Jr., 785

espadaña, 455

Et in Arcadia Ego (Poussin), 661

etching: printmaking by, 24–25; of Rembrandt, 412, *413*

Etruscans and Etruscan art, 153–59, 185: architecture, 154–56; bibliography, 185–86; painting, 158–59; sculpture, 156–59

Euaenetus: medallion, *138,* 139

Eugène Delacroix (Tournachon), 742, *742*

Euphronios: kylix, 136–38, *137*

Eva Prima Pandora (Cousin the Elder), 389, *389*

Evans, Arthur, 94

Evans, Walker, 749 *n.*

Evening Glow of the Ando (Harunobu), 588, *588*

Evergood, Philip, 725

ex voto pictures, 457

Exekias: amphora, *135,* 136; kylix, *136,* 136

Expressionism, German, 700, 719–20, 721, 724: Rodin and, 752–53

Expulsion (Masaccio), 293, *298,* 332–33

Expulsion of Heliodorus (Raphael), 362–63, *363*

Expulsion of the Money Changers (El Greco), 393 *n.*

Fabriano, Gentile da, 310: *Adoration of the Magi,* 310

fabrics (*see* textiles; weaving)

façade, west, of Gothic cathedral, 48–49

Façade of Rouen Cathedral (Monet), 11, *12*

Falconet, Etienne, 426

Falling Water (house), Pennsylvania (Wright), 777–78, 777

Fan K'uan, 558: *Travelers among Mountains and Stream,* 558

fan vaulting, 280

Fang tribes, Gabun: ancestor figures, *637,* 638

Farbman, M. S., 482 *n.*

Farnese Palace, Rome, 361, *361,* 369: gallery frescoes, 404, 405

Fauves, 693, 695–701, 719

Feast of Herod (Donatello), 294, 296

Federal style in United States, 469

Feininger, Lyonel, 780

Feke, Robert, 473: *Isaac Royall and His Family,* 473

Fenton, Roger, 742

Ferber, Herbert, 762: "*. . . and the bush was not consumed,*" 762

Fête Champêtre (Giorgione), 353, *354*

feudalism, 228–30: Gothic, 243; Japanese, 581–87

Ficino, Marsilio, 288, 322

Fiedler, Konrad, 28 *n.*

Fiesole, Giovanni da (*see* Fra Angelico)

Fiesole, Mino da, 319

Fighting Temeraire (Turner), *679, 680*

figure stones, 36

Filarete (Antonio Averlino), 358: doors of St. Peter's, Rome, 358 *n.;* Ospedale Maggiore, Milan, 358 *n.*

Finding of the Body of St. Mark (Tintoretto), *372,* 373–74, 404

Fiorentino Il Rosso (*see* Rosso, Fiorentino Il)

firing, in pottery-making, 19

Firth of Forth bridge, 772

Flake tradition, of toolmaking, 35–36

Flamboyant style in French Gothic architecture, 280

Flanders, 382, 408 (*see also* Low Countries)

flints, 33–37, *36*

Florence, Italy, 271–72, 287–329, 342–45, 358, 371

Florence cathedral, 273, *301:* Cantoria, *311,* 312; dome, 300; doors, 295; *Gates of Paradise,* 296: detail, *297*

flying buttress, *243,* 248, 256–57

Flying Fish, Cretan, 97, *98*

Flying Warehouse (*Shigisen Engi*), 579–80, *579*

Focillon, Henri, 28 *n.*

folk art: in Hispanic America, 457; in Latin America, 694; in United States, 726, 729, 730 (*see also* genre painting; primitives)

Fontainebleau, school of, 377, 388

Fontainebleau palace: decorations, 367; sculpture, 388

Font-de-Gaume cave, 40

Fonte Gaia (Jacopo della Quercia), 292
Forbes, E. L., 289 n.
form, 5–10: light and, 11
formal analysis, 5
Forsyth, George H., 220 n.
forum, Roman, 155, 170
Forum of Trajan, 170: plan, 171
Fountain of Neptune, Florence, 371
Fouquet, Jean, 338–40: Madonna and Child with Angels, 340; Marriage of the Virgin, 338; Pietà, 340
Four Gospels, book cover, 20, 223
Four Sages of Mount Shang (Shóhaku): detail, 586, 586
Fowling Scene, Theban tomb, 67–68, 67
Fox Trot A (Mondrian), 708–09, 709
Fra Angelico, 302–03, 310 n., 312, 338: Virgin and Child Enthroned, 303, 304; Visitation, 303
Fragonard, Jean-Honoré, 430
France and French art, 218: architecture, 224–27, 230–34, 245–49, 255–59, 262–63, 280–81, 385–87, 420–25, 768, 772, 779–80, 782–84; Baroque, 420–23, 425–30; bibliography, 284–86, 443; Carolingian, 220–27; 18th-century, 441; Gothic, 243–65, 280, 282–84; influence of, on Russia, 486; map, 190, 244; metalwork, 223–24, 253–54, 261; 19th-century, 651–77, 751–53, 763–64, 768–72, 779; painting, 221–23, 239–40, 265, 281, 283, 338–40, 377, 388–90, 426–31, 441, 651–77, 695–99, 701–05, 711; Renaissance, 338–40, 377, 385–90; Rococo, 423–25, 430–31, 438; Romanesque, 229–42; sculpture, 235–39, 249–51, 259–61, 264–65, 281, 387–88, 425–26, 751–53, 756, 763–64; stained glass, 250–53, 261; 20th-century, 695–99, 701–05, 711, 779–80, 782–84
Francesca, Piero della, 305–07, 309, 329, 338: Baptism of Christ, 305; Resurrection of Christ, 307; Visit of the Queen of Sheba to Solomon, 306
François Vase, 134, 135
Frankfort, Henri, 47 n., 59 n., 72 n.
Fray Palavicino (El Greco), 393
free-standing sculpture, 17 (see also sculpture)
French colonial art, 458–63: bibliography, 475
frescoes, 21: Aegean, 97–98, 97, 98; Baroque, 404–05; Byzantine, 208, 210, 212, 213; Etruscan, 155, 158, 160; Italian, 276–79, 297–300, 303–07, 324, 330, 346; Maya, 600–01; Mexican, 730, 731; Roman, 162–67, 164–67; Spanish, 392 (see also murals)
Fresnaye, Roger de la, 701 n.
Friesz, Othon, 696 n.
frieze, Greek, 111: on altar of Zeus at

Pergamon, 141, 144, 145; Doric, 115–16; Ionic, 117; of Parthenon, 127–29 (see also architectural ornament; relief sculpture)
Frieze of Animals, Paleolithic, 42
Froebel, Friedrich, 780
Fromentin, Eugène, 408 n.
Fry, Roger E., 42 n., 681 n.
Fuji above Storm (Hokusai), 589, 589
Fujiwara period of Japanese art, 579–80
Fuller, George, 688
Fulrad's church, St. Denis, 225: plan, 224
functional architecture, 774
Funeral of Phocion (Poussin), 428, 429
funerary sculpture, 281–82 (see also mausoleum of Halicarnassus; sarcophagi)
funerary urn, Dolciano, 156, 157
furniture: English colonial, 463; French, 423, 424; French colonial, 461, 462; Northwest Coast Indian, 624–25, 625
Futurism, 705–06, 720 n.

Gabo, Nahum, 760–61: Kinetic Construction, 761; Linear Construction, 760
Gainsborough, Thomas, 441: Morning Walk, 441
Galerie des Glaces, Versailles, 422, 423
Galerie des Machines, Paris, 772, 773
Gallego, Fernando, 342
gallery: corbeled, Cretan, 98, 99; Hagia Sophia, 200; Romanesque, 231, 235 (see also tribune)
Galloping Horse (Muybridge), 744–45, 745
Gandhara Buddha, 521, 522, 548
garbha griha of Hindu temple, 523, 524, 525
Garden of Venus, called Primavera (Botticelli), 323
gardening, landscape, Romantic Naturalism and, 771
gardens: Chinese, 567; Islamic Persian, 501–02; 17th-century French, 422–23, 425
Gardner, Alexander, 742
Gare Saint-Lazare, Paris (Cartier-Bresson), 748, 749
gargoyles, Gothic, 259
Gates of Paradise (Ghiberti), 296–97: detail, 297
Gattamelata (see Erasmo da Narni)
Gaudi, Antonio, 775: Casa Milá, 776
Gauguin, Paul, 667, 673–77, 698, 700, 756: Maternity, 675, 698; The Yellow Christ, 674
Gaulli, Giovanni Battista (called Baciccio), 405: Triumph of the Name of Jesus, 404
Geese of Medum, 50, 52–53
Gellée, Claude, 427–30, 684: Egeria, 429

of the Virgin, 392; *Cardinal Guevara,* 393; *Expulsion of the Money Changers,* 393 *n.; Fray Palavicino,* 393; *View of Toledo,* 20, *21,* 394; *Virgin with Sts. Ines and Tecla,* 392

Greece and Greek art: Archaic style, 108, 117, 119, 121, 123, 135, 145, 149; architecture, 110–17, 140–41; bibliography, 150–53; Classic style, 109–10, 113–16, 118–31, 138, 145, 149–50; Geometric style, 108, 117, 132–34, 149; Hellenistic style, 140–50; map, *106;* metalwork, 138–39; painting, 131, 147–49; pottery, 131–38; sculpture, 117–31, 142–47

Greek coins, 138–39, *138*
Greek drama, 107–08, 125–26
Greek Orthodox Church (*see* Eastern Orthodox Church)
Greek Revival, in United States, 470 (*see also* Classic Revival; neoclassicism; Romantic Classicism)
Greuze, Jean Baptiste, 441: *Village Betrothal, 442*
Gris, Juan, 701 *n.,* 707
Grodecki, Louis, 252 *n.*
groin vault, 169, *169, 173,* 175: Romanesque, 231–32 (*see also* vaults and vaulting)
Gropius, Walter, 780
Gropper, William, 724
"Group of Seven," 728–29
Grousset, René, 502 *n.*
Grünewald, Matthias, 378, 700: *Crucifixion, 378*
Guadalajara, University of, frescoes, 732
Guaranty Building, Buffalo, 774, *775*
Guatemala, 452: pre-Columbian, 594, 603
Gudea, statue of, 76, *76*
Guernica (Picasso), 704–05, *706–07*
Guesclin, Bertrand du, tomb of, 281, *282*
Guido di Pietro (*see* Fra Angelico)
guilds: in Italy, 290; in Low Countries, 331
Gupta style, India, 533, 551

Habakkuk (Donatello), 294, *295*
Hadrian, bust of, 179, *179*
Hadrian's villa, 175: plan, *175*
Hagia Sophia, Constantinople, 7, 199–200, 207, 500: "Beautiful Gates," 214; capitals, 205; exterior, *198;* interior, *199;* mosaics, 210; plan, *200*
Hagley Park, Worcestershire, 440: Doric portico, *439;* sham Medieval ruin, *439*
Haida Indians, 623
Halicarnassus, Mausoleum of, 143, *143*
Hallenkirche, 269
Hals, Frans, 409–10, 412: *Archers of St. Adrian, 409;* Governors of the St. Eliza-

beth Hospital, 410; *Laughing Cavalier, 409*
Hampton Court, 433
Han dynasty, 546–47
Han Kan, 555: *Horse, 556*
Hand of God (Rodin), 752
Handball (Shahn), 725, *725*
haniwa, 571, *572*
"hard" style, of German Renaissance, 340–41
Harding, Chester, 683 *n.*
Hardouin-Mansart, Jules, 422: Invalides chapel, *421*
Harihara, Prasat Andet, Cambodia, 535, *535*
harmonic façade of Romanesque church, 233
Harnett, William, 685
harp, Sumerian, 78, *79*
Harpignies, Henri, 693
Harris, Lawren, 728
Harrison Gray Otis house, Boston, 469: dining room, *470*
Harrowing of Hell, The, Ka'riye Djami, Istanbul, 212, *213*
Hartigan, Grace, 728
Hartley, Marsden, 720, *721*
Harunobu, Suzuki, 588: *The Evening Glow of the Ando, 588*
Harvester Vase, Aegean, 101, *102*
Hasegawa Tōhaku, 585: *Cryptomeria Trees, 585*
Hassam, Childe, 690, 691 *n.*
Hassan, Sultan, tomb of, 499: plan, *500*
Haterii, tomb of the, 177
Hatshepsut, Queen, temple of, 58, 60–61, *60*
Hawaii, 647: Ku, statue of, *646*
Hawes, Josiah Johnson, 739: *Lemuel Shaw, 740*
hawk's head, Egyptian, 57, *57*
Hay Wain, The (Constable), 678, *678*
Heade, Martin Johnson, 684
Heckel, Erich, 699 *n.*
Heiji Monogatari, illustrations of, 581, *582*
Hellenic style: in Byzantine art, 208; in Early Christian art, 191–92, 203, 205–07; in Gandhara Buddha, 521; in Roman art, 159–60, 177 (*see also* Antiquity; Greece and Greek art; Classic art of Greece)
Hellenistic Age, 140–50
helmet, Sumerian, 78, *79*
Henning, John, calotype of, *741*
Henri, Robert, 691, *692*
Henry VII's chapel, Westminster Abbey, 280, *280*
Hera, temple of: Olympia, 112, *113;* Paestum, 112, *112;* Samos: plan, *109*
Hera of Samos, 8, *116,* 117
Heraion temple, 111

Herakleitos, 127, 149

Herakles: Temple of Aphaia, 124, *124;* Temple of Zeus, 126, *126* (*see also Hercules and Antaeus*)

Herakles Strangling the Serpents (Pompeii), 166, *167*

heraldic art, of Northwest Coast Indians, 623

heraldic design: Assyrian, 82; in Romanesque art, 238; Sumerian, 78–79

Herculaneum, 163, 164: excavations at, 469, 651, 766

Hercules (*see* Herakles)

Hercules and Antaeus (Pollaiuolo), 321

Hermes with the Infant Dionysos (Praxiteles), 142, *142*

Herrera, Juan de, 391, 446: Escorial, *391*

Herreran style, 446, 447, 452

Herschel, John, 740: photograph of, *744*

Hesi-ra, panel from mastaba, 49, *50*

Hesselius, Gustavus, 471

High Court Building, Chandigarh, India, 783, *783*

high relief, sculpture in, 16 (*see also* relief sculpture)

Hildebrand, Adolf, 28 *n.*

Hildesheim, cathedral of, bronze doors, 226, *226*

Hildesheim Treasure, 183, *184*

Hill, David Octavius, 740–41: *John Henning and Alexander Ritchie, 741*

Hilliard, Nicholas, 436

Hinduism and Hindu art: in India, 506, 512, 522–31; in southeast Asia, 534

Hindustan (*see* India)

Hinks, Roger P., 223 *n.*

Hippodamos, 141, 154

Hiroshige, 589

Hispanic American art, 454–58

Hissarlik, excavations at, 94

historical painting, 19th-century American, 683–84

Hittites, 80

Hogarth, William, 436–37: *Breakfast Scene, 437*

Hōitsu, 586

Hokke-kyō (Lotus Sūtra) fan, 578, *578*

Hokke-kyō scrolls, 578

Hokusai, 589: *Thirty-six Views of Mt. Fuji: Fuji above Storm, 589*

Holbein the Younger, Hans, 378, 381, 436: *Ambassadors, 382; Dance of Death, 381*

Holland (*see* Dutch painting; Low Countries)

Holt, Elizabeth G., 236 *n.*, 325 *n.*, 369 *n.*

Holy Family, called the *Doni Tondo* (Michelangelo), 344, 349–50, *349*

Holy Rosary chapel, Vence (Matisse), 698–99, *699*

Holy Sepulchre, Jerusalem, 199

Holy Trinity cathedral, 486

Home Insurance Company building, Chicago, 773

Home of the Heron (Inness), 684, *685*

Homer, epics of, 107

Homer, Winslow, 685, 688–89, 720–21: *Northeaster, 689*

Hooch, Pieter de, 412–13, 427: *Pantry Door,* 412–13

Hood, Raymond, 774: Chicago Tribune Tower, 774; Daily News building, 774; McGraw-Hill building, 774

Hopewell hawk effigy pipe, *618*, 622

Hopewell Indians, 622–23, 630

Hopi jar, Sikyatki ware, *621*

Hopper, Edward, 722, 723: *Early Sunday Morning,* 724

Horace, 159

Horizontal Spines (Calder), *760*, 761

horror vacui, 218: Islamic, 495

Horse (Han Kan), 555, *556*

horse statuette: Early Classic, 121, *121;* Geometric style, 5

horseshoe arch, Islamic, 493, *494*

Horta, Victor, 775: People's Palace, 775

Horus, temple of, *61*

Hōryūji temple, near Nara, 577, *577:* murals, 574–75

Hosios Lucas, mosaic bust of Christ, 211, *211*

Hotel de Soubise, Paris, upper salon, *423*

Houdon, Jean Antoine, 426: *George Washington,* 426; *Louise Brogniart,* 425; *Voltaire, 425*

house (*see* domestic architecture)

Houses of Parliament, London (Barry), 767, *767*

Hovenden, Thomas, 685 *n.,* 691: *Breaking Home Ties,* 691

Howe, George, 775

Hsia Kuei, 561, 564, 581, 582, 584

Hsieh Ho, 553

Hsii Wei, 565: *Grapevine, 565*

Huang Kung-wang, 563: *Landscape,* detail, *563*

Hudson River school, 684

hue, 12

Huguet, Jaime, 342

Hui Neng, portrait of (Liang K'ai), *561,* 562

Hui-tsung, 559

human figure, treatment of: Assyrian, 82; Byzantine, 211; Cretan, 97; Egyptian, 49–50, 67; Greek, 118; Michelangelo's, 351; in 16th-century Mannerism, 362; Sumerian, 75–76

humanism, Renaissance art and, 288, 289, 291, 323, 337, 348

Humayun, tomb of, *506, 507, 508*

Hundred Years' War, 338

Hunt, William Holman, 681 *n.*

Hunters, Magdalenian, *42*

406, 416–17, 420, 422, 426, 432, 434
480, 485; map, *154, 190, 290;* painting,
274–79, 282, 297–300, 302–12, 321–
29, 343–57, 362–63, 366–67, 369–74,
402–05, 441, 705–06, 712–13; revival
of, 768; sculpture, 292–97, 312–14,
319–21, 343, 348–49, 371–72, 401–02,
706, 758; 16th-century Renaissance,
342–77; 20th-century, 705–06, 712–13,
758, 775 (*see also* Etruscans and Etruscan art; Roman empire and art)
Itō Jakuchū, 586
ivory carvings: Byzantine, 213, *214;* Carolingian, 223, *223;* Early Christian, 204–
05, *205;* High Gothic, 262

Jackson, William Henry, 742–43
Jacopo della Quercia, 292, 348, 351: *Allegorical Figure,* 293; *Expulsion,* 292,
292, 298; *Fonte Gaia,* 292; Ilaria del
Caretto, tomb of, 292
jade carving: Ch'ing dynasty, 567; Chou
dynasty, 545, *545;* Oceanic, 645; Sung
dynasty, 563
Jainism, in India, 515
jamb, 237 *n.*
James Stuart (Van Dyck), 408, *408*
Jane Avril (Toulouse-Lautrec), *25*
Japan and Japanese art: architecture, 570,
572, 575–77, 585, 589–90; bibliography,
591; Buddhism, 533, 572–75; influence
on Homer, 689, 721; influence on Impressionists, 665, 667, 672; influence on
Whistler, 686–87; literature, 578; map,
571; metalwork, 571; painting, 574–75,
577–89; pottery, 570–71, 584; prints,
587–88; sculpture, 570, 571–74, 580–
81; Zen Buddhism, 582–83
Japanese prints, 587: perspective in, 9
Japanese woodcuts, 24
Java, Indian art in, 534–35
Jawlensky, Alexei von, 699 *n.*
Jeanneret-Gris, Charles Edouard (*see* Le
Corbusier)
Jefferson, Thomas, 468–69, 767: Monti-
cello, 468; state capitol, Richmond, Va.,
467, 468; University of Virginia, *468–69*
Jenney, William Le Baron, 773: Home In-
surance Company building, 773
Jeremiah (Donatello), 294, *295*
Jeremiah (Michelangelo), 352, *353*
jewelry: Achaemenian, 88–89, *89;* Barbar-
ian, 218–19, *219;* Egyptian, 69, *69;* Mix-
tec, 605; Navaho, 628–29
John Henning and Alexander H. Ritchie
(Hill and Adamson), 741, *741*
Johnson, Eastman, 683 *n.,* 685
Johnson, Philip C., 785
Johnson Wax Company building, *765, 778*
Jomon culture in Japan, 570–71

Jones, H. S., 10 *n.*
Jones, Inigo, 432, 466: Banqueting Hall,
Whitehall Palace, *433*
Jones, S. H., 130 *n.*
Jones, W. H. S., 149 *n.*
Joseph in Egypt (Il Pontormo), 366–67,
366
Joshua Roll, detail, *202, 203*
Ju Peon, 566
Juárez, Juan Rodríguez, 457
Judgment of Cambyses (David), 337
Judith and Holofernes (Donatello), 312
Justinian, 191, 199
Justinian and Followers, mosaic, San Vi-
tale, *201,* 202: detail, *Plate 2*

Ka, 48, 49
Kabuki theater, 586, 587
Kahnweiler, D. H., 707 *n.*
Kaigetsudō family, 587
Kailāsha, Ellora, 527
Kamakura period of Japanese art, 580–81
Kandinsky, Vassily, 700, 714 *n.,* 780: *Im-
provisation, 1912, 701*
Kane, Paul, 693
K'ang-hsi period, porcelains in, 566
Kanō Sanraku, 585
Kanō school of Japanese painting, 584
Kao, 582
Ka'riye mosque, Constantinople, fresco,
212, *213*
Karle, India, cave sanctuary, 519–20, *519:*
detail of façade, *521;* plan, *520*
Karnak, temples of, 61
Kassites, 79–80
Kazan cathedral, St. Petersburg, 486, *486*
Kelmscott Chaucer, 682: title page, *682*
Kelmscott Press, 682
Kensett, John Frederick, 684 *n.*
Kenzan, 586
Kermess (Village Carnival) (Rubens),
407, *407*
Kertch vases, 147, *148*
Khafra: Pyramid of, 51–53, *52, 54;* statue
of, 53–56, *54,* 118
Khajuraho temples, India, 529, *530*
Khan, Kublai, 563
Khmers (*see* Cambodia)
Khonsu, temple of, 61–63, *61*
Khufuw, Pyramid of, 50–51, *52, 53,* 54
Kichijoten, Shōsōin, Nara, 575, *575*
Kinetic Construction (Gabo), *761*
kiosks, Islamic, 507, *508–09*
Kiowa shield, 627, *628*
Kirchner, E. L., 699 *n.*
Kiss, The (Rodin), *752*
kiva, Pueblo, 619, *620*
Kiyomasu I, 587
Kiyonaga, 588

Lescot, Pierre, 387: Louvre façade, *386*
Le Secq, Henry, 741
Leslie, C. R., 678 *n.*
Lethaby, W. R., 200 *n.*
Le Vau, 422; Louvre, east façade, *421*
Lever House, New York, 775
Levine, Jack, 724
li, Chinese pottery, 542, 544
Li Chao-tao, 557
Li Ch'êng, 558
Li Lung-mien, 559
Li Ssu-hsün, 557
Liang K'ai, 561–62, 582: *The Sixth Patriarch Tearing up a Sūtra, 561*
Lie, Jonas, 690 *n.*
light, 11–14: treatment of: by Bellini, 353; by Cézanne, 670; by Dutch genre painters, 413–14; by della Francesca, 306; by Giorgione, 353–54; by El Greco, 393–94; by Impressionists, 662, 663; by Turner, 679–80; by Veneziano, 305
lighting, architectural, 16: Early Christian, 201; in Gothic cathedrals, 246, 248; Roman, 175, 176; in Romanesque churches, 234 (*see also* clerestory windows; stain glass)
Ligorio, Piero, 359 *n.*
Lima, Peru, 447
Limbourg brothers, *Très Riches Heures,* 280, 283, *283*
Limburg-an-der-Lahn cathedral, 268
limners, English colonial, 464, 470
Limoges enamels, 261–62
Lincoln (Saint-Gaudens), 752
Lindisfarne Gospels, *217,* 219
line, 8: in drawing, 22
Linear Construction (Gabo), 760, *760*
"Linked Ring," 747, 748
lintel, *16,* 237 *n.* (*see also* post and lintel construction)
Lion Gate, Mycenae, *96,* 97, *98–99*
Lipchitz, Jacques, 757–58, 763: *Man with Mandolin, 758; Sacrifice II, 763*
Lippi, Filippino, 298 *n.*
Lippi, Fra Filippo, 288, 309–12: *Adoration of the Christ Child, 311, 312; Madonna and Child, 310*
Lippold, Richard, 762
Lisbôa, Antônio Francisco (see Aleijadinho, O)
Lissitzky, El, 710: *Proun 99, 710*
lithography, 25: of Daumier, 658–59 (*see also* graphic arts)
Liuthard, 223: *Crucifixion, 223*
Lochner, Stephan, 340: *Madonna in the Rose Garden, 340*
Lomas Rishi cave, India, 517: entrance, *516*
Lombardo, Pietro: Vendramin Palace, 316, *317*
London Bridge (Derain), 695, *696*

London public buildings, 19th-century, 770
London Zoo, Penguin House, 10, *11*
longitudinal-plan church, 400–01 (*see also* Baroque art)
Lorenzetti, Ambrogio, 278: *Good Government,* detail, 278–79, *278*
Lorenzo Monaco, 302
Lorenzo the Magnificent, 290, 322–23, 348 (*see also* Medici)
Lorrain, Claude (*see* Gellée, Claude)
Lotus Sūtra fan, 578, *578*
Loudon, J. C., 771
Louis XIV of France, 398, 420, 422–23, 426
Louis XVI of France, 651
Louise Brogniart (Houdon), *5, 425, 426*
Louisiana, French colonial architecture in, 461–62
Loup, Jean le, 258 *n.*
Louvain, Flanders, 331
Louviers, Church of Notre Dame, 281, *281*
Louvre, Paris, 10, 387: façade (Lescot and Goujon) *386;* façade (Perrault, Le Vau, Le Brun), *421,* 422
Low Countries, art of: Baroque (17th-century), 406–08; 15th-century, 330–38; 16th-century, 382–85 (*see also* Dutch painting)
Lucca cathedral, 235
Luks, George B., 691
Luncheon of the Boating Party (Renoir), 664–65, *665,* 667
Lung-men cave temples, 549
luster, 19; luster ware, 504, *504*
Luxe, Le, II (Matisse), 697–98, *697,* 753
Luxor, Egypt, temples, 61
Luzarches, Robert de, 258 *n.*
Lysippos, 146: *Apoxyomenos, 143, 144*

Ma'at in Egyptian art, 47
Mace, A. C., 59 *n.*
Macedonian dynasty, 208, 215
McGraw-Hill building, New York, 774
Machu Picchu, Peru, 613–14, *614*
McIntire, Samuel, 469
Macke, August, 699 *n.*
Maddelena Doni (Raphael), 345 *n.*
Maddox, Richard Leach, 745
Madeleine, La (church), Vézelay, 232
Maderna, Carlo, 359 *n.,* 399: façade of St. Peter's, 398
Madonna and Child (Epstein), 754, *754*
Madonna and Child (Fra Filippo Lippi), *310*
Madonna and Child (Michelangelo), 287, 345 *n.,* 348–49
Madonna and Child with a Goldfinch (Raphael), 343–44, *345*

Maurer, Alfred, 719
Mauryan period in Buddhist India, 515–17
mausoleum of Halicarnassus, frieze, 143, *143* (*see also* sarcophagi; tombs)
Maya culture, 593, 594–602, 615: influence on Wright, 776
Ma Yüan, 561, *561; Bare Willows and Distant Mountains, 560*
Mazzola, Francesco (*see* Parmigianino, Il)
meaning in art, 26–28
medallion: coin by Euaenetus, *138,* 139; in Persian carpets, 504–05
media of painting, 20–22
Medici, 290, 301, 303, 312, 322–23, 348
Medici-Riccardi Palace, Florence, 315, *316,* 368: paintings for, 310
Medici tombs (Michelangelo), 363–65, *364*
Medieval art, 217–86: bibliography, 284–86; Early, 217–27; Gothic, 243–84; Pre-Raphaelite Brotherhood and, 681–82; Renaissance and, 330–31, 333, 339; revival of, 766–68; Romanesque, 228–42 (*see also* Carolingian art; Gothic art; Romanesque art)
Mediterranean (Maillol), 756, *756*
Mediterranean world, map, *190*
Meeting of the Waters Fountain (Milles), 755, *755*
megaliths, Neolithic, 44
megaron, Mycenaean, 98, *100*
Melancholia I (Dürer), 380, 381
Melanesian culture and art, 641, 642–44
Memling, Hans, 337
Mena, Pedro de, 415: *St. Francis, 416*
menhirs (megaliths), 44
Meniñas, Las (Maids of Honor) (Velázquez), 418, *418*
Mercury (Bologna), 371, *371*
Mérida, Carlos, 730
Merz Picture 19 (Schwitters), 711, *711*
Mesolithic Age, 43
Mesopotamia, 72: influence on India, 512–13 (*see also* Babylonian art)
Messina, Antonella da, 353, 354
Mestrovic, Ivan, 756
metal, modern sculpture in, 762 (*see also* bronze, use of)
metalwork, 19–20: Achaemenian, 88–90; Aegean, 102–03, *103;* Andean, 612–15; Babylonian, 77–79; Barbarian, 218–19; Byzantine, 213–14; Chinese, 543–46, 557; Early Christian, *189,* 206; Egyptian, 57, 68, 69; French, 223–24, 253–54, 261; German, 240, 253, 261; Gothic, 253, 261–62; Greek, 138–39; Islamic, 497, 503, *504;* Japanese, 571; Roman, 183; Romanesque, *Plate 3,* 240–41, 242, *242;* Russian, 485
metaphysical painting, 712–13

Metcalf, Willard L., 690 *n.*
metope, Greek, *110,* 111: Doric, 115–16
Metzinger, Jean, 701 *n.*
Mexico and Mexican art: colonial, 444–47; 19th-century, 693–95; pre-Columbian cultures in, 593–94, 602–08, 615; 20th-century, 729–31
Mexico cathedral, Mexico City, 447
Mexico City, 444
Michelangelo Buonarroti, 318–19, 325, 342, 344, 345 *n.,* 348–52, 359–60, 363–66, 367, 376, 377, 398: *Battle of the Cascina,* 344; *Bound Slave (Unfinished),* 5, 6; *David,* 348; Farnese Palace, 361; *Holy Family,* called the *Doni Tondo,* 344, *349; Jeremiah, 353; Last Judgment,* 363; Laurentian Library, 363, *365; Madonna and Child,* Bruges, *287,* 345 *n.;* Medici tombs, 363, *364;* St. Peter's, Rome, 359–60; Sistine chapel ceiling, 324, *350–53; Temptation and Expulsion of Adam and Eve, 352*
Michelozzo di Bartolommeo, 312, 315, 368: Medici-Riccardi Palace, *316*
Micoquean phase, toolmaking in, 35
Micronesian culture and art, 641, 647
Middle American cultures and art, 594–608: bibliography, 616; map, *594*
Middle Eastern art, 72–93: Achaemenian Persian, 86–90; Assyrian, 79–84; Babylonian, 72–79; bibliography, 93; Chaldean, 84–86; Sassanian Persian, 90–93
Middle Kingdom, Egypt, 57–58, 70
Mies van der Rohe, Ludwig, 781–82, 784: German Pavilion, Barcelona, *781:* plan, *15;* Illinois Institute of Technology, *781*
Mi Fei, 559: *Landscape, 559*
Milan, Italy, 327, 358
Miller, Sanderson, *Hagley Park, 439*
Milles, Carl, 755–56: *The Meeting of the Waters Fountain,* 755
Millet, Jean François, 657–58, 663: *The Gleaners,* 657
Milne, David, 728–29
Mimbres bowl, 621, *621*
Mīnākshi temple, Madura, 531
minaret, 494, *495*
Minerva Medica, sculpture, 180
Minerva Medica, temple of, 176
Ming dynasty, 564–66
miniatures: Byzantine, 212; Early Christian, 201, 203–04; Persian Islamic, 502–03 (*see also* manuscript illumination)
Minoan art (*see* Aegean art)
Minos, palace of, 95, 96
Miracle of the Penitent Son (Donatello), *313,* 314
Miraculous Draught of Fish (Witz), *341*
Mirak, 502–03: *Laila and Majnum,* illustration for, *503*

oil painting, 22
oil paints: Flemish development of, 330; use of, in High Renaissance, 354, 356
O'Keeffe, Georgia, 722–23
Old Kingdom, Egypt, 47–57, 69
Old Market Woman, 145, *146*
Old Testament Trinity (Rublëv), 483, *484*
Olmec culture, 602, 615
Olympia, Greece, 124–25, 149–50
Olympia (Manet), 661
Olympiad, 107
open form, 7–8
Or San Michele, Florence, statuary, 293, *293, 294*
Orcival, Notre Dame, 233, *234*
orders, Greek architectural, *110,* 111
Ordination (Poussin), 427, *428*
organic architecture, modern, 771, 776, 784
Orientalizing style of Greek art, 134, 149
Orley, Bernaert van, 383: *Virgin and Child,* 383
ornament, architectural (*see* architectural ornament)
ornamentation: in Etruscan sculpture, 157–58; in Greek sculpture, 117; in Romanesque sculpture, 238–39 (*see also* architectural ornament; decoration; manuscript illumination)
"Ornate" style of Roman wall painting, 166, *166*
Orozco, José Clemente, 724, 730, 731–32
Orvieto cathedral, 273
Ospedale Maggiore, Milan (Filarete), 358 *n.*
O'Sullivan, T. H., 742
Ottonians, 226
Oud, J. J. P., 709 *n.*
Ouro Preto, Brazil, 453

pagoda, 567–68
Paine, R. T., 587 *n.*
painting, 20–22: Aegean, 97–98; Alberti's theories of, 302; Barbarian, 219–20; Baroque, 402–15, 416–19, 426–30, 436; Byzantine, 209–12; Canadian, 693, 728–29; Carolingian, 224; Chinese, 546–47, 550, 552, 553–57, 558–66; Dutch, 408–15, 416–19, 426–30, 436; Early Christian, 201–04; 18th-century, 440–41; Egyptian, 50, 66–68; English, 239–40, 267–68, 282, 436–38, 440–41, 677–82, 728–29; English colonial, 470–74; Etruscan, 158–59; French, 221–23, 239–40, 265, 281, 283, 338–40, 377, 388–90, 426–31, 441, 651–77, 695–99, 701–05, 711; genre, 412–14, 427, 431, 487; German, 282, 340–41, 377–82, 699–700, 711, 717–18; Gothic (*see* stained glass); Greek, 131, 132–38,

147–49; Hispanic American, 455–57; in India, 5, 31–33; Islamic, 494–97, 502–03; Italian, 274–79, 282, 297–300, 302–12, 321–29, 343–56, 362–63, 366–67, 369–74, 402–05, 441, 705–06, 712–13; Japanese, 574–75, 577; Latin American, 693–95; Maya, 600–02; 19th-century, 651–95; North American Indian, 620, 627, 629; Paleolithic, 39–42; purpose of, 327; Renaissance, 297–300, 302–12, 321–29, 331–56, 362–63, 366–67, 369–74, 377, 381–85, 388–90, 391–94; Rococo, 430–31, 437–38; Roman, 164–68; Romanesque, 239–40; Russian, 481–85, 487, 709–10, 717–18; South American, 450–52; Spanish, 240, 281, 341–42, 377–78, 391–94, 416–19; 20th-century, 695–731; in United States, 683–93, 718–28; (*see also* manuscript illumination; miniatures)
Pakistan, 511: map, *512*
palaces: Achaemenian Persian, 86–88, *87, 88;* Assyrian, 79–84, *81–84;* Cretan, 94–96, *95, 98, 99;* Inca, 613; Islamic, 494, 498, 506; Maya, 595; Mexican, 604; Renaissance, 315–18, *361,* 368–69, 375; Roman, 175; Sassanian Persian, *91, 91*
Palaeologi, 208, 211, 215
Palazzo del Te, Mantua (Giulio Romano), 368, *368*
Palazzo Massimo alle Colonne, Rome (Peruzzi), 368–69, *369*
Palazzo Valmarano, Vicenza (Palladio), 375, *375*
Palazzo Vecchio, Florence, 274
Paleolithic art, 33–42: in China, 542
Palestine, map, *190*
Palladio, Andrea, 370, 374–76, 377, 432, 435, 468, 487: Palazzo Valmarano, *375;* Villa Rotonda, *376,* 468
Pallava kings, 525
Palma da Majorca cathedral, 270, *271*
Panofsky, Erwin, 27 *n.,* 246 *n.,* 252, 335
Pantheon, Rome, 173–74, *174,* 469: plan, *15*
Pantry Door (de Hooch), 412–13
Papuan Gulf area sculpture, 642, *643*
Paradise cults of Buddhism, 549–50, 580
Paradise of Amitābha, Tun-huang caves, 553, *554*
Paris Boulevard (Daguerre), 738, *739*
Paris Exhibition, 772
Parmigianino, Il (Francesco Mazzola), 372: *Madonna del Collo Lungo,* 371
Parrhasius, 147
Parson Capen House, Topsfield, Mass., 464–65, *464*
Parthenon, Athens, 113–16, *114:* frieze, 17, 127–29, *128–29;* plan, *109, 113,*

plantation house, American Southern, 461–62, *462*

plaster, use of, in Islamic art, 495, 497 (*see also* frescoes)

Plateresque style of Spanish architecture, 390: in Mexico, 446; in South America, 452

plating in metalwork, 20

Plato, 140

Pleistocene period, 33–35

Pliny, 10

pointed arch, 231, 247, *247*: Islamic, 493, *493*, 507

pointillism, 667

Poliziano, Angelo, 323

Pollaiuolo, Antonio, 321–22, 336, 345: *Apollo and Daphne, 321; Battle of the Nudes,* 321; *Hercules and Antaeus,* 321

Pollock, Jackson, 727: *Number 29, 727*

Polonnāruwa, Ceylon, 533

Polyeuktos, head of Demosthenes, 146, *147*

Polygnotus, 131

Polyklcitos, 129–30: canon of, *130 n., Doryphoros,* 130, *130*

Polynesian culture and art, 641, 644–47

Polyphemus Hurling Rocks at Acis (Carracci), *403*, 404

Pompeii, 164–67, 192: excavations at, 469, 651, 766; plan, *154*

Pont du Gard, 169, *169*

Pontormo, Il (Jacopo Carucci), 366–67, 370, 376: *Deposition,* 367; *Joseph in Egypt, 366*

porcclain, 18–19: Chinese Ming, 566; Persian pottery and, 504 (*see also* ceramics; pottery and pottery-making)

Poro Secret Society masks, 639, *639*

Port of La Rochelle (Corot), 658, *658*

Porta, Giacomo della, 359 *n.*

portal, 237

portico of Greek temple, 111

Portinari Altarpiece (van der Goes), 336, *337*

Portland Vase, 184, *184*

Portrait of a Man (Rembrandt), 410, *410*

Portrait of a Young Man (Bronzino), 370–71, *370*

Portrait of Gertrude Stein (Picasso), 702, *702*

Portrait of Miss Alexander (Whistler), 686–87, *687*

portrait sculpture: Etruscan, 158; Greek, 146; Renaissance, 319–20; Roman, *153*, 177–80, *177–80*, 185

portraiture: Cézanne's, 671; Dutch Baroque, 409–12; English 18th-century, 440–41; Flemish Baroque, 407–08; French, 389, 426; 19th-century American, 683–84, 687; photographic, 741,

742; in seaboard colonies, 471–74; Spanish Baroque, 418–19

Portugal and Portuguese art: influence in Brazil, 452–53; in Renaissance, 342

Posada, José Guadalupe, 729–30: *Calavera: Don Quixote, 729*

Poseidon (or Zeus), Early Classic, 121, *122*

post and lintel construction, *16*: Cretan, 96; of Egyptian temple, 63–64; Greek, 111; Roman 168, 170, *171*, 172, *172*

posters of Toulouse-Lautrec, 667

Post-Impressionists, 667–77, 693: influence in 20th century, 695, 701

pottery and pottery-making, 18–19: Aegean, *94*, 101–02, *102*, *103;* Andean, 608–10, *610*, 615; Chinese, 542, *542*, 557, 562; Egyptian, 57; Greek, 131–38, *131–37*; Japanese, 570–71, 584; Maya, 601–02, *602;* Neolithic, 43–44, *44*, 542, *542*, 570–71; North American Indian, 621; Roman, 184 (*see also* ceramics)

Poussin, Nicolas, 427–28, 661, 668, 671, 673: *Et in Arcadia Ego,* 661; *Funeral of Phocion,* 429; *Ordination, 428*

Powell, John, 742

Pratt, Matthew, 474 *n.*

Praxiteles, *Hermes with the Infant Dionysos,* 142, *142,* 143

pre-Columbian culture and art, 592–617: architecture, 593–600, 603–04, 607, 608–09, 611, 612, 613; bibliography, 616–17; metalwork, 605, 612–15; painting, 600–02; pottery, 601–02, 608–10, 615; sculpture, 596–98, 600, 603, 605–08 (*see also* North American Indian culturc and art)

prehistoric art, 33–46: bibliography, 46

Prendergast, Maurice B., 690, 691 *n.*, 729

Pre-Raphaelite Brotherhood, 681–82

Prescott, W. H., 444 *n.*

Presentation of the Virgin (Tintoretto), 373

primary colors, 13

Primaticcio, Francesco, 377, 388–89

Primavera (*see Garden of Venus*)

primitive art, 632–48: African Negro, 633–39; bibliography, 648; influence, 675, 695, 702, 757; Oceanic, 640–48; sculpture, 633–39, 642–47

primitives, 19th-century American, 689–90

printing, development of, 288–89

printmaking, 24–25 (*see also* book illustration; engraving; etching; woodcuts)

Procession of Mammoths (Magdalenian), 40

program in architecture, 16

Proletarian Victim (Siqueiros), 730, *730*

proportion, 10: in Renaissance architecture, 301, 315–17; da Vinci's study of, 326

Propylaea, 113: plan, *113*

prostyle temple, *109:* Etruscan, 155

Protestant Reformation, 367

Protestantism: Dutch, 408; English, 432

Protogenes, 147

Proun 99 (El Lissitzky), 710, *710*

Psalter of St. Louis, 265

psychological effect: of architecture, 15; of color, 14; of line, 8

Pucelle, Jean, 265: *Belleville Breviary, 264*

Puebla cathedral, Mexico, *446:* high altar, *446*

Pueblo Bonito village, Chaco Canyon, 620

Pueblo Indians, 618–21, 630

Puget, Pierre, 425

Pugin, A. N. W., 769: Houses of Parliament, 767

putto motif, 320 *n.*

pylon of Egyptian temple, 62

pyramid temples: Maya, 595, 599; pre-Columbian Mexican, 607

pyramids, 49, 50–53: of Khafra, 51–54, *52, 54;* of Khufuw, 50, *52, 53, 54*

Quattro Santi Coronati (Nanni di Banco), 293, *293*

Queen Mary's Psalter, 268

Quetzalcoatl, temple of, Teotihuacan, 603, *603*

quillwork, Plains Indian, 627

Quirigua monolith, 597, *598*

Quito, Ecuador, 451–52

Rabi's Daurani, tomb of, 509

Raft of the Medusa (Géricault), 654, *655*

Raigō paintings, 580

"Railroad style" of architecture, 769

Raimondi, Marcantonio, 377 *n.*

Rain, Steam and Speed (Turner), 680

Rainaldi, Carlo, 400–01: Santa Maria in Campitelli, *401;* plan, *401*

"raised cottage" style, 460–61

raking cornice, *110:* Doric, 116

Ranier de Huy, 254

Ranofer: relief on tomb of, 50, *51;* statue of, *54, 56*

Rape of the Daughters of Leucippus (Rubens), *406,* 407

Raphael, 324, 325, 342–48, 356, 359 *n.,* 362–63, 368, 370, 376, 427, 665: *Belle Jardinière,* 345 *n., Cowper Madonna, 345; Deposition of Christ,* 357; *Disputà,* 346–47; *Expulsion of Heliodorus, 363; Maddalena Doni,* 345 *n.; Madonna and Child with a Goldfinch,* 343–44, *345; Madonna del Cardellino,* 345 *n.; Marriage of the Virgin, 344;* School of

Athens, 9, 23, 347

Rastrelli, B. F., 486: Peterhof, *486–87;* Tsarskoe Selo, 486; Winter Palace, 486

Ravenna mosaics, *Plate 2 (see also* San Vitale; Sant' Appollinare in Classe)

Ray, Man, 710 *n.*

Raynal, Maurice, 705 *n.*

Rayonnant style, 262, 267, 268, 280: revival of, 767

realism: of Courbet, 661; Dutch Baroque, 408–15, 715; of Eakins, 688; in Early Gothic sculpture, 251; of The Eight, 691; in English colonies, 472–74; in Greek painting, 147; in Greek sculpture, 145; in Japanese art, 580–81; Late Gothic, 330; in Low Countries, 331–35; in Roman painting, 165 (*see also* naturalism)

Reclining Figure (Moore), 762, 763

Red Horses (Marc), 700

Red House, Bexley Heath, 768

Redon, Odilon, 756

Refined Gothic art, 261–79

Reform Club building, London, 768

regionalist painting in Latin America, 694 (*see also* "American scene" painters)

Reims cathedral, 258: *Annunciation* in, 7; *Visitation* in, 8; west façade, 7, *264,* 272

Reindeer, Magdalenian, 40, *41*

reindeer-horn weapons, Magdalenian, 37, 38

Rejlander, O. G., 743: *Two Paths of Life, 744*

relief: in pottery-making, 19; printmaking by, 24

relief sculpture, 16: Andean, 608, 611; Cambodian, 538; Chinese, 547; Early Christian, 204–06, *204–06;* Etruscan, 157–58, *159;* Gothic, 249–51, *250–51;* Greek, 121–29, *123;* in India, 518–20, *518–19, 521,* 523–31; Islamic, 495; Maya, 596, 599–600; Renaissance, 294–97, *296, 297, 313,* 314, 387–88; Roman, 180–85, *181–83;* Romanesque, 236–39, *237–40 (see also* architectural ornament; frieze, Greek)

religion: Babylonian, 73–74; Cretan, 95, 97; Egyptian, 47, 48, 59; Greek, 105, 107; Persian, 86, 90; Shintō, 575–77 (*see also* Buddhism; Early Christianity; Eastern Orthodox Church; Hinduism; Protestantism; Roman Catholic Church)

Rembrandt van Rijn, 385, 398, 410–12: *Portrait of a Man, 410; Self-Portrait,* Plate 6; *Six's Bridge, 413; Supper at Emmaus (ca.* 1630), *411; Supper at Emmaus* (1648), *412; Two Women Teaching a Child to Walk, 413*

Remington, Frederic, 685 *n.*

Renaissance art, 287–396: architecture,

San Antonio church, Padua, altar relief, *313*, 314
San Carlo alle Quattro Fontane, church, 399: dome, *400;* plan, *400*
San Esteban Rey church, Ácoma, 455, *456*
San Francesco church, Arezzo, frescoes, 306
San Francesco church, Rimini, 317
San Francisco church, La Paz, 450
San Francisco church, Quito, 451: interior, *451*
San Giobbe church, Venice; Bellini's altarpiece, *353*
San Lorenzo church, Florence: Medici tombs, 363, *364;* sacristy, 301, *302*, 315
San Lorenzo church, Potosí, 450
San Marco church, Florence: altarpiece, 303, *304;* frescoes, 303
San Miniato church, Florence, 235
San Petronio church, Bologna, relief from, 292
San Satiro church, Milan, 358
San Sebastian and Santa Prisca church, Taxco, 447, *447*
San Sebastian church, Cuzco, 449
San Vitale church, Ravenna, 197: apse, *196;* capital, *205;* mosaic, *201*
San Xavier del Bac church, Arizona, 454–55
San Zaccaria church, Venice, Bellini's altarpiece, 353
Sanchi, India, stupas at, 517–18, *517*, *518*
sanctuaries, cave (*see* cave temples)
sand painting, Navaho, 629
Sangallo, Antonio da, 359 *n*., 361
Sangallo, Giuliano da, 318 *n*., 359 *n*.
Sant' Ambrogio church, Milan, 234
Sant' Andrea church, Mantua, 318
Sant' Apollinare in Classe church, Ravenna, *196*, 198: mosaics, *193;* sarcophagus, *204*
Sant' Apollonia convent, Florence, fresco, 303–04, *304*
Santa Croce chapels, Florence, frescoes, 277
Santa Felicita church, Florence, altarpiece, 367
Santa Lucia de' Magnoli church, fresco, *305*
Santa Maria degli Angeli church, Florence, 318 *n*.
Santa Maria della Grazia church, Milan, 358
Santa Maria delle Carceri church, Prato, 318 *n*.
Santa Maria in Campitelli church, Rome, 400: interior, *401;* plan, *401*
Santa Maria in Cosmedin basilica, Rome, *195*, 196
Santa Maria Maggiore church, Rome, mosaic, 192, *192*, 202

Santa Maria Novella church, Florence, *Trinity*, 300, *300*
Santa Sophia cathedral, Kiev, 478
Santa Sophia cathedral, Novgorod, 478
Santa Sophia, Constantinople (*see* Hagia Sophia)
Santiago de Compostela church, Spain, 235
Santo Spirito church, Florence, 318: interior, *315;* plan, 318, *318*
Sanzio, Giovanni, 343
Sanzio, Raphael (*see* Raphael)
São Francisco church, Ouro Preto, *453*, 454
sarcophagi: Early Christian, 204–05, *204;* Etruscan, 157, *157* (*see also* funerary sculpture)
Sargent, John Singer, 687: *The Picnic*, 22; *The Wyndham Sisters*, 687
Sargon II, palace of, 79, *80*, 81
Sarmatian art, 89–90, 217
Sarto, Andrea del, 346, 367
Sassanian Persian art, 90–93: Islamic art and, 494, 496
Savoie Villa, Poissy-sur-Seine, France, 782
Savonarola, 323, 352
scale, 10
Schevill, F., 290 *n*.
Schinkel, Karl Friedrich, 768–69: Altes Museum, *769*
Schliemann, Heinrich, 94
Schmidt-Rottluff, Karl, 699 *n*.
Schöngauer, Martin, 334, 341
School of Athens (Raphael), 9, 23, 362–63, *347:* composition of, *23;* perspective of, *9*
Schwitters, Kurt, 710 *n*., 711: *Merz Picture 19*, *711*
scientia and *ars*, 245, 248
Scopas, 143
Scorel, Jan van, 383
Scott, Geoffrey, 783
Scott, Gilbert, 770: Albert Memorial, *770*
screen painting, Japanese, 585
scroll painting: Chinese, 553, 559; Japanese, 578–83
sculpture, 16–18: Achaemenian, 87–88; Aegean, 98; African Negro, 633–39; Andean, 608, 611; Assyrian, 82–84; Babylonian, 75–79; Barbarian, 220; Baroque, 401–02, 415–16, 425; Byzantine, 212–13; Early Christian, 204–06; Egyptian, 49–59, 65–66, 69; English, 267, 754–55; Etruscan, 156–59; French, 235–39, 249–51, 259–61, 281, 387–88, 425–26, 751–53, 756, 763–64; German, 240, 269–70, 753–54; Gothic, 249–51, 259–61, 264–65, 267, 269, 272–73, 280, 281–82; Greek, 10, 117–31, 142–47; Hispanic American, 455–56, *457;* Hittite, 80; of India, 512–13, 516, 518–22,

523–31; Islamic, 494–95; Italian, 292–97, 312–14, 319–21, 343, 348–49, 371–72, 401–02, 706, 758; Japanese, 570, 571–74, 580–81; Maya, 596–98, 600; 19th-century, 751–53; North American Indian, 622–25; Oceanic, 642–47; Paleolithic, 42; Renaissance, 292–97, 312–14, 319–21, 343, 348–49, 363–65, 371–72, 387–88, 391; Rococo, 425–26; Roman, 177–83; Romanesque, 235–39; Sassanian, 91; South American, 449, 452, 454; Southeast Asian, 533–38; Spanish, 391, 415–16; 20th-century, 706, 754–63; United States, 755, 757–62 (*see also* relief sculpture; woodcarving)

Scythian art, 89–90, 217

seaboard colonies (*see* English colonial art)

seals: Babylonian, 76–77, *76;* Mohenjo-Daro, India, 513–14, *514*

Seated Scribe, Egyptian Old Kingdom, *56,* 57

Seated Youth (Lehmbruck), 7, *7*

Second Empire style in 19th-century architecture, 768

Second Golden Age of Byzantine empire, 208

secondary colors, 13

Seip Mound, Ohio, 622

self-awareness in Renaissance art, 287, 314 (*see also* individualism)

Self-Portrait (Rembrandt), *Plate 6,* 410–11

Selinus, Temple B at, plan, *109*

semiprecious material, Roman work in, 185 (*see also* cloisonné; gem carving)

Semites: Assyrian, 79; Babylonian, 73

Semitic style: in Byzantine art, 208; in Early Christian art, 191–92, 205–07

Seneca Indian masks, 630

Sens cathedral, France, 266

Sepik River style of Oceanic art, 642, *642*

Septimus Severus: arch of, 182, *182;* tomb of, 177

Serlio, Sebastiano, 377

Sesostris III (*see* Amenemhat III)

Sesshū, 582–83: *The Four Seasons,* 582; *Landscape,* 583

Settignano, Desiderio da (*see* Desiderio)

Setting the Bow Net (Emerson), *746,* 747

Sety I, temple decorations of, 65, 66

Seurat, Georges, 667–68, 677: *Sunday Afternoon on Grand Jatte Island,* 668

Seven Apostles Watching the Ascension of Christ (Mantegna), 12, *13*

Severe style (*see* Early Classic style)

Severini, Gino, 706 *n.*

Seville, Spain: cathedral, 270; town hall, 391

sgraffito, 19

Shahn, Ben, 725: *Handball,* 725

Shaka Triad (Tori Busshi), 572, *573*

Shang dynasty, 543–44

Sharaku, 589

Shaw, Lemuel, daguerrotype of, 738, *740*

shedding, 26

Sheeler, Charles, 722–23

Sheep and a Goat (Chao Meng-fu), 563, *564*

Sheikh el-Beled, Egyptian Old Kingdom, *56,* 57

Shen Chou, 564–65: *Landscape with Farm Buildings, 564*

Shigisen Engi, *The Flying Warehouse,* 579–80, *579*

Shih-t'ao, 566

"Shingle style," 773, 776

Shinn, Everett, 691

Shintō religion, 575–77

Shirlaw, Walter, 686 *n.*

Shōden, Ise shrine, Japan, 576, *576*

shoguns, 581 (*see also* feudalism, Japanese)

Shōhaku, 586: *The Four Sages of Mount Sheng* (detail), *586*

Shop Window, Paris (Atget), 747, *747*

Shōsōin, Nara, Japan, 575

Shōtoku Taishi, portrait of, 575

shrines, Shintō, 575–77

Shūbun, 581

Shwe Dagon pagoda, Burma, 533

Siam, Indian art in, 535

Siege of Tenochtitlan (Rivera), 731, *731*

Siena, Italy, 271: baptismal font, 294, *296;* cathedral, 273

sign, 27

Signing of the Declaration of Independence (Trumbull), 683

Signorelli, Luca, 324

śikara (tower) of Hindu temple, 523, 524–25, 530, 538

Sikyatki ware, 621, *621*

silhouette, 8

silver point, 23

silverwork: Inca, 613, *614;* Navaho, 628–29, 631; Sassanian, 92, *92* (*see also* metalwork; niello metalwork; *repoussé*)

Simonson, Lee, 484 *n.*

Singing Gallery (*see Cantoria*)

Siper, A., 587

Siphnian Treasury, Delphi, frieze, 121, *123*

Siqueiros, David Alfaro, 730: *Echo of a Scream,* 731; *Proletarian Victim,* 730

Sir John Herschel (Cameron), 744, *744*

Sistine Chapel, Rome: frescoes, 324; Michelangelo's ceiling, 324, 350–52, *350–53*

Śiva, 513, 523, *528*

Śiva as Natarāja, Lord of the Dance, India, 530, 531

Six's Bridge (Rembrandt), 412, *413*

Thomson, Tom, 728
Three Clowns (Rouault), 697, *697*
Three Fates, Parthenon, 127, *127*
Three Marys at the Tomb (Duccio), 275
Three Musicians (Picasso), 703–04, *704*
Throne of Maximianus, Ravenna, 205, *205*
Thutmose, mask of a man, *63*, 65
Tiahuanaco culture, 610–12, 615, *616*
Tickhill Psalter, 267–68, *268*
Tiepolo, Giovanni Battista, 405: *Apotheosis of the Pisani Family, 405*
Tigris-Euphrates valley (*see* Middle Eastern art)
tile, glazed, use of: Chaldean, 85–86; Islamic, 498, 500, 502 (*see also* glazing)
timber, use of: Chinese, 567–68; English colonial, 464–65; French colonial, 459–60; Japanese, 576, 589–90; *590;* Russian, 479–80
time, Chinese attitude toward, 541–42
Ting ware, 562, *562*
Tintoretto, Jacopo Robusti, 373–74, 377, 392, 404, 407, 668: *Ascension of Christ, 374; Finding of the Body of St. Mark, 372; Last Supper,* 374; *Presentation of the Virgin,* 373
Tiryns, 96: palace walls of, 98, *99*
Titian, 325, 343, 355–58, 373, 392, 407, 427: *Assumption of the Virgin, 356; Deposition, 357; Venus of Urbino, 358*
Tlingit Indians, 625–26
To be looked at with one eye, close to . . . (Duchamp), 711–12, *712*
Toba Sōjō, animal caricatures, 580, *580*
Todaiji temple, Japan, 577
Tokugawa period of Japanese art, 585
Toledo, Juan Bautista de, 391: *Escorial, 391*
Toledo cathedral, 270
Tolsa, Manuel, high altar, Puebla cathedral, *446*
Toltec culture, 606, 615
tomb art: Babylonian, 73; Chinese T'ang, 557, *557;* Egyptian, 48–57, 59–65, 67–68
Tomb of the Baron, 158, *160*
Tomb of the Leopards, *155,* 156, 158–59
Tomb of the Shields, 159, *161*
tombs: beehive, 99, *100;* Chinese, 547, 547–48, 555; Egyptian, 59, 60, 65, 67–68; Etruscan, 154, *155,* 156, 158–59, *160;* Islamic, 499, 506, 507, *507,* 509; pre-Columbian Mexican, 603–05 (*see also* mastaba; mausoleum of Halicarnassus; pyramids; sarcophagi; stupa; tholos; tumulus)
tonality, 12
tondo, 344 *n.*
toolmaking: Neolithic, 43; Oceanic, 641–42; Paleolithic, 35–37
toranas (gateways) of Buddhist stupa, 518

Torcello cathedral, mosaic, 211, *212*
Toreador Scene, Cretan, 97, *98*
Tori Busshi, 572: *Shaka Triad, 573;* Yashuki, sculpture of, 572
Torres Straits mask, 642, *643*
Torre-Tagle palace, Lima, 448, *448*
torus of Ionic column, 116
Tosa, Mitsunobu, 584
Tosa school of Japanese painting, 581, 584
totem poles, 623–24; *624*
totems, 623–24, *626*
t'ou, bronze, Chou dynasty, 545
Toulouse-Lautrec, Henri de, 666–67, 719: *At the Moulin Rouge, 651; Jane Avril, 25*
Tour, Georges de la, 426: *St. Sebastian, 426*
Tournachon, Gaspard Felix, 742: *Eugène Delacroix, 742*
towers: Carolingian, 225; in Gothic cathedral, 248–49; Romanesque, 233; of Wren's churches, 433 (*see also* minaret; śikara)
town plans, Etruscan, 154–55 (*see also* city planning)
Toyokuni I, 589
Trajan, Column of, relief, 180–82, *182*
transept: of Early Christian basilica, *194, 195;* Gothic (plan), 254–55
Transfiguration, apse of Sant' Apollinare, 193–94, *193*
Transfiguration, church of the, Kizhi, 479–80, *479*
Travelers among Mountains and Stream (Fan K'uan) 558–59, *558*
Treasury of Atreus, 99, *100*
Treasury of the Athenians, Delphi, plan, *109*
Très Riches Heures (Limbourg brothers), 280, 283, *283*
Treves, Marco, 710 *n.*
tribune in Gothic cathedral, 248, *249*
Tribute Money (Masaccio), 299, *299*
triforium passage in Gothic cathedral, 248, 249, 256–57
triglyphs, Doric, *110,* 115–16
Trinity Church, Boston (Richardson), 773
Trinity with the Virgin, St. John, and Donors (Masaccio), 300, *300*
triptych, Byzantine, 213
Triumph of the Name of Jesus (Gaulli), 404, *405*
Trojan Horse, Roman, *164,* 165–66
trompe-l'oeil painting, 685
Trumbull, John, 683: *Battle of Bunker Hill, 683; Battle of Yorktown,* 683; *Signing of the Declaration of Independence,* 683
Tsarskoe Selo (Rastrelli), 486
Tula, Mexico, 600, 606

tumulus: Etruscan, *155, 156;* Japanese, 572 (*see also* tombs)

Tung Ch'i-ch'ang, 565

Tung Yüan, 558

Tun-huang sanctuaries, 550–51, *552:* Paradise paintings, 553, *554*

tunnel vault, Romanesque, 321, *232* (*see also* vaults and vaulting)

Tura, Cosimo, 309 *n.*

Turkey, Islamic art in, 492, 500

Turner, Joseph M. W., 662, 677, 679–80: *The Fighting Téméraire, 679; Rain, Steam and Speed,* 680

Tut-ankh-amen: effigy of, 69, *70;* tomb of, 59, 68

Twachtman, John H., 690, 691 *n.*

20th-century art: architecture, 709, 774–85; bibliography, 734–36, 764, 785–86; Canadian, 728–29; Dutch, 707–09; English, 756, 762; French, 695–99, 701–07, 711–12, 756, 782–84; German, 699–700, 711, 716–18, 779–82; Italian, 705–06, 712–13, 758, 775; Latin American, 729–32, 784; painting, 695–731; photography, 749; Russian, 709–10; sculpture, 756–64; Spanish, 775–76; United States, 718–28, 757–62, 774–85

Two Paths of Life (Rejlander), 734, *744*

Two Women Teaching a Child to Walk (Rembrandt) 412, *413*

tympanum, 237 *n.*

Tzu-chou pottery, 562

Uaxacutun, Guatemala, 596, *596*

Uccello, Paolo, 309–10: *Battle of San Romano, 309,* 310

Uffizi courtyard, 373, *373*

Uji Bridge, Momoyama period, *584,* 585

ukiyo-e style, 587

Underwood, Paul, 212 *n.*

Unique Forms of Continuity in Space (Boccioni) 758, *758*

Unité d'Habitation, Marseilles, France (Le Corbusier), *782,* 783

United Nations' Secretariat, New York City, 775

United States art: architecture, 767–79, 781–82; 19th-century, 683–93, 752, 767–74, 779; painting, 683–93, 718–28; sculpture, 752, 755, 757–63; 20th-century, 718–28, 755, 757–63, 774–79, 781–82 (*see also* English colonial art; New France)

universities in Gothic times, 244–45

University of Guadalajara, frescoes, 732

University of Salamanca, portal, 390, *390*

University of Virginia, Charlottesville, 468–69, *468–69*

Unkei, 580

Upanishads, 514–15

Ur-Nammu, stele of, 75, *75*

Ursuline Convent, Three Rivers, 459, *459*

Uspenski cathedral, Moscow, iconostasis, *482*

Utamaro, 588

Utrecht Psalter, 222–23, *222*

Utrillo, Maurice, 696

Uxmal, Yucatan, 598–99, *599*

Vaast, Jean, 263

Valencia, Spain, 416

Valley of the Kings, Egypt, 60

value, 11–12, *13*

Vanbrugh, John, 434–35, 766; Blenheim Palace, *435*

Vanderlyn, John, 684

Van Dyck, Anthony, 407–08, 436, 471: *James Stuart, 408*

van Eyck, Hubert, 332 *n.*

van Eyck, Jan, 330, 332–34, 336, 340: *Adam and Eve, 333; Adoration of the Mystic Lamb* (Ghent Altarpiece), *332; Annunciation,* 334; *Arnolfini Wedding,* 334; *Madonna of the Canon van der Paele,* 334

Van Gogh, Vincent, 667, 671–73, 676, 677, 700, 707, 724: *Wheatfield with Blackbirds, 674; Woman Rocking a Cradle* (Mme. Roulin), 673

Vannuci, Pietro (*see* Perugino, Il)

Van Orley, Bernart, 383: *Virgin and Child,* 383

Vantongerloo, Georges, 709 *n.,* 760: *Construction* $y = 2x^3 - 13.5x^2 - 21x,$ *759*

Vaphio Cups, Aegean, 102, *103*

Vasari, Giorgio, 291 *n.,* 297–98 *n.,* 299, 354, 367, 369 *n.,* 370, 373, 376: Uffizi courtyard, *373*

vase painting, Greek, 147–48

vases (*see* ceramics; pottery and pottery-making)

Vasquez, Gregorio, 457

Vatican, Rome: Raphael's paintings in, 346; Sistine chapel, 324, *350–53*

Vau, Louis Le (*see* Le Van, Louis)

vaults and vaulting, 168–69: barrel, 74, 154, 168–69, *168, 169, 173,* 175, 231, 232; corbeled, 595; cross: 168–69, *168, 169, 173, 173;* fan, 280, *280;* groin, 169, *169, 173,* 175, 231–32; Islamic, 494; ribbed, 232, 234, 246–48, *246, 247* (*see also* arch; clerestory windows)

Vedder, Elihu, 686

Vedic religion, 514

Velázquez, Diego, 398, 417–19: *Innocent X, 419; Las Meñinas* (Maids of Honor), *418; Surrender of Breda,* 417

Vendramin Palace, Venice, 316, *317*

Veneziano, Domenico, 304–05, 309, 329: *Madonna and Child with Saints,* 305

341: *Bladelin Altarpiece, 336; Descent from the Cross, 335*
Whaler of Nantucket (Roszak), *761, 763*
Wheatfield with Blackbirds (Van Gogh), 7, *673, 674*
When the Morning Stars Sang Together (Blake), 680, *680*
Whistler, James Abbott McNeill, 686–87: *Portrait of Miss Alexander, 687*
White on White (Malevich), 710
Whitehall Palace, Banqueting Hall, 432, *433*
Whitehead, A. N., 192 *n.*, 677 *n.*
Whittemore, Thomas, 210 *n.*, 212 *n.*
Wild Bull Hunt, temple of Ramesses III, *64*, 66
William of Sens, 266
Wilson, Richard, 677
Winchester manuscripts, 240
Winckelmann, J. J., 651, 766
Winged Victory [*see Nike* (or *Victory*) *of Samothrace*]
Wingert, Paul, 637 *n.*, 641
Wingless Victory, temple of, plan, *109*
Winter Palace, Russia (Rastrelli), 486
Witz, Conrad, 340–41: *Miraculous Draught of Fish*, 341
Wohlgemuth, Michael, 334
Wölfflin, Heinrich, 8 *n.*, 28 *n.*, 329
Woman Rocking a Cradle (Van Gogh), 672–73, *673*
Wood, Grant, 725–26: *American Gothic*, *726*
woodblock, Japanese, 587
woodcarving: African Negro, 636–37; Egyptian, 68; Islamic, 495, 497; Northwest Coast Indians, 622–25; Oceanic, 642–47 (*see also* sculpture)
woodcuts, 24: of Blake, 681; of Dürer, 380; German 16th-century, 380–82; Japanese, 587 (*see also* printmaking)
woof (*see* weft)
Woolly Rhinoceros, Magdalenian, 40
Woolworth building, New York City, 774
Wordsworth, William, Constable and, 679
World War I, influence of, on art, 710
Wren, Christopher, 433: Hampton Court, 433; St. Mary-le-Bow, 434; St. Paul's cathedral, 435
Wright, Frank Lloyd, 771, 776–79, 783, 784: *Falling Water, 777;* Imperial Hotel, 776; Johnson Wax Company building, 765; Robie House, 777; *Taliesin West, 778*
Wu Chen, 564
Wu Tao-tzu, 556
Wu tomb, relief from, 547
Wu Wei, 564
Wyant, Alexander, 684
Wyndam Sisters, The (Sargent), 687, *687*

Xenophontos monastery, Mt. Athos, interior of, 208, *210*
Xerxes, 86

Yakushi, sculpture of (Tori Busshi), 572
Yamato-e style, 579, 581, 584
Yang Shao pottery jar, *542*
Yellow Christ, The (Gauguin), 674, *674*
Yen Li-pen, 555, 575: *Portraits of the emperors, 555*
Yin-ching ware, 562
Young Woman at a Casement (Vermeer), 414, *414*
Youthful Bacchus (Caravaggio), 403, *403*
Ypres, Flanders, 331
Yüan dynasty, 563–64
Yucatan, 593–96
Yung-cheng, 567
Yün-kang cave temples, 549, *550*

Zapotec culture, 603–05, 615
Zen Buddhism: Chinese, 561–62; Japanese, 582–83
Zeus (or Poseidon), Early Classic, 121, *122*
Zeus: temple of, Olympia, 112, *113:* metope, 126, *126;* pediments, 124–26, *125;* temple of, Pergamon, 141: frieze, 144, 145
Zeuxis, 147
ziggurat: Assyrian, 81; Babylonian, 73, 74
Zorach, William, 757